Adobe®
Acrobat® 5 PDF
Bible

Adobe®
Acrobat® 5 PDF
Bible

Ted Padova

Hungry Minds™

Best-Selling Books • Digital Downloads • e-Books • Answer Networks • e-Newsletters • Branded Web Sites • e-Learning

New York, NY ◆ Cleveland, OH ◆ Indianapolis, IN

Adobe® Acrobat® 5 PDF Bible

Published by
Hungry Minds, Inc.
909 Third Avenue
New York, NY 10022
www.hungryminds.com

Library of Congress Control Number: 2001090712

ISBN: 0-7645-3577-3

Printed in the United States of America

10 9 8 7 6 5 4 3 2 1

1B/RV/QW/QR/IN

Distributed in the United States by Hungry Minds, Inc.

Distributed by CDG Books Canada Inc. for Canada; by Transworld Publishers Limited in the United Kingdom; by IDG Norge Books for Norway; by IDG Sweden Books for Sweden; by IDG Books Australia Publishing Corporation Pty. Ltd. for Australia and New Zealand; by TransQuest Publishers Pte Ltd. for Singapore, Malaysia, Thailand, Indonesia, and Hong Kong; by Gotop Information Inc. for Taiwan; by ICG Muse, Inc. for Japan; by Intersoft for South Africa; by Eyrolles for France; by International Thomson Publishing for Germany, Austria, and Switzerland; by Distribuidora Cuspide for Argentina; by LR International for Brazil; by Galileo Libros for Chile; by Ediciones ZETA S.C.R. Ltda. for Peru; by WS Computer Publishing Corporation, Inc., for the Philippines; by Contemporanea de Ediciones for Venezuela; by Express Computer Distributors for the Caribbean and West Indies; by Micronesia Media Distributor, Inc. for Micronesia; by Chips Computadoras S.A. de C.V. for Mexico; by Editorial Norma de Panama S.A. for Panama; by American Bookshops for Finland.

For general information on Hungry Minds' products and services please contact our Customer Care department within the U.S. at 800-762-2974, outside the U.S. at 317-572-3993 or fax 317-572-4002.

For sales inquiries and reseller information, including discounts, premium and bulk quantity sales, and foreign-language translations, please contact our Customer Care department at 800-434-3422, fax 317-572-4002 or write to Hungry Minds, Inc., Attn: Customer Care Department, 10475 Crosspoint Boulevard, Indianapolis, IN 46256.

For information on licensing foreign or domestic rights, please contact our Sub-Rights Customer Care department at 212-884-5000.

For information on using Hungry Minds' products and services in the classroom or for ordering examination copies, please contact our Educational Sales department at 800-434-2086 or fax 317-572-4005.

For press review copies, author interviews, or other publicity information, please contact our Public Relations department at 317-572-3168 or fax 317-572-4168.

For authorization to photocopy items for corporate, personal, or educational use, please contact Copyright Clearance Center, 222 Rosewood Drive, Danvers, MA 01923, or fax 978-750-4470.

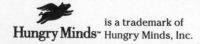

About the Author

Ted Padova is the Chief Executive Officer and Managing Partner of The Image Source Digital Imaging and Photo Finishing Centers of Ventura and Thousand Oaks, California. He has been involved in digital imaging since founding a service bureau in 1990.

Ted has taught university and higher education classes for over fifteen years in graphic design applications and digital prepress. Currently he teaches classes in Scanning and Halftoning, Adobe Photoshop, and Adobe Acrobat at the University of California, Santa Barbara and the University of California, Los Angeles.

Ted has contributed to over a dozen computer books as a technical editor, co-author, and author, including *Adobe Photoshop Look and Learn (Version 6.0)*, *Web Design Studio Secrets*, and *Adobe Photoshop 4.0 Bible* (technical editor); *Adobe Photoshop Tech Support* (co-author); and *Acrobat PDF Bible* (author), all published by Hungry Minds, Inc. (formerly IDG Books Worldwide).

Credits

Preface

The last version of the *Acrobat PDF Bible*, covering Acrobat 4.0, was the first of a comprehensive publication on Adobe Acrobat. The book did well at the resellers, and there were many online comments as well as e-mail received from readers all over the world. As time passed and I received more comments and criticisms, I thought about all the things I wished I had included in that first version and some things that I wished I had handled differently.

When I began the *Adobe® Acrobat® 5 PDF Bible*, I studied the comments I received from readers and made an effort to revise the book according to what readers asked for. This current edition covers almost all of what Acrobat 5.0 can do for you and it covers material according to what readers wanted in a new edition.

If revisiting the *Adobe® Acrobat® 5 PDF Bible*, it is my sincere hope you like the new additions and the style for which it is written. If you're new to the publication, then I hope you like the style and content and can find answers to all your Acrobat questions.

What Is Adobe Acrobat?

The reason many people first dismiss the thought of spending any energy on Adobe Acrobat is due to a lack of understanding of what Acrobat is and what it does. This, in part, is due to the fact that people jump onto the World Wide Web and download the free Adobe Acrobat Reader software. When acquiring Acrobat Reader, many folks think the viewing of PDF documents with Reader is the extent of Acrobat.

As I explain in Chapter 1, Reader is only one small component of Acrobat. Other programs are included in the suite of Acrobat software that provide you with tools for creating, editing, viewing, navigating, and searching Portable Document Format information. In Chapter 1, I offer an explanation of Adobe Acrobat and provide a little background on the product evolution. If you are not certain what Acrobat is, look over the first chapter to gain more understanding for how a book of such length can cover the product.

About This Book

This book is written for a cross-platform audience. Users of Windows 95, Windows 98, or Windows NT, Windows 2000, and Macintosh users will find references to these operating systems. Acrobat does work with MS-DOS and UNIX operating systems; however, coverage for these systems is limited. You'll find an equal devotion to performance only within Windows and the Macintosh OS.

For the most part, using Acrobat on either platform with regard to most of the features is identical. However, there are some distinct differences in a few features related to working with Acrobat on either Windows or the Macintosh. When such differences are addressed, separate references are made. If a topic is addressed and a screen illustration is provided without reference to a distinct difference running under different operating systems, you can expect the same options to appear on your system.

PDF Workflows

The definition of a *workflow* can mean different things to different people. One of the nice features of working with Acrobat is the development of a workflow environment. Quite simply, workflow solutions are intended to get out of a computer what the computer was designed for: productivity in a more automated fashion. If you go about editing page-by-page and run manual tasks to change or modify documents, it could hardly be called a workflow solution. Workflows enable office or production workers a means of automating common tasks for maximum efficiency. Batch processing documents, running them through automated steps, and routing files through computer-assisted delivery systems are among workflow solutions.

To help delineate a production workflow from manual methods, I have a specific icon appearing before a body of text that will alert you of a potential workflow proposition. PDFWorkflows are addressed throughout the book. When you see the PDFWorkflow icon, expect to see features to help you create automation in your environment.

The Book Contents

Almost all of what you can do with Acrobat is contained within the chapters that follow. I have made an effort to try to address many different uses for all types of users. This book covers Acrobat features and how to work with Adobe Acrobat and companion products. Individual industries, such as office occupations, digital prepress, multimedia, and Web publishing are covered. Regardless of what you do, you should be able to find some solutions for your particular kind of work. Whether you are an accounting clerk, a real estate sales person, a digital prepress technician, a Web designer, or a hobbyist who likes to archive information from Web sites, there's a reference to your needs and Acrobat will provide a solution.

To simplify the navigation of discovering Acrobat, I broke up the book into six separate sections. There are a total of 20 chapters that address Acrobat features and some individual purposes for using the software. The six sections include:

Part I: Welcome to Adobe Acrobat. To start off, I offer some history of Acrobat and toss in a few of my own opinions about the computer industry and evolution of companies and products. I should probably offer a disclaimer and say that where you find such opinions, they are my own and in no way reflect the publisher or any software or hardware manufacturer. I then go on to explain Acrobat and what you get when you buy the software — yes, the complete Adobe Acrobat software does require purchase. If you haven't yet purchased Acrobat, you can find a detailed description of using the free Adobe Acrobat Reader software and how to use Acrobat Search that is also distributed free from Adobe Systems. You can then browse the rest of the book to see if you can find features related to the other Acrobat software that would interest you in making the purchase. Part I covers viewing, navigation and understanding the Portable Document Format. By the time you finish Part I, you should be able to quickly find information and understand how Acrobat is embraced by many organizations, governments, and institutions throughout the world.

Part II: Creating PDF Documents. Viewing and navigation limits you to observe documents created by others. There are many different ways to create a PDF document and all these means are thoroughly covered in Part II. I start out discussing the easy methods for creating simple PDF files that might be used by office workers and travel through much more sophisticated PDF file creation for more demanding environments. In addition, many application software manufacturers are supporting PDFs through direct exports from their programs. The advantages and disadvantages of using all these methods are discussed.

Part III: Enhancing PDF Documents. This section covers the tools, menu commands, and features of using Adobe Acrobat 5.0. In this section, I cover the editing, modifications, and enhancing PDF files for many different purposes. Adding links, movies, sounds, comments, bookmarks, thumbnails, and all of the new features of Acrobat 5.0 are covered.

Part IV: Acrobat Publishing. This section covers distribution of PDF files in some of the more common means available to us today. I begin with distribution of PDF files on the Web and working with PDFs and Web browsers. Workgroup activity and sharing information through Internet connections is also covered. New industries emerging are focused on content distribution, so I move on to discuss eBooks and creating eBooks in PDF format. For the interactive elements of PDF distribution, you'll find the chapter on Acrobat Forms helpful. Anyone interested in distribution will also want to know something about authenticating documents and archiving them. I cover digital signatures and archiving through CD-ROM replication in the last chapter in this section.

Part V: Cataloging and Scanning. Using Acrobat Scan, converting scans to text through Optical Character Recognition (OCR), and then creating search indexes in Acrobat Catalog are all covered in this section.

Part VI: Advanced Acrobat Applications. I start this section out with simple printing of PDF files to desktop devices, and then move on to more complicated output in the form of digital prepress. For the advanced users, I included a special chapter on programming, particularly with JavaScript and cover how Acrobat handles JavaScript specifications. The last chapter covers plug-ins. Although all third party manufacturers do not have a demonstration product available on the accompanying CD-ROM, you can find Web addresses where software, products, and solutions can be found.

Appendix

The appendix describes the contents of the CD-ROM accompanying this book. A description of the items and some issues related to how the products are installed or references to where you'll find information and in what directories is found here.

The CD-ROM at the Back of the Book

In the back of the book you find a CD-ROM. The CD is a hybrid CD-ROM that can be viewed by Windows or Macintosh users. The CD-ROM contains some demonstration products that are either stand-alone applications or Acrobat plug-ins. Many developers have made contributions of their products and offer you a chance to try out their software. In several instances, the products are fully functional for a limited time. In other cases a single feature, such as saving a file, printing a file, or displaying text or an icon on a printed page will occur. Regardless of the limitation, the product can be thoroughly tested. Third-party manufacturers are an important asset to working with Adobe Acrobat. If you have some specialized needs, most often you can find a developer who provides a solution. Try out these products and visit the developer's Web sites to learn more of what Acrobat can do with add-on software.

Staying Connected

About every five minutes new products and new upgrades are distributed. If you purchase a software product, you will find a revision not too long after release. Manufacturers are relying more and more on Internet distribution and less on the postal delivery. With Acrobat, the third party products and almost any other software product, you should plan on making routine visits to manufacturer's Web sites. Anyone who has a Web site will offer a product revision for downloading or offer you details on acquiring the update. You should follow some basic steps to keep you updated on Acrobat.

Registration

Regardless of whether you purchase Acrobat or download the free Acrobat Reader software, Adobe Systems has made it possible to register for either product. You can register on the World Wide Web or mail a registration form to Adobe Systems. If you develop PDF documents for distribution, Adobe likes to keep track of this information. You will find great advantage in being a registered user. First, update information will be sent to you, so that you'll know when a product revision occurs. Second, information can be distributed to help you achieve the most out of using Acrobat. Who knows, some day you may be requested to provide samples of your work, which might get you a hit from the Adobe Web site. By all means, complete the registration. It will be to your benefit.

Web Sites to Contact

The first Web site to frequent is the Adobe Web site. Downloads for updates will be found when Acrobat components are revised. You can also find tips, information, and problem solutions. Visit the Adobe Web site at: www.adobe.com.

A Web ring is sponsored by pdfZone. Participants in the Web ring are individuals and companies that promote information and solutions for the PDF community. In addition, pdfZone publishes articles of interest, news, and hosts an extensive list of third party developers. You can find them at: www.pdfzone.com.

Acrobat tips can be found on many Web sites and all you need do is search the World Wide Web for Acrobat information. The best source you can find for information as well as a comprehensive collection of third party plug-ins is available at planetPDF. You can visit them at: www.planetpdf.com.

If learning more about Acrobat is your interest, you can find regional conferences sponsored by DigiPub Solutions Corporation. If you want to meet and discuss PDF issues with some of the world's experts, look for a conference in your area. You can find information at: www.pdfconference.com.

Content distribution is a new emerging industry, and PDF is king of the content developers and distributors. If you have a burning desire to become an author, then eBooks and eMatter can be a great avenue. The premiere Web site hosting eMatter for PDF downloads is MightyWords. A site totally dedicated to ePapers and eBooks, you can find them at: www.mightywords.com.

Whatever you may desire can usually be found on some Web site. New sites are developed continually, so be certain to make some frequent searches.

Contacting Me

If, after reviewing this publication, you feel some important information was overlooked, you can contact me and let me know your views, opinions, hoorahs, complaints, or provide information that might get included in the next revision. (If it's good enough, you might even get a credit line in the acknowledgments!) By all means, send me a note. E-mail inquiries can be sent to: ted@west.net.

If you happen to have some problems with Acrobat, keep in mind, I didn't engineer the program. Inquiries for technical support should be directed to the software manufacturer(s) of any products you use. This is one more good reason to complete your registration form.

There you have it — a short description of what follows. Don't wait. Turn the page and learn how Acrobat can help you gain more productivity with its amazing features.

Acknowledgments

I would like to acknowledge some of the people who have contributed in one way or another to make this edition possible. Mike Roney, my Acquisition Editor at Hungry Minds; my Project Editor, Katharine Dvorak; and my copyeditor, Jerelind Charles; as well as all the Hungry Minds crew of editors and production staff. Rick Hustead and Ray Hennessy for art contributions. Doug Lochner of where2go.com Karl DeAbrew and Kurt Foss of planetPDF; Carl Young of DigiPub Solutions Corporation; and Chris MacAskill and Judy Kirkpatrick of MightyWords.

Two special people helped make this edition much better than any other publication I have written and I can't say enough about their great contributions. Much thanks to Barbara Obermeier for carefully getting to the minutia of the tech edit job. She cursed me for the length of Chapter 6, but waded through every dialog box and line of text. Thanks, Barbie…you're the best.

Not being a programmer by profession, I needed a little help when it came to Chapter 19 and all the sophisticated programming stuff. My search was analogous to a motion picture producer who wants only a single actor in his/her film. No one else will do, it can only be one special person. When I began my search, my special individual in mind was Kas Thomas. In my mind, no other person on the planet would do. Fortunately, Kas said yes. I can't say enough about Kas. He's an expert programmer who addresses all user levels. This book is just a little bit better, all because of Kas's contribution.

Finally, I want to acknowledge all the users around the world who have written to me over the last two years and offered their praise and criticisms. You all contributed in making this edition more improved and comprehensive.

Contents at a Glance

Contents

Part III: Enhancing PDF Documents — 387

Part V: Catologing and Scanning 613

Chapter 17: Converting Scans to Text 659

Part VI: Advanced Acrobat Applications   665

Chapter 18: Printing and Digital Prepress 667

Chapter 19: Programming 687

Welcome to Adobe Acrobat

Getting to Know Adobe Acrobat

What Is Adobe Acrobat?

If, after perusing your local bookstore, you decided to lay down your money at the counter, carry away this ten-pound volume, and take it to bed with you tonight, you'd probably already know something about Adobe Acrobat. Heck, why else would you buy this book? If you're at the bookstore shelf and you haven't bought it yet, then you're probably wondering how in the world anyone could write so many pages for such a simple application. After all, isn't Acrobat that little thingy you download from the Adobe Web site?

Assuming you know little about Acrobat, I start with a brief description of what Acrobat is and what it is not. As I explain to people who ask about the product, I usually define it as the most misunderstood application available today. Most of us are familiar with the Adobe Acrobat Reader software, which is a product from Adobe Systems Incorporated that you can download free of charge from the Adobe Web site (www.adobe.com/acrobat). You can also acquire the Adobe Acrobat Reader from most of the installation CD-ROMs for other Adobe software. You can even acquire Acrobat Reader from other users, as long as the Adobe licensing requirements are distributed with the installer program. The Acrobat Reader, however, is *not* Adobe Acrobat. Acrobat Reader is a component of a much larger product that has evolved through several iterations.

History of Adobe Acrobat

When Acrobat was first released (as version 1.0), users could obtain the Acrobat Reader software for viewing and printing documents saved in Portable Document Format (PDF). Adobe released this product to help the growing user base view documents created on different platforms. The PC user, for example, could view a PDF file that was created on a Macintosh or UNIX workstation, and vice versa. The Acrobat Reader was free and enabled the viewing and printing of a document while maintaining that document's integrity. Fonts, graphics, design, and layout were all preserved in a PDF file so that the end user could view and print a document without needing any of the fonts, links, or applications from which the document was created.

The other two applications released in Version 1.0, Acrobat Distiller and Acrobat Exchange, were software items that had to be purchased from Adobe Systems. Acrobat Distiller enabled users to create a PDF document from a PostScript file printed to disk. Virtually any file created by an application with the capability to print to disk could be converted to PDF. After a PDF was created, it could then be edited in Acrobat Exchange.

As the product evolved, Release 2.1 was referred to as Acrobat Pro. The Acrobat Reader was still a free application distributed by Adobe Systems, but Acrobat Pro was a bundle of several applications that had to be purchased from Adobe. Acrobat Pro included Acrobat Distiller and Acrobat Exchange and it introduced a new application known as Acrobat Catalog that enabled the end user to create searches from multiple PDF files and provided an organized index of all the words used in documents.

With the release of 2.1, Acrobat Exchange, among other enhancements, also enabled the end user to add security to PDF files, which prevented other users with Exchange from modifying the documents.

With the release of Version 3.0, Adobe dropped the reference to Acrobat Pro, and simply called the Acrobat suite of software *Adobe Acrobat*. This terminology may appear somewhat confusing if you haven't followed the product closely during its evolution, as many users refer to Acrobat Reader as Adobe Acrobat. Keep in mind: The Reader is *not* Adobe Acrobat. The Reader software is still distributed free by Adobe Systems, but it is limited to only viewing and printing PDF files. For performing all of the editing tasks and adding bells and whistles to PDF documents, you need Adobe Acrobat, which consists of the complete complement of Acrobat products. The Adobe Acrobat release included all of the previous modules that were part of the 2.1 release, with new additions, Acrobat Capture and Acrobat Scan, added to the bundle.

Release of Adobe Acrobat 4.0 added further confusion to what we were to call some of the components. Adobe Acrobat was used to refer to the suite of applications, but Acrobat Exchange was simply referred to as *Acrobat*. The remaining applications of Reader, Catalog, Distiller, and PDFWriter were included in the bundle.

Enter Acrobat 5.0

Our new release of Adobe Acrobat has kept the name of Acrobat to refer to what we earlier referred to as Exchange. To centrally locate other functions, Adobe eliminated PDFWriter and added a means of creating PDFs from within Acrobat 5. Additionally, Acrobat Catalog is now a plug-in and also accessible from within

Acrobat. You'll find the new release of Adobe Acrobat includes just two separate applications: Acrobat and Acrobat Distiller.

Regardless of what you call it, Adobe Acrobat has grown into a sophisticated tool that provides many capabilities for organizing, displaying, and printing documents. Adobe Acrobat remains multi-platform and has achieved a high level of respect and performance in office, Web integration, and publishing environments.

Both Acrobat and the Distiller application in version 5.0 are designed to work in tandem to create and modify documents for on-screen viewing, Web publishing, and printing to suit most end user desires. This book covers all of the features of Adobe Acrobat. To perform the exercises contained herein, you need to purchase the complete Adobe Acrobat software, which has a street price of $295 as of this writing. If you work through all the chapters and develop a strong command in using Adobe Acrobat, I think you'll agree that the program is one of the best buys available in the computer software market.

What's PDF?

PDF, short for *Portable Document Format*, was developed by Adobe Systems as a unique format to be viewed through Acrobat viewers. As the name implies, it is portable, which means that the file you create on one computer can be viewed with an Acrobat viewer on other computers and on other platforms. For instance, you can create a page layout on a Macintosh computer and convert it to a PDF file. After the conversion, this PDF document can be viewed on a UNIX, DOS, or Windows machine. Multi-platform compliance (to enable the exchange of files across different computers, for example) is one of the great values of PDF files.

So what's special about PDF and its multi-platform compliance? It's not so much an issue of viewing a page on one computer created from another computer that is impressive about PDF. After all, such popular programs as Microsoft Excel, Microsoft Word, Adobe PageMaker, and Adobe Illustrator all have counterparts for multi-platform usage. You can create a layout on one computer system and view the file on another system with the same software installed. For instance, if you have Adobe PageMaker installed on a Macintosh computer and you create a PageMaker file, that same file can be viewed on a PC with PageMaker running under Windows.

In a perfect world, you may think the capability to view documents across platforms is not so special. Viewing capability, however, is secondary to document integrity. The preservation of the contents of a page is what makes the PDF format so extraordinary. To illustrate, let's say you have a PageMaker document created in Windows using fonts generic to Windows applications. After converted to PDF format, the document, complete with graphics and fonts intact, can be displayed and printed on other computer platforms.

This preservation can come in handy in business environments, where software purchases often reach quantum heights. PDF documents eliminate the need to install all applications used within a particular company on all the computers in that company. For example, art department employees can use a layout application to create display ads and then convert them to PDF so that other departments can use the free Reader software to view and print those ads for approval.

The benefits of PDF viewing were initially recognized by workgroups in local office environments for electronic paper exchanges. Today, we have much more opportunity for global exchange of documents in many different ways. As you look at Acrobat 5.0 and discover some of the new features now available for document collaboration, comparing documents and preparing PDFs for electronic readers, you'll see how Acrobat and the PDF format have evolved with new technologies.

Document repurposing

The evolution of the computer world has left extraordinary volumes of data on computer systems that were originally designed to be printed on paper. Going all the way back to UNIVAC, the number crunching was handled by the computer and the expression was the printed piece. Today, forms of expression have evolved to many different media. No longer do people wish to confine themselves to printed material. Now, in addition to publishing information on paper, we use CD-ROMs, the Internet, and file exchanges between computers. Sometimes we use motion video, television, and satellite broadcasts. As cable TV evolves, we'll see much larger bandwidths, so real-time communication will eventually become commonplace. And the world of tomorrow will introduce more communication media. Think of outputting to plasma, crystal, and holograms, and then think about having a font display or link problem with one of those babies!

Technology will advance, bringing many improvements to bandwidth, performance, and speed. To enable the public to access the mountains of digital data held on computer systems in a true information superhighway world, files will need to be converted to a common format. A common file format would also enable new documents to be more easily *repurposed*, to exploit the many forms of communication that we use today and expect to use tomorrow. As an example of how we might repurpose a document for one avenue to another, Figure 1-1 illustrates the process of repurposing a QuarkXPress file into a document suitable for viewing on the Web.

Where does Adobe see PDF heading? Adobe Systems and many software and hardware manufacturers expect most of our document exchanges today to be in PDF format. Adobe is using PDF as core technology for all new versions of its software. PostScript 3, new layout applications, and the flagship programs offered by the company all support PDF compliance. AGFA, a division of the Bayer group, has built a complete PDF workflow solution with its Apogee system. Scitex is corroborating with Adobe Systems in offering seminars throughout the country on how their imaging systems will work with PDF and PostScript 3. And the list goes on. As all these companies expand their existing equipment and software to take advantage of PDF, new documents will be hosted in PDF format, and old data will be converted to PDF.

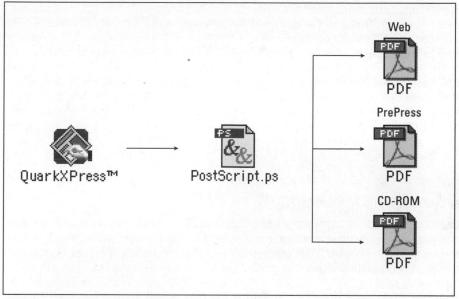

Figure 1-1: From an authoring application, the document is printed to disk as a PostScript file. With the Distiller JobOptions settings, the PostScript file designed for prepress is repurposed for screen and Web displays.

Adobe Acrobat is still in infancy now, but it will continue to evolve, as will other technologies. Currently, the best program for both document exchange and document repurposing is Acrobat, because it excels at creating a document, with or without multimedia elements, that can be printed, viewed on a computer screen, seen on the Web, and replicated on CD-ROM. What's more, with a vast number of third party manufactured plug-ins, all those records created years ago can be converted to PDF format. Document repurposing is one of the true values of using Adobe Acrobat. Throughout this book, I show you how to create PDF files with an eye toward document repurposing.

PDF and PostScript

On January 24, 1984, Apple Computer released the Macintosh computer. Not an impulsive buyer, I waited until January 26 to purchase my first Mac. I remember one of my earlier uses of the Mac involved submitting documents that contained about thirty fonts and several graphics to California government offices in Sacramento. I frequently received calls from people wanting to know how I put the little "choo-choo trains" on my memos. Although crude, the emphasis on the visual gained the response I needed for attention to my message.

If all the Macintosh computer could do was print on an ImageWriter I dot-matrix printer, it would have died alongside the Osborne portable, and Mr. Gates would own much more of the world than he does now. The credibility of the Macintosh was not realized with the hardware (certainly not at 128K RAM and a single 400K floppy drive), nor was it with MacPaint and Habadex. In 1985, Apple Computer introduced the Macintosh-LaserWriter connection. With 13 built-in fonts and a hefty $6,500 price tag, the LaserWriter, based on true Adobe PostScript, was one of the great products of the era. With this introduction, the world of desktop publishing was born.

Today, the de facto standard of almost all printing in the graphics industry is PostScript. Ninety-nine percent of North America and about seventy-five percent of the rest of the world uses PostScript for all high-end output. Adobe developed this page description language to accurately display from your computer screen to what the final printed output would look like. If graphics and fonts are included in your files, then PostScript is the only show in town. The Adobe PostScript language was responsible for the rise of so many software and hardware manufacturers. If you stop and think about it, PostScript ranks up there with MS-DOS and Windows in terms of its installed base.

One feature of successful software programs is that they run on a wide variety of hardware, giving users some choice when it comes to hardware. The most successful software published today is MS-DOS and Windows. This software is successful because it permits a lot of flexibility. Windows is not restricted to a single manufacturer's hardware. Scads of companies are producing Intel-, AMD-, and Cyrix-based machines, and they all include Windows with the purchase of the hardware. The Apple Mac OS, until recently, was only able to run on Apple-produced hardware. This limitation may have been one of the reasons that prevented Apple from enjoying the same success as companies, such as Microsoft.

PostScript also allows for flexibility in working with different hardware. With its device-independent structure, PostScript can accommodate many different printers, all with different resolution capabilities. For example, you can print to a 300-dpi PostScript laser printer or to a 3600-dpi imagesetter with the same flavor of PostScript. PostScript printing requires a raster image processor (RIP), which can be either a hardware device or software. The RIP converts the image on-screen to a bitmap page that can be printed on a PostScript printer. In other words, what you draw on your computer screen is defined in a language different from that used by your printer, and PostScript is like a language conversion utility in that it "translates" the screen image for printing.

Integrity of data is critical when printing files. A glitch or hiccup can blow out a font or graphic on the printed page. Software applications compliant with PostScript experience much fewer problems because data integrity is adhered to strictly. This, in fact, is another advantage of using Adobe Acrobat. One of the applications used to convert your screen files to PDF is Adobe Acrobat Distiller. Distiller is like a PostScript engine in that it adheres strictly to PostScript conventions. In almost all cases, if you can distill a file with Acrobat Distiller, you can print the file on a PostScript device. As you read through this book, you learn how and when to use Acrobat Distiller.

Adobe Acrobat Components

When you purchase a software product, you probably already understand something about the product, what it does, and how you intend use it. If you pick Adobe Photoshop or Microsoft Excel off the shelf, you already know that you want to work on image editing or number crunching. Some add-ons may be available for the product, but you're well aware that you have a single application, sophisticated as it may be, to tackle your digital needs.

With Adobe Acrobat, it's a little different. In previous versions of Acrobat, we had several different executable applications to perform different functions. Some separate features have been added to Acrobat as commands in menus. Although there has been no sacrifice to the features offered by the complete Adobe Acrobat software, the individual applications include:

✦ Acrobat Reader

✦ Acrobat 5.0

✦ Acrobat Distiller

✦ Acrobat Capture

✦ Acrobat Messenger

The separate applications above offer you a multitude of features to create, edit, and use with various electronic documents. Although some of the former applications have been changed to plug-ins accessible from within Acrobat, they almost appear as though they are separate programs. To give you an idea of the highlights of Acrobat features, take a look at the brief descriptions that follow.

Plug-ins

In addition to the distinct applications available with Adobe Acrobat are plug-ins developed by Adobe Systems and many third-party manufacturers. (*Plug-ins* are software components often created by third-party vendors to add more functionality to software applications.) Adobe includes several plug-ins on the installation CD-ROM that you can use with Acrobat and Acrobat Reader. After you install Adobe Acrobat, the Scan, Catalog, and Search plug-ins are also installed. I offer you a large list of plug-ins as well as a description of each and the manufacturer who supplies them in Chapter 20.

Acrobat viewers

Until recently, three Acrobat viewer applications could be used to view PDF documents: Acrobat Reader, Acrobat 5.0, and another version of Acrobat called Acrobat Business Tools. Acrobat Business Tools was recently dropped from the line of Adobe products and no longer is available. As I mentioned earlier, Acrobat Reader is the free application that you can acquire from the Adobe Systems Web site. You can also find the Acrobat Reader software on many application installation CD-ROMs. Adobe Systems and many other software manufacturers include documentation, updates, and the latest news about a product in PDF format. To view the PDF files, you need to install an Acrobat viewer. Therefore, the Reader software is often included on CD-ROMs.

Note End users can also distribute the Acrobat Reader software. Adobe Systems permits you distribution rights as long as you comply with their distribution policy, which requires the licensing documents and information to be distributed with the installation utility.

Acrobat Reader, because it is a free application, is limited in use. You cannot edit or save PDF files with Acrobat Reader. It is designed to enable you to view a PDF document on-screen or to print a PDF file.

If you want to edit or create PDF files, you need to purchase Adobe Acrobat, which includes the Acrobat 5.0 software. Acrobat 5.0 takes off where Reader and the Business Tools edition end. Acrobat performs all the tasks of viewing files with the same tools as Acrobat Reader, but it goes a step further in enabling you to change, edit, secure, and customize PDF files. Acrobat is not just a viewer — it's the heart of the Adobe Acrobat applications. To help you understand the differences between these two viewers, I describe the Acrobat Reader software separately in Chapter 3 and devote the remainder of the book to using Acrobat. If you are an author of PDF files that you intend to distribute, knowing some of the limitations of the Reader software may help you guide other users as to what they can and cannot do with the Reader software. Look over Chapter 3 to get an idea of what limitations may be encountered.

Acrobat Search

When you open a PDF document in an Acrobat viewer, you can invoke a Find command to search for a keyword, as shown in Figure 1-2. The viewer then searches through the pages and stops at the first occurrence of the searched word it finds (see Figure 1-3). This is fine if you have a single document open and need to search for the content within the open document. If you have several PDF files and want to search all documents for a keyword or words, you need Acrobat Search. Like Acrobat Reader, Acrobat Search is a free plug-in, and it can be used with all Acrobat viewers.

Acrobat Search is a powerful search engine that goes beyond searching for keywords. You can search with operators or Boolean expressions and narrow searches to specific requirements, as I discuss in Chapter 2.

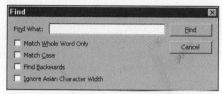

Figure 1-2: When the Find command is invoked, the search is limited to the open PDF document.

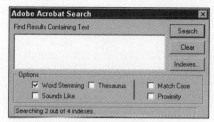

Figure 1-3: When Acrobat Search is used, it searches multiple PDF documents and reports in a result window a list of the PDF documents where the searched word(s) is found.

Note

When you acquire Acrobat Reader from the Adobe Web site, pull off the Reader from a CD-ROM, or acquire it from another user, you will find an installer for Reader and an installer for Reader + Search. If you elect to use the latter, both Acrobat Reader and Acrobat Search will be installed. If you cannot invoke a search of several PDF files at one time, you need to acquire Acrobat Search and install it.

Open as Adobe PDF

PDFWriter has been eliminated from Adobe Acrobat in Version 5.0. Rather than offer a separate application for creating PDFs with the PDFWriter software, Adobe has added a new menu command in Acrobat to convert many different image formatted files, HTML, and text files to PDF.

Open as Adobe PDF serves as the replacement for the PDFWriter software. The item is a menu command that converts many different file formats to PDF and drops them in the Acrobat application window. Converting documents via this menu command is much more limiting than using the separate Acrobat Distiller software. These limitations are discussed in Part II where I discuss converting files to PDF.

Acrobat Distiller

Adobe Acrobat Distiller is the more sophisticated conversion application. Distiller creates PDF documents from PostScript files. To use Distiller, you need to first print a file from your application document to disk as a PostScript file. Opening the printed PostScript file in Acrobat Distiller begins the conversion process. Distiller appears to be a simple utility when you first use it, but in reality, it is a very sophisticated application.

Many users opt to use the Open as Adobe PDF menu command because of its simplicity and the capability to create a PDF in a single step. However, you should be aware that Acrobat Distiller provides many more features that are preferred for many file types. (I cover creating PDF files and when to use Distiller over Open as Adobe PDF in Chapters 4 and 5.)

Acrobat Messenger

Acrobat Messenger is a tool to help office workers distribute documents quickly to remote offices and locations. With Acrobat Messenger you can use a scanner or copier, convert the documents to searchable PDFs, and e-mail them to clients or remote offices. It's a single solution for office workers needing quick and efficient means of distributing documents.

Acrobat Catalog

Earlier in this chapter I mentioned Acrobat Search and the powerful search capabilities you have available to you with Adobe Acrobat. The internal search available after you open a PDF document is executed with a Find command in an Acrobat viewer. This type of search, which can only be performed on the single open file, is further restricted by a limited set of search attributes. When you invoke a search using Acrobat Search, your Acrobat viewer searches through an index file containing key words extracted from a PDF document or several PDF documents. Index files are created with Acrobat Catalog.

In all earlier versions of Acrobat, Catalog was a separate executable application. With Version 5.0 of Adobe Acrobat, the Catalog program appears as a plug-in and is executed from a menu command in Acrobat.

In addition to developing search indexes from single or multiple PDF documents, Acrobat Catalog enables you to add more PDF files to the index and purge old data. Catalog can be designed to automatically build search indexes from PDF documents and keep them updated on a local workstation or remote server. I discuss all the features of using Acrobat Catalog in Chapter 15.

Acrobat Capture

Paper Capture, which was a command in Acrobat, executed a plug-in that converted raw scans to text via an Optical Character Recognition (OCR) program. Paper Capture has been eliminated from Acrobat 5.0. Adobe markets a separate and much more sophisticated product called *Acrobat Capture* that is sold apart from Adobe Acrobat. For industrial strength OCR conversion, Acrobat Capture is well suited for PDF workflows where scans need to be converted to text. I discuss using Acrobat Capture in Chapter 14.

Acrobat Scan

Acrobat Scan is a plug-in that must be present in the Acrobat plug-in folder when you install Adobe Acrobat, otherwise you won't have access to Acrobat Scan. After you launch Acrobat, the Scan plug-in becomes accessible through a menu command. Scan uses TWAIN (Technology With An Important Name) to access your scanner software, permitting you to scan a document from within Acrobat. After the document is scanned, it appears in the Acrobat window as a PDF. Configuring a scanner and invoking the Scan command are discussed in Chapter 16.

Acrobat Forms

Forms design and implementation was improved in Acrobat 4.0. All the features of creating forms and the wonderful ability to use JavaScript code with forms fields are still available with Acrobat 5.0. Acrobat 5.0 has introduced a new Fields palette and added much more to the JavaScript implementation. In Chapter 13, I walk you through forms creation and offer some tips for those who may be less inclined to do complex programming. If you're worried about the programming code, take a look at Chapter 11 for some ideas on how to make the programming a little easier. For advanced users, I created a separate chapter of JavaScript and programming. Chapter 19 covers some new additions to the JavaScript implementation in Acrobat.

Collaboration

A new feature introduced in Acrobat 5.0 permits you to collaborate on documents from remote locations. Workgroups scattered all over the planet can access a PDF file on the Internet and submit notes and comments directly to a server. Other authorized individuals can access notes and respond with their own messages. Collaboration introduces a new method of working with PDF documents among remote workers. I cover these new features in Chapter 11.

Digital Signatures

Digital Signatures were introduced in Version 4.0 of Adobe Acrobat. This feature enables you to digitally sign documents for authentication and legal purposes. You'll want to keep an eye on legislation as it moves through your country and governing bodies as many different legal systems are moving toward acceptance of digitally signed documents. I offer you a detail of Digital Signatures in Chapter 14.

Web Capture

Introduced in Version 4.0 of Acrobat, Web Capture is also a plug-in and a truly remarkable feature. Web Capture enables you to convert as much as entire Web sites to a PDF document or multiple PDF documents. If you need to have material accessible locally and wish to catalog and search information, you can use Web Capture to convert the HTML documents to a PDF, use Acrobat Catalog to create a search index, and store the files on your computer. I discuss using the Web Capture command in Chapter 4.

Web Buy

Web Buy was an added feature introduced after the initial release of Acrobat 4.0 and became available for both Reader and Acrobat users during the minor 4.0.5 upgrade. Web Buy offers the end user an opportunity to download secure documents typically found in the growing eBook market. File encryption locks files to hardware serial numbers preventing unauthorized distribution. If you are a publisher or want to control content, you may be interested in looking at the PDF Merchant program offered by Adobe. For end users, Web Buy is a must if you expect to download content that uses this type of encryption. A discussion of Web Buy can be found in Chapter 12.

In addition to the separate items described here, Acrobat remains unique in offering you just about everything but the kitchen sink. You still find bookmarks, thumbnails, articles, movies, sound, text editing, annotations, and more available with Acrobat 5. All the editing features of Acrobat are covered in Chapters 7 to 10.

Nomenclature

The use of the term *Acrobat* instead of the formerly named *Acrobat Exchange* and the use of *Adobe Acrobat* to refer to the complete suite of applications has created a little confusion among users. For the purposes of this text, I refer to Adobe Acrobat as the complete software you purchase from Adobe Systems. The term *Acrobat* or *Acrobat 5.0* is used to identify the application program Adobe refers to as Adobe Acrobat 5.0. Acrobat Reader may often be referred to as *Reader* and Acrobat Distiller will often be referred to as *Distiller*. Hence, when I suggest Adobe Acrobat, I'm talking about both Acrobat and Distiller and all the other components you find on the CD-ROM when you make the purchase. If you're upgrading from Version 3.x or below, then think of my references to Acrobat as what you once knew as Acrobat Exchange.

With regard to Acrobat Catalog, keep in mind that Catalog is not a stand-alone executable application in Adobe Acrobat 5.0. Catalog is now a menu command that opens a dialog box enabling you to create search indexes. References to the menu command are called *Catalog* or *Acrobat Catalog*. Acrobat Scan follows a similar example as Acrobat Catalog. These are all plug-ins and accessed through Acrobat. So, keep in mind, they may be referred to as if they are stand-alone applications, but all are executed from within Acrobat.

Acrobat viewers are the programs that can open and display PDF files. Acrobat, Acrobat Reader, and the Acrobat Reader from the Business Tools edition are all Acrobat viewers. Anytime an Acrobat viewer is referenced, I'm referring to one of these applications.

What's New in Acrobat 5.0?

Every time we see a software upgrade moving from 1.0 to 2.0, or in this case from 4.0 to 5.0, we expect to see major changes and improvements in the software product. Sometimes the changes are subtle and require us to poke around to find new enhancement features, and sometimes big changes are obvious immediately when the program is launched.

Acrobat 5.0 has both. After you launch the program, you immediately see a change in the user interface. This change is obvious. Poke around and you find new enhancements hidden in menus and palettes. Acrobat 5.0 has been upgraded to take advantage of many new user demands and a few things Adobe threw in that you may not have hoped for. Some of the more prominent new changes and the chapters that cover them are listed in this section.

User interface

The first feature you notice after launching Acrobat 5.0 is the new user interface. No Tool palette is present with Acrobat 5.0. What was found in Acrobat 4.0 for other tools is now placed at the top level Toolbar. In the Window menu, you find a menu option for Toolbars. If any tools disappear from the Toolbar, choose from the submenu options to regain access to the tools.

Tabs appear at the far left side of the Acrobat application window that is now used to expose the palettes within the Navigation pane. You can choose from the Window menu to open a palette or select one of the tabs on the left side of the document window.

PDF Version 1.4

The PDF version has been upgraded as well as Acrobat. Now in Version 1.4, the PDF format takes great advantage of newer technologies across the Adobe product line. With Acrobat 5.0 and the PDF 1.4 format, seamless integration with applications, such as Photoshop 6.0, Illustrator 9.0, and Adobe InDesign offers much more data integrity and compatibility. In Chapter 6, I cover integration with Adobe programs and those marketed by Microsoft, Corel, Quark, and Macromedia.

New palettes

Whether located in the Navigation pane or accessed from the Window menu, several additional palettes are introduced in Version 5.0:

   ✦ **Info:** This palette displays an Info window displaying the X, Y coordinates and Width and Height axes of the mouse cursor in the document window. This palette will be helpful when designing forms.

   ✦ **Fields:** This tab displays all of the form fields contained in the current PDF file. If form fields have been created on a hidden template, they will be displayed in this palette even though the fields may not appear in the open document window.

   ✦ **Tags:** The Tags palette offers a variety of means of tagging words, text blocks, and pages in PDF files with structure and marking the content of the documents. I cover the Tags palette and all its features in Chapter 9.

   ✦ **Comments:** Comments is a new term used for what was previously called *Annotations*. All of the Acrobat 4 Annotation tools are still available in Acrobat 5.0; however, the Navigation pane now refers to Annotations as Comments.

New tools

The E-Mail tool, added to the Toolbar, invokes the same command as you would invoke with the File ➪ Send Mail Command.

Tables defined in the original text document can be selected with the Table Formatted Text Selection tool for copying and pasting into other applications or the selected table can be saved in several different formats. This feature is available only on Windows.

New menu commands

Open as Adobe PDF enables you to convert many different image files from within Acrobat to PDF as well as text and word processor documents saved as text. For a fast method of converting these files to PDF, doing it from within Acrobat is easy.

Going the other way, at times you may want to convert a PDF to an image format for Web use or even printing. You can use the **Extract Image As** command to export to

JPEG, PNG, or TIF. The EPS Export option from this menu command has been eliminated. See the Save As command for exporting to PostScript or EPS format.

Acrobat 5.0 offers many new export formats. From the **File ➪ Save As menu** command, you can export to EPS or PostScript. You can also save files in TIFF, JPEG, PNG, and Rich Text formats.

A marvelous new feature in Acrobat 5.0, **Collaboration**, enables you to exchange annotations on a PDF document in a workgroup. Exchange annotations, review remarks from others, and do it all over the Internet or on local servers with your business partners across town, across the world, or across the room.

A new **Batch Sequence** command is offered where sequence operations that you select from a menu of vast choices can be added to your sequence list. Run a sequence for adding bookmarks, signatures, or a bunch of other operations and have that sequence appear in the file menu. After you select the sequence you created, you're off and running to edit a single PDF document or a folder full of PDFs.

Document security has been greatly improved in Acrobat 5.0. The encryption method has been extended to 128-bit encryption and offers many more alternatives for protecting your PDF files.

Spell check has been added to Acrobat 5.0. You can check spelling on form fields and comments. Spell checking is not limited to a single language. You can check spelling in 16 different languages plus eight different English variations. In addition, you can edit dictionaries to add new words.

Acrobat Catalog is no longer a separate executable program. The Tools ➪ Catalog command invokes Acrobat Catalog that appears as a separate dialog box from within Acrobat.

Although a separate executable program, **Distiller** can be launched from within Acrobat via a menu command.

Digital Signatures has been simplified to some degree and new menu commands have been offered to help you digitally sign electronic document files.

The JavaScript console and editing and debugging tasks have been improved. A new **Set Document Actions** feature enables you to run a JavaScript while closing, saving, and printing PDF files.

New improved enhancements have been added to the **Compare** function. A dialog box is opened when you launch the command from the Tools menu and offers you choices for the degree of comparison between documents.

Proof The Proof Setup command enables you to choose from a color profile list for printing your PDFs using a Color Management System. Choose from any one of the available profiles or create a new profile from programs, such as Adobe Photoshop.

After a profile is saved to the Windows: System Color folder (AppleSync for Macintosh), the new profile appears in the list when Acrobat is relaunched.

Proof Colors enables you to view on your monitor a close resemblance of the printed piece. Change the Proof Setup to a different profile and the color is adjusted on-screen if this menu option is selected for soft proofing files.

Preferences have been moved from the File menu to the Edit menu. Preference settings have been expanded to include settings for new features and the list of different preference groups has been expanded.

Microsoft Office integration

New features have been added to the ease of creating PDFs from Microsoft Office applications. The Create PDF function has given way to new menu commands for creating a PDF, creating and e-mailing a PDF, and viewing a PDF immediately after creating it from one of the Office applications. New toolbar icons are now provided to accommodate these features.

Printing

The Print dialog box now includes an Advanced button that, when selected, opens a dialog box to offer several new print options including trim marks, transparency levels, and omitting images for proof printing.

Understanding PDF Workflows

In what seems a very long time ago on the computer technology timeline, the advent of single-user workstations gave rise to the buzzwords *paperless office*. What we have come to learn over the past two decades is that computer systems are generating more paper than ever before. Somehow, the world population has not yet learned to work in a digital environment without paper. (I suspect it will be a long time before people can get away from the need to have something in their hands to carry around and to pile up on their desks.) In the office world, it's not the absence of paper that is important to us, but the ability to find information and then generate output to printing devices in a form and style that is easily legible. Organization of files and rapid retrieval is the first step to take before we can start saving more trees.

Automating digital workflows

In complex office environments, data is assembled and regurgitated in partial digital workflows; intra-office departments share data through multi-user systems or individual applications capable of sharing files. Users have been working with these partial digital workflows for some time. Advances with storage devices and network systems have helped move automation along. Even so, we computer users remain islands, so to speak, isolated because we haven't been able to bridge all systems and data structures.

What has been needed for some time is a tool that ignores application software variances and hardware differences to communicate information among workers, whether they be in a local office, remote facility, or across the globe. In an office that uses PDF, all these components can come together, for Adobe Acrobat ignores cross-platform problems and becomes the common denominator for data flow originating from almost any application.

If you work in a large office and have a network administrator, someone else likely handles the technical issues related to your network. You probably don't have to worry about keeping the network alive, configuring systems, and handling all the problems that come with these complex hardware systems. If you are a small office worker, the idea of setting up a network may be frightening and intimidating. If you want to have more of a digital workflow in your office, you may be puzzled as to where to begin. Here I try to dispel some of this confusion by taking you through various fundamentals of network configuration, which will help you in implementing Adobe Acrobat.

Local area networks

If you have two computers and a printer attached to both, you have a *local area network* (LAN). Networks have two components that enable printing and/or file sharing: hardware for creating connections and software for controlling the data flow. Network hardware involves a connection interface referred to as a *transceiver* (the most common of which is Ethernet) and cabling to connect the transceivers. To connect two computers and a printer, you need a transceiver on each device. Some devices, such as printers, as well as all newer Macintoshes, have Ethernet transceivers built in. PCs require the installation of an Ethernet board. With respect to the Macintosh, LocalTalk provides a transceiver alternative, but it is about 43 times slower than Ethernet and today almost nonexistent.

Network cabling is needed to connect the Ethernet transceivers. The type of cabling you need depends on the type of connectors you have on the Ethernet boards and whether you use other hardware devices. In a simple network environment, you can use coaxial cable (which resembles cable TV cabling) with a BNC connector and daisy chain the connectors on the boards. In this type of environment, you need to terminate each end of your network using a device, called a *terminator* that clips on the open end of the BNC connector. Coaxial cable has one significant problem in network architecture. If one cable is damaged or the connection is not correctly made, all computers and devices attached to the network lose access to all other network devices.

A better solution is to use a *hub*, a hardware device to which each unit on a network is connected via cabling with RJ-45 (telephone) clips. These clips plug into ports on the hub, and hubs can be purchased with 4, 8, 16, or more ports. You can also connect several hubs by bridging them. When you purchase Ethernet cards, you can find many that have BNC connectors for coaxial connections and RJ-45 receptacles.

Ethernet is also available in different speeds or capacities. 10Base-T Ethernet permits data transmissions of 10,000,000 bits per second (bps). This may seem fast, but it all depends on the amount of data you exchange with other devices or the size of the files you send off to a printer. If all you do is traffic PDF documents, 10Base-T works well, because PDF files are compressed and the file sizes are generally small. If your PDF documents are large, or you perform remote processing for distilling PDF files or cataloging them, this speed may not be fast enough for you. However, 10Base-T networks are inexpensive: You can purchase hubs for $20 or less on the low end.

Ethernet also comes in 100Base-T, which transmits data at 100,000,000 bits per second, or ten times faster than 10Base-T. As of this writing, the price of 100Base-T Ethernet has dropped remarkably: What a few years ago cost $800 to $1,000 can now be purchased for less than $100. If trafficking large amounts of data is a common practice in your environment, 100Base-T Ethernet would be the only way to go.

Cabling for Ethernet is an important consideration. 10Base-T networks can operate on two-pair wiring (four individual strands), whereas 100Base-T requires four-pair wiring (eight individual strands) called *Category 5* or *CAT5* wiring. The difference in the price of the wiring is incidental to the amount of labor required to rewire a network if you decide to upgrade from 10Base-T to 100Base-T Ethernet. If you go about installing a network in your office, my suggestion is to wire it with CAT5 and be done with it. When the receptacles are properly connected to the wiring, you can run either 10Base-T or 100Base-T on the same wiring.

Servers

On a network, a *server* is a computer that typically contains large amounts of storage space and software installed to permit network traffic to flow to and from it. Servers can be one of many types of computers, and it doesn't matter which platform it runs on; you can access a server of another flavor if you have the proper software installed. For example, if you operate on a Macintosh network, your server can be a Macintosh computer, a PC, a UNIX workstation, or a DEC Alpha. All the Mac files that you save to the server will be accessible to all Macintoshes on your network regardless of the type of server you elect to purchase.

Speed and cost will dictate which system you ultimately decide to use. Perhaps one of the cheapest solutions is an Intel-based PC running Microsoft Windows NT. Windows NT has network software built into the operating system. On Macintosh-based networks, I prefer to use the Miramar Systems MacLan Connect running under Windows NT or Windows 2000. It's easy to install and supports all of the file and print sharing you need.

Servers can play a variety of roles in a network environment. Among the possible uses for a server include the following:

✦ Store files shared in the environment.

✦ Contain the host network software.

✦ Link to output devices (printers, film recorders, imaging equipment).

✦ Link to media storage devices (Jaz drives, fixed and removable drives, tape drives, optical media).

✦ Link to multiple CD-ROM or DVD drives.

✦ Link to modems or Internet routers.

✦ Link to RIPs in imaging service centers.

The fundamentals of a network can be as basic as a single workstation and a single server. More complex networks can contain multiple servers, each performing special tasks. For example, you can have a single server behave as a print server and another server dedicated to file sharing. You can break up your office environment with dedicated servers for sharing departmental data. You can password protect server access, so that the office administration may access all servers and all files, whereas department personnel may only access individual servers or specific directories within a given server. Figure 1-4 shows an example of a local area network connecting client workstations, a server, and a printer.

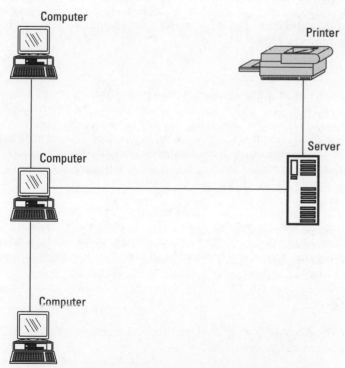

Figure 1-4: Local area networks are commonly connected by Ethernet cabling and may include client workstations, a server, and one or more printers or other output devices.

Servers are intended to be shared by people or devices. All computers connected to a network are known as *clients*, which have access to the network through the sharing software of the server(s). *Devices* are the noncomputer peripherals on the network either directly connected to the server or connected through the cabling mentioned earlier.

Wide area networks

Local area networks are contained in a single office and connected with network cables. A *wide area network* (WAN) enables network clients in one office location to connect to a server at another office location. (Figure 1-5 shows an example of a wide area network.) The location may be across town, across the country, or across the world. These systems are connected by dedicated telephone lines through which data is transmitted, like a telephone call. Remote terminals not connected to the network can't access the dedicated phone lines.

Multiple servers can be connected in each office or a single server in one office may connect to a single server or multiple servers in another office. Wide area networks allow for centralization. A good example would be a centralized accounting system. All accounting receivables and payables as well as all other accounting operations can be performed at the home office, whereas transactions are conducted online from the remote offices. As each transaction is performed, the data immediately updates the central accounting files.

Intranets

Intranets are a more recent addition to network topology. Intranets feature a server and modem or Internet router. These systems are usually password protected to prevent unauthorized access. Remote users dial into the modem or an Internet IP address and gain access to the intranet from other offices or from computers in the home. Depending on the number of users expected to access the system at any given time, an office may have a single modem to permit single-user access, or a router, which controls access traffic via several modems.

An Intranet can work the same way as a local area network. If you decide to access a drive on a server, output a file to a printer, or view the contents of a CD-ROM, you can do so via an Intranet. After you're in with the proper password, you can have all the same privileges as anyone physically connected to the network at the office.

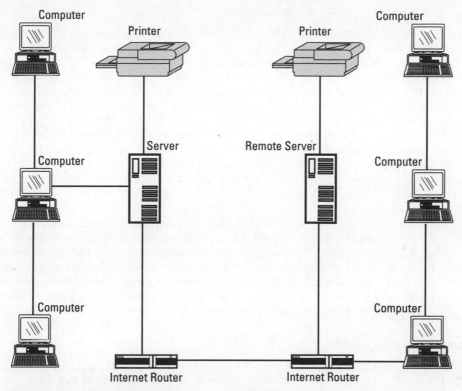

Figure 1-5: Wide area networks rely on dedicated phone lines or the Internet to connect remote workstations.

PDF as a standard

Stop for a moment and think about the mountains of software applications and different environments out there designed to help people exchange information. If you have just prepared a budget in Microsoft Excel and want to post the spreadsheet on a server either through direct or remote access, anyone wanting to see your spreadsheet will need Excel. The same holds true for other documents created in word processing software, illustration software, page layout software, and dedicated vertical market applications.

Imagine the software requirements for the personnel who approve budgets, display ads, corporate memos, building site improvements, legal documents, publications, and so on! The cost of licensing software to many different individuals in a company can quickly become prohibitive. As mentioned before, what is needed is a common denominator that enables all documents to be exchanged and viewed by all people involved in corporate decision making.

Cost-effective uses of Adobe Acrobat

PDF has many advantages in regard to developing a common viewing platform. For those who need to make notes and edit PDF files, the site licensing of Adobe Acrobat is integral. However, because all files can be reduced to PDF, only a single application site license is needed for the development of PDF documents. This aspect alone will make many office software purchases more cost effective. Compare a multi-user license of a single product to three, five, or ten different site licenses. Moreover, purchasing Adobe Acrobat may not be necessary for all personnel in an office. In some cases, the lower cost Business Tools version will accommodate many office environments. In other circumstances, if viewing a file prior to board and staff meetings or retrieval for later use is the main goal of certain employees, having them use the Acrobat Reader for such thereby increases cost effectiveness.

Caution   Adobe has specific licensing requirements that must be adhered to in regard to creating PDFs and distributing them in work environments. Certain restrictions do apply when producing PDFs under some conditions. At times it may be necessary for those viewing PDFs to purchase a site license or multiple copies of either the Business Tools edition or Adobe Acrobat. For further details, be certain to read the licensing agreement contained on your installer CD-ROM. If questions aren't answered suited to your purpose, contact Adobe support.

PDF as a standard

PDF has been adopted as a standard for many different environments. For example, the IRS posts all its tax forms on its Web site in PDF format so that you do not need to run down to the post office to find forms for tax preparation. (However, you may still want to have Acrobat Reader on hand well in advance of tax time. On April 14, 1999, over 190,000 people pounded the Adobe Web site to download Acrobat Reader.) In addition to the government's adoption of the PDF standard, Web integration is rapidly growing for display of PDF and file downloads where document integrity is important. Many software manufacturers are choosing PDF as the format to use for online guides, help files, and technical documents on CD-ROMs containing new software releases. Browse the Internet and you often find documents, employee application forms, and other content available for PDF downloads. In isolated markets, PDF has had wide acceptance.

If you look at the professional business applications software, almost every major software manufacturer has supported PDF exports and many accept importing PDF. The wide acceptance of the format by different companies throughout the world has additionally contributed to the development of PDF as a standard.

The struggle still goes on however. You can find new emerging technologies, such as the fast growing eBook market struggling to adopt a new standard. Microsoft continues to promote proprietary technologies and file formats, such as Microsoft Word, PowerPoint, and ASCII text that can be found as alternatives to PDF.

Adobe has not rested on its laurels though. With the new features included in Acrobat 5.0, we're coming closer to a universal standard. PDF acceptance is still a growing market and few manufacturers can claim the number of installed users as we find with the Acrobat Reader software. Today, we can accept the fact that PDF has found its way to all avenues of document distribution and we can claim PDF as a standard.

Adobe Acrobat in the publishing market

Associated Press, as well as many newspaper chains and affiliates around the world, have adopted PDF as a standard. If you submit a display ad to AP, you better know how to create a proper PDF file. PDF was a logical choice for publishing giants. Anyone who serves the digital imaging industry will tell you fonts and image links are major problems. With a bazillion fonts and images not delivered with lay-out documents, newspapers and magazines have longed for a standard. In these environments, PDF rules. With font and image embedding as well as file compression, one nightmare of the publishing world has almost vanished.

End users aren't the only factions of the communications industry who have embraced PDF. In 1997, AGFA introduced PDF as the standard in their advanced RIP and server architecture. AGFA has built a multimillion-dollar system around PDF and sees it as the new standard for imaging. Solutions for color separations, OPI comments, and impositions have all been added to PDF workflow. In addition to AGFA, other high-end device manufacturers, such as Scitex, Harlequinn, and Linotype-Hell have all provided integrated PDF workflow in their systems.

In the publishing industry, PDF is becoming a standard, and it won't be long before all graphic designers and advertising artists will be required to submit PDF-only files to commercial printers and imaging centers. Other industries also seem to be moving in the direction of a PDF standard. Government offices are embracing PDF as a format for distributing documents.

Perhaps the greatest accolade to PDF is the new operating system developed by Apple Computer. The Mac OS X operating system includes PDF support at the operating system level. All applications running under the new System X by Apple can produce PDFs on-the-fly for screen views, file exchanges, and printing. It's a new revolution in operating systems and all completely integrated with PDF.

If you're wondering whether to choose PDF as a standard in your office, be assured that many industries and individuals have already adopted it as their standard. Reaching critical mass may take more time, but the PDF model should continue to grow as a standard for many new additional markets.

PDF workflow solutions

To fully take advantage of Adobe Acrobat, one needs to think in terms of solutions to digital file problems. I don't know about you, but I always tend to spend a significant part of my day searching through mountains of paper on my desk, file cabinets, and around the office at key locations where more paper piles exist. If all the telemarketers and originators of junk mail could simply send out PDF files, I could easily find what I want when I decide to make a purchase. Unfortunately, I don't have much control over the junk mail, but I do where my own digital files are concerned.

Office solutions

Office administration is an easy target for PDF workflow solutions. Think about the management meeting where people are discussing an employee policy that was delivered via memo to staff. If you have a well-organized system in place, the memo is probably located in a logical spot in the personnel policies manual. If not, you begin searching. The same holds true for the display ad for that charity event last year, the memo from the president, the consumer satisfaction survey conducted two years ago, the last CAD drawing of a new widget, or almost any form of data or correspondence that originated on someone's computer.

Take Widget Company as an example. The company consists of four departments, administration, accounting, marketing, and production, as illustrated in Figure 1-6. All the departments use computers and specific software. In some cases, off-the-shelf software is used, and in other cases, vertical market applications are used. All the computers are networked to a single server.

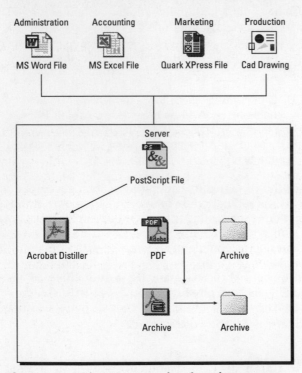

Figure 1-6: Widget Company has four departments networked to a single server. The departments print PostScript files to a server running Acrobat Distiller and Acrobat Catalog. Distiller creates PDF documents that are then added to the search index.

The administration usually posts memos on the employee bulletin board, but in some cases, a memo may be printed and delivered to all employee mailboxes. A particular memo needs to be retrieved by an employee in production. Because the memo appeared three months prior, it has vanished from the bulletin board and cannot be found among the mountains of paper on the employee's desk.

Fortunately for Widget Company, they have adopted a PDF workflow that requires all employees to archive memos, policies, and procedures to the server in PDF form. The files are printed in PostScript to a hot folder known in Acrobat Distiller terms as a *watched folder* on the server. The server keeps Acrobat Distiller operating in the background. After a PostScript file hits a watched folder, it is automatically distilled and placed in an out folder. The out folder files are monitored by the network administration and placed in the archive data folder. As soon as a file hits the archive data folder, Acrobat Catalog is used to update the search index and include the new PDF keywords. The production worker invokes a search and finds the memo in question. That employee may review the document online or print the PDF file. In either case, the amount of time to retrieve the information is a fraction of the time it takes to shuffle through those piles of paper.

Office environments can manage documents easily by creating similar workflows. Regardless of the size of your office, a PDF workflow enables you to store and retrieve information in an efficient and cost-effective way.

Publishing solutions

Publishing solutions can begin with office environments and be applied to high-end service centers, publication houses, and all forms of commercial media. In a publishing environment, the art department, design firm, or ad agency creates a document for advertising or a campaign. The material can be a display ad, brochure, catalog, or any communication piece that will eventually be printed on press. The final document will ultimately be created in a layout application, such as Adobe PageMaker, Adobe InDesign, QuarkXPress, or Adobe FrameMaker. After the document has been created and approved, the file can be printed to disk as a PostScript file, ready to be distilled in Acrobat Distiller for PDF file creation. Distiller affords you many choices for font embedding, compression, and sampling methods for graphic images. For prepress purposes, the sampling and compression will be different from requirements for Web, screen, and various composite color output. Because all the sampling can be controlled in Distiller, PDF files suitable for different purposes can be created from the same PostScript file.

In a traditional prepress workshop, the native files are delivered either to a RIP or OPI server. In a PDF workflow environment, application documents are printed to disk as PostScript files and distilled in Acrobat Distiller, where all OPI comments, job tickets, and prepress instructions are preserved.

Publishing has not been restricted to print anymore. Today, we retrieve much content from the Internet. Whether it be published PDF documents or HTML files, Acrobat affords us the opportunity to wade through the searches and helps us to find information quickly. By using the Web Capture feature in Acrobat, Web pages through entire Web sites can be captured and converted to PDF. After being converted, these files can be catalogued and searched for information. As the Web grows each week holding more content, our searches become more difficult. When information is needed from archived material, Acrobat shines.

Content is paramount to most of us. We live in a world where we are bombarded with mountains of information. Getting the right information in condensed form is important to those with limited time. With regard to digital content, we can search for information and have individualized documents assembled from many different sources and delivered electronically to us. Whether it be newspaper articles or citations from different publications, PDFs can be created and tailored for individual readers. As we move along the technology road, these avenues will soon become commonplace and the printed works will eventually move aside in favor of a new publishing market.

From print to Web

Document distribution is a major concern for many companies hosting Web sites. Product catalogs, consumer information, new product announcements, company information, and more all need distribution. Almost all these examples are typically produced for print or other viewing. Press releases go to the media, catalogs are distributed to the public, and announcements often occur at trade shows. Original designs for these items are performed in application layout programs. The requirements for the documents that ultimately wind up at a commercial print shop are much larger than would be efficiently used for distribution on the Internet. All those CMYK color files should be in RGB, and the image resolution needs to be reduced from 300 to 72 pixels per inch (ppi). The fonts need to be embedded in the files so that other users don't need the same font sets. In a PDF workflow environment, the repurposing of the file for Web content can be automated with Adobe Acrobat. The alternative to repurposing the file in Adobe Acrobat is to go back and manually recreate the files. As you can see, PDF workflows reduce costs and save time.

Summary

✦ Adobe Acrobat is a multi-faceted program, including Acrobat Reader, Acrobat 5.0, and Acrobat Distiller with many plug-ins offering unique and separate features.

✦ PDF, short for Portable Document Format, was developed by Adobe Systems and was designed to exchange documents between computers and across computer platforms while maintaining file integrity.

✦ Acrobat 5.0 has introduced many new features and boasts a major upgrade. Acrobat Catalog and access to Acrobat Distiller are now contained within Acrobat. Paper Capture has been eliminated from Adobe Acrobat and the Capture program is a stand-alone application requiring separate purchase.

✦ Document repurposing is a term used to describe the process of adapting documents created for one purpose to be suitable for other uses.

✦ PostScript is a page description language used for output to various types of imaging devices — from desktop laser printers to high-end professional devices — and it serves as a standard for the digital imaging industry.

✦ PDF workflows are automated processes used to create PDF documents and traffic jobs commonly found on networks and Intranets.

✦ Networks most often include at least one server and one or more clients. Networks enable the exchange, imaging, or transfer of digital data files.

✦ PDF has become a standard document format used in many different industries and is expected to grow as a universally accepted standard.

✦   ✦   ✦

Viewing and Searching PDF Files

The Acrobat Viewer Tools

If you are one of the many hundreds of thousands of people who have downloaded the Acrobat Reader software from the Adobe Web site (www.adobe.com), then moving around a PDF file may already be familiar to you. If you haven't yet used an Acrobat viewer, you'll want to carefully look over the pages in this chapter to learn how you can navigate, view, and search PDF documents. If you're a seasoned user, maybe you'll want to browse a bit to see tool changes and the new user interface introduced in Acrobat 5.0. Regardless of where you are in Acrobat skill, knowing the Acrobat viewer environment and navigating a document is a fundamental task, and the more you know, the faster you can move around in Acrobat viewers.

Acrobat Reader and Acrobat are both Acrobat viewers that have tools for file handling, navigation, viewing, and basic tools for creating selections. Both programs also offer plug-in support, although the Reader plug-ins are considerably fewer and much less capable than those found with Acrobat. Throughout this chapter, the focus is on working with the tools and plug-ins common to both programs. The emphasis is on using the Reader software, but occasionally I throw in some features specific to Acrobat. When Acrobat specific items are addressed in this chapter, I mention the feature being specific to Acrobat. In most cases, if you only have the Reader software you can use all the tools as they are covered here.

Like other Adobe applications, Reader and Acrobat offer the user different means to accomplish the same ends. Something as simple as navigating through an open file can be handled through several tools, commands, and keyboard modifiers that achieve the same result. As we move forward and examine the tools common to both viewers, keep in mind that the same task can be accomplished through several methods.

The viewer work area

Before I can begin to explain tools and viewing PDF files, you need to understand some terms used as identifiers in the Reader and Acrobat application window. Pulling off a Toolbar from the Command bar will be difficult for you if you don't know what the *Command bar* is. Therefore, I want to be certain that you understand the terms as I supply them in this chapter and throughout the remaining chapters. Figure 2-1 shows a document opened in Acrobat Reader.

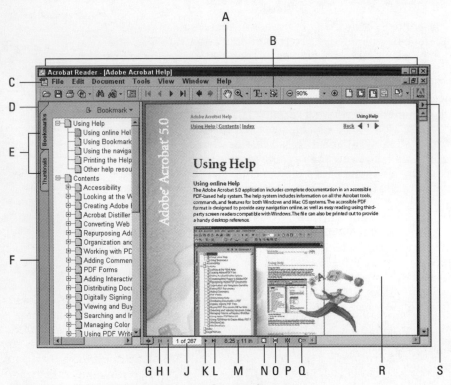

Figure 2-1: A PDF file opened in Acrobat Reader 5.0.

The work area includes the menus and Toolbars, the Navigation pane, and the Document pane. The status bar and pop-up menus add to the controls available for viewing and navigating PDF files. As shown in Figure 2-1, the individual controls include:

- ✦ **A**   Command bar
- ✦ **B**   Toolbar
- ✦ **C**   Menu bar
- ✦ **D**   Palette menu
- ✦ **E**   Tabs
- ✦ **F**   Navigation pane
- ✦ **G**   Navigation pane button
- ✦ **H**   First Page button
- ✦ **I**   Previous Page button
- ✦ **J**   Current Page
- ✦ **K**   Next Page button
- ✦ **L**   Last Page button
- ✦ **M**   Page size
- ✦ **N**   Single Page button
- ✦ **O**   Continuous Page button
- ✦ **P**   Continuous – Facing Page button
- ✦ **Q**   Document is encrypted
- ✦ **R**   Document pane
- ✦ **S**   Document pane menu

Tools

In Reader and Acrobat, the Toolbars (B) available to you in the top level Command bar (A) can be organized and relocated. You can move the tools around the Command bar, or you can tear them off and reposition groups of tools anywhere in the Document pane (R). For Microsoft Office users, you'll find this behavior similar to Office applications. Understandably, Acrobat has many more tools than you find with Reader. A brief rundown on the tools specific to Acrobat appears here, while details of tools not available in Reader are addressed in later chapters.

Acrobat Reader tools

Acrobat Reader's primary use is viewing PDFs. You can print from Acrobat Reader, and you can fill in Acrobat PDF Forms. However, any new data added to a PDF cannot be saved from the Reader software. No true editing tools are within Reader, so that Reader has many limitations for those who want to seek more from PDF usage. Reader's Command bar includes all of the tools identified in Figure 2-2.

All of the tools from the Reader Command bar are also available in Acrobat. For almost every tool displayed in Figure 2-2, the tool behavior is identical to using the same tool in Acrobat. As you shall see, Acrobat expands the Command bar and includes more tools unique to Acrobat features. Within the Command bar for both Reader and Acrobat, you find tools, buttons, and menus. Any of the items listed below with the term *tool* can be thought of as a tool. Other icons behave like tools but simply invoke an action similar to a menu command. Regardless of what you call them, the resources available in the Reader Command bar include:

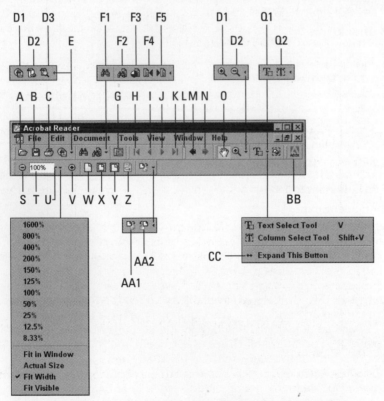

Figure 2-2: The Acrobat Reader tools displayed in the Reader Command bar.

✦ **A**   **Open tool.** Click the Open tool to open a PDF file.

✦ **B**   **Save a Copy tool.** In Reader, you can save a copy of the open PDF document. Any information supplied in the PDF is not saved in the copy. Only an exact duplicate of the original file is created.

✦ **C**   **Print tool.** Click this tool to print the PDF. Reader's Print dialog box opens where page ranges, the destination printer, and the like can be selected.

✦ **D**   **Adobe Web Hosted Services tools**. These tools access the Adobe Web site to perform different functions. When the toolbar is expanded, three tools appear, identified as D in Figure 2-1. (To expand the tools, see E in the following section.) The tools reading left to right include:

   • **D1**   **Create PDF.** This tool is used to open the Adobe Web site where the Create PDF Online is a Web hosted service by Adobe to create PDF documents for the Acrobat Reader user. You have a free trial period to test the service. After the free trial, you will be charged for creating PDFs with the Web hosted service. Files are uploaded to the Adobe Web site where the PDFs are created. After the files are converted, you then download the PDFs.

   • **D2**   **Paper Capture.** This tool launches the Adobe Web site and takes you to the Create Adobe PDF Online Web hosted service. Scanned image files are converted with OCR (Optical Character Recognition) software to convert image scans to text.

   • **D3**   **Search PDF.** This tool launches the Adobe Web site and takes you to the Search Adobe PDF Online demonstration service. A search can be invoked to find information on all the PDF files contained on the Adobe Web site and view a summary before downloading the PDF. It is intended for demonstration only, and the service is free to visitors.

✦ **E**   **Open tool group menu/collapse tool group.** The down pointing arrow opens a drop-down menu where other tools within the group can be selected. In addition, a menu option exists for expanding the tool group so that all tools are in view in the Toolbar. After a group has been expanded, a left pointing arrow is displayed adjacent to the tool group. Clicking this arrow collapses the tools and returns to the default display.

✦ **F**   **Search tools.** After the tool group for the search tools is expanded, five tools appear to assist in finding information in a PDF file. From left to right, they include:

   • **F1**   **Find tool.** The Find tool is limited to searching for keywords in an open PDF file.

   • **F2**   **Search tool.** The Search tool is used to search indexes created by Acrobat Catalog for information contained in multiple PDFs.

- **F3**   **Search Results tool.** The Search Results tool opens a dialog box where results of a search are displayed. A list of all the PDF files in hierarchical order according to frequency of occurrence is displayed in the list.

- **F4**   **Next Highlight tool.** Navigates to the next highlighted found word(s).

- **F5**   **Previous Highlight tool.** Navigates to the previous highlighted found word(s).

✦ **G**   **Show/Hide Navigation Pane tool** (F6). Opens the Navigation pane on the left side of the application window to display palette tabs for bookmarks and thumbnails. In Acrobat, additional palette tabs are located in the Navigation pane. (At times, for simplicity, I make reference to this tool as the Navigation Pane tool.)

✦ **H**   **First Page tool.** Takes the user to the first page in the PDF file.

✦ **I**   **Previous Page tool.** Takes the user to the previous page. When the first page is in view, neither the First Page tool nor the Previous Page tool is operative.

✦ **J**   **Next Page tool.** Takes the user to the next page in the PDF file.

✦ **K**   **Last Page tool.** Takes the user to the last page in the PDF file. When the last page is in view, neither the Last Page tool nor the Next Page tool is operative.

✦ **L**   **Toolbar Anchor.** The vertical lines for each tool group can be dragged to reorganize the tools in the Toolbar or tear them out of the Toolbar for relocation anywhere in the document window.

✦ **M**   **Go to Previous View tool.** This tool takes the user to the last view displayed in the document window. If the last view was a different document than the one displayed, it opens the previous document and displays the last view.

✦ **N**   **Go to Next View tool.** After the Previous tool has been used, the Next View tool becomes active. Clicking the tool moves you forward to the next view.

✦ **O**   **Hand tool** (H). Pressing H on the keyboard can activate the tool. The Hand tool is used to move the document around the Document pane.

✦ **P1**   **Zoom tool** (Z). Use to zoom in on the PDF page. Pressing Z on the keyboard accesses the tool.

✦ **P2**   **Zoom Out tool.** Use to zoom out to display a smaller view of the PDF page. Pressing Shift + Z can access the tool. If the Zoom Out tool is active, pressing Shift + Z toggles between the Zoom Out and Zoom In tool.

✦ **Q1** **Text Select tool** (V). Press the V key to access the tool. Use to select text in blocks or non-contiguous groups. Dragging across multiple columns selects text in all columns horizontally across the page.

✦ **Q2** **Column Select tool** (Shift + V). If the Text Select tool is active, Shift + V selects the Column Select tool. Shift + V toggles the tool selection back and forth. This tool enables user-defined selections by permitting you to draw a selection around the text to be selected.

✦ **R** **Graphics Select tool.** A marquee selection can be created anywhere in the PDF document around either text or graphic elements. When copied and pasted, the pasted data is a graphic element.

✦ **S** **Zoom Out.** Clicking the minus button (-) in the Toolbar zooms out of the document page. Zooms are in increments equal to the preset zoom levels displayed in item T below.

✦ **T** **Zoom Percent.** A field box is available for user supplied zoom levels. Enter a value between 8.33% and 1600%. After the new value is supplied in the field box, press Enter (Return on Macintosh) or the Enter key on the numeric keypad. The zoom takes effect only after you press one of these keys.

✦ **U** **Preset View menu.** Selecting the down pointing arrow opens a menu where preset views can be selected. Figure 2-2 displays the menu and preset views.

✦ **V** **Zoom In.** Clicking the plus (+) button zooms in at increments consistent with the preset views.

✦ **W** **Actual Size** (Control + 1/Command + 1). Displays the zoom view at 100 percent. Pressing the key modifiers provides the same display.

✦ **X** **Fit in Window** (Control + 0/Command + 0). Displays the document completely within the Document pane regardless of the size the application window is viewed.

✦ **Y** **Fit Width** (Control + 2/Command + 2). Displays the document page at the width of the page to the edges of the Document pane.

✦ **Z** **Reflow Page to Window.** Reflows the contents of a page to fit the width of the window.

✦ **AA1** **Rotate View Clockwise.** All pages in the PDF document are rotated 90 degrees clockwise.

✦ **AA2** **Rotate View Counter-clockwise.** All pages in the PDF document are rotated 90 degrees counterclockwise.

✦ **BB** **Visit Adobe on the World Wide Web**. Clicking this button launches a Web browser, creates an Internet connection, and navigates to the Adobe Web site where Adobe Acrobat product information is displayed. From the Web page, you can navigate to other pages containing upgrade information, tips, articles, and other related Acrobat information.

✦ **CC**   **Expand This Button.** A menu is displayed after any down pointing arrow is selected. The menu command Expand This Button expands a tool group so that all tools within the group appear in the Toolbar.

Acrobat tools

Acrobat is the editing application and as such provides many more tools than Acrobat Reader for modifying PDF documents. The viewing and search tools are the same as Reader's counterparts, as are a few of the miscellaneous tools used for opening files, saving, printing, and rotating. However, unlike Reader, Acrobat also includes the tools illustrated in Figure 2-3.

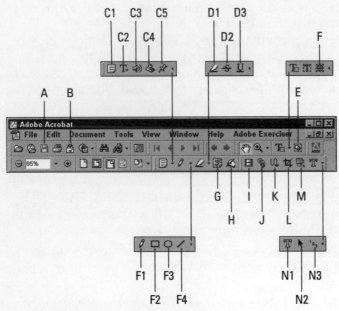

Figure 2-3: The Acrobat 5.0 tools displayed in the Acrobat Command bar.

✦ **A**   **Open Web Page tool.** Clicking the tool opens a dialog box where a URL can be supplied for converting Web pages to PDF files.

✦ **B**   **Save tool.** The tool exists for both Reader and Acrobat. In Acrobat, files changed can be saved while Reader is capable of only saving a copy of the PDF.

✦ **C**   **E-mail tool.** The open PDF file is automatically attached to an e-mail message. Clicking the tool launches your e-mail application and attaches the file.

✦ **D**   **Comment tools.** Formerly called Annotations tools, the first of three groups is now referred to as Comment tools. All of the expanded Toolbars include the menu option for expanding the Toolbar, such as those illustrated in Figure 2-1. Collapsing the Toolbars also works the same in Reader. The Comment tools include:

- **D1**   **Note tool** (S). Press S on the keyboard, and the Note tool becomes active. Notes appears in small windows with a title bar. The title bar color and author name contained within the title bar can be user defined.

- **D2**   **FreeText tool** (Shift + S). Press Shift + S on the keyboard, and the FreeText tool becomes active. All the remaining tools can be toggled with the Shift + S keyboard modifiers. Text comments can be created without note windows by using this tool.

- **D3**   **Sound Attachment tool** (Shift + S). Audio sounds can be used for comments and attached to the PDF.

- **D4**   **Stamp tool** (Shift + S). Stamp icons can be added to the PDF from a source of icons provided with the installation of Acrobat. User designed icons can be created and used as stamp icons. Comments can be added in note windows to the icon symbols.

- **D5**   **File Attachment tool** (Shift + S). An external file created in any application program can be attached to the PDF.

✦ **E**   **Text MarkUp tools.** Similar to what we may do in an analog world, these tools are designed to highlight and markup text. Among this group exist:

- **E1**   **Highlight tool** (U). Works much like a yellow marker. Highlight text and attach a note comment to the highlight.

- **E2**   **Strikeout tool** (Shift + U). Drag across text, and a strikeout line appears through the selected text. A note can be attached to the strikeout line.

- **E3**   **Underline tool** (Shift + U). The selected text appears underlined. A note attachment can be added to the underlined text.

✦ **F**   **Table/Formatted Text tool** (V) (Windows only). In addition to the Text Select tool and the Column Select tool common to both Reader and Acrobat, another tool exists in this group in Acrobat. The tool is only available to Acrobat running under Windows. Formatted text and columns can be selected, copied, and pasted in other applications while preserving tabs and indents.

✦ **G**   **Graphic Comment tools.** The third group among the Comment tools is the Graphic Comment tool group. All of the tools can have notes attached to the markup. Among these include:

- **G1**   **Pencil tool** (N). The Pencil tool draws free form lines.

- **G2**   **Square tool** (Shift + N). The Square tool draws squares and rectangles.

- **G3   Circle tool** (Shift + N). The Circle tool draws circles and ellipses.

- **G4   Line tool** (Shift + N). The Line tool draws straight lines.

✦ **H**   **Spell Check Form Fields and Comments.** Spell checking is limited to text created in Acrobat with the Comment tools and the Form tool.

✦ **I**   **Digital Signatures tool** (D). Digital signatures are added with the Digital Signature tool.

✦ **J**   **Movie tool** (M). Movie files can be imported in the PDF file with the Movie tool.

✦ **K**   **Link tool** (L). The Link tool enables hyperlinks created from a PDF file to link to other pages, other files, menu options, World Wide Web links, and more.

✦ **L**   **Article tool** (A). Article threads can be created in a PDF file to enable end users to follow contiguous reading of articles across multiple pages.

✦ **M**   **Crop tool** (C). PDF pages can be cropped individually or within page ranges.

✦ **N**   **Form tool** (F). The Form tool is used to create a form field where many different form actions and descriptions can be defined.

✦ **O**   **TouchUp tools.** For editing within Acrobat, the TouchUp tools offer some simple editing features. Among the editing tasks you can perform are:

- **O1   TouchUp Text tool** (T). Text can be edited in single horizontal lines only. Select the tool and click a line of text to make the text editable.

- **O2   TouchUp Object tool** (Shift + T). All objects can be selected as well as blocks of text. Click an object and you can move the object around the PDF page. Select an object and hold the Control key (Option key on a Mac) down and double-click. An external editor launches where edits can be made and dynamically update the PDF file.

- **O3   TouchUp Order tool** (Shift + T). If tagged PDFs are not reflowed in the order that you want, use the TouchUp Order tool to reflow text to change the order in which elements are reflowed on a document page.

Releasing tools from the Toolbar

Regardless of whether you use Reader or Acrobat, tools can be reorganized and broken away from the Command bar. You can customize your working environment by reorganizing the tools as you like. For example, if navigating through PDF documents is easier for you with the navigation tools positioned at the bottom of the page, you can tear off the tools from the Command bar and relocate the tool group anywhere you desire within the application window. To remove a tool group from the viewer Command bar, select the tool group anchor (the vertical line to the left of the tool group) and drag away from the Command bar. Figure 2-4 displays tool groups after they have been removed from the Command bar.

Dragging anywhere from within the tool group Toolbar can move a tool group. The problem you encounter is no room between the tool and the background display of the Toolbar. Other than the tool group anchor appearing in a tool group, not much real estate is available for selecting the Toolbar. Therefore, position the cursor over the anchor (vertical line), click and drag, and you'll easily be able to move a group.

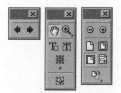

Figure 2-4: Viewing tools can be removed from the Command bar and dragged to any location within the application window.

After removed from the Command bar, the tool group behaves like a floating palette. The palette can be dragged around the document window by the Title bar. However you cannot *dock* the group back into the Command bar when dragging the Title bar. To dock the group back in the Command bar, you need to move it by dragging on the anchor.

Grouping tools

Tool groups can be combined together to form a single group. In essence, you can create your own toolbox in the application window. To combine several groups into a single floating palette, drag one group on top of another group and release the mouse button. Figure 2-5 shows several tool groups merged together within a single floating palette.

Figure 2-5: Multiple tool groups removed from the Command bar can be combined into a single group within the application window.

Context-sensitive menus

Acrobat makes extensive use of context-sensitive menus. In regard to tool groups and floating palettes, you quickly want to learn the ease of using context-sensitive menus. If you want to view your floating palette with the tools displayed horizontally instead of vertically, a context menu selection can easily accommodate you.

To open a context-sensitive menu, press the right mouse button (Control + Click on the Mac). In opening a context-sensitive menu specific to the viewing of a palette, you must click below the title bar (Windows) or top of palette (Macintosh). Clicking the title bar will not offer you the same viewing options. Figure 2-6 displays the two context-sensitive menus resulting from clicking below the title bar and on the title bar.

Figure 2-6: The context-sensitive menu displayed on the left side of the figure shows choices when opening a context menu after the cursor is placed below the title bar on a floating palette. The display at right shows the menu options (Windows only) after the context menu is opened from selecting the title bar. On the Macintosh, no context-sensitive menu opens after clicking the top of the palette.

Docking tools

Relocating a tool group back in the Command bar is referred to as *docking*. To dock a group back in the Command bar, select the anchor (vertical or horizontal line) appearing in the floating palette and drag the group on top of the Command bar. If you drag from the title bar in the floating palette, the group will not be docked in the Command bar.

If you want to relocate docked groups, you can move them around the Command bar and reorganize their order. You can also create several levels of Toolbars by placing one group below another. Doing so, however, expands the Command bar and results in less viewing area for your PDF documents.

Navigating and Viewing PDF Documents

Page navigation in an Acrobat viewer is handled by several means. You can scroll pages with tools and keystrokes, click hypertext links, and use dialog boxes to move through multiple documents and individual pages. Depending on how a PDF file is created and edited, you can also follow Web links and articles through different sections of a document. Acrobat viewers have many navigation controls. In this chapter, you first take a look at some of the navigation tools and later explore hypertext links and Web links.

Navigation tools

Navigation tools are located in the Acrobat viewer Command bar and in the viewer Status bar. As in many other applications, icons for these navigation tools resemble the buttons on VCRs, CD players, and tape recorders, which when pressed move you through the media (see Figure 2-7). For the most part, the icons will be familiar if you've ever dealt with video frames in applications on your computer or worked a VCR. A few subtle differences are in the Acrobat viewer navigation tools, however, so take a look at each of the navigation items.

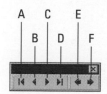

Figure 2-7: The Acrobat viewer Toolbar navigation tools assembled in a floating palette.

The tools for navigation in an Acrobat viewer include the following:

✦ **A**   **First Page:** In the current active document window, this tool returns you to the first page in the file.

✦ **B**   **Previous Page:** Used to move back one page at a time.

✦ **C**   **Next Page:** Used to scroll forward through pages one page at a time.

✦ **D**   **Last Page:** Moves you to the last page in the document.

✦ **E**   **Go to Previous View:** Returns you to the last view displayed on your screen. Whereas the four preceding tools are limited to navigation through a single open document, the Go to Previous View tool returns you to the previous view even if the last view was another file. Go to Previous View tool is only available from tools in the viewer Toolbar.

✦ **F**   **Go to Next View:** Behaves as the Go to Previous View tool except it moves in a forward direction. Use of the Go to Previous View and Go to Next View tools can be especially helpful when navigating links that open and close documents. The Next Page and Last Page tools confines you to the active document, whereas these last two tools retrace your navigation steps regardless of how many files you have viewed. You can find Go to Next View tool only from within the viewer Toolbar.

✦ **G**   **Page *n* of *n*:** The display only appears in the viewer Status bar shown previously in Figure 2-1. This tool is editable, so you can change the current page number by entering a new value. After you press the Enter key (Return on the Mac), the Acrobat viewer jumps to the page number you supplied in the field box.

If you select the Document menu, the same navigation choices are available as menu commands, as shown in Figure 2-8.

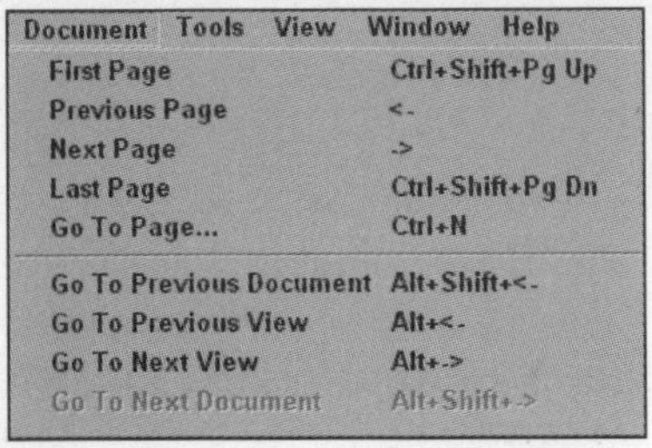

Document	Tools	View	Window	Help

First Page	Ctrl+Shift+Pg Up
Previous Page	<-
Next Page	->
Last Page	Ctrl+Shift+Pg Dn
Go To Page...	Ctrl+N
Go To Previous Document	Alt+Shift+<-
Go To Previous View	Alt+<-
Go To Next View	Alt+->
Go To Next Document	Alt+Shift+->

Figure 2-8: The Document menu in Acrobat Viewers offers menu commands similar to the tools and status bars.

Notice in Figure 2-8 the same six navigation items are listed among the menu commands. In addition, each of these navigation items has corresponding keyboard modifiers that produce the same action. The keystrokes for page navigation are listed in Table 2-1.

Table 2-1
Page Navigation Keyboard Modifiers

Navigation	Windows	Mac
First Page	Control + Shift + PgUp or Home or ALT + D, then F	Home
Previous Page	Control + PgUp or up arrow* or ALT + D, then R	PgUp or up arrow*
Next Page	Control + PgDn or down arrow* or ALT + D, then N	PgDn or down arrow*
Last Page	Control + Shift + PgDn or End or ALT + D, then L	End
Go To Page (number)	Control + N or ALT + D, then P	Command + N
Go Back to Document	ALT + Shift + left arrow or ALT + D, then K	Command + Shift + left arrow
Go Back	ALT + left arrow or ALT + D, then B	Command + left arrow

Navigation	Windows	Mac
Go Forward	ALT + right arrow or ALT + D, then O	Command + right arrow
Go Forward to Document	ALT + Shift + right arrow ALT + D, then W	Command + Shift + right arrow

* When the view is set to Fit in Window, the keystrokes move you to the next or previous page. When partial page views appear, the keystrokes scroll the page.

The Go to Page Control + N command (Command + N on the Mac) opens a dialog box and enables you to supply a value, just as you would in the Status bar field box. If you choose Document ➪ Go To Page, the same dialog box appears that enables you to enter the page number you want to visit. If you want to move to page 199 in a 299-page document, press Control + N (Command + N on the Mac) or choose Document ➪ Go To Page and enter 199 in the dialog box.

Context-sensitive menus used with tools

Context-sensitive menus provide another means of navigation. Just as I mentioned when we looked at tools from the viewer Command bar, you bring up context-sensitive menus by pressing the right mouse button (Control key and clicking the mouse button on a Mac). Context-sensitive menus are specific to a tool. If you have the Hand tool selected and you right-click (Control + click on the Mac), a pop-up menu appears that enables you to navigate through the PDF document (see Figure 2-9). Additionally, you can use this menu to change page views or invoke the Find command to perform a search. (I discuss using the Find command later in this chapter.)

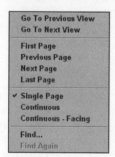

Figure 2-9: Context-sensitive menus appear by pressing the right mouse button (Windows) or Control + Click (Macintosh). Menu options change according to the tool used.

Scrolling

Anyone familiar with window environments is no stranger to scrolling. Fortunately, this is a standard for how scrollbars should behave among computer platforms and among various computer software manufacturers. Page scrolling works the same in an Acrobat viewer as it does in Microsoft Word (or any other Microsoft product for that matter), or any illustration, layout, or host of other applications that you may be familiar with. Drag the elevator bar up and down or left to right to move the document within the active window. Click between the elevator bar and the top or bottom of the scrolling column to jump a page segment. The arrow icons at the top, bottom, left, and right sides allow you to move in smaller segments in the respective directions.

Note   When dragging the elevator bar up or down in a multiple-page PDF file, a small pop-up tool tip will display a page number associated with the elevator bar position as well as the total number of pages in the document. The readout will be in the form of "*n* of *n* pages." The first number dynamically changes as the elevator bar is moved between pages.

Windows users find an Acrobat viewer opens in the same manner that they expect any other application on their computers to open. By default, the open PDF file occupies the entire Document pane. If you size the application window, the PDF pages will be sized within the Document pane. The application window by default appears on top of a background that prevents your view of the desktop or concurrent running applications. As is the case with many other Adobe applications, sizing down the application window displays the background desktop or any application windows running concurrently.

Macintosh users find the appearance of the Acrobat viewers similar to layout applications with pasteboards. You can size the pasteboard down and reveal other application windows or the Desktop.

Regardless of which platform you work with, some views in an Acrobat viewer maintain the same relative position within the application window as you size them. For example, if you choose View ⇨ Fit in Window and size the application window down, the page will be sized within the new window dimensions as a Fit in Window view. The same holds true for the Fit Width and Fit Visible views. As an application window is sized, you'll find the keystroke navigation and scrolling to work the same as it does in a full-size window.

Zooming

As you view an open document, you often have a need to zoom in and out of the page. Like many other applications, Acrobat viewers provide you with the ability to zoom by use of one of the Zoom tools. The Zoom tools permit views from 8.33 percent to 1,600 percent of a document page. The Zoom tools are selected from the viewer Zoom Toolbar contained within the application's Command bar.

Two tools are available for zooming. By default the Zoom In tool appears in the viewer Toolbar. If you select the down pointing arrow adjacent to the right of the tool, a drop-down menu will appear revealing the Zoom Out tool. Depending on the tool you use, click and you invoke a zoom action.

Zooms can also occur by selecting the Zoom Out or Zoom In icons in the viewer Toolbar (represented by a + and – symbol) or editing the zoom percentage field in the Command bar. Click the down pointing arrow, and the preset drop-down menu appears. In addition, the zoom percentage readout is editable. You can edit the zoom percentage by typing in a value within the acceptable range of 8.33 to 1,600 percent.

Like many commands and features in Acrobat, you may choose from several alternatives for viewing at different zoom magnifications. A menu command also provides zooming in and out of your PDF document. After you choose View ⇨ Zoom To, the Zoom To dialog box appears, enabling you to enter a zoom value or make any of the same choices available in the Command bar. You can press Control + M (Command + M on Macintosh) to open the dialog box and bypass the menu selection (see Figure 2-10).

In addition, the View menu contains choices for Zoom In and Zoom Out and these commands also have keyboard modifier equivalents. Press Control + (plus sign) [Command + (plus sign) on the Macintosh] for zoom in and Control - (minus sign) [Command - (minus sign) on the Macintosh] to zoom out. It may seem redundant and unnecessary, but Adobe has afforded you the opportunity to use any of the commands, keyboard modifiers, or menus to achieve the same results.

Figure 2-10: The Zoom To dialog box enables the user to specify magnification levels between 8.33 and 1,600 percent in 1 percent increments.

Page views

The page views for Actual Size, Fit in Window, and Fit Width are static views that you want to access frequently when navigating through a PDF document. Acrobat viewers provide several ways to change a page view. As with the Zoom tool, Acrobat viewers include three tools in the Command bar, as shown in Figure 2-11, for the selection of these views:

✦ **Actual Size:** Displays the PDF page at actual size (a 100 percent view).

✦ **Fit in Window:** Displays the page at maximum size to fit within the viewer Document pane. If the Acrobat viewer window is sized up or down, the Fit in Window view will conform to the size of the Document pane.

✦ **Fit Width:** The data on a PDF page is displayed horizontally without clipping. If the page is large and data only appears in the center of the page, the page will be zoomed to fit the data. The white space at the page edges is ignored.

⬜⬛⬛   **Figure 2-11:** Page view icons for Actual Size, Fit in Window, and Fit Width

Other choices for zoom magnification are also available from the View menu. The View menu enables you to zoom in and zoom out at preset zoom values, or you may use the modifier keys Control/Command + – (minus) or Control/Command + + (plus) for zooming out or in on the PDF window. These modifier keys remain consistent with many other Adobe applications.

As you become familiar with moving around PDF documents, you'll no doubt want to access different views in a much faster manner than moving the mouse cursor and clicking a page tool, selecting a menu item, or clicking the magnification button. Use of modifier keys will help you fly through the page views. For the Acrobat viewers, the first key modifiers you want to commit to memory are the page view and zoom modifiers that are listed in Table 2-2.

Table 2-2
Page View Keyboard Modifiers

View	*Windows*	*Mac*
Fit in Window	Control + 0 (zero) or ALT + V, then F	Command + 0 (zero)
Actual Size	Control + 1 or ALT + V, then A	Command + 1
Fit Width	Control + 2 or ALT + V, then W	Command + 2
Fit Visible	Control + 3 or ALT + V, then V	Command + 3
Full Screen Mode	Control + L or ALT + V, then U	Command + L
Zoom In	Control + + (plus) or ALT + V, then I	Command + + (plus)
Zoom Out	Control + – (minus) or ALT + V, then O	Command + – (minus)
Zoom To Size	Control + M or ALT + V, then M	Command + M
Show/Hide Navigation Pane	F5	F5
Show/Hide Menu Bar	F9 or ALT + W, then M	F9
Show/Hide Command bar	F8	F8

The Show/Hide Menu Bar in Table 2-2 toggles displays of the top level menu. If you inadvertently hide the menu bar, you'll need to remember how to regain it with the keyboard modifier. The equivalents for the keystrokes are found in the Window menu. However, if the menu bar is hidden, the only way to bring it back is by using the F9 keystroke.

> **Note**
>
> If you run an application concurrently with Acrobat that also uses the same "F" keys, you may want to reassign the F key in your other application. For example, if you use Corel Capture in Windows, don't use an F-key, such as (F9). Acrobat does not always supersede another application's modifier key when the programs run concurrently.

The views you choose conform to the monitor attached to your computer. If you have a 13-inch monitor, the Fit in Window view for a file will be displayed much smaller than it would be on a 19-inch monitor. Therefore, any PDF file saved with a fixed view of its actual size appears zoomed in on a small monitor. If you open several PDF files successively, you may want to change views immediately to find the information that you want. Using the keystrokes on your keyboard help you quickly establish the view you desire.

Full-screen views

Among other uses, Acrobat viewers can serve as a slide or presentation program. On-screen presentations typically have been the work of programs, such as Microsoft PowerPoint and Adobe Persuasion. (Persuasion, which was inherited by Adobe from Aldus Corporation years ago, was updated once by Adobe Systems and then discontinued. Adobe apparently saw no need to manufacture two programs that closely resemble each other.) Although Acrobat lacks many features of a dedicated presentation application, such as templates, an outliner, full-featured text editing, and page size defaults for film recorders, it can be effective in creating presentations as well as output to film recorders. As a screen presentation application, Acrobat can be used in Full Screen mode with automated slide navigation and displays that hide tools and menu bars.

To enter Full Screen mode to display a PDF document at full-screen size, choose View ➪ Full Screen or press Control + L (Command + L on a Mac). When Full Screen is chosen, the menu bar and the Acrobat Command bar is hidden. Acrobat's different viewing choices can be changed in the preferences dialog box. If you choose Edit ➪ Preferences ➪ Full Screen (or Control/Command + K), the Full Screen Preferences dialog box shown in Figure 2-12 opens, enabling you to control the behavior of the Full Screen view.

> **Note**
>
> The Preferences have been relocated in Acrobat 5.0 to the Edit menu. The dialog box for General Preferences now includes multiple choices from a list of preferences. To edit preferences within a given area, select the respective name in the left column to view the corresponding options appearing on the right side of the dialog box.

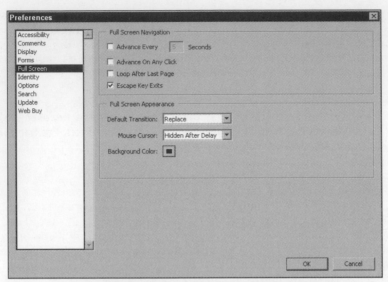

Figure 2-12: The Full Screen Preferences in Acrobat Reader are selected from the list on the left. The dialog box then enables you to edit the behavior of the Full Screen view from the options appearing to the right of the list.

The options in this dialog box include the following:

✦ **Advance Every *N* Seconds:** For auto advancing of PDF pages, you can enter a value between 1 and 32767 seconds. Realistically a range of 1 to 60 seconds would be used in most circumstances. After a value is entered, the Acrobat viewer advances to the next page after the specified delay time passes.

✦ **Advance On Any Click:** When enabled by clicking the checkbox, the viewer advances to the next page after the mouse button is clicked.

✦ **Loop After Last Page:** When the checkbox is disabled, the Acrobat viewer stops at the last page. If enabled, the first page appears upon advancing after the last page, and the viewer continues to loop through the document for another cycle.

✦ **Escape Key Exits:** You should plan on keeping this checkbox enabled at all times. Pressing the Esc key returns you to a page view and exit the Full Screen mode. If the checkbox is disabled, you need to remember other key equivalents to exit Full Screen view. In Windows, press Control + L. On the Macintosh, you can press Command + . (period) or Command + L.

✦ **Background Color:** You can choose from several preset color values or select the Custom option from the pop-up menu to gain access to your system color palette. When the system color palette is opened, you can choose any available color for the background. The background appears at the edges of the PDF page when in Full Screen view. Typically, the background color appears on the left and right sides of the PDF page.

✦ **Default Transition:** As you navigate through PDF pages in Full Screen view, the pages can be viewed with transition effects, such as dissolves, wipes, venetian blinds, and so on. A number of transition choices appear in the pop-up menu, which is shown in Figure 2-13. If you choose No Transition from the menu choices, the pages will advance without transition effects.

Blinds Horizontal
Blinds Vertical
Box In
Box Out
Dissolve
Glitter Down
Glitter Right
Glitter Right-Down
No Transition
Random Transition
✓ Replace
Split Horizontal In
Split Horizontal Out
Split Vertical In
Split Vertical Out
Wipe Down
Wipe Left
Wipe Right
Wipe Up

Figure 2-13: The Default Transition pop-up menu enables you to choose from many preset page transition effects that can be viewed in Full Screen mode.

✦ **Mouse Cursor:** The Mouse Cursor pop-up menu provides three choices for altering cursor behavior. You can choose Always Visible, which keeps the mouse cursor in view as the pages are advanced; Always Hidden, which hides the mouse cursor upon entering Full Screen view and keeps it hidden when pages are advanced; or Hidden After Delay, which hides the mouse cursor during the transition and reappears when you move the cursor across the screen.

Note   Full Screen view preferences are the same for both Acrobat viewers.

Full Screen mode is obviously designed for presentations and automated viewing of PDF files. You can display a PDF on an overhead projection screen to facilitate the delivery of a presentation. Or you can save PDF files from Acrobat complete with automatic delivery of the Full Screen mode — together with transitions and automatic advances. You can also save the PDF document to an external media cartridge or CD-ROM and distribute it to other users for viewing in Acrobat Reader.

What about viewing PDFs on the Web in Full Screen mode? This is a good question and one that certainly deserves an answer. In Chapter 11, I talk about the many ways to work with PDFs and viewing in Web browsers. One of the means of Web viewing PDFs is *Inline viewing*, which displays the Acrobat Command bar within the Web browser. If a PDF is saved to open in Full Screen Mode, the display on a Web page will hide the Command bar in Netscape Navigator just as it would in an Acrobat viewer. In Microsoft Internet Explorer, the Command bar is not hidden. Transitions and auto scrolling of pages are not available in either browser.

More page views

The default display in an Acrobat viewer is restricted to viewing one page at a time. You can fit the whole page in the Document pane, zoom in, or change to the Fit Width or Actual Size views, which continues to display a single page. In addition to single-page views, Acrobat viewers enable you to see your PDF pages in a continuous page display or side by side, much like you would see pages displayed in a layout program. To access these views, use the display choices in the status bar or choose the appropriate menu commands. The choices include the following:

✦ **Single Page:** The Single Page command can be chosen from the status bar or by choosing View ➪ Single Page. This command is most often the default view when you open a PDF file. The Single Page view has hard breaks and only displays the selected page in the viewer Document pane. If you scroll pages, the next page snaps to view within the Reader or Acrobat window (see Figure 2-14).

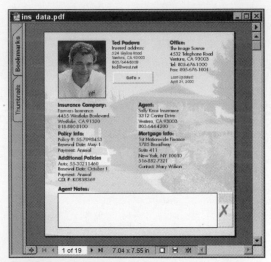

Figure 2-14: Single Page view is the default view when you open a PDF document. This display only shows a single page regardless of the zoom level.

✦ **Continuous:** Choose the Continuous command from the status bar or by choosing View ➪ Continuous. This display shows the current PDF page and any partial pages preceding or following the current page, with no hard breaks between pages (see Figure 2-15).

Figure 2-15: Continuous view displays the current PDF page and any partial pages before or after the page in view.

✦ **Continuous — Facing Pages:** The Continuous — Choose the Facing command from the status bar or by choosing View ➪ Continuous-Facing. The display shows continuous facing pages, similar to what you may see in programs, such as QuarkXPress, Adobe PageMaker, Microsoft Word, Claris Works, and so on (see Figure 2-16).

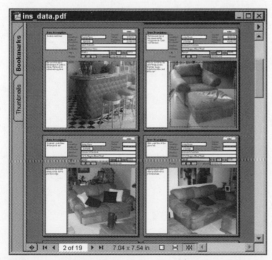

Figure 2-16: Continuous — Facing view displays pages facing each other like a book layout.

At times, the Continuous view can be helpful when searching through PDF files to find graphic images. However, you can find text in much easier ways as shall be demonstrated a little later in this chapter. The Continuous — Facing view provides a much larger display than does the Thumbnail view, even on smaller monitors. At times, this view can be quite helpful. Changing the page display only affects your monitor view. If you decide to print the PDF file, the printed pages will consist of single-page printouts, just as you see in the Single Page view.

Note   A PDF author can control the default view. You can choose to have end users open a PDF file in any one of the previous three viewing options, which I explain how to do in Chapter 7. Controlling this behavior is only available with Acrobat.

Multiple document viewing

If you open a PDF file and then open a second PDF, the second file hides the first document that you opened. If several more PDFs are opened, the last opened document will hide all the others. Fortunately, the Acrobat viewers have made it easy for you to choose a given document from a nest of open files. If you choose the Window menu, all open documents appear by name in a list at the bottom of the menu. The Acrobat viewer places a check mark beside the current active document. As you close files, they disappear from the menu.

The Window menu affords you some other viewing options, which include Cascade, Tile Vertically, and Tile Horizontally. Cascading windows display the open documents overlapping so that you can see the right edges of each of the open files (see Figure 2-17). They are offset from each other on your screen. You can easily click any of the document windows to make that file the active document. When you choose Window ➪ Tile ➪ Horizontally, the PDF files appear in individual windows stacked on top of each other, as shown in Figure 2-18. Window ➪ Tile ➪ Vertically displays the PDF files in individual windows placed side by side, as shown in Figure 2-19. If you have more than three documents open at one time, the display for Tile Horizontally and Tile Vertically will appear identical.

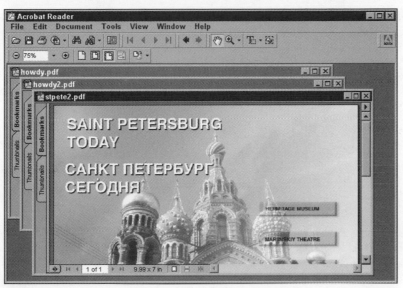

Figure 2-17: Three open documents in Cascade view

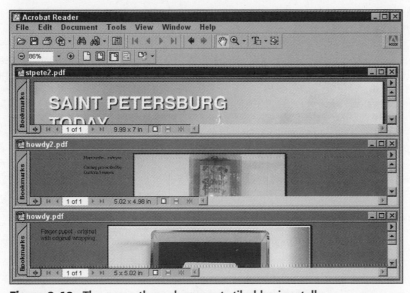

Figure 2-18: The same three documents tiled horizontally.

Figure 2-19: The three files tiled vertically.

The Navigation Pane

The first of many linking options is available when you open the *Navigation pane*. To open the Navigation pane, position the cursor over the Navigation Pane tool in the Command bar (refer to Figures 2-1 and 2-2 earlier in this chapter) or press F5. Depending on which viewer you use, different tabs are displayed in the Navigation pane.

Acrobat Reader defaults to the following two tabs:

✦ **Bookmarks:** In Reader, Bookmarks appear in the Navigation pane. The Bookmarks tab is the front view and any bookmarks created in the PDF file is displayed in a list aside the tab. A bookmark may take you to another page, another view, or invoke an action when chosen (see Figure 2-20). Bookmarks can only be created in Acrobat. (I cover creating and editing Bookmarks in Chapter 9). Reader does not support creating Bookmarks. If created in Acrobat however, they are visible in all Acrobat viewers.

✦ **Thumbnails:** To view thumbnails, click the Thumbnails tab on the far left of the Acrobat viewing screen. Thumbnails can be displayed as large images or small icons. Figure 2-21 illustrates the view when small thumbnails are displayed. For both bookmarks and thumbnails, choosing the small down arrow at the top of the pane can open a palette menu. From this palette menu, a choice for viewing small or large thumbnails is available.

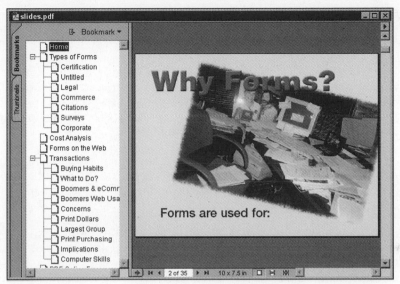

Figure 2-20: PDF document displayed with Bookmarks in Page view.

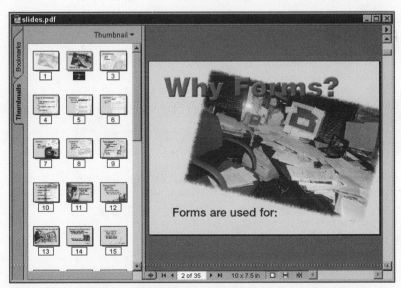

Figure 2-21: PDF document displayed with small Thumbnails.

Reader includes another palette that can be docked in the Navigation pane: the Articles floating palette, which appears when you choose Window ➪ Articles. Drag the Articles palette to the Navigation pane and it will be docked and assume the same appearance as the other two tabs.

✦ **Articles:** Article threads created in Acrobat can be displayed in Reader. An article thread is used to follow a logical sequence of text through PDF pages for easy navigation. After Articles are created, they are listed in the Articles palette.

Many times, a document will be viewed without the Navigation pane opened. When viewing a PDF without the Navigation pane in view, the document is said to be in a *Page Only* mode. In Acrobat, the default view of either having the Navigation pane open or in Page Only can be controlled when saving the file.

In Acrobat, the Navigation pane appears with four tabs. Bookmarks, Thumbnails, and Articles are available, such as those in Reader, and five additional tabs offer you editing capabilities not found in Reader. (The additional tabs and their editing in Acrobat are discussed in Chapters 8 through 10.)

Tear-away palettes were introduced in Acrobat 4.0. Acrobat 5.0 continues to offer you an ability to customize your working environment. You can pull out any of the tabs away from the Navigation pane. Each repositioned item becomes a floating palette. Both Acrobat and Reader afford you this opportunity. The advantage of removing a tab from the pane is the Navigation pane can be closed while the floating palette remains in view. If you want a single palette displayed, it can be relocated to any position in the application window you desire, thus providing a little more real estate for viewing the PDF contents. In Figure 2-22, all the tabs are removed from the Navigation pane in Reader. To move a palette away from the pane, you can click the tab and drag it away. Conversely, dragging a palette tab to the pane places the palette within the pane. Click any tab to bring the window forward.

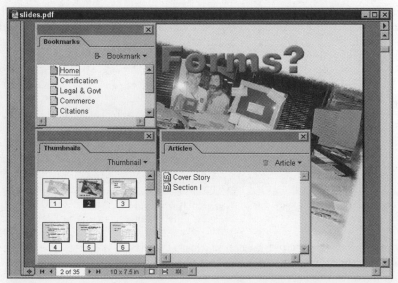

Figure 2-22: All of the tabs are removed from the Navigation pane and Window menu and relocated in the Reader window.

You can close the Navigation pane with the same actions used to open the pane. Click the Show/Hide Navigation Pane icon in the Toolbar or press F5 to close the pane.

Navigating PDF Documents

It seems like eons since Apple Fellow Bill Atkinson developed a great application called *HyperCard*. HyperCard introduced navigation buttons, referred to as *hypertext references* that you could place on a card in a document. These buttons provided dynamic navigation through a series of cards or files and also provided actions executable for all kinds of commands. HyperCard was a Mac product, and even though some attempts were made at reproducing the application for Windows in the early days, it never quite made it in the Windows camp.

I suppose it's easy for us armchair software critics to talk about the past and criticize companies for mistakes made in marketing, production, and technology. We could really bash IBM and Xerox for blowing it in the computer world. Imagine if Xerox PARC got all those wonderful new developments to market or IBM burned in a little more proprietary code in ROM when they manufactured the PC? We would have an IBM and Xerox world, and Microsoft would be a small development company catering to both. Even PostScript would be part of Xerox, and chances are, Chuck Geschke and John Warnock might still be working there.

One of the big mistakes Apple made was not advancing HyperCard to real-world publishing. Bill Atkinson, with great ingenuity, paved the way with MacPaint and subsequently, HyperCard. Unfortunately, Bill was a pixel guy and never got beyond those early developments to what publishers really needed. In the early HyperCard days, I remember begging Bill and the gang to just let me use a few PostScript fonts with the product. If Apple had continued with some foresight and pushed the development of HyperCard in the direction of publishing along with multimedia, Danny Goodman would be your author instead of me, and this book would be the *HyperCard Bible*. HyperCard could have been developed to do all the things Acrobat does, and it could have been the basis for all Web browsers.

I won't dwell anymore on the mistakes, for Apple did indeed bring the technology of hypertext to the masses. It began with HyperCard and subsequently became part of many other applications, particularly in the multimedia market. The introduction of hypertext was a vision by many to explore new methods for searching for knowledge. In a traditional learning world, we explore knowledge in a linear fashion. Reading a novel is linear. We start at the first page and read through each page sequentially. In a hypertext world, we click buttons to go wherever we desire — exploring the facts according to our interests. The Internet is probably the greatest manifestation of hypertext usage we have today. Imagine what it would be like if hypertext wasn't around, and we had to navigate the Net in a linear fashion. Let's face it — Zuma would never have gotten a single hit!

HyperText links

In an Acrobat viewer, hypertext references enable you to move around the PDF or many PDFs much like surfing the Net. You've probably become so accustomed to clicking buttons on your desktop computer that the navigation is almost common-place and needs little instruction. Invoking the action is nothing more than a click with the mouse. What the actions do in Acrobat is simply remarkable. To gain an understanding of how Acrobat has employed hyperlinks, the following sections describe all of the link actions as they can be created in Acrobat and executed in either viewer.

Buttons

Hypertext references, or *buttons,* are easily identified in a PDF document. As you move the mouse cursor around the document window, a hand icon with the forefinger pointing upward displays as the cursor is positioned over a button. You click, and Presto! The action associated with the link is executed. Links can be made for a number of different actions in a PDF file, some of which include the following:

✦ **Views:** A link can be made to any of the views discussed earlier in this chapter. You can click a button and zoom in or out of a page.

✦ **Pages:** Links can be made to another page in a PDF file or another PDF document.

✦ **Bookmarks:** A bookmark is a hypertext reference taking you to a page, a view, another PDF document, or invoking a page action. Bookmarks can assume all attributes of a link.

✦ **Destinations:** You can set destinations within a PDF document or between PDF documents and have them listed in a palette. Click a destination, and it takes you to the page associated with the link. Unlike bookmarks, destinations can be sorted in the Destinations palette by name or page numbers.

✦ **Thumbnails:** Thumbnails are also hypertext references and can navigate your view to the page represented by the thumbnail by double-clicking the thumbnail.

✦ **Comments:** Comments (formerly known as Annotations in earlier versions of Acrobat) are also links. When you create comments in a document, they are listed in the Comments palette in Acrobat. Double-clicking the comment name in the palette takes you to the page where the comment exists.

✦ **Execute a menu item:** A link can be made to execute almost all the commands on menus. Click a button and menu options for printing, saving, opening files, and more can be executed.

✦ **Import data:** A link can be made to import data in an Acrobat form. This type of link is limited to Acrobat, as you cannot import data into Acrobat Reader.

✦ **Play a movie:** Links can exist to movie files. After you click a movie frame, the movie plays.

✦ **Sounds:** A link can be made to a sound file. After executed, the sound plays.

✦ **Read an article:** A link can be made within an article. You can navigate through an article and follow the article easily through a PDF file. This type of link corresponds to a common feature in newsletters and magazines, where a story begins on page 1 and continues on page 4 and the reader is given a reference to the page on which the story continues. In Acrobat, you can click the end of the last column appearing in an article, and you immediately are taken to where the article continues on another page.

✦ **Reset a form:** Acrobat provides great opportunity with forms development, as discussed in Chapter 13. You can create buttons by using the Form tool to create links that assume the same attributes as those used with the Link tool.

✦ **Show and hide fields:** Once again in forms, you can use a link to display or hide a data field.

✦ **Submit a form:** Also with forms, you can use a button to submit form data to a Web server for posting on a Web site.

✦ **World Wide Web link:** A link can be made to a Uniform Resource Locator (URL), which opens your browser window and connects you to the specified URL.

✦ **JavaScript actions:** A link can invoke a JavaScript routine from within a form field, a link, a bookmark, or a page action.

Cross-document links

A button linking one PDF document to another is a known as a *cross-document link*. When you click a button that opens a second document, by default your original document closes and the second document opens. This feature was a great new addition when Acrobat 3 was introduced. In earlier versions of Acrobat, when additional documents opened, you had all these open documents to deal with. Whether a document closes when a link to another document is executed is determined in the Acrobat viewer preferences. When you choose Edit ⇨ Preferences ⇨ General ⇨ Options, the Options area of the Preferences displays a check mark at the bottom of the dialog box to toggle Open Cross-Doc Links in Same Window (see Figure 2-23).

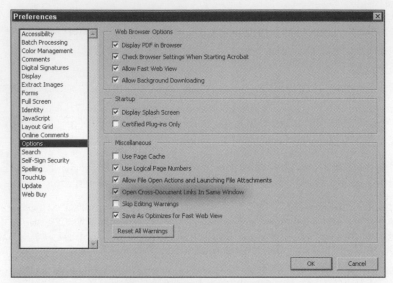

Figure 2-23: The Preferences dialog box enables you to control the behavior of cross-document linking.

In Figure 2-23, the Open Cross-Doc Links In Same Window item is enabled. When the item is enabled, every time you click a link that opens another PDF file, the document containing the link closes. Disabling this button keeps all documents open. You can explore the differences in viewing PDFs with cross-document links by following a few sequential steps:

STEPS: Cross-document Linking

1. **Choose Edit ⇨ Preferences ⇨ General in an Acrobat viewer.** Verify the Open Cross-Doc Links In Same Window option in the General Preferences ⇨ Options dialog box has a check mark beside it. If it does not, click the checkbox.

2. **Choose File ⇨ Open.** You can use any file of choice that you know has a cross-document link. If a PDF file with such a link is not available, use one of the files contained on the CD-ROM accompanying this book. In the Tutorial:eBooks folder, open the file titled *welcome.pdf*. This file has link buttons that open additional files contained in the same folder.

3. **Click a link.** If you use the welcome.pdf file, click one of the four links on the page. All links appear in blue text.

4. **Select Window on the menu bar to reveal its pull-down menu.** At the bottom of the menu is a list of all open files. Notice that only the file you currently have open appears.

5. **Choose File ⇨ Close.** To close an open document window you can also use Control + W (Command + W on Macintosh) or click the close button in the top right corner of the document window (top left corner on Macintosh).

6. **Choose Edit ⇨ Preferences ⇨ General.** Since you last visited the Options, the default should display the Options setting in the General Preferences dialog box. If it does not, select Options from the list on the left side of the dialog box.

7. **Disable the Open Cross-Doc Links In Same Window option.** Click the checkbox to disable the item. Notice that the check mark disappears.

8. **Choose File ⇨ Open.** Open the same document you used earlier.

9. **Click the link item.** Use the same link as used in Step 3 above.

10. **Choose Window on the menu bar to open the pull-down menu**. Notice the original file is open as well as the second file.

In this example the preference setting was immediately changed without the need for quitting the application. Many of the Acrobat viewer preferences can be changed without needing to quit the program and relaunch it for the new preferences to take effect.

The preference setting for cross-document links will be important to you when creating PDF files. By having files close upon the opening of additional files, the end user will become less confused about following a navigation sequence. Keep in mind the cross-document preference is only effective when using hypertext links. If you elect to choose File ⇨ Open and open another document while a PDF is in view, opening the second document will not close the original file.

Acrobat-only features include many other opportunities to create hyperlinks to PDF pages, files, and more. Among the palettes that you find only in Acrobat where some form of hyperlink can be created include the following:

Bookmark links

Earlier in this chapter, I showed you a list of bookmarks in the Navigation pane (refer back to Figure 2-20). Each of these bookmark items are also hypertext links. Bookmark links are similar to button links in that they are created as links and can assume the same attributes. Most often bookmarks will be navigational items for finding sections or headings in a given PDF file.

To select a bookmark, move the cursor to the bookmark in question and click. Notice that the bookmark text becomes underlined when the cursor is placed over that bookmark in the Navigation pane. Acrobat informs you which bookmark will be used by displaying a line under the text. The action associated with the bookmark is applied after the mouse button is clicked.

Bookmarks have options available via a context-sensitive menu appearing when you right-click the mouse button (Control + Click on the Mac) in the Navigation pane when the Bookmarks tab is selected. Similar options appear when you choose the down arrow at the top of the Bookmarks pane to open the palette menu. These options afford you viewing bookmarks by finding the current bookmark, showing the location of a bookmark, and hiding the Navigation pane after selecting the bookmark. An icon to the right of the arrow also finds the current bookmark (see Figure 2-24). If you are on a page in a document that has been bookmarked, clicking this icon highlights the associated bookmark.

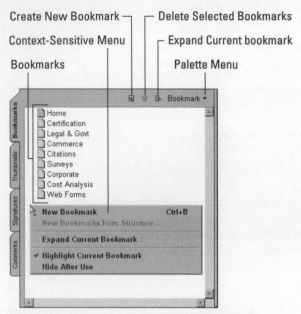

Figure 2-24: When a context-sensitive menu is opened in the Bookmark pane, the menu options appear the same as choices available from the palette menu. Be certain to open the Context menu without selecting a bookmark. If a bookmark is selected and a context menu opened, the menu options will appear different.

Note   I cover bookmarks in much more detail in Chapter 9. It is important to note now, however, that many of the floating palettes and panes in Acrobat viewers have palette menus that make additional options available to you. As you browse through the new version of Acrobat, look for the pull-down menus and other icon symbols that all offer you more options.

Thumbnails

Thumbnails can also be viewed in the left column of the open PDF file. Typically thumbnails, which are mini-representations of pages, enable you to quickly see page content. Thumbnails are also hypertext links. After you double-click a thumbnail, the page view changes to the page corresponding to that thumbnail. Unlike buttons and bookmarks, you don't need to create the link items. The Acrobat viewer automatically links all thumbnails to their respective pages.

Like bookmarks, thumbnails also use a palette menu to provide more options. In this case, your choices are to view large or small thumbnails. And, like bookmarks, many more options are available to you in Acrobat than in Reader. Acrobat offers many different capabilities for using Thumbnails when editing PDFs that I explain in Chapter 9.

Tip　　When PDF files are intended for display in Acrobat viewers Version 5.0 and greater, do not embed thumbnails when creating the PDF file with Acrobat Distiller. Thumbnails add approximately 3K per page to the PDF file. With Acrobat viewers 5.0 and greater, thumbnails are generated on-the-fly when the PDF is opened without the need for embedding.

Form Fields

For people designing Acrobat Forms, you'll appreciate the new addition to the Navigation pane for the Fields palette. Like the lists of bookmarks and annotations, this pane lists all the fields in the document. Form fields can be created as hyperlinks to PDF pages, files, and many other links. Also available only in Acrobat, I cover forms and fields in Chapter 13.

Destinations

At first it may seem that destinations have little difference from bookmarks. Though they are similar, the destinations feature enables you to specify any destination and give it a name. A destination name can then be identified within a document or paragraph where specified. The advantage over bookmarks comes with the capability to sort destinations by name or page number. In addition, you can do some spiffy programming to find destinations when creating form fields as I explain in Chapter 13.

World Wide Web links

If you're not a Web enthusiast, and you're sick and tired of the mere mention of Web issues with every application that you purchase, hold on—Acrobat's interaction with the Web is entirely different from that of other applications that try to appeal to all people. Personally, I think that it's ridiculous to put HTML hooks in layout and illustration programs, as there are so many better applications out there for Web publishing. But with Acrobat, we have another animal. Web links are the one solution that indeed serve you well by being all things for all purposes—well, at least for document viewing and exchanges.

Talking about any kind of link without talking about the World Wide Web is hard. After all, the Web *is* link mania. Therefore, it's no surprise that Acrobat has the additional capability to connect you to a Web site by the simple click of a button. When you encounter a Web link, Acrobat provides you some immediate feedback that a Web link will be executed before you click the mouse button. As the cursor is positioned over a Web link, a small *w* appears inside the hand icon. Additionally, the tool tip display will indicate the URL you are about to launch when you click the mouse button. After you click the mouse button on a Web link, Acrobat launches your Web browser and finds the URL associated with the link. Acrobat remains open in the background as the Web browser appears and the Web page in question is loaded. If you have limited memory, be certain to not select a Web link without sufficient memory to keep your Acrobat viewer and your Web browser open at the same time.

Tip   If you don't have sufficient memory to select a Web link and keep both the Browser and an Acrobat viewer open together, you can copy and paste the URL from Acrobat to your Web browser. When the URL is identified in text in the PDF window, select the Text Select tool in the Acrobat Toolbar in Acrobat or Reader. Drag across the text. Choose Edit ⇨ Copy and copy the text to the clipboard. Quit the Acrobat viewer and launch your Web browser. Paste the text into the URL Location field. When you use the Text Select tool in Acrobat 5.0, the Acrobat viewer assumes you want to edit text and not invoke a link action.

Using the Find Tool

Before getting into the specifics of the Find tool, look at the difference between find-ing information versus searching for information in a PDF file. When you execute a *find* operation in an Acrobat viewer, the operation is performed on an open docu-ment. You can look through the open file to find keywords you enter in a dialog box. A *search*, on the other hand, does not require a file to be open in the Acrobat viewer. Searches can be performed on multiple PDF files by invoking the Search Query.

The Find and Search tools appear in the Acrobat viewer. You need to think of these tasks as the responsibility of tools rather than commands. If you look at the Edit menu, you'll notice the Find and Search items listed in the menu. As tools, both are also included in the viewer Toolbar. Selecting the left pointing arrow expands the Search tools as illustrated in Figure 2-25.

A   C   E
   B   D

Figure 2-25: The Find tool and the Search tools viewed after the Toolbar is expanded include (A) Find; (B) Search; (C) Search Results; (D) Previous Highlight; and (E) Next Highlight.

The responsibility of the Find tool is to locate keywords in the active PDF docu-ment. If you use the Search tool to conduct a search and locate a keyword in an open file, a search index will need to have been created with Acrobat Catalog. Creating Search indexes are covered in Chapter 15.

Find tool dialog box

Executing a find can occur by either clicking the Find tool or by choosing Edit ⇨ Find or using Control + F (Command + F on a Mac). When you select either, the Find dialog box opens in which you can establish attributes of the word or words to be found. The Find dialog box enables you to select from the following options (see Figure 2-26):

✦ **Match Whole Word Only:** If the checkbox is disabled and you search for a word, such as *on*, then *on, one, online*, and so on will be found. If the checkbox is enabled, only the word *on* will be found.

✦ **Match Case:** If enabled, the found words will be case-sensitive. For example, searching for *WWW* returns only *WWW* and not *www*. If disabled, the Acrobat viewer disregards letter case and will find both *WWW* and *www*.

✦ **Find Backwards:** If your current view is page 28 and the checkbox is enabled, the Find tool will search backward from page 28. Disabling the checkbox causes Find to search from the current page forward. When the Acrobat viewer reaches the end of the document, you are prompted to either stop or continue searching the remaining pages.

✦ **Ignore Asian Character Width:** This option only applies to the Japanese language version of Acrobat. It enables the user to distinguish between full and half width Kana characters. If enabled, the found words will match exactly what is entered in the Find dialog box.

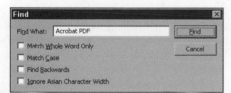

Figure 2-26: The Find dialog box offers four attribute settings to aid you in finding words in an open PDF document.

Find Again

After you find a word in a PDF file, the Acrobat viewer stops at the first found occurrence. The word is highlighted on the page where it was found. You can continue searching with the same attributes identified in the Find dialog box by selecting the Find Again command. Choosing Edit ⇨ Find Again or choosing the Find Again button in the Find dialog box accesses the Find Again command. Find Again only appears in the dialog box after a word has been found.

If you want to quickly navigate through found words, you'll want to use the modifier keys for Find and Find Again. The Control + F (Command + F on a Mac) keys open the Find dialog box. Pressing Control + G (Command + G on a Mac) invokes the Find Again command. If you attempt to find a word not found in the open PDF document, the Acrobat viewer will open a dialog box and inform you the word cannot be found.

Using Acrobat Search

Whereas the Find tool is limited to the open document and operates similarly to find commands found in word processors and layout applications, the Acrobat Search tool is a much different animal. To use Acrobat Search, you need to have the Search plug-in installed on your computer. If you only have Acrobat Reader installed, you won't be able to use Acrobat Search. When installing Reader, be certain to select the Search and Index option in the Installer dialog box. If you have Adobe Acrobat, Acrobat Search will be installed by default.

Acrobat Search enables you to search multiple PDF files with a host of attributes available enabling you to narrow your search more specifically than with the attributes of the Find tool. To use Acrobat Search, you need to have a search index available on your hard drive or a server, or on an external media cartridge or CD-ROM. The search index file must be identified in the Available Indexes dialog box. By default, when you install Adobe Acrobat or Reader + Search and Index, the Acrobat help index file is identified for you.

All about index files

Index files need to be loaded and active in order for Acrobat Search to find keywords. Indexes are created with Acrobat Catalog, which I cover in Chapter 15. However, there are some index files you can already use. You'll find an index file loaded when you install Adobe Acrobat, and you can find some index files on the CD-ROM accompanying this book. To use an index file, you need to add it to an Available Index list.

Adding index files

To add an index file to the search engine, you need to load the Acrobat Search application. After you open an Acrobat viewer, the viewer is loaded into memory. If you select the Search tool from the viewer Toolbar, you'll notice that your computer hesitates a moment. This hesitation is due to the Search application loading in additional memory. Depending on the speed of your computer and the available RAM, it may take a few moments for the Search application to load.

Index identification is accessed by choosing Edit ➪ Search ➪ Select Indexes (Control + Shift + X) or (Command + Shift + X on a Mac). When you choose this command, you experience the same delay as when choosing the Search tool in the Acrobat viewer Toolbar. Anything associated with the Search commands requires Acrobat Search to load into memory. If the Indexes command is chosen, the Index Selection window will open, as shown in Figure 2-27.

Figure 2-27: The Index Selection window opens after you choose Edit ➪ Search ➪ Select Indexes. From this window you can add or remove different index files.

The Index Selection dialog box provides options for loading and removing index files as well as activating an index. Notice in Figure 2-28 the index file listed in the Available Indexes list. For the index to be active and available to Acrobat Search, the checkbox for the index must be enabled. If you disable the checkbox of a particular index, Acrobat Search will not search through that index. If no indexes are enabled, Acrobat Search will return no results because it won't search any file.

You can add indexes to the Index Selection dialog box by clicking the Add button at the bottom of the window. After you click Add, a navigation dialog box opens and you can navigate your hard drive, CD-ROM, or server to find an index to be loaded. If an index is trashed or relocated on the drive, Acrobat Search won't be able to find the index. The index name will appear grayed out in the Index Selection dialog box, indicating Acrobat Search cannot locate the file. In this case, you need to delete the item and click the Add button. Navigate to the new location of the index file and add it to the Available Indexes list.

Dialog Boxes versus Windows

The terms *dialog box* and *window* have different meanings. A dialog box in most applications offers you an ability to exercise more options associated with a given function. Behavior of dialog boxes often restricts the user from gaining access to the document page while the dialog box is open. Windows, on the other hand, imply the user can work in one window, and then switch to another window without closing either. In working with Acrobat viewers, dialog boxes often enable you to perform a task in the document while the dialog box remains open. All references throughout this book shall mention both dialog boxes and what may appear like a window as dialog boxes. It may frequently look like a window, but for simplicity, I call them dialog boxes.

Removing indexes

If an index is to be eliminated from searches, you can deactivate the index by disabling its checkbox. In a later Acrobat session, you can go back and enable indexes listed in the Index Selection dialog box. You should always use this method rather than deleting an index if you intend to use it again. At times, however, you may want to delete an index file. If the index will no longer be used, or you relocate your index to another drive or server, you may want to completely remove the old index. If this is the case, select the index file to be deleted and click the Remove button. Indexes may be enabled or disabled after you select Remove. In either case, the index file is removed without warning.

If you inadvertently delete an index, the index can always be reloaded by selecting the Add button. Placing index files in a directory where you can easily access them is a good idea. To avoid confusion, try to keep indexes in a common directory. Acrobat doesn't care where the index file is located on your hard drive or server — it just needs to know where the file is located. If you move the index file to a different directory, be certain to reestablish the connection in the Index Selection dialog box.

Index information

When a number of index files are installed on a computer or server, the names for the files may not be descriptive enough to determine which you want to search. If more detailed information is desired, the information provided by the Index Information dialog box may help identify the index needed for a given search.

Index information may be particularly helpful in office environments where several people in different departments create PDFs and indexes are all placed on a common server. What may be intuitive to the author of an index file in terms of index name may not be as intuitive to other users. Index information offers the capability for adding more descriptive information that can be understood by many users.

Fortunately, you can explore more descriptive information about an index file by clicking the Info button in the Index Selection dialog box. When the Info button is clicked, the Index Information dialog box opens, displaying information about the index file as shown in Figure 2-29. Some of the information displayed requires user entry at the time the index is built. Acrobat Catalog automatically creates other information in the dialog box when the index is built. The Index Information dialog box provides a description of the following:

✦ **Title:** The user supplies title information at the time the index is created. Titles usually consist of several words describing the index contents. Titles can be searched, as detailed later in this chapter, so the title keywords should reflect the index content.

✦ **Description:** Description can be a few words or several sentences containing information about the index created. (In Figure 2-28, the description was supplied in Acrobat Catalog when the index was created.)

✦ **Path:** The directory path where the index file is located on a drive or server is displayed with the last item appearing as the index filename.

✦ **Last Built:** If the index file is updated, the date of the last build is supplied here. If no updates have occurred, the date will be the same as the created date.

✦ **Created:** This date reflects the time and date the index file was originally created, and is therefore a fixed date.

✦ **Documents:** Indexes are created from one or more PDF documents. The total number of files from which the index file was created appears here.

✦ **Status:** If the index file has been identified and added to the list in the Index Selection dialog box, it will be Available. Unavailable indexes appear grayed out in the list and described as Unavailable.

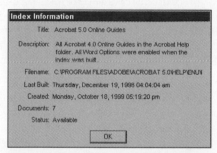

Figure 2-28: The Index Information dialog box appears when you select the Info button in the Index Selection dialog box.

If you launch an Acrobat viewer and open the Index Selection dialog box without an active index, invoking a search will open a warning dialog box indicating no documents were found that match the search query. Acrobat does not inform you that it doesn't have an active index to search. If you attempt a search and get this warning dialog box, be certain to click the Indexes button in the Adobe Acrobat Search dialog box to verify the index or indexes you intend to search have been enabled.

Using the Acrobat Search dialog box

As soon as you have an index file loaded and enabled, you can go about the business of creating a search. Searches are handled in Acrobat viewers by either accessing the Search tool through the viewer Toolbar or by choosing Edit ➪ Search ➪ Query (Control + Shift + F) or (Command + Shift + F on a Mac). Notice that the Search command in the Edit menu has a submenu with several choices for conducting searches, as shown in Figure 2-29. The lower half of the submenu will be grayed out until you perform at least one search.

Query...	Ctrl+Shift+F
Select Indexes...	Ctrl+Shift+X
Results...	Ctrl+Shift+G
Word Assistant...	Ctrl+Shift+W
Previous Document	Ctrl+Shift+[
Previous	Ctrl+[
Next	Ctrl+]
Next Document	Ctrl+Shift+]

Figure 2-29: The Search commands are listed in a submenu available by choosing Edit ⇨ Search.

When you first start using Acrobat Search, it may be a bit confusing as to which submenu command to select to perform the search. The easiest way to go is to choose the Search tool in the viewer Toolbar. After you click the tool, the Query dialog box appears after the Search application is loaded. As you start using the submenu commands, keep in mind that *Query* is synonymous with *Search*.

When you either choose the Acrobat Search tool from the viewer Toolbar or choose Edit ⇨ Search ⇨ Query, the same dialog box opens. Like the dialog box discussed with the Index Selection, this dialog box affords you the opportunity to select menu commands and tools while it is open. When you open the Adobe Acrobat Search dialog box, you'll immediately notice the many different data fields available for user input. As you can see in Figure 2-30, the number of search fields are much greater than those provided with the Find command.

Figure 2-30: The Adobe Acrobat Search dialog box provides opportunity to search on many different data fields.

 Note

The default view of the Adobe Acrobat Search dialog box does not display all options as viewed in Figure 2-30. What is displayed in the dialog box is determined in the Search Preferences. Choose Edit ⇨ Preferences ⇨ General. In the Preferences dialog box, select Search from the list appearing on the left side of the dialog box. Under the Query item, you see four checkboxes. When all checkboxes are enabled, the view in the Adobe Acrobat Search dialog box appears as shown in Figure 2-30.

This dialog box looks like a maze and thus deserves some detailed explanation. All those fields are probably intimidating if this is your first pass through searching PDF indexes. Beginning at the top of the Adobe Acrobat Search dialog box, the items include:

✦ **Find Results Containing Text:** The box below Find Results Containing Text is for user entry of keywords for what to search. The words you enter here are not limited to single words, but can also include operators or Boolean expressions that I discuss a little later in this chapter.

✦ **With Document Info:** The four items listed below the With Document Info heading apply to information supplied when the PDF document was created. When you create a PDF file, you have the opportunity to supply this information. When you view PDF files created by someone else, you can observe the document information supplied by the PDF author. To view document information, choose File ⇨ Document Properties ⇨ Summary. The Document Summary dialog box opens and displays document information, including information specific to the four fields listed in the Query dialog box, as shown in Figure 2-31. In Acrobat Reader, no changes are permitted, and you can't proceed in Reader until the dialog box is closed. In Acrobat, some of the fields in the Document Summary dialog box can be edited, thus behaving more like a window than a dialog box.

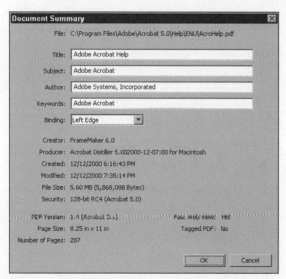

Figure 2-31: The Document Summary dialog box displays document information, including fields for document title, subject, author, and keyword. The field contents can be searched with Acrobat Search with any viewer and edited only in Acrobat.

- **Title:** The content for this field is supplied by the user who, at the time the PDF is created, identifies a title for the PDF.

- **Subject:** The Subject field, which is user supplied, generally contains keywords to identify a common subject. For example, if you had a number of PDF files for the human resources department in a company, you might indicate in the Subject field keywords associated with human resources.

- **Author:** Typically, the author of the PDF supplies this field at the time the document is created. The contents of this field may be the name of a person or a department. If a company changes personnel frequently, a better choice would be to have a department or facility name appear in the Author field.

- **Keywords:** You can add any number of words for the keyword field up to a maximum of 255 characters. Keywords are usually additional descriptors, not included in the Title or Subject fields, which relate to the PDF contents and make it easy for users to search for words they expect to find in a given document. If a PDF file for an employee handbook is created, for example, the subject field might include "employee handbook." The keywords may include "benefits," "salary," "vacation," "grievances," and so on.

✦ **With Date Info:** These fields show the dates for file creation and last modification for a PDF, as was mentioned earlier in the discussion on index document information. You can search on the date fields and narrow the date by using the after and before fields. Entering date data in any of the date fields is easy. You can supply a month, day, or year in a single field, and Acrobat supplies the remaining fields. For example, if you enter 4 in the first available field, Acrobat will enter the current day and year from your system clock (date fields follow a mm/dd/yy syntax). Enter a year, and Acrobat will enter the current month and day, and so on. All the date fields are Y2K compliant, so don't worry about any legacy files. Just make certain that your operating system is also Y2K compliant. The up and down arrows in the date field boxes increase or decrease the respective selection. Select the year and click the down arrow, and the year decreases. The same holds true for the day and month fields.

  - **Creation after:** If a date is supplied in this field, Acrobat Search finds all PDFs in the index file created after that date.

  - **Creation before:** To the right of the Creation after date field, the word *before* appears beside a date field. If you enter a date field in the Creation after field box and another date in the before field box, Acrobat Search will find all PDFs created within the specified date range.

  - **Modification after:** This field works similar to the Creation after date field. Enter a value, and Acrobat Search finds PDFs with modification dates after the field entry. If you have several similar files, all created on the same date, and you modified one of those documents a few months ago, searching on this field helps you narrow down your search.

- **Modification before:** If you enter a date in this field, which appears to the right of the Modification after field, Acrobat Search looks for all PDFs modified before your specified date.

✦ **Options:** The five option items listed in the Options box frame also help you narrow down a search. Clicking the checkboxes beside each respective option enables these items.

- **Word Stemming:** If you want to search for all words stemming from a given word, enable this option. Words, such as *header* and *heading*, stem from the word *head*. If you type in *head* in the Find Results Containing Text box and select the Word Stemming option, all PDFs containing the search criteria from the word stem will be listed.

- **Sounds Like:** This option is a crude attempt at finding words that sound like other words. This option is really not dependent on a rhyming scheme; for example, Acrobat Search can find words, such as *fix*, *fx*, *fox*, and so on for the search entry *fog*. Words, such as *dog*, *log*, and *hog* won't be found.

- **Thesaurus:** When the Thesaurus option is used, Acrobat Search can find synonyms for the searched word. If you search for *lower* with Thesaurus enabled, the returned results include words, such as *down*, *lower*, *below*, *beneath*, and so on.

- **Match Case:** Case-sensitive searches are the same with Acrobat Search as with the Find command. When Match Case is enabled, only identical case-matched words are returned in the results.

- **Proximity:** Proximity is a powerful tool when performing searches. If you want to search for two independent words that may appear together in a given context — for example, *Acrobat* and *PostScript* — the proximity option can find the two words if they appear within three pages of each other in a PDF.

✦ **Searching:** At the bottom of the Query dialog box, a display appears that provides feedback on the index file currently being searched. If a single index file is loaded, the name of the index file appears in the dialog box. If more than one index file is loaded, the readout in the dialog box appears as "Searching x out of y indexes" — where x equals the number of indexes searched and y is equal to the total number of index files loaded.

After you establish the search criteria, click the Search button. Acrobat Search lists all the occurrences of files that fit the criteria specified in the Query dialog box. This list appears in another dialog box — the Search Results dialog box.

Understanding search results

The Search Results dialog box lists all the PDFs where at least one occurrence of the searched word(s) appears. The order displayed in the Search Results dialog box is according to a relative reference scheme based on the percentage of occurrences of the found word(s) to the number of words in the document. After you click Search in the Query dialog box, the Search Results dialog box appears (see Figure 2-32).

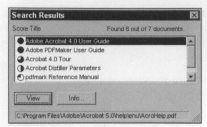

Figure 2-32: The Search Results dialog box is displayed after searching for *PDF*. The documents are listed in a relative ranking order.

Notice in Figure 2-32 the first two items appear with a solid circle to the left side of the title of the PDF file. The name is not the filename, but the name the PDF author supplied for the Title field in the Document Properties dialog box when the PDF was created or modified.

The next two names in the Search Results dialog box appear next to circles with a ³/₄ fill. In this example, the first two items have a higher order of relative ranking than the last four items. This is to say the percentage of occurrences of the word *PDF* (which was the searched word) to the total number of words in the first set of files is higher than the last four files. Keep in mind the relative ranking is based on percentages; for example, a file with 10 found occurrences out of 100 words will have a higher order of ranking that 1,000 found occurrences out of 100,000 words. The former is 10 percent, whereas the latter is 1 percent.

Relative ranking is displayed with five different icons. Ranking goes from the highest order (circle with a solid fill) to the lowest order (circle without a fill), as shown in Figure 2-33.

Figure 2-33: Beginning from left to right, the solid circle indicates the highest order of ranking, whereas an empty circle indicates the lowest ranking.

Acrobat Search enables you to use Boolean expressions and operators for conditional statements — for example, *word1* OR *word2*, where OR is a Boolean expression. When using such conditions, the relative ranking of these expressions is always higher than ordinary searches based on a single word.

When you conduct a search with the Proximity option, the closer the two words are, the higher the ranking. For example, if the two words in question appear on the same page in a PDF file, that file would have a higher order of ranking than one in which the words appear three pages apart from each other.

Viewing search results

When the Search Results dialog box displays the list of PDFs in which your word or words have been found, you can open the PDF or display its document information. Sometimes it may be handy to view document information, especially if the title, subject, author, or keywords fields can help you narrow your search. To display the document information, click the Info button in the Search Results dialog box and the Document Info dialog box appears, as shown in Figure 2-34.

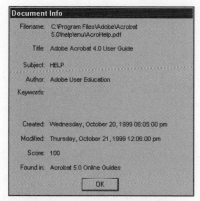

Figure 2-34: Document Info is displayed when you select the Info button in the Search Results dialog box.

If you want to open a PDF file from the Search Results dialog box, select the file from the list and either click the View button or double-click the title. In this example, I searched for the word *PDF*. From the list of titles, I opened the Acrobat 5.0 Online Guide. After the file is opened, all occurrences of the found word are highlighted throughout the document.

After you've opened a PDF file from the Search Results list; if you want to continue finding more occurrences of a given word in that open PDF file, you can select the Next Highlight tool in the Acrobat Toolbar, choose the Edit ⇨ Search ⇨ Next menu command, or use Control +] (Command +] on Macintosh). Any one of these three methods take you to the next highlight in the open document. In addition, you can also use the Find command.

Search preferences

Earlier, when you got your first look at the Adobe Acrobat Search dialog box (refer back to Figure 2-31), all the provisions for search criteria were displayed. The appearance of this dialog box can be customized according to preference settings you enable in the Acrobat Search Preferences dialog box. Even if you have a large monitor, the Search dialog can become overbearing and you may need to move it around your monitor screen in order to examine the results of a search. The customization of the Search dialog box as well as the dialog box behavior is handled by choosing Edit ➪ Preferences ➪ General. After the General Preferences dialog box appears, choose Search from the left column (see Figure 2-35).

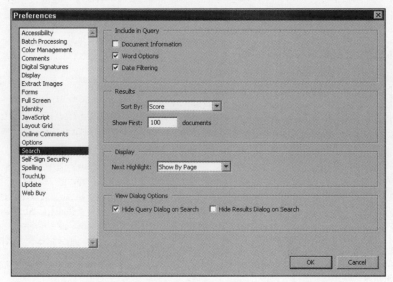

Figure 2-35: The Search Preferences appear as an option in the General Preferences dialog box.

The Search Preferences options include the following:

✦ **Include in Query:** The items described in the Include in Query area enable you to customize the Adobe Acrobat Search dialog box after you choose the Acrobat Search tool or choose Edit ➪ Search ➪ Query.

✦ **Document Information:** All fields with Title, Subject, Author, and Keywords appear in the Adobe Acrobat Search dialog box. When disabled, these fields are hidden.

✦ **Word Options:** At the bottom of the Adobe Acrobat Search dialog box Word Options include Word Stemming, Sounds Like, Thesaurus, Match Case, and Proximity. The checkboxes are visible for these selections when this item is enabled in the preferences.

✦ **Date Filtering:** All the date fields including the date created and date modified fields are visible in the Adobe Acrobat Search dialog box.

• **Sort By:** This pull-down menu has a number of choices that you select to specify the order for the display of the PDFs in the Search Results dialog box. The pull-down menu items include those listed here:

• **Author:** The sort results appear as an alphabetical list according to the first word in the Author field.

• **Created:** The PDF files are listed according to creation date, going from the most recent date at the top of the list to the least current date.

• **Creator:** *Creator* refers to the program that created the original document before the PDF was generated. For example, a program such as Adobe Illustrator, that can export files to PDF format, would be identified as the Creator. The sort results in a list of PDF files in alphabetical order according to Creator.

• **Keywords:** The sort results appear as an alphabetical list according to the first word in the Keywords field.

• **Modified:** The PDF files are listed according to the date they were last modified, going from the most recent date of modification to the least current.

• **Producer:** The Producer is the application or driver that created the PDF file. Producers can be applications, such as Acrobat PDFWriter or Acrobat Distiller, along with the version number and platform used. The sort results in a list of PDF files in alphabetical order according to the Producer; however, you won't see the Producer identified in the Search Results window. Producer information is available in the Document Info dialog box after you open the PDF in an Acrobat viewer.

• **Score:** The default is Score, which lists the occurrences in the relative ranking for the total number of found words.

• **Subject:** The same applies for subject as it does for title. The order of display is in alphabetical order according to the subject specified in the document information. Like subjects are grouped together.

• **Title:** The same relative ranking is indicated by the respective icon adjacent to titles listed in the Search Results dialog box, only the files are listed in alphabetical order by title rather than in ranking order. Essentially, those files with the same titles are nested together.

✦ **Display:** In this category is the **Next highlight** pull-down menu, which provides the three choices, which are listed as follows:

• **Show By Page:** The searched word(s) are displayed on the first page of the viewed file. If only one occurrence of a found word exists, the single word is highlighted. If several words are found with the first occurrence on the same page, all words are highlighted. All subsequent pages with the same word are likewise highlighted.

- **Show By Word:** The first found word is highlighted when a file from the Search Results list is viewed. Any other occurrences on the same page are not highlighted.

- **No Highlighting:** No words are highlighted if a file is viewed from the Search Results window.

✦ **View Dialog Options**. Two checkboxes offer how to handle the dialog box after the search has been invoked. They include:

- **Hide Query Dialog on Search:** The Query dialog box can remain open thus permitting additional searches. If you want the Query dialog box to close after invoking a search, enable this checkbox.

- **Hide Results Dialog on Search:** When enabled, the Search Results dialog box disappears after you view one of the listed documents. If you choose File ➪ Open and open a PDF file, the Search Results dialog box remains open. Only after you view one of the listed items by clicking the View button or double-clicking a listed file does the dialog box close.

Automount Servers (Mac only): Despite the fact that Adobe Acrobat is one of the best cross-platform applications, it holds some advantages specifically for Mac users and others specifically for Windows users, depending on the task to be performed. As you view all that Acrobat has to offer, I'll make some distinctions when one system offers an advantage over another. These distinctions are not based on bias, but empirically there are advantages of using one system over another for various duties. With regard to the automounting of servers, this advantage goes to the Mac. There is no opportunity to automount servers on Windows, as you can see back in Figure 2-36. When Automount Servers is enabled, all indexes identified on a server or servers on your network will be mounted by Acrobat Search. This can be handy if you forget to mount a server and need to search an index located on a remote server. If a server is not mounted, Acrobat Search will display the index file grayed out in the Index Selection dialog box. In a true PDF workflow environment, you may have one or more servers containing PDF documents for your company.

As you can see, the preference settings for Acrobat Search help you customize and narrow your searches. If you elect to eliminate from view the many options available in the Adobe Acrobat Search dialog box, you can use keystrokes in the Find Results Containing Text box. You can eliminate all options from view and still enter keystrokes to create searches with all the options. I explain these keystroke equivalents in the following sections, where I show you how to use operators and Boolean expressions with Acrobat Search to make searches truly powerful.

Operators

Operators are conditions that require matching the field type to the found word or field contents. If a word is contained in the document title, the condition is <word *contained* in title>. If the word searched is not contained in the title, the condition does not exist and no results are returned. If the word is contained in the title, the condition does exist, and you will find those documents meeting the condition listed in the Search Results dialog box.

You can use a number of operators with Acrobat Search to aid you in finding precisely the information you want. By using operators, you begin to tap the power of Acrobat Search. Operators and Boolean expressions, as you see a little later in this chapter, make Acrobat Search a powerful search engine. Look over Table 2-3 and mark this page. You'll want to use these operators regularly for plowing through your stack of PDF files.

Table 2-3
Using Operators with Adobe Acrobat Search

Operator	Meaning
= (equal sign)	**Equals:** The word or words match exactly the field for text, numerics, and date. The field type appears first, followed by the equal sign (=) and then the word(s). *Example:* Title = Adobe Acrobat
~ (tilde)	**Contains:** The word or words are contained in the field. *Example:* Subject ~ Help
!=	**Does not equal**: The word or words are not contained in the field. *Example:* Subject != Help
!~	**Does not contain:** The word or words are not contained in the field. *Example:* Title !~ Acrobat
<	**Less than:** The value is less than the field contents. This operator applies to date and numeric fields only. *Example:* Created < 9/24/01
<=	**Less than or equal to:** The value is less than or equal to the field contents. This operator applies to date and numeric fields only. *Example:* Created <= 9/25/01
>	**Greater than:** The value is greater than the field contents. This operator applies to date and numeric fields only. *Example:* Modified > 10/30/01
>=	**Greater than or equal to:** The value is greater than or equal to the field contents. This operator applies to date and numeric fields only. *Example:* Modified >= 10/25/01
*	**Wildcard character:** Matches zero, one, or more characters. *Example:* w*d returns *wood, wild, world.*
?	**Wildcard character:** Matches only a single character. *Example:* t*n returns words like *ton, tan, ten.* Woods like *took, town,* and *then* will not be returned.

When you use operators, they will be entered in the Query dialog box in the Find Results Containing Text box. If you want to find all PDFs from the Acrobat online files that are designed as help guides, you might search the Subject field for the word *help*. If you have all the options disabled and your search dialog box is minimized, you can supply the attributes of your search without the aid of the options in view. In this example, you would enter *Subject ~ help*.

The returned list displays all the PDFs where occurrences of the word exist. Each of the fields you hide in the Search Preferences dialog box has a keyword associated with its field name. You can minimize the Adobe Acrobat Search dialog box and use the keywords if you want. The Adobe Acrobat Search dialog box size will be reduced to provide more viewing space on your monitor. The syntax for supplying the keywords in the Find Results Containing box include the following:

Title	Title field
Subject	Subject field
Author	Author field
Keywords	Keywords field
Created	Document Creation date
Modified	Document Modified date

Entering any of the preceding items by using keywords enables you to search the respective field contents. The syntax must be precise. If an error or warning dialog box is opened when you invoke the search, be certain to carefully review the syntax. In addition to field and date items, you can also use identifiers to specify which of the five options you want to use to modify your search. The five option items and their corresponding identifiers are listed in Table 2-4.

Table 2-4
Search Options Identifiers

Identifier	*Meaning*
/st	**Word Stemming:** All found words stem from the searched word.
	Example: go /st returns words like *going, gone.*
/so	**Sounds Like:** All found words sound like the searched word.
	Example: fog /so returns words like *fix, fx, fog* (remember, this option doesn't necessarily return words that rhyme with the searched word).
/th	**Thesaurus:** All found words are synonyms to the searched word.
	Example: publish /th returns words like *author, write, issue.*

Identifier	Meaning
/ca	**Match Case:** All found words exactly match the case of the searched word.
	Example: www /ca returns *www*, not *WWW*.
/pr	**Proximity:** Proximity is used with Boolean expressions and requires two words to be in close proximity of each other.
	Example: WWW AND PDF /pr returns files containing both the words *WWW* and *PDF* within close proximity.

More power in Acrobat Search is available when you use operators with Boolean expressions. Boolean expressions offer more opportunities to create searches with conditional requirements.

Boolean expressions

The Boolean operators AND, OR, and NOT allow you to specify conditions existing between words or fields for narrowing your search. For example, if you want to search the Title field for the word *Adobe* and you want all PDFs except those created by Adobe Developer Relations, you can enter (Title ~ Adobe) AND (Author !~ Developer). The search seeks all files with the word *Adobe* contained in the Title field and all files where the word *Developer* is not contained in the Author field (see Figure 2-36).

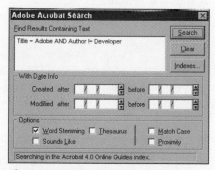

Figure 2-36: Search criteria are entered in the Adobe Acrobat Search dialog box using a Boolean expression.

In Figure 2-36, notice the syntax for the statement to create the search. You can also use parentheses, such as: (Title ~ Adobe) AND (Author != Developer). These characters are optional. The search can easily be accomplished without the parentheses, and the same results will occur. They sometimes are used to help easily view the search criteria and can be helpful if you accidentally create a syntax error. If you find using parenthetical statements simplifies the task, by all means use them.

Acrobat viewer immediately reports any syntax error you may create in the Search dialog box after you select the Search button.

You should try to get some practice creating different searches. The more you practice, the more effective you become in using them. To help you get started, you can follow along with this example for creating a search with Boolean expressions:

STEPS: Using Acrobat Search with Operators and Boolean Expressions

1. **Launch an Acrobat viewer.** You can use either Acrobat Reader or Acrobat. (With Reader, be certain the Search and Index are installed).

2. **Select the Indexes button in the Adobe Acrobat Search dialog box.** You should verify the Acrobat 5.0 online guides or help files are available in the Available Indexes list and the index is active (an X should be placed in the checkbox).

3. **Click OK.** The Index Selection dialog box disappears.

4. **Choose Edit ⇨ Preferences ⇨ General and then select the Search item from the list.** In the Search Preferences dialog box, disable all the options (Document Information, Word Options, and Date Filtering should be disabled). Disabling the options reduces the size of the Adobe Acrobat Search dialog box so that you can see more of the document behind the dialog box. As the dialog box is reduced and hides all the options, you need to use operators for searching in place of the options not currently in view.

5. **Click OK.** The Search Preferences dialog box disappears.

6. **Click the Search tool in the Acrobat Command bar or choose Edit ⇨ Search ⇨ Query.**

7. **Enter the search criteria in the Find Results Containing Text box in the Adobe Acrobat Search dialog box.** Enter Title ~ Adobe AND Title !~ Help AND Created >= 10/1/98. This search asks for all files that show the word *Adobe* in the Title field, exclude the word *Help* in the Title field, and were created on or after October 1, 1997.

8. **Click the Search button.** Acrobat Search returns the Search Results window.

9. **Click the View button.** The PDF file is opened in the Acrobat viewer and the first page of the document is displayed.

You'll notice multiple expressions can be used when creating your searches. If you find a dialog box opens indicating Acrobat Search cannot understand your search criteria, you have made an error with the syntax. Be certain you carefully review the entry in the Find Results Containing Text box. The Boolean expressions are not case-sensitive. I prefer to use capital letters to easily distinguish the expression from the other text. What is important though is being certain that you have a space between the operators and the text (in other words, Title ~ Adobe and not Title~Adobe).

Try using several other searches. You have some wonderful opportunities to learn about Acrobat's search capabilities with the Adobe online help guides. Try to become familiar with these. The online help guides will aid you in finding information that can help you learn more about Adobe Acrobat.

Word Assistant

The last menu item in the Search submenu not yet discussed is Word Assistant. After you choose Edit ⇨ Search ⇨ Word Assistant, the Word Assistant dialog box appears, as shown in Figure 2-37. Assistant enables you to search through your selected index files to find matches to the word you enter in the field box. A button on the right, labeled Indexes, opens the Index Selection dialog box. You must have an index active for Assistant to return results as a list appearing below the pop-up menu.

Figure 2-37: The Word Assistant dialog box has a field box for a word entry and a pop-up menu. The option selected is the Thesaurus assistant.

The pop-up menu contains three items: Stemming, Sounds Like, and Thesaurus. You enter a word in the field box and select one of the three choices from the pop-up menu. The dialog box is used to aid you in finding words matching one of the three conditions available in the pop-up menu. When you search with Assistant, a list of matches appears in the dialog box list. Double-click a word in the list, and it is copied to the field box. After the word is in the field box, the word can be copied to the clipboard by choosing Edit ⇨ Copy and subsequently is pasted in the Query dialog box.

Summary

✦ Acrobat viewer tools are located in the viewer Command bar. Tool groups can be undocked and arranged in the application window. They can be nested together to form custom palettes according to user needs.

✦ Viewing PDF documents is handled with a number of tools, menu commands, and keyboard modifiers. When you view PDF files in the Full Screen mode, you can create an online presentation and automate page navigation.

✦ The navigation tools enable page navigation through an open document and between documents. You can return to previously viewed pages by going forward and back to retrace your steps.

✦ Hypertext links enable navigation to views, other documents, and a variety of menu commands. Dynamic linking enables you to view documents in a nonlinear manner. Bookmarks, thumbnails, and destinations add additional navigation opportunities.

✦ Links can be made to the World Wide Web whereby a button can open a Web browser and connect you to a specific URL.

✦ The Find tool works with open documents to create searches within a PDF file. The Find Again command finds additional occurrences of a searched word or words.

✦ Acrobat Search can search on index files created with Acrobat Catalog. Search indexes must be loaded in the Index Selection dialog box. The searches can be complex, including various options, keywords, operators, and Boolean expressions. Word Assistant provides options for searching word criteria related to word stems or similarity in sound, and for thesaurus lookups.

✦   ✦   ✦

Using Acrobat Viewers

Understanding the Reader Environment

Because Adobe Acrobat has so many components with distinct features, it might be a good idea to tackle them one at a time, starting with Acrobat Reader. If you purchased Acrobat, all of what you do here in the Reader application will be the same in Acrobat 5.0. Acrobat has more bells and whistles than Reader does, and I discuss these starting in Chapter 4. If you haven't purchased Acrobat, then this chapter will introduce you to all of what Acrobat Reader has to offer. If you don't currently have Reader 5.0, you can install it from the CD-ROM accompanying this book.

Like any other windowing application, Acrobat Reader makes use of tools (see Chapter 2 for information about the Reader tools), menu commands, and a set of preferences that help you customize the application environment. With Reader, the environment controls are handled by menu commands that include Document Properties and Preferences. These menu commands help users customize the application for personal working conditions. This chapter first takes a look at the Document Properties and Document Security commands and then moves on to the Preferences command.

Document Properties

The Document Properties commands give you access to information regarding the contents and attributes of a PDF file. You can quickly access document information to learn some particulars of a PDF file, which may help you when searching for a file that fits a certain profile. Among the document properties are two menu commands that provide information about PDF files: Document Summary and Document Security.

Document Summary

When a PDF file is created from many applications, either by using an export to PDF from an application or distilling a PostScript file with the Acrobat Distiller, you may have an opportunity to add document properties. In some cases the ability to provide the document properties may not be available at the time the PDF is created. PDF creators do supply some information and other information needs to be user supplied. When information cannot be supplied at the time the PDF is created, the PDF can be edited in Acrobat where the additional information can be added to the Document Summary.

Chapter 2 introduced a brief look at document information when searches were performed on the Title, Author, Subject, and Keywords fields. The field data for these items is user definable. You can elect to supply the information at the time the PDF is created with some PDF producers, or you can add and modify information when the PDF is viewed in Acrobat. Document Properties can neither be altered nor saved from the Reader application.

Note   The File menu contains a menu command for Save a Copy from within Acrobat Reader. When a copy is saved, it's an exact duplicate of the original. No edits can be made with Reader and any information that can be supplied, such as filling in form data fields, won't be saved after choosing File ➪ Save a Copy.

What you can do in Reader is view document information. Of course, it must be supplied by the author of the PDF or by an amendment with Acrobat, but once the information is there, you can see it. To access the document properties, choose File ➪ Document Properties ➪ Summary. The Document Summary dialog box opens and displays the document information for the open file, as shown in Figure 3-1.

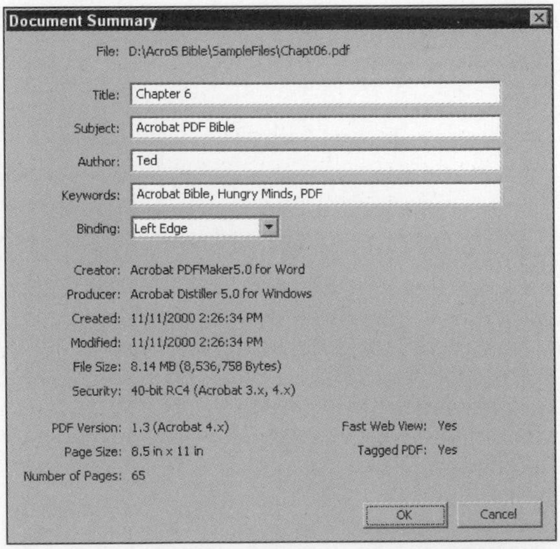

Document Summary	✕
File:	D:\Acro5 Bible\SampleFiles\Chapt06.pdf
Title:	Chapter 6
Subject:	Acrobat PDF Bible
Author:	Ted
Keywords:	Acrobat Bible, Hungry Minds, PDF
Binding:	Left Edge

Creator:	Acrobat PDFMaker 5.0 for Word
Producer:	Acrobat Distiller 5.0 for Windows
Created:	11/11/2000 2:26:34 PM
Modified:	11/11/2000 2:26:34 PM
File Size:	8.14 MB (8,536,758 Bytes)
Security:	40-bit RC4 (Acrobat 3.x, 4.x)

PDF Version:	1.3 (Acrobat 4.x)	Fast Web View:	Yes
Page Size:	8.5 in x 11 in	Tagged PDF:	Yes
Number of Pages:	65		

[OK]   [Cancel]

Figure 3-1: The PDF author supplies the Document Properties for a PDF file, which cannot be edited with the Acrobat Reader software.

When you examine the Document Summary dialog box, several data field boxes appear; however, these are fixed and not editable. The contents within the field boxes can be edited and changed in Acrobat only. The PDF creator supplies the remaining information, which cannot be edited.

If PDF files are created without the user supplying information in the appropriate data fields, the PDF creator leaves all fields empty except the Title field. The Title field defaults to the filename of the authoring application.

If you open the Document Summary dialog box in Acrobat, you can change the data for the Title, Subject, Author, and Keyword fields. Although Acrobat offers this capability, you'll most often want to supply data at the time the PDF is created. In a true PDF Workflow environment, proper identification of the files will prevent you from spending much time appending information to the Document Summary dialog box. Because these fields can be searched, you want to ensure all fields are completed with identifying information.

The information below the field boxes is supplied at the time the PDF is created. Information about the Creator, Producer, when Created, and Modified are all explained in Chapter 2. In addition to these, the Document Summary dialog box offers information on the following:

✦ **File Size:** The size of the PDF file is reported. Modifications and updates that may occur in Acrobat reflect changes in file size if data is added or deleted from the file.

✦ **Security:** If security has been applied to the PDF, it will be reported with the level of encryption. None indicates the file is not encrypted. 40-bit RCA (Acrobat 4.0) signifies the security applied is 40-bit encryption. 128-bit RCA (Acrobat 5.0) indicates 128-bit encryption has been applied.

✦ **PDF Version:** PDF versions are reported as 1.2 for Acrobat 3.0 compatibility, 1.3 for Acrobat 4.0 compatibility, and 1.4 for Acrobat 5.0 compatibility.

✦ **Page Size:** The physical dimensions of the first PDF page in the file is reported. If the first page is smaller or larger than other pages, only the first page dimensions are supplied among the properties.

✦ **Number of pages:** The total number of pages in the PDF is reported.

✦ **Fast Web View:** Acrobat 5.0 can optimize PDFs to reduce file sizes with greater file reductions than earlier versions of the PDF format. In reducing file sizes, Acrobat can remove repeated elements, such as background text, line art, and images and replace them with pointers where the first occurrence of the background elements appear. The file is also restructured to produce page-at-a-time downloading from Web servers. If the Fast Web View optimization was used in producing the PDF, it is reported here.

✦ **Tagged PDF:** File tagging for accessibility, which I explain in Chapter 8, can be added to PDFs. If the PDF has been created with file tags, it will be so indicated in the properties dialog box.

Fonts

The next item you can choose to view for document properties is the font data. Reader permits you to examine the fonts contained in the PDF file by choosing File ➪ Document Properties ➪ Fonts. After you choose the command, the Document Fonts dialog box shown in Figure 3-2 appears.

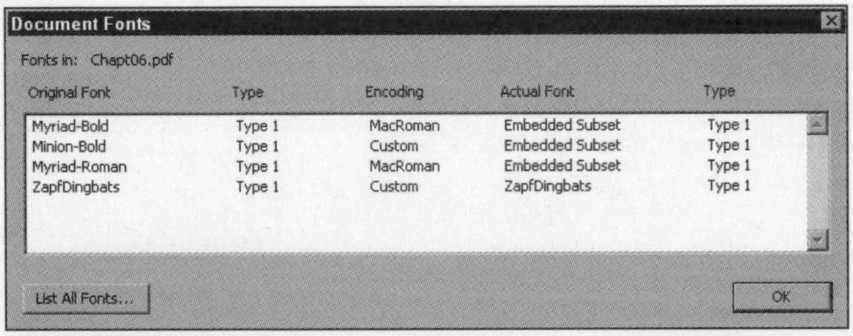

Original Font	Type	Encoding	Actual Font	Type
Myriad-Bold	Type 1	MacRoman	Embedded Subset	Type 1
Minion-Bold	Type 1	Custom	Embedded Subset	Type 1
Myriad-Roman	Type 1	MacRoman	Embedded Subset	Type 1
ZapfDingbats	Type 1	Custom	ZapfDingbats	Type 1

Document Fonts

Fonts in: Chapt06.pdf

List All Fonts...   OK

Figure 3-2: The Document Fonts dialog box lists the fonts contained within a PDF file.

Font information is specific to the page being viewed and not the entire document. If you open a PDF with Times Roman appearing on page 1 and Helvetica on page 2, the first font listed in the Document Fonts dialog box will be Times Roman. Until Reader views another page with another font, you'll see only the fonts that appear on page 1 listed. If Times and Helvetica appear on page 1, both will be listed in the Font Info dialog box.

You can't navigate the pages while the Document Fonts dialog box is open. To view another page, click OK in the Document Fonts dialog box and then use the navigation tools to see another page. Choosing File ➪ Document Fonts again retains the name of the font or fonts viewed on page 1 and adds the additional fonts found on the next page to the list in the Document Fonts dialog box.

As you can see in Figure 3-2, the original fonts from page 1 (Myriad-Bold, Minion-Bold, Myriad-Roman, and Zapf Dingbats) appear in the font list. When I scrolled to page 2 and viewed the Document Fonts, the additional fonts were supplied in the font list (see Figure 3-3). As you move through the pages and view the font information, any additional font names are appended to the list.

Note

Fonts are listed in the order in which they are encountered on a PDF page and the order of the PDF pages. Notice in Figure 3-2 Myriad appears before Minion and both appear before Zapf Dingbats. The list displays the first font encountered on the page, then the next, and so on. The display therefore ignores the alphabetical order.

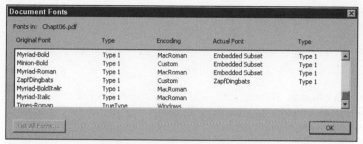

Figure 3-3: I scrolled the pages, viewed another page in a PDF file, and then opened the Document Fonts dialog box to get this list.

Reader handles this method of display for you so that there won't be a burden generating a font list for the whole document every time you open the Document Fonts dialog box. If a PDF file has an inordinate number of fonts, it may take a few moments to display all the fonts. Rather than defaulting to a display of all fonts, Reader provides those fonts encountered as pages are read. You do have an opportunity to view all fonts in a PDF by selecting the List All Fonts button in the Document Fonts dialog box. If you click this button, all fonts used in the open document will be displayed in the list.

Note

After all of the fonts are listed, the List All Fonts button becomes grayed out. If you close the PDF file and later reopen it, Reader won't remember the font list. If you want to view all the fonts again in the Document Fonts dialog box, click List All Fonts again.

At the top of the font list appear several categories describing the fonts, as listed here:

✦ **Original Font:** The font(s) used in the original document.

✦ **Type** (second-column heading): The font type of the described font. If the font is a Type 1 font, it will be indicated here. TrueType will be specified if used, as well as multiple master fonts.

✦ **Encoding:** The method of encoding used. Most often you see MacRoman, Windows, or Custom for the encoding method.

✦ **Used Font:** The reference to the font used in Reader. If you have the font installed in your system, the used font (or *actual* font) will be the same as the font chosen when the PDF was created, in which case you won't see any item denoted in the column. If you do not have actual fonts installed, a substitute font will be used, in which case you'll see the name of the substituted font. These fonts appear as Adobe Sans or Adobe Serif.

✦ **Type** (fifth-column heading): The font type for the substitute font used. Typically, you see Type 1 listed.

Font information is helpful if you want complete integrity of your PDF file output. When a PDF is created, the fonts may be substituted for similar fonts, as illustrated in Figures 3-4 and 3-5. Depending on the font and the font size, the substitution may not display the font as designed with the actual font. If you have the same fonts installed on your computer as those listed in the Document Fonts dialog box, you'll know which fonts to load when such data integrity is paramount to printing the file without font substitution. The only way to determine what fonts are contained in the PDF file is via the Document Fonts dialog box.

Figure 3-4: If the actual font(s) are installed or embedded in the PDF file, the display and printed file includes the original fonts.

Figure 3-5: If the font is not installed or not embedded, font substitution is used. With script fonts, the substitution is less accurate than with serif and sans serif fonts.

Caution

Fonts have been one of the primary problems encountered with accurate displays and printing of digital documents. In as much as Acrobat has greatly improved font handling, still some problems are periodically experienced with font embedding and reporting information about the fonts contained in the document. You can sometimes experience viewing the Document Fonts dialog box and find no listing for a font that may be embedded in the PDF. Furthermore, at times you can also find fonts listed as being embedded and still experience font substitution when printed. About the only thing you can do is try to keep records of fonts that are presenting problems and create some workarounds. Reinstallation of a font, creating outlines, having the font loaded when you print, and other workarounds may be your only solution.

Security information

Users of previous versions of Reader and Acrobat will immediately notice the Document Security information has been moved from the Document Properties (formerly called Document Info) submenu to a menu item directly under the File menu. After you choose File ⇨ Document Security, a dialog box appears supplying information about any encryption contained in the file (see Figure 3-6). Now in Version 5.0 of Adobe Acrobat, Document Security has radically changed and offers you many more features for protecting your content. The methods of Standard security are discussed here and an amplified section on 128-bit encryption is addressed in Chapter 7.

PDF authors can secure documents in Acrobat or at the time of distillation. Security can be handled at several levels: A document can be secured from viewing, different levels for resolution output, only available for specific digital signatures, and secured against changes by another Acrobat user. If a document is secure, you need a password to open it. When using Acrobat Reader, if you are prompted for a password, you need the password to open the file. If you can open a file without a password, the means of determining encryption is to visit the File menu and select Document Security. After you open the dialog box, the following items are listed for the 40-bit security options:

✦ **Security Method:** Several methods are available to Acrobat 5.0 users for encrypting PDF files. The most frequently used is the Acrobat Standard Security. Additional options can be controlled from Acrobat or during Distillation for securing Web Buy files and with Digital Signatures (both of which are discussed in Chapter 7). The method that the PDF author used is listed in this field.

✦ **User Password:** A PDF author can secure a document at two levels when using the Standard Security Method. One level is for a user to gain access to the PDF. If you want a user to open a secure file without access to changing the document, then two separate passwords would be used. *User Password* is the password used to open the document. If security has been added to open a PDF file, the User Password item appears with Yes adjacent to it. If no password protection is used, the User Password item appears with No in the field.

If you can open the PDF in Reader, obviously you have the open password or the file is not secure for viewing.

✦ **Master Password:** A second level password is listed in this field. If the PDF author uses two levels of security, both the User Password field and the Master Password field is listed with Yes adjacent to the respective level. Master Password is only used by Acrobat users to gain access to changing security and editing PDFs. In Reader, you can examine the passwords used, but the Master Password cannot be accessed.

✦ **Printing:** Files can be secured at various levels for printing and output. If the PDF author wants you to view the file but not print it, then the file can be secured against printing. This item is denoted with Not Allowed if it has been secured without printing privileges.

✦ **Changing the Document:** Changes to documents involve all the authoring capabilities of Adobe Acrobat. If users are to view and/or print a PDF file, but not change it, disabling this item ensures that no alterations to the PDF file can be made. With respect to Acrobat Reader, because no changes are permitted with the Reader application, it won't matter if this item is accessible or not.

✦ **Content Copying or Extraction:** If you want to prevent an end user from copying or extracting any data, a security option is available to prevent a user from copying text or image data. The permission is listed in this field. Reader is capable of copying data; therefore, this item is important to Reader users.

✦ **Authoring Comments and Form Fields:** End users can be prevented from changing comments and form fields. If changing is not allowed, it is listed in this field. Form fields cannot be changed in Reader, so the encryption has no effect for the Reader user.

✦ **Form Field Fill-in or Signing:** You can prevent users from filling in forms and digitally signing them. If not allowed, it is listed in this field. Reader users can fill in forms but not digitally sign them. In this regard, form fill-in is important to the Reader user.

✦ **Content Accessibility Enabled:** This option is one area where Reader outshines Acrobat. Adobe has been committed to providing products for the visually and motion challenged. Reader supports accessibility for custom readers for people with these limitations much more than Acrobat. If the content is accessible for screen readers, it is so indicated.

Note   The Document Security dialog box appears with the same information on Windows and Macintosh computers. In as much as the information supplied for Content Accessibility can be viewed in the Properties dialog box on a Macintosh, content delivery with screen readers is currently only supported on Windows.

✦ **Document Assembly:** Document Assembly has to do with page handling features in Acrobat, such as inserting, deleting, creating bookmarks and thumbnails. With both Reader and Acrobat, Document Assembly items also include page rotations. If no Document Assembly is permitted, it is so stated.

✦ **Encryption Level:** Acrobat 5.0 has introduced 128-bit encryption. Earlier versions were limited to 40-bit encryption. With a higher encryption level, other features, such as the choices for printing levels and digital signatures were made possible. What level used for securing the PDF is listed in this field. (For 128-bit encryption options, see Chapter 7.)

You can disable/enable one or more of the security options listed in the Security dialog box only in Adobe Acrobat. Reader won't have access to many operations with or without security. Reader can however, assess the protection applied to the PDF by opening the Document Security dialog box. When you open a PDF and attempt to edit, change, or print it from Acrobat, and you find the task to be unavailable, choosing File ⇨ Document Security is a good idea. The Document Security dialog box appears as illustrated in Figure 3-6.

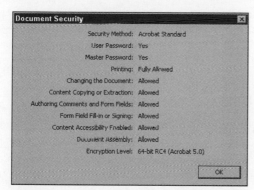

Figure 3-6: The Document Security dialog box displays all secure operations in the open PDF file.

This dialog box provides a starting point for troubleshooting printing or editing problems. As a first step, check the Document Security dialog box to see whether the PDF is secure. If it is not, your inability to perform a task is related to something going on with the Acrobat viewer or printer.

Modifying Preferences

Chapter 2 covers the preference settings for Full Screen view and Acrobat Search. The remaining preferences help users customize the Acrobat viewer environment for viewing, editing, and navigating through PDF files. Like any other application on your computer, examining preference settings when you first start using a program is always a good idea. All the preferences discussed in this chapter in reference to Acrobat Reader are identical to those available in Acrobat. (Additional preference settings unique to Acrobat are introduced when I discuss Acrobat preferences in Chapter 7.)

Earlier versions of Acrobat placed a host of preference settings in submenus under the File menu. With the advent of many more features, Adobe has organized preference settings in one compact menu where different settings are grouped together in a single dialog box. From a list of categories on the left side of the dialog box of the Preferences, you can choose which category to modify by selecting the respective name for a given preference group. After it's selected, the right portion of the dialog box changes to correspond to the settings you want to edit.

Choose Edit ➪ Preferences to access the Preferences settings. Depending on any additional plug-ins installed on your computer, you may see additional items appearing below the Preferences. The first preference category listed in the Preferences dialog box is Accessibility. Of all the preference categories, the attribute choices for Accessibility are different between Windows and Macintosh versions of Reader, as shown in Figures 3-7 and 3-8.

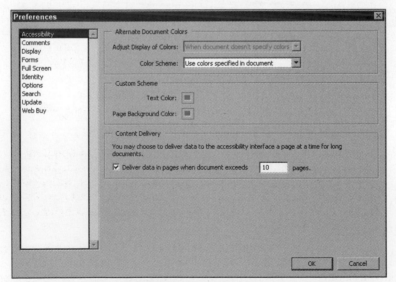

Figure 3-7: The Accessibility Preferences dialog box as viewed from Acrobat Reader 5.0 in Windows includes a category identified as Content Delivery.

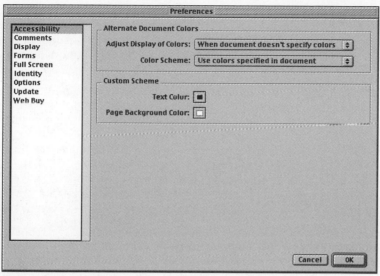

Figure 3-8: The Accessibility Preferences dialog box as viewed from Acrobat Reader 5.0 on the Macintosh does not include Content Delivery.

Accessibility preferences

Adobe Systems is committed to providing accessibility for the vision and motion challenged with tools and resources to make digital content more available. Screen readers operating on Windows computers enable people with such physical challenges to gain access to PDFs with audio support and without the need for using a mouse. The PDF files need to be designed with the intent of making it accessible. Structure, alternative text for figures, and tags are all supplied in Acrobat at the time of authoring the document. Acrobat Reader offers retrieval of PDF files with accessibility to a greater extent than Acrobat.

When a document has been designed to support Accessibility, the following preferences enable user control over accessibility attributes:

✦ **Adjust Display of Colors:** Two choices are available from the pop-up menu. The default is the setting When document doesn't specify colors. This setting displays the PDF in the Acrobat viewer as you may expect it to appear. All the original content and design will be unaltered. If the display contains black text on a white background, you can change colors for both by making choices for the Color Scheme.

The second choice is: Always, overriding document colors. Colors for text and background can be changed to preset color values, Windows System colors (Windows only), or custom colors that are user defined. From the pop-up menu, you have three choices. Use colors specified in document will not change the appearance of the PDF file and leaves the document as you would normally see the content in an Acrobat viewer. Use custom scheme is the second choice. Custom color choices change text and background color according to choices

made in the Custom Scheme listed below this pop-up menu. The last choice is:
Use Windows Colors (Windows only). Windows colors can be changed in the
Control Panel by selecting the Display Properties. Make adjustments for the
properties, and the color scheme will appear consistent with the Windows
settings.

✦ **Text Color:** Colors can be changed for text in accessible documents to the
color scheme identified above. For Windows colors, the Windows System colors are used. On the Mac, clicking the swatch immediately opens a dialog box
with color models on the left side of the dialog box and sliders on the right.
Custom colors selected above relate to the custom color choices for text
made here respective to the choices in your operating system. Click the color
swatch in the dialog box and a pop-up menu appears (Windows only) for
choices between preset values and a custom selection. Choose Custom from
the pop-up menu (Windows) or a swatch (Macintosh), and the system color
palette opens. The color identified in the palette is used for text.

✦ **Page Background Color:** Handling page background color is identical to the
item above. Click the swatch for preset colors or select Custom to open the
Windows System color palette (Windows only). Click a swatch (Macintosh)
and custom color choices can be made.

✦ **Content Delivery** (Windows only): The delivery of a PDF file to a screen
reader is currently only supported on Windows computers that support the
Microsoft Active Accessibility Interface. If the checkbox is disabled, the entire
document can be sent to the reader all at once. Enabling the checkbox delivers the number of pages as user defined in the field box one page at a time.

Comments preferences

In earlier versions of Acrobat, notes and comments were referred to as *Annotations*.
In Adobe Acrobat 5.0, what was formerly known as Annotations is now referred to
as *Comments*. The preferences for comments enable you to change the appearance
of comments created in Acrobat (see Figure 3-9). In Reader these include:

✦ **Font:** You can change the font by choosing the Font pull-down menu. Any
available fonts listed in the menu can be used for the text appearance within
comment notes. Font choices are not restricted to the Base 14 fonts as we had
available in earlier versions of Acrobat. Now in Acrobat 5.0, you can choose
any font loaded in your system to display comments text.

✦ **Font Size:** Font sizes are available from a pop-up menu that lists fixed sizes. In
addition, you can supply a value for a font size not listed among the fixed
sizes by entering a user defined point size.

Display preferences

What was formerly defined as Preferences in earlier versions of Acrobat has now
been consolidated in the Display preferences. If you're looking for some of those
preference settings you're familiar with, many will be found in this dialog box. The
Display preferences are placed in three categories. These are categorized as
Display, Smoothing, and Magnification (see Figure 3-10).

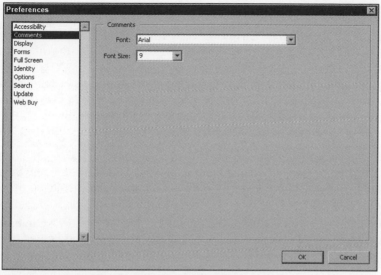

Figure 3-9: The Comment Preferences dialog box provides choices for changing the display of fonts and font sizes with comments created in Acrobat or Reader.

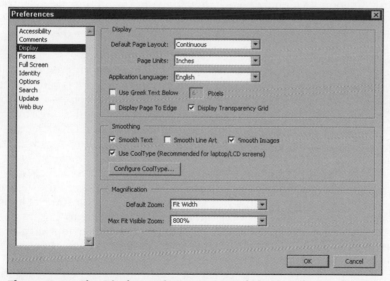

Figure 3-10: The Display preferences control viewing choices for PDF documents on your monitor or laptop computer.

Display

Display is the first of the three categories. These preferences handle page viewing in the Acrobat viewer and include:

✦ **Default Page Layout:** The default is Continuous Pages. You can change to a new default by selecting either the Single Page or Continuous - Facing options from the pull-down menu. Either of these two options displays PDF files in the layouts discussed in Chapter 2. After you change the viewing default, all sub-sequent documents will be displayed accordingly until you change the preferences to another view. This preference setting is not dynamic. You need to make a choice from the pop-up menu appearing in the Preferences dialog box and close any open PDF files. When you open a document after a new Default Page Layout change has been made, that document will be displayed according to your choice.

✦ **Page Units:** You can view the page dimensions in one of the three choices available: points, inches, or millimeters. The dimensions are indicated in the status bar in both Reader and Acrobat and also in the Crop dialog box in Acrobat only. This setting is dynamic. The minute you exit the dialog box, the new units of measure will be reflected in the status bar.

✦ **Application Language:** Acrobat ships with multiple language support. The application language you choose upon installation will be the default language used. If you install multiple languages, you can elect to choose another language from the pop-up menu choices. Changing options in this menu causes all menus, dialog boxes, and windows to display in the language chosen. You must quit the Acrobat viewer and relaunch the application for the new language changes to take place.

✦ **Use Greek Text: Below [___] Pixels:** When you have a value entered in the Below___Pixels field, text will be "greeked" when the page view is reduced to display a font size below the given field entry. *Greeked text* displays as a gray bar; the characters of which are illegible. Greeked text is used to improve screen refreshes and help you navigate through pages faster. Greeking text has no effect on printing a file — regardless of the display, the pages will print with complete font integrity. Entries for the data field range between 0 and 99, with many applications using 6 points as a minimum for the default. When you enter 0, no greeking of text occurs, no matter how small you size the viewer window. A good candidate for this would be screen dumps for tutorial hand-outs or Web graphics. If you desire no greeking, set the value to 2 or less or disable the checkbox. When you enter 99 in the data field, the font display in your viewer window will need to be larger than 99 pixels for the characters to be displayed without greeking. Greeking text is also dynamic. You can make any change in the field box and have the view reflected when you return to the viewer window.

✦ **Display Page to Edge:** This preference setting was introduced with Acrobat 3.01 and was only available in Acrobat Exchange 3.01. When Acrobat 3.0 was introduced, distilled PDFs were not clipped according to the printer driver's page dimension. This detail was actually a bug in the program. However, when Acrobat was upgraded, Adobe reinstituted the bug based on requests from users. When Display Page to Edge is enabled, the Acrobat viewer honors the page clipping provided by the driver. If disabled, a thin white border may appear around the edge of the PDF page created by the printer driver. To eliminate the white border, be certain the checkbox is enabled.

✦ **Display Transparency Grid:** Acrobat 5.0 supports true transparency. The PDF 1.4 format maintains integrity of transparent effects created from other applications, such as Photoshop 6.0 and Adobe Illustrator 9.0 as I explain in Chapter 6. In Acrobat, comments can be viewed with various levels of transparency. A comment appearing on top of page content or a comment icon may display the comment note as transparent where the background data can be seen through the note. In Figure 3-11, the checkbox in the Display Transparency Grid for Preferences is enabled. Figure 3-12 shows the same comment when the item is disabled.

Figure 3-11: Display Transparency in the Preferences dialog box is enabled. The note appears as transparent where the comment icon can be seen in the background.

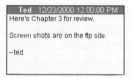

Figure 3-12: When Display Transparency Grid is disabled, the note appears opaque resulting in hiding the background data.

Smoothing

The second category appearing in the Display Preferences dialog box controls text and image viewing on computer monitors and laptop computers. These include:

✦ **Smooth Text:** Produces an anti-aliased effect that smoothly renders the edges of text (see Figure 3-13), minimizing the contrast between foreground and background elements. The result is usually a more improved appearance. When you disable the checkbox, fonts will be displayed with jagged edges (see Figure 3-14). This preference is dynamic; that is, you can change the view while a PDF is open, and when you return to the document window, the new view takes effect.

Figure 3-13: The PDF file is viewed while the preference setting for Smooth Text is enabled. Notice the smooth appearance of the edges.

Figure 3-14: The checkbox for Smooth Text is disabled. The text now appears with obvious jagged edges.

✦ **Smooth Line Art:** This item refers to vector art that can be created in programs, such as Adobe Illustrator, Macromedia FreeHand, or CorelDraw. Vector art objects can also be viewed with an anti-aliased effect as the above example with anti-aliased text. Enable the checkbox for smoother appearances of vector art.

✦ **Smooth Images:** The same holds true for images that you might export from Adobe Photoshop. Enable the checkbox to provide a smoother rendition of raster based images.

✦ **Use CoolType (Recommended for laptop/LCD screens):** Yet another battle is brewing in the digital war for global dominance with this one over typeface technology for handheld devices and eBooks. The primary contenders are Adobe with its CoolType technology and Microsoft with its ClearType technology. These new typeface designs are intended to display text on LCD (liquid crystal display) and handheld readers in resolutions equivalent to 200 dpi. If viewing PDFs on one of these devices, be certain to enable the checkbox.

✦ **Configure CoolType:** When the checkbox above is enabled, you can make a choice for the appearance of text by selecting the Configure CoolType button. After you click the button a dialog box opens, as shown in Figure 3-15.

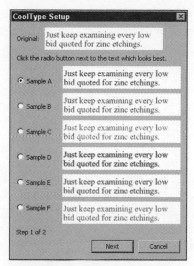

Figure 3-15: Clicking the Configure CoolType button opens a dialog box where a choice for the display on LCD and hand held devices can be made. From the examples, you can click the radio button adjacent to the display that looks best.

In the dialog box, you have more choices accessible by clicking the Next button. After the button is selected, more choices appearing in Figure 3-16 are displayed.

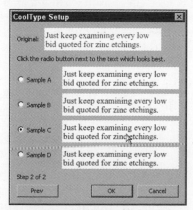

Figure 3-16: Additional choices for CoolType displays are available by selecting the Next button in the first dialog box.

Magnification

The final category in the Display Preferences involves choices for the zoom level when viewing PDF files. These include:

✦ **Default Zoom:** The default is Fit Width, which fits the width of the data displayed on the PDF page. If your monitor is either small or large, and you want to view all documents at another size, the pull-down menu offers many different choices. Sizes ranging from 8.33 to 1,600 percent are available as well as the options Fit in Window, Actual Size, Fit Width, and Fit Visible. The Fit in Window, Fit Width, and Fit Visible options are the same as those discussed in Chapter 2. Changes you make to the default magnification are not dynamic. Any change requires you to close an open PDF file and reopen it for the new view to take effect.

✦ **Max Fit Visible Zoom:** This option enables you to describe the maximum amount of magnification for the Default Zoom selected. For example, if you want to fit only the visible data in a PDF file on-screen but want the magnification to be no greater than 400 percent, you would select 400% from the Max Fit Visible Zoom pop-up menu. In such a case, the page view would never exceed 400 percent. The default for Acrobat viewers is 800 percent, which zooms in on the window. At times, you may navigate through articles or pages in a PDF file and find the zoom to be too high for comfortable viewing. In such cases, return to the Preferences dialog box and select a new Max Fit Visible Zoom default. Changes made to this option are dynamic. When you edit the Max Fit Visible Zoom and return to the open window, the new change takes immediate effect.

Forms preferences

A new preference dialog box has been introduced in Acrobat 5.0 for controlling some behavior with forms. Acrobat Reader can take advantage of filling out form data and automatic controls for calculating data fields take effect from within Reader. As soon as a form is completed in Reader, the only way to preserve the data locally is to print the form. After you exit Reader all the data will be lost and you have no provision for saving the edited file. Among the preference choices for working with forms in Reader are shown in Figure 3-17 and listed as follows:

✦ **Auto Calculate Field Values:** Scripts used in the form design for auto calculations can be suppressed or enabled. When enabled, auto calculations are performed dynamically as data is entered in respective form fields. You may want to suppress the calculations in order to move through the form faster without the computer needing to compute each field as data is entered. Deselect the checkbox and enter the data. When you return to the preferences and enable the checkbox, the data fields are dynamically calculated.

✦ **Show Focus Rectangle:** When the mouse cursor is positioned over a field, a small rectangle icon appears on the mousedown click. If the focus rectangle is to be eliminated from view, deselect the checkbox.

✦ **Highlight Form Fields:** Users of Acrobat 5.0 will immediately notice a helpful rectangle appear after clicking on a form field. When a field is clicked, a rectangle is displayed showing you the area occupied by the data field. After entering data and leaving the field, the rectangle disappears. To eliminate the appearance of the rectangle, deselect the preference choice.

✦ **Highlight Color:** When Highlight Form Fields is enabled above, the highlight color can be changed to a custom color. Such as the other color scheme choices in preferences mentioned earlier, there are preset value choices (Windows) and custom color settings (Windows and Macintosh). Click the swatch to change color as described earlier in this chapter.

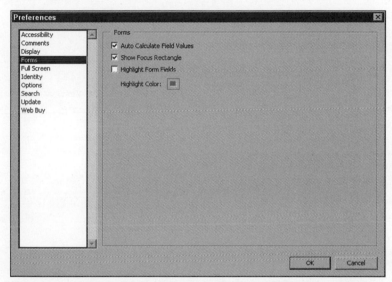

Figure 3-17: The Forms preferences offer four settings for working with PDF documents with form fields.

Identity

In the Preferences dialog box, the next item appearing in the list at the left of the dialog box is Full Screen preferences. (These preference settings are discussed in Chapter 2.) The next settings following Full Screen preferences is Identity. Identity is a new preference item in Acrobat 5.0 and is used for personal information with form fields. (See Figure 3-18.) The following options are provided in the Identity preferences dialog box:

✦ **Name:** The real name of the user is supplied in this field.

✦ **Company Name:** An optional choice for company name is provided in this field.

✦ **E-Mail Address:** The user e-mail address is supplied in this field.

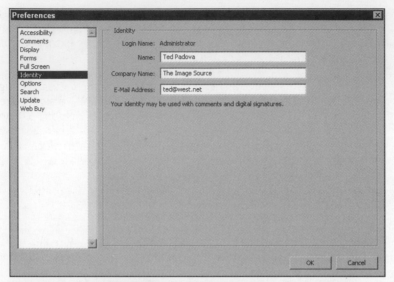

Figure 3-18: Identify preference settings enable you to establish identifying information that is used with form fields only in Reader.

Options preferences

Options preferences have three categories: Web Browser Options control how PDFs with Web links to URLs are viewed; Startup determines if the Acrobat Splash Screen will be viewed and plug-ins used when the program is launched; and the Miscellaneous settings offer miscellaneous choices for viewing PDFs. (See Figure 3-19.)

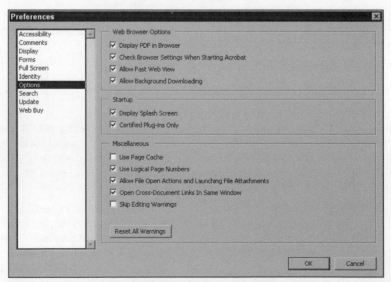

Figure 3-19: Options preferences offer a miscellaneous group of settings to control Web browser viewing, startup attributes, and viewing choices.

✦ **Display PDF in Browser (Windows)/Auto-configure Browser (Macintosh):**
When the checkbox is enabled, selecting a PDF posted on a Web server displays the PDF as an inline view in Web browsers. If the dialog box is disabled, the browser preferences for PDF viewing will be used.

In earlier versions of Acrobat, the display of PDFs when accessing them through Web browsers was handled in individual Browser preferences dialog boxes. Handling PDFs in this manner was often confusing. Now in Acrobat 5.0 and Reader 5.0, Acrobat viewer handles the disposition of PDF files when accessed from a Web browser. When Display in Browser is disabled, you can elect to save the PDF to disk or view it in a viewer as opposed to inline PDF viewing.

✦ **Check Browser Settings When Starting Acrobat:** If Web browser settings are improperly set for tasks, such as Web Buy, a dialog box prompts you to change them when this preference setting is enabled.

✦ **Allow Fast Web View:** Web servers with byte serving capabilities can download single PDF pages as they are viewed in the Web browser with Inline viewing (that is, Display PDF in Browser (Win)/Auto-configure Browser (Mac)). Rather than wait for the entire PDF file to download from the server, only the page viewed is downloaded. Save files with Fast Web Views to take full advantage of faster viewing.

✦ **Allow Background Downloading:** When viewing PDF files on the Web, you can have a requested page download to your computer, and the remainder of the PDF document will also be downloaded. If this preference setting is disabled, only the requested page is downloaded.

✦ **Display Splash Screen:** When enabled, the Acrobat splash screen comes into view while the viewer is loading. Disabling this option eliminates the screen from view when the viewer application is launched.

✦ **Certified Plug-ins Only:** Acrobat plug-ins certified by Adobe are the only plug-ins loaded after the program is launched and when the checkbox is enabled. Those third party plug-ins not certified will be inaccessible during the Reader session. To use Web Buy, the option must be enabled. Changing the mode requires you to quit the viewer and relaunch it for the change to take effect.

✦ **Use Page Cache:** When enabled, the Page Cache requires more system memory, but the viewing of PDF pages move faster as pages are loaded to the cache. The next page in logical order is loaded in the cache, thus occupying more memory. Disabling the option conserves RAM on your computer and slows down the page viewing.

✦ **Use Logical Page Numbers:** In Acrobat, you have the ability to renumber pages and create sections. If, for example, you have a 20-page document, and you specify the first page to be designated page 10, the document pages will be numbered 10 to 29. When you open the PDF file in Reader and disable Use Logical Page Numbers, the pages appear in their original numbered form (that is, pages 1 to 20). If you enable the preference setting, the status bar will show something, such as 10 (1 to 20), indicating the new first page number has been changed to 10, but you are viewing the first page out of a total of 20 pages.

✦ **Allow File Open Actions and Launching File Attachments:** Provides a warning dialog box when attempting to open a secure file from another application via a link in the PDF document. The warning dialog box enables you to cancel the operation.

✦ **Open Cross-Document Links In Same Window:** When this option is enabled, document links are opened in a single window to minimize the number of windows open at any given time. When disabled, a new window opens whenever a link is accessed. When you have the Open Cross-Document Links In Same Window preference enabled, you can temporarily disable it by holding down the Control/Option key when clicking the link. When viewing PDF files from other authors, check that this setting is enabled. Many authors will assume that you have the Cross-Document Links In Same Window preference enabled, as this will help you navigate through their PDF files with much less confusion. (Cross-document links are reviewed in Chapter 2 in the discussion on navigating PDFs via hypertext links.)

✦ **Skip Editing Warnings:** Just about any action you attempt to do in regard to editing PDFs opens a warning dialog box. When this checkbox is enabled, the warning dialog boxes are not opened. Because you can't perform any true editing tasks in Acrobat Reader, this preference setting will not have much meaning. In Acrobat you may use it frequently.

✦ **Reset All Warnings:** Clicking the button returns you to all the default settings.

Update preferences

Update preferences keep you connected with Adobe Systems and all updates that may be hosted online at their Web servers. Choices made in this dialog box enable you to routinely connect to the Adobe Web site to check for new updates and changes for all Acrobat components. In the dialog box, the date of the last checks made for Adobe Acrobat updates and Web services updates are displayed, as shown in Figure 3-20.

✦ **Check for Updates:** Three choices are offered from the pop-up menu. You can elect to have weekly connections, monthly connections, or set up a manual connection. The third choice is user determined for when an update is made. When Manual is selected, you need to click either of the two buttons appearing below the pull-down menu.

✦ **Update Acrobat Now:** Any changes to Acrobat or Reader components, plug-ins and documentation can be updated when selecting the button. Regardless of the choice selected above, clicking the button connects you to the Adobe Web site and updates Acrobat or Reader.

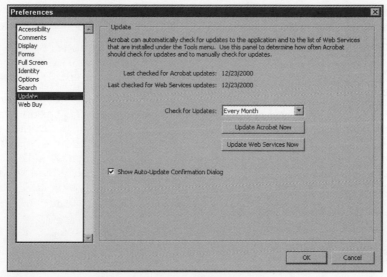

Figure 3-20: Update preferences enable you to keep connected with Adobe for updating plug-ins and Acrobat components.

✦ **Update Web Services Now:** All Adobe Web services that have changed can be updated by selecting this button. If you subscribe to Create PDF Online, for example, any change in the Web hosted service will be updated.

✦ **Show Auto-Update Confirmation Dialog:** When enabled, a dialog box appears showing confirmation for all updated services.

Web Buy preferences

Web Buy was first introduced during the Acrobat 4 life cycle and appeared as a free update in Version 4.05 of Acrobat and Reader. Web Buy is specifically designed for content protection in the growing eBook market. Companies using the secure PDF Merchant program of Adobe can host PDF files on Web sites and have files uniquely encrypted to each individual user's hardware devices. When a PDF file is downloaded to your computer, the serial numbers of your hardware devices encrypt the file. After encrypted, the PDF can only be viewed on your computer and thus prevents unauthorized distribution. The preference settings enable you to activate Web Buy and select the devices to be used for the encryption. (See Figure 3-21.)

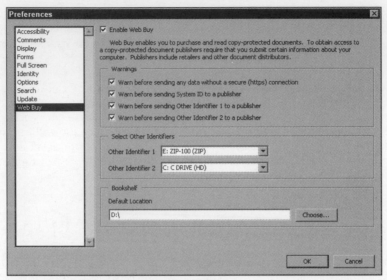

Figure 3-21: Web Buy preferences enable you to activate Web Buy and determine what hardware is used for encryption.

✦ **Enable Web Buy:** The checkbox is used for enabling Web Buy. When the checkbox is deselected, you are not able to download eBooks that have been secured with a Web Buy feature.

✦ **Warn before sending any data without a secure (https) connection:** If a server is not secure, a warning dialog box opens informing you that you are about to provide your hardware keys to a server not using security.

✦ **Warn before sending System ID to a publisher:** When enabled, a warning dialog box appears informing you that your computer System ID will be submitted to a server that is not secure.

✦ **Warn before sending Other Identifier 1 to a publisher:** Other Identifiers can be hard drives or removable media devices attached to your computer. The hardware serial numbers are used for encryption. When the Identifier 1 item listed below is used for encryption, a warning dialog box opens.

✦ **Warn before sending Other Identifier 2 to a publisher:** Identical to the previous setting, this item relates to the Identifier 2 listed below and likewise will open a warning dialog box when enabled.

✦ **Other Identifier 1:** This pull-down menu enables you to select from a list of drives attached to your computer as a second level identifier. (Note: The first level identifier is your computer). In Figure 3-21, notice this identifier is a Zip disk. External media devices can be used as identifiers. To use the external device, a cartridge must be inserted in the device.

✦ **Other Identifier 2:** This pull-down menu enables you to select from a list of drives attached to your computer as a third level identifier.

✦ **Default Location:** As soon as you commence using Web Buy and begin a download, the PDF is saved to the folder identified here. If you want to change the location, open the preferences and reassign the folder by selecting the Choose button.

When you use Web Buy, the identifiers specified in the Web Buy preferences dialog box are used for encrypting a PDF file that you download. Unique serial numbers from your computer's hardware and drives become part of the encryption. If you attempt to move an encrypted PDF to another computer, the file will not open. This encryption method guarantees publishers protection of their content and prohibits copyright infringement. More about using Web Buy is discussed in Chapter 12 where I discuss PDFs and eBooks.

Opening, Saving, and Printing PDF Files

To add a little more consistency across computer applications, Adobe added tools in the Command bar in both Reader and Acrobat for opening and printing files. The Open tool appears first in the Command bar and is used for opening files. Clicking this button produces the same navigation dialog box that appears when you choose File ⇨ Open.

Next to the Open tool is the Save a Copy tool. In Reader, you can save a copy of the open PDF file. In Acrobat, the Save tool enables you to update any edits and save the updates with the tool much like you would with the File ⇨ Save command. Keep in mind that when using Reader, even though you can fill in form data, saving a copy does not preserve the data entries.

The third tool in the top of the Command bar is the Print tool. Clicking this tool launches the Print dialog box, the same as if you had chosen File ⇨ Print. Although a bit redundant, the icons for these tool buttons are familiar to computer users of many applications, including most of the Microsoft products (see Figure 3-22).

 Figure 3-22: The Open, Save a Copy, and Print tools as they appear in Acrobat Reader.

Making Text and Graphics Selections

Up to this point, we've looked at tools in Reader for views and displays, navigation, finding and searching text, and Web links. As you examine the Reader Command bar, notice that only three editing tools are available. Reader, as a viewer, cannot create or modify text. You can, however, select both text and graphics in Reader. The three tools that appear as editing tools are the Text Select tool, the Column Select tool, and the Graphics Select tool. When the tools are expanded, they appear, as shown in Figure 3-23.

Figure 3-23: When the Text Select tool is expanded in the Reader Command bar, the three editing tools appear as illustrated.

Text Select tool

The Text Select tool appears in the Reader Command bar to the right of the Zoom tool. To select the tool, move the cursor to the tool and click it or press the V key on your keyboard. Press the Shift + V key on your keyboard to toggle between the Text Select tool and the Column Select tool.

Use of this tool behaves a little differently than similar text tools in other applications. When you click a word with the cursor in a PDF document, the entire word is selected. You can't select individual characters. Multiple words can be selected by dragging through a line of text or down several lines of text to select the text in a paragraph. All the text on a page can be selected by choosing Edit ➪ Select All. Select All is available regardless of the tool you have selected from the Reader Command bar. When using the Text Select tool, it doesn't matter if the text is contained in a contiguous block. Reader selects all the text on the page when you drag from top to bottom or vice versa. You needn't be concerned about selecting the first word when you drag across the page either. All text is selected even if you drag from an area where no text appears and move the cursor up or down.

To select a horizontal line of text, drag the Text Select tool across the line of text to be selected. You can start the cursor position from outside the first characters to be selected and drag across the line. All text in the line will be selected as you drag the mouse cursor, as shown in Figure 3-24.

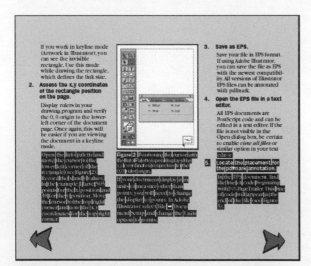

Figure 3-24: When the Text Select tool is dragged across a line of text, all the text in a horizontal line is selected. Multiple lines can be selected by dragging up or down the page. Acrobat viewers make no distinction between single and multiple columns.

Tip   If you want to select text across multiple pages, zoom out so that multiple pages can be viewed in the Document pane. You can view the pages as Single pages or Facing pages. Click the Text Select tool from the Acrobat viewer Command bar and drag down the pages. If you want to select text on more pages than can be seen in the Document pane, change the view to Continuous. With the Text Select tool, click the mouse button and drag down to the bottom of the Document pane. Pages will scroll to the end of the document while the text is selected.

Column Select tool

Acrobat viewers don't interpret text the way word processors or text editing applications do. The viewers handle text more like clumps spattered across the page. If you want to select a column of text, the Text Select tool is not the ideal choice. Dragging this tool down the column selects not only the text in the column but also the text in adjacent columns, as shown in Figure 3-24. The Column Select tool behaves more like a selection marquee that restricts text selection to the area confined within the marquee. If you want to select a column of text, use the Column Select tool and draw a marquee around the text column (see Figure 3-25).

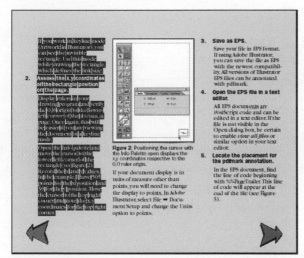

Figure 3-25: By using the Column Select tool, you drag a marquee around the text to be selected. When the mouse button is released, all text within the marquee is selected.

When using either the Text Select tool or the Column Select tool, you can temporarily toggle to one or the other by pressing the Control key (Option on a Mac). If, for example, your current tool is the Text Select tool, pressing Control (Option) enables the Column Select tool. Using the modifier keys eliminates the need to return to the Command bar.

Copying and pasting text

If you want to move text from a Reader page to a word processor, you can select the text and copy it to your system clipboard. After copied to the clipboard, the text can be pasted into any document that supports text. Pasted text will not always retain formatting with complete integrity. Even though text does not convert to ASCII text, in which all formatting attributes are lost, you may lose some tabs and paragraph formatting. Depending on the application you use, more or less of the formatting will be retained when pasted into a new document. If colors have not been identified in the resultant document, an application supporting text colors different from those in the Reader file may use a close proximity of a particular color identified in the pasted text.

Note   If either the Text Select tool or Column Select tool is used to attempt to copy text and the Edit ➪ Copy command is grayed out, the PDF file may be encrypted. If the Copy command is inaccessible, check the Document Security.

To see how copying and pasting text works, perform the following simple copy and paste operation so that you can examine the results. If you have Microsoft Word or another word processor, use it for the example. If you do not have a word processor, you can use a layout application or text editor.

STEPS: Copying Text in Reader and Pasting in a Word Processor

1. **Launch Reader and Microsoft Word.** If you do not have enough memory to keep both Reader and your word processor open concurrently, launch Reader.

2. **Choose File ➪ Open.** Open a PDF file of your choice. Ideally, using a file with multiple columns of text is best. If such a file is not handy, look in the Tutorial folder on the CD-ROM accompanying this book and open the epslinks.pdf file.

3. **Navigate to a page with multiple columns of text.** In my example, page 1 has text in three columns.

4. **Click the Text Select tool and drag through the text.** Beginning at the top of the page, drag down and across the page to select the text, as shown in Figure 3-26.

5. **Choose Edit ➪ Copy.** The text is copied to the clipboard.

6. **Choose Window ➪ Show Clipboard (Windows only).** Examine the clipboard. You should see the text from the selection appear in the clipboard window. Observe the text and note formatting has not been retained. Before pasting in the word processor, viewing the clipboard is a good idea, as shown in Figure 3-27. On the Macintosh, you won't have access to the Clipboard in Acrobat. After selecting text, click the Desktop background to access the Finder. Choose Edit ➪ Show Clipboard.

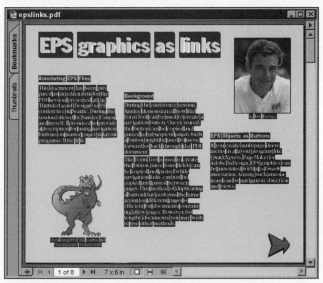

Figure 3-26: All the text on a single PDF page is selected when you choose Edit ➪ Select All.

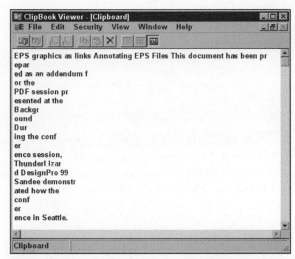

Figure 3-27: After it's copied to the Clipboard, the text can be viewed when opening the Clipboard Viewer in Acrobat (Windows) or returning to the Finder and choosing Edit ➪ Show Clipboard (Macintosh).

7. **Open your word processor.** If you have Microsoft Word launched, select Word from the application selections in the top-right corner of your screen (Mac) or from the status bar (Windows). If you don't have a word processor loaded in memory, quit Reader and launch your word processor.

8. **Choose Edit ⇨ Paste.** If your word processor opens with a new document window, you can paste the clipboard contents immediately (see Figure 3-28). If you need to create a new window, choose File ⇨ New. After a new document is displayed, choose Edit ⇨ Paste.

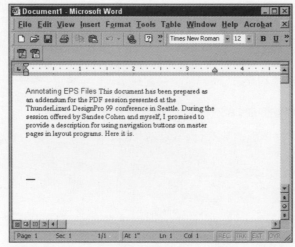

Figure 3-28: The clipboard contents appear in the new document window. All of the column formatting was retained in the pasted text.

In Microsoft Word, most of the text formatting is retained. Fonts displayed in the Word toolbar may show substituted font names from Adobe multiple master fonts. The text appears with colors either identical to the values in the Reader file or with a color range similar to the colors in the original Reader file.

Copying and pasting graphics

Graphics selections in an Acrobat viewer are handled similarly to the text selections made with the Column Select tool. The Graphics Select tool behaves like some utilities used for screen dumps. Mainstay Capture for the Macintosh or Corel Capture for Windows enable you to define the area of the screen to be captured by dragging open a marquee. Whereas capture utilities save the defined region to disk or the clipboard, the Graphics Select tool in the Acrobat viewer merely selects the marquee contents. From there, you need to copy the selection and paste it into an image editing application. Regardless of which method you use, you can't raise the resolution of the captured area above 72 pixels per inch (ppi). At best, this tool enables you to use graphic selections for screen or Web views. Printing the selections on almost any kind of output device requires a higher resolution image.

When you select the Graphics Select tool and place the cursor in the Acrobat document window, the cursor changes to a plus (+) symbol, indicating the Acrobat viewer expects you to create a marquee. Click and drag to open a marquee around the image you want to select. When you release the mouse button, a marquee is displayed, but the contents will not appear to be selected (see Figure 3-29). The traditional "marching ants" do not appear, and the selection is not highlighted. Though this behavior is different from almost any other type of selection you may create in any application, the image you want actually has been selected.

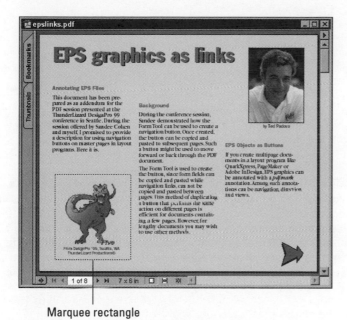

Marquee rectangle

Figure 3-29: When you create a selection with the Graphics Select tool, a marquee rectangle defines the selected area.

To copy the selection contents, use the same method described for text selections: Choose Edit ➪ Copy to place the image contents on the clipboard. Files copied to the clipboard use your system native file format. On Windows, the file format for clipboard information is Windows Metafile (WMF); on the Macintosh, the format is PICT. After copying the data, you can display the clipboard contents and view your copied file data through accessing the Clipboard, as I mentioned earlier (see Figure 3-30).

Figure 3-30: You can view graphics copied to the clipboard by choosing Window ⇨ Show Clipboard (Windows) or returning to the Finder and choosing Edit ⇨ Show Clipboard (Macintosh).

Copied graphics can be edited in image editing programs, such as Adobe Photoshop. Photoshop enables you to create a new document with the default size determined from the clipboard contents. If you copy a graphic in an Acrobat viewer, launch Photoshop, and then choose File ⇨ New, the dimensions for width and height will be supplied from the clipboard image's width and height.

The physical dimensions of the new Photoshop window will conform to the data on the clipboard. As you view the New dialog box in Photoshop, notice the default resolution is 72 ppi. You may be tempted to pump up the resolution in an attempt to capture a high-resolution image. Unfortunately, the Metafile or PICT format won't give you the same results as an EPS graphic from a vector editing program. If you change the resolution in the new document and then paste the clipboard contents, the image will appear severely bitmapped and not usable for any application. The best you can hope for is keeping the copied image at its original size and resolution.

Using context-sensitive menus

In Chapter 2, I discuss the use of context-sensitive menus. You can use context-sensitive menus with the Text Select tool, the Column Select tool, or the Graphics Select tool. When any of the three tools are positioned in the PDF window, click the right mouse button (Windows) or hold the Control key down (Macintosh) to open a pop-up menu. With the Graphics Select tool you have three options (see Figure 3-31):

✦ **Copy:** Selecting this option copies the marquee contents to the clipboard. If a marquee has not yet been created with the Graphics Select tool, the Copy option will be grayed out.

✦ **Select All:** If you choose Select All from the pop-up menu, a marquee is created around the PDF page. The entire page can then be copied to the clipboard by choosing Edit ⇨ Copy or by bringing back the context-sensitive menu and choosing Copy.

✦ **Print:** When Print is chosen, the Acrobat viewer opens the Print dialog box. At first you might think the contents of a graphic selection will print after you select Print from the context-sensitive menu. Making this choice only brings up the Print dialog box. When printed, the entire PDF page or pages specified in the dialog box will print.

Figure 3-31: The context-sensitive menu for the Graphics Select tool offers three menu options: Copy, Select All, and Print.

If you use either the Text Select tool or the Column Select tool, the options available from the context-sensitive menu are Copy and Select All in Reader. If you have Acrobat, an additional item for creating a bookmark appears in the menu. You can select text on a page and add a bookmark to it. (Bookmarks are discussed in Chapter 9.) Print is not an option when using the menu with either of the text tools.

Using the Online Help Commands

Online help for all the Acrobat components is available through a menu command. On both platforms, Help menus appear after the Window menu in an Acrobat viewer. Whatever system you use, an online guide is available to you.

These help menu commands perform two different types of assistance. When you open one of the Acrobat components (Reader, Acrobat, or Distiller), an online guide menu item appears in the menu respective to your system software. When you select this menu item, a PDF document installed with Adobe Acrobat opens in an Acrobat viewer related to the application from which you are choosing the guide. For example, if you have Acrobat Distiller open and select Acrobat Guide, the Acrohelp.pdf file opens in the default Acrobat viewer. If you access Acrobat Help from Acrobat or Reader Help from Acrobat Reader, a help guide opens in the respective viewer.

When you open Reader and select Reader Help, the Reader.pdf file opens. This file is installed on your computer in the Reader folder created during the installation of Acrobat Reader. If you install Adobe Acrobat and Reader, the Reader .pdf file is installed in a subfolder called Help. If you choose Help ⇨ Purchase Adobe Acrobat, the Acrobat.pdf file opens, and a page describing Acrobat appears. Links from this page to the Adobe Web site take you to information related to Acrobat.

The Reader.pdf is your online user manual for the Adobe Acrobat Reader software. Because Reader is distributed free from Adobe Systems, there are no printed user manuals. All the support for Reader is contained in PDF documents. Even when you purchase Adobe Acrobat, many documents and references are contained in online guides that are installed in the Help folder. If you can use the many different search capabilities of Acrobat Search, as examined in Chapter 2, you'll find support for Adobe Acrobat much easier in the online guides than you could possibly find in printed publications. In addition to the searches you may use with an online guide, you'll find an elaborate set of bookmarks that further your capability to find help fast.

If you have Adobe Acrobat installed, the Help folder inside your Acrobat folder will contain many different help files. The help file respective to the application you are using will be accessible in the Help menu, or you can choose File ➪ Open from an Acrobat viewer and open any of the PDF files contained among the help guides. An index file is also included in the Help folder with hypertext links to pages in all the PDF online guides respective to the information being sought.

Accessing the Adobe Web Link

Like most of the other Adobe applications, you can access the Adobe Web site while in Reader by clicking Visit Adobe on the World Wide Web tool in the Command bar. You need an Internet connection to take advantage of the Web link, whether it be a simple dial-up connection or a faster method. The tool is represented as the far right icon in the Reader and Acrobat Command Bar and connects you to the Adobe Acrobat Web page. Click this icon and your Web browser will launch.

Tip   Adobe maintains an excellent Web site that is intuitive and easy to navigate (www.adobe.com). As you work with Acrobat or any other Adobe product, revisiting the Web pages related to your application is a good idea. Upgrade information, new features, new releases of software, tips, technical information, and help are all available. Many of the tips and technique files are PDFs. You can download the PDFs and store them in a support documentation folder on your hard drive. Create a search index and rebuild the index as new files are added. When a search is invoked with Acrobat Search, you have immediate access to helpful tips.

As Acrobat evolves and becomes updated, you will need additional documentation for changes and upgrades. Because the Adobe Web site can offer you updates faster than printed documentation, you'll find this method a useful tool in keeping you up to date with Acrobat products.

Registering Acrobat Reader

Registration for Acrobat Reader has not always been clear and straightforward. In earlier versions you had direct links to where a registration for the Reader product could be made. In later versions, registration appeared after the product shipped and was often overlooked by many users. As of this writing, a product registration form exists on the Adobe Web site. When you visit the Acrobat Web page, click the

Registration button at the top if the Web page. You are taken to the page where Acrobat Reader registration can be completed. Because Reader requires no serial number at the time you install it, the 160,000+ people who download it weekly have often overlooked registration.

Adobe Systems doesn't require you to register the software in order to launch it on your computer, but taking a moment to complete the registration is advisable. After the information is in the Reader user data bank, you'll be updated on information related to Acrobat software. If you choose to do so on the Web site, you are added to the Adobe e-mail list, through which you can receive electronic information about the product and upgrades to it.

Registration of Acrobat Reader is somewhat volatile. Adobe may not have a registration form immediately available after the release of Acrobat Reader 5.0 or they may eventually eliminate Reader registration. The only way to be certain whether it will appear if not immediately accessible is to routinely visit the Web site.

Getting help from Adobe on the Web

When the Visit Adobe on the World Wide Web tool is selected from the viewer Command bar and you open the Acrobat Web page, five links to Acrobat specific information appear at the top of the Web page. Keep in mind, Web sites are volatile and continue to change. The next time you visit the Adobe Web site, the links may provide different information. The five options available as of this writing are described here.

Support

The support Web page deals with support for Acrobat — technical support in particular. Here you can browse a Web page detailing the top ten problems with Acrobat performance; reach a tech support e-mail center where you can e-mail questions that are answered by the Adobe technical support staff within 24 hours; or peruse the frequently asked questions page, where common problems and solutions are displayed. Like many other Web pages, the customer support site may be updated periodically, thereby offering more solutions for your Acrobat performance.

Related products

When the related products button is selected, a Web page opens where products working in concert with Acrobat are listed. Other Adobe software, plug-ins, third party solutions, books, and references are listed. If looking for a particular solution with Acrobat, be certain to view this page periodically.

User forums

User forums exist for all Adobe products. Here you can click a button for any Acrobat product and join a forum where information is shared between users and experts. If keeping up with Acrobat development and solutions is important to you, be certain to join a forum and visit it regularly.

ePaper

At the top-level view of the Adobe Web site are buttons linking you to categories, products, the Adobe home page, and other avenues. Among those items listed in this group is a button for ePaper. ePaper contains information almost exclusively related to Acrobat. New developments in protecting digital content, distributing it, product hardware support and other related items are linked to the ePaper page.

Tutorials

Tutorials are one of the true values in browsing the Adobe Web site. From the Acrobat Web page, you are taken to a page where tips and techniques are provided by different Acrobat experts, as well as Adobe Acrobat engineers and product support people. The tips change periodically, so be certain to visit often. Immediately after you upgrade to Acrobat 5.0, be certain to check out these pages. New features will be provided in easy to follow step-by-step instructions.

Buy now

If you haven't upgraded to Acrobat 5.0, the Adobe Web site offers an opportunity to make a direct purchase from Adobe. Both new purchases and upgrades can be made from this Web page.

Summary

✦ The Reader environment is controlled through menu commands for document information and preferences. You can change preferences to suit your individual needs when viewing PDFs in Acrobat Reader.

✦ Text selections are made with the Text Select tool. Columns of text are selected with the Column Select tool. With either tool, selected text can be copied and pasted into other application documents.

✦ Graphic image selections can be made with the Graphics Select tool, which is located on the Command Bar in an Acrobat viewer. Graphics, such as text, can be copied. The copied images can be pasted into an image editor.

✦ Online help guides are installed with Acrobat Reader and Acrobat 5.0. Help can be selected from the Help menu, which opens a help guide in an Acrobat viewer.

✦ Web links to the Adobe Web site offer additional help and information about Adobe Acrobat. You can view the Adobe Acrobat home page and navigate through a site related to information about Acrobat. Among other information is a special link to pages that offer tips and techniques in using Acrobat.

✦   ✦   ✦

Creating PDF Documents

Converting Documents to PDF

How PDFs Are Created

The very first element you should understand about Acrobat
is the way PDF files and pages within a PDF document are *not*
created. Shortly after the release of the previous version of
the *Adobe Acrobat PDF Bible*, I received an e-mail message
from a woman who was definitely at wit's end. Her e-mail message detailed complete frustration and exasperation for
attempting to create templates where PDF pages would be
originated and edited. She was a sophisticated computer user,
but had never looked at Acrobat until shortly before she sent
me the e-mail. Her assumption was that, like any other program, one simply needed to go to the File menu and choose
New to create a new file. After all, almost any other computer
program supports this common interface.

With Acrobat however, one needs to think in terms of converting some form of digital data to PDF. Unfortunately, you still
have no means of *creating* a PDF from scratch in Acrobat 5.0.
With Acrobat, you must have something already created in
order to *convert* your data to the Portable Document Format.
After the woman who sent me her e-mail message understood
this fact, the frustration was relieved, and I suspect she's out
there somewhere blissfully converting digital content to PDF.
I haven't heard from her since, so I imagine that things have
worked out quite well.

The seasoned Acrobat user will immediately notice that the PDFWriter utility has been eliminated from the Acrobat 5.0 bundle. In improving the ability to create PDF files, Adobe has offered newer solutions that hopefully you'll find much easier to use when converting application documents and various file formats to PDF. The tools now available with Acrobat 5.0 are handled through direct conversion from within Acrobat, through printer drivers, and through Acrobat Distiller. In addition, many other application programs support saving or exporting documents directly to the PDF format.

Acrobat 5.0 offers a new menu command called Open as Adobe PDF. When the file is opened in Acrobat 5.0, it is essentially converted from the host application format to the Portable Document Format. Only specific file types can take advantage of the menu option from within Acrobat, as we momentarily explore.

Printer drivers have been created that support converting an open application document to PDF through the application's Print command. To exercise this operation, you should further your understanding of Acrobat Distiller, as I explain in Chapter 5. Printing to PDF uses attribute settings established in Acrobat Distiller. You don't need to address Distiller to create the PDF, but you do need to understand it when making choices for how many attributes will be used in producing the file.

Yet another means of creating PDF files is through many different exports from other applications. An increasing number of programs now support PDF creation either by saving in the PDF format or exporting the application document to PDF. The flagship programs and major business applications all include means of exporting to PDF, and I cover the most popular programs used today in Chapter 6.

Converting paper documents and digital camera files to PDF can also be accomplished through the Acrobat Scan plug-in. Using Acrobat Scan, as I explain in Chapter 16, offers an easy means of converting any paper document and digital camera images to PDF.

If none of the above methods suits your workflow, Adobe offers yet another solution. An online service at the Adobe Web site provides a means for creating PDFs on the Adobe Web site. At the end of this chapter, we look at using the service.

PDF files can be created from almost any data residing on microcomputers, minicomputers, and mainframes. Because the software running on these systems varies so greatly, there is an obvious need to develop many methods for converting an application document to PDF. Part of the process is covered in this chapter. To become completely literate in PDF file creation, you'll also need to become familiar with the next two chapters. For now, start slow and look at creating PDFs from within Acrobat.

Opening as Adobe PDF

Acrobat 5.0 has introduced a new command from within the program, called Open as Adobe PDF, which is used to convert certain file formats to PDF. These file formats are limited to a select few and won't satisfy your needs if creating PDFs from applications software that either doesn't support the proper format or cannot be recognized by Acrobat.

For image and text files, Open as Adobe PDF can be accomplished from within Acrobat by choosing File ➪ Open as Adobe PDF. The same results also occur if you drag a file on top of the Acrobat application icon or a shortcut (application alias on Macintosh). In both cases Acrobat converts the file to PDF as long as the file format is supported by Acrobat.

Converting image files

When the Open as Adobe PDF command is executed, a dialog box appears, as shown in Figure 4-1 (Window) or Figure 4-2 (Macintosh). In the dialog box, a button for Settings opens the Conversion Options dialog box where file compression for certain formats can be established. Only the image formatted files offer conversion options.

Figure 4-1: When choosing File ➪ Open as Adobe PDF on Windows, the Open dialog box appears. In this dialog box is a button for Settings where the amount of file compression can be assigned to the imported file.

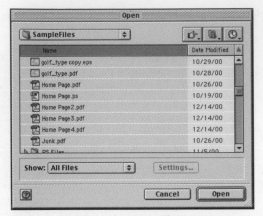

Figure 4-2: When choosing File ➪ Open as Adobe PDF on the Macintosh, the dialog box appears with the same options as viewed in Windows.

From the Open dialog box, first select a file type and then click Settings to determine the amount of compression for any of the image format files. (See Figure 4-3.) The Settings button is only available for image files. Text and HTML file types won't have any control over the attributes of the file converted to PDF.

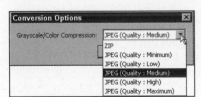

Figure 4-3: After clicking the Settings button, the Conversion Options dialog box opens where file compression can be assigned to image format files.

For all of the image formats listed here, the Settings are identical. From the Conversion Options, you can select either Zip compression or different levels of JPEG compression. Zip compresses files without any image degradation but the compression won't be as great as the alternative JPEG choices. JPEG compression is available at five different levels. The more compression used, the more image degradation appears in the final PDF. The best way to determine what level of compression to apply is to experiment and view results on your monitor. Selecting different compression settings and viewing the results helps you determine what level to assign for various output needs.

Open as Adobe PDF supports the following image formats that all offer the same conversion options:

✦ **BMP:** Bitmap (BMP) is a file format that can be saved from Adobe Photoshop. Bitmap is also commonly referred to as a *color mode* in Photoshop. As a color mode, the file can be saved in other file formats. For example, a 1-bit bitmap image can be saved as a TIFF formatted file. In regard to Acrobat, the bitmap file format that is capable of rendering images in 1-bit, 4-bit, 8-bit, and 24-bit color depths can all be opened as PDF. Furthermore, a bitmap color mode saved as any of the following compatible formats can also be opened as a PDF.

✦ **CompuServe GIF:** Graphic Interchange Format (GIF) by CompuServe was developed years ago to port image files to and from mainframes and micro-computers. GIFs remain a popular format for Web graphics, and in the later version of GIF89a, supports interlacing. If using Photoshop, you can either save in the CompuServe GIF 87 format or use the Photoshop Save for Web command and choose the GIF89a format. Regardless of what format is used, Acrobat can import either as a PDF. Interlacing, as would be used with Web browsers, won't be supported in PDF files.

✦ **JPEG:** Joint Photographic Expert Group (JPEG) images are also used for Web graphics and file exchanges on the Internet. JPEG compression is a *lossy* com-pression scheme and will degrade images rapidly when compressed at high levels of compression. These files are already compressed. Adding further compression with the PDF conversion options won't add to the compression. In as much as the Settings button will be active in the Open dialog box, you can't get more compression out of the file when converting to PDF.

✦ **PCX:** PCX files are native to the PC and were commonly used as an extension for PC Paintbrush. Adobe Photoshop can export in PCX format, but today it is rarely used for any kind of image representation. The advantage you have in opening PCX files in Acrobat is when converting legacy files saved in this for-mat. Rather than use a two-step operation of opening a PCX file in an image editor and saving in a more common format for file conversions, Acrobat can import the files directly.

✦ **PICT (Macintosh only):** The Apple Macintosh equivalent to the previous PCX is the PICT (Picture) format native to the Macintosh. Photoshop supports PICT file exchanges in both opening and saving. Acrobat however, only sup-ports the format for conversion to PDF via the Open as Adobe PDF command. On Windows the format can be seen when in the Open dialog box, but attempting to open the file in Acrobat under Windows produces an error with a warning dialog box.

✦ **PNG:** Portable Network Graphics (PNG — pronounced *ping*) is a format enabling you to save 24-bit color images without compression. The format was designed for Web use and is becoming more popular among Web designers. Older Web browsers need a special plug-in to view the images, which has slowed its wide acceptance in the user community. Interestingly enough, PNG images are saved from image editors without compression, yet Acrobat can apply image compression when converting to PDF. All of the compression options in the Conversion Options dialog box can be used with PNG images to reduce file sizes.

✦ **TIFF:** Tagged Image File Format (TIFF) is by far the most popular format among the print people regardless of platform. TIFF files originate from image editors and scans. When scanning text, you can save as a TIFF format, import the file in Acrobat, and then proceed to convert the image file to rich text with Acrobat Capture, as I explain in Chapter 17.

Converting HTML files

Acrobat also supports non-image formatted files in two categories with the Open as Adobe PDF command. The first of these two categories is HTML files. Web page designs can be converted to Acrobat PDF easily in Acrobat 5.0 through the Open as Adobe PDF command. Navigate a hard drive or server, find the HTML (HyperText Markup Language) file, and open it. After the Open button is clicked in the Open dialog box, Acrobat converts the HTML file complete with active links, images, and text to PDF. All text in the PDF file is preserved and can be copied and pasted as described in Chapter 3.

Only a single HTML file can be opened at one time with the Open as Adobe PDF command. If another HTML file is opened when one file is active in Acrobat, a dialog box will appear enabling you to create a second PDF file or append the new document to the open file, as shown in Figure 4-4.

Figure 4-4: If a PDF is open in the Acrobat Document pane, any new HTML files opened can be converted to PDF in a second document file or appended to the open document.

The new PDF may be one page or several pages depending on the number of standard 8.5-x-11-inch pages the HTML file spans. All the links both external and internal are preserved in the PDF file. When the PDF page is viewed in Acrobat and a link is selected, a dialog box appears where the viewing options can be determined. Figure 4-5 shows the dialog box that determines the viewing options. Checking the box eliminates the dialog box from appearing when clicking subsequent links.

The Specify Weblink Behavior dialog box offers options for viewing the linked destination in either Acrobat or the default Web browser. If Acrobat is selected, the linked HTML file will be converted to PDF.

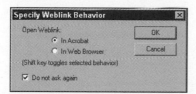

Figure 4-5: When a link is selected on a PDF page converted from HTML, the Specify Weblink Behavior dialog box opens. In this dialog box, you have choices for viewing the next HTML document in Acrobat or the default Web browser.

If the Do not ask again checkbox is enabled in the Specify Weblink Behavior dialog box and you later want to change viewing options, open a context-sensitive menu. With the mouse cursor placed over a link, right-click the mouse button (Control + Click on a Mac). A context-sensitive menu opens, as shown in Figure 4-6.

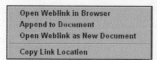

Figure 4-6: Position the mouse cursor over a link on the PDF page in Acrobat and right-click (Control + Click on a Mac) to open a context-sensitive menu. From the menu choices, the viewing behavior can be determined.

When viewing the PDF and navigating through links from multiple HTML files appended to a PDF, two different appearances of the mouse cursor appear when placed over a link. If a link to another HTML document has been converted to PDF, the cursor appears as a hand with the forefinger pointing upward. The icon is as you would find with any Acrobat links, as shown in Figure 4-7. If, on the other hand, the destination for a link has not yet been appended to the PDF, the cursor icon appears with a + (plus) symbol inside the hand icon, as shown in Figure 4-8. In addition, the link location is displayed in a tool tip below the cursor.

Figure 4-7: When the destination for a link has been appended to the PDF, the cursor appears as a hand with the forefinger pointing upward.

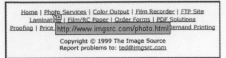

Figure 4-8: If the destination for the link has not yet been appended to the PDF, the cursor appears with a + (plus) symbol inside the hand icon. The URL location also is displayed as a tool tip.

 Tip   Web designers interested in protecting digital rights may want to use PDFs saved with encryption for client proofing. An entire Web site can be supplied as a PDF file complete with URL links to pages on the site and external links to other sites. When encrypted, the recipient can be prevented from copying source code, text, and images.

Converting text files

The final format that can be converted with the Open as Adobe PDF command is text files. These file types must be saved as ASCII text either with or without control brakes and other formatting acceptable to the text only format. Word processor files originating from programs, such as Microsoft Word, and saved as an application format cannot be converted through the Open as Adobe PDF command. As ASCII text, most of the document formatting will be lost.

If you have a PostScript file and want to convert it to a PDF, even though the PostScript file is ASCII text, it cannot be converted without some editing. Acrobat will read the first line of text in the PostScript file and interpret the instruction as opposed to text only. The first line of PostScript files are generally a comment line, but Acrobat won't ignore the comment and will produce an error when these files are opened with the Open as Adobe PDF command. A warning dialog box appears, as shown in Figure 4-9.

In the dialog box, you find a button to enable copying the text to the clipboard. If you click this button, only the text up to the error is copied. The remaining text in the document won't be copied to the clipboard. In the case of PostScript files, only the first line will be copied.

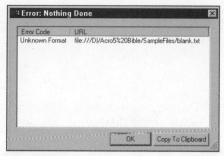

Figure 4-9: A warning dialog box appears when attempting to convert PostScript files to PDF with the Open as Adobe PDF command.

If you want to convert PostScript file text to PDF with the Open as Adobe PDF command, the first line of text needs to be edited. You can add a word or characters to the first line of text and then press the Enter key (Return on a Mac) or just eliminate the ! (exclamation mark). Acrobat will encounter the first line and interpret the file as ASCII text. Instructions in the rest of the file will be ignored and the file will be successfully converted to PDF. In Figure 4-10, I edited the first line of text in Microsoft Word and supplied the text *New Line*. The file was then saved as text only from Microsoft Word and opened in Acrobat.

Figure 4-10: If PostScript files need to be converted as text only to PDF, edit the first line of text by supplying any desired text or delete the ! (exclamation mark). Save the file as text only from a word processor and then open in Acrobat.

The above procedure is only intended to convert any PostScript code for viewing the code in a PDF. If you want to create a PDF from PostScript files, then Acrobat Distiller would be used, as I explain in Chapter 5.

Multiple file conversions

Open as Adobe PDF can be used to convert multiple files from either the same file format or different formats. If files are of the same format then conversion options can be selected for all the image formats. If two files of different formats are selected in the Open as Adobe PDF dialog box, the Settings button for addressing conversion options won't be available.

For converting files of the same image type, choose Open as Adobe PDF from Acrobat. In the Objects of type pop-up menu (Show on a Mac), select the file format to be converted. A display of all the common file types will be displayed in the Open dialog box. To select multiple files in a contiguous list on Windows, select the first file and then depress the Shift key to select the last item in the list. All files will be selected between the first and last selection. On a Macintosh, use Shift + Click to select individual files.

To select files in a noncontiguous group, click a file and then press the Control key and click a second file (Windows). On the Macintosh, hold the Shift key down while clicking successive files in a noncontiguous group. In Figure 4-11, a noncontiguous group of files is selected on Windows.

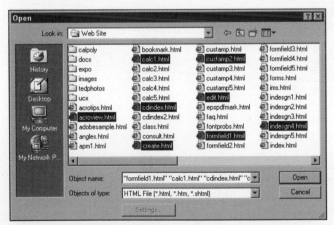

Figure 4-11: Clicking a file in the Open dialog box and Shift + Clicking files in a contiguous group (Windows only) opens multiple files. Noncontiguous selections require Control + Clicking (Shift + Click on a Mac).

To select files of different types, choose All Files (*.*) from the Objects of type pull-down menu. On the Macintosh, choose All Files from the Show pull-down menu. Multiple selections are made with the same modifier keys described above. After the files are converted and appear in the Acrobat Document pane, they will be converted to separate PDF files.

Drag and drop

Another method of opening files as PDFs from Acrobat is by dragging and dropping files either to the application icon or a Shortcut (Alias) of the application icon. When a document file is dragged on top of any one of these two items and the mouse button is released, the file(s) will be converted to PDF.

In Windows, you can also drag files to the Document pane either with a PDF document open and in view or to an empty window. To illustrate the ease of converting files by drag and drop on Windows, follow these steps:

STEPS: Dragging and dropping document files on the Acrobat Document pane in Windows

1. **Place multiple files in a folder.** Copy or place a number of files in a common folder. The file types must be one or a combination of the same file types listed earlier in this chapter.

2. **Launch Acrobat.** Launch the application.

3. **Resize the application window.** To see both the application window and the folder where the files to be converted, both windows should be in view.

4. **Place both the application window and the folder in view.** I sized my application window down and placed my folder containing some files to be converted adjacent to each other, as shown in Figure 4-12.

5. **Select the files to be converted.** To select a contiguous group of files, hold the Shift key down while clicking the files. For a noncontiguous group, Control + Click for each file to be selected in the group.

6. **Drag the files to the Document pane in the Acrobat application window.** After all files are selected, I release the modifier keys and drag the files to the Document pane. When the cursor is placed over the pane, I release the mouse button. The files are then converted and appear in a single PDF document. (Notice in Figure 4-12, the status bar reads 2 of 2. This reading is the result of dragging two files to the Document pane.)

The same results apply to files dropped on the program icon in the Acrobat folder or a Shortcut (Alias on a Mac) made from the application icon. On the Macintosh, you have to use either the application icon or an alias to produce a similar drag and drop effect. Dragging a file to the Acrobat Document pane on the Macintosh won't produce a PDF file conversion.

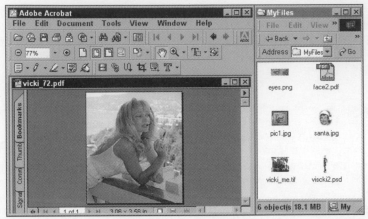

Figure 4-12: The Acrobat application window is sized down and the folder where the files to be converted is placed adjacent to the window.

Tip

If converting any of these file types is a common practice in your workflow, create a Shortcut (Alias) of the Acrobat application icon and place it on your desktop. When you drag the files to the Shortcut (Alias), Acrobat launches and the files will be converted to PDF. All the files converted will appear in a single PDF document. This method works for both Windows and Macintosh users.

Printing to Acrobat Distiller (Windows)

In Chapter 5, I cover all the details of working with Acrobat Distiller. The specifics on settings and operations to use with Distiller are all found in the next chapter. Our task at hand is not to control Distiller's options but to merely understand that often the Distiller application can work in the background to create a PDF file. This can occur with some file exports from applications as discussed in Chapter 6 or by using the Acrobat Distiller printer in Windows. When Adobe Acrobat is installed under Windows, a printer driver for Acrobat Distiller is part of the installation.

Printing to the Acrobat Distiller printer selection in the Print dialog box creates PDFs from application files. Virtually any application can take advantage of using the Acrobat Distiller Printer. When the print command is executed for the Acrobat Distiller printer, a file is printed to disk as a PostScript file and Distiller is automatically launched. Distiller subsequently creates a PDF from the application document and then returns you to the application document window. The process is transparent to the user; other than the momentary pause for producing the file, you may not even know it all happened.

To create a PDF with the Acrobat Distiller printer, choose File ⇨ Print from the application where the host document is in view. The Print dialog box appears, as shown in Figure 4-13. Among the list of printers in the dialog box you will see the Acrobat Distiller printer. Select this printer from the icons appearing under the Select Printer item.

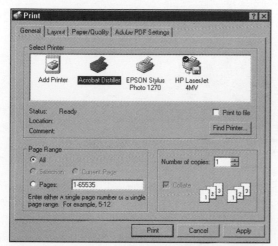

Figure 4-13: From the host document application, choose File ⇨ Print to open the Print dialog box. Select the Acrobat Distiller printer (shown here in Windows 2000) from the icons appearing under Select Printer.

At the far right of the Print dialog box, notice a checkbox for Print to file. Be certain to leave this checkbox disabled when converting to PDF. If Print to file is enabled, you can later convert the print file with Acrobat Distiller, but you'll need to perform a two-step operation by first printing the file to disk and then later launching the Distiller application. When the checkbox is disabled, Acrobat Distiller automatically launches, converts the file to PDF, and returns you to the host application.

When you click the Properties button, a number of tabs offer other dialog boxes where different attributes for the print output can be chosen. You can make selections as you would for any file to be printed on your desktop printer for facets, such as page size, orientation, and so forth. At the far right of the tabs, an item denoted as Adobe PDF Settings appears only when the Acrobat Distiller printer is selected. Click this tab to make changes for handling PDF files. Figure 4-14 shows the Adobe PDF Settings in the Print dialog box.

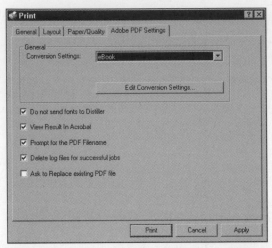

Figure 4-14: From the Print dialog box, click the Properties button and then click the Adobe PDF Settings tab to address options for creating the PDF file.

To determine attribute settings for the PDF and how it will be handled during and after creation, choices are made in Adobe PDF Settings dialog box. Among the items to be addressed are:

✦ **Conversion Settings:** The conversion settings are used to determine the kind of output results suited for different destinations. Displays on monitors, printing to desktop printers, and printing for high-end digital prepress all use different conversion settings. All the settings are covered in Chapter 5. For many PDF uses, you'll want to leave the default at eBook, as shown in Figure 4-14. These settings are optimally established for PDF viewing on monitors, exchanging files with others, and using PDFs for the Web. If you want to print PDFs, then look at Chapter 6 where the conversion options are discussed.

✦ **Edit Conversion Settings:** This button opens another dialog box where the Distiller Job Options can be addressed. For a complete description of Job Options, look at Chapter 5.

✦ **Do not send fonts to Distiller:** When enabled, the fonts will not be included in the PDF file. If the Acrobat Distiller application is monitoring a fonts folder as I describe in Chapter 5, the fonts will be embedded in the PDF file. If Distiller cannot find the fonts and the checkbox is enabled, fonts will not be embedded in the resultant PDF.

✦ **View Result in Acrobat:** After the PDF is created, the default Acrobat viewer is launched and the PDF is displayed in the Document pane.

✦ **Prompt for PDF Filename:** If the checkbox is enabled, you will be prompted for a filename and location for the PDF. This checkbox should be enabled at all times so that you know where the files are saved. If the checkbox is disabled, the PDFs will be nested in the Acrobat folder and usually more difficult to find.

✦ **Delete log files for successful jobs:** Every time Distiller is used, it creates a log file where errors in creating a PDF will be written. If a file is successfully converted, there is no need to keep the log file. Enabling this checkbox deletes the file only for PDFs that have been created successfully.

✦ **Ask to Replace existing PDF file:** If you convert a document to PDF, make an edit and print to Acrobat Distiller again, the new PDF file will overwrite the previous one if the default name is used. In the event you want to keep several versions of edited documents, keep this checkbox enabled. When Distiller encounters a filename already residing in the destination folder, you are prompted with a warning dialog box.

After all the settings have been selected in the Adobe PDF Settings dialog box, click the Print button. The PDF is produced. If you select View Result in Acrobat, the default Acrobat viewer launches and the PDF is displayed in the Document pane.

Create Adobe PDF (Macintosh)

For Macintosh users, the process of printing to a printer driver for PDF file conversion is very similar to Windows. To successfully convert application documents to PDF, Adobe recommends the LaserWriter 8.7 driver or higher when using Acrobat 5.0. This driver is available on the installation CD-ROM when you install Adobe Acrobat.

Although the process is very simple and quite similar to Windows, the setup and configuration can sometimes be a bit confusing. Much of the confusion has to do with the version of the operating system and the printer drivers installed. Add to this some extra configuration toggles and the easy PDF conversion can sometimes become overwhelming. Fortunately, after you muddle through the configuration steps, creating PDFs will be seamless and easy to perform. For many different operating systems and the use of different printer drivers and PPD selections, you have alternatives for almost any configuration steps you perform. As we explore the setup, I cover some of the alternatives you can use.

Selecting the printer

Making the right choice for a printer is the first step in the configuration process. Here you have a couple of alternatives. You can choose the LaserWriter 8.7 printer driver recommended by Adobe in which case you need to have System 8.6 or above installed. Users of System 8.1 and 8.5 need to use another printer driver. The universal axiom with whatever system you use is that the printer driver must be a PostScript printer. The most common choices available to you include one of two options:

✦ **LaserWriter 8.7:** With System 8.6 and above, you can open the Chooser dialog box and select the LaserWriter 8.7 printer driver. After selecting the LaserWriter 8.7 printer driver, select a PostScript local printer or one on your network. In the Chooser is a button for Setup, as shown in Figure 4-15. Click the button, and your system should auto configure the printer with the proper PostScript Printer Description (PPD) file. Close the dialog box and the new driver now becomes your default.

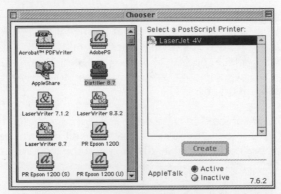

Figure 4-15: In the Chooser dialog box, when you select a printer in the right panel, the Setup button becomes active. Clicking this button enables you to select a PostScript Printer Description (PPD) file. In the Chooser dialog box, note the name of the LaserWriter 8.7 was changed to Distiller 8.7. This change is a personal choice. If you want to change printer driver names, use names descriptive of the kind of driver that is used.

✦ **AdobePS:** The AdobePS printer driver can be downloaded from the Adobe Web site or you may already have it installed on your computer. If using a Mac OS prior to System 8.6 or if you have any problems with the LaserWriter 8.7 driver, select this printer. Click a PostScript local printer or one on your network, and then click the Setup button.

Tip

The PPD selected for the printer is a device PPD and includes all the information, such as color handling, page sizes, font information, and so forth for the device you use. When creating PDFs, using the Acrobat Distiller PPD rather than the device PPD is often more desirable. To create a second printer driver and assign the Acrobat Distiller PPD to the driver, open the System:Extensions folder and select the LaserWriter 8.7 driver. Duplicate the driver by pressing Command + D. Rename the driver with a name that's descriptive. In Figure 4-15, I named a duplicate driver Distiller 8.7. Select the new driver in the Chooser and click the Setup button. In the next dialog box, click the Select PPD button, as shown in Figure 4-16. Another dialog box appears where the PPD selection can be made. Find the Acrobat Distiller PPD and select it, as shown in Figure 4-17. Click Open and then click OK. The new printer driver now uses the Acrobat Distiller PPD.

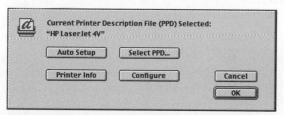

Figure 4-16: To assign a PPD for the new printer driver, click the Select PPD button.

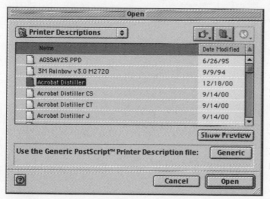

Figure 4-17: From the list of PPDs in your System Folder, select the Acrobat Distiller PPD.

Page setup

After the printer has been selected, you're ready to print a file from an application. Before selecting the Print dialog box, you need to visit the Page Setup dialog box. Here you find some important toggles to configure. In virtually every application, choose File ⇨ Page Setup to open the Page Setup dialog box. Under the Printer item, a pull-down menu exists where PostScript Options can be selected. Choose PostScript Options from the pull-down menu and the display appears, as shown in Figure 4-18.

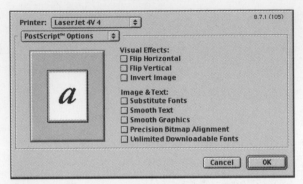

Figure 4-18: In the PostScript Options dialog box, choices for font handling and text and image smoothing can be made. Disabling all the checkboxes before printing PostScript or converting to PDF is important.

By default, the first three items under Image & Text are checked. Substitute fonts, Smooth Text, and Smooth Graphics should all be deselected. If text and graphics smoothing is enabled, both will be anti-aliased with tiny pixels in contrast areas adding to file size and printing time. Anti-aliasing won't be needed to produce quality prints and is more of a burden than asset. After disabling the checkboxes, click OK.

Printing the file

Depending on which driver is used, the Print dialog box appears differently. Both will be used to create the PDF, however the attribute choices vary a little. The choices include:

✦ **LaserWriter drivers:** For either the LaserWriter 8.7 driver or even earlier drivers, you may not have an option for Create Adobe PDF displayed in the pop-up menu below Printer. If this is the case, select the option denoted as Save as File from the pop-up menu. When Save as File is selected, choose Acrobat PDF for the Format, as shown in Figure 4-19. From within the dialog box, you can make some choices for image and text handling. All of these options are addressed in Chapter 5 when I cover the Distiller JobOptions. If you are using the default settings, then click Save and the file will be printed as a PostScript file and subsequently distilled with Acrobat Distiller.

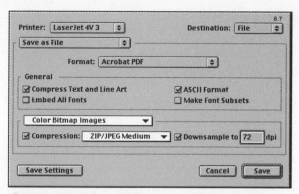

Figure 4-19: Select Adobe PDF from the Format pull-down menu. After the selection is made and the file printed, a PDF is created.

✦ **AdobePS driver:** If a Create Adobe PDF option is not available in the Print dialog box when using another printer driver, then your best bet is to use the AdobePS driver. This driver affords you the capability of using JobOptions assigned to the Distiller application. When you choose File ➪ Print, the Create Adobe PDF option is available in the Printer pull-down menu, as shown in Figure 4-20.

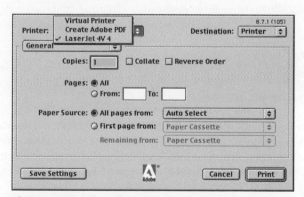

Figure 4-20: The AdobePS printer driver includes a Create Adobe PDF pull-down menu option.

Click the OK button and another dialog box appears, as shown in Figure 4-21. This dialog box enables you to make choices for JobOptions and how the PDF viewing will be handled. Leave the default for eBook enabled. Choices for viewing the PDF appear in the second pop-up menu. After all the selections have been made, click Save and the PDF is created.

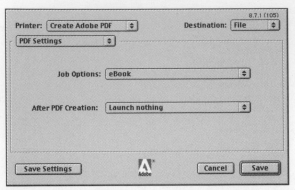

Figure 4-21: After selecting Create Adobe PDF in the
Print dialog box and clicking the Print button, another
dialog box appears where JobOptions and viewing
can be chosen.

Drag and drop printing

All of the many controls used to configure printers and Create Adobe PDF on the
Macintosh leaves one to wonder how the claim of being easier to use than a
Windows machine could be made. Compared to printing to the Acrobat Distiller in
Windows, the maze of controls on the Macintosh is a bit more complicated. The
configuration goes to Windows, but once configured, the ease of drag and drop
printing is advantaged on the Macintosh. To use drag and drop printing, you do
have to be certain one more configuration control has been made. Make sure that
you open the Extensions Manager by choosing Apple Menu ➪ Control Panels ➪
Extensions Manager. In the Extensions Manager dialog box, scroll down to the
Desktop printer options, as shown in Figure 4-22. Be certain the Desktop Spooler
and Desktop PrintMonitor are enabled.

A printer for Create Adobe PDF should appear on your desktop when the
Extensions are enabled. To create a PDF from any application document, drag the
document file to the top of the printer icon. If the host application is not open, it
will be launched automatically and the file will be printed and distilled. The PDF
produced by the Create Adobe PDF printer is saved to the Desktop.

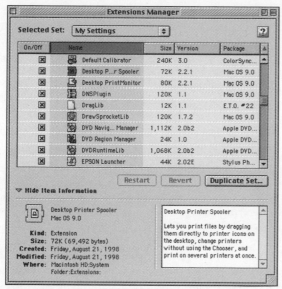

Figure 4-22: For a printer to be placed on the Desktop, enable the Desktop printer extensions in the Extensions Manager.

Note   To use the drag and drop method of creating PDFs with the Create Adobe PDF printer, you must have the application from which the document was created.

Creating PDFs from Web sites

Acrobat introduced a means of converting Web sites to PDF in Version 4.0 called Web Capture. The first implementation was only available in Windows. After the release of Acrobat 4.05, Web Capture was provided in the Macintosh version. The menu command, Open Web Page, enables the user to convert Web pages to PDF. It may be a bit redundant but you also have a submenu available for Web Capture by choosing Tools ➪ Web Capture. The first command in the submenu is also termed Open Web Page. And, like many other Acrobat features, a third method exists for invoking the same command. When a preference setting for the Web Capture preferences is enabled, the Open Web Page tool appears in the Command bar used for invoking Web Capture.

With a complex set of preferences and tools, Web Capture provides different options for converting Web pages, a Web site, or multiple sites to PDF. A captured Web site converts HTML, text files, and images to PDF, and each Web page is appended to the converted document. Whereas the Open as PDF command converts HTML files on a hard drive or network, Web Capture can be performed either locally on a single computer or through an Internet or Intranet connection. Conversion to PDF from Web sites can provide many opportunities for archiving information, analyzing data, creating search indexes and many more uses where information needs to reside locally on computers.

Web site structure

To understand how capturing a Web site and converting the documents to PDF is handled, you need a fundamental understanding of a Web page and the structure of a site. A Web page is a file created with HTML. There is nothing specific to the length of a Web page. A page may be a screen the size of 640×480 pixels or a length equivalent to several hundred letter-sized pages. The page content usually determines size in terms of linear length and amount of space needed to display the page. PDF files, on the other hand, have fixed lengths up to 200 inches x 200 inches. You can determine the fixed size of the PDF page prior to converting the Web site from HTML to PDF. After the PDF page size is determined, any Web pages captured will adhere to the fixed size. If a Web page is larger than the established PDF page, the overflow will automatically create additional PDF pages. Hence, a single Web page converted, may result in several PDF pages.

When Web sites are designed, they typically follow a hierarchical order, as shown in Figure 4-23. The home page rests at the topmost level where direct links from this page will occupy a second level. Subsequently, links from the second level will refer to pages at a third level, and so forth.

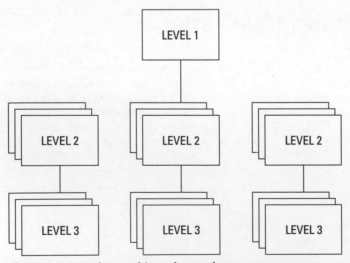

Figure 4-23: Web page hierarchy can have many pages at multiple levels. The volume of Web pages at any level other than the first level can be extensive.

When pages are captured with Acrobat, the user can specify the number of levels to convert. Be forewarned, though, even two levels of a Web site can occupy many Web pages. The number of pages to convert and the speed of your Internet connection determine the amount of time needed to capture a site.

Captured pages structure

One or more levels can be captured from a Web site that is user defined in the Open Web Page dialog box. PDF pages can be converted and placed in a new PDF file or appended to an existing PDF file. One nice feature with Web Capture is that it can seek out and append only new pages that have not yet been downloaded.

As soon as pages are converted to PDF, they can be viewed in Acrobat or linked directly to a Web browser for viewing on the Internet. Among the file types that can be converted to PDF include the following:

✦ **HTML documents:** HTML files can be converted to PDF. The hypertext links from the original HTML file is active in the PDF document as long as the destination documents and URLs have also been converted.

✦ **PDF documents:** Although not converted to PDF because they already appear in the format, PDF pages can be downloaded with Web Capture.

✦ **Text files:** Any text-only documents contained on a Web site, such as an ASCII text document, can be converted to PDF. When capturing text-only files, you have the opportunity to control many text attributes and page formats.

✦ **JPEG images:** Images used in the HTML documents can also be captured and converted to PDF. JPEGs may be part of the converted HTML page. When captured, they can be part of a captured HTML page and can also appear individually on PDF pages.

✦ **GIF images:** GIF images, as well as the last image in an animated GIF, can also be captured when converting a Web site. GIFs, like JPEGs, appear in the HTML file and can also appear on separate PDF pages.

✦ **FDF/XFDF:** Form Data Files (FDF) can also be converted to PDF. If Form Data appears in a database file, the entire file is converted.

✦ **Image maps:** Image maps created in HTML can be converted to PDF. The links associated with the map are active in the PDF as long as the link destinations are also converted.

✦ **Password-secure areas:** A password-secure area of a Web site can also be converted to PDF. To access a secure site however, you need the password(s).

✦ **HTML attributes:** Pages containing frames, tables, background and text colors, PDF, and HTML forms can be converted. All the attributes are preserved in the PDF document.

Accepted file types and links

If a Web page link to another Web page or URL exists, the link is preserved in the converted PDF document. Links to pages, sites, and various actions work similarly to the way they do directly on the Web site. If a PDF document contains a link to another PDF document, the converted file won't preserve the link. When the site is converted, the captured pages reside in a single PDF document. To maintain PDF links that open other PDF documents, the destination documents need to be captured as individual pages or extracted and saved from the converted pages.

Links to another level are also inactive if they have not been converted during the capture. Individual linked pages can be appended to the converted PDF document by viewing Web links and opening a dialog box. Selections for converting individual links are made available. One or more links can then be appended to the converted document. Specifics on how to accomplish this task are explained when you look at appending links a little later in this chapter.

JavaScripts cannot be downloaded when capturing a Web site. For executed animation, such as an animation from a GIF file or other programming application, the download only contains the last image in the sequence. A mouseover effect that changes an image is preserved in the converted PDF document as long as both the original image and the image associated with the mouseover are downloaded. Additionally, sounds contained in documents can be captured.

For Web pages that contain non-English characters, you need to have the appropriate resources loaded to download and convert the files. Japanese characters, for example, require installation of the Far East language files and additional system files.

Bookmarks in converted pages

After a Web site has been converted to PDF, you can edit the document in Acrobat like you would any other PDF. Links to pages become editable links — that is, their properties can be changed and modified. When a site has been converted to PDF, all the PDF pages contain bookmarks linked to the respective pages, as shown in Figure 4-24. The first bookmark is a regular (unstructured) bookmark that contains the name of the server from which the site was captured. All bookmarks appearing below the server name are structured bookmarks linked to the converted pages. With the exception of specific Web applications, these bookmarks can be edited and modified just as any other bookmarks created in Acrobat. Additionally structured bookmarks can be used for page editing by moving and deleting the bookmarks and associated pages. For a more detailed discussion on structured bookmarks, see Chapter 9.

Figure 4-24: A captured Web site converted to PDF displays the Web server name as a normal bookmark at the top of the list. All bookmarks below the server name are structured bookmarks linked to the converted pages. The bookmark names refer to HTML filenames, PDF document names, and URLs.

Converting Web pages to PDF

To begin capturing Web pages, choose File ➪ Open Web Page. The alternative methods, such as selecting Tools ➪ Web Capture ➪ Open Web Page or clicking the Open Web Page tool in the Command bar can also be used to produce the same dialog box. Regardless of the command used, the Open Web Page dialog box appears, as shown in Figure 4-25.

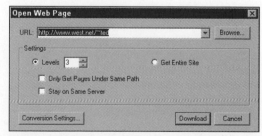

Figure 4-25: If you select the Open Web Page command from any of the three methods used to capture a Web page, the Open Web Page dialog box appears.

In the Open Web Page dialog box, various settings can determine many different attributes for how the Web page will be converted to PDF and how they will appear in the Acrobat Document pane. The first level of controls is handled in the Open Web Page dialog box. Additional buttons in this dialog box open other dialog boxes where many more settings can be applied. If this is your first attempt at capturing a Web page, then leave the default values in the dialog box, as shown in Figure 4-25 and supply a URL in the first field box. Click the download button and watch the page appear in Acrobat. Above all, verify that the Levels field box is set to 1. Entering any other value may keep you waiting for some time depending on how many pages are going to download.

Depending on the site, the number of different links from the site to other URLs and the structure of the HTML pages, there will often be a need to wade through the maze of dialog boxes that control settings for the PDF conversion from the HTML files. You needn't memorize all these, but just use the following as a reference when capturing Web pages.

Settings in the Open Web Page dialog box

The controls available to you in the Open Web Page dialog box begin with the URL that you supplied previously when downloading the first Web page. This field box determines the site at which the pages are hosted that are to be converted. After the URL is entered, the remaining selections include:

✦ **Levels:** Appended pages can contain more than one level. The URL link may go to another site hosted on another server or stay on the same server. Select the levels to be downloaded by clicking the up or down arrows or enter a numeric value in the field box.

Caution   A Web site can have two levels of extraordinary size. If the Home page is on the first level and many links are contained on the Home page, all the associated links will be at the second level. If downloading with a slow connection, the time needed to capture the site can take quite a long time.

✦ **Get Entire Site:** If the radio button is selected, all levels on the Web site will be downloaded.

✦ **Only Get Pages Under Same Path:** If this option is enabled, all documents will be confined to the directory path under the selected URL.

✦ **Stay on Same Server:** If links are made to other servers, they will not be downloaded when this option is enabled.

✦ **Conversion Settings:** Clicking Conversion Settings opens another dialog box (see Figure 4-26) where attribute choices for various file types can be made.

✦ **Download**: Clicking this button commences the download and conversion to PDF.

✦ **Browse:** Clicking this button enables you to capture a Web site resident on your computer or network server. Click Browse and a navigation dialog box opens where you can find the directory where HTML pages are stored and capture the pages.

Although it may not be entirely practical, Web designers more comfortable with WYSISWYG (What You See Is What You Get) HTML editors over layout applications may find it beneficial to create layout assemblies in their favorite editor. You can't get control over image sampling, but a layout for screen display can be accomplished. Create the layout in a program, such as Adobe GoLive, Microsoft FrontPage, or Macromedia DreamWeaver. After you're finished with the pages, launch Acrobat and choose File ➪ Open Web Page. Click the Browse button in the Open Web Page dialog box and navigate to your HTML files. Click the Select button and your pages convert to PDF. These pages can be sent as an e-mail attachment to a colleague or printed to your desktop printer. Sounds a little crazy, but some people just don't like to leave familiar ground.

Caution

Even though you may browse to a folder on your hard drive and convert a local Web site to PDF, any external links will launch your Internet connection and capture pages on anoth er site. If you only want local pages to be converted, be certain to click the button Stay on Same Server in the Open Web Page dialog box.

General conversion settings

Clicking the Conversion Settings button in the Open Web Page dialog box opens a second dialog box. Two tabs are visible in the Conversion Settings dialog box where file conversion attributes and page layout settings can be supplied. The General tab deals with the file attribute settings as shown in Figure 4-26.

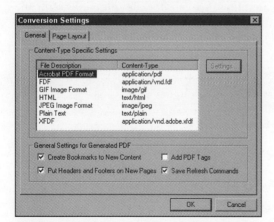

Figure 4-26: The Conversion Settings dialog box offers controls for file types and how they are converted to PDF.

At the top of the dialog box, a list of file types is displayed in the File Description column. Each file type can be selected in the list. Only the file types for HTML and Text offer more options by selecting the Settings button on the right side of the dialog box. If a file type other than HTML or Plain Text is selected, the Settings button will not be active. At the bottom of the dialog box, four General Settings for Generated PDF include checkboxes for the following:

- **Create Bookmarks to New Content:** When enabled, pages converted to PDF have structured bookmarks created for each page captured. The bookmark name uses the page's title as the bookmark name. If the page has no title, Acrobat will supply the URL as the bookmark name.

- **Put Headers and Footers on New Page:** A header and footer is placed on all converted pages if this option is enabled. A header in the HTML file consists of the page title appearing with the <HEAD> tag. The footer retrieves the page's URL, the page name, and a date stamp for the date and time that the page was downloaded.

- **Add PDF Tags:** The structure of the converted PDF matches that of the original HTML file. Items, such as list elements, table cells, and similar HTML tags are preserved. The PDF document creates structured bookmarks for each of the structured items. A tagged bookmark can then link to a table, list, or other HTML element.

- **Save Refresh Commands (Windows)/Save Update Commands (Macintosh):** When enabled, a list of all URLs in the PDF document converted is saved. When the capture is refreshed, these URLs are revisited and new PDF pages are converted for additional pages added to the site. If appending new pages to the PDF, this item must be enabled for Acrobat to update the file.

Returning to the top of the dialog box, the two items where additional settings can be edited include HTML and Plain Text files. When HTML is selected in the File Description list and the Settings button clicked, a dialog box opens for HTML Conversion Settings, as shown in Figure 4-27.

Figure 4-27: If HTML is selected in the File Description list and you click the Settings button, the HTML Conversion Settings dialog box opens.

Two tabs are in the HTML Conversion Settings dialog box. The first group of settings handles the attributes assigned to the page layout. These include:

✦ **Default Colors:** Assigns new default color for Text, Background color, Links, and Alt Text colors with user-identified colors. A set of preset colors as well as an option for custom colors can be selected from a palette appearing after clicking the swatch.

✦ **Force These Settings for All Pages:** HTML pages may or may not have assigned color values for the items listed previously. When no color is assigned for one of these items, the Default Colors defines these elements with the colors selected previously. If this checkbox is enabled, all colors, including HTML assigned colors will change to the Default Colors above.

✦ **Background Options:** These include settings for the background colors used on the Web page, tiled image backgrounds, and table cells. When these checkboxes are enabled, the original design is preserved in the PDF document.

Tip

If table cells, background colors, and tiled background images appear distracting when reading Web pages either in a browser or converted to PDF, disable the checkboxes before converting to PDF. The original design will not be preserved, but the files will be easily legible for both screen reading and when printed.

✦ **Line Wrap:** Enables you to choose a maximum distance for word-wrapping the text in an HTML file. When the <PRE> tag is used in HTML, the text is preformatted to preserve line breaks and indents. The field box for this option enables controlling the maximum length for text lines in inches.

✦ **Convert Images:** Converts images contained in the HTML as separate PDF pages. If the option is disabled, the JPEG and GIF images will not be converted to separate PDF pages, but will appear on the HTML converted page.

Tip

To produce faster downloads, disable the Convert Images checkbox. The number of pages to be converted maybe be reduced significantly thereby reducing the amount of time to capture a Web site.

✦ **Underline Links:** Displays the text used in an <A HREF...> tag with an underline. This option can be helpful if the text for a link is not a different color than the body copy.

After the Layout settings have been chosen, click the Fonts tab to open the Fonts portion of the HTML Conversion Settings dialog box. The display appears, as shown in Figure 4-28.

Figure 4-28: When you select the Fonts tab in the HTML Conversion Settings dialog box, another dialog display appears where font choices can be made.

Options for font handling include:

✦ **Body Text, Headings, and Fonts for Pre-Formatted:** (Used with the `<PRE>` tag in the HTML file). These properties can be changed globally by selecting the Fonts tab in the HTML Conversions dialog box. Click the Choose Font button for the respective item to display your installed system fonts and select a font to be used during conversion, as shown in Figure 4-29.

✦ **Embed Platform Fonts:** Fonts used to view the pages are embedded when the checkbox is enabled. The file sizes are larger with embedded fonts, but file integrity is preserved. Embedded fonts ensure display and print of the PDF documents precisely as seen in the Web browser.

After choosing all the settings for how HTML files will be converted, click the OK button in the HTML Conversion Settings dialog box. The dialog box disappears and returns you to the Conversion Settings dialog box. The second group of settings can be established for Plain Text documents. Select Plain Text in the File Description list and click the Settings button, as shown earlier in Figure 4-26. The Text Conversion Settings dialog box appears, as shown in Figure 4-30.

Figure 4-29: When Choose Font is selected from any of the three font representations, a dialog box appears where a system font and point size can be selected. The chosen font appears as the default for the respective text in the converted PDF.

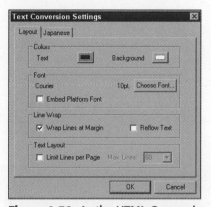

Figure 4-30: In the HTML Conversion Settings dialog box, select Plain Text in the File Description list and click the Settings button. The Text Conversion Settings dialog box appears where settings can be applied for ASCII text file conversion to PDF.

Choices in this dialog box are similar to the choices available in the HTML Conversion dialog box for the Color, Font, and Line Wrap items. Line Wrap behaves similarly to the Pre-Formatted text discussed earlier. One additional item has been added to this dialog box:

✦ **Text Layout:** For large bodies of text the number of lines on the page can be limited. Depending on point size, the standard number of lines on an 8.5 x 11 letter size page is 66. The default in Acrobat is 60 if the checkbox is enabled. You can make a choice for the number of lines by editing the field box only after selecting the checkbox.

After making changes in the Page Layout dialog box for Plain Text documents, click the OK button. Again you return to the Conversion Settings dialog box.

Page Layout Conversion Settings

All of the settings discussed on the previous few pages were related to the General Conversion Settings. Once again in the Conversion Settings dialog box, another option is available for handling page layout. Click the Page Layout tab and another dialog box appears, as shown in Figure 4-31.

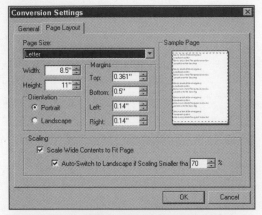

Figure 4-31: The Page Layout options are available from the Conversion Settings dialog box when you select the Page Layout tab.

Page layout attributes enable you to force long HTML pages into more standard page sizes for viewing or printing. If an HTML page spans several letter pages, you can determine where the page breaks will occur and the orientation of the con- verted pages. Many options are available in the Page Layout section of the Conversion Settings dialog box and they include:

✦ **Page Size:** A pull-down menu with default page sizes provides selections for a variety of different sizes. Acrobat supports page sizes from 1-inch square to 200-inches square. You can supply any value between the minimum and maxi- mum page sizes in the Width and Height field boxes to override the fixed sizes available from the pop-up menu.

✦ **Margins:** The amount of space on all four sides of the PDF page before any data appears can be set in the four Margins field boxes.

✦ **Sample Page:** The thumbnail at the right side of the dialog box displays a view of how the converted page will appear when sizes are established for the Width, Height, and Margin settings.

✦ **Orientation:** Choices for Portrait or Landscape orientation are selected from the radio button options. If a site contains all Web pages that conform to screen sizes, such as 640 x 480, you may want to change the orientation to Landscape.

✦ **Scaling:** Once again, because HTML documents don't follow standard page sizes, images and text can be easily clipped when converting to a standard size. When this option is enabled, the page contents are reduced in size to fit within the page margins.

✦ **Auto-Switch to Landscape if Scaling Smaller than:** The percentage value is user definable. When the page contents appear on a portrait page within the limit specified in the field box, the PDF document is automatically converted to a landscape page. The default is 70 percent. If the default value is used, any page scaled lower than 70 percent is auto-switched to Landscape as long as the orientation is selected for Portrait.

If your workflow is dependent on capturing Web pages routinely, then you'll want to use the same conversion settings for most of your Web captures. For educational facilities, government agencies, research institutes, and large corporate offices, there may be repeated needs for archiving research information found on the Web.

Unfortunately, Acrobat makes no provision for saving and loading Web Capture settings established in all of those dialog boxes discussed in the preceding pages of this chapter. To develop a workflow suited to organizations or workgroups, your one alternative may be setting up a single computer dedicated to the task of capturing data from the Web. The computer needs to be licensed for Acrobat, but using a single computer will ensure that all Web Captures are performed with the same Conversion Settings. Users can retrieve the PDF files captured across a network or Intranet with either Acrobat or Reader installed.

Download status

After all settings have been made in all the dialog boxes for the options to be used when converting Web sites to PDF, you can revisit the Open Web Page command from any one of the three methods discussed earlier. As pages are downloaded and converted to PDF, a dialog box appears displaying the download status. After the first page is downloaded, the dialog box, shown in Figure 4-32, disappears when running Acrobat under Windows. On the Macintosh, the Download Status dialog box remains in view during the entire download.

Web Capture places the converted PDF in memory and uses your hard drive space as an extension of RAM. The PDF will not be saved to disk until you perform a Save or Save As function. If your computer crashes or you quit without saving, the file will be lost and you'll need to capture the site again.

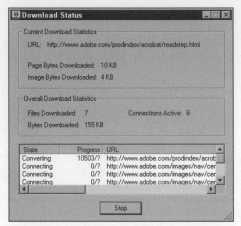

Figure 4-32: The Download Status dialog box appears momentarily and then disappears as Acrobat continues to download pages and then convert them to PDF.

On Windows the dialog box will remain open, but will appear behind the PDF pages being converted as the download continues. If you want to bring the Download Status dialog box to the foreground, choose Tools ➪ Web Capture ➪ Bring Status Dialogs to Foreground (Windows only). The dialog box remains in the foreground while Acrobat continues to convert pages. If you want to have the Download Status dialog box remain in the background and you still want to observe whether the download progress is occurring, the globe in the Open Web Page tool in the Acrobat Command bar spins while the download is in progress.

On Macintosh computers, if the Window Shade is collapsed, the Download Status dialog box will continue to be visible. You can toggle the Window Shade by clicking in the top-right corner of the application window to open and collapse the window.

Appending pages

When a PDF file is open in the Document pane, pages can be appended from URL links by choosing Tools ➪ Web Capture and then selective choices made from the submenu commands. Pages can also be appended by opening a context-sensitive menu. To open a context-sensitive menu, the cursor must be positioned over a structured bookmark when you right-click (Control + Click on a Mac) the mouse button. Figure 4-33 displays the submenu options from the Tools menu.

Figure 4-33: When choosing Tools ⇨ Web Capture, the submenu options for appending pages appear.

Choices for appending pages to the open PDF can be made through the following selections in the submenu command:

✦ **Append Web Page:** Selecting this option opens a dialog box where attribute choices can be made. The dialog box for Append Web Page, as shown in Figure 4-34 offers the same choices as originally displayed in the Open Web Page dialog box. When appending pages, you can change the attribute choices for all the options discussed earlier.

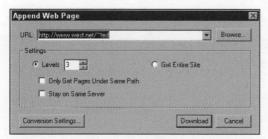

Figure 4-34: The Append Web Page dialog box offers the same options as the Open Web Page dialog box.

✦ **Append All Links on Page:** When this submenu option is selected, no dialog box appears before the download commences. All Web links to other HTML pages are converted and appended to the PDF. Conversion settings are used from the last options choices made in the Open Web Page dialog box. If the conversion settings need to be changed for links to other pages, you can use the View Web Links dialog box explained in the next section.

✦ **View Web Links:** A dialog box opens when the menu command is selected. In the Select Page Links to Download dialog box, all Web links are listed according to the URL, as shown in Figure 4-35.

The list contains an icon displayed at the far left of the URL listing informing you that a link exists to the URL. Each item in the list can be selected. After it's selected, the Properties button on the right side of the dialog box becomes active. Click the Properties button and another dialog box opens, as shown in Figure 4-36.

Notice that in this dialog box all the options for conversion settings appear within the three tabs. These settings options are the same as those described when using the Open Web Page command.

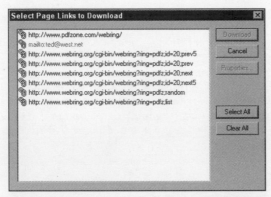

Figure 4-35: If you select the View Web Links in the Web Capture submenu, the Select Page Links to Download dialog box opens where a list of all Web links in the PDF appear.

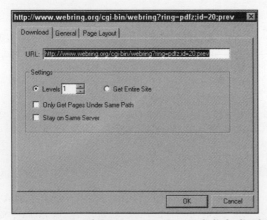

Figure 4-36: The Properties for each link display a dialog box where appended pages conversion options can be determined.

✦ **Page Info:** A dialog box appears displaying information about the current page viewed in the PDF file. As you scroll through pages, the Page info changes according to the page viewed. The information supplied in the dialog box, as shown in Figure 4-37, includes the original URL, title of the page, creation date, a description of the content, and the preferred zoom level for viewing.

When a context menu is opened from a structured bookmark, the menu options appear, as displayed in Figure 4-38. The two choices from the menu commands for appending pages to the PDF include Append Next Level and View Web Links. These menu commands offer the same options as those described when choosing the same Web Capture submenu commands.

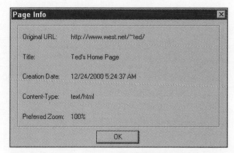

Figure 4-37: Page Info is dependent on the page viewed in the PDF. As you scroll pages, the dialog box reflects the information on the respective page. While the dialog box is open, page scrolling is not permitted.

Figure 4-38: When the cursor is placed over a structured bookmark, the context menu options provide choices for appending pages to the PDF.

Tip   Clicking a link in the PDF page can also append Web pages. If the link destination is not contained in the PDF, the URL will be contacted and the page appended to the PDF. When the cursor is positioned over a link, the cursor displays a hand icon and index finger pointing upward. If a link has not yet been converted, the icon displays a plus (+) symbol inside the hand, and a tool tip displays the URL where the link can be found. If the link has been converted to PDF, no plus (+) symbol and no URL display will appear.

Refreshing Web pages

Refreshing pages is used to update a previously captured site. If content has changed, the updated pages will be downloaded. Any pages remaining constant without changes are ignored. To update a PDF file created with Web Capture, choose Tools ➪ Web Capture ➪ Refresh Pages. The Refresh Pages dialog box appears, as shown in Figure 4-39. To update pages with the Refresh Pages command, the Conversion Settings in the original Open Web Page dialog box must have the Save Refresh Commands checkbox enabled, as shown earlier in Figure 4-26.

Figure 4-39: The Refresh Pages dialog box offers options for converting pages to be updated in the open PDF file.

Updates occur according to options selected in the Refresh Pages dialog box. You have two choices for comparing the page to be downloaded with a page in the PDF document. These include:

✦ **Compare Only Page Text to Detect Changed Pages:** If you are interested in only changes made to the text on Web pages, then click this checkbox. Acrobat will ignore new graphics, colors, backgrounds and other nontext elements.

✦ **Compare All Page Components to Detect Changed Pages:** When enabled, this option downloads and converts pages where any change has occurred.

If you want to selectively update different page links, then click the Edit Refresh Commands List button in the Refresh Pages dialog box. Another dialog box appears, which is similar to the one used with the View Web Links command. When the Refresh Commands List dialog box opens, as shown in Figure 4-40, all links are selected by default.

Figure 4-40: When you open the Refresh Commands List dialog box, all Web links contained in the PDF are selected by default.

If you want all links to be updated, leave the default alone and proceed with the download. If selected links are to be updated, click the desired link to update. For multiple links, hold the Shift key down as the links are selected. For noncontiguous selections in the list, hold the Control key down (Command key on a Mac) and click links to be included in the update. Click OK and exit the Refresh Pages dialog box. The download will commence, and the Download Status dialog box will disappear. To view the status on Windows, bring it to the front by choosing Tools ➪ Web Capture ➪ Bring Status Dialogs to Front.

Tip

Comparing Web pages for obvious changes prior to refreshing the page can occur by visiting the Web page in your browser. In Acrobat, choose Edit ➪ Preferences ➪ Web Capture. In the Web Capture Preferences, as shown later in this chapter in Figure 4-42, select In Web Browser from the Open Weblinks pop-up menu. Click OK and click the URL link in the PDF file. The Web page opens in your Web browser. Compare this page to the PDF page to determine any discrepancies before downloading the pages.

Locate Web addresses

If you have a PDF file that has been converted from a document where a URL is identified in text, Acrobat can convert the text to a Web link. The text must have the complete URL listing including http://. As soon as the Web link is converted, you can click the link and append pages by using Web Capture. For PDF authors, you may also create Web links for end users when distributing files to others.

To create Web links on pages where URLs are identified, choose Tools ➪ Locate Web Addresses ➪ Create Web Links from URLs in text. A dialog box opens, as shown in Figure 4-41.

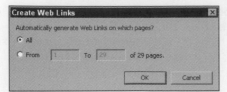

Figure 4-41: The Create Web Links dialog box enables you to create Web links from text for user defined page ranges in the open PDF file.

In the dialog box, you can specify page ranges where the links will be created. Acrobat performs this task quickly and creates all links where the proper syntax has been used to describe the URL. If you want to delete links from a PDF document, open the Remove Links dialog box by selecting Tools ⇨ Locate Web Address ⇨ Remove Web Links from document. The same dialog box appears where page ranges can be user supplied for eliminating Web links.

Preferences for Web Capture

The Web Capture preferences are available by choosing Edit ⇨ Preferences ⇨ Web Capture (see Figure 4-42). The attribute settings further identify Web Link behavior as well as options available for converting a Web site to PDF.

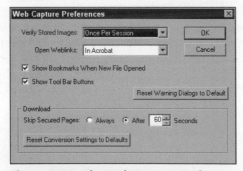

Figure 4-42: The Web Capture Preferences dialog box opens after choosing Edit ⇨ Preferences ⇨ Web Capture.

The choices appearing in the Web Capture Preferences dialog box include:

✦ **Verify Stored Images:** From the pull-down menu, options are available for verifying images stored on a captured Web site Once Per Session, Always, or Never. When the default setting, Once Per Session, is selected, Acrobat checks the Web site to see if stored images have changed on the site. If changed, the new files are downloaded.

✦ **Open Weblinks:** You can elect to open Weblinks in either Acrobat or the default browser. When the browser is used, clicking a Web link in the converted PDF document launches the browser and opens the URL for the associated link. Regardless of whether links are a result of captured pages or authored PDF files, the view will appear in the Web browser.

Regardless of which option you elect to use for opening Web links, you can use the alternate method by pressing the Shift key and clicking the link. For example, if the preference setting is used to display the link in the Web browser, Shift + Click displays the link in Acrobat and vice versa.

✦ **Show Bookmarks When New File Opened:** When this option is enabled, the converted PDF file is displayed with the Navigation pane open and the structured bookmarks appearing in the Bookmarks tab. When this option is disabled, the Navigation pane is closed, but the bookmarks will still be created.

✦ **Show Tool Bar Buttons:** The top left of the Command Bar is the Open Web Page button. When this item is enabled, the button is displayed. If you deselect the checkbox, the tool disappears from the Command bar.

✦ **Reset Warning Dialogs to Default:** When you first capture a site in an Acrobat session, a warning dialog box appears, informing you the operation may take a long time to complete. An option in the dialog box enables you to eliminate the warning during subsequent downloads. To regain access to this or other warning dialog boxes, enable Reset Warning Dialogs to Default. The next time the same command is invoked, a warning dialog box reappears.

✦ **Skip Secured Pages:** Secured areas of a Web site can be downloaded, but you must have permission to access the password protected areas. If you inadvertently attempt to download a secure area, you can elect to always skip secured pages or skip secured pages at specified intervals ranging between 1 and 9999 seconds.

When you enter a secure area of a Web site, Acrobat provides an opportunity to supply a login name and/or password. The dialog box shown in Figure 4-43 automatically opens for secure sites.

Acrobat will continue to try to gain access to a secure site until the time interval established in the Web Capture Preferences dialog box has been reached. In the dialog box that appears when you try to download secured pages, the time remaining in the specified interval is displayed. When no access is granted, an error dialog box opens, displaying an error message and the URL where the access attempt was made.

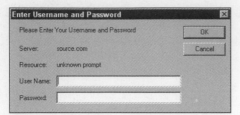

Figure 4-43: When attempting to capture Web pages on a secure site, you need to access the site with a username and password.

✦ **Reset Conversion Settings to Defaults:** Clicking this button resets all options in the Conversion Settings dialog boxes back to the default positions when Acrobat was first installed.

Capturing a Web site

The number of options available for converting Web pages to PDF documents and controlling the behavior of Weblinks may seem overwhelming when you first attempt to capture a site. There is no substitute for practice. The more you use the tools and options discussed earlier, the more proficient you'll become at converting Web sites to PDF documents. To help simplify the process, take a look at some steps for converting Web pages. To perform these steps, you need to be working in Acrobat 5.0 and have an Internet connection established.

STEPS: Capturing a Web site

1. **Set the Web Capture preferences.** Before attempting to capture a site, review all of the preference settings. To open the Web Capture Preferences dialog box, choose Edit ➪ Preferences ➪ Web Capture. In the dialog box, click the Reset Warnings to Default button and click Reset Conversion Settings to Default. Use the Acrobat default settings for this capture. Click OK after making the changes.

2. **Click the Open Web Page tool.** Because the default preference settings include showing the Open Web Page tool in the Command bar, you should see the globe icon appear on the top left of the Command bar. Click the globe icon to display the Open Web Page dialog box. Note: As the cursor is placed over the tool, a tool tip displays Open Web Page.

3. **Enter the URL for the site to be captured in the Open Web Page dialog box.** You can use any site on the World Wide Web. If you have a company Web site, use the URL for your site. If not, pick a site. The URL must be complete, so verify the address before proceeding.

4. **Enter the number of levels to capture.** If working with a modem connection, you should first attempt to capture only a single level, especially if you are not familiar with the site structure. If you have a faster connection, try capturing two levels. Enable the options for downloading files under the same path and staying on the same server.

5. **Stay on the same server.** In the Open Web Page dialog box, enable the checkbox for Stay on Same Server. The settings made in the Open Web Page dialog box should appear, as illustrated in Figure 4-44.

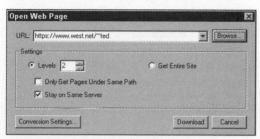

Figure 4-44: The Open Web Page dialog box displays two levels to be captured and the Stay on Same Server checkbox is enabled.

6. **Click the Conversion Settings button in the Open Web Page dialog box.** You can elect to use the Acrobat default settings or make some choices for bookmark attributes and how the HTML and plain text files will be converted. When the Conversion Settings button is clicked, the Conversion Settings dialog box appears.

7. **Add PDF Tags.** Three of the four checkboxes at the bottom will be enabled. Add to the enabled checkboxes the Add PDF Tags and place a checkmark in the box. With tags we can add new structured bookmarks that will be linked to all the page content. Click OK in the Conversion Settings dialog box to return to the Open Web Page dialog box.

8. **Capture the site.** You can navigate to the other options for Conversion Settings, but at this point just look at capturing the Web site with the remaining conversion options at the default values. Click the Download button to begin downloading the site.

9. **View the download progress.** If your connection is slow and it appears as though the computer is sluggish, files are continuing to download. You can easily determine whether files are downloading by observing the globe for the Open Web Page tool. To display a progress dialog box on Windows, choose Tools ➪ Web Capture ➪ Bring Status Dialogs to Foreground.

10. **Stop the progress.** If an inordinate amount of time passes and you want to stop the download, click the Stop button in the Download Status dialog box. Acrobat displays all PDFs converted from Web pages before the Stop was invoked.

11. **View the PDF file.** Examine the number of pages and scroll through the document. Open the Navigation pane and view the bookmarks.

12. **Add New Structured Bookmarks.** Because you enabled the Add PDF Tags option, you can create new structured bookmarks that will be linked to the PDF content. With the Navigation pane open, select the pull-down menu and choose New Bookmarks from Structure.

13. **Click the top-level bookmarks.** The bookmarks can be opened or closed by clicking the plus (+) symbol (right pointing arrow on a Mac) to open the nest of bookmarks. Collapsing them is accomplished by selecting the minus (-) symbol (down pointing arrow on Macintosh). Collapsed bookmarks appear, as displayed in Figure 4-45. When collapsed, click the new bookmarks. You should be able to navigate to different pages when selecting the bookmarks.

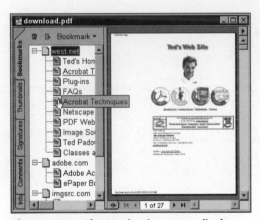

Figure 4-45: The Navigation pane displays the new Structured Bookmarks viewed in a collapsed position.

Regardless of whether you downloaded the entire site or stopped the download progress, you end up with the converted pages appearing in Acrobat. The PDF document can be edited or saved for further use. If you save the file, appending Web pages can be accomplished in other Acrobat sessions at a later time. If you performed the preceding steps, save the file to use it later for working through some editing steps.

Create Adobe PDF Online

As a service to its users, Adobe offers a Web hosting implementation of creating PDFs. You can find the service by logging on the Adobe Web site at `http://cpdf1. adobe.com`.

Note Keep in mind URLs may change as Web sites are updated. If the Web address above doesn't work after you try it, use the Adobe Web site search engine (`www.adobe.com`) to find the Create PDF Online service.

When you arrive at the Web page for Creating PDFs online, you will be asked to login as either a registered user or a guest. Guests can use the service three times to test it without charge. After that, Adobe requires a monthly fee of $9.95 (U.S.) for continuing use. If you're trying the service for demonstration, you'll need to fill out a license agreement and then proceed to the area where you can upload files for PDF conversion.

Accepted file formats

The first detail you want to make certain is that the file formats for the files you want to convert are accepted by the Create Adobe PDF Online service. The file formats that are acceptable include:

✦ **Microsoft Office:** Microsoft Word (.doc) files, Microsoft Publisher (.pub), Microsoft Excel (.xls), Rich Text Format (.rtf), and Text (.txt) files are supported.

✦ **Web Pages:** All HTML pages (.htm, .html, .shtml) are supported.

✦ **Adobe Formats:** Adobe Illustrator native (.ai), InDesign (.indd), FrameMaker (.fm), and PageMaker (.pm, .pm6, .p65) are supported. Because these products include exports or saves to PDF, it would be rare for someone to use the service unless you had document files in your archives without the applications supporting them.

✦ **Corel WordPerfect Office Formats:** WordPerfect (.wpd). This particular service might be helpful for service centers printing on different devices that don't carry Corel WordPerfect in the software library. Rare as it may be, some end users may need books printed that were created in WordPerfect.

✦ **PostScript Formats:** PostScript (.ps, .prn) and Epcapsulated PostScript (.eps) are supported.

✦ **Image Formats:** Windows bitmap (.bmp), GIF (.gif), JPEG (.jpg), PNG (.png), RLE (.rle), and TIFF (.jpg) are supported.

Why subscribe?

The first question that will no doubt be on every reader's mind is why would I pay for this service? After all, if you purchased this book you probably have Acrobat and can use all of its methods and tools to create your own PDFs. In most cases you may never have need for the service, but you may have need for referring colleagues, offices, departments, or satellite facilities to take advantage of the service. For those who need volumes of data converted to PDF, especially from large text files, the service can be quite valuable. When you stop to think that at $9.95 (U.S.) monthly, it would take more than two years to reach the cost of purchasing Acrobat. If a company needs nothing more than archives of data converted to PDF, then it may make sense to use the Create PDF Online service.

Another reason why one may want to subscribe is when converting document formats from many different applications. If you don't own FrameMaker, PageMaker, Corel WordPerfect, or Microsoft Office, then purchasing all the software applications to convert documents to PDF will certainly be a costly proposition. In this regard, it would take more than ten years to pay for all that software compared to costs of the online service — not to mention the needed learning curve to understand how to properly export files.

In either case, there are some viable reasons why someone might want to subscribe to the Adobe online service. If it's not needed now, keep it in mind in case you ever need it or have a need to refer others.

How it works

After logging in as either a guest for the three free trial services or as a registered user, you upload one of the accepted file formats to the Adobe Web site. Files must be within 50MB of storage space and they must not take longer than 15 minutes of processing time to convert. Fifteen minutes is actually a long time when converting large documents with Acrobat Distiller and many files of substantial size can be converted in much less time.

After the PDFs have been created, you receive an e-mail attachment or a message informing you where the file can be downloaded. The files you download will be PDFs converted from your documents.

Summary

✦ PDFs are created from existing digital files. There is no provision in Acrobat to create a new page or document from the File menu.

✦ The Acrobat Open as Adobe PDF command can convert many existing image file formats, ASCII text files, and HTML files to PDF.

✦ The Acrobat Distiller printer is installed in Windows at the time of the Acrobat installation. When converting open documents to PDF from Windows applications, you can select the Acrobat Distiller from a Print command. The file will be printed to disk as PostScript and Acrobat Distiller will automatically launch, convert the PostScript to PDF, and return you to the application document window.

✦ Create Adobe PDF on the Macintosh is accessed through a Print command or by dragging and dropping on the Desktop printer icon. Files are printed to disk and distilled in Acrobat Distiller transparent to the user.

✦ The Open Web Page command can convert Web pages online or locally from HTML files on hard drives or network servers.

✦ A host of different conversion settings can be user defined for setting many options on how Web pages will be converted and how the content will be organized.

✦ Structured bookmarks and tags offer extensive opportunities for editing and navigating PDF files.

✦ Create Adobe PDF Online is a Web hosted service provided by Adobe Systems for converting many different document formats to PDF.

✦   ✦   ✦

Using Acrobat Distiller

Why Use Acrobat Distiller

Whereas other means of creating PDF files, such as using the Acrobat Open as PDF command is straightforward and quite easy, using Acrobat Distiller to create PDF files requires some thought and use of a complex set of controls. Because of the complexity of Acrobat Distiller, the range of opportunities for many different purposes exists. Although complicated at times, Distiller affords us several means of automating PDF generation and the attributes associated with creating a PDF file.

With Distiller's handling of many more controls, PDF file creation can be used for all document display and printing needs. You may remember back in Chapter 1 the discussion on document repurposing. If you think now that you will need a file for internal office use and later want to employ that document for some other purpose, you may need to go back to the original application document and reprint the file to PDF. If this is the case, you'll be involved in duplicating unnecessary steps. To develop a true PDF workflow, using Acrobat Distiller will at times provide a much better solution.

In using other tools for creating PDFs, such as printing to the Acrobat Distiller printer driver on Windows or using the Create Adobe PDF on the Macintosh, you need to know something about Distiller's settings. You may never launch Distiller in your workflow, but it may be used in the background when you create PDFs from many different means. Whenever Distiller is introduced in the process, you will be better served by knowing all the controls and options the Distiller application affords you when producing PDFs.

Acrobat Distiller is like a PostScript engine. Theoretically, if a page can be distilled, it can be printed. The Acrobat Distiller application is used to convert PostScript files or files saved as Encapsulated PostScript (EPS) to PDF. In essence, it's a conversion utility. The only use it has is to convert either of these two file types to a PDF file.

With Distiller, you can add prepress controls and file attributes that can assist you in developing a PDF workflow for output to many different printing devices. The entire PDF workflow can be handled in many different automated ways with Acrobat Distiller. In addition, some files and file types cannot be used with the Acrobat Open as PDF command and require the use of Distiller. Some of the reasons you would use Acrobat Distiller for creating PDFs include:

✦ **Digital prepress:** For all printing output in digital prepress, approximately 90 to 95 percent of the computer-using U.S. population is married to PostScript. About 75 percent of the computer users the world over use PostScript for all digital print needs. Distiller uses PostScript rather than the clipboard or screen to create the PDF file. To keep the integrity of the PDF file on par with the print file, always use Distiller. Exceptions to this rule are when using programs that are built on core PDF architecture, as I explain in Chapter 6.

✦ **EPS graphics:** One of the file formats not available for converting to PDF from within Acrobat is the EPS format. For vector art files and other application document files saved as EPS, you need Distiller to convert to PDF. If an EPS file is linked to a document or embedded, likewise you'll need Distiller to convert to PDF.

✦ **Sophisticated publishing applications:** Some applications programs, such as layout, illustration, and image editors are optimized to take advantage of PostScript printing. Some of these programs in newer releases export directly to PDF. When PDF export is not available, use Distiller where PostScript integrity is needed.

✦ **Compression controls:** Bitmap resampling is much more limited with the Acrobat PDF conversion and even some applications that can export to PDF. Distiller uses downsampling and subsampling, as well as different methods of resampling. When you need to exercise more control over the sampling methods of images, always use Distiller.

✦ **Automated PDF development:** If you want to have files automatically converted to PDF, you can set up a watched folder and have your PostScript files converted to PDF. If you get in the habit of creating PostScript files for printing devices, your files can serve a dual purpose: to be sent to a PostScript printer and to be distilled into a PDF file.

✦ **Automatic image color conversion:** Distiller provides you an opportunity to convert CMYK (Cyan, Magenta, Yellow, and Black) color images to RGB (Red, Green, and Blue) for screen viewing. If you want to repurpose a catalog for Web publishing, Distiller will automate all the necessary steps needed to properly create the PDF file.

✦ **Concatenating PDF Pages:** If you have different document files that need to be converted to a single PDF file, Distiller can concatenate individual PostScript files into a single PDF file with multiple pages.

✦ **OPI and prepress controls:** With Distiller, you can preserve Open Press Interface (OPI) comments, overprints, halftone frequencies, and transfer functions, and preserve or remove undercolor removal (UCR) and gray color removal (GCR).

✦ **Monitor viewing color conversion:** Distiller provides the capability to convert color spaces to device-dependent or device-independent color.

Distiller's only worth on the planet is to convert PostScript and EPS files to PDF documents. To use Distiller, you must start with either an EPS or PostScript file. Before you can examine all the controls available with Acrobat Distiller, you need to begin with an understanding of PostScript.

Understanding PostScript

Adobe PostScript is a *page description language* — that is, it describes the text and images on your monitor screen in a language. A raster image processor (RIP) performs the interpretation of this language. Whereas PostScript is the language, the RIP behaves like a compiler. The RIP interprets the file and converts the text and images that you see on your monitor to a bitmap image in dots that are plotted on the printing device. In the office environment, you won't see a RIP independent of a PostScript laser printer that you use — but it exists. It's built into the printer. With high-end devices, such as imagesetters, platesetters, large format ink-jet printers, on-demand printing systems, high-end composite color devices, and film recorders,

About Imaging Devices

Imagesetters are high-end devices ranging from $10,000 to over a $100,000 and are usually found in computer service bureaus and commercial print shops. Imagesetters use laser beams to plot the raster image on either sheet-fed or roll-fed paper or film. The paper is resin coated, and both paper and film require chemical processing through a developer, fix, and wash much like a photographic print. A commercial printer uses the material to make plates that are wrapped around cylinders on a printing press. These prepress materials are an integral part of offset printing, and almost all printing performed today is handled from a form of digital output to material that is used to create plates for presses.

Direct-to-plate and direct-to-press systems bypass the prepress materials and expose images on either plates that are used on print cylinders or directly to the press blankets where the impression receives the ink.

On-demand printing is a term describing machines that bypass the prepress process by taking the digital file from a computer directly to the press. Depending on the engineering of the output device, the consumable materials may consist of toner (as used in copy machines) or ink (as used on printing presses).

the RIP is often a separate component that may be either a hardware device or software operating on a dedicated computer.

One of the reasons PostScript has grown to its present popularity is its device independence. When you draw an object on your computer, the resolution displayed by your monitor is 72 pixels per inch (ppi). This image can be printed to a 300 dots per inch (dpi) laser printer or a 3,600 dpi imagesetter. Through the device independence of PostScript, essentially the computer says to the printer, "Give me all you can." The printer responds by imaging the page at the resolution it is capable of handling. When the file is ripped, the laser printer RIP creates a 300-dpi bitmap, whereas the imagesetter RIP creates a 3,600-dpi bitmap.

With all its popularity and dominance in the market, PostScript does have problems. It comes in many different dialects and is known as a *streamed* language. If you have a QuarkXPress file, for example, and import an Adobe Illustrator EPS file and a Macromedia EPS file, you'll wind up with three different flavors of PostScript — each according to the way the individual manufacturer handles their coding. If the same font is used by each of the three components, the font description will reside in three separate areas of the PostScript file when printed to disk. PostScript is notorious for redundancy, especially with fonts.

As a streamed language, PostScript requires that the entire code is processed by the interpreter before the image bitmap can be created. Ever wonder why you need to wait while the RIP is churning for an endless amount of time only to eventually end up with a PostScript error or RIP crash? PostScript can't begin plotting the bitmap image until the entire PostScript stream has been interpreted.

PDF, on the other hand, is like a database file — it has a database structure. PDF eliminates all redundancy with file resources. Fonts, for example, only appear once, no matter how many iterations are used in imported EPS files. In addition, PDF takes all of the dialectical differences of PostScript and converts them to a single dialect. Whereas a PostScript file containing many pages requires the entire file to be downloaded to the RIP and ultimately printed, a PDF file is page independent in that each individual page can be imaged. In short, PDF is much more efficient than PostScript.

Using PostScript and Acrobat Distiller should not be thought of as restricting output to professional printing devices. For any kind of PDF usage, becoming familiar with PostScript and using the Distiller application will often be a preferred solution. Even when you don't exercise a print command through many different methods of creating PDFs, a file will indeed be printed first to PostScript and then distilled with Acrobat Distiller.

Creating PostScript files

In some ways, a PostScript file is very similar to a PDF file. If, for example, you create a layout in Adobe PageMaker, Adobe FrameMaker, or QuarkXPress with images and type fonts, the document page can be printed to disk as a PostScript file. In doing so, you can embed all graphic images and fonts in the file. If you take your file to a service center, the file can be downloaded to a printing device. To ensure proper printing, though, you need to be certain the PostScript Printer Description (PPD) file was properly selected for the output device. Assuming you created the PostScript file properly, the file will print with complete integrity.

On desktop printers, printing to a PostScript file is just like printing to a device. On printers in commercial imaging centers, many different requirements need to be considered that are not typically found on a desktop printer. Some of the considerations that need to be understood when printing PostScript files for high-end devices include the following:

✦ **PPD device selection:** Whenever printing a PostScript file for direct download, always be certain to choose the proper PPD file. PPD files for imaging equipment can be obtained from imaging centers or from Web addresses. You first need to know the device name; for example, an AGFA SelectSet Avantra25 is a specific printing machine. You need the PPD for an Avantra25 to properly prepare the PostScript file, which will include specific parameters for the printer, such as page dimensions, screening, and media length.

Note The PPD selection that you make for a specific output device is only used when a file is to be imaged on the device in question, and no other repurposing of your document is needed. The PPD selection in the preceding example is used only to send a PostScript file to an imaging center for output on a particular device.

Tip PPD files are ASCII text files. In cross-platform environments where a PPD file is installed on one platform and you do not have access to the same PPD file for another platform, the file can be copied across platforms. Be certain to copy the PPD file to the required directory when adding new PPD files for printing devices. In Windows 2000, the directory is: WinNT\system32\spool\drivers\w32x86 (See Figure 5-1). On the Macintosh the folder is: System Folder: Extensions: Printer Descriptions (See Figure 5-2).

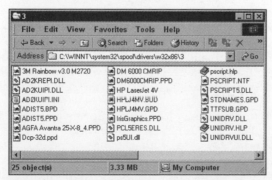

Figure 5-1: The w32x86\3 folder on Windows 2000 stores PPDs.

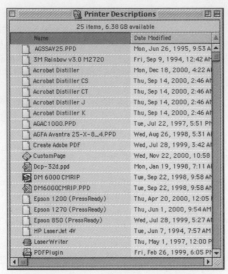

Figure 5-2: The Printer Descriptions folder stores PPDs on a Macintosh.

✦ **Acrobat Distiller PPD:** When document repurposing and PDF workflows are important and your file may be used for output to several devices or for many purposes, always use the Acrobat Distiller PPD. If, for example, you want to image a file to a laser printer and use a PPD specific to your device, and then you want to image the same file on a color printer, the PPD you may have used for the laser printer could exclude color information. You would need to reprint the job's PostScript file to disk, and then distill it again for the color output. If you use the Acrobat Distiller PPD, you can print the PDF file to both the laser printer and the color device. When Distiller is installed, the Acrobat Distiller PPD will also be installed.

When files are distilled with Acrobat Distiller to create PDFs for almost all imaging equipment, always opt to first try the Acrobat Distiller PPD. Problems may arise if you use device PPDs, especially with large format printers. For example, if you want PowerPoint slides to be printed to a large format inkjet printer, the printer's PPD may clip the final PDF created with Acrobat Distiller. To ensure page size accuracy and color control, use the Acrobat Distiller PPD. If you experience any problems with printing the PDF, you can then go back to the device PPD if necessary.

✦ **Page size:** With desktop printers, you often have only one page size. With printers that have multiple trays or interchangeable trays, you select the appropriate page size for the tray used. With imaging equipment, you need to be certain the page size is properly selected to include all image data and printer's marks. Assume for a moment a document is created in the standard page size for a letter (8.5-x-11-inches) page. However, when printer's marks (registration and color bars) are included, it turns out the page area needs to be defined larger than a letter page to accommodate the printer's marks. In the Paper Size area of the dialog box shown in Figure 5-3, the word *Custom* appears, indicating the page size is a custom size. The thumbnail on the right in Figure 5-3 from Adobe PageMaker shows how the page will fit within the defined size. In this example, all data and printer's marks will print within the defined page. If your page size is too small, some clipping of the data will occur when printed or when a PDF file is generated.

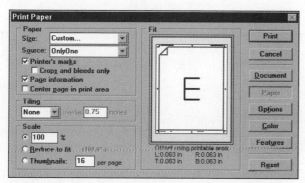

Figure 5-3: The paper size in the Adobe PageMaker Print Paper dialog box is defined as Custom to include the printer's marks and page information.

✦ **Font inclusion:** You may need to specifically tell the host application to include fonts in the PostScript file. If the file is printed at a service center, you definitely need to include the fonts in the file you submit for output. If you distill the file in Acrobat Distiller, the fonts need to be loaded on your system in order to embed the fonts in the PDF file. When you have options in Print dialog boxes for font inclusion, always choose to embed the fonts.

✦ **Screening:** Halftone frequencies, or *line screens*, can be printed at different settings. With desktop printers the maximum line screen available for the device is often the default. Six-hundred-dpi laser printers, for example, most commonly use a maximum line screen of 85 lines per inch (lpi). With imaging equipment, you need to first know the requirements of the commercial printer and take his/her advice depending on the paper, press, and prepress material. Therefore, if your file ultimately will be printed at 133 lpi, this value must be entered in the Print dialog box for the application creating the PostScript file.

Screening can also be a particular type relative to the printing device and RIP. Stochastic screening, Crystal Raster, AGFA Balanced Screens, and others are available from a PPD selection for a particular device. For these settings you need to contact your service center for the precise screening options needed for inclusion.

✦ **Color:** Will the file be color separated or composite? If separations are to be printed, you must make certain all identified colors are named properly in the host document. Often an option is in a Print dialog box to specify whether the file will be separated. As you view the color list, verifying all colors appearing are those you specified in the document is imperative. If a spot color is in the current document, the color won't print unless it is an identified color in the Print dialog box. In as much as you may view preseparated colors to determine if they will be printed properly, you should always send a composite color PDF file to an imaging center and let them do the separations. If you want to be certain of proper printing, you can print separations as PostScript files to disk, distill the files, and view them in an Acrobat viewer. Each of the separated pages will be included in one PDF file so that you can check knockouts, overprints, and colors. Use a separated file to preview the results only, then go back and create a composite PDF to send off to your service center.

Encoding

Encoding comes in two flavors: Binary and ASCII. Binary encoding will result in smaller files and print faster on PostScript Level 2 and PostScript 3 devices. As a default, you want to use binary encoding when the option is available in the Print dialog box from the host application. In some cases, you may need to have ASCII as a choice. This will be rare, and you should be informed by an imaging center if ASCII is preferred.

PostScript levels

PostScript originated in 1976, and later it was updated to a version called Interpress at the Xerox Palo Alto Research Center (PARC). Interpress was designed for output to early laser printers. Xerox abandoned the project, and two of the staff at Xerox PARC — John Warnock and Chuck Geschke — decided to take it forth and develop it. In 1981, Warnock and Geschke formed Adobe Systems, and PostScript was their first product.

On March 21, 1985, the digital print revolution was founded when Apple Computer, Aldus Corporation, Adobe Systems, and Linotype collaborated on an open architecture system for electronic typesetting. Later that year, Apple Computer introduced the LaserWriter printer, that came with a whopping 13 fonts fried into the printer's ROM chips and a price tag of $6,500. If you were outputting to a PostScript device in 1987, when Adobe Illustrator first appeared, you may still be waiting for that 12K Illustrator file to spit out of your laser printer. PostScript Level 1 was a major technological advance, but by today's standards it was painfully slow. Many in the imaging world remember all too well those countless times at 3:00 a.m. waiting for the final file to print after ripping over eight hours.

In 1990, Adobe Systems introduced PostScript Level 2, which was a more robust version of PostScript and a screamer compared to the first release. In addition to speed, PostScript Level 2 provided these features:

Encoding and PostScript Levels

You may find contradictory recommendations for the encoding method and PostScript level depending on recommendations from software vendors and hardware manufacturers. In some instances, Level 2 or 3 and binary encoding may not work with some applications or software utilities. Level 2 and 3 PostScript handle color much better than Level 1 and provides for separating spot colors. Most often Level 2 or 3 PostScript and binary encoding will be the preferred choice when creating PostScript files. As a matter of rule, always use binary encoding and Level 2 or 3 for creating a PostScript file. If you encounter problems, use the alternative settings.

✦ **Color separation:** In earlier days, color was preseparated on Level 1 devices. PostScript Level 2 enabled imaging specialists to separate a composite color file into the four process colors, Cyan, Magenta, Yellow, and Black (CMYK). Also, there was support for spot color in PostScript Level 2.

✦ **Improved font handling:** In the early days of PostScript imaging, there were more font nightmares than you can imagine. Font encoding for PostScript fonts only handled a maximum of 256 characters. Other font sets, such as Japanese, have thousands of individual characters. PostScript Level 2 introduced a composite font technology that handled many different foreign character sets.

✦ **Compression:** Getting the large files across a 10-Base-T network was also burdensome in the Level 1 days. PostScript Level 2 introduced data compression and supported such compression schemes as JPEG (Joint Photographic Expert Group, LZW (Lempel-Ziv-Welch), and RLE (Run Length). The files are transmitted compressed, which means they get to the RIP faster, and then decompressed at the RIP. In a large imaging center, the compression greatly improved network traffic and workflows.

In 1996, Adobe introduced PostScript 3 (note *Level* has been dropped from the name). Perhaps one of the more remarkable and technologically advanced features of PostScript 3 is the inclusion of Web publishing with direct support for hypertext markup language (HTML), PDF, and Web content. PostScript 3 also provided us with the ability to create In-Rip separations. When you send a PDF file to an imaging center using PostScript 3 Rips, you can deliver composite color files that can be sent direct to the RIP and are separated at the imaging device.

The options for different output needs can be found in either the application Print dialog box or from options selected in print driver dialog boxes. The most common choices for the kind of output you desire are listed in Table 5-1.

Table 5-1
Print Options According to Output Device

Output Device	PostScript Printer Description (PPD)	Page Size	Font Inclusion	Screening	Frequency	Encoding
Screen/Web	Distiller	Default	Yes	N/A	N/A	Binary
Laser Printer*	Distiller					
Device	Default*	Yes	N/A	Yes	Binary	
Desktop Color	Distiller	Default**	Yes	N/A	N/A	Binary
Commercial InkJet	Distiller	Custom	Yes	N/A	N/A	Binary
Imagesetter* Platesetter*	Distiller	Custom	Yes	Yes	Yes	Binary

*Always first use the Acrobat Distiller PPD. If problems are encountered, switch to the device PPD.

**If output is smaller than standard sizes and crop marks are to be included, the page size might be selected as a smaller size than the default. For desktop printers supporting tabloid and larger sizes, custom page sizes fitting within the maximum page size can often be used, especially with bleeds.

Creating PostScript Files from Web Pages

If your world is confined to Web page design and use, then perhaps none of the previous discussion on high-end imaging is of interest to you. Perhaps you want a little more utilitarian purpose with your work and want to restrict your Acrobat usage to Web documents. Fortunately Acrobat is a tool that can be used by almost any computer user in almost any given environment. Acrobat has the capability to convert entire Web sites to PDF as was discussed back in Chapter 4. However, there may be times when you don't need to convert a Web site or a partial Web site but you want to pick selective pages from Web sites and have those pages converted to PDF. If a question comes to mind as to why you would want to convert Web pages to PDF, then first look at some sound reasoning in this regard.

Why convert Web pages to PDF

The Web has vast volumes of data that people are increasingly relying on for digesting information. A virtual library of resources exists from the office or home. Regardless of your occupation or special interest, there's bound to be information that will be helpful when the need for research exists. This sea of information on the Web has become a behemoth of disorganized content that becomes frustrating when you want to narrow down on a special topic or category.

As you poke around the maze of Web sites and find a page that needs to be referenced, you may add a bookmark to your browser. This is fine for targeting sites that you want to return often for review of information. However, if you are conducting research and navigate through complex searches to find the right pages, there may be hundreds available that relate to your task at hand. Bookmarking each page will create a collection of listings about as disorganized as your Web search. Even if you take time to place them in a logical hierarchy in your browser and footnote each one, the content won't be easy to search for selected topics.

Imagine a second scenario. You convert all relative Web pages to PDF and then create a search index of all the PDFs related to your topic of interest. When you later find additional sites that provide useful information, you add more PDFs to your folder and then update the search index. When you want to find information, you can use Acrobat Search with all its strong features of operators, Boolean expressions, and proximity, as I explained in Chapter 2. When you're in a hurry and want to target the right information for your purpose, invoking a search will get you there much faster than logging on the Web and browsing your bookmarked sites. What's more, if your Internet connection is down or the target site is down, you won't be hindered by the need to have a connection. All your PDFs will reside locally on your hard drive or possibly a network server.

As an example, say you want more information on creating Acrobat forms. You can visit a host of Web sites where articles, samples, and related information exists. You could potentially find hundreds of sites offering information helpful in assisting you to prepare a form for your office. You might be looking for that one JavaScript that's needed to calculate sales tax. You've forgotten the formula and want to find an example. I guarantee that if you start following a string of bookmarks to Web sites, you'll spend much time in finding the one example you need. If you use Acrobat Search, you could enter **[sales tax AND JavaScript /pr]** in the Adobe Acrobat Search window. The Search Results dialog box will display the PDFs according to the most frequent occurrences of your search criteria.

For anyone conducting research, using PDFs converted from Web pages and using Acrobat Search is an efficient means of finding information quickly.

Caution

Web sites can contain copyright information that may restrict your use. Some documents and Web pages may be restricted to individual use and prohibit access on servers and intranets. Before capturing pages and making them accessible to others, be certain to review the copyright information. When in doubt, send an e-mail to the site manager or Webmaster.

Printing Web pages to PostScript

As you browse Web sites, you can pick and choose different pages containing the content useful for your task. Rather than interrupt your navigation through Internet searches and following a trail of links, you can print pages to disk as PostScript files. When you finish your Internet search, you can then open the Distiller application and convert the PostScript to PDF. If you want a single PDF created from pages of multiple Web sites, Distiller will provide the ability to do so, as I explain a little later in this chapter when discussing concatenation (see "Concatenating PostScript Files").

Note   Acrobat does provide a means of downloading a single Web page and converting the identified page to PDF all from within Acrobat, as was discussed in Chapter 4. When browsing Web sites in a Web browser and using Acrobat to convert individual pages to PDF, you need to continually work between your Web browser and Acrobat. In as much as you can copy and paste URLs from the Web browser to the Acrobat Open Web Page dialog box, printing to PostScript and later distilling files is often a much faster solution — especially with slower connection speeds. Furthermore, exercising a print command produces a printed PostScript file much faster than waiting for Acrobat to produce the PDF.

Creating the PostScript from sources such as Web pages is an easy task and you needn't be concerned with many of the file attributes discussed earlier for imaging environments. As an example, follow these steps to first create the PostScript files and a little later in this chapter, I cover using the Distiller application. Because the print dialog boxes vary considerably between Windows and Macintosh systems, I present steps for both platforms. If you're a Macintosh user, jump to the next set of steps. Windows users can begin with the following:

STEPS: Creating PostScript from Web Pages on Windows

1. **Open a Web page in Microsoft Internet Explorer or Netscape Navigator.** Any page you want to use will work. If you have a Web site, you can navigate to your own home page.

2. **Choose File ➪ Print.** Choose either the Acrobat Distiller printer driver or a PostScript printer from the Print dialog box. Be certain to avoid using a non-PostScript printer driver.

3. **Check the Print to file checkbox.** If you have a printer with a Port defined for File: you won't need to check the checkbox. If uncertain, enable this checkbox, as shown in Figure 5-4.

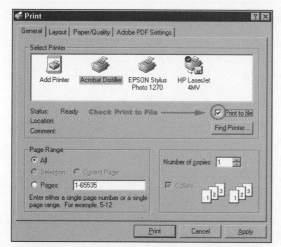

Figure 5-4: The Acrobat Distiller printer driver is selected in the Print dialog box and the checkbox for Print to file is enabled.

Note When the Acrobat Distiller printer driver is selected and you disable the Print to file checkbox, your file is printed to disk and automatically distilled with Acrobat Distiller. In this example, we're going to hold off distillation of the PostScript files to eliminate any disruption with our Web browsing.

4. **Select the Page Size.** Web pages vary in size greatly. A Web page may be equal to a standard letter page, or a single Web page may be equal to many standard letter pages. Additionally, the physical width of the Web page may exceed a standard letter page width in which case the data will be clipped if the orientation or page size is not set properly. If your page viewed in the browser appears to be wider than a standard letter page, you can print a Landscape page. To alter the page orientation, select the Layout tab in the Print dialog box. Page orientation choices can be chosen from this dialog box, as shown in Figure 5-5.

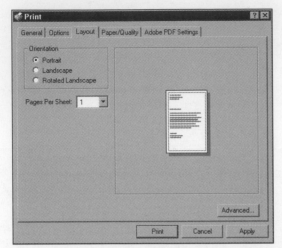

Figure 5-5: Page orientation choices are available after selecting the Layout tab in the Print dialog box.

5. **Click the Print button.** You can set many other toggles in the various tab settings within the Print dialog box, however the defaults should work fine for creating the PostScript file. After you click the Print button, a dialog box appears enabling you to name the PostScript file and select the destination folder on your hard drive. Provide a name and select the folder where the PostScript file is to be saved (see Figure 5-6).

Figure 5-6: The Print To File dialog box appears after selecting the Print button. In this dialog box, you determine filename and location for the PostScript file.

Note The default extension in Windows for files printed to disk is .prn. All Adobe applications use a file extension of .ps. To keep parody with Adobe defaults, use the .ps extension for all your PostScript files. This extension can be added in the File name: field box in the Print To File dialog box illustrated in Figure 5-6.

Poke around the Internet and create a few more PostScript files. You can save these to a folder and later use the files when I discuss using the Acrobat Distiller application.

STEPS: Creating PostScript from Web Pages on the Macintosh

1. **Open a Web page in Microsoft Internet Explorer or Netscape Communicator.** Any page you want to use will work. If you have a Web site, you can navigate to your own home page.

2. **Choose Apple Menu ➪ Chooser.** In the Chooser dialog box, select a PostScript printer. You needn't have the printer online, but a PostScript printer driver must be selected, as shown in Figure 5-7. Select the printer and click the close box in the top-left corner.

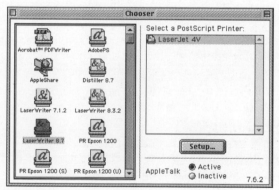

Figure 5-7: In the Chooser dialog box, select a PostScript printer driver. In this figure, I select the LaserWriter 8.7 printer driver.

3. **Choose File ➪ Print from your Browser menu.** In the Print dialog box, you have several selections to make that include:

   • **Save as File:** The pull-down menu below the Printer pull-down menu offers a number of menu options. Select the Save as File option from this menu, as shown in Figure 5-8.

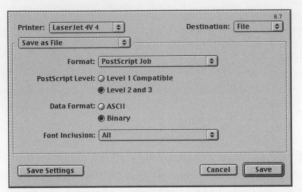

Figure 5-8: The Print dialog box offers many options for selecting attributes of the print file. To successfully execute a print to file, you need to make the appropriate selections.

- **Format:** From the pull-down menu, select PostScript Job.

- **PostScript Level:** For all PostScript files related to this example, use the Level 2 and 3 selection.

- **Data Format:** Select Binary encoding. If you use Level 1 Compatible selection for the PostScript Level, then you use the ASCII encoding option.

- **Font Inclusion:** Be certain to select the All option from the pull-down menu. While the Base 13 fonts won't be necessary, you can include them without experiencing any problems.

- **Destination:** Set this destination to File from the available menu options. It may seem redundant, but if you don't check file here, the document will be sent to your printer instead of a PostScript file.

- **Save Settings:** This setting is optional, but if you are using the same print driver and printing several files to disk, the settings you save in the Print dialog box become new defaults and you won't need to set all the toggles again.

4. **Select the Save button in the Print dialog box.** After you click the Save button, a dialog box opens prompting you for a filename and location where the PostScript file is to be saved (see Figure 5-9).

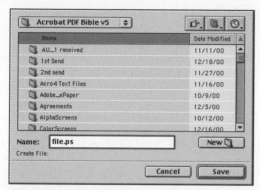

Figure 5-9: After clicking Save in the Print dialog box, another dialog box appears where you can provide a name for the PostScript file and choose a destination folder.

5. **Provide a name and choose the location.** Enter a name for your PostScript file and save it to a folder where you can easily revisit the file. Try to print several more files and keep these handy when we look at using the Acrobat Distiller application.

You have many different ways to create PDF files as you already observed back in Chapter 4, and as you shall also see in Chapter 6. Not all of these means may be suitable for work groups and specific applications. If, for example, you are an accounting clerk and you need to create a PDF of an invoice or a financial statement, you may not have an opportunity to export to PDF from your accounting software and you may not have the Distiller application installed locally on your hard drive. In this example and many more instances, you need to create a PostScript file that will be distilled later in the Acrobat Distiller application. For PDF Workflows, you may have the Distiller application running on a network server where all your PostScript files will be converted to PDF. In almost all instances, if one means of creating a PDF is not available, you can rely on creating PostScript files that can be later converted to PDF via the Acrobat Distiller application. In many instances, using the method of first printing to disk as PostScript and then leaving the distillation process for a later session is handier. As soon as you begin printing to disk, it becomes part of your natural workflow. So, practice and become proficient. You will use this process many times.

Acrobat Distiller Preferences

When you first launch Acrobat Distiller, it looks like a fairly simple application. Examining the menus immediately tells you there's not much to do in the File menu. This menu is limited to opening a file, addressing preferences, and quitting the program. Nothing else is offered in this menu. The Edit menu options of earlier versions of Acrobat offered the traditional Cut, Copy, and Paste commands; but these commands didn't work, and were always grayed out.

Now in Acrobat 5.0, it makes more sense to eliminate the menu from the Distiller application, which is exactly what Adobe has provided in the new release. Distiller's real power is contained in the Settings menu. The commands listed in this menu offer all the control for determining how PDFs will be created. The Settings menu has four choices for changing various attributes. In addition to these settings, the Preferences located in the File menu help you customize some Distiller startup and output options.

Older versions of Preferences options for Distiller were located in the Distiller menu. In Acrobat 5.0, Preferences were moved to the File menu. When you choose File ➪ Preferences, a dialog box will appear. The options available are listed among three groups that include Startup Alerts, Output Options (Windows), and Log Files, as shown in Figure 5-10. (Preferences available for the Macintosh are shown later in this chapter in Figure 5-11.)

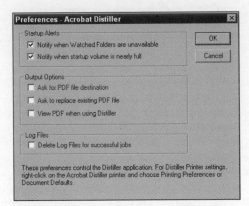

Figure 5-10: Choose File ➪ Preferences on Windows to access Acrobat Distiller Preferences. Preferences enable you to customize startup and output options.

Startup Alerts

The two items listed in this section of the dialog box have to do with your initial startup upon launching the Distiller application.

✦ **Notify when Watched Folders are unavailable:** This command enables Distiller to monitor a folder or directory on your computer or network server to automatically distill PostScript files placed in watched folders. (Setting up watched folders is discussed later in this chapter.) In an office environment, you can have different users create PostScript files and send them to a server for automatic distillation.

✦ **Notify when startup volume is nearly full:** Distiller needs temporary disk space to convert the PostScript files to PDF documents. If the available hard disk space on your startup volume becomes less than 1MB, Distiller will prompt you with a warning dialog box. Leaving this preference setting enabled is always a good idea. The amount of temporary space required by Distiller is approximately twice the size of the PostScript file being distilled.

Output Options

Output options relate to what you intend to do with the PDF both in terms of where it will be located and what to do after it has been produced by Distiller.

✦ **Ask for PDF file destination (Windows):** This is a handy new feature with Acrobat 5.0. In older versions, every time you distilled a PostScript file, the new PDF was created in the same directory as the PostScript file. This feature offers more user control for choosing a destination folder and supplying a name in a dialog box before the PDF is created.

✦ **Ask to replace existing PDF file (Windows):** Another new feature in Acrobat 5.0, selecting this option warns you if a PDF of the same name exists in the folder where the new PDF will be created. If you want to use different Job Options and create two PDF files, you may forget that you have a PDF with a filename the same as the new one you are creating. With this option, you are warned if Distiller attempts an overwrite of your existing file.

✦ **View PDF when using Distiller (Windows):** After the PDF has been created, the default Acrobat viewer is launched and the PDF is displayed in the Document pane.

Acrobat viewers are auto launched according to the order of installation. The last Acrobat viewer you installed on your computer becomes the default viewer. If you have installed Acrobat first and Reader last, Reader will become the default viewer. When you select the viewing options in the Distiller Preferences dialog box, the PDFs are displayed in Reader. If you want to have all your PDFs viewed in Acrobat while both viewers are installed on your computer, install Reader first and Acrobat last.

Log Files

Log files describe the sequence of steps used to produce the PDF file. This section offers a choice on what to do with the log file.

✦ **Delete Log Files for successful jobs:** A log file is an ASCII text file detailing the distillation process. If an error is produced during distillation, the Log file will record the error even though the PDF may not be created. Viewing the Log file can be helpful in debugging problems with files not successfully being converted to PDF. If the PDF is successfully created, there would be no need to keep the log file on your computer. By default, you want to enable this checkbox to eliminate the clutter.

Macintosh only

On the Macintosh, several items listed previously are not available, as shown in the Preferences dialog box on the Macintosh (see Figure 5-11). One item not included with the Windows version of Distiller is:

✦ **Restart Distiller after PostScript fatal error (Macintosh):** When distilling a file, you may encounter a PostScript error. A fatal error closes Distiller. If the checkbox is enabled, Distiller will automatically relaunch. Relaunching Distiller is particularly important in network environments where you may have a server automatically distilling files in the background. If Distiller is closed, all your PDF workflow tasks will come to a halt. Be certain to enable this option when using Distiller on a network.

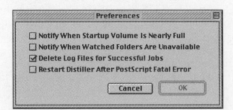

Figure 5-11: The Preferences dialog box on the Macintosh offers fewer choices than Windows preferences and one item not found in the Windows settings.

As you can see, the preferences focus primarily on what to do with your PDFs and choices for viewing options. More specific preferences related to PDF development are available via a group of settings known as Job Options.

Job Options

Distiller's Job Options provide controls for the resultant PDF files. With Distiller you have extensive control over settings that are not available when using the Acrobat Open as Adobe PDF menu command or when you export directly to PDF from other applications software. Job Options attribute control is handled in two ways. First, you can choose various preset options by selecting one of the preset Job Options choices from a pull-down menu in the Distiller window. The other choice available to you is to open the Job Options window by choosing Settings ➪ Job Options. After you open the Job Options window, five tabs containing specific settings for several categories enable you to customize many options to specify how the PostScript file will be distilled.

Preset Job Options

The Job Options pull-down menu in the Distiller window was a welcomed addition when introduced with Acrobat Distiller 4.0. Acrobat 5.0 has expanded the Job Options to include another setting, and Adobe has also offered you another preset for the Job Options that ship with the Installer CD-ROM. To change a Job Option from one preset to another, choose the pull-down menu for Job Options in the Distiller window, as shown in Figure 5-12. Choices for the preset conditions include the following:

✦ **eBook:** When PDF files intended for file exchanges between users who view and print to desktop printers is needed, the eBook Job Options will satisfy the most common needs. Unless printing to commercial devices, use the eBook settings as your default around the office.

✦ **Press:** The preset settings associated with this option are established for the highest-quality images to be produced for high-end digital prepress and printing. The lowest levels of compression and downsampling are used to preserve image quality.

✦ **Print:** The preset settings for this option are established for output to printing devices, such as desktop color printers, laser printers, and similar devices where color separations are not produced.

✦ **Screen:** The preset settings associated with this option are established for screen views and Web graphics. Screen Job Options use a higher level of compression and downsampling on files than you would choose to use with printed graphics.

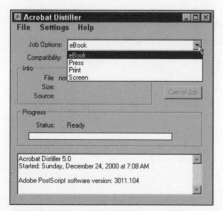

Figure 5-12: The Distiller window enables you to choose from one of four preset conditions for Job Options. Click the down arrow to the right of the Job Options setting to display the presets.

If one of these preset conditions comes close to producing the type of PDF you want to create, but it doesn't exactly meet your needs, go ahead and select that preset option and then choose Settings ➪ Job Options to open a dialog box where changes can be made as needed. After you finish editing the Job Options settings to your satisfaction, you have an opportunity to save your own custom preset file that can be accessed at a later time. Custom preset files are saved from the Job Options window. You can choose from five tabs in the Job Options dialog box that offer you all the attribute choices for creating your PDFs, which are discussed next.

General Job Options

If you need to make any changes in the Job Options settings from one of the preset options, or you need to create a new set of Job Options settings, choose Settings ➪ Job Options to open the Job Options dialog box, which is shown in Figure 5-13.

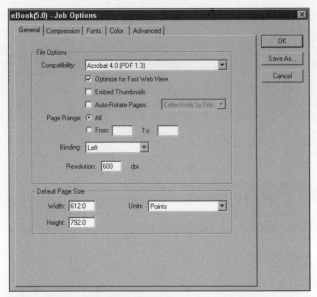

Figure 5-13: The first Job Options settings that appear after you choose Settings ➪ Job Options are those under the General tab.

The first of five tabs appear, labeled "General," which covers the following general controls:

✦ **Compatibility:** You encounter this option first in the General Job Options dialog box. You have a choice between 3.0, 4.0, and 5.0 compatibility. If you elect to use 3.0, the PDF version you create is PDF version 1.2. All users of Acrobat

3.0 are able to use PDFs with Acrobat 3.0 compatibility. If your files will be exchanged among users who have not yet upgraded to an Acrobat viewer later than version 3.01, then use this compatibility version. Your second choice is Acrobat 4.0 compatibility that offers version 1.3 of the PDF format. The newest setting is the Acrobat 5.0 compatibility that offers you PDF 1.4 format. Choices made from these options relate to the Acrobat users you exchange files with and the kind of work you do. You may need to use any one of the three choices for one use or another. If you experience problems with either viewing or printing, redistill the PostScript file with another compatibility setting. The different compatibility settings and what features are supported are listed in Table 5-2.

Table 5-2
Acrobat Compatibility Differences

Acrobat 3.0	Acrobat 4.0	Acrobat 5.0
Supports PDF version 1.2	Supports PDF version 1.3	Supports PDF version 1.4
Acrobat viewers 3.0 and later can open PDF files.	Acrobat viewers 3.0 and later can open PDF files.	
Minor viewing problems with earlier viewers may be experienced.	Acrobat viewers 3.0 and later can open PDF files.	
Some viewing problems with earlier viewers may be experienced.		
Page size is limited to 45 in x 45 in.	Page size is available up to 200 in x 200 in.	Page size is available up to 200 in x 200 in.
Document conversion is limited to 32,768 pages.	Only RAM and hard drive space limit document length.	Only RAM and hard drive space limit document length.
Color conversion supports CalRGB (Calibrated RGB).	Color conversion supports sRGB.	Color conversion supports sRGB.
ICC Profile embedding supported.	ICC Profile embedding supported.	ICC Profile embedding supported.
DeviceN color space is converted to an alternate color space.	DeviceN color space is supported.	DeviceN color space is supported.
Smooth shading is converted to images.	Smooth shading is supported.	Smooth shading is supported.
Patterns display at 50% but print correctly.	Patterns display accurately and print correctly.	Patterns display accurately and print correctly.

Continued

Table 5-2 (continued)

Acrobat 3.0	Acrobat 4.0	Acrobat 5.0
Places halftone information in the PDF.	Only places halftone information when the Preserve Halftone information is selected in the Color Job Options.	Only places halftone information when the Preserve Halftone information is selected in the Color Job Options.
Transfer Functions are supported.	Transfer Functions are not supported.	Transfer Functions are supported.
Masks do not display or print properly.	Masks are supported in viewing and printing.	Masks are supported in viewing and printing.
Photoshop 6.0 layers and transparency not supported.	Photoshop 6.0 layers and transparency not supported.	Photoshop 6.0 layers and transparency supported in Saves as PDF from Photoshop only.*
Illustrator 9.0 transparency is simulated.	Illustrator 9.0 transparency is simulated.	Illustrator 9.0 transparency is preserved in Saves as PDF from Illustrator only.*
Cannot embed double-byte fonts.	Can embed double-byte fonts.	Can embed double-byte fonts.
TrueType fonts cannot be searched.	TrueType fonts can be searched.	TrueType fonts can be searched.
Supports 40-bit encryption.	Supports 40-bit encryption.	Supports 40-bit encryption and 128-bit encryption.

*Distilling files from Photoshop and Illustrator will not support transparency.

✦ **Optimize for Fast Web View:** An optimized PDF file is smaller than one created without optimization. All files intended to be used for screen views, CD-ROM replication, and Web usage should all be optimized. Generally, almost any printing device also accepts optimized files. As a default, keep this option on. Acrobat optimizes files by eliminating repeating elements and supplying pointers to where the first occurrence can be found in the file. Optimization also prepares files for page at a time downloading from Web servers. If byte-serving capability exists on a server, the optimized files will download pages as they are viewed.

✦ **Embed Thumbnails:** Thumbnails add about 3K per page to your PDF file. Thumbnails are helpful when editing PDF files in Acrobat or when browsing PDF files on-screen. However, because they create larger files, you want to eliminate thumbnails when producing PDF files for Web use or sending your PDF files across the Internet for output to printing devices. If using Acrobat 5.0, thumbnails are displayed on the fly regardless of whether they have been embedded. Any legacy PDFs created with older PDF formats are also displayed with thumbnails without embedding when viewed in an Acrobat 5.0 viewer.

✦ **Auto-Rotate Pages:** You can have pages automatically or individually rotated during distillation. Choices from the pull-down menu include Collectively by File and Individually. When Collectively by File is selected, Acrobat analyzes the text in the file and rotates pages based on the orientation of the majority of the text in the entire file. When Individually is chosen, each page is rotated based on the majority of text on a given page. If the checkbox remains disabled, no auto-rotation will occur. Figure 5-14 shows a page where the layout was designed with the text rotated in the design. When distilled in Acrobat without auto-rotation, the page is viewed as it was designed. Figure 5-15 displays the same layout converted to PDF with the Auto-rotate checkbox enabled in the General Job Options.

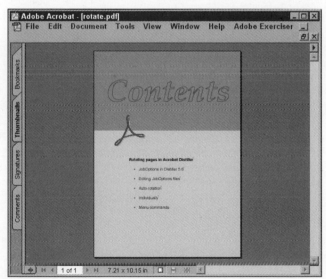

Figure 5-14: When Auto-rotate is disabled, the PDF is produced as it was originally designed without rotation regardless of the orientation of the text.

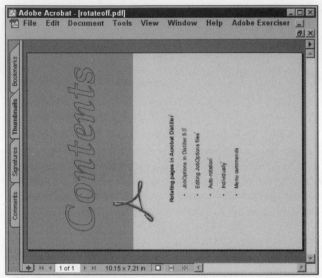

Figure 5-15: When Auto-rotate is enabled, the text is analyzed for orientation. If the predominant text orientation is rotated, the PDF is rotated so that the text appears in legible form.

Tip

Users of Acrobat 4.0 can control auto-rotation even though the Job Options in this version does not support it. The Job Options files are ASCII text files and can be opened in a simple text editor or word processor. Open a joboptions file in WordPad (Windows) or Simple Text (Macintosh) from the Distiller/Settings (Windows) or Distiller:Settings (Macintosh) directory. Find the line of code beginning with /AutoRotatePages / PageByPage (see Figure 5-16). Change this line from /PageByPage to /None to disable auto-rotation. To enable page rotation, change /None to /PageByPage. Save the file under a new name with the .joboptions extension to the Settings folder. The next time you open Acrobat Distiller the new Job Options will appear in the pull-down menu.

Figure 5-16: Acrobat 4.0 does not have auto-rotation control among the Job Options. Auto-rotation can be enabled or disabled by editing a .joboptions file in the Settings folder.

✦ **Page Range:** Auto-rotate pages (described previously) is a new addition to Acrobat 5.0 as well as this most welcomed item. You can choose to create a PDF within a specified range of pages from a PostScript file that has been printed to disk from a document containing many pages. If one page is having trouble converting to PDF, you can eliminate it from distillation by choosing a specified page range.

✦ **Binding:** This setting relates only to viewing pages in an Acrobat viewer with Continuous-Facing layouts and with thumbnails. By default, the binding is left-sided.

✦ **Resolution:** Settings for Resolution affects only vector objects and type in EPS files. The ranges between 72 and 4000 dpi are available. A handy tool tip has been added that displays the range when you click in the field box. Lower resolution settings may create banding with gradients when files are printed. For desktop printing, use a resolution of 600 dpi. For high-end commercial printing, set the resolution to 2400 dpi. The higher resolution setting only adds about 3K to the file size.

✦ **Default Page Size:** In older versions of Distiller, this preference setting was located in the Advanced Job Options. Now in Acrobat Distiller 5.0 it has been relocated to the General Job Options dialog box. Setting page sizes in these field boxes only applies to distillation of EPS and PostScript files where page boundaries are not specified. Whatever you enter in the field boxes when distilling PostScript files is ignored if the page boundary is included in the file. If you want to trim a page size or create a larger page size for an EPS file, you can establish the dimensions in the field boxes for width and height. The Units pull-down menu enables you to choose from four different units of measure.

Compression

Compression and sampling of images is managed better with Acrobat Distiller than some other methods used to create PDFs. With the Open as Adobe PDF command, for example, you have no options for sampling as exists with Distiller. You have much control over how much compression and methods of downsampling within this dialog box. To open the Compression Job Options dialog box, click the Compression tab to the right of the General Job Options. Compression and sampling choices are available for four different image types that include the following:

Distiller's Downsampling Threshold

Users of Acrobat 3.x may have noticed that PDF files distilled with Acrobat Distiller 3.x produced smaller file sizes than when distilled with Acrobat Distiller 4.x. The reason for the difference in file sizes is due to Distiller's Downsampling Threshold. In Acrobat Distiller 3.x, the threshold was established at 1.0. In Acrobat Distiller 4.x and Acrobat Distiller 5.0, the threshold is 1.5.

The translation for the threshold setting of 1.5 means that if you choose 300 dpi as your downsampling amount, the file is actually downsampled to 450 dpi (300 X 1.5 = 450). Editing the Job Options in a text editor can change this setting. To do so, you need to open a Job Options file in a text editor and change three lines of code. Search for:

```
/ColorImageDownsampleThreshold 1.50

/GrayImageDownsampleThreshold 1.50

/MonoImageDownsampleThreshold 1.50
```

Change each of the above values from 1.50 to 1.00 and save the file as text only to your Distiller:Settings folder. When you downsample subsequent images with these settings, the downsampling amount for color, grayscale, and monochrome bitmaps will be the same as the value you supply in the Distiller Job Options Compression dialog box.

Color images

The first category handles color images used in your original file. You have choices for the sampling method and the amount of compression to be used. These include:

✦ **Bicubic Downsampling to [__]:** A checkbox and pull-down menu appear as your first choices. Bicubic Downsampling is the default setting for all preset Job Options except the Screen preset, which uses the Average Downsampling setting. Bicubic downsampling uses a weighted average to determine the resampled pixel color. The algorithm is much more mathematically intensive, and as a result, this method takes the longest time to complete distillation when files are downsampled. The upside is that it produces the best image quality for continuous tone images. With this method as well as the other two choices for resampling images, there are two field boxes where the amount of sampling can be user specified. The values range between 9 and 2400 dpi. The for images above field box enables you to choose when an image will be resampled. For example, in Figure 5-17, only images above 225 dpi will be resampled.

✦ **Average Downsampling to:** From the pull-down menu, the first item listed is Average Downsampling to. When you resample an image by downsampling, the average pixel value of a sample area is replaced with a pixel of the averaged color. The field boxes to the right of the sampling method can be used for user determined sampling amounts the same as used above with the Bicubic method.

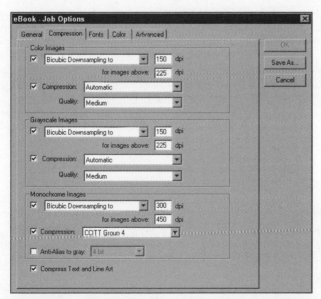

Figure 5-17: Distiller provides many more compression controls than some other PDF creators. In the Compression settings, you can make choices for the type of sampling and the amount of compression to be applied to images.

✦ **Subsampling to [__]:** The final item in the pull-down menu is Subsampling to. When Subsampling is specified, a pixel within the center of the sample area is chosen as the value applied to the sample area. Thus, downsampling noted above replaces pixels from averaged color values, whereas the subsampling replaces pixels from a given color value. Of the two methods, subsampling significantly reduces the amount of time to resample the image. Because all that averaging is taking place with downsampling, the calculations are more extensive, thereby increasing the distillation time. Subsampling, however, may result in more problems in the printed PDF file. Unless you have a large single-color background, you are better off choosing Bicubic downsampling when printing to hard copy.

✦ **Compression:** Acrobat Distiller has a choice for automatic compression in the Compression tab of the Job Options dialog box. In Figure 5-17, note a checkbox for Compression. When this checkbox is selected, you can open the adjacent pull-down menus by selecting the down arrows. The first pull-down menu enables you to select the Automatic, JPEG, or ZIP compression option. When Automatic is selected, Distiller will examine each image and automatically determine which compression to use (that is, either ZIP or JPEG). If the image to be compressed has large amounts of a common color value, ZIP compression will be used. If the image consists of smooth transitions of color — such as a continuous tone photograph, JPEG compression will be used. If you want to apply the same compression to all images, you can select either the JPEG or ZIP options. Doing so eliminates any decision making by Distiller about the type of compression to be applied.

✦ **Quality:** After the compression type is selected, you have one of five choices for the amount of compression to be applied. *High* quality relates to less compression, whereas *Minimum* quality relates to high compression. For high-end prepress, use the High quality setting (that is, Maximum). For desktop color printers, use Medium quality; and for Web, screen, or CD-ROM replication, use *Low* quality. The Minimum setting might be used in some cases with screen or Web graphics, but when viewing continuous tone photographs, they will often appear visibly degraded. You might use this setting to transfer files quickly across the Internet for client approvals, and then later use a higher setting for the final production documents.

Grayscale

All of the choices you have for color images are identical for grayscale images. You can elect to use different settings for color and grayscale images by toggling through all the options. When the final PDF is produced, the sampling and compression for your images appears respective to the choices made for each image type.

Monochrome images

Monochrome images include only two color values: black and white. Photoshop line art is a monochrome image. This is not to be confused with line art as we define it with vector art applications. The sampling methods available to you for monochrome images are identical to those described for color images.

Compression settings, however, are much different. The Compression settings include:

✦ **CCITT Group 3:** Fax machines use the International Coordinating Committee for Telephony and Telegraphy (CCITT) Group 3 compression. The images are compressed in horizontal rows, one row at a time.

✦ **CCITT Group 4:** CCITT Group 4 is a general-purpose compression method that produces good compression for most types of bitmap images. This compression method is the default and typically the best method for bitmap images.

✦ **ZIP:** ZIP compression is more efficient than earlier versions of Acrobat that used LZW compression. Zip achieves approximately 20 percent more compression. ZIP should be used when large areas of a single color appear in an image.

✦ **Run Length (RLE):** The Run Length format is a lossless compression scheme particularly favorable to bitmap monochrome images. You can run tests yourself for the compression method that works best for you. Typically CCITT Group 4 handles most of your needs when compressing these images.

✦ **Anti-Alias to gray:** Bit map images appear pixelated either on-screen or in some cases when printed. By using anti-aliasing, the image is rendered with a smoother appearance. The amount of anti-aliasing can be selected from the pull-down menu that becomes active when the checkbox is enabled. Choices are for 2, 4, and 8 bits that produce 4, 16, and 256 levels of gray respectively. If using anti-aliasing with scanned type, small point sizes may appear blurry when anti-aliased, especially with higher gray levels.

Line art

Line art definition in this window relates to vector artwork and not raster bitmaps. Line art would typically be vector artwork created in illustration programs. Also included in this category is text.

✦ **Compress Text and Line Art:** Text and line art uses Zip compression that is lossless and won't degrade vector images or type. You see virtually no difference in files printed compressed or uncompressed with this setting. By default, always keep this checkbox enabled. If you select Optimized for Fast Web View in the General Preferences, text and line art will be compressed automatically even if this checkbox is disabled.

Guidelines for sampling images

Acrobat handles all the sampling appropriate for your output needs as long as image sampling is equal to or greater than the requirements for the output. If image resolution is lower than the output needs, Distiller won't be able to upsample images to provide the necessary resolution. Even though Distiller can effectively downsample images, a few rules should be observed.

First, the resolution for all images in a layout or design should be sampled at the highest output requirement. For example, if prepress and commercial printing is to be used, then the image sample needs a resolution to support commercial printing. In this regard, you want to sample images in Photoshop at the needed resolution. Don't rely on Distiller to downsample images during distillation. The time you save can add up if converting many files with high-resolution images. When you open the Job Options and select the Compression tab, deselect the checkmarks for sampling.

Use the second rule when repurposing images. If you have a PostScript file that has been printed for a higher order of output, such as the commercial printing discussed previously, then you don't need to create a second PostScript file for another output requirement. Use the same PostScript file and now check the sampling appropriate for the output. If using the previous example and you now want to create a PDF for screen views, enable the sampling checkboxes and set the resolution to 72 dpi.

Font embedding

The distinctive advantage of using the Portable Document Format is to maintain file integrity across computers and across platforms. One of the greatest problems with file integrity is the handling of fonts. Therefore, Distiller provides the ability to embed fonts within the PDF so that the end user won't need font installations to view and print PDF files. The Fonts tab, as shown in Figure 5-18 offers control on font embedding during distillation.

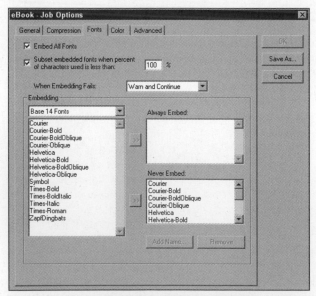

Figure 5-18: The Distiller Job Options dialog box with the Fonts tab selected displays the control over font embedding available to you during distillation.

✦ **Embed All Fonts:** Unless you have a specific reason to not embed fonts, this option should always be enabled. As you may recall from the discussion of font embedding in Chapter 3, some fonts don't do well with font substitution. For all PDF documents to be printed, especially those that are to be sent to an imaging center, always embed the fonts when licensing agreements permit you to do so.

There are many different font manufacturers, and the permissions for use of fonts from these manufacturers vary considerably. To legally include font embedding in a PDF file, you need to know whether the manufacturer provides the permission for inclusion. Adobe original fonts that are owned by Linotype-Hell, International Typeface Corporation, AGFA, AlphaOmega, Bigelow & Holmes, Fundicion Typografica Neufville, and Monotype Typography, Ltd., as well as those in the Adobe library, can be used for font embedding without written releases. Fonts with licensing restrictions will often appear with an explanation of the limitations of use. If in doubt, you'll need to check with the manufacturer or distributor to inquire as to whether you can legally distribute PDF files that include certain fonts. Failure to do so may result in a copyright violation.

✦ **Subset embedded fonts when percentage of characters used is less than [__]:** Some PDF producers provide you an opportunity to subset both PostScript and TrueType fonts. The difference between the subsetting in Distiller as opposed to other producers is your ability to determine when a font is subset. With Distiller, you can specify when you want subsetting to occur. The subsetting percentage has to do with the percentage of *glyphs* (special renderings) in the font. If 100 percent is selected, Distiller includes all information necessary to draw all the glyphs in the font. Lower percentages determine what characters among the set are embedded. When using Type 3, TrueType, and CID fonts, they are always embedded regardless of what value is supplied. (For font format descriptions, see table 5-3 later in this chapter).

✦ **When Embedding Fails:** This pull-down menu offers three choices. Choose Ignore to ignore a failed font being embedded, in which case distillation will continue. The Warn and Continue option displays a warning and then continues distillation. Choose Cancel to cancel the distillation if a font embedding error occurs. When sending files off to service centers for imaging or when font substitution is not desired, you may want to use the Cancel option as your default. If the PDF is not created, you won't inadvertently forget there was a problem with font embedding.

✦ **Embedding:** The left side of the dialog box lists all fonts available for embedding. Distiller can monitor font locations on your computer. If several font locations exist, the only fonts displayed in the list are those in the currently selected folder being monitored. By default, you see the Base 14 fonts listed. If you want to view the font list from a monitored folder, click the pull-down menu and select the folder. Monitored font directories can be identified in the Settings menu, as discussed a little later in this chapter. Regardless of what is listed in the Embedding list, Distiller can embed fonts that were included in the PostScript file or all the folders listed for monitoring. The font to be embedded must be present in either the PostScript file or a monitored folder.

✦ **Always Embed:** A list of fonts for always embedding appears to the right of the Embedding list. You add fonts to this list by selecting them from the Embedding list and clicking the right-pointing chevron (double arrows). You can select multiple fonts by pressing the Control (Windows) key or Shift (Macintosh) key and clicking all the fonts to be included. If the fonts are listed in a contiguous display, use Shift+Click to select them. After selecting the font(s), click the right-pointing chevron. A good use for the Always Embed list may be for a font that appears in your company logo. Regardless of the type of document you are creating, you may want to always include your corporate font set in all your documents to avoid any font substitution.

The design of TrueType fonts enable the type designer the ability to prevent font embedding. These fonts can be moved to the Always Embed list, but if designed without embedding permissions, they will fail to embed in the PDF. Font embedding errors are reported in the log file that can be viewed in a text editor. If a PDF is produced, you can choose File ⇨ Document Properties ⇨ Fonts to determine whether the font was embedded.

✦ **Never Embed:** This list operates the same way as the Always Embed list. You can select fonts to be eliminated from the set of monitored fonts or fonts contained in a PostScript file. One use for this list may be to eliminate Courier, Times, Helvetica, and Symbol (the Base 13 fonts). Because these fonts ship with Acrobat and are usually burned into ROM chips on most PostScript devices, you rarely have a problem either viewing them or printing documents with these fonts included. Because every user of Acrobat Reader has the Base 13 fonts installed, you can reduce some file size by eliminating them from the PDF files that you create.

The Base 14 fonts are sometimes referred to as the Base 13 + 1 fonts. The Base 13 fonts consist of Courier, Helvetica, Times, and Symbol. Courier, Helvetica, and Times include Roman, bold, italic, and bold italic thus resulting in four fonts for each family plus the thirteenth font being Symbol. The extra font added to the base set is Zapf Dingbats. You should plan on embedding this font and do not include it in your Never Embed list. PostScript RIPs do not include Zapf Dingbats in ROM.

You may find contradictory information related to what a vendor refers to as the Base 13 fonts. Some technical documentation refer to other fonts included in the Base 13 set, such as Arial, while technical documents from the same vendor may use the above named fonts in separate technical documents. By the most common standards, the Base 13 set includes only: Courier, Helvetica, Times, and Symbol. Don't deviate from this as you may experience font problems if fonts outside this list are not embedded.

✦ **Add Name:** Fonts can be added to the Always Embed list or the Never Embed list by entering the font name in a separate dialog box. To add a font name, you must first deselect the Embed All Fonts checkbox, and then click the Add Name button. A dialog box appears where you need to type the name precisely as the font is identified. Two radio buttons exist for determining where the font will be added. Select either the Always Embed list or Never Embed list as needed. Click Done, and the font appears in the appropriate list.

Font names must be accurate. To ensure accuracy for the name you enter in the Add Font name dialog box, open a PDF file in an Acrobat viewer containing the font to be described. Choose File ⇨ Document Properties ⇨ Fonts. If the font is included in your PDF file but not displayed in the font list, click the List All Fonts button. Under the Original Font heading, you will see the font name as it should appear when you add the name in the Add Font name dialog box. Make note of the name, including all case sensitivity and special characters. Return to your Add Font name dialog box and enter the name exactly as it appeared in your viewer's font list.

✦ **Remove:** If you add a font name to either the Always Embed list or the Never Embed list, and you want to delete that name, select the font name to be deleted and click Remove. Fonts can't be removed from the Embedding list. The only time Remove is enabled is when you select a font name in either the Always Embed list or Never Embed list.

The priority used by Distiller to decide whether to embed a font in the PDF follows an order to resolve ambiguity. Distiller views the Never Embed list as having the highest order of priority. If a font is placed in the Never Embed list, it will not be embedded even though the same font may be added to the Always Embed list.

Font types

Any PDF author will tell you the continuing problem with file displays and prints as well as producing PDFs is font handling. People swear at times that they have enabled all the appropriate controls for font embedding and PDF file creation, yet the resultant PDF either displays or prints with font substitution. Gathering as much knowledge as you can with regard to font evolution, design, engineering, and proper use will help you understand how to overcome problems and provide solutions for your workflow. To gain a little more understanding, look at the following font types, formats, and their characteristics.

✦ **Type 0:** Type 0 (zero) is a composite font format composed as a high level font that references multiple font descendents. Type 0 fonts use an OCF (Original Composite Font) format that was the first effort of Adobe in attempting to implement a format for handling fonts with large character sets. A good example of a font using a large character set is Asian Language font types. Today, the OCF format is not supported.

✦ **Type 1:** By far the most popular PostScript font today is the Type 1 font. These are single-byte fonts handled well by Adobe Type Manager (Windows and Macintosh) and all PostScript printers. Type 1 fonts use a specialized subset of the PostScript language, which is optimized for performance. For reliability, use of Type 1 fonts present the fewest problems when embedding and printing to PostScript devices.

✦ **Type 2:** Type 2 fonts offer compact character description procedures for outline fonts. They were designed to be used with the Compact Font Format (CFF). The CCF format is designed for font embedding and substitution with Acrobat PDFs.

✦ **Type 3:** Type 3 fonts are PostScript fonts that have been used with some type stylizing applications. These fonts can have special design attributes applied to the font such as shading, patterns, exploding 3D displays, and so on. The fonts can't be used with ATM (Adobe Type Manager) and they often present problems when printing to PostScript devices. They should never be used when creating PDF files.

✦ **Type 4:** Type 4 was designed to create font characters from printer font cartridges for permanent storage on a printer's hard disk (usually attached by a SCSI port to the printer). PostScript Level 2 provided the same capability for Type 1 fonts and eventually made these font types obsolete.

✦ **Type 5:** This font type is similar to the Type 4 fonts but used the printer's ROM instead of the hard disk. PostScript Level 2 again made this format obsolete.

✦ **Type 32:** Type 32 fonts are used for downloading bitmap fonts to a PostScript interpreter's font cache. By downloading directly to the printer cache, space is saved in the printer's memory.

✦ **Type 42:** Type 42 fonts are generated from the printer driver for TrueType fonts. A PostScript wrapper is created for the font making the rasterization and interpretation more efficient and accurate. Type 42 fonts work well with PDFs and printing to PostScript printers.

✦ **OpenType Font Format:** OpenType is a recent joint effort by Adobe Systems and Microsoft to provide a new generation of type font technology. OpenType makes no distinction between Type 1 and TrueType fonts. Font developers have a much easier way of porting font designs to a single format in production and mastering as well as across platforms. The OpenType format is supported with font embedding and distillation. Fonts eventually produced with this technology should be as reliable as you find with Type 1 and Type 42 fonts listed previously.

✦ **Compact Type Format:** CFF is similar to the Type 1 format but offers much more compact encoding and optimization. It was designed to support Type 2 fonts but can be used with other types. CFF can be embedded in PDFs with the PDF Version 1.2 format and Acrobat 3.0 compatibility. Fonts supporting this format are converted by Distiller during distillation to CFF/Type 2 fonts and embedded in the PDF. When viewed on-screen or printed, they are converted back to Type 1 that provides support for ATM and printing with integrity.

✦ **CID-keyed Fonts:** This format was developed to take advantage of large character sets particularly the Asian CJK (Chinese, Japanese, and Korean) fonts. The format is an extension of the Type 1 format and supports ATM and PostScript printing. Kerning and spacing for these character sets are better handled in the OpenType format. On the Macintosh, a utility called Make CID is found in the Distiller: Xtras folder. For Asian TrueType or Type 1 OCF formats, use the utility to convert the fonts to CID keyed fonts. The first time Distiller is launched with the Asian character set installed, you will be prompted to convert any of these fonts found in monitored folders. If you want to manually convert the fonts, you can double-click the application icon. On Windows, the Make CID application won't be available. Converted fonts can be copied across platforms and Distiller running under Windows processes PostScript files created under Mac OS that have references to the character widths.

When distilling PostScript with Acrobat Distiller, font embedding and substitution is allowed, as described in Table 5-3.

Table 5-3
Distiller Handling of Font Embedding and Subsetting According to Type Format

Font	Never Embed	Always Embed	Subset
Type 1	Yes	Yes	Yes
Type 2	No; Always embedded		No; Always subsetted
TrueType Type 42	Yes	Yes	No; Always subsetted
CID Font Type0	Yes	Yes	No; Always subsetted
CID Font Type1	No; Always embedded		No; Always subsetted
CID Font Type2	Yes	Yes	No; Always subsetted
OpenType*	Yes	Yes	No; Always subsetted

*OpenType is only supported with Distiller 5.0.

Color Job Options

Adobe has been working on developing standard color viewing and file tagging for color spaces for some time. Releases of the latest software products continue to support sophisticated color-handling methods. Latest releases of products, such as Illustrator 9 and Photoshop 6, have color control options consistent with the new color handling features in Acrobat 5. When making choices for color handling, your first decision to make is whether to convert color. After your conversion choice, you move on to working spaces and profile assumptions. If you tag a file for conversion, what profiles will be embedded in the document? Under the Color management Policies settings, you can choose to control many conditions for prepress operations as well as on-screen viewing. As you view the Color tab in the Job Options dialog box, examine each of the controls available for color handling (see Figure 5-19).

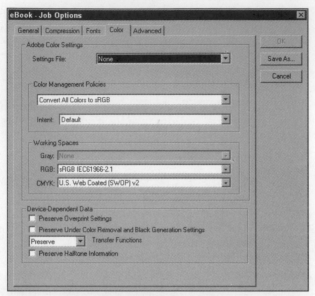

Figure 5-19: The Color tab of the Job Options dialog box handles the color profile management.

Adobe color settings

Working with a color management system requires you to make some decisions about how the color is viewed on your computer monitor and on the final output medium. In some cases, the monitor view and output medium will be the same, such as Acrobat viewer files on-screen and Web files. The first of these decisions appear among the choices in the pull-down menu for Settings File. The choices available to you include None, prepress defaults, Photoshop emulation, and defaults for Web graphics. When None is selected from the pull-down menu, the Color Management Policies and Working Spaces can be edited for custom choices. If any of the other choices are made, the options below the pull-down menu will be grayed out. When color management and profile embedding is controlled by other programs, such as Photoshop, leave the setting to None and turn off all color management for the choices that are described next.

Color Management Policies

If None is selected in the Settings File pull-down menu, the options for Color Management Policies and Intent will be active. If any other choice is made from the aforementioned settings, these items will be grayed out. Choices for the Color Management Policies are different depending on what compatibility choice is selected in the General Job Options. Acrobat 3.0 compatibility offers different options than the 4.0 and 5.0 compatibility. As we look at the policies choices, the settings change according to the compatibility selection made.

✦ **Leave Color Unchanged:** The menu item appearing in the Color Management Policies should be enabled if you presume all color handling in the PostScript file is defined for your specific needs. No color conversion occurs and device-dependent colors remain unchanged. When sending files to color-calibrated devices, this option should be used. The presumption is the device will specify all color handling and the file will not be tagged for color management.

✦ **Tag Everything for Color Management:** When the Acrobat 4.0 or 5.0 compatibility setting is made in the General Job Options, a color profile selected in the Working Spaces below is used to Tag Everything for Color Management, which embeds an ICC profile for the images, artwork, and text. The printed PDF file maintains the integrity of any documents containing embedded profiles; however, the view on your monitor screen will assume the color viewing space of the assumed profile selected respective to choices from the Working Spaces. When Acrobat 3.0 compatibility is chosen, the option changes to Convert Everything for Color management and no ICC profiles are embedded. Device-dependent color spaces for all color modes will be converted to device independent color spaces of CalRGB, CalGray, and Lab.

✦ **Tag Only Images for Color Management:** The same holds true as noted in the preceding entry except only raster images are tagged with color management according to the same compatibility options selected in the General Job Options. Text and vector objects remain unaffected.

✦ **Convert All Colors to sRGB:** Selecting this option converts all colors to sRGB. The RGB and CMYK color images are converted. When using Acrobat 3.0 compatibility, the RGB and CMYK images are converted to CalRGB (Calibrated RGB). The sRGB setting is used for screen and Web images. The file sizes are smaller and screen redraws appear faster. Grayscale images are unaffected by choices made for color tagging and conversion.

Below the first pull-down menu is another pull-down menu used for the Intent for how color is mapped between color spaces. Choices for Intent include:

✦ **Default:** The color output device and not the PDF file handles the Intent. By default, device handling most commonly uses a Relative Colormetric intent.

✦ **Perceptual:** Perceptual (Images) has to do with the mapping of pixels from one gamut to another. When you select this item, the image is mapped from the original pixels to the color gamut of the printer profile. All out of gamut colors are remapped.

✦ **Saturation:** Saturation (Graphics) maintains relative saturation values. If a pixel is saturated and out of the color gamut of the printer, it will be remapped preserving saturation but mapped to the closest color within the printer's gamut.

✦ **Absolute Colormetric:** Disables the white point matching when colors are converted. With no white point reference, you will notice a change in brightness values of all the remapped colors.

✦ **Relative Colormetric:** Preserves all color values within the printer's gamut. Out of gamut colors are converted to the same lightness values of colors within the printable gamut.

Working Spaces

Profile management for working spaces involves your decisions for embedding profiles for the color space while viewing your images on-screen. If a color space is defined for a given image and viewed on one monitor, theoretically it can be viewed the same on other monitors if the color profile is embedded in the image. Working space definitions can only be applied to images tagged for color management. Either of the two tagging options above must be selected for a working space to be defined.

✦ **Gray:** Selecting None from this menu prevents grayscale images from being converted. The Dot Gain choices affect the overall brightness of grayscale images. The default is Adobe Gray with a dot gain of 20 percent. Lower values will lighten the image while values above 20 percent will display grayscale images darker. Gray Gamma choices may be used for images viewed between computer platforms. A gray gamma of 1.8 is suited for Macintosh viewing while the higher 2.2 Gamma is better suited for Windows.

✦ **RGB:** If you use a color calibration system or monitor profile, the respective profile can be selected from this pull-down menu. Choices available to you will depend on profiles installed on your computer. If you have created custom profiles from Adobe Photoshop and saved them to your Color folder (Windows) or ColorSync folder (Macintosh), they will appear as menu options. Default RGB profiles from Photoshop appear here after Photoshop is installed on your computer. The default option is sRGB IEC61966-2.1. If in doubt, use this option. This option is becoming an industry standard and generally good for matching color between display and color output devices.

✦ **CMYK:** CMYK profiles also appear according to those stored in the respective folder according to platform, as mentioned previously. Profile tagging is uniquely applied to images according to the color mode of the image. Thus, the Gray options are only applied to grayscale images. RGB choices are applied to only RGB images while the CMYK choices tag only CMYK images. When using CMYK output for prepress, you may have a profile embedded in the CMYK images. You can select None for this setting while changing the Gray and RGB working spaces which preserves the color for output while enabling you to tag the other color modes for screen views. It is unlikely that you would use RGB and CMYK images together for prepress, but you can set up the Job Options for consistent display of files regardless of the color mode used. For those who aren't using a CMS in your workflow and you haven't performed any level of sophisticated color calibration, make the choice for US Web Coated (SWOP) as your default profile.

Device Dependent Data

All options available under the Device Dependent Data are applied to images intended for prepress and printing. Whatever choices are made here will have no effect on screen views.

✦ **Preserve Overprint settings:** Overprints manually applied in applications, such as illustration and layout programs are preserved when you enable this option. Overprinting only has an effect when your files are color separated or possibly when you print composite color to proofing machines that display trapping problems from files printed as separations. If your workflow is consistent and you don't deviate between creating overprints and relying on a service center to perform them, then you can leave this item as a default for your high-end output needs. Enabling the checkbox has no effect on images where overprints are not present.

✦ **Preserve Under Color Removal and Black Generation Settings:** If you made changes to undercolor removal or black generation settings in Photoshop, these changes will be preserved when the file is distilled. Disabling the checkbox eliminates any settings made in Photoshop.

✦ **Preserve Transfer Functions:** If you embed transfer functions in Adobe Photoshop, you can preserve them by selecting Apply from the pull-down menu. If transfer functions have not been saved with your Photoshop file, it won't matter if Apply is used. Use Apply when you intentionally set them up in a Photoshop image and you have the settings confirmed by your printer. You can eliminate transfer functions set in a file by selecting Remove from the pull-down menu.

✦ **Preserve Halftone Information:** Preserving the halftone information does not disturb halftone frequencies embedded in documents, as well as custom angles, spot shapes, and functions specified. Depending on the service center you use, they may want to have you set halftone information in the PostScript file and preserve them in the PDF. For PostScript 3 devices, PDFs can be delivered straight to the imagesetter and will print at the halftone frequency preserved in the file. Service centers using PostScript Level 2 RIPs won't care if the halftone frequency is preserved or not. They have to manually set the frequency every time they print a PDF.

Advanced Job Options

The final tab in Distiller's Job Options dialog box, Advanced, enables you to make settings for other miscellaneous attributes. The controls listed in this dialog box greatly distinguish Acrobat Distiller from other PDF producers. When you choose the Advanced tab in the Job Options dialog box, the settings shown in Figure 5-20 appear.

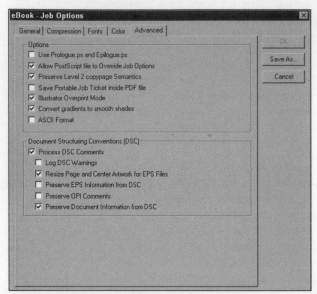

Figure 5-20: The Advanced Job Options offer a group of miscellaneous settings often not available with other PDF producers.

Advanced Job Options contains a variety of options for job ticketing, document structure, and other items not found in the previous dialog boxes. These include:

✦ **Use Prologue.ps and Epilogue.ps:** Two files, named `prologue.ps` and `epilogue.ps`, are located in the Acrobat5:Distillr:Data folder when you install Acrobat. To use the files, you must move them to the same folder as the Acrobat Distiller application and both files must reside together in this location. The files contain PostScript code that is appended to a PDF file when it is created with Distiller. By default, the files do not contain any data that will affect distillation. They serve more as templates where you can write code that will be appended to the PDF. The `prologue.ps` file can be used to append information to the PDF, such as a note, cover page, or job ticket information. The `epilogue.ps` file is used to resolve PostScript procedure problems.

Note
Both of these files can be edited; however, you need to be familiar with the PostScript language to effectively change the files. When relocating the files, be certain to place a copy in the Distiller folder and leave the original in the Data folder, especially if you decide to edit either file. You can also use the files with watched folders, as explained a little later in this chapter. When using watched folders, place the `prologue.ps` and `epilogue.ps` files at the same directory level as the In and Out folders.

✦ **Allow PostScript file to Override Job Options:** If you are certain the PostScript file you printed to disk has all the settings handled properly for output, enabling this option allows the PostScript file to supersede any changes you make in the Distiller Job Options dialog box. Disabling the checkbox allows all Distiller Job Options specifications to take precedence.

✦ **Preserve Level 2 copypage Semantics:** This setting has to do with semantic differences between PostScript Level 2 and PostScript 3. If you are imaging to PostScript Level 2 devices, enable this option. If printing to PostScript 3 devices, disable this option. If you are sending files to an imaging center, ask the technicians which level of PostScript is used on their devices.

✦ **Save Portable Job Ticket inside PDF File:** Job tickets contain information about the original PostScript file and not the content of the PDF file. Information related to page sizes, page orientation, resolution, halftone frequencies, trapping information, and so on is some of what is contained in job tickets. When printing PDF files, enable this option. If you produce PDF files for screen, Web, or CD-ROM, you can eliminate job ticket information.

✦ **Illustrator Overprint Mode:** Overprints assigned in Adobe Illustrator can be preserved when the checkbox is enabled when applied to CMYK images. To eliminate overprints from Illustrator files, disable the checkbox.

✦ **Convert gradients to Smooth Shades:** This feature only works with Acrobat 4.0 compatibility and greater. Gradients are converted to smooth shades and appear much smoother when rendered on PostScript 3 devices. The appearance of the gradients is unaffected when viewed on-screen, but they have noticeable differences when printed.

✦ **ASCII Format:** By default, files are Binary encoded. If you want to use ASCII encoding, enable this checkbox.

✦ **Process DSC Comments:** Document structuring comments (DSC) contain information about a PDF file. Items, such as originating application, creation date, modification date, page orientation, and so on are all document structuring comments. To maintain the DSC, enable this option. Because some important information, such as page orientation and beginning and ending statements for the prologue.ps file are part of the document structure, you want to keep this item as a default.

✦ **Log DSC Warnings:** During distillation, if the processing of the document structuring comments encounters an error, the error is noted in a log file. When you enable this checkbox, the log file is created. You can open the log file in a word processor or text editor to determine where the error occurred. Enable this option whenever document structuring comments are processed.

✦ **Resize Page and Center Artwork for EPS Files:** In earlier versions of Acrobat, distillation of a single-page EPS file, created from programs, such as Adobe Illustrator, Macromedia FreeHand, or CorelDraw, would use the EPS bounding box for the final page size. Many problems occurred when distilling EPS files directly as opposed to printed PostScript files. At times, a user would experience clipping and lose part of an image. With this option, you have a choice between creating a PDF with the page dimensions equal to the artwork or having the artwork appear on the size of the original page you defined in your host application. When the checkbox is enabled, the page size is reduced to the size of the artwork, and the artwork is centered on the page. When the checkbox is disabled, the entire page appears consistent with the page size definition from the host application.

✦ **Preserve EPS Information from DSC:** This item is similar to the Process DSC option. If your file is an EPS file, enabling this checkbox will preserve document structuring comments.

✦ **Preserve OPI Comments:** Open Press Interface (OPI) is a management tool used by many high-end imaging centers to control production. An OPI comment may include the replacement of high-resolution images for low-resolution FPO (*for position only*) files used in a layout program. OPI comments can include many different issues related to digital prepress, such as image position on a page, crop area, sampling resolution, color bit depth, colors (in other words, CMYK, spot, and so on), overprint instructions, and more. If outputting to high-end imaging devices at service centers using OPI management, enable this option.

✦ **Preserve Document Information from DSC:** Document information items, discussed earlier in this book, include such elements as title, subject, author, and keywords. Enabling this option preserves document information.

Many of the controls available in the Advanced tab are further amplified when I discuss prepress and printing in Chapter 18. At this time, it is important to realize that Acrobat Distiller provides you with many more controls for establishing attributes with PDF document creation and permits flexibility in designing PDF files for specific purposes. With all these toggles and checkboxes, becoming confused and feeling overwhelmed is easy. Fortunately, Acrobat can help make this job a little easier for you. If you work in an office environment where a network administrator sets up all the controls for your PDF workflow, you can load preset custom Job Options. If you are the responsible party for establishing Job Options, you can create different custom settings, save them, and later load them in the General Job Options. Either way, you won't have to go back and reread this chapter every time you want to distill a file for another purpose.

✦ **Save As:** The Save button captures all the settings you make for all the Distiller Job Options and opens a dialog box that defaults to the Settings folder. Provide a filename and click the Save button to create a new Job Options set. In Figure 5-21, I named a new set MySettings.joboptions.

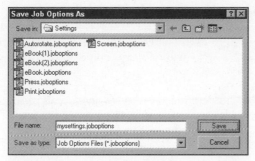

Figure 5-21: After you select the Save button, a navigation dialog box opens enabling you to supply a name and find a location for the new settings to be saved. By default, the new file is saved to the Settings folder. The files must reside in this folder in order to appear in the General Job Options dialog box.

Font Locations

Font embedding, as described earlier in this chapter, occurs with Distiller Job Options when a font is contained in the PostScript file or loaded in the system with a utility, such as Adobe Type Manager. If fonts reside neither in the PostScript file nor loaded with ATM, then Distiller offers another method for handling fonts that may escape you. Under the Settings menu, choose Font Locations. The Acrobat Distiller – Font Locations dialog box opens, as shown in Figure 5-22.

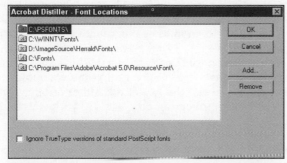

Figure 5-22: Distiller can monitor fonts installed on your hard drive when listed in the Acrobat Distiller-Font Locations dialog box.

In this dialog box, you can add folders of fonts that instruct Distiller to look in the identified folders when a font is neither contained in the PostScript file nor loaded in the system memory. Monitored font folders are listed in the window shown in Figure 5-22. To add a new folder, click the Add button. To remove a folder, select it in the list and click the Remove button.

A checkbox at the bottom of the dialog box enables you to resolve some problems that may occur when a TrueType font has the same name as a PostScript font. To eliminate embedding TrueType fonts with the same names as PostScript fonts, check the box at the bottom of the dialog box.

Watched Folders

Watched folders enable you to automate distillation of PostScript files in a business or production environment. PDF workflows can be easily developed by hosting a server on a network where Acrobat Distiller is continually running in the background and *watching* a folder or many folders for the introduction of new PostScript files. When Distiller encounters a new PostScript file, the file can be distilled in the background while foreground applications are running. The resulting PDF files can be automatically moved to another folder or directory, and the PostScript files can be either preserved or deleted automatically.

Licensing restrictions

Before moving on to working with watched folders, please look over this section carefully and try to understand the proper use and authorization of working with watched folders on networks. Adobe Systems grants you license for working on a single computer when installing Acrobat. When you create PDFs on your computer, you can distribute them to anyone who uses an Acrobat viewer. Therefore, the PDFs you create can legitimately be distributed to anyone who acquires the free Acrobat Reader software.

Creating PDFs, whether locally or on a network, assumes that you have complied with the proper licensing agreements for use of the Acrobat Distiller application. Ambiguity arises when using the Distiller application on networks with watched folders. If you set up a watched folder on a network where multiple users can access the watched folders, you need a site license to use the Acrobat Distiller application. Because multiple users would use Distiller, site licensing or individual purchases of the product is required.

Therefore, the licensing policies in this regard are related not to distribution; but rather, how the PDFs are created. As we move through the discussion on watched folders, keep in mind that when I make mention of using watched folders on networks, I'm assuming you are compliant with the proper licensing agreements.

Creating watched folders

Watched folders can be individual folders, hard drive partitions, or dedicated hard drives. When you choose Settings ➪ Watched Folders, a dialog box appears enabling you to establish preferences for the watched folders and distillation attributes.

The options available in the Watched Folders dialog box include the following:

✦ **Watched folders list:** The list window displays all folders you have identified to be watched. The name of the watched folder appears in the list as well as the directory path. In Figure 5-23, notice the directory is D:\ and the folder name is Acro5 Bible as might be viewed in Windows. On the Macintosh, the name of your drive (for example, Macintosh HD) appears first in the list followed by the folder name(s).

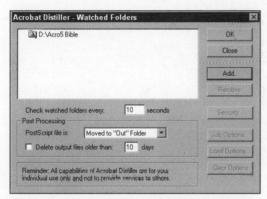

Figure 5-23: The Watched Folders dialog box establishes the Watched folder preferences. When you open the Acrobat Distiller–Watched Folders dialog box, a reminder for the licensing restrictions appears at the bottom of the dialog box.

✦ **Check Watched Folders every [__] seconds:** This user-definable field accepts values between 1 and 1000 seconds. When Distiller monitors a watched folder, the folder is examined according to the value entered in this field box.

✦ **PostScript file is:** Distiller automatically treats the PostScript file according to the options available in this pull-down menu. You can choose the Deleted menu item that will delete the PostScript file after distillation; or choose Moved to "Out" folder, that will move the PostScript file to a folder entitled Out. If you intend to repurpose files for different use, be certain to keep the PostScript file.

✦ **Delete output files older than [__] days:** If you elect to keep the PostScript files in the Out folder, they can be deleted after the time interval specified in this field box. The acceptable range is between 1 and 999 days.

✦ **Add:** To create a watched folder or add to the current list of watched folders, click the Add Folder button. When you click the button, a navigation dialog box appears. Depending on the platform that you use, the dialog boxes offer some different options, as shown in Figure 5-24 for Windows and Figure 5-25 for the Macintosh.

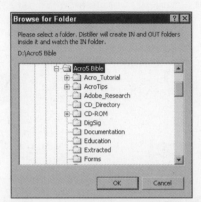

Figure 5-24: The Browse for Folder dialog box on Windows doesn't provide an opportunity to create a new folder. Folders must first be created on the Desktop or nested in other folders before it can be identified as a watched folder.

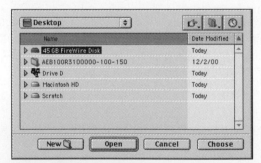

Figure 5-25: On the Macintosh, the button used for New creates a new folder from within the dialog box opened after clicking the Add button in the Watched Folders dialog box. After the folder is created, it can be selected by clicking the Choose button and subsequently used as a watched folder.

To add a folder to the watched folders list, the folder must first be created before clicking the Add button (Windows) or created by selecting the New button (Macintosh). Folders, as well as partitions and drives, can be added to your list. On a network, remote folders, partitions, and drives can also be added to the list. If you want to select a folder similar to the one displayed in Figure 5-23, select a folder after clicking the Add button. If you want to have the entire hard drive watched, select the drive designation (C:\, D:\, E:\, and so on in Windows or Macintosh HD, Hard Drive, and so on with a Macintosh) and click the OK button in the Browse for Folder dialog box.

✦ **Remove:** To delete watched folders, select the folder name in the watched folders list and click the Remove Folder button. If a folder is moved on or deleted from your hard drive, the next time you launch Distiller, you will see a warning dialog box appear notifying you that Distiller cannot find the watched folder(s). Removal of watched folders must occur in the Acrobat Distiller-Watched Folders (Windows) or Watched Folders (Macintosh) dialog box. If you inadvertently deleted a watched folder, you need to delete the folder name in the watched folders list. Return to your desktop and create a new folder; then return to the dialog box and add the new folder to the list.

✦ **Security:** Security can be established for the PDF files distilled. Adding security during distillation is handy for multiple files created in PDF Workflow environments. If the Acrobat 3.0 or 4.0 compatibility option is selected in the current General Job Options dialog box, the security level will be limited to 40-bit encryption. If Acrobat 5.0 compatibility is selected in the General Job Options dialog box, 128-bit encryption will be used.

✦ **Job Options:** The Job Options button becomes active when you select a watched folder name in the watched folders list. With a folder name selected in the list, clicking the Job Options button will open the Job Options dialog box. You can apply different Job Options to different watched folders. If, for example, you print PostScript files to disk and have them distilled for high-end output and Web page design, you will want compression and color modes distinctive for the output sources. You can set up two watched folders and have the same PostScript file distilled with the different Job Options. Setting Job Options here will override Distiller's defaults and apply new options to the specific watched folder where the attributes are established.

✦ **Load Options:** Selecting this button opens the Settings folder where your Job Options are stored. Any Job Options you created or the presets can be selected and used for the watched folder.

✦ **Clear Options:** This button in the Watched Folders dialog box can only be used after the Job Options button is selected and the Job Options for the watched folder have been changed from Distiller's defaults. After the Job Options have been changed from the Job Options control, an icon appears adjacent to the folder icon and directory path in the watched folders list, as illustrated in Figure 5-23. The symbol indicates the Job Options have been changed from Distiller's defaults. When you select the name in the list and click the Clear Options button, the icon changes back to the view displayed in Figure 5-26.

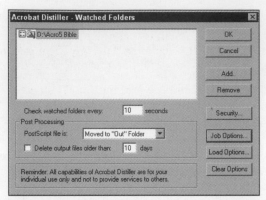

Figure 5-26: When custom Job Options settings are made for a watched folder, an icon appears adjacent to the folder icon displayed in the watched folders list. (Notice the icon added to the left of the folder.)

Watched folders greatly help your PDF workflow and assist you in automating the smallest office environment to large offices with multiple networks and servers. When you install Acrobat Distiller on a server, the burden of PDF creation is dedicated to the server and relieves individual workstations.

In identifying watched folders, you need only have the directory or folder created on a hard disk. After you identify the watched folder, Distiller automatically creates the other folders needed to execute distillation from watched folder files. The In folder created by Distiller are monitored. When a PostScript file is copied or written to the In folder, the distillation commences according to the interval that you establish in the Watched Folder settings dialog box. Files can be *dropped* into the In folder, or you can print to PostScript from within an application directly to the In folder.

Watched folders work well in cross-platform environments, too. To use a watched folder from one platform and have the distillation performed on another platform, you need to have the computers networked and have software installed that enables you to communicate between two or more computers on your network. To give you an idea of how easy cross-platform networking and remote distillation is, I walk you through the steps I used in my home office in the following exercise.

STEPS: Creating Watched Folders for Network Distillation

1. **Network topology.** On my network, I have a Pentium running Windows 2000 Workstation, and two Mac G4s. To communicate between the Macs and the PC, I use Miramar Systems PC MacLan software (www.miramarsystems.com). PC MacLan provides one of the best applications for cross-platform network communication (see Figure 5-27).

2. **Launch the server software.** I open PC MacLan in Windows.

3. **Grant privileges.** After launching PC MacLan, I identify the Users and Groups, which grants privileges to users. In this example, I use my login information and password already established for my computer access, as shown in Figure 5-28.

Figure 5-27: PC MacLan software is opened on the PC to enable file sharing and communication between PCs and Macs.

Figure 5-28: The Users and Groups dialog box enables me to establish file-sharing privileges.

4. **Create shared volumes.** I need to let PC MacLan know which drive(s) are to be shared. On my Pentium, I have two internal drives installed. The drives are identified as C:\, and D:\. I identified my D:\ drive where all my documents are saved.

5. **Start the file sharing.** After I have the privileges and volumes identified, I start the server software by clicking the icon to start PC MacLan.

6. **Create a folder to be watched.** The Folder to be watched can be created either before or after the server is running. PC MacLan will display new documents and folders after your server connection has been established. In this example, I created the folder after the server software was running.

7. **Log on to the network.** On a Macintosh, I choose Apple ➪ Chooser to open the Chooser dialog box and select AppleShare, which displays the computer that is currently being shared (see Figure 5-29). I select the PC MACLAN workstation, and click OK in the Chooser dialog box.

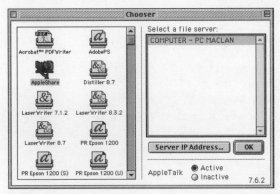

Figure 5-29: Network connections and file sharing are built into the Macintosh operating system. Addressing network communications is handled in the Chooser by selecting AppleShare.

8. **Launch Acrobat Distiller.** The watched folder can be identified either before or after the network connection. In this example, I first established my network connection, and now I need to set up the watched folder.

9. **Create a watched folder.** The folder I created earlier is just a folder or directory on my hard drive. To make this folder a watched folder, I need to choose Settings ➪ Watched Folders and select the folder to be watched. When the Acrobat Distiller - Watched Folders dialog box appears, I click the Add button, which opens the Browse for Folder dialog box shown in Figure 5-30.

   I select the folder and click OK in the dialog box. When I return to the Watched Folder dialog box, the new folder name is displayed in the watched folder list.

10. **Examine the watched folder.** When I return to my desktop and open the Acro5 Bible folder, I double-check it to be certain Distiller has created the subfolders necessary to make this a watched folder, as shown in Figure 5-31. If you find the In and Out subfolders within the watched folder, you know Distiller will monitor this folder.

Figure 5-30: My drive D displays the folder list, which includes my Acro5 Bible folder.

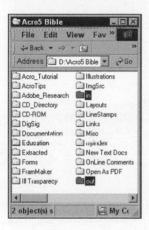

Figure 5-31: After I open the watched folder, the In and Out folders, automatically created by Distiller, appear. Verifying that the folders have been created assures me Distiller has identified the folder as a watched folder.

11. **Printing the PostScript file.** I can drop a PostScript file into the In folder, and within 10 seconds (as determined in the watched folder settings) the file will be distilled. I can also print a PostScript file directly from my Macintosh to the In folder inside the Watched Folder. As soon as the PostScript file is in the In folder, Distiller will commence distillation at the interval specified in the Acrobat Distiller – Watched Folders dialog box. In this example, I print a PostScript file directly to the In folder.

12. **Examine the In folder.** After distillation is complete, I open the Out folder to check its contents. From observing the folder, I can see the new PDF file created and the PostScript file were moved from the In folder to the Out folder. In addition, there is a file named <*name*>.log (where *name* is the name of the PostScript file distilled) that Distiller created as a log file as it progressed through the Job Options (see Figure 5-32).

Figure 5-32: The original PostScript file, the new PDF file, and a log file created by Distiller is visiblewithin the Out folder.

If you elect to delete the PostScript file in the Watched Folder settings dialog box, Distiller will delete the PostScript file after the PDF is created. Also, the new PDF file will be moved to the Out folder according to the time interval you established in the Watched Folder settings dialog box.

Multiple files can also be placed in the In folder and distiller creates PDFs in the order in which they are displayed as a list in the In folder. If an application is running in the foreground, Distiller will continue to convert PostScript files to PDF in the background.

Security

Security can be applied either at the time of distillation or later from within Acrobat after the PDF has been created. In as much as this feature appears under the Settings menu in Distiller, all the features discussed here are the same as those you may use when saving files from within Acrobat. Either way you secure documents, one of the great enhancements new to Acrobat 5.0 includes more improved methods of security.

When using security, I would pass on to you a few words of caution. Many years ago I created a HyperCard stack and secured it. Shortly thereafter I tried to open it knowing I had used a password similar to my father's birth date. To this day I can't open that stack. Security has been downright frustrating to me. The moral of this story: If you use security, make a note of all your passwords and store them safely. And, I'd like to caution you on one more thing. I have about 20 different notes with passwords around somewhere. Where, I don't know. I always figured passwords need to be somewhat secret, so I tried to think of hiding places where they would not easily be found. Well, they're secure all right — even I can't find them. Therefore, if you record your passwords, keep them in a logical place you frequent.

Enough about the pitfalls of losing security passwords — check out how Distiller handles security. To access the Security settings, choose Settings ⇨ Security in Acrobat Distiller. After you select the Security item from the pull-down menu, a window appears where your security options are established. If you have Acrobat 3.0 or 4.0 compatibility selected in the General Job Options dialog box, then the Acrobat Distiller – Security dialog box, as shown in Figure 5-33 is displayed. If

or 4.0 compatibility selected in the General Job Options dialog box, then the Acrobat Distiller – Security dialog box, as shown in Figure 5-33 is displayed. If Acrobat 5.0 compatibility is selected, the dialog box for 128-bit encryption offers different options, as shown in Figure 5-34.

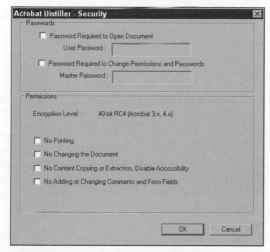

Figure 5-33: With Acrobat 3.0 and 4.0 compatibility, the document security provides 40-bit encryption.

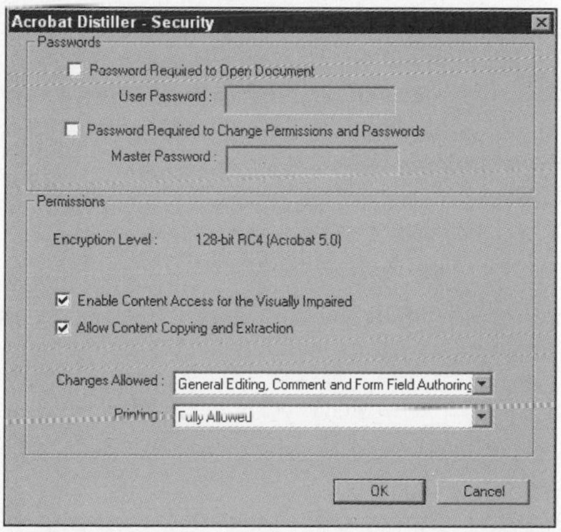

Figure 5-34: With Acrobat 5.0 compatibility, the document security provides 128-bit encryption.

When using either encryption level, two categories appear in the dialog box. Passwords are identical when using either level. Permissions change according to the level selected when making choices in the pull-down menu for Encryption Level. First, look at 40-bit encryption and then later move to understanding the Permissions options for 128-bit encryption.

Passwords

With either or both encryption levels, you have two password options:

✦ **Password Required to Open Document:** This option is a field box where you can add a security password that controls viewing PDF documents. If a password is supplied, anyone with an Acrobat viewer will need the password in order to open the document.

✦ **Password Required to Change Permissions and Passwords:** Acrobat makes a distinction between viewing PDF files and editing them with regards to password protection. Whereas the first item deals with viewing, this field box is used to prevent users from changing the original file or using commands as listed in the Permissions section with either encryption level. You can supply two different passwords in the two field boxes. If you want to have all users allowed to open a PDF file without entering a password but do not want anyone to change your document; you can eliminate a password from the first field box and only provide a password to prevent changes.

Permissions for 40-bit encryption

When 40-bit encryption is selected for Encryption Level, as shown in Figure 5-33, you can choose from four items to prevent access for users without passwords. These include:

✦ **No Printing:** If the Password Required to Change Permissions and Passwords field box contains a password, and you enable the checkbox for printing, the user will need to open the PDF file with the password required to change permissions. If not, no printing is allowed.

✦ **No Changing the Document:** When enabled, this checkbox prevents any changes in document editing and saving updates to the file.

✦ **No Content Copying or Extraction, Disable Accessibility:** This item is used to prevent any copying of data and pasting into other applications. When enabled, the TouchUp tool, Text Select tool, Column Select tool, and Graphics Select tool are all disabled in Acrobat viewers. Any Accessibility contained in the document for access to the PDF structure is disabled when the checkbox is selected.

✦ **No Adding or Changing Comments and Form Fields:** The behavior of Comments (formerly called Annotations) is different than text selections, thus this item is separate from the option for Changing the Document. When enabled, no note changing or form field editing can occur.

Permissions for 128-bit encryption

Keep in mind, you must change the compatibility to Acrobat 5 when using 128-bit encryption. If 128-bit encryption is selected for Encryption Level, as shown in Figure 5-34, choices for Permissions include:

✦ **Enable Content Access for the Visually Impaired:** When enabled, Accessibility is provided in the Acrobat viewer. The document structure can be copied, which is required to provide access with readers.

✦ **Allow Content Copying and Extraction:** This item is separate from the item listed previously where the content access is need for Accessibility, but the file can still be protected from access to the content with the Acrobat tools. If using Acrobat Catalog, you'll want this feature deselected. Catalog needs access to the content to create the search index. After it's created however, the security can be changed in Acrobat after distillation and cataloging.

Changes allowed

Several choices appear in a pull-down menu for the type of permissions to be allowed for changing a PDF document in Acrobat. These choices include:

✦ **None:** When enabled, no editing or saving of the PDF file can be made with Acrobat. No forms filling or digital signatures can be used.

✦ **Only Document Assembly:** Document assembly involves features, such as adding, replacing, deleting or rotating pages. When enabled, these editing tasks can be performed. Comments, links, articles and other similar editing features cannot be used.

✦ **Only Form Field Fill-in or Signing:** No changing of the document is permitted. Users without password access for changing the PDF is limited to filling in form data and digitally signing the document.

✦ **Comment Authoring, Form Field Fill-in or Signing:** This option prevents users from changing a document, but permits comments to be created, edited, and deleted as well as form fills and digital signatures.

✦ **General Editing, Comment and Form Field Authoring:** All editing features but document assembly is enabled.

Printing allowed

With 128-bit encryption, Acrobat has offered a new alternative for people involved with prepress and printing. You can allow the end user alternatives for proofing low resolution print files or allow access to printing at high resolution. The choices from this pull-down menu include:

✦ **None:** No printing is permitted.

✦ **Low Resolution (150dpi):** PostScript printing is not permitted. The PDF prints as an image in which case all fonts print as raster data and loose their PostScript attributes. The ultimate resolution of the image is undesirable for high-end output.

✦ **Fully Allowed:** High resolution and PostScript printing is permitted. Graphic artists who want to have clients print a low-resolution file for proofing and a high resolution file to be printed by an imaging center can offer the same PDF to both sources. For clients, a User password can be provided that prevents the end user from access to the security options. Clients would be restricted to the low resolution printing if so enabled in the security options. The service center can be provided the master password that allows them access to changing the security, thus enabling technicians an opportunity to change printing permissions.

After entering the password(s) and selecting the various options, click the OK button. When you return to the Distiller window, all files are distilled with the security settings enabled for both encryption levels.

Caution   When using security with Acrobat Distiller, be certain to always recheck your Distiller Security settings and/or your watched folders. If you begin distilling files with security, Acrobat offers no warning. You can often inadvertently add security to files where you do not want it. If you need to change secure PDF files to nonsecure PDF files, you'll need to open the files in Acrobat and save them without security. The process is easy to perform with the new batch processing commands in Acrobat 5.0, however, you may forget passwords if you don't revisit the security options often.

Working with Non-Roman Text

Acrobat provides great support for text created from character sets foreign to U.S. English and other Roman text alphabets. Eastern languages, such as Russian, Ukrainian, and similar languages based on forms of Cyrillic characters require proper configuration for font access and keyboard layouts. When configurations are made and the fonts accessed in the document layout application, be certain to embed the fonts in the PostScript file or have Distiller monitor the font's folder of the character set used. As is the case with any font embedded in the PDF, the document will be displayed without font substitution. In Figure 5-35, I used a Cyrillic font in Microsoft Word. The file was printed PostScript to disk and font embedding was used in Distiller's Job Options.

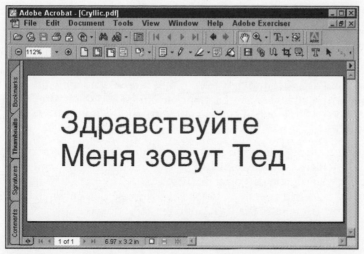

Figure 5-35: When fonts are properly configured from character sets foreign to Roman characters, the fonts can be embedded and viewed without font substitution.

Eastern language support is provided by Acrobat but requires much more in regard to configuration and proper installation of the Asian Language Support option (Windows) or the Asian Language Kit (Macintosh). As long as the language support respective to your platform is installed with the Acrobat installer, files can be printed as PostScript and embedded in the PDFs. Viewing PDFs with embedded Asian languages, such as Chinese, Simplified Chinese, Japanese, and Korean (CJK) are displayed without font substitution.

When installing Acrobat for use with these languages, you need to use the custom installation and include the language support with the other Acrobat components. After the support has been installed, font problems need to be resolved when printing to PostScript occurs. For PostScript fonts, fewer problems are experienced. TrueType fonts require special handling depending on the platform and type of fonts used. Special documentation for managing PostScript and TrueType fonts is included in the Acrobat documentation. For specific handling of Eastern Language support and TrueType fonts, review the documentation thoroughly before attempting to convert PostScript files to PDF.

Accessing Acrobat Distiller

After all the controls have been established in the Job Options dialog boxes, you're ready to use the Distiller application. Files that can be distilled need to be PostScript files printed to disk or EPS files. You can access the Distiller several ways after the files have been created. These methods include:

✦ **Open from Distiller.** Find the application on your hard drive and double-click the application icon to launch Distiller. When the Distiller application window opens, choose File ➪ Open. Navigate to the file you want to convert to PDF and select it in the Acrobat Distiller – Open PostScript File dialog box. Only a single file can be opened at one time. If the Preferences have been set up to ask for a filename or ask to replace a PDF (on Windows), a navigation dialog box will open where filename and destination can be supplied. After a file has been converted to PDF, you can choose File ➪ Open and open another PostScript or EPS file.

✦ **Drag and Drop to the application icon.** Either the application icon or a shortcut (alias on Macintosh) of the application can be used for drag and drop distillation. In this regard, you can drag multiple PostScript files, EPS files or a combination of both to either icon. Release the mouse button when the files are placed over the icon and Distiller launches and subsequently converts the file(s) to PDF.

✦ **Drag to the application Window.** A single file or multiple files can be dragged and dropped on the application window. Launch Distiller to open the application window. Select a single file or multiple files and release the mouse button after the files have been dragged to the window. All files will be converted as individual PDFs.

✦ **Launch Distiller from within Acrobat.** Distiller can be opened from within Acrobat by choosing Tools ➪ Distiller. When the menu command is selected, the Distiller application launches. From the file menu, PostScript and EPS files can be opened or files can be dragged to the Distiller window.

✦ **Print to Acrobat Distiller (Windows).** As described in Chapter 4, Distiller will be used when a print command is selected from an authoring application. When the Acrobat Distiller printer driver is used, Distiller automatically launches and converts the open document to PDF.

✦ **Use the Run command (Windows).** PDFs can be created with Distiller by accessing the Run command from the Windows status bar. Select Run and supply the directory path first for Distiller, and then the path for the files to be converted. Syntax must be exact. Pathnames need to be contained within quotation marks and a space needs to separate the pathname for Distiller and the pathname for the file(s) to be converted. Filenames with spaces need to be contained within quotation marks. Entering the pathname, filename, and having each file separated by commas can distill multiple files. In as much as Acrobat offers you this capability, you'll often find drag and drop methods much easier.

✦ **Create Adobe PDF (Macintosh).** When selecting Create Adobe PDF from a print dialog box on the Macintosh, Distiller launches and converts the open document to PDF.

✦ **Exporting to PDF.** From many application programs, such as Microsoft Office, illustration, and layout programs as discussed in Chapter 6, Distiller will be launched and produce a PDF. When distillation is complete, the user will be returned to the application document window. Some programs bypass Distiller when saving directly to PDF as is also discussed in Chapter 6.

✦ **Watched folders.** As described earlier in this chapter, copying a PostScript or EPS file to the In folder of a watched folder creates distillation at the interval specified in the Acrobat Distiller - Watched Folders dialog box. Distiller must be launched before distillation of files from watched folders occurs.

When Distiller is used in all of the above circumstances other than the use of watched folders, the current Job Options set as the default will be used to produce the PDF. That is to say, if Distiller is launched and the eBook settings appear in the pull-down menu, the Job Options associated with eBook will be used to create the PDF. When using watched folders, the Job Options associated with the watched folder will be used to produce the PDF. If no Job Options are assigned to the watched folder, the current default settings will be used.

Concatenating PostScript Files

Suppose you have several documents that you want to convert to a single PDF file. All these documents can be of a single application type (for example, a bunch of Microsoft Excel spreadsheets). Or the documents may come from many different applications (for example, PageMaker, Microsoft Word, Microsoft Excel, QuarkXPress, and Photoshop). In either case, if we want to create a single PDF document from all those separate files, the task of combining them in Acrobat could take a little time. Admittedly, a batch command would not take much time, but the advantage of creating a single PDF from multiple PostScript files is having only one font subset included in the document. With separate files, there is the presence of a different subset for each page. By creating a multiple page PDF at the time of distillation, your resultant PDF will be smaller in size.

Acrobat Distiller reads PostScript code and as such, you can have Distiller begin its job by looking at a PostScript file that includes instructions to concatenate, or join together, all PostScript files in a given directory. If you attempt to write this code from scratch, you'll need to be fluent in PostScript. For those of us with much more limited skills, Adobe has made it easier to perform the task.

When Acrobat is installed, a folder entitled Xtras include two files with PostScript code that are used for concatenating distilled files into a single PDF file. The PostScript code is generic and needs to be edited in a text editor. Edits to define the directory path for your files and the specific filenames of the PostScript files to be distilled need to be identified.

The `RunFilEx.ps` and `RunDirEx.ps` files installed in the Xtras folder inside your Distiller folder concatenates PostScript files — the former concatenates files that you specify and the latter includes all the files in a specified directory whose names include a common extension. These two files need to be edited individually, so you can examine both.

Combining files by name

The Fil in `RunFilEx.ps` is your first clue that this file is used for concatenating PostScript files by filename, each of which you specify. When using this file, you must tell Distiller specifically which files (by exact name) will be distilled. To edit the file for entering user-supplied filenames, open the `RunFilEx.ps` document in a text editor, as shown in Figure 5-36. If using the Macintosh, you can edit this file in Simple Text. In Windows, use Windows Notepad or WordPad.

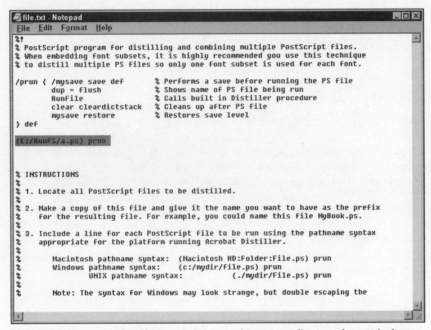

```
% !
% PostScript program for distilling and combining multiple PostScript files.
% When embedding font subsets, it is highly recommended you use this technique
% to distill multiple PS files so only one font subset is used for each font.

/prun { /mysave save def        % Performs a save before running the PS file
        dup = flush             % Shows name of PS file being run
        RunFile                 % Calls built in Distiller procedure
        clear cleardictstack     % Cleans up after PS file
        mysave restore          % Restores save level
} def

(E:/RunPS/a.ps) prun



% INSTRUCTIONS
%
% 1. Locate all PostScript files to be distilled.
%
% 2. Make a copy of this file and give it the name you want to have as the prefix
%    for the resulting file. For example, you could name this file MyBook.ps.
%
% 3. Include a line for each PostScript file to be run using the pathname syntax
%    appropriate for the platform running Acrobat Distiller.
%
%       Macintosh pathname syntax:  (Macintosh HD:Folder:File.ps) prun
%       Windows pathname syntax:    (c:/mydir/file.ps) prun
%            UNIX pathname syntax:          (./mydir/File.ps) prun
%
%       Note: The syntax for Windows may look strange, but double escaping the
```

Figure 5-36: Open the file `RunFilEx.ps` in a text editor, such as Windows NotePad or WordPad (SimpleText on the Macintosh) to supply filenames for distilling in Acrobat Distiller.

After `RunFilEx.ps` is opened, the PostScript code for instructions on procedures in concatenating files from user-supplied names is displayed. All lines of code beginning with a % symbol are comment lines that do not supply instructions to Distiller. These comments are provided to explain the procedures.

RunFilEx.ps in Windows

The syntax for directory paths in the PostScript code is different between Windows and the Macintosh, and on Windows varies somewhat from standard DOS syntax. When you open the `RunFilEx.ps` file in Windows WordPad or a text editor, the sample lines of code demonstrate directory paths and filenames for Macintosh users. The comments below the code provide a guideline for proper syntax when using Windows. In Figure 5-36, notice the comment line for Windows pathname syntax located toward the bottom of the figure. In Windows, identify your drive as a standard drive letter (for example, C:). After the drive letter, use a forward slash instead of a backslash to separate the drive name from the directory name. Nesting occurs in Windows the way it does below in the Macintosh example, but be certain to use forward slashes to separate the folder names. The filename should include the name and extension as it was written.

When describing drive, directory, and filenames, case sensitivity is not an issue. Any of these identifiers can be either upper or lowercase. In Figure 5-36, I used my E: drive and a directory labeled RunPS. Only the file a.ps will be distilled, as it is the only file identified in the code. Notice the filename was changed from RunFilEx.ps to File.txt, as can be seen in the top-left corner of Figure 5-36. The filename was changed when the file was saved to disk and I provided a new name.

RunFilEx.ps on the Macintosh

The same file and location is used on the Macintosh as observed in the previous section with Windows. When the RunFilEx.ps is opened in a text editor, the complete directory path, as described above with Windows, needs to be supplied. In Figure 5-37, a description of a Macintosh directory path and filenames are shown.

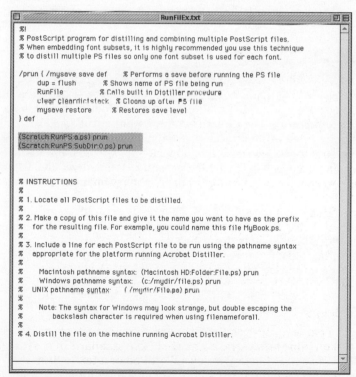

```
%!
% PostScript program for distilling and combining multiple PostScript files.
% When embedding font subsets, it is highly recommended you use this technique
% to distill multiple PS files so only one font subset is used for each font.

/prun { /mysave save def      % Performs a save before running the PS file
        dup = flush           % Shows name of PS file being run
        RunFile               % Calls built in Distiller procedure
        clear cleardictstack   % Cleans up after PS file
        mysave restore        % Restores save level
} def

(Scratch:RunPS:a.ps) prun
(Scratch:RunPS:SubDir:0.ps) prun




% INSTRUCTIONS
%
% 1. Locate all PostScript files to be distilled.
%
% 2. Make a copy of this file and give it the name you want to have as the prefix
%    for the resulting file. For example, you could name this file MyBook.ps.
%
% 3. Include a line for each PostScript file to be run using the pathname syntax
%    appropriate for the platform running Acrobat Distiller.
%
%    Macintosh pathname syntax:  (Macintosh HD:Folder:File.ps) prun
%    Windows pathname syntax:    (c:/mydir/file.ps) prun
% UNIX pathname syntax:    ( /mydir/File.ps) prun
%
%    Note: The syntax for Windows may look strange, but double escaping the
%        backslash character is required when using filenameforall.
%
% 4. Distill the file on the machine running Acrobat Distiller.
```

Figure 5-37: The highlighted lines of code indicate the hard drive name (Scratch) and directory path followed by the filenames to be distilled.

It is critical to precisely code the directory path and filename(s) for Distiller to recognize the location and files to be distilled. The name of your volume (that is Macintosh HD, Hard Drive, and so on) would be the name you have provided for your hard disk. By default, many Macintosh hard drives are labeled Macintosh HD. If you have named your hard drive another name, enter it exactly as found on your Desktop. In Figure 5-37, you can see I have a secondary hard drive I named Scratch, which appears as the first item in the highlighted code following the open parentheses. After the hard drive name, enter a colon (:) followed by a folder name. Folders are not necessary, but it is recommended you save the files to a folder inside your hard drive. Folders can be nested as long as you follow the proper syntax (in other words, Hard Drive:FolderA:FolderB:FolderC, and so on). The last entry for each line of code will be the filename. In Figure 5-37, I named two files a.ps and 0.ps.

From Simple Text or any other text editor, save your file as text-only. Save the file with a descriptive name — you needn't use the RunFilEx.ps name of the original file. Be certain the file is a copy of the original, so that you can return to the Xtras folder and find this file again when needed.

To convert the named files in the RunFilEx.ps file, you need to open the newly edited file in Acrobat Distiller. You can drag the file on top of the Distiller window on either platform, or launch Distiller and choose File ⇨ Open. The instructions in the PostScript code will direct Distiller to the files you listed for conversion to PDF.

Combining files in folders

The second file in the Xtras folder used for concatenating PostScript files is RunDirEx.ps. Whereas RunFilEx.ps requires you to name all the PostScript files to be distilled, this file uses a wildcard character to distill all files with a common extension in a specified directory. The directory path for either the Mac or Windows uses the same syntax as illustrated previously; however, instead of filename(s), a wildcard character followed by the extension for the filenames is used. The wildcard is the standard asterisk (*), which is used to indicate all files with the same extension that you specify in the line of code for the pathname.

In Figure 5-38, I specified my D: hard drive on my Windows computer and the ClientFolder directory. Acrobat Distiller distills all the files with a .ps extension. On either platform, follow the same syntax described earlier. In this example for Windows, I used: /PathName (D:/ClientFolder/*.ps). I then saved the file as MyFile.txt to the same directory.

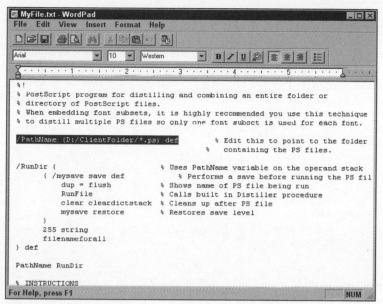

Figure 5-38: Following `/PathName` in the `RunDirEx.ps` file, enter the path and *.extension for all the files to be included in the distillation.

Distillation and page order

After the `RunFilEx.ps` or `RunDirEx.ps` file has been edited, it becomes the file that will be opened in Acrobat Distiller. This file tells Distiller where to go and which files to convert to PDF. The file can be located in any directory on your hard drive, because it instructs Distiller where to go to find the files for distillation. If the file is saved in the same folder where the files to be distilled are stored, it is important to provide a different extension for this filename from the extension of the files to be distilled when using `RunDirEx.ps`. If you name the file `MyFile.ps` and include it in a directory with a number of files also having a .ps extension, the PostScript code file for combining the other files will be included in the final PDF file. The default filenames you find in the Xtras folder have .ps extensions, and changing them to a .txt extension to avoid confusion is a good idea.

When `MyFile.txt` (or whatever name you have supplied for the file) is run, the page order occurs in the same order as an alphameric character set. To help simplify understanding how the page order is applied, view your files in a folder as a list. Be certain the order is not date, type, or anything other than an alphabetical order. The order you view will display the same page order as the resulting PDF.

In Figure 5-39, the top of the list begins the page order. In my example, the 0.ps file is the first page in the PDF file, followed by 2.ps, and so on. All eight pages will be distilled if the RunDirEx.ps file is used and will include all files ending in .ps in the ClientFolder directory.

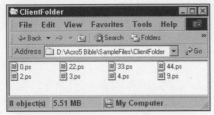

Figure 5-39: PostScript files in a Windows directory are viewed as a list with the files arranged by name.

Note   As you examine the list in Figure 5-39, notice that 49.ps is followed by 9.ps. If you want these files to be consecutively ordered, the file naming has to follow some different rules. Both Distiller and your operating system arrange the files according to the characters in left-to-right (dictionary) order. If two files have the same first character, the second character is examined and the file placed in the list accordingly. In this example, Windows doesn't care about 49 being larger than 9. It looks at the 4 in 49 and sees it as a lower order than 9.

To rearrange your files in the order you want to have them appear in an Acrobat viewer, rename them before distillation, taking into consideration the first character will be the highest order of priority. For this example, I renamed my files, as illustrated in Figure 5-40. After the PDF file is produced, the page order matches my new order as viewed in the folder.

Figure 5-40: I renamed the files in the ClientFolder directory by including a zero (0) in front of the single digit filenames so that the two digit filenames follow in numerical order.

Tip

Because Distiller and your operating system order alphameric characters the same, view your folder contents as a list before distilling the files. The list order you see will be the same order of the page numbers in the final PDF document.

Combining PostScript files on networks

If you want to develop a PDF workflow and use a server to collect all your PDF files on a local area network, some simple guidelines need to be followed to produce PDF documents. Whereas files can be printed to disk on remote systems and drives that are cross-platform, Distiller can't follow cross-platform directory paths. Therefore, if you use RunDirEx.ps and want to distill files in C:\MyFolder*.ps, Distiller running on a Macintosh won't be able to execute instructions for following cross-platform directory paths. This also applies to Windows users who may want to use a file describing directory paths on a Macintosh. Distiller can be used cross-platform to distill files on remote drives, and the RunDirEx.ps file will work between two computers running the same operating system. Using Distiller and RunDirEx.ps on networks have the following capabilities and limitations:

✦ **Running Distiller across platforms:** Distiller can open PostScript files on local hard drives and across platforms. PDF files from distillation can be saved to local hard drives and across platforms. For example, by using Distiller on a Macintosh, you can open a PostScript file on a PC and save it to either computer's hard drive.

✦ **RunDirEx.ps across platforms:** RunDirEx.ps cannot be run across platforms where directory paths are specified for one platform while distilling on a different platform. For example, you can't open from a Macintosh the RunDirEx.ps file that resides on a PC with directory paths specified for the PC. The alternative solution would be to run Distiller on the platform consistent with the path identity or set up watched folders where the RunDirEx.ps file is introduced into a watched folder.

✦ **RunDirEx.ps in a common platform:** Distiller can open the RunDirEx.ps file that resides on one computer where the directory path includes files on another computer of the same platform. The RunDirEx.ps file can be located on either computer, the destination of the PDF can be saved to either computer, and the path to find the .ps files can be on either computer.

To understand how files can be concatenated across two computers on the same platform, here are some steps I used to produce a single PDF document from files located on another computer running the same operating system on my network.

STEPS: RunDirEx.ps **and Networked Computers**

1. **Create the PostScript files.** I created PostScript files from several application document windows and stored them on my G4 computer.

2. **Edit the** `RunDirEx.ps` **file.** I opened the `RunDirEx.ps` file from my Xtras folder inside the Acrobat folder (in Windows, the path is Acrobat5\Distillr\Xtras). The path directory on my G4 computer is G4 System:Documents:RunPS:*.ps. The hard drive name is G4 System, and I want to distill all files in the RunPS folder (see Figure 5-41).

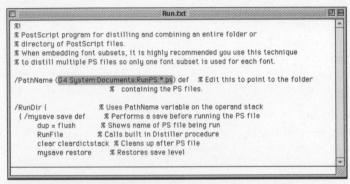

Figure 5-41: I edit the `RunDirEx.ps` file in Simple Text and save it to a Macintosh G3 Desktop as `Run.txt`.

3. **Open the** `RunDirEx.ps` **file in Acrobat Distiller.** The file is saved on a Mac G3 computer on my network and I also run Acrobat Distiller from the G3. In Distiller, I choose File ➪ Open and navigate to the Desktop level to find the file I saved as `Run.txt`.

4. **Name and identify the file destination.** I rename the file `Run.txt` to `Run.pdf` and identify the RunPS folder on the G3 System computer as the destination, as shown in Figure 5-42.

5. **Distill the** `Run.txt` **file.** After you click the Save button, Distiller's progress is displayed in the Distiller window, shown in Figure 5-43. The directory path is displayed for each file distilled. My `Run.txt` file was opened in Distiller on my Mac G4. The file asked Distiller to find the .ps files in the RunPS folder on the G3 computer and saved the concatenated PostScript files in a single PDF document on the G3.

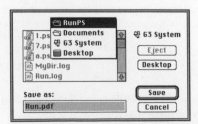

Figure 5-42: The second dialog box appearing in Distiller is used to identify the filename and destination.

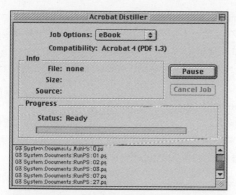

Figure 5-43: Distiller's window displays
the job progress and includes the directory
path for all files opened and distilled.

6. **Examine the destination folder.** After I open the RunPS folder on the G3 computer, the Run.pdf is found along with the log file.

Most often it won't be necessary to run Distiller on your local computer to distill
files on another computer. The option exists if you need it, but in many cases, you'll
find a better solution to be setting up watched folders and having Distiller run on
the computer where the files are located. If you give a little thought to setting up
the network for creating PDF files, the workflow can be seamless.

The introduction of using Acrobat Distiller can be handled in many different ways
as discussed in all the previous pages in this chapter. Additional access to Distiller
can also be found when exporting to PDF from many application programs. These
features as well as adding more opportunity with pdfmark operators are discussed
in Chapter 6.

Summary

✦ At times, Acrobat Distiller can be the preferred method of converting documents to PDF. As an alternative to other PDF creation methods, the Distiller
application offers many ways to set attributes in the resultant PDF file.

✦ PostScript is a streamed language that can contain many different dialects and
is often redundant in describing page elements for imaging. PDF is a much
more efficient file format, as it is structured like a database that offers logical
order and eliminates redundancy.

✦ When creating PostScript files, the preferred PPD to use the Acrobat Distiller
PPDs, unless specific output needs require use of a device PPD.

✦ Printing Web pages to PostScript can often be a faster solution for producing PDFs from different URLs than using the Acrobat Open Web Page command.

✦ Distiller Preferences enable you to establish settings for file naming and over-writing (Windows) and rebooting Distiller after a fatal crash (Macintosh).

✦ Acrobat Distiller has many Job Options that behave like preferences enabling you to control font compression, image compression, color, and high-end digital prepress output.

✦ Additional font monitoring can be established in the Distiller Settings menu for identifying different font locations on your computer.

✦ Watched folders enable you to establish PDF workflows that automate the PDF creation process. Watched folders can be contained on local or remote storage systems in network environments. Use of network watched folders with multiple user access requires strict compliance with the Adobe licensing agreements.

✦ Acrobat enables you to supply security passwords at the time of distillation. New features in Acrobat 5.0 expand security to 128-bit encryption levels.

✦ Eastern language character sets and Asian text are supported font embedding features as long as font formats and font management are properly configured.

✦ Access to Acrobat Distiller is supported from within Acrobat 5.0, by using shortcuts or aliases, printer drivers and through a variety of drag and drop procedures.

✦ PostScript files can be joined in a single PDF document by using either the RunFilEx.ps or RunDirEx.ps PostScript file supplied on the Adobe Acrobat Installer CD-ROM. RunFilEx.ps is used to concatenate files by filename, and RunDirEx.ps is used to concatenate all files within a folder that have the same extension.

✦　　✦　　✦

PDF Exports and Imports

Application Programs Exporting to PDF

The last two chapters discussed PDF file creation using Adobe Acrobat and Acrobat Distiller. If you've read those chapters, you've learned when to use Distiller over other methods. Yet another means of creating PDF files is with direct exports from application software programs. Adobe Systems has been implementing PDF support for some time in many of its design applications and other vendors are continually providing support. Early methods for creating these exports were fairly simple in that they were similar to the way PDFWriter generated PDF files. Current methods rely on more sophisticated approaches that offer control over font embedding, compression, and advanced Job Options.

It stands to reason that the software manufacturer that has implemented the best PDF integration with other programs is Adobe Systems. The new PDF support for Illustrator 9.0, InDesign 1.5, and Photoshop 6.0 are applications all developed around core PDF architecture. The integration of PDF between these programs is now seamless and offers opportunity to create, edit, and import PDFs with consistent reliability.

Other software manufacturers are also adding more support with every program upgrade. Manufacturers, such as Corel Corporation, Macromedia, and Quark, Inc., also implement PDF support in their recent program releases. At times, there may be a need to create PostScript files and use Distiller with one program or another. Most often though, you'll find the advanced, professional application software well suited and often preferred in producing PDF files.

With all of the different ways of creating PDFs, it may become somewhat overwhelming to decide which method you should choose when working in programs. The decision becomes more difficult if you work in some programs that support PDF exports and other programs that don't. Add to this the occasional need for legitimate conversion to PDF from within Acrobat, and the other times that you definitely need to use Distiller. What you require is a formula and maybe an understanding of the PDF "food chain" to come up with an ordered approach to PDF development. Among the considerations you should make in setting up your PDF workflows are the following:

✦ **Consistency:** Regardless of which method you use, try to be consistent when creating PDF documents from a given application. If you use a program, such as Adobe Illustrator to generate PDFs, and sometimes print files to Acrobat Distiller, other times distill EPS files, and occasionally use the PDF export feature of Illustrator, eventually you'll wind up with some unexpected results. Try to assess your output needs and the reliability of the producer application. Be consistent and use the same method when creating PDFs from the same program.

✦ **Export and Save to PDF:** If PDF exports and saves always satisfy your needs from a given application, always use the Export to PDF command from within the software in question — especially those programs that have been developed with core PDF architecture. When you know the reliability of a program's export to PDF to satisfy file integrity, use the export method. This is particularly important from those more recent Adobe programs supporting PDF Version 1.4.

✦ **Use Acrobat Distiller:** For programs that don't effectively satisfy PDF file creation for all output needs always use Acrobat Distiller. If you have some documents that require distilling and others that don't, try not to go back and forth between two or more methods of creating PDF files. Make an effort to always use Distiller for everything with these programs. You'll become more fluent in printing PostScript as well as more experienced in predicting output results.

✦ **Open as PDF:** Last on the PDF "food chain" is Open as PDF from within Acrobat for those file formats that are supported. Use this command when converting files for office use but not high-end imaging. If you never go to prepress and high end printing, then be consistent with an easy method that supports your PDF needs.

In some instances PDF support is not limited to exports. Some applications can also import PDF files. Because Acrobat is not a full-featured editor, importing PDF files into some other applications can be useful for page editing and alterations. Ideally, you would return to the application that produced the PDF file for major editing changes, but at times you may find it helpful to import PDF files into another program where minor editing can be accomplished. This is particularly true in a situation where you are the recipient of a PDF file created by another person and you do not have the producer application or the original document. In such cases, you could open the PDF file in a program, such as Adobe Illustrator, make your edits, and create another PDF file.

Acrobat and Adobe Photoshop

Adobe Photoshop Version 4.0 introduced support for exports and imports of PDF documents. You could save a Photoshop image directly in PDF format and open the file in an Acrobat viewer. Importing PDF files, however, was only limited to those files that were originally saved from Photoshop. If a PDF was created from another application through PDFWriter, Acrobat Distiller, or an export to PDF, Photoshop couldn't open it. Version 5.5 of Adobe Photoshop included much better support for PDF and permitted opening multiple page PDFs as well as files from any PDF producer. The newest iteration of Photoshop (Version 6.0) now demands that you use PDF as a file format when preserving vector art and type in a format other than Photoshop's native .psd format. It's the only game in town if you don't want vector objects and type to be rasterized (converted from objects to pixels) by Photoshop.

Exporting to PDF from Photoshop

Creating a PDF file from Photoshop is nothing more than choosing the format from the Save dialog box. Photoshop supports many different file formats in opening and saving documents. In earlier versions prior to Photoshop 6.0, all layers had to be flattened before saving as a PDF file. In Version 6.0, you can preserve layers and vector art. When you save a layered file from Photoshop 6.0 as a PDF and open it again in Photoshop, all layers will be retained. Type and vector art work the same way. You can create type without rasterizing it and save the file as a PDF. Later, if you want to edit the file, you can reopen it and edit the type.

With either a multi-layered Photoshop image, a Photoshop document, or a flattened image, access to the PDF format is handled with the Save As command. In Photoshop 6.0 choose File ⇨ Save As. The Save As dialog box, shown in Figure 6-1, provides many options for preserving the Photoshop file integrity while saving in PDF format.

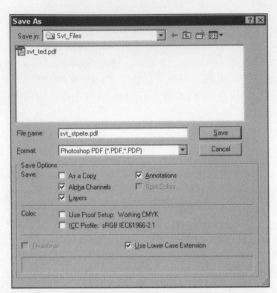

Figure 6-1: Exporting directly to PDF is handled in the Save or Save As dialog box in Photoshop. In Photoshop 6.0, multi-layered files can be saved as PDF.

The options available in the Save As dialog box include:

✦ **File name:** As with any Save dialog box the filename and destination are supplied in the Save (or Save As) dialog box. Note Save In at the top of the dialog box and the File name field in Figure 6-1.

✦ **Format:** From the pull-down menu, you can choose many formats for layered documents and documents containing vector art. However preserving both can only be achieved with either the native format of Photoshop or the Photoshop PDF format.

✦ **As a Copy:** If using the Save As command, the file you use will be a copy of the original document presuming that you use a different filename than the original. If you open a PDF file and select Save As, you can click the As a Copy checkbox to duplicate the file. The filename is automatically extended to include the word copy after the filename and before the extension.

✦ **Alpha Channels:** The PDF format also retains all Alpha Channel data. Use of Alpha Channels is restricted to Photoshop when you reopen the file in Photoshop. In Acrobat, the use of Alpha Channel data won't be useful.

✦ **Layers:** Saving as a Photoshop PDF also preserves all layers. When the file is reopened in Photoshop, access to all layer data is available.

✦ **Annotations:** Text notes can be created in Photoshop 6.0 much like the Comment in Acrobat. When a Note Comment is created, it is preserved in the PDF file. If you open the PDF in Acrobat, the Comment Note can be edited or deleted. Audio annotations can also be created in Photoshop and exported to PDF. The audio comments can be played in Acrobat.

✦ **Spot Colors:** If a Spot Color is included in the Photoshop file, the Spot Color can be preserved when saved as a PDF.

✦ **Use Proof Setup:** Proof viewing can accommodate different monitor viewing options according to profiles selected in the Save As dialog box. If a profile is saved with the Photoshop PDF and later viewed in Acrobat, the color will be displayed according to the profile selected.

✦ **ICC Profile:** The current profile used for the respective color mode can be embedded in the PDF file.

✦ **Thumbnail:** Thumbnails are created for Photoshop format images. No Thumbnail preview can be obtained with the PDF format.

✦ **Use Lower Case Extension:** Filenames default with an extension. PDF files automatically have a .pdf extension added to the filename. When the checkbox is enabled, the extension appears in lower case.

After enabling all checkboxes for the file attributes and then clicking Save, Photoshop opens a second dialog box where the compression to be used with the PDF file is determined. Figure 6-2 shows the PDF Options dialog box.

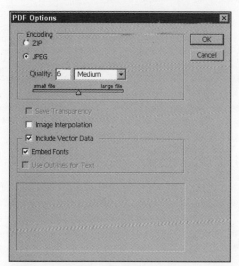

Figure 6-2: After clicking the Save button in the Save As dialog box, the PDF Options dialog box appears.

The first of two choices available to you in the PDF Options dialog box is the encoding method:

✦ **Zip:** Zip compression is lossless. Files are not compressed as much as you have available from JPEG, but the data integrity will be optimal. Zip compression is usually preferred for images with large amounts of a single color.

Acrobat 5.0 has eliminated use of LZW compression in favor of the more efficient Zip compression. No access to LZW compression exists in either Photoshop 6.0 or Acrobat 5.0.

✦ **JPEG:** JPEG (Joint Photographic Expert Group) compression in this dialog box corresponds to the compression amounts we observed in Chapter 5. Depending on your output, the compression amount corresponds to the examples discussed in Chapter 5.

✦ **Save Transparency:** A single layer image may have transparency on the layer. If you select Save Transparency, the PDF viewed in Acrobat will appear with the transparent area white — regardless of the background color that you used in Photoshop. Whether Save Transparency is enabled or not; when the PDF is opened in Photoshop, the transparency will be preserved. If the PDF is opened in another program, such as Adobe Illustrator, the transparency is preserved when the checkbox is enabled. If the checkbox is disabled, then Illustrator will not honor the transparent area.

✦ **Image Interpolation:** Anti-aliasing is created for lower resolution images. If you use higher compression on files, you can somewhat improve appearances by using interpolation.

✦ **Include Vector Data:** Vector data may be in the form of vector objects or type. When either is used, the data is not rasterized. Vector data and type are preserved in the PDF and recognized by Acrobat and Photoshop. Figure 6-3 shows a PDF with vector data saved from Photoshop.

✦ **Embed Fonts:** Font embedding occurs much like it does with Distiller. If you create a Photoshop file and preserve the type layer, embedding the font eliminates another user from needing the font if the file is opened in Acrobat.

✦ **Use Outlines for Text:** Text is converted to outlines (or paths) when exported to PDF.

Many designers have resolved themselves to always convert type to outlines regardless of the program or fonts used. This habit has been developed due to many continuing font problems found when using service centers. Converting type to outlines is not a panacea for resolving all the problems. Fonts converted to outlines puts undo burden on raster image processors (RIPs) and imaging equipment, not to mention desktop printers. You should avoid converting to outlines whenever possible and reserve the procedure for only those fonts where a known problem exists. In addition to experiencing some printing problems, type will not be anti-aliased when converted to outlines, thereby degrading type appearances when viewed on-screen in an Acrobat viewer.

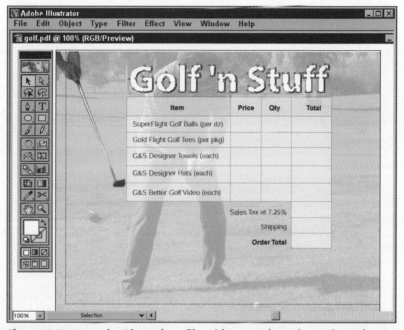

Figure 6-3: I saved a Photoshop file with a type layer from Photoshop as a PDF. The PDF was opened in Illustrator where the type was converted to outlines. Although not preserving all type attributes, the text was not rasterized.

PDF and color modes

Photoshop provides a number of choices for the color mode used to express your image. You can open files from different color modes, convert color modes in Photoshop, and save among different formats available for a given color mode. File formats are dependent on color modes, and some format options are not available if the image data is defined in a mode not acceptable to the format. (See Table 6-1 for Photoshop PDF exports supported by the Photoshop color modes and relative uses for each mode.) Color mode choices in Photoshop include the following:

✦ **Bitmap:** The image is defined in two colors: black and white. In Photoshop terms, images in the bitmap mode are referred to as line art. In Acrobat terms, this color mode is called monochrome bitmap. Bitmap images are usually about ⅛ the size of a grayscale file. The bitmap format can be used with Acrobat Capture for scanning text and recognizing the text in a scan.

✦ **Grayscale:** This option is your anchor mode in Photoshop. Grayscale is like a black-and white-photo, a halftone, or a Charlie Chaplin movie. You see grayscale images everywhere, including the pages in this book. I refer to this as an anchor mode because you can convert to any of the other modes from grayscale. RGB files cannot be converted directly to either bitmaps or duo-tones. You first need to convert to grayscale and then to either of the other two modes. From grayscale, although the color will not be regained, you can also convert back to any of the other color modes. Grayscale images significantly reduce file sizes — they're approximately ⅓ the size of an RGB file, but larger than the bitmaps discussed previously.

✦ **RGB:** For screen views, multimedia, and Web graphics, RGB (red, green, blue) is the most commonly used mode. This mode has a color gamut much larger than CMYK and is best suited for display on computer monitors. A few printing devices take advantage of RGB — for example, film recorders, large inkjet printers, and many desktop color printers. In most cases, however, this mode is not used when printing files to high-end output devices, especially when color separating and using high-end digital prepress.

✦ **CMYK:** The process colors of Cyan, Magenta, Yellow, and blacK are used in offset printing and most commercial output devices. The color gamut is much narrower than RGB; and when you convert an image from RGB to CMYK using mode conversion command of Photoshop, you usually see some noticeable dilution of color appearing on your monitor. When exporting files to PDF directly from Photoshop or when opening files in other applications and then distilling them, you should always make your color conversions first in Photoshop.

✦ **Lab:** Lab color in theory encompasses all the color from both the RGB and CMYK color spaces. This color mode is based on a mathematical model to describe all perceptible color within the human universe. In practicality, its color space is limited to approximately 6 million colors, about 10+ million less than RGB color. Lab color is device-independent color, which theoretically means the color will be true regardless of the device on which your image is edited and printed. Lab mode is commonly preferred by high-end color editing professionals and will color-separate on PostScript Level 2 devices. With PDF however, you don't want to use the Lab color mode. Photoshop can export to PDF from Lab, and you can place Lab EPS files in other applications. However, after you convert the final document to PDF, the lab images won't separate properly whether you export the document from Acrobat as EPS or use some commercial third party print plug-ins.

✦ **Multichannel:** If you convert any of the other color modes to Multichannel mode, all the individual channels used to define the image color will be converted to grayscale. The resultant document will be a grayscale image with multiple channels. With regard to exporting to PDF, you will likely never use this mode.

✦ **Duotone:** The Duotone mode can actually support one of four individual color modes. Monotone is selectable from the Duotone mode, which holds a single color value in the image, such as a tint. Duotone defines the image in two color values, Tritone in three, and Quadtone in four. When you export to PDF from Photoshop, all of these modes are supported.

✦ **Indexed Color:** Whereas the other color modes, such as RGB, Lab, and CMYK define an image with large color gamuts up to millions of colors, the Indexed Color mode limits the total colors to a maximum of 256. Color reduction in images is ideal for Web graphics where the fewer colors significantly reduce the file sizes. You can export indexed color images directly to PDF format from Photoshop.

Table 6-1
Photoshop Color Modes

Color Mode Separations	Export to PDF	Screen View	Print Composite	Print
Bitmap	Yes	Yes	Yes	No
Grayscale	Yes	Yes	Yes	No
RGB	Yes	Yes	Yes*	No
CMYK	Yes	No	Yes	Yes
Lab	Yes	Yes	Yes	No**
Multichannel	Yes	No	No	No
Duotone	Yes	Yes	No	Yes
Indexed	Yes	Yes	No	No
Spot Color (DCS 2.0)	No	No	No	No
16-bit	No	No	No	No

* In most cases, CMYK is preferred.

** Not from PDF files (but Lab can be separated from other applications).

Compression and color modes

When you choose File ⇨ Save or File ⇨ Save As and choose PDF as the format, the PDF Options dialog box appears after you make your choices in the Save (or Save As) dialog box. As I mentioned earlier, compression was discussed in Chapter 5. Because Photoshop does not have an automatic choice for compression types, you should know that there are different compression choices depending on the color mode of the Photoshop image. Table 6-2 includes the compression types available according to the color mode of the image to be exported.

Table 6-2
Compression Methods According to Color Mode

Color Mode	Export to PDF	Compression Type
Bitmap	Yes	No compression option
Grayscale	Yes	JPEG/ZIP
RGB	Yes	JPEG/ZIP
CMYK	Yes	JPEG/ZIP
Lab	Yes	JPEG/ZIP
Duotone	Yes	JPEG/ZIP
Indexed	Yes	ZIP only
Multichannel	No	N/A

Acquiring PDF files in Photoshop

PDF documents may be composed of many different elements depending on the design of the original file. If you design a page in a layout program for which you create text, import Photoshop images, and also import EPS illustrations, the different elements retain their characteristics when converted to PDF. Text, for example, remains as text, raster images, such as Photoshop files remain as raster images, and EPS illustrations remain as EPS vector objects. Although the images, text, and line art may be compressed when distilled in Acrobat Distiller, all the text and line art remain as vector elements. In Photoshop, if you open an illustration or text created in any program other than Photoshop, the document contents will be rasterized and lose their vector-based attributes. Photoshop rasterizes PDF documents much as it does with any EPS file.

In Photoshop 6.0, you have several methods of handling PDF imports. PDF documents to be opened in Photoshop are handled with the File ⇨ Open command, File ⇨ Place command, File ⇨ Import command, and through a File ⇨ Automate command. Each of the methods offers different options, so take them one at a time.

Opening PDF files in Photoshop

When you choose File ⇨ Open, the Open dialog box permits you to choose from among formats in a pull-down menu for Files of type. Three file formats listed reference PDF documents, as shown in Figure 6-4.

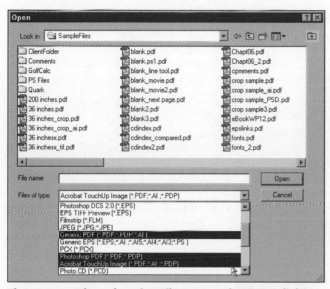

Figure 6-4: When choosing File ⇨ Open the Open dialog box offers three PDF file formats.

✦ **Generic PDF:** Any PDF file from any producer application can be opened in Photoshop. Files other than those saved from Photoshop are rasterized by the Photoshop Generic Rasterizer.

✦ **Photoshop PDF:** PDFs originating from Photoshop and those containing layers where vector art and/or type will be preserved and appear on different layers when opened. If the PDF was not produced from Photoshop and this file type is selected, Photoshop will automatically switch to the Generic PDF and prompt you for rasterizing attributes.

✦ **Acrobat TouchUp Image:** When working on a PDF in Acrobat, you have an opportunity to edit a raster or vector based object in Photoshop or an illustration program. (See Chapter 8 for more about updating with the TouchUp Object tool). Using the TouchUp Object tool, hold the Control key down (Option Key on a Mac) and double-click the object. The respective image is opened in one of the supporting applications. The object you open is saved as a TouchUp Image. If you save the file and reopen it in Photoshop, this format will recognize the fact that the image was exported from a PDF file.

Placing PDF files in Photoshop

Instead of opening a PDF file through the File ➪ Open command, you can use File ➪ Place to add a PDF within an open Photoshop document. Placing PDFs also requires rasterization. The advantage of using Place instead of Open is the placed PDF won't fully rasterize until you finish scaling it. You can place the file and size it up or down in the Photoshop document window. When finished scaling, press the Enter (Windows) or Return (Macintosh) key. Pressing the key lets Photoshop know you have accepted the size. At that point the image is rasterized. The disadvantage of using Place over the Open command is that you have no control over resolution and color mode. The PDF is rasterized at the same resolution and mode for where the document is placed.

Importing PDF files in Photoshop

When you choose the File ➪ Import command, a submenu appears. The first option is PDF Image. When PDF Image is selected from this submenu, navigation is similar to using the Place command. The file you import however won't be a PDF document. Photoshop searches for images contained in the PDF file and permits you to selectively import a single image or all images found in the document. You can navigate thumbnail views before electing to import an image and see a thumbnail in the PDF Image Import dialog box by clicking the forward and back arrows. Navigation can also occur by selecting the Go to image button in the PDF Image Import dialog box, as shown in Figure 6-5.

Figure 6-5: The PDF Image Import dialog box displays thumbnails of each image contained in a PDF file. Clicking the arrows or the Go to image button handles navigation.

When you select the Import all images button, another dialog box appears enabling you to enter a number. Unfortunately, you need to know the order of the images to choose the right number. The last button in the PDF Image Import dialog box enables importing all images. As each image is imported, they appear in separate document windows in Photoshop.

The size and resolution of the images imported into Photoshop hold their original values. Because these images are already raster objects, the Photoshop rasterizer won't be used. Photoshop does not determine the color mode, resolution, and physical size. They are imported with the same attributes as they were distilled.

Working with multi-page PDF imports

File ➪ Automate ➪ Multi-page PSD to PDF is a command similar to a Photoshop Action in that it automatically opens PDF files, rasterizes them in Photoshop, and saves the file to a destination directory specified by the user. When you select this command in Photoshop, a dialog box opens that enables you to determine the same rasterizing characteristics as used with the Open command. When you select this menu command, the Convert Multi-page PDF to PSD dialog box shown in Figure 6-6 appears.

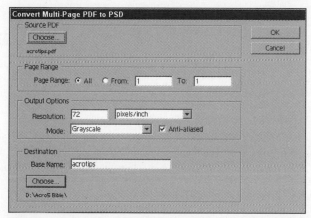

Figure 6-6: The Convert Multi-page PDF to PSD command enables conversion of several pages within a PDF file to be acquired in Photoshop.

The dialog box offers several choices for automating the sequence that include:

✦ **Choose:** Clicking the Choose button at the top left of the dialog box selects the source PDF file, as shown in Figure 6-6. Photoshop can't use multiple PDF files as a source. You are limited to opening a single PDF document. The document, of course, can have multiple pages.

✦ **Page Range:** You can select all pages in the PDF or a range of pages. The page range choices require you to know ahead of time the number of pages in the PDF file to be converted. If you select pages by clicking the From radio button and choosing a range outside the PDF page range, a warning dialog box will appear indicating the problem. For example, if you attempt to select pages 21 to 22 in a 20-page PDF file, pages 21 and 22 will be out of range. Photoshop opens a warning dialog box to inform you the first page it attempts to convert is out of range. If you attempt to convert pages 18 to 22 in the same example, Photoshop will convert pages 18 through 20 and then open another dialog box informing you that not all pages within the specified range exist in the PDF document.

✦ **Output Options:** These options are the same as the ones for single-page conversions. You can choose the resolution, color mode, and whether anti-aliasing will be used. One option you do not have available in the dialog box is the capability to choose size and proportions. If you want to size the PSD files, you can set up a Photoshop Action to open the saved files and resize them with values used in creating the Action.

✦ **Base Name:** The base name that you specify appears in the filename for the saved PSD files. If you use a name, such as MyFile, Photoshop will save the PSD files as `MyFile0001.psd`, `MyFile0002.psd`, `MyFile0003.psd`, and so on. Photoshop adds the 000n and .psd extension to the filename that you supply as the base name.

✦ **Destination:** The destination typically is a folder or directory selected by clicking the Choose button below the item denoted as Destination. You can highlight a directory name in the hierarchy list and click the Select button, or you can open a directory in the hierarchy list and click the Select button.

Rasterizing PDF files

For those conversion methods that require rasterization, such as the Open command discussed earlier, Photoshop opens a dialog box where user defined rasterization attributes will be supplied. If you have a multi-page document and you use the Open command, the first dialog box to appear is the Generic PDF Parser dialog box, as shown in Figure 6-7.

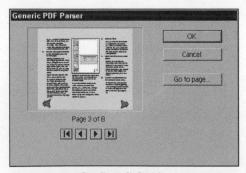

Figure 6-7: The first dialog box appearing when a multiple page PDF is opened in Photoshop is the Generic PDF Parser.

The Generic PDF Parser dialog box is the same as the PDF Image Import dialog box. The method of selecting a given page from within the multi-page document is exactly the same as discussed earlier when we looked at importing PDFs with the

File ➪ Import ➪ PDF Image command. After navigating to the desired page, click OK and another dialog box appears, as shown in Figure 6-8.

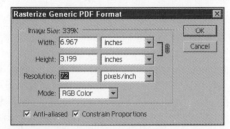

Figure 6-8: After selecting a page in a multi-page PDF file, the Rasterize Generic PDF Format dialog box appears where the rasterization attributes are supplied.

If a single page PDF file is opened, the Generic PDF Parser dialog box will not appear. Regardless of whether you select a page within a range of pages or a document with only one page, Photoshop wants some information before it rasterizes the PDF page. The rasterization attributes to be determined include:

✦ **Width/Height:** The physical size of the final Photoshop image can be determined by changing the width and/or height of the rasterized image. The default size of the original PDF document appears in this dialog box.

✦ **Resolution:** The default resolution regardless of the size is 72 ppi. You can choose to supply a user-defined resolution in this dialog box. If the original raster images were at a resolution different than the amount supplied in this dialog box, the images will be resampled. Text and line art are rasterized according to the amount that you define in the dialog box without interpolation.

✦ **Mode:** The color mode can be selected from the pull-down menu that includes choices for Grayscale, RGB, CMYK, and Lab color. The default is CMYK regardless of whether any color is in the original PDF file.

✦ **Anti-aliased:** This option is used to smooth edges of text, line art, and images that are interpolated through resampling. If you disable this option, text will appear with jagged edges. Text in PDF files rasterized in Photoshop looks best when anti-aliased, and the display is more consistent with the original font used when the PDF was created.

✦ **Constrain Proportions:** If you change a value in either the Width or the Height field and the Constrain Proportions option is enabled, the value in the other field (Height or Width) will automatically be supplied by Photoshop to preserve proportional sizing. When the checkbox is disabled, both the Width and Height are independent values — that is, they have no effect on each other. If you elect to not preserve proportions, the PDF page appearing in Photoshop after rasterizing will likely be distorted.

One problem you may encounter when rasterizing PDF documents in Photoshop is maintaining font integrity. Photoshop displays a warning dialog box when it encounters a font not installed on your system, which presents problems when you attempt to rasterize the font. If such a problem exists, the font may be easily eliminated from the document or changed after opening in Photoshop by addressing the type layer.

When files are password protected, users are prevented from opening a PDF file in Photoshop or any other application. If you attempt to open a secure document, a warning dialog box will appear. The warning dialog box indicates the PDF is password protected and needs to be unprotected before opening. If you encounter such a dialog box, open it in an Acrobat viewer and check the security settings, as discussed in Chapter 2.

If you want to convert catalogs and lengthy documents to HTML-supported files, the PDF to PSD conversion can be useful. You can set up Actions in Photoshop to downsample images, convert color modes, and save copies of the converted files in HTML-supported formats.

Using Comments with Photoshop

Photoshop 6.0 supports use of the annotations Notes tool — now referred to as Comments in Acrobat 5. You can create a note in Photoshop much like you do in Acrobat. The note is an object and won't be rasterized with any other Photoshop data. You can delete the annotation at any time by selecting the note icon and pressing the Backspace (Windows) or Delete (Macintosh) key.

Annotations from PDF files can also be imported into Photoshop. You must use the Comment Note tool as Photoshop does not support the other comment types available in Acrobat. If a Note is contained in a PDF document and you want to import the Note in Photoshop, choose File ⇨ Import ⇨ Annotations. Photoshop can import an annotation only from PDF formatted files.

In addition, Photoshop can also import Form Data Format files. Data exported from Acrobat in FDF format can be chosen as another import format from the File ⇨ Import ⇨ Annotations command. Data from FDF files are contained in an annotation text note.

Audio annotations enable you to add voice comments to a file. Using a recording application and microphone connected to your computer, you can create an audio comment. Select the Audio Annotation tool in Photoshop, click in the document window, and then click the Start button in the Audio Annotation dialog box. The recording is contained as an annotation and can be played in Acrobat when the file is saved with the Annotations checkbox enabled in the Save or Save As dialog box.

Acrobat and Microsoft Office Applications

Maybe working with images isn't your cup of java. Perhaps you look to the staples of computer software and confine your work to using Office applications, such as Microsoft Word, Excel, PowerPoint, and occasionally throw in a little Microsoft Publisher now and then when the artistic flare inspires you. Fortunately, Adobe and Microsoft have worked well together in helping us out when converting the Office applications documents to PDF. You can use all the methods described in Chapter 5, such as printing PostScript and Distilling files with Acrobat Distiller; but if you are searching for an easier method, Adobe offers a few gems on the Acrobat Installer CD-ROM to help you out.

Keep in mind that virtually any program that is capable of printing can have the document files converted to PDF via the Acrobat Distiller application. The references to Microsoft Office are not necessarily a bias. People may use many other applications for text entry, data handling, or presentations. However, Microsoft Office applications do have a distinct advantage as Adobe and Microsoft have corroborated heavily on PDF integration with the Office products. Given the fact that PDF file creation is seamless with these applications and they do command the largest market share in their respective markets, I stick to the Office applications for word processing, spreadsheets, and presentations.

On Windows, Microsoft Word, Excel, and PowerPoint accommodate a macro developed by Adobe Systems called PDFMaker. When the PDFMaker macro is installed in Office applications in Office 97 and higher, the PDFMaker macro appears in the toolbar for all three applications. When installing Acrobat and the Office products, be certain to first install all the Office applications. The Acrobat Installer automatically detects the Office applications and installs the PDFMaker macro.

On the Macintosh, working with Office applications requires you to use an alternative method for creating PDF files. The easiest method is to use the Create Adobe PDF printer driver, as I described in Chapter 4. After installing Acrobat, the Create Adobe PDF printer driver should be installed on your system. If you have any trouble with the driver, visit the Adobe Web site (www.adobe.com) and download the AdobePS printer driver.

Microsoft Word

Of all the Office applications, Microsoft Word gives you great support for PDF file creation. Microsoft Word is the only word processing application that provides access to the structural data of the document. The *Metadata* of the Word document, such as titles, heads, tables, paragraphs, figure captions, and so on, can be converted to tagged bookmarks. Tagged bookmarks, as I explain in greater detail in Chapter 11, give you much more control over the PDF content. You can navigate to the element structures, move, copy, extract, and delete pages through menu commands in the Navigation pane.

PDFMaker offers several tools to control PDF file creation from within Microsoft Word. After you install Acrobat and later open Word, two Acrobat icons appear on the far left side of the toolbar. The first of these two icons is the Convert to Adobe PDF macro. Clicking this icon opens a dialog box where the filename and destination will be supplied. Enter and name and then choose a destination. Then click the Save button and the PDF is created.

The second icon is Convert to Adobe PDF and Email. This tool performs the same function as the Convert to Adobe PDF tool and then adds the resultant PDF as an e-mail attachment. The user defined default e-mail application automatically launches and the PDF attached to the message you send. Figure 6-9 shows an e-mail attachment created from the Convert to Adobe PDF and Email tool.

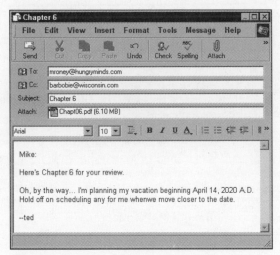

Figure 6-9: After clicking the Convert to Adobe PDF and Email tool in Microsoft Word, the PDF is created and automatically placed as an e-mail attachment in Microsoft Outlook Express.

The third item installed in Microsoft Word with the PDFMaker macro is a menu. At the far right side of the top menu bar, the Acrobat menu appears after installing Acrobat. The first two choices in the menu activate commands that execute the tools mentioned previously. The third menu item enables you to view the PDF after it has been created with PDFMaker. The last item appearing in the menu is the Change Conversion Settings command. When the command is selected, a dialog box appears where Job Options can be established and choices for how the structure in the Word document will be converted in the PDF file.

Changing Conversion settings

PDFMaker can print the Word document to disk and then convert it through Distiller's Job Options. Before the file is printed, various choices for Job Options can be determined without leaving Word. When you choose Acrobat ⇨ Change Conversion Settings, the Acrobat PDFMaker 5.0 for Microsoft Office dialog box appears. In the dialog box, five tabs offer attribute choices for how the PDF is to be created, which are described next.

Settings

The Settings options enable you to choose from Job Options appearing in a pull-down menu. In Figure 6-10, the Print Job Options from Distiller was selected from the pull-down menu. If none of the existing Job Options are suitable, clicking the Edit Conversion Settings opens the Distiller Job Options dialog box. All Job Options settings discussed in Chapter 5 are accessible. When finished editing the Job Options, a dialog box appears prompting you to save the new Job Options.

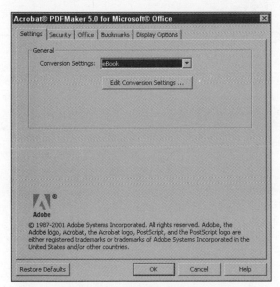

Figure 6-10: The first choices appearing in the Acrobat PDFMaker 5.0 for Microsoft Office dialog box enable you to select Job Options for creating the PDF file.

Security

After the Settings have been determined, click the Security tab. Security options are available for 40-bit encryption when the Job Options are set to Acrobat 3 and Acrobat 4 compatibility, as shown in Figure 6-11. If 128-bit encryption is needed, you must change the Acrobat compatibility to Acrobat 5.0 in the Job Options dialog box accessed through the Settings tab.

Job Options

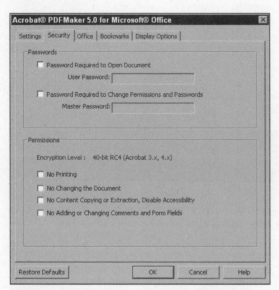

Figure 6-11: PDF files can be encrypted with 40-bit encryption when Acrobat 3 or Acrobat 4 compatibility is used. To access 128-bit compatibility, change the Job Options from the Settings tab to Acrobat 5 compatibility.

Office

What sets the Microsoft Office applications apart from other PDF creators is handled in the Office dialog box, shown in Figure 6-12. The Office dialog box is where you determine what structure is retained in the PDF file.

Figure 6-12: PDFMaker offers many features from Office applications not available from other PDF creators.

The features that can be preserved include the following:

✦ **Convert Document Info:** Many of the choices in the Office dialog box are intuitive and self-explanatory. Other settings require a little more explanation. The first setting is obvious. Document properties are preserved when the checkbox is enabled.

✦ **Convert Cross-Document Links:** If cross document links exist in the original file, they will be preserved and result in hyperlinks to other files also converted to PDF.

✦ **Convert Internet Links:** Any URL contained in the Word file are preserved as a URL link and accessible in Acrobat.

✦ **Link Destination Magnification:** When a link is selected, the link destination appears in the Acrobat Document pane. The view magnification can be determined from the pull-down menu. You can choose from five preset values. In Figure 6-12, the default is Fit visible.

✦ **Save File Automatically:** The document must be saved before the PDF can be created. If the checkbox is enabled, Word will save the document without warning. If disabled, a dialog box will appear to prompt the user to save the file.

✦ **Comments ⇨ Notes:** Notes can be converted to annotation Comments that appear in a text note in the PDF file.

✦ **Text Boxes ⇨ Article Threads:** Text body copy defined with a style can be converted to an article thread. When different styles are used, the article threads are unique to each style.

✦ **Page Labels (e.g., iii, A-1):** The labeling for page numbers is preserved from the numbering system used in the Word document.

✦ **Cross-References & TOC Links:** Any cross-references, such as Table of Contents and indexes, have links to their respective destinations. These links are preserved in the PDF file when enabled.

✦ **Footnote and Endnote Links:** Bookmark links are supplied for all footnotes and endnotes.

✦ **Embed Tags in PDF (Accessibility, Reflow):** Document structure tags are preserved. Accessibility meeting Microsoft accessibility standards for visually challenged and developmentally disabled that is contained in the Word document is preserved in the PDF. Reflowing text enables the Acrobat user to use the Reflow text tool. The PDF can have the text reflowed to fit copy wrapping lines and fitting margins.

Bookmarks

In the Bookmarks dialog box, shown in Figure 6-13, two items determine what bookmarks are created in the PDF file. These include:

✦ **Convert Word Headings to Bookmarks:** Word headings can be converted to bookmarks. In the box below the enablers, a list of all headings and styles contained in the Word document, appear. Click the box under the Bookmark column to determine what heads are to be converted to Bookmarks.

✦ **Convert Word Styles to Bookmarks:** Style sheets that are user defined can be selected for converting to bookmarks. Scroll the list of elements and place a checkmark for the styles you want to have converted.

In addition, as in the Office dialog box where link magnification was determined, all the bookmarks can also be tagged with a zoom magnification from the pull-down menu if the Bookmark Destination Magnification checkbox is selected.

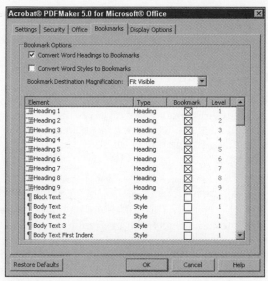

Figure 6-13: The Bookmarks dialog box offers two choices for determining what bookmarks are to be created in the PDF file.

Display Options

In the Display Options dialog box, shown in Figure 6-14, a number of choices are available to determine what attributes are to be assigned to the PDF display.

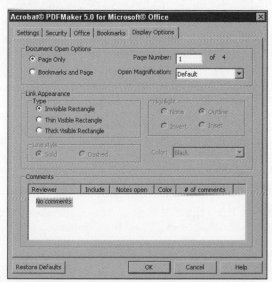

Figure 6-14: The Display Options include many features for the appearance of the PDF and the associated links and bookmarks.

Among the options in the Display Options dialog box are the following:

✦ **Page Only:** When the radio button is selected, the PDF file opens in Page Only mode.

✦ **Bookmarks and Page:** The PDF opens with the Navigation pane exposed and all the bookmarks visible.

✦ **Page Number:** The status bar in the Acrobat viewer displays the page numbers of the pages in view. The number supplied here can begin at a value determined by the user. If, for example, page one is identified as 10 in this dialog box, the readout in the status bar will appear as 10 (1 of n). Where n is equal to the total number of pages.

✦ **Open Magnification:** If you want the PDF to be opened in a Fit in Window view or perhaps 100% view, make the choice from the pull-down menu. In many cases, you find choices from the menu listings to be preferable over the Default view shown in Figure 6-14. When Default is used, the view opens based on the end user default view settings. In some cases, the PDF pages may be zoomed in or out depending on what a user has specified as his/her default view.

✦ **Type:** Under the Link Appearance features are three choices for the appearance of links. Invisible will display no rectangle around the link. The only indication that a link is present is when the user places the cursor over the link. Doing so changes the cursor to a hand with the forefinger pointing upward. The other two choices display a rectangle around the link with either a thin or thick keyline.

✦ **Highlight:** When a link is selected, a highlight is visible when selecting three of the four choices. None produces no highlight.

✦ **Line Style:** A Line displayed over a link can appear as solid or dashed from the two choices available. If no line is specified from the Type choices, then neither line style can be selected.

✦ **Color:** Lines can be assigned a color from the pull-down menu choices. If no line is specified among the Type choices, the Color options will not be available.

✦ **Comments:** Various attributes can be assigned to the notes appearing in the PDF file. Choices exist for the reviewer name, whether to include the comment, whether it appears open or closed, a choice for color in the note title bar, and the number of comments contained in the file for the note in question.

After all the options have been chosen from the dialog boxes for PDFMaker, click the OK button appearing in any of the dialog boxes. When the Convert to Adobe PDF tool or menu option is selected, the file begins its conversion. Depending on the length of the document and the structure contained in it, the conversion may take a little time. A progress bar appears while PDFMaker works away. In the progress dialog box, a button appears where the details of the conversion progress can be observed. Click the button and the display appears, as shown in Figure 6-15.

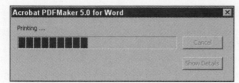

Figure 6-15: When you click the Show Details button in the Progress bar, the button description changes to Hide Details. A scrollable window displays the conversion progress as PDFMaker converts the Word document to a PDF.

Viewing the PDF

When Convert to Adobe PDF is accessed via the tool in the toolbar or the menu option in the Acrobat menu, a dialog box appears where the filename and destination can be determined. Supply a name and destination and the file is saved as a PDF. The PDF can be viewed immediately by choosing Acrobat ➪ View Results in Acrobat or by later opening it in an Acrobat viewer. When the PDF is open in Acrobat, click the Navigation pane tool to open the bookmarks. If the file has been successfully converted and the structure preserved, the display should appear, as shown in Figure 6-16.

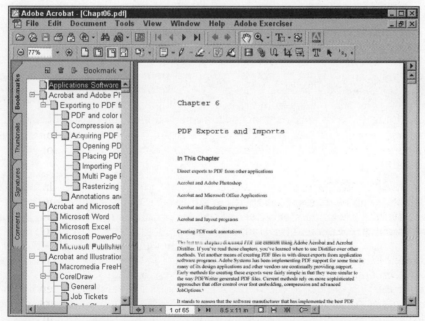

Figure 6-16: The final PDF document is opened in an Acrobat viewer. The bookmarks are all created with the structure defined when the Change Conversion Settings menu choice was selected in Word.

Printing Microsoft Word documents

Microsoft Word is a powerful application and is used by many different industries for creating documents for many different purposes. Because of Word's capability for page layout and integration of graphic elements, tables, and a variety of other means of expressing content, users often design documents on their computers with little regard to the output device where the file will be printed. If the task of printing a Word file is destined for a desktop printer, few problems are ever experienced. When the output goes to professional devices, problems most often will occur.

Book layout is a good example of where the designer may not need the tools available with high-end layout programs, such as Adobe InDesign, Adobe PageMaker, Adobe FrameMaker, or QuarkXPress. If hundreds of pages of text need to be printed, most often there's not a need to place all the Word text in a layout program. However, getting the Word file to a digital copy machine, imagesetter, or other similar device where controls for creating crop marks, halftone frequencies, or other settings are needed cannot be accomplished by Word's print features. In such cases, a work around is needed.

Fortunately, when a PDF is produced either through PDFMaker or printing a file to disk and distilling in Acrobat, all the controls needed to print to professional devices can be employed from within Acrobat and with the use of additional plug-ins. For exercising more control over printing PDFs with features, such as crop marks, you need additional resources. Plug-ins that work with Acrobat and Adobe's own plug-in Adobe InProduction can accommodate professional printing needs. (For more detail on using plug-ins for professional printing and Adobe InProduction, see Chapter 18.)

Caution   One limitation in regard to professional output from Office applications is when color separations are needed. Word and Excel should never be used to produce process color separations from artwork or photographic images. If spot color is used for text, you can use Acrobat and third-party tools to produce spot color separations.

Microsoft Excel

The PDFMaker can also be used with Microsoft Excel. Features described with Microsoft Word for Settings, Security, and Display are the same with Excel as you find with Word. Excel doesn't have a Bookmarks dialog box as does Word, and the Options dialog box offers different choices than the Options selected in Word (see Figure 6-17).

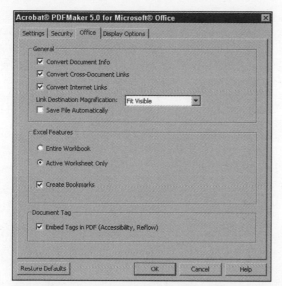

Figure 6-17: Microsoft Excel offers different Office features than Microsoft Word. Bookmarks for Excel are specified in the Office tab.

All the features in the Office tab are the same as those found in Word with the exception of the area noted as Excel Features. The choices for the first two items determine how many PDF pages will be created. If Active Worksheet is enabled, only the active Excel spreadsheet will be converted to PDF. The other option for Entire Workbook converts all pages in the Workbook.

If bookmarks are desired, the checkbox for Create Bookmarks needs to be enabled. All other features in the Office dialog box are the same as those discussed with Word Options earlier.

Microsoft PowerPoint

For presentations, no manufacturer can claim as much market share as Microsoft with its PowerPoint product. PowerPoint is so extensively used, people are creating everything from slides and presentations to large format inkjet prints with PowerPoint. If you're into presentations, then PowerPoint rules.

I have the good fortune to speak at the annual regional PDF conferences sponsored by DigiPub Corporation (www.digipubcorp.com). At the first conference in June 2000, PDF experts from around the world gave presentations to several hundred

PDF evangelists. What amazed me at the conference as I sat in some presentations orchestrated by my colleagues was that every presenter used a PowerPoint presentation to deliver his/her talks on Acrobat. Perhaps no greater accolade can be made of PowerPoint than having the world's top Acrobat experts all delivering PDF seminars with PowerPoint presentations.

Using PowerPoint to develop a presentation is understandably a wise choice for anyone authoring a visual aid to assist in the delivery of a lecture. With PowerPoint's outline and great text handling features, it is well suited for creating presentations quickly and painlessly. Yet PowerPoint can also be used as a foundation for creating an Acrobat presentation. All of the slides can be created in PowerPoint, converted to PDF, and then have other features specific to Acrobat added later. In my presentation at the PDF conference, I needed to open documents in other applications and then move forward to the next slide in Acrobat. With the Acrobat file attachment feature, I easily launched other applications, opened documents, and automatically had Acrobat move to the next slide. In addition to adding some Acrobat features, the slide presentations were delivered to the PDF conference organizers complete with font embedding and compression. All of the handouts were printed without problems, and the copy shop only needed Acrobat Reader to print the presentation.

If extending presentation opportunities from PowerPoint to Acrobat is your intent, then using PDFMaker, which also appears in the PowerPoint toolbar, can easily create a PDF. As the options are viewed in the dialog box appearing when you choose Acrobat ➪ Change Conversion Settings, choices appear similar to those available with Microsoft Excel. Converting to PDF can occur from PowerPoint by either using PDFMaker or printing the file to PostScript and distilling in Acrobat Distiller.

Not many people convert PowerPoint presentations to PDF, but printing PowerPoint slides to large format inkjets or large sized desktop color printers is becoming increasingly popular. With desktop printers you may have no problem printing directly from PowerPoint. If you have one of the consumer grade desktop printers that produce prints 22 inches or 44 inches long some problems with image clipping and producing the desired size may occur. If this is the case, you need to convert the PowerPoint slides to PDF for printing. The methods used to produce a PDF for desktop printing will be the same methods as those who may print to large format devices for 60-inch wide by 72 or more inches long.

Depending on the version of PowerPoint used, PDFMaker may not work. With more recent upgrades of Microsoft Office you may effectively create PDFs for printing oversized prints. In an effort to include all PowerPoint users, I describe the necessary steps needed to produce a PostScript file and then distill it in Acrobat Distiller.

Printing PowerPoint slides as PostScript files

In PowerPoint, choose File ➪ Print. The Print dialog box appears, as shown in Figure 6-18. The first choice to be made is the printer driver. Invariably if a device printer driver is selected, the PowerPoint slide(s) will be clipped if a preset page size is not selected from the Printer Properties dialog box. Most printers only have preset sizes without the ability to print a custom size. If you use an E size (large format) output there may be a waste of paper if the image size doesn't quite fit the E size measurement. The only driver that consistently produces custom pages without clipping the data is the Acrobat Distiller driver. Be certain to choose this driver for all large format output from PowerPoint.

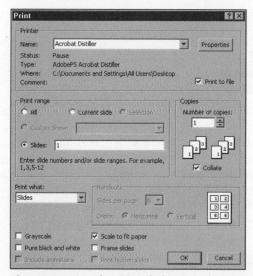

Figure 6-18: In the Print dialog box, be certain to select the Acrobat Distiller printer driver for all large format printing from PowerPoint.

Also in the Print dialog box, select Print to file and Scale to fit paper. If the final print from a 10-x-7.5-inch slide is to be produced on 40-x-30-inch media, the Scale to fit paper checkbox will take care of sizing the output to the desired page size. Just be certain to keep the Width and Height measurements proportional.

When the checkboxes are selected in the Print dialog box, click the Properties button. The Acrobat Distiller Document Properties dialog box appears, as shown in Figure 6-19.

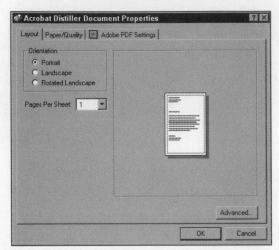

Figure 6-19: The document properties provide selections for orientation and media choices.

Users of earlier versions of Acrobat and PowerPoint need to set the paper orientation to Portrait. Even if the slide is landscape and the output measures 40 x 30 inches, Portrait needs to be selected. Failure to do so clips the image data. Users of Office 97 and above and Acrobat 5.0 want to set the orientation to match the layout.

For setting up custom page sizes, select the Advanced button. When the advanced options are displayed, a dialog box, as shown in Figure 6-20 appears.

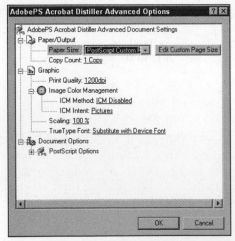

Figure 6-20: The Advanced options provide the feature to create a user defined page size.

Where Paper Size appears in the dialog box, select PostScript Custom Page Size from the pull-down menu. After the selection is made, a button to the right of the menu displays Edit Custom Page Size. Click this button and the Custom Page Size Dimensions can be provided, as shown in Figure 6-21. In my example, I use a size of 40 inches wide and 30 inches high. If using an earlier version of PowerPoint and Acrobat, be certain to supply the same values for width and height. Even though the dimensions will have a longer width than height and the orientation is Portrait, the file will be converted to PDF without clipping.

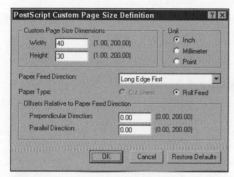

Figure 6-21: The Edit Custom Page Size button opens another dialog box where user defined dimensions for custom pages sizes can be supplied.

When finished with all the settings, click OK, and the PostScript file is produced. Distill the PostScript file in Acrobat Distiller to create the PDF. The only disadvantage with PowerPoint in producing large format prints is the inability to handle bleeds and crop marks. If the background appears on all edges of the slide, then the prints can easily be trimmed to the edges. If white is used for a background color, then you'll have to use a keyline on the slide or a plug-in that produces crop marks, which I explain in Chapter 18.

Microsoft Publisher

Microsoft Publisher began as a simple product designed to produce newsletters, fliers, brochures, and pamphlets on desktop printers. Some people in the user community began to take their Publisher files to service centers for output to film and commercial printing. Most service center technicians will tell you their greatest nightmares have often been from attempting to print Publisher files.

With the advent of Microsoft Publisher 2000, Microsoft has made several efforts to accommodate professional printing. The newest incarnation of Publisher supports all the controls needed to output to imagesetters and on-demand printing devices. Color separations, crop and registration marks, and halftone frequencies can all be established in Publisher's Print dialog box.

PDFMaker won't be available in the Publisher toolbar; therefore, the way to produce PDF files is to first print the file to disk as PostScript and then distill it in Acrobat Distiller. If all the print controls are correctly selected through Publisher's print dialog box, then you should have no problems producing files for high-end output. As many service centers are Macintosh based, the best way to get Publisher files to them is by delivering PDFs.

Acrobat and Illustration Programs

Illustration programs, at least the most popular ones, are vector-based applications. You can import raster data, such as Photoshop images, however, all you create in an illustration program is object-oriented art. Programs, such as Adobe Illustrator, Macromedia FreeHand, and CorelDraw are among the most popular, and they all have the capability to save files in EPS format as well as export (or Save) directly to PDF.

With programs such as Adobe Photoshop and Adobe Acrobat, little significant competition exists among manufacturers for market share. Photoshop clearly dominates the market in photo-imaging applications, and Acrobat has no worthy counterpart. Illustration programs, on the other hand, have some pretty fierce competition. CorelDraw has a tremendous share of the PC user market, and it clearly overshadows Illustrator and FreeHand. On the Mac side, most of the attempts of Corel have seen failure, which leaves the major market first to Adobe, then to Macromedia. Because these three companies are battling to keep current market share and gobble up more, the advances in feature-rich applications have been aggressive.

The competitive nature of the manufacturers of these products can present some problems for all end users. With each revision of illustration software, it appears as though the manufacturers are attempting to make the programs all things to all people. Each of these three illustration programs use a different dialect when exporting files in PostScript, which may impact your output for distillation in Acrobat Distiller. Add to this the difference in the way the PostScript coding is handled, and the addition of new whiz-bang features, and we wind up with some additional printing or distillation problems. Depending on which program that you use, you may want to reorganize the PDF creation "food chain" mentioned earlier in this chapter according to the strengths and weaknesses for each individual program.

Macromedia FreeHand

Whereas Adobe Illustrator has a weaker set of print controls, FreeHand has always excelled at printing files either as composites or color separations. FreeHand has great control over bleeds, too. Freehand documents can be printed to disk as PostScript files and distilled in Acrobat Distiller or exported directly from FreeHand to PDF. Obviously, with the Distiller application, you have much more control.

FreeHand permits user-defined compression control and font embedding, which makes it suitable for many PDF document purposes. To export a FreeHand document to PDF, choose File ⇨ Export ⇨ PDF. A dialog box appears where Options can be selected for the PDF conversion by selecting PDF from the Format pull-down menu and then click Options. All the PDF attributes are assigned in the Options dialog box (see Figure 6-22).

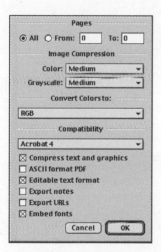

Figure 6-22: Macromedia FreeHand supports PDF exports and offers compression control and font embedding.

In the Image Compression settings, you have two pull-down menus from which color and grayscale image compression are determined. The amount of compression from the available choices is the same amount available with the Distiller Job Options. FreeHand supports color conversion as a choice from a pull-down menu below the compression settings. You have three choices that include RGB, CMYK, and RGB & CMYK. Depending on your output needs be certain to make the correct choice.

Tip   If you want screen images for CD-ROM replication, Web graphics, or file exchanges with other users, be certain to choose the Export command rather than Acrobat Distiller. Files printed to PostScript from FreeHand and later distilled from RGB colors don't retain the original color values as well as direct exports to PDF.

At the time of the release of Acrobat 5.0, FreeHand was only capable of exporting in PDF Version 1.3 format — that is, Acrobat 4.0 compatibility. By the time you get your version of Acrobat installed, it may support Acrobat 5.0 compatibility. If not, look for an upgrade soon. Macromedia has been on top of PDF support for their applications for some time, and I suspect they will continue to do so.

Below the compatibility choices are items easily understood from a quick glance at Figure 6-22. After all the choices have been made in the Options dialog box and the OK button is selected, you return to the Export Document dialog box, as shown in Figure 6-23. If you want to view your PDF file before you select the Export button, click the checkbox for Open in external application. When the checkbox is enabled, you decide what program displays the file by clicking the ellipsis (...). A dialog box appears, enabling you to navigate to your application choice for viewing the PDF. Immediately after selecting Export, the PDF is created and your viewer of choice displays it.

Figure 6-23: The Export Document dialog box offers an option to select a viewer for opening the exported PDF file.

CorelDraw

Whereas Adobe illustrator is the purest of the PostScript-compliant applications, CorelDraw has often been the most deviant. Some nuances with PostScript code have at times been a little problematic, but Corel has had a lot of experience in imaging and developing a strong contender in the Illustration application software market. Hence, it comes as no surprise that Corel 10 offers one of the most sophisticated PDF exports available from almost any application.

You won't find the Corel export buried among the Save formats or nested in a list of Export options; Corel has placed a separate menu item dedicated to PDF under the file menu. When you choose File ➪ Publish to PDF, the first of many dialog boxes opens (see Figure 6-24). The Publish to PDF dialog box contains several tabs, much like Distiller's Job Options, where file attributes are selected. The first of the tabs includes the General options.

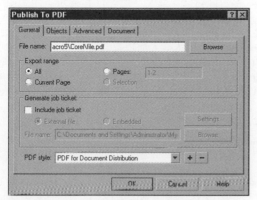

Figure 6-24: The Publish to PDF dialog box is the central navigation point from where all PDF file attributes are selected.

General settings

The PDF filename is supplied at the top of the dialog box in the General settings dialog box. Individual pages or a selection of the graphic elements can be exported as indicated in the Export range section of the dialog box. In addition to many Job Options discussed in Chapter 5 and earlier in this chapter, Corel offers yet another feature not provided by Distiller. Job ticket information can be included in the PDF either through an external file or from within CorelDraw. If you want to supply job ticket information, click the Include job ticket checkbox and select the Settings button.

Job Tickets

The first dialog box for Job Ticket Settings is used to supply all identifying client information. Use this dialog box for all your contact and billing data, as shown in Figure 6-25.

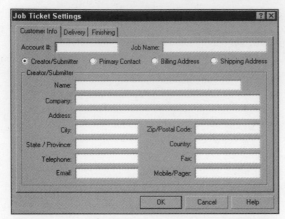

Figure 6-25: Identifying information is supplied in the Customer Info tab of the Job Ticket Settings dialog box.

Click the Delivery tab in the Job Ticket Settings dialog box and all information related to a job delivery method can be entered (see Figure 6-26).

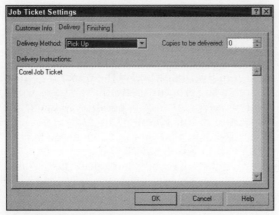

Figure 6-26: The Delivery tab contains fields where information related to delivery method is supplied.

The final tab is Finishing. For print shops needing information related to bindery and finishing, choices can be made in this dialog box. A special note area is available for custom finishing requests (see Figure 6-27).

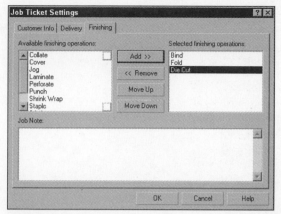

Figure 6-27: The Finishing tab includes all finishing
requests.

After you click OK, you are returned to the Publish to PDF general settings dialog
box. The last item in the General settings enables you to create a style for your Job
Ticket. Rather than toggle though all the dialog boxes every time you create a PDF,
you can capture settings. After the settings are captured, they appear in the PDF
style pull-down menu.

PDF Style

Because the PDF style option is included in the General settings, I mention it now.
However, when you create a style, you'll want to explore all settings among the
other tab choices before actually creating a style. Ultimately, when you return to
the General settings and are ready to create a style, click the + (plus) symbol. When
you select the + symbol, the Save PDF Style dialog box appears, as shown in
Figure 6-28.

Figure 6-28: PDF styles are added to
the Save PDF Style dialog box.

After a style as been added, it appears in the pull-down menu in the General settings
for PDF style. To delete a style, you must select it in the pull-down menu then click
the – (minus) button. A warning dialog box prompts you to confirm the deletion.

Objects settings

The next tab in the Publish to PDF dialog box includes control for image compression and font handling. Many of the same choices that you have with Acrobat Distiller Job Options appear the same in the Corel Objects settings, as can be viewed in Figure 6-29.

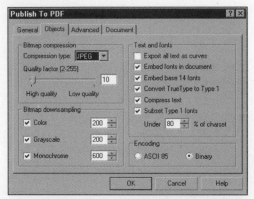

Figure 6-29: Corel offers similar control for image compression and font handling as found with Acrobat Distiller Job Options.

Advanced settings

The prepress control and color handling are made available in the Advanced settings, as illustrated in Figure 6-30. For color management, click the Set Profiles button. Most of what we find in Distiller for high end prepress is included in this dialog box except use of the `prologue.ps` and `epilogue.ps` files.

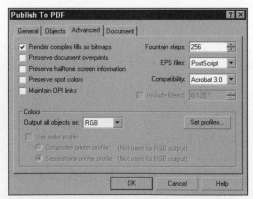

Figure 6-30: Advanced settings offer similar high-end prepress choices as found with Distiller's Job Options.

Document settings

The Document settings dialog box offers a little more than we find with Distiller Job Options, as shown in Figure 6-31. You can choose to add bookmarks and choose a display when the PDF is opened in an Acrobat viewer. When bookmarks and thumbnails are created, you can choose between opening in Page Only mode, with bookmarks or with thumbnails. In addition, you can choose to open in Full Screen mode.

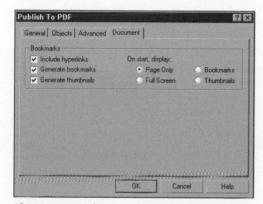

Figure 6-31: The Document settings provide control over viewing PDFs with bookmarks, thumbnails, and full screen views.

With all the features for PDF creation, CorelDraw direct exports can satisfy most of your PDF needs when using this program. If printing problems are experienced, you'll need to use the Print dialog box and print a PostScript file, and then distill it to create the PDF. This should be rare, as Corel has created a nice PDF export feature from their flagship program.

Adobe Illustrator

Now in Version 9.0 of the program, Adobe Illustrator — such as other Adobe programs — is built on core PDF technology. Illustrator has evolved to a sophisticated integration with PDF and supports through direct export, transparency, layers, blending modes, text, and filters. Further integration with the program in non-PDF workflows embraces exports for Web design where its current iteration now supports one-step optimization for formats, such as GIF, JPEG, PNG, SWF (Flash format), and SVG (Scalable Vector Graphics).

Illustrator's new, sophisticated illustration features include transparency. As the development of these new editing features became more sophisticated, there became a need for a more efficient file format to preserve file integrity. When files are saved directly in PDF format with Acrobat 5.0 compatibility, the native data is preserved. If you save an Illustrator 9.0 file as EPS, only a portion of the native data is preserved. EPS formatted files flatten artwork and convert transparent objects to opaque objects simulating transparency. Printing a file to PostScript and distilling in Acrobat Distiller yields the same results. Therefore, the best method of producing PDFs from Adobe Illustrator 9.0, especially when new editing features are used, is through direct saves to PDF.

Saving PDFs from Adobe Illustrator

Exporting PDF files from Adobe Illustrator is handled through the Save command. When you choose File ➪ Save, the format options available to you include the native Illustrator format, Illustrator EPS, and Adobe PDF. In Illustrator, choose File ➪ Save from a new document window. A dialog box appears that enables you to name the file, choose the destination, and select one of the formats just noted. When you select Acrobat PDF and click the Save button, the Adobe PDF Format Options dialog box opens where various PDF options appear, as shown in Figure 6-32.

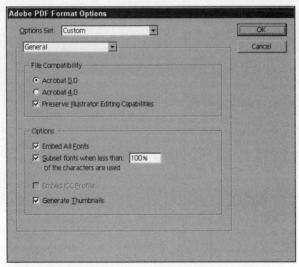

Figure 6-32: When you select the PDF format and click the Save button in the Save dialog box, the Adobe PDF Format Options dialog box opens enabling you to select PDF export options.

✦ **Options Set:** You have three choices available for PDF options from this pull-down menu. You can choose from Default, Screen Optimized, or Custom. Choices that you make here change the downsampling and compression options according to the output requirements.

- **Default:** When this option is selected, the Preserve Illustrator Editing Capabilities checkbox is enabled and compression settings are switched to Zip compression. Default also switches the format compatibility to Acrobat 4.0 and thereby flattens the image data.

- **Screen Optimized:** When Screen Optimized is selected, all compression is defaulted to screen resolutions and the compression method changes to JPEG compression. File sizes are larger when the Illustrator editing capabilities are preserved, so this checkbox is disabled for screen graphics. CMYK color in the Illustrator file is converted to RGB color.

- **Custom:** Custom doesn't necessarily hold a set of preset values. It is designed to accommodate custom options that you determine necessary for your output needs and it is used with Acrobat 5.0 compatibility. If you make any changes in either the options or the compression settings, Illustrator will automatically select the Custom options in the Options Set pull-down menu to inform you that a change from one of the presets has been made. For all formats, when files are saved with compatibility less than Acrobat 5.0, the artwork is flattened and the transparency is simulated. In the resultant PDFs, image elements are broken apart where simulated transparency is created. With Acrobat 5.0 compatibility, all vector objects retain their original attributes and appear as whole objects in the PDF file.

✦ **General:** The pull-down menu below the Options set offers two choices. By default, General is selected which is the display that you see in Figure 6-32. After making the choices in this dialog box, you advance to compression choices that are accessed by clicking the pull-down menu and selecting Compression.

✦ **File Compatibility:** Three choices are available in the File Compatibility section of the options dialog box. Here you can set the file compatibility and determine whether the PDF will retain the Illustrator editing capabilities.

  - **Acrobat 5.0:** Unless you have special needs for exchanging files with users of earlier versions of Acrobat, the Version 5.0 compatibility should be your default. Transparency created in Illustrator 9.0 is only preserved with the Acrobat 5.0 compatibility.

  - **Acrobat 4.0:** For the rare circumstances where Version 4.0 compatibility is needed, the choice can be made here. Be aware that any objects created with transparency flatten the artwork and convert all type to outlines when a transparent element has been created in the file.

  - **Preserve Illustrator Editing Capabilities:** This is a great new feature with Adobe Illustrator 9.0. For those who have attempted to edit PDF files in Illustrator, you know there have been many problems with nested grouped objects, masking, and handling text. With this new feature, PDF files can be preserved in terms of their editing capabilities after being saved as PDF and reopened in Illustrator. For all but screen and Web graphics, enabling this checkbox should be your default.

✦ **Options:** The Options section of the dialog box includes choices for font handling and color management.

- **Embed All Fonts:** Font Embedding is available with Illustrator's direct save to PDF. Some fonts, such as protected Japanese fonts, can't be embedded in the PDF.

- **Subset fonts when less than [   ]:** Font subsetting is handled the same as Acrobat Distiller. One feature you may notice with Illustrator is that the font subset defaults to 100 percent when selecting the Screen Optimized Option Set. This default is the same as Distiller, however, you may want to change the value when saving PDFs for the Web. Using lower values helps economize space especially when hosting long text documents, such as newsletters or product catalogs.

- **Embed ICC Profile:** For the checkbox to be active, you must have an ICC profile identified and available for embedding. If no color management is used in the Illustrator file, the checkbox will remain grayed out. To select color profiles, open the Edit ➪ Color Settings menu. After determining your color management policies, you can save the PDF with the selected profiles embedded. Color management must be controlled before you attempt to save the file. If you need to embed a profile and the option is grayed out, cancel out of the dialog box and choose your profile. Return to the Adobe PDF Format Options dialog box and then select the color management options.

- **Generate Thumbnails:** Because creating thumbnails increases file size, the Screen Optimized Options Set disables the checkbox. If using the Default Option Set, Generate Thumbnails is enabled. For most output needs, you'll want to create PDFs without thumbnails. If print is your intended output and you select the Default options, disable this checkbox.

✦ **Compression:** Compression settings for all image types are the same in Illustrator as found with Acrobat Distiller, as shown in Figure 6-33. Compression settings, such as font subsetting, can be changed from the defaults associated with the choices that you make in the PDF Options Set. If you want to use a different level of compression or manually set the compression type, you can make those changes here. Also, the downsampling amounts can be established in this dialog box. While the Compression options are in view, you can change the PDF Options Set and make your choices according to the attributes of the PDF file to be created.

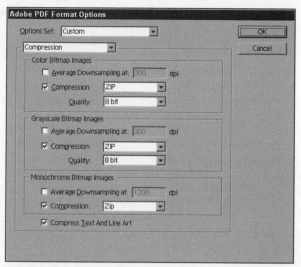

Figure 6-33: Selecting Compression from the pull-down menu where the default setting General appears brings up controls for compression.

After you click OK in the PDF Format Options dialog box from either the settings for General or Compression, the document is saved in PDF format. From Illustrator, the file is converted to PDF directly, and Distiller won't be introduced in the background.

Note

Notice that you have no options for viewing the PDF and no opportunity to supply document information in the PDF Format Options dialog box within Adobe Illustrator. In addition, you have no provisions for Job Ticketing, such as those features offered by CorelDraw.

Converting EPS files to PDF

Let me begin by saying that in many circumstances, saving a file as an Illustrator PDF is better suited to your workflow than distilling EPS files. However, some exceptions may require you to produce PDFs from EPS files. If you want to use some of Distiller's Advanced Job Options, convert legacy EPS files in a batch, concatenate legacy EPS files, create PDFs with a compatibility earlier than Acrobat 4.0, or add PDFMark annotations as explained at the end of the chapter, all these circumstances require distillation.

One of the easiest methods of producing PDF files with Acrobat Distiller is convert-ing EPS files. You don't need to worry about PPD selection, advanced print controls, page sizes and all the other toggles we explored when printing a file to PostScript. EPS files can be dragged and dropped onto the Distiller alias or application window. Distillation is performed with the last Job Options selected in Distiller.

Theoretically you can produce PDFs from any file saved in the EPS format. At times, however, you may experience some problems depending on what flavor of PostScript a given software manufacturer uses. Files exported from CorelDraw, FreeHand, QuarkXPress, and a host of other programs all handle their EPS exports a little differently. Sometimes an EPS file produced by one of these programs may not successfully distill. If an EPS export won't distill properly, you can import it into Illustrator and save as an Illustrator EPS. Many times the rewriting of the EPS for-mat from Illustrator overcomes problems when attempting to convert to PDF. Regardless of whether you import an EPS and resave it from Illustrator or create original artwork in the program, Adobe Illustrator EPS files consistently give you the fewest problems when using Acrobat Distiller.

In earlier versions of Acrobat and Illustrator, we had many problems with page sizes, bounding boxes, page clipping, and preserving crop marks. With Illustrator 9.0 and Acrobat 5.0, these problems have been eliminated. If you need bleeds and crop marks to appear in the final PDF, both programs successfully handle them. To examine a workflow where distillation of EPS files is needed, take a look at the steps to produce PDFs from an Illustrator EPS file containing bleeds and crop marks:

STEPS: Distilling EPS files with Bleeds and Crop Marks

1. **Create the Illustrator artwork.** I created a design in Adobe Illustrator. In the illustration, I use a layer for type, a layer for transparency, and a separate layer for the background. Figure 6-34 shows the image and the palettes used.

2. **Create crop marks.** The illustration has a bleed; therefore, I extend the art-work beyond the page boundaries to accommodate the bleed area. I then choose Object ➪ Crop Marks ➪ Make to create the crop marks.

3. **Create a bounding box.** One problem Adobe Illustrator has in getting files to display crop marks when exported to other programs is that the EPS format doesn't honor the crop marks created from the menu command. EPS files are distilled from Illustrator EPS files with bounding box information and not page size definitions. To include the crop marks in the resultant PDF file, drag open a rectangle outside the crop marks so that all image data including crop marks is contained inside the rectangle. Set the rectangle attributes to no stroke and no fill. After the file is distilled, the rectangle is the new bounding box.

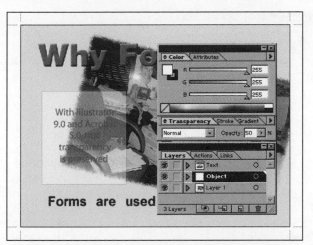

Figure 6-34: Acrobat 5.0 supports multiple layers and
transparency. I created the illustration with separate
layers for text, transparency, and the background image.

4. **Save the file in EPS format.** I wanted to use Distiller's Job Options so that the
   file is exported from Illustrator by choosing File ⇨ Save and choosing the
   Illustrator EPS format. After I save in EPS format, I lose some of the Illustrator
   file attributes, such as transparency. The EPS format flattens the data and creates an opaque image that simulated the transparent effect. All type is converted to outlines and lost the type attributes.

5. **Create Job Options suited for the output.** Launch Acrobat Distiller and
   choose the Print Job Options from the pull-down menu in the Distiller window.
   I change the compatibility to Acrobat 5.0. I open the Job Options dialog box,
   click the Advanced tab, and examine the Advanced Job Options. I verify the
   Resize Page and Center Artwork for EPS Files is enabled. For all EPS files, this
   option should be a default.

6. **Save the Job Options.** After I close the Job Options dialog box, Distiller
   prompts me for a name for the new Job Options. I enter Print_EPS as a name
   for the new Job Options setting and click the Save button.

7. **Distill the EPS file.** I drag the EPS file to the Distiller application window to
   produce the PDF. See Figure 6-35.

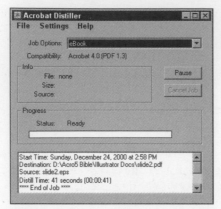

Figure 6-35: The Distiller window shows
the new Job Options setting used and
a report of the distillation time.

8. **View the PDF.** I open Acrobat and examine the PDF. Crop marks, bleeds, simulated transparency, and layer data are all visible in the PDF, as shown in
Figure 6-36.

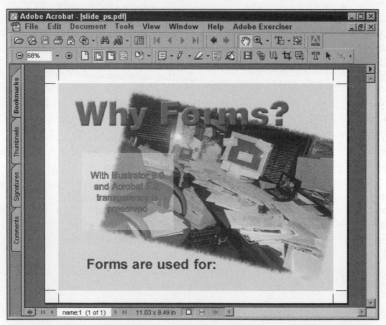

Figure 6-36: The final PDF document produces the PDF image as it
was designed in Illustrator including the bleeds and crop marks.

Some caveats exist when choosing a save as PDF from Illustrator versus an EPS export and distillation. If you want to retain editing capabilities in regard to text, files need to be saved as PDF whenever transparency is used. If you distill an EPS with text and transparency, you will no be able to edit the text. If you use crop marks without adding a bounding box to accommodate the crop marks and bleeds, saving as PDF will clip the document to the page boundary and ignore bleeds and crop marks.

Opening PDFs in Illustration Programs

All of the illustration programs mentioned previously can open PDF files. Opening a PDF in one of these programs provides access to individual page elements to one degree or another. The page elements can be changed, deleted, or edited to the degree that the program opening the PDF retains document integrity. Programs other than the illustration programs may offer PDF imports; however, they do not provide access to individual elements. Programs, such as Adobe InDesign, Adobe PageMaker, and QuarkXPress all enable you to import PDFs, but you won't be able to edit the document elements. The PDFs appear as grouped objects that can't be ungrouped.

In terms of editing PDFs, you'll find distinct differences between legacy files and PDFs created with programs, such as Illustrator 9.0 and Acrobat 5.0 compatibility. Regardless of which program you choose to edit legacy PDFs, you have problems with individual elements. Text does not retain precise formatting when opened in either CorelDraw or Illustrator. FreeHand may preserve text elements better than the other two programs. Colors may shift in either CorelDraw or FreeHand. Objects are nested with masks and groups in Illustrator. In short, you will have many problems when editing legacy files in any of the illustration programs.

Ideally, it would always be best to edit in the originating application and produce another PDF — especially when major changes are needed. If editing PDFs is important to your workflow, then perhaps one of the best solutions would be to use a third-party plug-in, such as Enfocus Software's PitStop. (See Chapter 20 for a list of third-party plug-ins and where to acquire them.)

PDF files are opened in all programs via the File ⇨ Open command. You have no special import commands or filters needed by any of the illustration programs to recognize a PDF file. When you choose File ⇨ Open to open a single-page PDF file, the document opens in the application window. If opening a multi-page PDF, a dialog box will appear enabling you to navigate to a specific page.

On opening the PDF file, you have access to all of the elements contained within the document. If you happen to have several illustration programs installed on your computer, you may want to compare opened PDF files between your applications. At one time or another, one program may preserve more document integrity. If vector objects need to be edited or type needs to be changed, simple edits may be performed by one of these programs.

Limitations with editing PDF files in illustration programs

If the need calls for editing PDFs in one of the illustration programs, you should be aware of some limitations that need to be overcome. As an example, I use Adobe Illustrator to demonstrate some of the limitations:

✦ **Text limitations:** All text — titles, headlines, body copy, and so on — lose text block attributes. A single line of text often is a noncontiguous grouping of characters. The text can be broken up both between words and within a given word on the same text line. These broken text blocks may be difficult to edit, especially if you make major copy changes. In some cases, it may be easier to re-create the text block (see Figures 6-37 and 6-38).

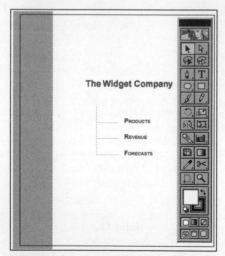

Figure 6-37: A PDF opened in Illustrator with text as it appeared in the original PDF document.

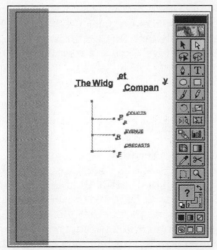

Figure 6-38: The text shown in Figure
6-37 was moved in Illustrator. Notice
the broken text blocks and noncontiguous
grouping of the text.

✦ **Font problems:** If fonts are not embedded in the PDF documents, font substitution will be used and any text changes will make use of the substituted
fonts. Those documents in which fonts have been embedded and subsetted
only contain the subset fonts. Edited text may appear in a font different than
the non-edited text in your document. In addition, character sets across platforms vary, and font characters may not offer an accurate substitution. When
you open a PDF in Illustrator, a warning dialog box appears if there are any
font problems.

✦ **Masked objects:** Some objects appear masked when you open a PDF file in
Adobe Illustrator. Although not a major problem, as you can easily unmask
the objects, care should be used when relocating objects contained within
a mask. If you attempt to move an object outside the mask boundary, it
disappears.

Tip

Overcoming text problems can be handled in Adobe Illustrator with a little work
around. Open a PDF in Illustrator and select the text to be edited with the Direct
Selection Tool. Choose Edit ⇨ Cut. Click the Type Tool and drag open a rectangle.
The text box appears with a blinking cursor. Choose Edit ⇨ Paste to paste the text
in the new rectangle. The text is now reformed with all paragraph attributes intact.
Word wrap works properly, and text is not broken throughout the text block.

As all programs continually upgrade, you'll see more implementation of supporting document integrity with PDF files. Illustrator 9.0 overcomes these limitations when saving in a PDF format and preserving editable text. As CorelDraw and Macromedia FreeHand experience new upgrades, I suspect we'll see some similar features in the new editions.

Acrobat and Layout Programs

Contenders in the high-end imaging arena with regard to layout applications are Adobe Systems and Quark, Inc. Adobe markets Adobe PageMaker, Adobe InDesign, and Adobe FrameMaker. The flagship program of Quark is QuarkXPress. Although Microsoft Publisher is a favorite among Microsoft Office users, it hasn't had much impact within the professional design market. As part of the Office suite, I placed the discussion of Publisher earlier in the chapter when we covered Office applications. The remaining layout programs are all suited for handling PDFs, so take a look at them individually.

With all of the layout programs listed here, you have options for both exporting and importing PDFs. With InDesign and FrameMaker, the export and import features are built into the applications. With PageMaker and QuarkXPress you need a plug-in or XTension, respectively. In each description, you look at both exports and imports.

Adobe InDesign

InDesign, such as Illustrator 9.0, was developed with core PDF architecture. Exporting to PDF is as reliable from InDesign as found with Illustrator saves to PDF and as good as you can get with Acrobat Distiller. With all its support for PDF and extraordinary design capability, InDesign has suffered greatly in the marketplace. Adobe has yet to convert either PageMaker or QuarkXPress users to the program in any significant numbers. Service centers and printers have not embraced the program due to many confusing printing controls and the unpopular acceptance of either the LaserWriter 8.6 or 8.7 driver on the Macintosh. The program is still young, so I expect we'll see more improvement as time goes by. From a design point of view, you can't beat many of the design and type handling features. If you're in the market for a layout application, keep your eye on this product as it matures.

Exporting PDF from InDesign

With InDesign, PDFs are created by accessing the File ➪ Export menu. Before you begin, be certain to select the latest printer driver recommended by Adobe. When the Export command is executed, the first of several screens appears in the Export PDF dialog box (see Figure 6-39).

Figure 6-39: Export PDF is the default dialog box that appears when you choose File ⇨ Export.

The first controls encountered are the PDF Options:

✦ **PDF Options:** The PDF Options available in the Export PDF dialog box include settings for font and image handling and some PDF attributes.

- **Subset Fonts below [ ]:** By default, fonts are embedded in the PDF document. InDesign permits font subsetting with user-defined amounts below percentages in this field box.

Tip

Font embedding can be problematic with any program and certain fonts that for one reason or another do not successfully embed in either the PostScript file or the PDF. One feature available with InDesign is the ability to convert fonts to outlines (or paths). If a font gives you trouble, try converting it to outlines. Use this feature sparingly and don't convert all fonts to outlines. Be selective and only use this feature with fonts having embedding problems.

- **Color:** Color management is handled from the Color pull-down menu. Choices include Leave Unchanged, RGB, and CMYK. If you intend to embed a profile, the color management policies have to be established in the Color Settings dialog box. To enable color management, choose File ⇨ Color Settings before selecting the Export command. InDesign enables you to set application specific color management or controlling color at the document level. From the Color Settings menu, a submenu appears where these choices are made.

- **Imported Graphics:** The first of the choices for handling imported images is the resolution setting. High Resolution preserves the resolution of raster images. Low resolution downsamples the images. For greater control over image sampling, a separate dialog box containing image sampling and compression is available.

- **Omit:** For proof printing where text needs to be carefully examined, images can be omitted. Choices are available for the three image types (EPS, PDF, and Bitmap Images) listed in Figure 6-39.

- **Options:** The three checkboxes include choices for generating thumbnails, optimizing PDFs, and viewing the final PDF in an Acrobat viewer. Similar to many other PDF producers, these checkboxes offer the same options.

✦ **Compression:** After the PDF Options have been chosen, select the pull-down menu where PDF Options is listed or click the Next button at the top-right side of the dialog box. Compression settings are handled in the Compression dialog box, as shown in Figure 6-40.

All compression options are identical to those found with Acrobat Distiller. When compression choices have been made, select Pages and Page Marks from the pull-down menu or click the Next button. The Pages and Page Marks dialog box appears, as shown in Figure 6-41.

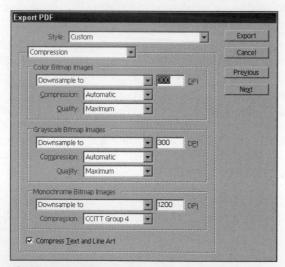

Figure 6-40: You can access compression choices by selecting Compression from the pull-down menu at the top of the dialog box or clicking the Next button on the top-right side of the dialog box.

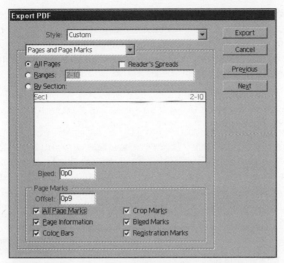

Figure 6-41: The Pages and Page Marks dialog box opens when the respective item is selected from the pull-down menu or the Next button is clicked.

✦ **Pages and Page Marks:** This dialog box contains all the settings for page ranges to be exported to PDF and any printer's marks that will appear in the PDF.

- **Page range:** All Pages appears as the default. You can also select a range of pages according to sections if so defined in the InDesign document. A checkbox for Reader's Spreads enables the pages to be printed as spreads.

- **Bleed:** If the document contains a bleed, you can supply a bleed amount. The default is 0p0, which indicates no bleed. If your document unit of measure is in inches and you want to specify points for the bleed, enter 0pn where n is the amount of the bleed in points. A bleed amount of 0p18 translates to zero picas and 18 points.

- **Offset:** For roll fed papers and film, you may need to offset the document from the paper/film edge. This offset amount prints the document the same distance from the edge as it is user defined. The same syntax for points units of measure is used as explained previously.

- **Page Marks:** All the checkboxes in this section of the dialog box refer to printer's marks. If you have bleeds, then crop marks will be a necessity to trim the page to the right size.

Note Perhaps the clumsiest aspect of either Exporting to PDF or printing a file from InDesign is the way page sizes are handled. If you want crop marks and bleeds to appear either in the final PDF or the printed page, you need to exit either the Export PDF or Print dialog box and use the Page Setup dialog box. InDesign makes no provision for custom page sizes when exporting or printing from the respective dialog boxes. Furthermore, if you don't use the recommended printer driver, custom page sizes won't be available.

✦ **Security:** After selecting the Pages and Page Marks, adding security to the PDF can be obtained by selecting Security from the pull-down menu or clicking the Next button. The Security options in the latest version of InDesign only offer 40-bit encryption, as shown in Figure 6-42. As InDesign is upgraded above Version 1.52, I suspect we'll see support for encryption consistent with Acrobat 5.0. All features accessible in this dialog box are identical to the 40-bit encryption described in Chapter 5.

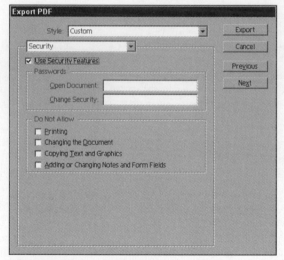

Figure 6-42: As of this writing, only the 40-bit level of encryption is available with InDesign.

Defining PDF styles

After moving through the maze of options in the Export PDF dialog box, you may think that it would be a pain to revisit each dialog box every time you want to export a PDF file. Fortunately Adobe offers a nice solution. A PDF Style can be created that captures all of the settings made for export to PDF. To create a style, a separate command must be selected. InDesign offers no solution from within the Export to PDF dialog box to capture the settings made here. To create a new style, choose File ➪ Define PDF Style. A separate dialog box appears, as shown in Figure 6-43.

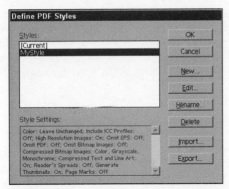

Figure 6-43: To create a style for capturing all export options, choose File ➪ Define PDF Style.

If a new style is to be created, click the New button appearing in the Define PDF Styles dialog box. When New is selected, all the dialog boxes explained previously will be available. After making the options choices, click OK. The new style is accessible when you choose File ➪ Export. All styles created appear from a pull-down menu at the top of the Export PDF dialog box.

Importing PDFs into InDesign

InDesign acquires images by using the File ➪ Place command. InDesign handles PDF documents just as InDesign handles other image files, such as Tiff and EPS. When File ➪ Place is selected, a navigation dialog box appears, as shown in Figure 6-44. In this dialog box are some important options to be addressed when placing PDFs.

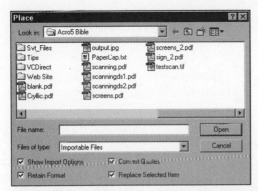

Figure 6-44: PDF files are acquired in InDesign by choosing File ➪ Place. The Place dialog box appears enabling you to select the PDF to be imported on the document page.

The most important of these checkboxes is the Show Import Options enabler. If not checked, only the first page of a multiple page PDF file will be imported. To selectively choose a page from within a multiple page document, the checkbox must be enabled. If a multi-page PDF is chosen for import and the checkbox is enabled, a second dialog box will appear. From the Place PDF dialog box shown in Figure 6-45, a user specified page can be selected.

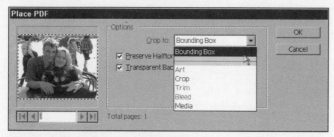

Figure 6-45: When multiple pages are contained in a PDF, the second dialog box appearing for Place PDF permits selective page acquisition.

In the Place PDF dialog box, options exist for Crop To, Preserve Halftone Screens, and Transparent Background.

✦ **Crop To:** The default is Bounding Box. The bounding box area is the same as the PDF page as you may see in an Acrobat viewer. Other options for cropping enable control over how much of the PDF can be placed.

- **Art:** Only art as defined by the PDF author will be placed, for example, clip art. Only the clip art will be placed while ignoring the text and other images.

- **Crop:** Only the area that is printed or displayed by the PDF will be placed. If the cropping in Acrobat eliminates data on the edges, what you see in the viewer will be the placed data while ignoring the cropped area.

- **Trim:** If bleeds and trim marks are contained in the PDF, only the final trim size will be placed, eliminating the bleeds and trim marks.

- **Bleed:** Contains the bleeds but ignores the trim marks. The size of the image will be a little larger than Trim above because it displays the bleed area that may exist outside the trim area.

- **Media:** Equal to the physical page size. If the page is defined as Letter and the image, bleeds, and trim marks are contained within the page, the entire page boundary will be displayed.

✦ **Preserve Halftone Screen:** If a halftone frequency was embedded in the PDF, it will be preserved in the InDesign file. You could have a single page print with the imported PDF at one screen value and the remaining InDesign elements printing at a different screen value if so desired.

✦ **Transparent Background:** Transparency will be created even if it wasn't defined in the PDF. A white page background appears as transparent when the checkbox is enabled.

Adobe PageMaker

Adobe PageMaker has an export command that permits export to PDF first by printing the file to PostScript, and then automatically launching Distiller in the background. With PageMaker, you also have a choice of holding off on the distillation by creating PostScript files that can be distilled later.

To export a PDF from PageMaker, you must have the Export PDF plug-in properly installed on your computer. This plug-in is available free for downloading from the Adobe Web site. As of this writing, the current Version is 3.01. With advanced features in Acrobat Distiller 5.0, you may want to frequently check the Adobe Web site for an updated version. After you install the plug-in, a menu command appears when you choose File ⇨ Export. The option available is Adobe PDF. This command only appears when the plug-in is available. If you don't see it, then the plug-in is not properly installed in the PageMaker plug-in folder.

Installing Export Adobe PDF Version 3.01

When you download version 3.01 of the Export Adobe PDF plug-in, you need to decompress the downloaded file. Double-clicking the file launches the installer utility and decompresses the files. On the Macintosh, you need to move the Export Adobe PDF.add file to your PageMaker folder and place it in PageMaker:RSRC:Plug-ins. This file must be in your plug-ins folder to export or import PDF files.

In Windows, when you decompress the file, find the Exppdf.add file and copy it to Pm65 (your PageMaker application folder)\Rsrc\<*language*>\Plug-ins folder. The <*language*> item denoted is the language you determined upon installation. If the language was USenglsh, then the directory path would be Pm65\Rsrc\USenglsh\Plug-ins.

You must copy these files to the respective folder on your system and restart PageMaker to have the plug-in take effect. If you run into any problems after installing the plug-in, trash the old plug-in and reinstall by following the preceding steps.

Using the PDF Export plug-in

When you choose File ➪ Export ➪ Adobe PDF from within PageMaker, the Export Adobe PDF dialog box, in which all the PDF attributes are controlled, will appear (see Figure 6-46). A maze of options are available in this dialog box — enough to make your head swim. If you have a handle on the Job Options in Acrobat Distiller, you've reduced your learning curve by about half. The remaining half of the settings that you will encounter are used for controls that aren't available from Distiller, some of which are specific to PageMaker. The first level of options deals with workflow distillation and printer styles. You can select from the following options:

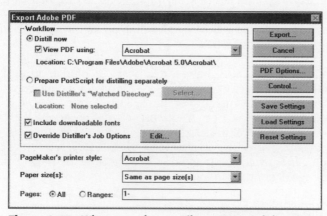

Figure 6-46: When you choose File ➪ Export Adobe PDF, the Export Adobe PDF dialog box, through which all PDF attributes and workflow is determined, appears.

✦ **Distill now:** The Distill now option will auto-launch Acrobat Distiller. When you select the Export button in the top-right corner of the dialog box, your PageMaker file will be printed to disk as a PostScript file and then distilled in Acrobat Distiller. Upon completion of distillation, you will be returned to the PageMaker document window.

✦ **Export PostScript file to distill later:** When the radio button is selected, the Distill Now option will be disabled. If the Export button is clicked with this option enabled, the file will be printed to disk as a PostScript file. You can develop PDF workflows by using watched folders and remote systems for distillation.

✦ **Printer Style:** Two choices are available. The default is Acrobat. This choice corresponds to the pull-down menu choices identified for PDF Style at the bottom of the dialog box (see PDF Style below). When a choice is made from PDF Style, the pull-down menu will return to Acrobat. The other choice available is Use Current Print Settings. When this item is selected from the pull-down menu, no PDF Style will be used. The settings in the Print dialog box will override the PDF Style choices.

✦ **Include all publications in book:** In PageMaker, you can create separate files to be contained within a book. When you're ready to index, develop a table of contents, or print, you can have PageMaker include all separate files into a logical book order via the Book command. When you choose Utilities ⇨ Book in PageMaker, a dialog box will appear that offers the opportunity to select the chapters to be contained in the book. When this option is enabled, all chapters identified as part of the book will be printed to disk as a PostScript file. If disabled, the current open document will be printed to disk.

✦ **Page Size(s):** Two choices are available from the pull-down menu. Same as current publication produces a page size equal to the page dimensions in the document. Same as printer style is your second choice. If a page size, such as LetterExtra, is included in the printer style, the larger page size will be used.

✦ **Pages:** The page range found here will be similar to the page range in the Print dialog box. All pages or a range of pages can be used.

✦ **PDF Style:** Printer styles can be created similar to those explained when using Adobe InDesign. After a style has been created, it will appear in the pull-down menu. A style can be selected from this menu or a choice for the current print options identified in the Print dialog box.

When all settings have been made for the General options, select from either the pull-down menu at the top of the dialog box or click the Next button. The Format & Fonts dialog box appears, as shown in Figure 6-47.

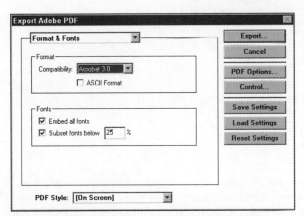

Figure 6-47: Selecting the Format & Fonts menu option from the pull-down menu or clicking the Next button opens the next dialog box where compatibility and font handling can be established.

✦ **Compatibility:** Choices for compatibility with the PDF Export plug-in in Version 3.01 is limited to Acrobat 2.01 and Acrobat 3.0 compatibility. If preparing PDFs where newer compatibility versions are not needed, you can choose the Acrobat 3.0 compatibility setting. If you need to have the file distilled with Acrobat 5.0 compatibility, you need to be certain that the Distiller Job Options are not overridden. (See Miscellaneous settings later described for overriding Distiller Job Options.)

✦ **ASCII Format:** The default is binary encoding. If ASCII encoding is needed, check this box.

✦ **Fonts:** Embedding and Subsetting are available and are handled the same as those options found in Distiller.

Select Compression from the pull-down menu or click the Next button. The compression settings appear, as shown in Figure 6-48.

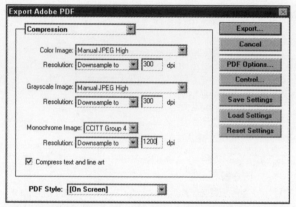

Figure 6-48: Selecting the Compression menu option from the pull-down menu or clicking the Next button opens the next dialog box where compression choices are made.

✦ **Color and Grayscale Images:** All choices for Color Image and Grayscale Image will appear similar to those used in Distiller. With the current PDF Export plug-in, there are a few exceptions. Acrobat 5.0 has abandoned use of LZW compression in favor of Zip compression. Zip is not available in the PDF Export 3.01 plug-in. If Automatic is selected from the pull-down menu for any of the three image types, compression automatically will be chosen between JPEG and LZW. If using Acrobat 5, use the Manual JPEG options.

✦ **Monochrome:** All choices for Monochrome bitmap images are the same as those found in Distiller's Job Options.

✦ **Compress text and line art:** Likewise, this option is the same as the Distiller Job Options.

Select Color Model from the pull-down menu or click the Next button. The color handling methods appear, as shown in Figure 6-49.

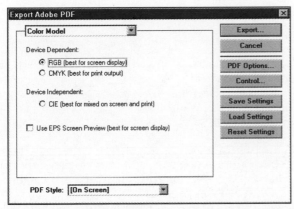

Figure 6-49: Selecting the Color Model menu option from the pull-down menu or clicking the Next button opens the next dialog box where choices for color handling can be made.

✦ **Device Dependent/Device Independent:** Ideally, it is best to let Distiller handle all the color management. The choices in the current plug-in are archaic and some are no longer used. If screen output is your destination, then a choice for RGB can be selected in the dialog box. For print, let Distiller Job Options control the color handling.

✦ **Use EPS Screen Preview (best for screen display):** If EPS images are imported into the PageMaker document, select this radio button. The appearance of the images will display on-screen much better.

Select Document Information from the pull-down menu or click the Next button. A dialog box appears, as shown in Figure 6-50 where document information can be supplied.

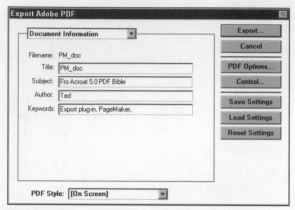

Figure 6-50: Selecting the Document Information menu option from the pull-down menu or clicking the Next button opens the next dialog box where Document Information can be supplied before distillation.

✦ **Document Information:** This feature accompanies the PageMaker Export to Acrobat PDF command. Title, Subject, Author, and Keyword fields can be supplied, as shown in Figure 6-50. When you choose File ⇨ Document Info ⇨ General in an Acrobat viewer, the document information supplied here will be visible in the General Document Information dialog box.

Select Hyperlinks from the pull-down menu or click the Next button. A dialog box appears, as shown in Figure 6-51 where document information can be supplied.

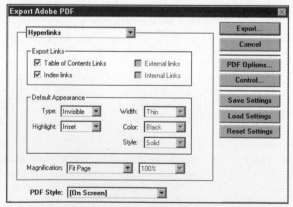

Figure 6-51: Selecting the Hyperlinks menu option from the pull-down menu or clicking the Next button opens the next dialog box where Hyperlinks to book-marks and indexes can be included in the PDF document.

In publication houses or companies that create publications, catalogs, newsletters, and other lengthy documents, the auto generation of hyperlinks produces PDFs for final distribution on CD-ROMs and Web-hosted documents. Controlling all the hyperlink activity in PageMaker can significantly reduce time spent creating links in Acrobat.

✦ **Hyperlinks:** The dialog box is divided into three categories — the first of which deals with hyperlinks. These controls are part of what pairs PageMaker to similar tasks handled by Microsoft Word. You can create auto-links to many different document items in a file, and these links will be visible in an Acrobat viewer. When you create a PageMaker publication and use some of these auto-linking settings, you will save much time by eliminating the need to create links in Acrobat. The hyperlinks that you can create are as follows:

- **Table of Contents Links:** PageMaker has an automatic generator for tables of contents. You identify TOC items in the PageMaker story editor, select a menu command, place the contents, and presto — your TOC has been generated. When this option is enabled for PDF exports, items in the table of contents included in the PageMaker file serve as hyperlinks to the pages where those items appear. If you work in a publishing environment where you produce print documents and CD-ROMs, you can develop a PDF workflow where watched folders are used to convert PDF files for both purposes. The links for the CD-ROM will have no effect on the documents developed for print; therefore, only a single PostScript file needs to be exported. Job Options for the watched folders can be developed to handle compression and downsampling for the respective output.

- **Index links:** The same capabilities for indexes exist as they do for tables of contents. When an index has been developed, the index items serve as hyperlinks to the pages where the words or phrases appear.

- **External links:** Links can be made to URLs on the World Wide Web from within PageMaker. If you create a Web link, enabling this option will preserve the link.

- **Internal links:** PageMaker has an internal hyperlink palette, which enables you to set up links from selected words or graphics to other pages in your document. When Preserve internal links is enabled, you can select from a number of different views, the same as those available in Acrobat viewers.

✦ **Magnification:** The default view is Fit Page. You can edit the view from the pull-down menu, or you can select from preset views. When you view the page magnification pull-down menu, you'll see the choices available. Only the Fit Top Left of Page and Fit Top Left choices enable you to edit the view magnification. The percentage pull-down menu will be inactive with the other three choices. If Fit Top Left of Page or Fit Top Left is selected, you can open the pull-down menu to select a preset view magnification or select Other and then enter a value between 12% and 800% in the field.

Note Acrobat 5.0 magnification is capable of zoom levels from 8.33% to 1600%. The PageMaker PDF Export plug-in relies on earlier versions of Acrobat Compatibility where the larger range of zoom levels was not available. If zooms lower than 12% or higher than 800% are desired, zoom magnifications will need to be edited individually in Acrobat.

Select Articles & Bookmarks from the pull-down menu or click the Next button. A dialog box appears, as shown in Figure 6-52 where articles and bookmarks can be created in the exported PDF.

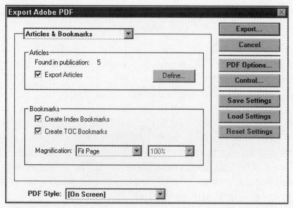

Figure 6-52: Selecting the Articles & Bookmarks menu option from the pull-down menu or clicking the Next button opens the next dialog box where articles and bookmarks can be preserved.

✦ **Export Articles:** When the checkbox is enabled, any articles that have been defined in the publication will be exported as article threads. To have an article exported, it must first be defined. Clicking the Define button creates an article definition.

To examine the article definition, click the Define button. The Define Articles dialog box, shown in Figure 6-53, opens.

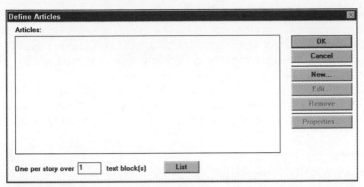

Figure 6-53: Clicking the Define button in the Export Adobe PDF dialog box opens the Define Articles dialog box.

When the Define Articles dialog box is opened, you won't find any items listed. The settings available in the dialog box include:

- **List:** (Lower center of dialog box) Clicking the List button will recognize the Stories in the publication. From within the publication you may create many article threads from different contiguous text blocks.

- **New:** Selecting the New button will prompt you with another dialog box designed to establish the article definition.

- **Edit:** When an article has been defined, you select it in the list, click Edit, and the dialog box where the article was originally defined will reappear. In this dialog box, you can make changes to the defined article.

- **Remove:** Selecting a defined article in the list and clicking the Remove button will eliminate the article thread. When the PDF file is created, only the defined articles existing in the list box will appear in the Acrobat viewer.

- **Properties:** When article properties have been created, clicking this button will display the Article Properties dialog box.

- **One per story over [*nn*] text block(s):** PageMaker Stories can have many different text blocks. If you have one or two-line text blocks, you may want to eliminate them from your list. You can limit the number of text blocks in a story by supplying a value in this field. For example, entering the value 5 in this field results in only a list of stories that contain six or more text blocks.

Clicking the New button in the Define Articles dialog box opens the PageMaker Stories dialog box, shown in Figure 6-54.

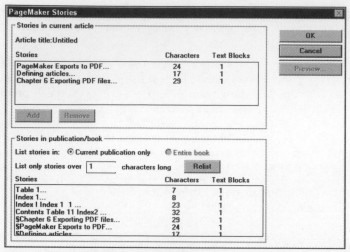

Figure 6-54: I listed all of the PageMaker Stories containing over one character to view all text blocks in the document.

- **Stories** (top of dialog box): When stories have been identified as articles and listed, the stories will appear in the box along with the number of characters and text blocks.

- **List stories in:** You can select the current publication or a book that has been defined just as you would when working with hyperlinks. The Entire book option will only be available if you have created a book publication.

- **List only stories over [*nnn*] characters long:** The default for the field box is 400. Any stories less than 400 characters will not appear in the Stories list. You can reduce the value in the field box to reveal shorter stories. If you change the value, you need to select the Relist button, and PageMaker will recalculate the list according to the stories containing the number of characters corresponding to the new value.

- **Stories** (bottom of dialog box): The list appearing in the lower Stories box is among those that can be defined as articles. To define an article, you must select a story listed in the lower box and add it to the upper list.

- **Stories in current article** (back to top of dialog box): From the Stories list in the lower box, you add a story or several stories to an article. All stories in the upper Stories list will become part of the article that you define. Whereas multiple stories can become part of an article thread, only one article thread can be defined at a time.

- **Add:** The Add button is used to place a story in the upper Stories list. Select a story in the lower box and click the Add button. You can also double-click a story name in the lower Stories list, and the story will appear in the upper Stories list.

- **Remove:** Clicking the Remove button will remove a selected story from the upper Stories list. A story must be selected before the Remove button will become active.

- **Preview:** When you select a story in either the upper or lower Stories list, the Preview button will become active. If you select Preview, a separate window will open to show you the story contents. You can preview the story before you define it as an article.

Often you have only a single story listed in the current article story list. If multiple stories are contained in the list, all stories are threaded in the article. When you click the OK button in the PageMaker Stories dialog box after listing a story or several stories, another dialog box appears for defining the article properties, as shown in Figure 6-55.

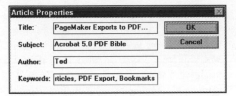

Figure 6-55: After an article has been defined and the OK button is clicked, the Article Properties dialog box opens.

- **Article Properties:** The fields for Title, Subject, Author, and Keywords are items searchable by Acrobat Search. Just as with the document information discussed in Chapter 2, all the search criteria apply to these fields.

Whenever creating articles in PageMaker, be certain to provide all the article property information. If you want to develop a true PDF workflow, the time you take supplying information for article properties will be much less than having to edit the properties in Acrobat.

After defining articles and clicking the last OK button in the Article Properties, you are returned to the Articles and Bookmarks section of the Export Adobe PDF dialog box. When the Export button is selected, the articles defined appear as article threads in the final PDF.

✦ **Create Index Bookmarks:** Bookmarks can be created from all your index definitions in much the same manner as TOC entries are created. To define index text, you open the Story Editor and select the line of text or the individual characters to be included in your index. After selecting the characters or word for the index item, choose Utilities ➪ Index Entry from within the Story Editor. A dialog box opens that enables you to make some choices about the attributes of the index entry. Among the choices in the Index Entry dialog box is a sort option. After sorted and exported to PDF, the entries will appear as bookmarks in the same order in an Acrobat viewer. As you define index entries in the Story Editor, the editor window will display a symbol indicating which items have been added to the index. To the left of each item will be a description of the index level corresponding to the entry.

✦ **Create TOC Bookmarks:** Table of contents items in PageMaker are defined in the Paragraph Specifications dialog box. When you choose Type ➪ Paragraph, this dialog box opens. Any words that you have highlighted can be included in the table of contents by selecting the option Include in table of contents.

✦ **Magnification:** When a bookmark is selected in the PDF file, the bookmarked page will be displayed at a magnification level consistent with what is selected from the pull-down menu. Choices include: Fit Page, Fit Contents, and Fit Top Left of Page.

Note   After you define all the TOC entries, you need to open the PageMaker Story Editor (Edit ➪ Edit Story) and choose Utilities ➪ Create TOC. PageMaker will calculate all the TOC entries and load the text gun that can be used to place the text on a page. After placing the text, the TOC items will be linked to the pages where the entries were defined. All these entries must be made before you begin to export to PDF. When the PDF file is created, bookmarks will be generated and hypertext links from the bookmarks will provide a connection to the respective pages.

Caution   TOC and indexes have a data structure invisible to the end user. When bookmarks are created in Acrobat, the data structure is used to create the bookmarks. If you cut and paste TOC and index entries, you will lose the data structure and bookmarks won't be created in the PDF. When editing text you can change fonts and point sizes, but be certain to avoid cutting and pasting these items.

After making all the choices for Articles & Bookmarks, select Note On First Page from the pull-down menu or click the Next button. The Note On First Page dialog box appears, as shown in Figure 6-56.

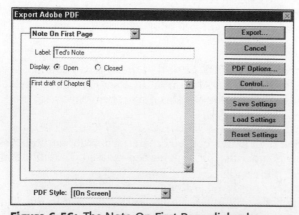

Figure 6-56: The Note On First Page dialog box provides an opportunity to create a note that appears on the first page of the PDF file.

✦ **Note on First Page:** Another nice feature with PageMaker is the ability to create a text note annotation that will appear in the resultant PDF file. Only one note can be added, and it will always appear on the first page in the PDF.

- • **Label:** The text added for Label will appear in the title bar of the text annotation note.

- • **Display:** Two choices are offered. Open will display the Note opened and the text contained within. Closed will display the text note annotation collapsed with only the comment icon in view.

- • **Text Block:** The large rectangular box under the Display choices is where the note contents are user supplied. Type a message in this box and it will appear as the note contents in the PDF.

After making all the choices for Note On First Page, select Advanced Options from the pull-down menu or click the Next button. The Advanced Options dialog box, appears, as shown in Figure 6-57.

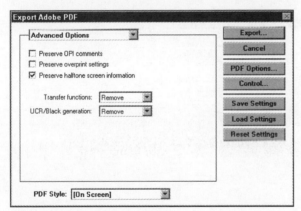

Figure 6-57: Advanced Options offer choices for prepress and printing attributes.

The Advanced Options include some of the controls and settings contained in Distiller's Color Job Options. These settings are used for files delivered to service centers and print shops and only apply to high-end digital prepress.

✦ **Preserve OPI comments:** For service centers using Open Press Interface (OPI), comments are preserved when enabling the checkbox. If no OPI comments are used, checking the box will have no effect on printing the final PDF.

✦ **Preserve overprint settings:** Overprints manually applied in applications, such as illustration and layout programs, will be preserved when you enable this option. Overprinting will only have an effect when your files will be color separated.

✦ **Preserve halftone screen information:** Preserving the halftone information will keep the frequency you specify in the PageMaker Print dialog box. For service centers downloading PDFs direct to PostScript 3 devices, they'll want the halftone frequency preserved. If you print to desktop color printers, it will have no effect on the printed results.

✦ **Transfer functions:** Three choices appear from the pull-down menu. If transfer functions have been embedded in a Photoshop image, Remove will eliminate them. Preserve will keep the transfer functions as long as they were embedded in the image. Apply will apply transfer functions.

✦ **UCR/Black generation:** If you made changes to undercolor removal or black generation settings in Photoshop, these changes will be discarded if Removed is selected or kept when Preserve is selected.

After making all the choices for Advanced Options, select Miscellaneous from the pull-down menu or click the Next button. The Miscellaneous dialog box appears, as shown in Figure 6-58.

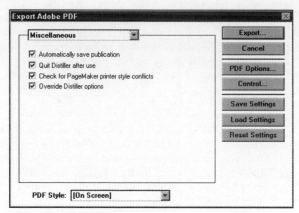

Figure 6-58: Miscellaneous options offer some additional settings, the most important of which is overriding the Distiller Job Options.

This dialog box contains a few miscellaneous items thrown together that don't fit all the previous options listed above. They include:

✦ **Automatically save publication:** PageMaker is notorious for prompting you to save a publication regardless of whether you have edited a page or not. You just look at the PageMaker file, and the program will prompt you for a save before closing the file or exporting to PDF. When this enabler is active, PageMaker automatically saves the document and then exports it to PDF.

✦ **Quit Distiller after use:** The PageMaker export to PDF procedure is a two-step process. After the PostScript file has been produced, Distiller will be launched in the background. If you want to quit Distiller after creating the PDF file, enable this option. If disabled, Distiller will remain open. The Distiller window may appear hidden behind a PageMaker document, but it will still be open. If you have several PageMaker documents to distill, leave the option disabled.

✦ **Check for PageMaker printer style conflicts:** PageMaker provides you the opportunity to capture all the attributes for printing to devices. The printing attributes are determined in the Print dialog box. You can select a PPD, page size, screening, and many other attributes in the Print dialog box and capture these settings to a printer style. When you want to use the same style, rather than return to the Print dialog box and make all the choices again, select the printer style and print. If there are any conflicts, such as selecting the wrong page size, PageMaker will open a warning dialog box when this option is enabled.

As a default, you should leave this option enabled. Any conflicts will be reported, which can save time in having to redistill files. You should be aware, however, PageMaker is notorious for reporting some problems that do not exist. When the option is enabled, you will commonly see a dialog box appear, informing you the blank pages will not print. Even when no blank pages exist nor are any bookmarks, articles, or hyperlinks established, the warning dialog box still appears. When you see the warning dialog box appear, click the Continue button, and your PDF will print properly — even a great PDF producer such as PageMaker has a few nuances.

✦ **Override Distiller options:** This option is one of the most critical. If you intend to create PDFs with Acrobat 5 compatibility, be certain to leave this box unchecked. If the checkmark is active, all the Job Options from Distiller that may be in conflict with the PageMaker options, such as compatibility, will be overridden by the PageMaker options. When using Acrobat 5.0 and PageMaker with the PDF Export 3.01 plug-in, most often you'll want this option deselected as a default.

When all options have been created, click the Export button and the file will first be printed as a PostScript file. If you have the Distill Now checkbox enabled in the General Options dialog box, Acrobat Distiller will automatically launch and distill the PostScript file. After completion of distillation, you will be returned to the PageMaker document window.

In cross-platform environments you may have a need to develop styles commonly used across platforms. All the settings and option choices in the Export Adobe PDF dialog boxes would be best used after the settings have been captured and saved as a style. The style settings you save can be transported across platforms. Therefore, a style set can be developed on a Macintosh, copied to a Windows computer, and used with PageMaker running under Windows. To illustrate how to create a style for cross-platform use, perform the steps that follow.

STEPS: Creating PDF Styles for Cross-Platform Use

1. **Create the style attributes.** From a PageMaker application document running on a Macintosh, I select File ⇨ Export ⇨ Adobe PDF. Using the 3.01 export plug-in, I set the attributes in the Export Adobe PDF dialog boxes to create a PDF document for output to high-end digital prepress. I use the Acrobat 3 format, subset fonts at 100 percent, set the image compression to the lowest JPEG compression, and make other choices for prepress considerations.

2. **Save the PDF style.** After all the attribute choices are made in the Export Adobe PDF dialog box, I select Save PDF Style from the pull-down menu in the export dialog box.

The Save PDF Style option from the pull-down menu can be selected from any of the views in the Export Adobe PDF dialog box. Provide a descriptive name when saving the style. If you work in Windows, the style name does not need to adhere to standard DOS conventions. In the example, I use Prepress PDF Style.

3. **Review the settings.** When the Save PDF Style pull-down menu choice is made, a dialog box appears with a list of all my attribute choices, as shown in Figure 6-59. I review the list and click the Save button.

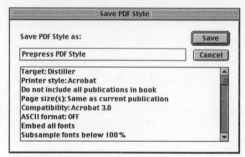

Figure 6-59: When you select Save PDF Style in any of the views of the Export Adobe PDF dialog box, another dialog box appears with a list of all your current attribute selections.

4. **Locate the** `PDFStyles.cnf` **file.** I locate my `PDFStyles.cnf` file in the Adobe PageMaker:RSRC:Plug-ins folder on my Macintosh computer.

5. **Copy the** `PDFStyles.cnf` **file to another computer.** I use Miramar Systems PC MacLan to network my PC and Macintosh and mount the PC Volume using AppleShare on my Macintosh. I open the destination folder on my NT workstation from the Macintosh mounted volume and navigate to PM65 (PageMaker directory)\Rsrc\Usenglsh\Plugins and copied my `PDFStyles.cnf` file to the plug-in folder.

6. **Select the PDF style in the Export Adobe PDF dialog box.** I launch PageMaker in Windows NT and open a PageMaker document. I then select File ➪ Export ➪ Adobe PDF. When the Export Adobe PDF dialog box appears, as shown in Figure 6-60, I select Prepress PDF Style, which is the name I provided when the style was saved on the Macintosh.

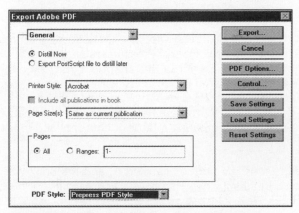

Figure 6-60: The style(s) that you create on one system can be used on another system when the `PDFStyle.cnf` file is copied to the PageMaker plug-ins folder.

QuarkXPress

QuarkXPress has been the premier choice of layout applications for design professionals on Macintosh computers. Quark, Inc., has paved its own road and traveled the digital highway in its own way. What has been accomplished in page layout for high-end design professionals has been magnificent, and one only needs to look at the incredible number of Quark XTensions to see the pinnacle of success accomplished by a company that has survived on a single product in a fiercely competitive world. For all intent and purposes, the company has literally maintained its dominance in page layout software prior to version 4.0 without a major revision for almost a six-year period. No other off-the-shelf product can claim such success.

On the Windows side, QuarkXPress has taken a back seat to Adobe PageMaker. More high-end professionals working in Windows tend to prefer PageMaker to QuarkXPress. Both programs are completely cross-platform and you find little difference between the two running on either platform. All the screens used in the earlier description of PageMaker were taken from a Windows computer. However, the choices available to Macintosh users are the same. In this section, you look at screen shots from the Macintosh point of view. Windows users will find the same options available when using QuarkXPress running under Windows.

Working with tables and indexes in QuarkXPress

PageMaker, as discussed earlier in this chapter, uses a plug-in to handle PDF export and import. QuarkXPress uses a similar plug-in technology referred to as XTensions. To export or import PDFs in QuarkXPress, you must acquire the PDF Filter XTension. The PDF Filter XTension can be downloaded free from the Quark Web site (www.quark.com). As of this writing, the XTension is in Version 1.51 and is supported by QuarkXPress Version 4.04 or higher.

We could muddle through a bunch of screen shots and look at the features included in the PDF Filter, but I'd rather offer the QuarkXPress users a more utilitarian purpose for using direct exports to PDF. Earlier in this chapter, I discussed the ability of PageMaker to include topic heads and index items as hyperlinks to pages in the resultant PDF file. Fortunately, QuarkXPress can perform the same tasks as PageMaker. Because QuarkXPress is a program heavily used by publication companies, I thought we might look at first creating a table of contents and index and then later export the file to PDF.

The text you're reading was laid out in QuarkXPress, and the book was entirely produced from Quark. In addition, we also have a PDF version on the CD-ROM accompanying the book. Now, all those production people don't want to struggle through the pages in the PDF file to create bookmarks and links, so I gave them a little hand in using automated features. If you create newsletters, pamphlets, short stories, or books, then you'll want to create a workflow that automates the creation of bookmarks and links when producing PDF files. In this regard, we'll look at creating bookmarks from topic heads and an index with hyperlinks that will appear in an exported PDF.

Identifying style sheets for a table of contents

In preparing a document of any substantial length, users often first create the text in a word processor, such as Microsoft Word and import the text in a layout program, such as QuarkXPress — at least this would be the most efficient method. In Word, your workflow is much easier if you create style sheets for all your headings, chapter heads, body text, figure captions, and the like. When in QuarkXPress, be certain to create a master page with an Automatic Text Box. On the master page be certain to create a link with the linking tool so that the text will autoflow.

Autoflow in QuarkXPress is easily handled by creating a Master Page with a Text Box. Open the master page and select the Linking tool from the QuarkXPress toolbox. Notice the link icon in the top-left corner of the master page. Click this icon and then click in the text box. All pages identified with this master page will autoflow the text. As new pages are needed, XPress automatically creates new pages.

When importing text, be certain to enable Include Style Sheets in the Get Text dialog box, as shown in Figure 6-61. All those styles defined in Word should be retained when the text is imported into XPress to develop an efficient workflow.

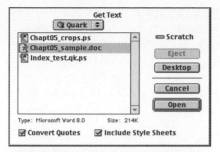

Figure 6-61: When importing text in QuarkXPress, be certain to check Include Style Sheets in the Get Text dialog box.

Assuming that you have a lengthy publication and the original Word document had several styles identified for major heads, subheads, and perhaps different chapters, these styles will all be contained in the QuarkXPress document when the Word file is imported. After importing the text, XPress needs to know what styles will be used to identify your eventual bookmarks in the Acrobat PDF file. To identify certain styles to be converted to bookmarks in the PDF, the styles need to be added to a List. In QuarkXPress, choose Edit ⇨ Lists to open the Lists dialog box for the open document. In this dialog box is a button appearing for New. Click this button to create a new List, as shown in Figure 6-62.

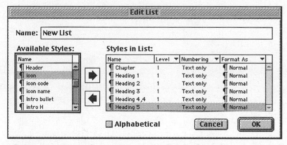

Figure 6-62: When New is selected in the Lists dialog box the Edit List dialog box will appear.

In the Edit List dialog box a display of all the styles included in the document will be listed under Available Styles on the left side of the dialog box. If you have styles for body copy, captions, callouts, quotes, and so on, you'll want avoid including them in the bookmarks appearing in Acrobat. The important items to include are topic heads, subheads, chapter titles, and other similar categorical items. In my example in Figure 6-62, I included Chapter and five levels of headings. To include a style in the styles list, select the style in the Available Styles list and click the right pointing arrow. The style name will be moved to the Styles in List box. All styles in the Styles in List box will be converted to bookmarks when exported to PDF.

After completing the selection of all styles to be included in your final document, add a name for the list in the Name field and click the OK button. When you return to the Lists box, the name of your list appears, as shown in Figure 6-63.

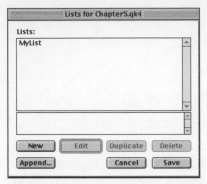

Figure 6-63: After clicking OK in the Edit List dialog box, you are returned to the List dialog box, where the name identified in the Edit List dialog box is displayed.

You can create several lists with many different attributes. QuarkXPress offers many features with table of content generation and indexing. The List box can be used to create a table of contents or many different tables. After completing all your work in the List box, click the Save button to save all edits.

Creating the table of contents

So far, we identified those styles that will be used to create bookmarks in the PDF and a table of contents in the QuarkXPress document. The generation of the table of contents needs to be our next task. Without generating the table of contents, no bookmarks will appear in the final PDF file.

To create a table of contents that you want to display in QuarkXPress, creating a new master with an autoflow text block is best. Create a new page and drag the new master page in the Document Layout palette to the top of the new page icon. This new master page will be a different master than the one you created initially to autoflow the text. It's not necessary, but it will often better suit your needs to create a separate master.

Choose View ➪ Show Lists. In the Lists palette, click the Update button. A list of all the items by the content of the heading styles will appear in the Lists palette. That is to say, the actual text used in any given style will appear in your list, as shown in Figure 6-64.

To generate a table of contents page, click the text block with the Content Tool. The Build button in the Lists palette becomes active. Click this button and a table of contents will be generated. If the contents spread across more than one page, QuarkXPress will automatically create additional pages as necessary.

Figure 6-64: When you click the Update button in the Lists palette, all the content of the styles identified appear listed in the palette.

Identifying index entries

Index entries can also be created as hyperlinks in the PDF file. You can create an index through the Quark index generator, and all the index items will link to the respective page in the PDF file. To create an index, each entry must be identified in the text of the document.

Note To create an index, the Index XTension must be present in the XTensions folder. If you don't have the Index XTension, you can download it free from the Quark, Inc. Web site (www.quark.com).

To create index entries, open the Index palette by choosing View ➪ Show Index. With the palette open, select a word to be included in your index and click the Add button, as shown in Figure 6-65.

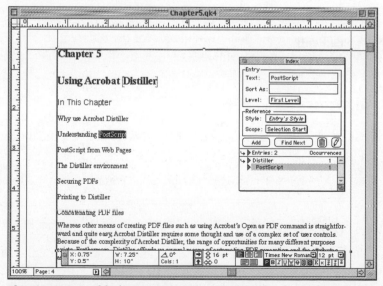

Figure 6-65: I added two entries to my index. The second entry was the highlighted word PostScript. After selecting the word, I clicked the Add button. The word is added to my index list.

Indexes created in QuarkXPress can be very complex. You can create up to four different levels. If you want a single level index with no sub categories, just move about the document and select words then click the Add button.

Building the index

After all index items have been identified, you need to build an index. To build the index, choose Utilities ➪ Build Index. The Build Index palette appears, as shown in Figure 6-66.

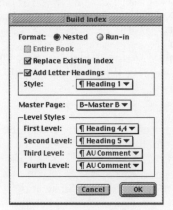

Figure 6-66: The Build Index palette is used to create the index from entries identified in the Index palette.

In the Build Index palette, you can make choices for styles to be applied to the index text when the index is generated. If you want a different type style than one used in the original Word document, you can identify a new style in Quark. After the style is created, it will appear in the pull-down menus for the different levels. When you click OK, the index will be created and placed on a new page at the end of the document.

Exporting QuarkXPress files to PDF

After the QuarkXPress file has been created and all the file components, such as table of contents and index have been developed, it's time to convert the file to PDF. If output to prepress is your wish, you can export to PDF from QuarkXPress or print a file to disk and distill it in Acrobat Distiller. However, if you want to prepare the PDF for viewing in Acrobat with bookmarks and links, you must use the Export PDF Filter.

QuarkXPress does not directly produce a PDF file. When using the Export PDF Filter, the file is printed to disk as a PostScript file and then Quark automatically launches Distiller. When distillation is complete, Distiller quits and you are returned to the Quark document window. To export the QuarkXPress document with the PDF Filter, choose Utilities ➪ Export as PDF. The Export as PDF dialog box appears, as shown in Figure 6-67.

For QuarkXPress to open the PDF Export dialog box, it must be able to find the Acrobat Distiller PPD. By default the PPD (PostScript Printer Description) is installed with Acrobat. If you reinstall software or QuarkXPress loses its directory path to the PPD, you'll need to be certain the PPD exists and Quark can find it. On the Macintosh, the PPD is installed in the System:Extensions:Printer Descriptions folder. On Windows, it should be placed in the WINNT\system32\spool\drivers\ w32x86 folder. Be certain that the PPD resides in the respective folder before attempting to export to PDF from QuarkXPress.

PPDs are ASCII text files. They are completely cross platform and can be copied between Macintosh computers and Windows computers. If you are a Windows user who supplies output files to imaging centers by using Macintosh computers, ask for the PPDs for their devices or visit the Web site for the manufacturer respective to the output device used and download it off the Web. Copy the PPDs to your WINNT\system32\spool\drivers\w32x86 folder, and they can be selected from any program by using the PPDs placed in this directory.

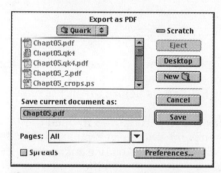

Figure 6-67: The Export as PDF dialog box can only be accessed after the PDF Filter XTension has been installed. This XTension is available free from the Quark, Inc. Web site (www.quark.com).

PDF export preferences

Before exporting the file, accessing the preferences where all the PDF attributes are assigned is important. To open the PDF Export Preferences dialog box, click the Preferences button in the Export as PDF dialog box. The PDF Preferences contain four tabs for different categories similar to the Distiller Job Options dialog box. The first settings include the Document Info, as shown in Figure 6-68.

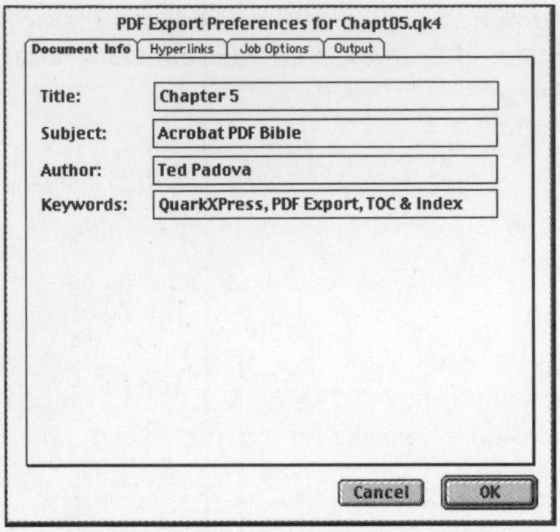

Figure 6-68: Document Info is supplied in the exported PDF file by entering information for the Title, Subject, Author, and Keywords fields.

✦ **Document Info:** The document information for the field boxes, shown in Figure 6-68, correspond to the Document Properties as displayed in an Acrobat viewer. Enter the information for these field boxes before the PDF is created.

After Document Info has been supplied, click the Hyperlinks tab to open the Hyperlinks dialog box. This dialog box provides the necessary options that will ensure your bookmarks and index entries will be included as hot links in the PDF file (see Figure 6-69).

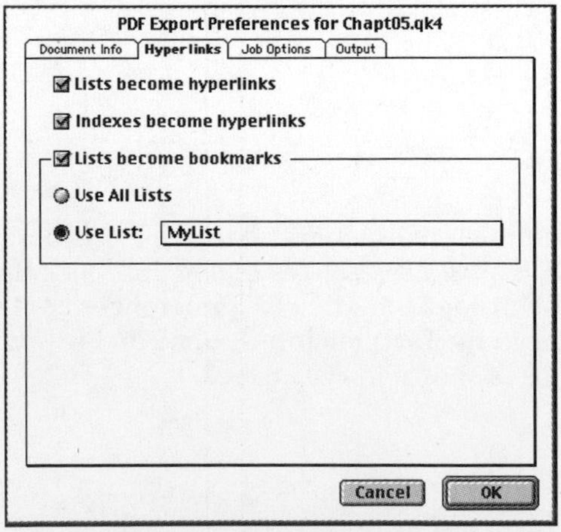

Figure 6-69: Including lists and indexes from this dialog box is critical in order for the bookmarks and index links to appear in the final PDF.

✦ **Links become hyperlinks:** For all the items identified in the Links dialog box in QuarkXPress to become referenced links in the PDF, this checkbox must be enabled.

✦ **Indexes become hyperlinks:** When the index was created in QuarkXPress, the index was added at the end of the document. If this checkbox is enabled, each index entry will link to the source in the body of the publication.

When viewed in an Acrobat viewer, the link will be created around the page number and not the index name. At times it may appear as though the links are not present if you don't position the cursor directly over the page number. If selecting index links becomes awkward for the end user, you may need to edit the link rectangles in Acrobat and expand them.

✦ **Lists become bookmarks:** A table of contents will be generated from the list if you elect to do so in QuarkXPress. The table of contents will link to the heads where they appear in the body of the publication when the Links become hyperlinks checkbox above is enabled. If you want to additionally turn all the table of contents items into bookmarks that will be displayed in the Acrobat viewer navigation pane, enable this item.

✦ **Use All Lists:** If enabled, all lists identified in QuarkXPress will be used.

✦ **Use List:** If multiple Lists have been created, you can select from the pull-down menu any single list to be included. In the example created above, I had only one list, therefore, Use All Lists or Use List would produce the same results.

After Hyperlinks options have been selected, click the Job Options tab to open the Job Options dialog box. This dialog box provides Job Options choices that can be used to override Distiller's Job Options. The options available to you are shown in Figure 6-70.

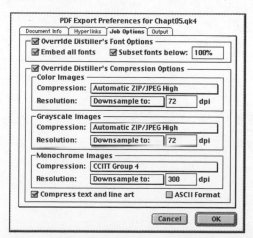

Figure 6-70: The Job Options dialog box offers many options choices that can be assigned in this dialog box and override Distiller's Job Options.

✦ **Override Distiller's Font Options:** If the checkbox is enabled, the Font Options for embedding and subsetting will override Distiller's Font Job Options. If you want to change Font Job Options, I would recommend you handle it in Distiller. If the Font embedding and subsetting is produced by Quark, writing the PostScript file could take much longer because all the subsetting is handled before it gets to Distiller. A 50-page document could conceivably become a 200MB file when printed as PostScript. The PDF will be infinitely smaller, but it will take some time to write large files to disk.

✦ **Override Distiller's Compression Options:** You can choose to handle image compression and downsampling in Quark by selecting the checkbox. All the compression and sampling available in this dialog box are the same as found with Distiller's Job Options.

✦ **Compress text and line art:** Also the same as Distiller's Job Options, compression for text and line art are handled the same.

✦ **ASCII Format:** The default is binary encoding. If ASCII is needed for some reason, it can be enabled in this dialog box. Neither of the two items at the bottom of the dialog box require a checkbox to override Distiller's Job Options. If either is checked, the Job Options in Distiller will be overridden.

After completing the Job Options settings, click the Output tab. The Output Job Options handles color and prepress concerns, as shown in Figure 6-71.

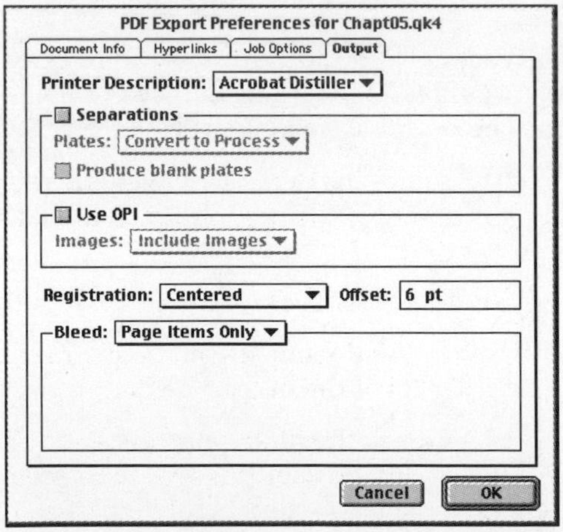

Figure 6-71: The Output Job Options control all prepress attributes.

If PDF viewing on-screen or Web is your output objective, then most of what is contained in this dialog box will be of no concern. The default PPD selected will be the Acrobat Distiller PPD and it should be left alone for any screen output.

✦ **Printer Description:** All PPDs accessible to QuarkXPress will appear from the pull-down menu. As mentioned in Chapter 5, in almost all cases, you should use the Acrobat Distiller PPD. If creating output to a device where the device PPD will better serve your needs, make the appropriate selection from the PPD choices.

✦ **Separations:** The file will be printed as separations if this checkbox is enabled. If prepress proofing on-screen is needed, check this box. If screen output or final files delivered to an imaging center is the purpose, leave the checkbox disabled.

✦ **Produce blank plates:** If you are screen proofing, separations enable this checkbox. Any blank pages produced in the PDF will also be printed at the service center. You may be charged for blank plates printing so that you'll want to know if a color is identified for a separation where it is not assigned to any data in the file. In all other cases, disable the checkbox.

✦ **Use OPI:** If you want a proof printed to a laser printer, you can check this box and omit images when proofing text. The print time will be much faster when images are omitted. If your service center uses an OPI server, you can elect to omit either TIFF or EPS or both TIFF and EPS files that will be replaced by the server. For OPI server issues, contact your service provider.

✦ **Registration:** A very nice feature with the QuarkXPress method of producing PDFs, registration and crop marks can be printed without exercising any reassignments to page sizes. Quark sees the page size and automatically increases it to accommodate printer's marks in the final PDF. If you have bleeds and want to print to any device, use Registration. The default will be Off. You have two other choices that include Centered and Off Center. Either of the latter two choices will produce registration marks.

✦ **Bleed:** You have three choices for handling bleeds. These include:

  • **Page Items Only:** Any bleed items in the document will be printed as wide as the bleed area within the limits of the output media.

  • **Symmetric:** When Symmetric is selected, the dialog box expands to include a field box where an amount can be user defined. Whatever amount is supplied in the field box will be applied to all four sides of the document page. See Figure 6-72.

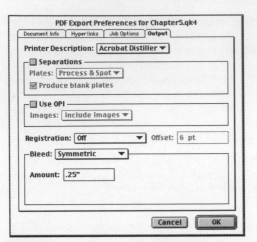

Figure 6-72: The Amount field box is displayed after selecting Symmetric in the Bleed pull-down menu. The amount supplied in this field box will extend the PDF page boundary to include an equal bleed area on all four sides of the document page.

- **Asymmetric:** When Asymmetric is selected, the dialog box expands as in using Symmetric bleeds except four field boxes will be displayed. Whatever amount is supplied in the individual field boxes will be applied to each respective side in the document page (see Figure 6-73).

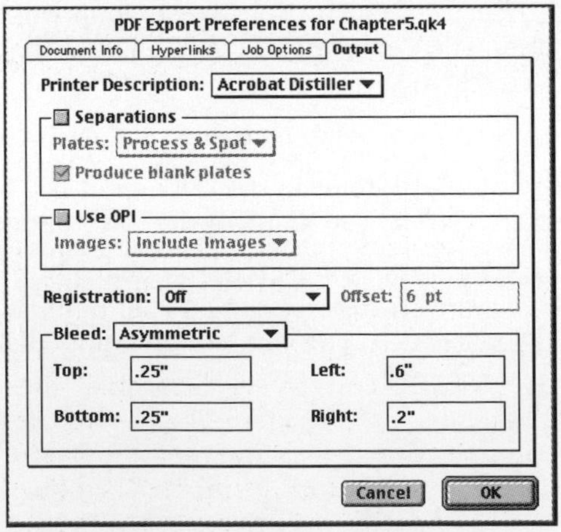

Figure 6-73: Asymmetric bleeds enables you to assign different bleed compensation for each side of the document page.

When completing all the Export Options settings, click the OK button. The file will be printed to PostScript. When the file completes writing to disk, QuarkXPress launches Acrobat Distiller. When Distiller finishes, the program quits and returns you to the QuarkXPress document. In the example illustrated, I created a PDF with bookmarks and index entries. The final PDF displayed in Acrobat 5.0 is shown in Figure 6-74.

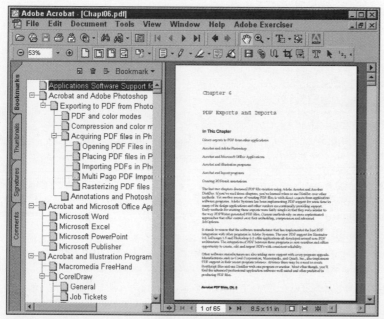

Figure 6-74: When the Navigation pane is opened and the Bookmarks tab is selected, all the entries from my List in QuarkXPress were converted to bookmarks.

Application preferences

All the preferences set up in the PDF Export filter relate to the attributes of the PDF file to be created. Other preferences are established when you install the program. The PDF Export filter must know where Distiller resides so that it can effectively launch Distiller when producing the PDF. When you first install the XTension, QuarkXPress prompts you to locate the Distiller application. If you move Distiller or reinstall another version, you need to let Quark know where the new Distiller application can be found. These settings are not handled by the PDF Export filter. To reassign the Distiller application to work with the filter, Application Preferences need to be changed. When you choose Edit ⇨ Preferences ⇨ Application, the Application Preferences dialog box will appear. In the dialog box are several tabs. The tab denoted as PDF will offer additional preference choices, as shown in Figure 6-75.

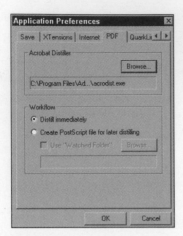

Figure 6-75: PDF Application Preferences enable you to find any newer installations of Distiller on your hard drive and other choices not found with the PDF Export filter.

In the Application Preferences dialog box are some preference choices you don't have available with the PDF Export filter. These include:

✦ **Acrobat Distiller:** At the top of the dialog box within the Acrobat Distiller designation, a browse button appears. Click this button and you can relocate the Distiller application. The directory path of the current assignment appears below the button.

✦ **Workflow:** The area defined as Workflow offers choices in regard to the handling of the distillation. These include:

- **Distill immediately:** This button is the default setting when you install the PDF Export filter. QuarkXPress immediately launches Distiller after completing the writing of the PostScript file.

- **Create PostScript file for later distilling:** If you want to Postpone distillation, select this radio button. This option is similar to what we observed when using PageMaker.

- **Use "Watched Folder":** An item independent of the setting above, you can choose to send the PostScript file to a Watched Folder. If this checkbox is enabled, the PostScript file will be sent to the Watched Folder you designate by selecting the Browse button and navigating to one of Distiller's Watched Folders. Distiller will be auto launched according to the interval determined in the Watched Folder settings.

After making the necessary choices, click the OK button. If QuarkXPress is having trouble locating the Distiller application, you'll need to return to the Application Preferences and reassign the location.

In addition to Application Preferences, Quark also offers selection of preference settings without navigation through the PDF Export dialog box. If you choose Edit ⇨ Preferences, one of the submenu choices will appear for PDF Export. Selecting the preference choices from the menu command offer identical preference choices as discussed earlier when examining the PDF Export filter.

Importing PDFs into QuarkXPress

The PDF Export Filter must be installed in order to import PDFs into QuarkXPress. Acquiring PDFs in a layout in Quark is handled the same way as you import graphics. Click the Rectangle Picture Box Tool from the QuarkXPress toolbox and drag open a picture frame. With the frame selected, choose File ➪ Get Picture. All the PDF documents within a given directory appear available for import. Select a PDF and click Open. The Get Picture dialog box appears, as shown in Figure 6-76.

Figure 6-76: The Get Picture dialog box displays all PDF documents available for importing into QuarkXPress when the PDF Filter is properly installed.

At the bottom-left corner of the dialog box appears a field box for PDF Page. If you want to open a PDF with multiple pages, you can navigate to a page within the document by supplying the respective page number in the field box. QuarkXPress only permits a single PDF page to be imported in the Picture Box. For multiple image placement, you need to create separate Picture Boxes for each imported PDF page. As you supply different page numbers, a thumbnail preview will appear displaying the page contents for the respective page.

Click the Open button when the desired page is in view. QuarkXPress places the PDF page in the Picture Box much the same as any graphic image.

Adobe FrameMaker

Adobe FrameMaker has been the choice for technical documents and publications produced by many publication designers and companies. The user guides you see shipping with all the Adobe software are created in Adobe FrameMaker. The Adobe award winning publications, such as the Classroom in a Book series, are all printed from FrameMaker files. FrameMaker doesn't have the installed user base to match PageMaker or QuarkXPress, but the product does have significance among those who produce substantial publications and technical documents.

FrameMaker handles both an export to PDF in which case Distiller is introduced in the process and importing PDFs. FrameMaker combines many of the features from Microsoft Word, Adobe PageMaker, and QuarkXPress all into a single PDF producer that rivals most other application programs. If you are in the market for a software program for creating long documents, technical manuals, books, or briefs, you can find none better than the easy-to-use feature-rich application of Adobe FrameMaker. For the FrameMaker user, you will be well advised to export documents to PDF for digital imaging and portability. Because FrameMaker exists more often in the commercial publications market, average consumer use is quite limited.

FrameMaker appears to be a simple program when first looking at the user interface, but it offers a robust set of tools that enable you to deliver HTML content, XML tags, and PDF structure to the PDF files exported. In looking at the PDF exports from FrameMaker, you examine structured PDFs and leave the other features for those who may want to visit the program's documentation.

Export to PDF from FrameMaker

Like the other layout applications discussed earlier, FrameMaker supports style sheets created in Microsoft Word. If you import text files created in a word processor, the styles that are imported can be used by FrameMaker and also when exporting to PDF. To create a PDF file from FrameMaker, choose the File ➪ Print command. The Print Document dialog box appears, as shown in Figure 6-77.

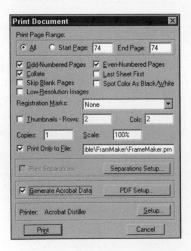

Figure 6-77: FrameMaker creates PDF files when the Print Document dialog box is accessed by choosing File ➪ Print.

In the Print Document dialog box are a number of controls for setting different print attributes similar to other applications discussed earlier. With regard to exporting to PDF, the items of most concern include:

✦ **Print Only to File:** If you want to print the file to disk as a PostScript file, select this checkbox. If the checkbox is deselected, Distiller will be introduced immediately. The file will be printed to disk, distilled, and return you to the FrameMaker document window.

✦ **Generate Acrobat data:** This checkbox needs to be enabled if you want to export the PDF with tags and structure. Disabling the checkbox will produce a PDF without structure.

✦ **PDF Setup:** Clicking the PDF Setup button will open the PDF Setup dialog box where all the structure attributes will be established.

✦ **Printer (Setup):** The Setup button for the Printer item will open the printer driver selected in the Page Setup command accessed through the File menu. If Acrobat Distiller is selected, options for page sizing and PDF Output described earlier in this chapter can be accessed.

The distinctive controls for FrameMaker with respect to exporting PDFs are handled in the PDF Setup dialog box. When you click the button for PDF Setup in the Print Document dialog box, the PDF Setup dialog box opens. Access to the PDF Setup dialog box can also be opened by choosing Format ➪ Document ➪ PDF Setup. PDF Setup appears in a submenu with other options used for optimizing the exported PDF file. Either way that you access the PDF Options dialog box, the settings are the same and they include:

Bookmarks

The first of the settings encountered in the dialog box control bookmarks to be added in the PDF file, as shown in Figure 6-78. Like other PDF producers noted earlier, bookmarks can be established from styles identified in the document. Two lists offer a view of the styles to be included. To move a style, select it in a list and click the respective arrow to move between lists. Below the lists is an option for nesting bookmark levels. You can select a bookmark in the Include Paragraph list and move the level left or right by clicking the chevrons located below the list. Organized levels for parent/child bookmarks can be supplied by successive clicks on the left or right chevron.

Like PageMaker, FrameMaker enables you to create Article threads. The FrameMaker advantage is the ability to use styles for creating articles without a need for defining each article manually just as one has to do with PageMaker. When the checkmark for Articles is enabled, all paragraphs in the FrameMaker document will be supported with Article threads. Two options exist for defining articles according to text within frames or text throughout the document by columns. These choices appear in the pull-down menu adjacent to the Articles checkbox.

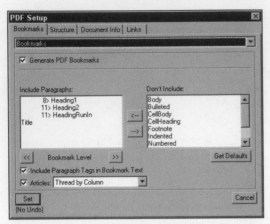

Figure 6-78: The first item displayed in the PDF Setup dialog box provides options for creating bookmarks in the exported PDF file.

Structure

After all the controls for bookmarks and articles have been created, click the Structure tab at the top of the PDF Options dialog box. These settings control the structure to be exported in the PDF, as shown in Figure 6-79.

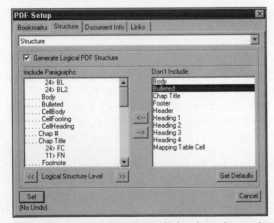

Figure 6-79: The Structure dialog box determines the structure to be exported in the PDF from FrameMaker.

The checkbox needs to be enabled for Generate Logical PDF Structure if the structure is to be created in the PDF. The list boxes below Include Paragraphs enable you to include or exclude styles in the document from which the structure will be developed.

Document Info

Clicking the Document Info tab accesses a separate dialog box for document information. Click this tab to open a dialog box, as shown in Figure 6-80.

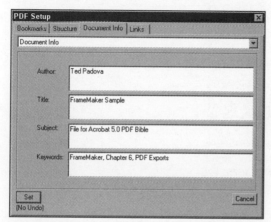

Figure 6-80: FrameMaker can export document information that is supplied in the Document Info dialog box.

Here you can add the Author, Title, Subject, and Keywords fields. These items will be accessible by Acrobat Search after the PDFs have been catalogued with Acrobat Catalog.

Links

The last of the dialog boxes appearing as a tab in the PDF Setup dialog box is used for creating named destinations. Named destinations behave similar to bookmarks in the PDF as I further describe in Chapters 10 and 13. To create named destinations, be certain to enable the checkbox for Create named Destinations for All Paragraphs, as shown in Figure 6-81.

When the last item is selected in the PDF Options, click the Set button to record all the settings made in the dialog boxes. You will be returned to the Print Document dialog box where the Print button, when selected, will invoke printing the file to PostScript. If you had File designated as the output source, the file will be saved to the directory where the FrameMaker document resides. If you set up the PDF Output options for prompting you for a name and destination in the PDF Output options from the Distiller printer driver, a dialog box will appear where the filename and destination can be supplied. A destination folder can also be chosen from the Format ⇨ Document ⇨ Optimize PDF ⇨ Options dialog box.

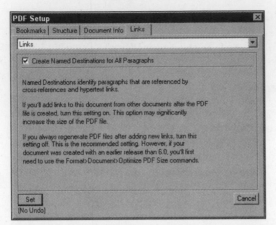

Figure 6-81: FrameMaker enables you to create named destinations to the PDF content exported from FrameMaker.

After the PostScript file has been converted to PDF, open the PDF document in Acrobat and choose Window ➪ Destinations. A floating palette will appear where the destinations can be viewed. To view destinations in the Palette, select the pull-down menu by clicking the down arrow and then select Scan Document or click the broken page icon in the palette. Acrobat will scan the document and list all the named destinations it finds in the palette, as shown in Figure 6-82.

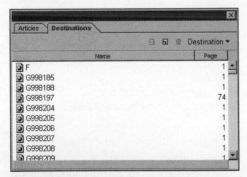

Figure 6-82: Named destinations exported from FrameMaker can be viewed in the Destinations palette by selecting the pull-down menu and choosing Scan Document or by clicking the icon appearing as a broken page at the top of the palette window.

Double-click a destination name in the palette to place the associated destination in the Document pane. Any items that you define with styles in FrameMaker, such as body text, tables, graphs, bullet items and the like are referenced as a destination. If you open the Navigation pane and select the bookmarks tab, from the pop-up menu, you can choose the command for New Bookmark from Structure. Acrobat then creates structured bookmarks from all the structured elements in the PDF. In Figure 6-83, I created bookmarks for an exported FrameMaker document from the PDF structure.

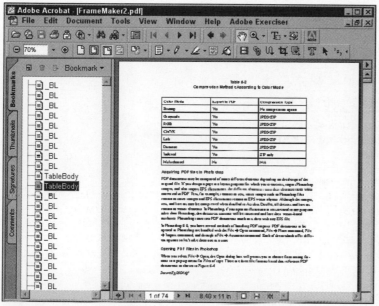

Figure 6-83: Bookmarks can be created from the PDF structure by selecting the pull-down menu from the bookmark pane and choosing New Bookmarks from Structure.

In addition to the named destinations, tags for Accessibility are also created in the PDF document when the PDF structure is exported from FrameMaker.

Importing PDFs in FrameMaker

FrameMaker supports PDF imports just as the other layout programs described earlier. When you import a PDF file into FrameMaker, it can be imported with a text wrap and inserted within the body copy on a page. To import a PDF file, choose File ➪ Import ➪ File. A navigation dialog box opens enabling you to select the destination and filename of the PDF to be imported. If a multiple page PDF is selected, FrameMaker will open a dialog box where pages can be scrolled to select the desired page for import. One nice feature of FrameMaker is all the thumbnail previews are much larger than any other application supporting PDF imports. You can easily examine detail on the PDF pages before importing. When the page in question is imported in FrameMaker, it will appear on the page in the application window. In Figure 6-84, I imported a PDF file created from Cyrillic text.

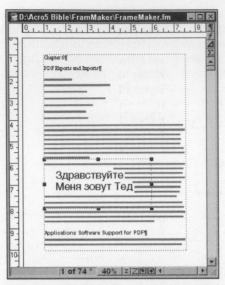

Figure 6-84: PDF files can be imported in FrameMaker with automatic text wraps.

PDFMark

If you're thumbing through the pages ahead wondering when I'm going to finish up this chapter, hold on—there is still more to work through when creating PDF files from various applications. All of what was discussed with regard to layout programs is fine if you are willing to learn one of the applications. In a perfect world, we would all be up to speed on the tools needed to produce documents with ease and clarity. Unfortunately, we don't live in a perfect world, and some programs don't support the many features available with InDesign, PageMaker, QuarkXPress, or FrameMaker.

So what do you do if you're not willing to take advantage of all of PDF export controls of the major layout applications? Fortunately, you have an option. It may not be easy, and you may need to poke around with some programming steps, but just about anything you can do to a PostScript file from programs supporting PostScript can also be accomplished by using a pdfmark annotation.

If you stop and think about it, anything you see as a graphic image on your screen could be created in a text editor by using PostScript programming code. You certainly wouldn't want to create graphics by code. It takes over 185 pages of raw text and over 100,000 characters in PostScript code just to create a page that has the word *text* on it when printed. Imagine what you might have to do just to draw an object, let alone an entire layout?

Fortunately, you don't have to begin editing a PostScript file by starting from scratch. You can supply edits to PostScript code in the form of annotations known as *pdfmark annotations*. A pdfmark operator can be used to identify a TOC entry, add a note to a PDF file, add a bookmark, create a transition, or add almost any kind of element you desire. You can add pdfmark annotations in two ways: You can write the code in a text editor and concatenate two PostScript files, or you can create an EPS file that can be placed on a page to create elements and effects that you want to appear in the PDF file. The EPS file that you place contains the pdfmark annotations needed to produce the desired effect. To see how all this works, first explore editing PostScript code and then look at placing EPS files with pdfmark annotations.

Annotating PostScript Code

Technical information on pdfmark annotations is provided in the Help files contained on your Acrobat Installer CD-ROM. When you install Acrobat and include all of the Help files in the installation, the PDFMARK.PDF document will be included in the Help folder. This document is the PDFMark Reference Manual provided by the Adobe developer team, and it explains how to use pdfmark annotations. For a complete review of pdfmark and the syntax used for adding notes, bookmarks, links, and many other features in PDF files, refer to the technical manual.

To help understand how annotating PostScript code is handled, take a look at adding a note to a PDF document during distillation. When working with Adobe PageMaker, a note can be added to the first page of the PDF when using the Export Adobe PDF command. The note will appear in the PDF in a fixed position on the first page. However, you cannot use this command to change the note position on page 1 or to have a note or several notes appear on pages other than page 1. Furthermore, when using programs such as QuarkXPress, Microsoft Publisher, or other applications, you won't have opportunities to create notes until you add them in Acrobat.

In a PDF workflow environment, you may want to set up files that can automatically create notes when distilling PostScript files with Acrobat Distiller. Whereas document information is limited to some description of the PDF file, notes provide you opportunities for adding descriptions to individual document pages. Furthermore, notes can be customized to display different colors and titles that can be set up to be unique for each individual PDF author. In a workflow environment, you can exercise control over who's adding note information and easily identify the contributors.

After you create a PDF file from a program, such as Adobe PageMaker, QuarkXPress, Microsoft Word, or any other application capable of generating multiple pages, you may want to have a note or several notes added to the PDF file. Notes can be added in Acrobat; however, individual authors need to have Acrobat loaded on their computers and add notes manually on the desired pages. By using pdfmark, you can create a separate PostScript file with the note contents and note color and specify the document pages on which you want the notes to appear. When you open the PDF in an Acrobat viewer, the note(s) will appear as you defined them.

Note attributes

To add a note with pdfmark, you need to be precise about coding the information in the PostScript file that you write, which will be concatenated with the document PostScript file. Several note attributes need to be addressed. Some of these attributes are required and others are optional. Table 6-3 describes the note attributes available for definition with pdfmark. In Table 6-3 several types are associated with the attributes:

✦ **string:** An alphanumeric string of characters. Typically strings include text (for example, the contents of the notes).

✦ **array:** A mathematical expression that consists of numeric values. A quadrant would be composed of four numeric values in an array to define the *x, y* coordinates of the opposite diagonal corners.

✦ **integer:** Always a whole number.

✦ **Boolean:** A conditional item. May be a switch, such as on or off, expressed as *true* for on and *false* for off.

✦ **name:** A specific reference to a procedure or call. Must be expressed as /Name. For example, Page /Next would proceed to the next page in a PDF document.

✦ **Required:** Not among the types already listed. You will find a reference to Required in relation to pdfmark semantics in the technical manual. When Required is indicated, a value for the procedure must be included.

✦ **Optional:** The opposite of Required. If an Optional reference is made, you don't need to include the procedure for the key in question.

	Table 6-3 **Note Attributes**		
Key	**Type**	**Options**	**Syntax/Semantics**
Rect	array	Required	Rect is an array describing the note boundaries beginning from bottom-left corner to top-right corner. Measurement is in points, with the page boundary at the lower-left corner defined as 0, 0 for the *x, y* coordinates. Syntax for the /Rect key is something such as [/Rect 117 195 365 387]. In this example, the lower-left corner of the note is 117 points to the right of the left side of the page and 195 points up from the bottom. The top-right corner of the note is 365 points from the left side and 387 points up from the bottom. The array data must be contained within brackets, as shown in the syntax example.

Key	Type	Options	Syntax/Semantics
Contents	string	Required	The contents string is what you want to appear as the note message. The maximum number of characters that you can include in the note is 65,535. The text string scrolls within the note boundaries. If you want to add paragraph returns, enter \r where the return should appear. An example of the syntax for the contents is /Contents (This is my first note with examples in using pdfmark annotations.) Notice that the text is contained within parentheses.
SrcPg	integer	Optional	By default, notes appear on the first page in the PDF file. Eliminate the SrcPg key, and the note will appear as you define using the Rect and Contents keys. If you have multiple pages, you can choose to place a note on any page in the document. An example of the syntax for SrcPg is /SrcPg 2, which specifies the note is to appear on page 2. When identifying a page in a PDF file, you should be aware all pages begin with page 1. Do not use page 0 as the first page when counting the pages.
Open	Boolean	Optional	By default, all notes appear open. If you want to have a note appear collapsed, you can use the Open key to do so. The syntax for closing a note is /Open false.
Color	array	Optional	Note colors can be determined prior to conversion to PDF. A three-character array is used with the acceptable values of 1 and 0 (zero). Eight total permutations are the color choices. An example of the syntax for the color array is /Color [1 0 0]. Notice that the array values must be contained within brackets.
Title	string	Optional	The title string appears in the title bar for the note. You can add any text up to 65,535 characters. If you want to be practical, you would limit the number of characters to display a short descriptive title. An example of the syntax for the Title key is /Title (My Personal Note). Notice that the text string is included within parentheses.
ModDate	string	Optional	The date can be described in terms of the month, day, year, hour, minute, and second. Any one or all of the above can be included. Unless you have a need for time stamping, use only the year, month, and day dates. Syntax is either yymmdd or yyyymmdd—for example, /ModDate (20100101) would be used to specify January 1, 2010. Notice that the date field is contained within parentheses and no spaces are entered between year, month, and day. When you view the note in an Acrobat viewer, the date stamp will not appear. You need to summarize the notes in the PDF to view the date.

Continued

Table 6-3 *(continued)*			
Key	**Type**	**Options**	**Syntax/Semantics**
SubType	name	Optional	A subtype will commonly not be used with notes. A subtype for something such as a link may look like /View [/xyz *n n n*], where the contents within the bracket is an array describing the view magnification. Another example is /View /Next, which specifies the next page will be viewed when the link button is selected.

Creating a pdfmark annotation

The keys and syntax described in Table 6-3 must be saved in a text file to be distilled by Acrobat Distiller. You can create a pdfmark annotation with a text editor or word processor. If using a word processor, be certain to save the file as text only. You can then combine the text file with the application document that is printed to disk as a PostScript file — just use the RunDirEx.txt file, discussed Chapter 5, to concatenate the two files. To see how all this is accomplished, walk through the steps to produce a note on page 2 in a two-page document.

STEPS: Using pdfmark to Add a Note to a PDF File

1. **Print a document to disk.** Create a two-page layout in an application, such as a layout program or a word processor. After creating the layout, print the file to disk. If using PageMaker and the Export Adobe PDF command, be certain to select the option Prepare PostScript for distilling separately and not the option Distill now. If using QuarkXPress, Microsoft Word, Publisher, or other application, print the file to disk as a PostScript file and save the file for later use.

2. **Add a comment.** Open a text editor and supply a comment line for your file. All comments begin with %. In my example, I use these three comment lines:

   % Custom Note pdfmark annotation

   % Created by Ted Padova

   % Places note on page 2

   Comments are optional. You don't need the comment line, but it will be helpful if you create many different files for pdfmark annotations. Try to use a comment line so that you can return to the file later and know what to expect after distillation.

3. **Define the note boundary.** Your first attempt to create a note and locate it precisely on a page may be awkward. If the coordinates are not supplied properly, your notes may not appear where you expect them. To aid you in the process, try to use a program, such as Adobe Illustrator that can provide you with information about coordinate values for an element created on a page. In my example, I used Illustrator 9.0 to determine where I wanted the note to appear and recorded the coordinates.

Note When recording coordinate values, do not use a rectangle boundary as your assessment device. The top-right corner of the rectangle will be the coordinates from lower left to upper right for the rectangle and not the page. You need to record coordinate values for the lower-left and upper-right corners respective to the page. To determine these values, use rulers and guides in your application program and read the coordinates from an info palette.

When I drew the guidelines in Illustrator, I used the Info palette to determine the coordinates for each x and y position. In Figure 6-85, the x, y position for the lower-left corner of the note can be read in the Info palette.

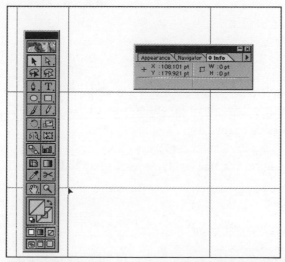

Figure 6-85: When assessing x, y coordinates, do not use elements as a measuring tool; use rulers and guidelines. The x position is measured from the left side of the page, and the y position is measured from the bottom of the page. Here, the x, y position is measured for the first x, y values.

4. **Enter the coordinates in the text file.** After you determine the coordinates for the note position, enter those values for your first line of code. In my example, I entered the following:

   [/Rect 108 200 360 360]

   You must include all the data within brackets [ ].

5. **Enter the note contents.** The next line of code will be the note content you want to appear when the note is open. Add text as you desire. In my example, I added the following line:

```
/Contents (This document was created by Ted Padova
The document was originally a multiple
page QuarkXPress file and
the note was added to page 2.)
```

 Note   All carriage returns used in coding the PostScript file are retained in the note text.

6. **Identify the source page.** If you only have a single-page PDF or you want to use the default placement of the note on page 1, you don't need to use the SrcPg value key. In my example, I decided to place the note on page 2, so I added the following line:

   /SrcPg 2

7. **Opening and closing notes.** If you want to collapse the note, use the Open key value and enter false. If you want to have the note appear open, you use the Open key and enter true. In my example, I used the Open key, as shown here, and entered true so that the note appears open when the note is viewed:

   /Open true

8. **Enter a title for the note.** The Title value key allows you to specify a string of text to appear in the note title bar. In my example, I included the following line:

   /Title (PDFMark Note)

   Be certain all the text to appear in the note title is included within the parentheses.

9. **Enter a color value for the note color.** The note adheres to the defaults set up in the Acrobat viewer unless you make changes, such as choosing another color for the note. To examine the colors available for the note, you can change the array values for the three data fields by toggling 1s and 0s and then distill each change. I wanted to change the note color for my example, so I included the following line:

   /Color [1 0 0]

   These values produced a red note.

10. **Date stamp the note.** Enter a date for a creation date for the note. The date can be viewed when you summarize notes in Acrobat. In my example, I included the following line:

    /ModDate (20001104)

    When the note is viewed as a summary, the date reads November 4, 2000 (11/04/00).

11. **Save the file as text only.** The file must be saved in text format and not as a native word processor file. In my example, I saved my file as note.ps (see Figure 6-86).

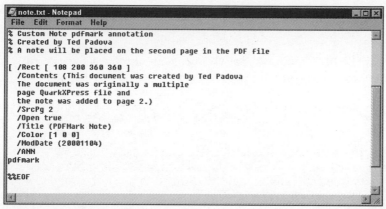

Figure 6-86: The final file is saved as a text-only file from Windows NotePad.

12. **Edit the** `RunDirEx.ps` **file.** Open the `RunDirEx.ps` file from the Acrobat Xtras folder in a text editor and edit it to include the directory path for the files to be distilled in Acrobat Distiller. In my example, I edited the file for the directory path where both my .ps files were saved and left the name at the default — remember, if you name this file with a .ps extension, it will be distilled and add another page to the PDF file. To avoid distilling the `RunDIREx.ps` file, always use an extension that is different from the extensions of the files you are distilling. Figure 6-87 shows the code that I supplied for my directory path and files to be distilled.

Figure 6-87: I included the directory path of the folder where my PostScript files were saved and saved the file as `RunDirEx.txt`.

13. **Distill the `RunDirEx.txt` file.** Open the new `RunDirEx.txt` file in Acrobat Distiller and save the PDF to a directory of your choice. In my example, I opened `RunDirEx.txt` in Acrobat Distiller.

14. **View the PDF in an Acrobat viewer.** In an Acrobat viewer, verify the note appears on the page where you expect it (see Figure 6-88).

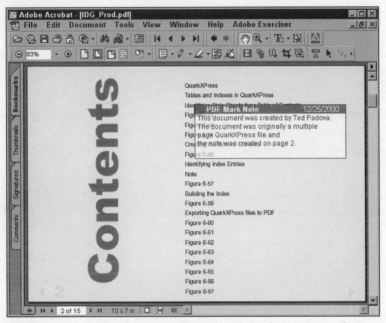

Figure 6-88: I opened my PDF file and navigated to page 2, where the note was successfully added to the page.

Tip   One excellent use of adding a pdfmark annotation to create a note is when producing many different PDF files for distribution. If you want to have identifying information included in all your PDFs, such as name, address, phone, fax, e-mail address, and so on, adding the annotation will save much time in your workflow. After the code has been written and saved to disk, it can be reused an infinite number of times without re-editing.

As a starting point for using pdfmark, you can find a template file installed with Acrobat Distiller. Look in the Acrobat 5.0: Distillr: Xtras (Windows) or Acrobat 5.0: Distiller: Xtras (Macintosh) folder. A file named `PDFMRKEX.PS` is an ASCII text file with instructions and comments set up for creating many different pdfmark annotations. You can copy and paste the desired annotations to a new text file for helping you write the proper code.

Annotating EPS files

The preceding exercise for creating a note for a single PDF document may seem laborious. You could easily open Acrobat and draw a note box, enter the text, and be done with it. However in a workflow situation where many PDF files are created with Acrobat Distiller and common information needs to be supplied in each document, the pdfMark annotation will speed up the workflow. In the last example, if you need a common note on 50, 100, or more files, the procedure explained will save you time.

Automating workflows are not necessarily limited to pdfMark annotations in external code. They can equally be applied to all PostScript documents. If you look at Adobe Illustrator in a text editor, you see nothing more than PostScript text. As such, Illustrator documents can also be edited with pdfMark annotations.

Presume for a moment that you want to have link buttons or instructions applied to pages in a layout program. In creating a button that links to another page, you could place the button on a master page in the layout program and, when clicked in Acrobat, it would navigate as instructed. We do have great opportunities with copying and pasting Form fields in Acrobat, but you can also develop some nice buttons in Illustrator and use them when creating your layouts. To understand the steps involved in creating such links, I use Adobe Illustrator to create a link in the following example and then I show you how to annotate the PostScript file.

STEPS: Creating EPS Links with pdfmark Annotations

1. **Create a link icon.** You can create an illustration anywhere on the Adobe Illustrator document page. After the illustration has been created, draw a box around the illustration. The box you draw will represent the hot spot for the link. When the cursor is moved over the rectangle that you define for the hot spot, the cursor will change to a hand icon with a pointing finger, indicating an active link is present. When you draw the rectangle, be certain to define the element attributes with no stroke and no fill (see Figure 6-89).

Tip

If you work in keyline mode (artwork in Illustrator), you can see the invisible rectangle. Use this mode while drawing the rectangle, which defines the link size.

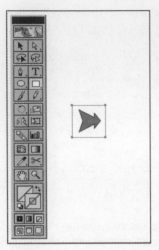

Figure 6-89: I created a brush stroke with one of the Illustrator 8 brush patterns and drew a rectangle around the shape. The rectangle attributes were defined with no stroke and no fill.

   2. **Set the zero point.** Display rulers in your drawing program and move the 0, 0 origin to the lower-left corner of the rectangle that you drew (see Figure 6-90). Again, this is easier if you are viewing the document in a keyline mode.

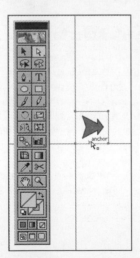

Figure 6-90: In Adobe Illustrator, I chose View ➪ Rulers to display my rulers. From the top-left corner of the ruler well, I dragged the point of origin to the lower-left corner of the invisible rectangle.

Caution

This next step is critically important. If you don't set the ruler origin and leave the default origin at the lower-left corner of your document page, the link won't appear when viewing the document in an Acrobat viewer.

3. **Record the link size.** The rectangle you draw will form the link boundary. Actually, you can make the link boundary larger or smaller than the rectangle, but keep in mind this rectangle is drawn as a guide to help you assess the link size. With the rectangle selected, view the element information. In Adobe Illustrator, the Info palette will display the size. Make a note of the physical size of the rectangle before exiting Illustrator.

> **Note** If your document display is in units of measure other than points, you will need to change the display to points. In Adobe Illustrator, choose File ➪ Document Setup and change the Units option to points.

4. **Save as EPS.** Save your file in EPS format. If using Adobe Illustrator, you can save the file as EPS with the newest compatibility. All versions of Illustrator EPS files can be annotated with pdfmark.

5. **Open the EPS file in a text editor.** All EPS documents are PostScript code and can be edited in the same manner as was the text file created in the pdfmark annotation example earlier. In this example, rather than creating a separate file, I annotate the EPS file exported from the illustration program.

6. **Locate the placement for the pdfmark annotation.** In the EPS document, find the line of code beginning with `%%PageTrailer`. This line of code will appear at the end of the file (see Figure 6-91).

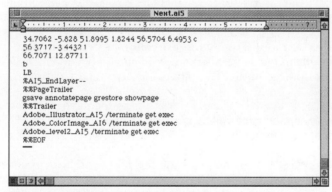

Figure 6-91: At the end of the EPS file, find the line of code beginning with `%%PageTrailer`.

7. **Enter PostScript code for the pdfmark annotation.** Immediately after the line `%%PageTrailer`, I entered the lines of code displayed in Figure 6-92.

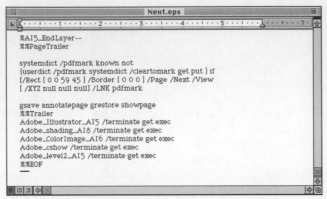

```
                              Next.eps
L    · · · 1 · · · · 2 · · · · 3 · · · · 4 · · · · 5 · · · · · · · · 7 ·

     %AI5_EndLayer--
     %%PageTrailer

     systemdict /pdfmark known not
     {userdict /pdfmark systemdict /cleartomark get put } if
     [/Rect [ 0 0 59 45 ] /Border [ 0 0 0 ] /Page /Next /View
     [ /XYZ null null null] /LNK pdfmark

     gsave annotatepage grestore showpage
     %%Trailer
     Adobe_Illustrator_AI5 /terminate get exec
     Adobe_shading_AI8 /terminate get exec
     Adobe_ColorImage_AI6 /terminate get exec
     Adobe_cshow /terminate get exec
     Adobe_level2_AI5 /terminate get exec
     %%EOF
```

Figure 6-92: With the EPS document open in a word processor, enter the lines of code for the pdfmark annotation as illustrated here.

Note   The /Rect line of code contains the array for the bounding area of the link. These values were recorded when you created the link in your illustration program. In my example, the link rectangle was 59 points wide and 45 points high. Therefore, the array values read 0 0 59 45, where 0 0 is the lower-left corner and 59 45 is the top-right corner of the rectangle. The /Page /Next value keys indicate the page destination for the link. If you want to supply a fixed page number, you can change this line to /Page *n*, where *n* will be the fixed page number.

8. **Save the file as text only.** From your text editor, be certain to save the file as text only. The file still has EPS attributes and can be opened in your illustration program or placed as an EPS graphic in a layout application.

Caution   If you reopen the file in Adobe Illustrator after adding the pdfmark annotation and save it, all the annotated code will be removed from the file. You need to reopen it in a text editor and rewrite the code.

9. **Place the EPS graphic.** You can place the EPS file saved from your text editor in any application that accepts EPS imports. Be certain to place the image and not *open* it in a PostScript editor. If using a layout application, you can place the EPS file on a master page. All subsequent pages in the final PDF document will display the graphic and retain the link attributes. In my example, I placed the EPS file on a PageMaker master page.

10. **Create a PDF document.** If you place the EPS in QuarkXPress, use the PDF Export filter. If using PageMaker, you can either print to disk as a PostScript file or Export the file to PDF.

11. **Test your links.** If all the code you entered was correct, clicking a link will advance you to the next page in an Acrobat viewer. When positioning the cursor over the link, you'll immediately notice the cursor change to a hand with the forefinger pointing upward (see Figure 6-93).

Figure 6-93: Each page in the final PDF file contains a link, which was defined on the master page in the layout application. When positioning the cursor over the graphic, the cursor shape will change, indicating a link is present.

As you may suspect, using pdfmark annotations for EPS links saves you much more time than creating them individually in Acrobat. Even with Form fields and the ability to duplicate links across pages, the design decisions you make while constructing the artwork may be better served by using the method described here. Almost infinite opportunities are available with pdfmark annotations. You can create libraries of buttons and place them in documents when needed for the actions you want to include in your PDF documents. As part of the files available to you with your Acrobat Installer CD-ROM, you will find a folder containing transitions. Transition effects are pdfmark annotations that enable you to create wipes, venetian blind effects, dissolves, and a host of other transition effects for screen viewing. In addition to the transitions, the Distiller:Xtras folder contains the pdfmrkEx.ps file, which provides some samples of different pdfmark annotations for creating document information, cropping specifications, bookmarks, articles, borders, links, and more. The single file contains PostScript code for various pdfmark annotations and comment lines describing each annotation.

Note   As of this writing it has not yet been determined if the transition files that were distributed with the Acrobat 3 installer will be included on the Acrobat 5 installer. If you cannot find the files, log on to my Web site at: `www.west.bet/~ted`. I have a link in my Acrobat Tips pages where the files can be downloaded.

Summary

✦ Adobe Photoshop can export directly to PDF. Photoshop 6 can open single and multiple PDF documents created by any producer and preserve text and vector art when exported to PDF.

✦ Microsoft Office applications, such as Word, Excel, and PowerPoint can export direct to PDF with the PDFMaker macro. Office applications can retain document structure and convert structured elements to bookmarks and links in exported PDFs.

✦ Illustration programs, such as Adobe Illustrator, Macromedia FreeHand, and CorelDraw can export directly to PDF. Adobe Illustrator 9.0 preserves transparency with native data.

✦ Adobe Illustrator can open PDF files and access all elements. Individual elements, such as text and vector objects can have the attributes changed in Illustrator.

✦ PageMaker supports PDF Export and Import through a plug-in available free from the Adobe Web site. PageMaker can create notes, bookmarks on indexes and tables of contents, article threads, and hypertext links as well as exercise control over Distiller's Job Options.

✦ QuarkXPress offers PDF support for importing and exporting PDFs through a free downloadable Quark XTension from their Web site. PDF structure will be preserved in a QuarkXPress export when using the plug-in.

✦ Adobe FrameMaker offers a robust set of controls for exporting and importing PDF files. FrameMaker offers all the features of PageMaker and QuarkXPress and additionally provides named destinations in the exported PDFs.

✦ `RunDirEx.ps` and `RunFilEx.ps` can be used to concatenate a PostScript file containing pdfmark annotations and multiple application document PostScript files.

✦ You can develop pdfmark annotations in independent text files, have them contained within a PostScript or EPS file, or save them as an EPS graphic and placed in an application document. These annotations can add many different features to a PDF document when those features are not supported in the authoring application.

✦   ✦   ✦

The Acrobat Environment

Using Acrobat Preferences

Acrobat is the center of the Adobe Acrobat universe. Distiller
and a few of the plug-ins that used to be executable applications
perform dedicated functions related to their respective duties.
Added to the Acrobat Reader software, these components are
specific to a single task and disciplined to execute duties within
a narrow scope. Acrobat, on the other hand, is the eclectic
workhorse in its capacity to perform many varied tasks, either
through core features or add-ons using additional plug-ins.
Through the addition of many different third-party plug-ins, the
capabilities of Acrobat are continuing to expand. As you begin
exploring Acrobat in this chapter, you first examine the Acrobat
environment and learn about the many different preferences
and document controls that can be customized.

Some preferences for Acrobat are identical to the preferences
in Acrobat Reader. Acrobat adds more to the preference settings, however, and the differences between the Reader and
Acrobat preferences are covered here. If you need to refer to
preference settings not amplified in this chapter, look back to
Chapter 3 for an explanation of preferences that are identical
between the two programs.

General preferences

Preferences in Acrobat, such as Reader, are accessed when
you choose Edit ➪ Preferences. A submenu appears where
several choices for different preference settings can be made.
Depending on installation of additional plug-ins, the number
of menu selections will expand. If no plug-ins are installed that
use preference settings, you'll see on Windows General, Table
Formatted Text, Web Capture, Internet Settings, and DocBox.

The Macintosh Preferences include General, Search, Web Capture, and Internet Settings. For both platforms, the first item is General, where a host of different settings are contained in a single dialog box.

Preferences are covered for Acrobat Reader in Chapters 2 and 3, where preference settings for Accessibility, Display, Forms, Full Screen, Identity, Search, Update, and Web Buy are discussed. All of these items have identical dialog boxes in Acrobat as they do in Reader. The remaining settings either have different options for the same items or additional preferences are unique to Acrobat. When you choose Edit ➪ Preferences ➪ General, the Preferences dialog box opens and the first item, Accessibility, is selected by default. Click the second item to display Batch Processing and the options in the right panel change, as shown in Figure 7-1.

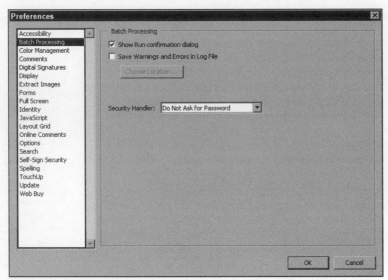

Figure 7-1: The Preferences dialog box contains a list of different items on the left side of the dialog box and the settings for a given selected item are contained on the right side. When Batch Processing is selected in the list, the options are displayed in the right panel.

Batch Processing

A new feature for batch processing documents with a variety of options has been added to Acrobat 5.0. Batch Processing enables you to automate many tasks in Acrobat and apply edits to PDF files stored on your hard drive without opening them individually. (I cover the use of the Batch Processing command in Chapter 9.) The preferences for batch processing set some global conditions and the batch sequences are established when accessing the Edit Batch Sequences command. Preferences include:

✦ **Show Run configuration dialog:** A confirmation dialog box opens before any batch sequence is run.

✦ **Save Warnings and Errors in Log File:** A log file is created to report any errors when a sequence is run. Log files are ASCII text and can be opened in a text editor or word processor. The filename is reported according to name, date and time.

✦ **Choose Location:** The location on your hard drive can be selected for where the log file will be saved by clicking the button to open a navigation dialog box where destination and filename are supplied.

✦ **Security Handler:** The type of security handler can be chosen from the pull-down menu. If Do Not Ask for Password is chosen and the file is secure, a dialog box will appear for password entry for each secure file in the batch sequence.

Color Management

Color Management preferences enable you to manage color viewing for PDF documents on-screen (see Figure 7-2). The color settings options are the same as those discussed with Distiller JobOptions in Chapter 5. Any ICC (International Color Consortium) profiles for devices, such as scanners, color printers, digital cameras, and so on, are available in the pull-down menus if installed in the proper location on your hard drive. See Chapter 5 and the Distiller Color JobOptions for more details on color management.

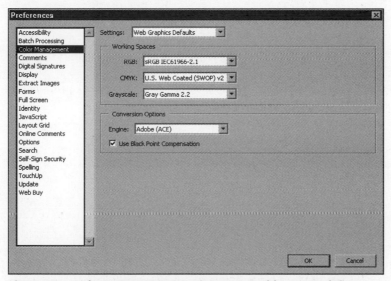

Figure 7-2: Color Management preferences enable you to define color working spaces for viewing images in an Acrobat viewer.

Comments

Formerly called Annotations in Acrobat 4.0, Comments preferences provides settings for viewing comment notes (see Figure 7-3).

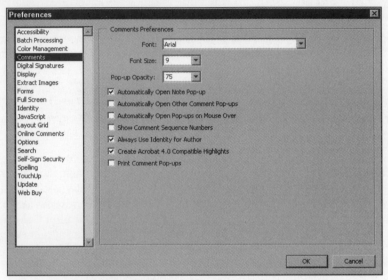

Figure 7-3: Comments include preferences for the display of comments and associated notes.

✦ **Font:** The pull-down menu displays all fonts loaded in your system memory. Any font used by your operating system can be selected to view text in comment notes.

✦ **Font Size:** The point size for the font selected from the Font option can be chosen from the available sizes in the pull-down menu.

✦ **Pop-up Opacity:** Note comment windows can be displayed with transparency. The acceptable range of the opacity is 0 to 100 percent.

✦ **Automatically Open Note Pop-up:** When enabled, the note window opens immediately when the comment is created.

✦ **Automatically Open Other Comment Pop-ups:** All Comment tools except the Note comment and the Text comment have their associated note windows appear immediately after the comment is created.

✦ **Show Comment Tooltips:** If the mouse cursor is positioned over a comment with the note window collapsed, the note window will open. If the cursor is moved away from the comment, the note window will close.

✦ **Show Comment Sequence Numbers:** A sequence number is displayed in the top left corner of the comment icon or note window when enabled. The number scheme will order the comments according to when they were created beginning with the first note created.

✦ **Always Use Identity of Author:** Places the name of the author as identified in the Identity preferences in the comment note title bar.

✦ **Print Comment Pop-ups:** Prints text notes for all comments containing text in the associated notes. When disabled, the comments won't be printed.

Digital signatures

The use of digital signatures offers more than an ability to sign a document. With digital signatures, you can ensure a PDF file has not been changed since you signed it, review the document since you last signed it, and review documents since other people last signed them. If any changes have been applied to a digitally signed PDF, you can ensure authenticity by comparing a current version of the file to those versions when the signatures were added. Chapter 14 covers more about other features available when using digital signatures.

In order to use the digital signatures feature in Acrobat, you must first choose a signature handler. Acrobat offers a default signature handler for basic self-signing purposes. Additional handlers can be added from third-party vendors. After you open the Digital Signatures preferences dialog box, the default handler is displayed, as shown in Figure 7-4.

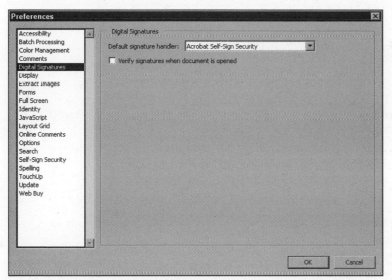

Figure 7-4: The default signature handler is the Acrobat Self-Sign Security handler. Third-party vendors can add additional handlers.

✦ **Default signature handler:** As additional handlers are added to the plug-ins folder, they appear in the pull-down menu. The handler selected here will be used when digital signatures are added to PDF files.

✦ **Verify signatures when document is opened:** When a digitally signed document is opened, the document is automatically verified for authenticity when the checkbox is enabled.

Extract Images

The single item in the Extract Images preferences relates to the minimum size an image must be in order to be extracted with the Extract Images command from the Export menu (see "Extract Images" later in this chapter). Choices from the pull-down menu are within a range of fixed sizes. The default, as shown in Figure 7-5, is 1.00 inches. If left at the default, all images 1-inch square and less would be eliminated when extracting from the PDF. If all images are to be extracted from the PDF, choose No Limit from the pull-down menu choices.

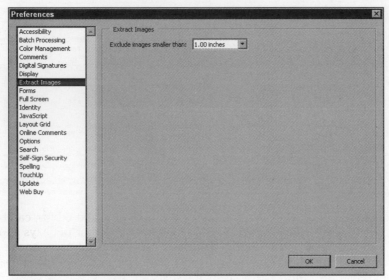

Figure 7-5: Extract Images eliminates images from being extracted according to the value selected in the preferences. The default value of 1-inch means that all images less than one inch will not be extracted when the Extract Images command is selected.

JavaScript

JavaScript, among other things, enables you to turn static forms into dynamic forms. The ability to use a scripting language adds interactivity and automation for forms designers and users. JavaScript can be either turned on or off in the JavaScript preferences, as shown in Figure 7-6.

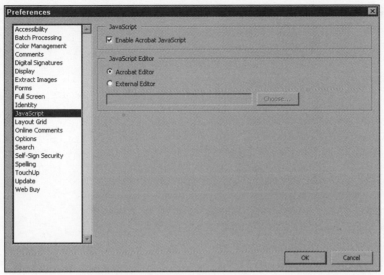

Figure 7-6: The JavaScript preferences controls JavaScript activation in Acrobat.

✦ **Enable Acrobat JavaScript:** When using forms in Acrobat, you want to keep this checkbox enabled. JavaScript usage is only available when enabled.

✦ **Acrobat Editor (Windows):** For JavaScript authors, you can choose to use the Acrobat internal editor where the JavaScript code is created and edited by selecting this checkbox.

✦ **External Editor (Windows):** An external editor, such as a text editor, can be used to write JavaScript code. When more control over larger displays and text formatting is desired, make this selection. When enabled, the Choose button becomes active. Clicking the button enables you to browse your hard drive and select the editor that you want to use.

Layout Grid

Layout grids can be helpful when designing Acrobat forms. The Layout Grid preferences enable you to determine the spacing and color of gridlines. The choices available in the preferences are shown in Figure 7-7.

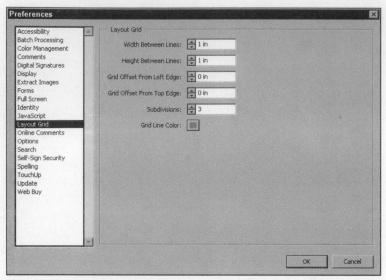

Figure 7-7: Layout Grid enables you to define the spacing for major and minor gridlines and to assign different colors to the gridlines.

✦ **Width Between Lines:** Major gridlines are established in the first and second options appearing in the Grid Layout preferences. The acceptable range is between .03 and 138.88 inches.

✦ **Height Between Lines:** The same as the previous option for the major gridlines. Establishes the width between the height of the lines.

✦ **Grid Offset From Left Edge:** Sets the first major gridline from the left side of the document page.

✦ **Grid Offset From Top Edge:** The grid offset origin is the top left corner of the document page. This setting provides the first gridline from the top of the page.

✦ **Subdivisions:** The previous settings are the major gridlines that appear with a darker shade of color. The subdivisions appear with a lighter shade of color. The number supplied here is the number of lines appearing between the major gridlines.

✦ **Grid Line Color:** The default color is blue. Clicking on the color swatch can change the color. On Windows, a pull-down menu is placed in view where preset or custom colors can be selected. On the Macintosh, the System color palette opens where custom colors can be defined.

Online Comments

One of the great new features with Acrobat 5.0 is collaboration where comments can be shared among workgroups. Chapter 11 covers sharing comments where collaboration on networks and the Web is addressed. Options you have in the preference settings for collaboration appear in Figure 7-8.

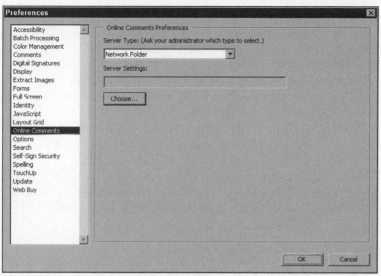

Figure 7-8: For collaboration to be active for sharing comments, the preferences must be properly established.

The pull-down menu below Server Type in the Online Comments dialog box provides several options for choosing a server. As explained in Chapter 11, all collaboration is handled through a Web browser. The connection types that can be used with collaboration include:

✦ **Database (Windows):** A database server can be used for collaboration. The server name and database as well as the protocols require setup by your network administrator.

✦ **Network Folder:** Different Acrobat users can share comments across networks. To share comments on a network, a Network Folder needs to be identified. When the item is selected, the Choose button enables you to navigate the network hard drive to select the shared folder. Network comments require viewing and editing within a Web browser, even though they are not hosted on a Web server.

✦ **None:** Online comments are submitted to a database or repository when uploading according to the connection type. These comments are delivered to the network folder, database, Web discussions or WebDAV folder according to the respective choices from the menu selections. Selecting None will not store the comments in a folder or database.

✦ **Web Discussions (Windows):** Comments can be shared online through the Internet. When using a Web Server, select this option and define the URL where the comments will be shared in the Server Settings dialog box.

✦ **Web DAV:** Web DAV servers can be used to share comments. If you know the server is a Web DAV server, select this option and supply the Server Settings information in the field box.

Options

A single item differs between Acrobat and Reader in the Options dialog box:

✦ **Save as Optimized for Fast Web View:** When using the File ➪ Save As command, Acrobat saves files optimized when the checkbox is enabled. Users of earlier versions of Acrobat will remember the Optimize option was contained in the Save As dialog box. This option no longer exists in this dialog box, as I explain later in this chapter. For optimization of PDFs, be certain to keep this checkbox enabled.

Self-Sign Security

The Self-Sign Security preferences enable you to encapsulate your signature in a format standardized by most security handlers. Two items are available in the Self-Sign Security preferences dialog box, as shown in Figure 7-9.

When the checkbox is enabled, the PKCS#7 format is used to encapsulate your signature. This setting offers a standard format easily recognized by others using different handlers. It is recommended that you enable the checkbox and use it as a default. The second checkbox is used to ignore expiration dates when signatures are verified.

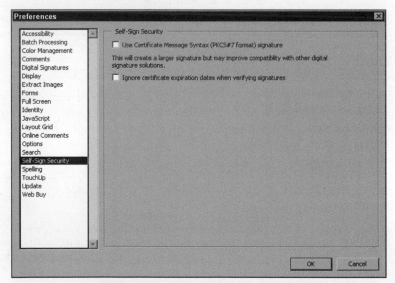

Figure 7-9: Selecting the first item available in the Self-Sign Security dialog box uses a syntax standardized by common security handlers.

Spelling

Spell checking is limited to comment notes and form fields created in Acrobat. Spell checking can't be used for checking text within the PDF when it was created. Options for spell checking appear in Figure 7-10.

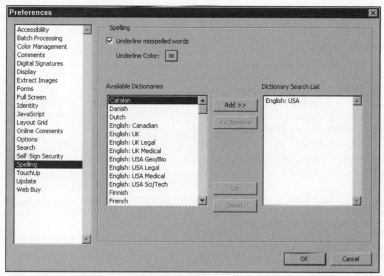

Figure 7-10: Spell checking can be performed on comment text notes and form fields only. Checking body text in the PDF is not supported.

✦ **Underline misspelled words:** All words found with spelling errors as compared to the installed dictionaries are underlined. With notes and form fields, the spell checking can be dynamic — as you type, the errors are displayed with underlines below misspelled words.

✦ **Underline Color:** The same color options appear when the swatch is selected as those color choices discussed previously. Click the swatch to select a color that you want to appear as the underline color when the checkbox above is enabled.

✦ **Available Dictionaries:** All the language support installed with Acrobat appears in a list. By default, the default language used is the only dictionary used for spell checking. For other language dictionaries to be used, find the language desired in the list on the left side of the dialog box. Select the dictionary and click the Add button to add it to the Dictionary Search List. The Up and Down arrows in the dialog box enable you to select which dictionary order is used first during a spell check. To remove a dictionary from the Dictionary Search List, select it and click the Remove button. At least one dictionary must be present in the Dictionary Search List. If a single item is listed, the Remove button is inactive.

TouchUp

The TouchUp preferences enable you to select external editors for raster image, vector image objects, and text blocks. Upon installation, Acrobat finds the most recent version of Adobe Photoshop and Adobe Illustrator and selects them as the default editors. Clicking the buttons, as shown in Figure 7-11, can change these default editors.

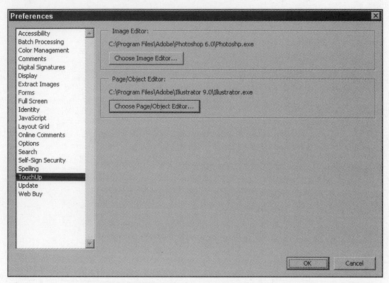

Figure 7-11: The TouchUp preferences enable you to select an image editor and object editor as tools to be used for updating the respective file types in a PDF. The Choose buttons enable navigation to select external editors.

✦ **Choose Image Editor:** A raster image editor is used for this option. Adobe Photoshop is the default. If using another editor, be certain Acrobat supports it as an acceptable external editor. To select a different editor, click the Choose button. A dialog box opens where you can navigate your hard drive and select the editor of choice.

✦ **Choose Page/Object Editor:** Page editors enable you to edit text blocks. When choosing to edit a text block, the entire text body will be placed in the external editor and can span many PDF pages. The object editor enables you to edit vector artwork. Any editors selected for this option must also comply with acceptable editors of Acrobat.

Chapter 8, where I discuss using the TouchUp tools, covers additional configuration for external editors and launching them.

Table/Formatted Text preferences (Windows)

A second selection appearing in the Preferences submenu offers settings for table formatted text in a PDF document. This option is only available to Windows users. When you choose Edit ➪ Preferences ➪ Table/Formatted Text, the dialog box appearing in Figure 7-12 opens.

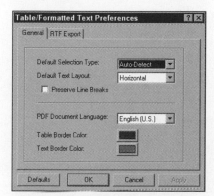

Figure 7-12: You access the Table/ Formatted Text Preferences by selecting the second submenu item from the Preferences menu on Windows only.

Table/Formatted Text Preferences determine how table data is exported from PDF documents for inclusion in word processors or spreadsheet applications. The preference settings include:

✦ **Default Selection Type:** Three choices are available from the pull-down menu. Choose Auto-Detect to determine data formatting automatically. The Auto-Detect option makes a choice for the data to be interpreted as text or as a table. Text is the second item and interprets all the data as text. The final selection interprets the data as a table whereas all table formatting is preserved.

✦ **Default Text Layout:** Two choices exist for the layout interpretation. Horizontal lays out Roman text in a horizontal format much like you view the table in Acrobat. Vertical lays out text created from Japanese fonts in a vertical format.

✦ **Preserve Line Breaks:** Original line breaks used in tables are preserved when enabled. Deselecting the checkbox ignores the original breaks.

✦ **PDF Document Language:** Four choices exist for specifying the language used when the table data was created. The options are English, French, German, and Japanese.

✦ **Table Border Color:** A keyline border is created around the table. Click the swatch to set a color other than the default displayed.

✦ **Text Border Color:** Within each cell appears a cell border. This option enables you to define the color to be used for the keylines around each cell.

The Table/Formatted Text Preferences includes a second set of options for RTF (Rich Text Format) exported data. Click the RTF tab to open the dialog box where these settings are defined, as shown in Figure 7-13.

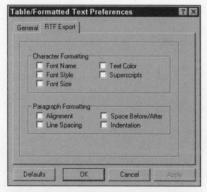

Figure 7-13: The RTF Export dialog box offers settings for how RTF formatted text is exported from tables.

✦ **Character Formatting:** The types of formatting listed in the checkboxes are preserved in the exported data when enabled.

✦ **Paragraph Formatting:** All items enabled with the checkmarks preserve the data as it was defined in the table.

Web Capture preferences

The next item available from choices in the Preferences submenu is for Web Capture preferences and the preference choice is available to both Windows and Macintosh users. For more detail on Web Capture and the preferences, see Chapter 4 where they are discussed at length. The preference settings in the Web Capture preferences are identical to the options settings that are covered in Chapter 4.

Internet Settings preferences

The Internet Settings Preferences need to be properly configured in order to use Web Buy. When Acrobat is first installed, you may have to visit this dialog box before you can obtain any PDFs through the Web Buy feature. To configure your Internet settings choose Edit ➪ Preferences ➪ Internet Settings. Depending on the platform you use, the dialog boxes will appear differently. In Windows, the dialog box displayed is the same dialog box used when configuring Microsoft Internet Explorer and choosing the Internet Options for your Windows Internet configuration, as shown in Figure 7-14. On the Macintosh, a dialog box appears, as shown in Figure 7-15.

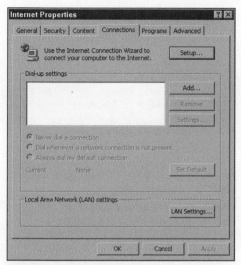

Figure 7-14: On Windows, choosing Edit ⇨ Preferences ⇨ Internet Settings opens the Internet Properties dialog box.

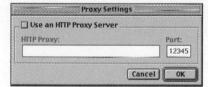

Figure 7-15: On the Macintosh, the Internet Settings preferences open the Proxy Settings dialog box.

Before attempting to change any settings, be certain your current Internet configuration cannot access Web Buy. You may have your configuration properly established to use all the Acrobat Internet access without any further configuration.

Those who work in an enterprise environment need to supply Proxy settings for access to Web Buy. Specifics on the configuration in these environments need to be supplied by your network administrator, Internet Services Provider (ISP), or Webmaster.

On Windows, if your Internet configuration is not handled by the Internet Settings in Acrobat, you need to create your configuration in Microsoft Internet Explorer (IE) through the Internet Properties dialog box displayed in Figure 7-14 for access to the Internet. You can change your Web browser, but only after you first set up your configuration in Internet Explorer. If you're using an earlier version of Microsoft IE and you don't have access to Internet Properties, you'll need to upgrade to a more recent version.

Note   For Windows users not involved in an enterprise environment, be certain to disable the Use proxy server item in the Microsoft Internet Explorer configuration dialog box. When you choose Tools ⇨ Internet Options, a dialog box appears for configuring Explorer. Click the Connections tab and select the LAN Settings button. A dialog box opens for the Local Area Network (LAN) Settings. Be certain to deselect Use a proxy server unless instructed by your ISP or Network Administrator. Enabling this checkbox keeps you on a local server and denies access to an Internet gateway.

DocBox preferences (Windows)

A plug-in from InterTrust is installed with Acrobat used for identifying hardware components where encryption will be retrieved from hardware serial numbers. In the DocBox preferences, you can choose what devices are used and a location for stored PDFs acquired from files downloaded from servers where the encryption method is used. When you choose Edit ⇨ Preferences ⇨ DocBox, the dialog box appearing in Figure 7-16 opens.

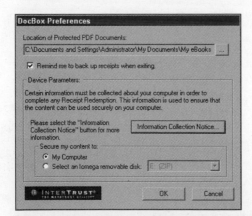

Figure 7-16: DocBox enables you to select what hardware devices are used for certain encrypted PDFs and select a location on your computer where the PDFs are stored.

In the dialog box, click the ellipsis (far top right side of the dialog) to open a navigation dialog box. From this dialog box, you determine where your stored PDFs will be located. If changing directories for stored files, you can revisit the dialog box and select a new folder.

The checkbox for Remind me to back up receipts when exiting opens a warning dialog box as a reminder for backing up receipts obtained from acquired content. The backup would typically be made to an external drive or media cartridge.

The bottom of the dialog box contains two radio buttons used for selecting the hardware components where the content will be secured. The My Computer selection uploads your Central Processing Unit (CPU) serial number to a fulfillment server that provides rights for accessing encrypted content. If you have an external media hardware device attached to your computer, the media cartridge serial number can be uploaded to the fulfillment server.

PDF Document Control

Whereas changes to preferences affect the Acrobat environment globally (that is, any PDF file you open after making various attribute changes will display those changes), document information is document specific. Many of the items available within the Document Properties submenu are informational, but some can be changed. Changes you make in the dialog boxes appearing from the submenu after choosing File ⇨ Document Properties can be saved with the PDF file. Subsequently opening the PDF document in an Acrobat viewer will display the PDF file with new defaults you created.

General

The first item in the Document Properties submenu is the Document Summary (see Figure 7-17). As mentioned in the discussion of Acrobat Reader preferences in Chapter 3, Document Summary fields for Title, Subject, Author, and Keywords cannot be changed in Reader. Because you can't save an edited PDF file from Reader, there is no need to make these fields editable. In Acrobat, the first four fields can be user-supplied and saved with the file. Remember, you can invoke searches on any of the field data in this dialog box (as first detailed in Chapter 2). Searches require building an index, which is covered in Chapter 15.

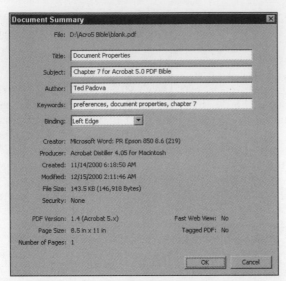

Figure 7-17: The Document Summary dialog box contains document information that can be supplied by the user in Acrobat. All changes in this dialog box can be saved and searched using Acrobat Search.

Document information can be supplied in many ways when PDF files are first created. You can enter data in the four fields with some PDF producer applications as discussed in Chapter 6, supply data with direct PDF exports from many programs, and even supply document information using pdfmark as covered in Chapter 6.

In some instances, you won't have an opportunity to enter document information when distilling PostScript files unless pdfmark is used. This information can't be supplied with the current version of Distiller. If you use programs without direct PDF export options and create PDF files by printing a PostScript file to disk and distilling the PostScript file, you'll need to add document information in Acrobat. If you use pdfmark annotations when distilling PostScript files, the data can be supplied at the time of distillation.

Open

When you save a PDF document, you can also save any changes to various attributes that specify how you want the PDF file to appear when viewed in an Acrobat viewer. The Document Open Options dialog box, accessed by choosing File ➪ Document Properties ➪ Open Options and shown in Figure 7-18, contains many different viewing parameters that can be changed:

Supplying Document Information in a PDF Workflow

If you use programs where document information can't be supplied at the time the PostScript file is created, you are best served by using pdfmark to hand code the information. Your workflow will move along faster when you can easily copy and paste redundant information to set up new PostScript code for the document information fields. The advantage of using pdfmark is it eliminates the need to resave the PDF from Acrobat, which alone can save quite a bit of time. The precise coding for supplying all document information acceptable for PDF files is illustrated here:

✦ `/Title (Acrobat PDF Document)`

✦ `/Author (Your Name)`

✦ `/Subject (This is a test document)`

✦ `/Keywords (author, title, subject, keywords, pdfmark)`

✦ `/Creator (PostScript code programmed)`

✦ `/ModificationDate (D:20000101184502)`

✦ `/DOCINFO`

✦ `pdfmark`

The preceding date field will result in January 1, 2000 at 6:45:02 p.m. Any of these fields can be eliminated. For example, if you want to use the system clock for time and date stamping, you can eliminate the `/ModificationDate` value. After coding the preceding information in a text editor, save the file as text only. Use the `RunDirEx.ps` file to concatenate the application document PostScript file and this file. When distilled with Acrobat Distiller, the information appears after you choose File ➪ Document Properties ➪ General.

✦ **Initial View:** The radio buttons on the left side of the Initial View section enable you to specify what appears on-screen when you initially open a PDF file. The Page Only option displays the open PDF document without bookmarks or thumbnails. The options Bookmarks and Page, and Thumbnails and Page display the PDF file with either bookmarks or thumbnails opened respectively in the Navigation pane. When you select one of these options and save the PDF document, the new display takes effect every time the PDF file is opened in an Acrobat viewer. This section also gives you the following choices for your initial view:

 • **Page Number:** The document opens on the page specified in the field box. The default is page 1 or the first page in the document. Any other page can be displayed as a new default by supplying a page number here.

 • **Magnification:** Magnification options are selected from the pull-down menu and correspond to those viewing options discussed back in Chapter 2.

- **Page Layout:** The Page Layout pull-down menu provides choices for Single Page, Continuous, and Continuous — Facing Pages (also discussed in Chapter 2). The default is Single Page view.

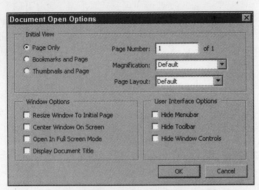

Figure 7-18: The Document Open Options dialog box enables you to establish viewing parameters that can be saved with the PDF document that set new viewing defaults when the file is opened in an Acrobat viewer.

✦ **Window Options:** Notice the options provided in this part of the dialog box appear beside checkboxes instead of radio buttons. Unlike a set of radio button options, which allow you to specify only one option in that set, you can enable any or all of the following options by clicking their respective checkboxes. If none of the options have been enabled, the PDF file will open at the default view with the Acrobat viewer window occupying a full screen.

- **Resize Window to Initial Page:** When you set a view, the contents of the PDF document is displayed in the Document pane and that pane is sized to fit the document. If, for example, you set the magnification to 50%, the document will be viewed at 50 percent and the Acrobat window will be sized down to fit around the page.

- **Center Window on Screen:** An image that is smaller than full screen will be centered on your monitor. Using the preceding example, the 50 percent window appears centered on-screen.

- **Open in Full Screen Mode:** Regardless of what you check in the other selections, the PDF file will open in Full Screen mode without menus or tools exposed. To bail out of this mode, press the Esc key or Control/Command + L.

✦ **User Interface Options:** Once again, the checkboxes for these options enable you to select one or more for combined effects. If you want to hide the Menubar, Toolbar, and Window Controls, enable all three checkboxes. You may want to create a PDF document for screen viewing by including all the navigational buttons within that PDF document. If you want to have the end user use buttons that you created and not the tools on the Toolbar, you may elect to have the Toolbar hidden upon opening the document in an Acrobat viewer.

The end result of enabling the various user interface options should not be confused with what you get in Full Screen mode. When the Menubar, Command bar, and Window Controls are hidden, you won't see the same view as when using Full Screen mode. The background color for the viewer window does not change as it does when viewing in Full Screen mode. If you enable the Hide Menubar option and save your PDF file, you won't have access to the menus with the mouse. You'll need to use keyboard modifiers when available. If you want to disable the Hide Menubar option, you must remember to use the F9 key to bring back the Menubar. After the Menubar has returned, you can choose File ⇨ Document Properties ⇨ Open to disable the option.

Fonts

The options for the Fonts in the Document Properties submenu are the same in Acrobat as they are in Acrobat Reader (refer back to Chapter 3 for specifics). Acrobat also offers you the same options for viewing font names, as discussed in Chapter 2. Users of earlier versions of Acrobat will notice that Fonts and Security has been changed only to Fonts in this submenu item. Security in Acrobat 5.0 is now handled under a separate command in the File menu, as I explain later in this chapter.

Trapping Key

The prepress preferences available through the Trapping Key dialog box are informational and permit you to inform imaging personnel whether prepress controls related to trapping are contained in a PDF file (see Figure 7-19).

✦ **Yes:** Informs anyone opening the PDF that trapping has been applied to the file. Trapping may be applied to the PostScript file prior to distillation or trapping controls may have been used in authoring applications.

✦ **No:** Informs the user that no trapping has been applied to the PDF.

✦ **Unknown:** The default setting is Unknown, which implies the PDF author is not certain whether trapping has been applied to the PDF document. If you are in doubt, always keep this setting at Unknown. Only use the No setting if you are the author of the application document and the PDF file and you are certain these controls have not been applied to the PDF.

Figure 7-19: The Prepress Options dialog box offers selections for supplying service centers information on trapping.

Index

The Index setting enables you to identify an index file for an open PDF file. After you associate an index with an open PDF document, you won't need to load the index in the Acrobat Search Window, as was discussed in Chapter 2. The index associated with your PDF document is volatile and is only available during a given Acrobat viewer session. When you quit the Acrobat viewer and reopen the file at a later time, you need to once again reassign the index with the open document. However, if you identify an index and then save your PDF file in Acrobat, the index file will be associated with that PDF file. In this regard, the index file won't need to be loaded in Acrobat Search whenever the PDF is opened.

By default, no index file is associated with a given PDF document at the time it was created. When you choose File ⇨ Document Properties ⇨ Index, the Select Index dialog box appears, as shown in Figure 7-20.

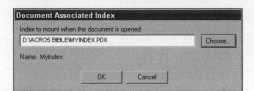

Figure 7-20: By default, no index file is associated with a PDF file, as indicated by the Document Associated Index dialog box shown here.

In the Document Associated Index dialog box, notice a button labeled Choose. When selected, a navigation dialog box opens. You can search your hard drive or network server to locate the index to be assigned to the document.

Index filenames default to .pdx when created with Acrobat Catalog. After you navigate to the directory and find the .pdx file you want to use with the open PDF document, select it and click the Open button. After clicking Open, you are returned to the Document Associated Index dialog box, which now displays the index filename and directory path for the index that you selected. Figure 7-20 displays the Document Associated Index dialog box after an index is selected.

Document Metadata

Document Metadata is embedded in PDF files. You can access metadata from legacy files as well as PDFs compatible with Acrobat 5.0. Metadata is the structural information of the document properties and is reported in XML (Extensible Markup Language) syntax when viewed in the Document Metadata preferences dialog box. When you choose File ⇨ Document Properties ⇨ Document Metadata, the Document Metadata dialog box displays the XML code according to *schema*, all the metadata contained in the document properties. The default view display each schema with the data visible, as shown in Figure 7-21. Clicking the down pointing arrow adjacent to the left side of the schema heading can collapse the information associated with each schema.

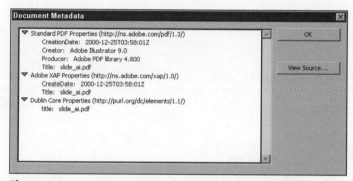

Figure 7-21: Document Metadata is displayed in a dialog box in XML code according to schema.

Because the metadata is contained in XML format, it can be extended and modified by using third party plug-ins. Editing code is simplified through copying and pasting the code. If you want to copy the code in a schema, select one of the headings in the Document Metadata dialog box and click the View Source button. The Metadata: Source View dialog box opens. In this dialog box, you can drag the cursor up or down to select the code, as shown in Figure 7-22 or press Control/Command + A to select all the code. On the Macintosh, you need to first click the mouse button in the Metadata: Source View dialog box, and then press Command + A to select all.

Figure 7-22: You can select the XML code in the Metadata: Source View dialog box by dragging the cursor up or down the window or pressing Control/Command + A to select all the code within a given schema.

After selecting the desired code, press Control/Command + C to copy it to the clipboard. If you view the clipboard, you should see the code appear in the clipboard contents, as shown in Figure 7-23. After it's on the clipboard, the code can then be pasted into an editor where you write your XML routines.

Figure 7-23: The XML code from the Metadata: Source View dialog box is copied by pressing Control/Command + C. After the Clipboard Viewer (Windows) is opened, the copied code appears within the clipboard window. After it's on the clipboard, the code can be pasted in an XML editor. The same results appear in the Macintosh clipboard after returning to the Finder and choosing Edit ➪ Show Clipboard.

Base URL

The Base URL (Uniform Resource Locator) feature is designed to make it easy to manage links to the World Wide Web. If URLs to a given site are created in a PDF file, each Web link needs the complete URL to access the respective Web page. The syntax needs to include: `http://www.mycompany.com/products.html`. In this example, if you supply: `http://www.mycompany.com/` in the base URL, then the Web link can be set up to include only `products.html`. In essence, Acrobat appends the name you specify on a Web link to the Base URL. To specify a Base URL, choose File ➪ Document Properties ➪ Base URL.

The complete URL address needs to be identified in the Document Base URL dialog box, as shown in Figure 7-24. Before you exit the file, be certain to save the updated changes. When creating links to the Web, you especially need to optimize your PDF files before uploading to a server. More details on the Web and Acrobat files are presented in Chapter 11.

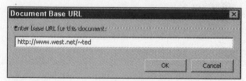

Figure 7-24: The Base URL is used to make it easy to manage hypertext links to the World Wide Web. When entering a URL, be certain to include the full URL information.

Tip When distributing PDF files on CD-ROM, you can enter the Base URL for your company in the Document Base URL dialog box. As you move through pages in the PDF file, add just the HTML filenames and path below the root of your Web address and create World Wide Web links with the Link tool. When the PDF file is saved, the Base URL is saved with the document.

Saving Files from Acrobat

Acrobat 5.0 has introduced support for different file format exports. These supports are all handled in the Save As dialog box. Now in Acrobat 5.0, you can save PDF files in many supported image formats, EPS, PostScript, as well as PDF. When you choose File ➪ Save As, the Save As dialog box opens, as shown in Figure 7-25 in Windows. Users of previous versions of Acrobat will immediately notice the absence of the Optimize checkbox. When you save files from Acrobat, optimization is now determined in the Preferences dialog box as discussed earlier in this chapter.

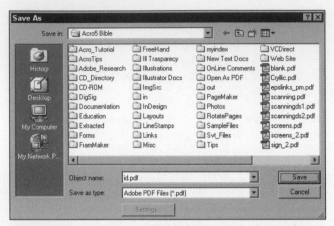

Figure 7-25: The Save As dialog box appears in Windows with a Settings button used to assign attributes for different file types.

File formats are accessible by choosing the Save as type (Windows) or Format (Macintosh) pull-down menu in the Save As dialog box. Click the down arrow (Windows) or up/down arrows (Macintosh) to open the pull-down menu and select the option for the file format desired. After the format is chosen, if different settings can be applied to the saved file, the Settings button becomes active.

Saving as Adobe PDF

Acrobat PDF files saved as PDF display the Settings button grayed out in the Save As dialog box. No settings can be applied to the PDF. Optimization and security features that appeared in the Save As dialog box in earlier versions of Acrobat are handled in other properties dialog boxes. The Save As dialog box may be used for saving a duplicate copy after providing another name in the Object name field (Windows) or Name field (Macintosh). If the file was not optimized, you can enable optimization in the preferences and select Save As to rewrite the file.

Saving as EPS

In earlier versions of Acrobat the Export submenu contained a command for exporting in Encapsulated PostScript format. Now in Acrobat 5.0, EPS files are created from PDFs by selecting the Save As command. After you select the EPS format, the Settings button becomes active. Clicking the Settings button opens the Encapsulated PostScript dialog box, as shown in Figure 7-26.

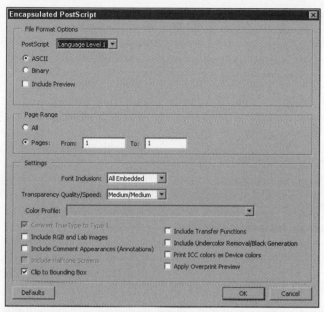

Figure 7-26: When selecting EPS as the format and clicking the Settings button, the Encapsulated PostScript dialog box opens, as shown here in Windows where different file attributes can be assigned.

When saving files in EPS format, you can select a number of settings for various attributes in the resultant file. These include:

✦ **PostScript:** The PostScript level can be selected from the pop-up menu. Choices for Language Level 1, Language Level 2, and Language Level 3 are among the menu options.

✦ **ASCII:** ASCII Encoding for Language Level 1 PostScript can be selected. If using other than PostScript Level I, select Binary encoding.

If exporting PDF files for importing into illustration programs or placing in layout programs for color separating or printing, use Language Level 1 and ASCII encoding. Higher PostScript levels and Binary encoding often return an error when attempting to open or place EPS files exported from Acrobat.

✦ **Binary:** When using Language Level 2 or Language Level 3, select Binary for the encoding method.

✦ **Include Preview:** A screen preview is exported with the EPS file when enabled. Failure to include the preview will display a gray box when the EPS is placed in another program. The file may print fine, but the preview will not display the image. On Windows, a single choice is available. On the Macintosh, you have choices for a PICT or TIFF preview.

Macintosh users who want to port EPS files from Mac OS to Windows should include a TIFF preview. Saving EPS files from Acrobat with PICT previews appear as gray boxes without the image previews when placing the EPS files in other applications. When using the TIFF options, the image displays with complete integrity.

✦ **Page Range:** Multiple page PDFs can have one, several, or all pages saved as individual EPS files. The page range for the pages to be saved as EPS is supplied in the field boxes.

✦ **Font Inclusion:** Choices for font embedding include None, All Embedded, and All. Preserving embedded fonts can be obtained by selecting All Embedded. If fonts are not embedded in the PDF, they can be embedded in the EPS file by selecting All. To embed fonts not embedded in the PDF, you must have the fonts loaded in your system memory.

✦ **Transparency Quality/Speed:** Five choices appear for quality performance similar to the JPEG compression levels discussed in Chapter 5. In regard to EPS files, any transparency used with programs, such as Illustrator 9.0 or Photoshop 6.0, appear with better quality when making the higher quality selections, but screen redraws are slower as quality is increased.

✦ **Color Profile:** From the pull-down menu, a color profile can be selected from the installed profiles in your system. If using a CMS, choose the desired profile. If profile management is not to be used, select Same As Source (No Color Management).

✦ **Convert TrueType to Type 1:** Any TrueType fonts used in the PDF will be converted to Type 1 fonts. If no TrueType fonts are contained in the PDF, the checkbox won't be active.

✦ **Include RGB and Lab Images:** When enabled these color modes will be included along with CMYK images. Failure to check the box results in an elimination of images in the EPS file for these color modes.

✦ **Include Comments:** If comments are included in the PDF, they are exported in the EPS file. In order to review any comments, an application acquiring the EPS file must be capable of handling comments.

✦ **Include Halftone Screens:** If halftone information was preserved in the PDF file, it is included in the exported EPS. If no halftone information is contained in the PDF, the checkbox remains inactive.

✦ **Clip to Bounding Box:** The Bounding Box is the area that includes all the page data without regard to the page size. If selecting this option, the EPS file will be exported at a size equal to the page data. When disabled, the page size will be included in the EPS.

✦ **Include Transfer Functions:** If Transfer Functions were included and pre-served in the PDF, they will be exported in the EPS when the file is saved. The same results also apply to Include Undercolor Removal, and Apply Overprint Previews.

✦ **Print ICC Colors as Device colors:** As the name suggests, ICC profiles embed-ded in the document print as Device colors.

Saving as JPEG

PDF files can be saved in several image formats, the first of which appears as JPEG from the file format options in the Save As dialog box. Saving PDF files as JPEG offers several options for file compression in the JPEG Options dialog box when opened from the Settings option, as described previously. Figure 7-27 displays JPEG Options.

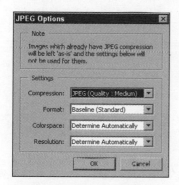

Figure 7-27: When selecting JPEG as the format and clicking the Settings button, the JPEG Options dialog box opens where compression and color information can be supplied.

Settings for JPEG exports include:

✦ **Compression:** The same compression options used in Distiller's JobOptions are available. The five settings range from JPEG (Quality: Minimum) to JPEG (Quality: Maximum).

✦ **Format:** Format options include Standard and Optimized Baseline as you find equal to the same options available in Adobe Photoshop. In addition, you have options for exporting as progressive JPEGs used for display in Web browsers.

✦ **Colorspace:** Files can be stripped of color if selecting the Grayscale option from the pull-down menu. Selecting the Color option preserves color contained in the image. Determine Automatically preserves all color and grayscale images. Unless any color conversion is desired, leave the default at Determine Automatically.

✦ **Resolution:** Image resolution can be fixed at sizes ranging from 72 dpi to 600 dpi. If the original PDF includes images at lower resolutions, the files will be interpolated through upsizing or downsampled when resolutions are lower than original sizes. Determine Automatically preserves original resolution of the PDF contents.

Save as PNG

PNG (Portable Network Graphics) format can be saved from Acrobat. When selecting the Settings option for PNG exports, the PNG Options dialog box appears, as shown in Figure 7-28.

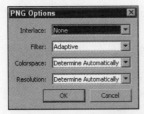

Figure 7-28: When selecting PNG as the format and clicking the Settings button, the PNG Options dialog box opens where you can assign file attributes similar to JPEG options.

Options for PNG, which are listed here, are similar to JPEG in regard to the Colorspace and Resolution settings. The first two choices are unique to the PNG format.

✦ **Interlace:** PNG files can be interlaced, such as GIF files for Web use. The choices are for no interlacing, in which case None is selected in the pull-down menu or Adam7. Adam7 provides interlacing similar to interlaced GIF images.

✦ **Filter:** The color palette used for the PNG color handling can be selected from a number of choices in the pull-down menu. The default is Adaptive that often produces the best results with continuous tone images. Selecting other options should be previewed on-screen and in Web browsers supporting PNG images. Through some careful testing, you can determine what setting offers the best results.

✦ **Colorspace:** All menu items for Colorspace are the same as JPEG with the addition of Monochrome. When selecting Monochrome, images are reduced to 1-bit bitmap images.

Save as PostScript

The PostScript option results in a file, such as those printed as PostScript to disk. When the PostScript file option is selected from the file formats, settings similar to the EPS format are available in the PostScript settings dialog box, as shown in Figure 7-29.

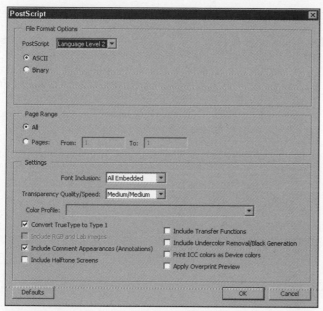

Figure 7-29: When selecting PostScript as the format and clicking the Settings button, the PostScript Options dialog box opens where file attributes similar to the EPS options can be assigned.

✦ **File Format Options:** The options available for file format are the same as those described with the EPS file options. For almost all circumstances, use Language Level 2 or Language Level 3 and Binary encoding. If you experience difficulty in converting back to PDF, use Language Level I and ASCII encoding.

The remaining options are the same as those found with the EPS choices. Using PostScript as the format provides you with an opportunity to create a PostScript file and convert it back to PDF with Acrobat Distiller. Using Distiller, you can select different JobOptions to repurpose your document.

Tip

If you have a PDF where images need to be downsampled or some other Distiller JobOption needs to be applied to the PDF, export it as a PostScript file, and then redistill in Acrobat Distiller after making JobOptions choices. If you need file content created in Acrobat, such as comments and form fields that can't be preserved when creating the new PDF file, be certain to keep your original file handy. In Acrobat, open the old file and choose Document ⇨ Replace Pages. Navigate to your new PDF file and select it as the file to use for replacing the pages. After the pages have been replaced, all your comments and form fields remain on the same respective pages. This method can be especially helpful when you need to downsample images that were distilled with higher resolution settings.

Saving as RTF

As explained earlier in this chapter, RTF (Rich Text Format) options are specified in a preference dialog box for tables in Windows. Table and columnar data need specific detail for exporting from Acrobat to preserve the formatting. With RTF saves from Acrobat, text dominant PDFs export with all formatting preserved when single columns are contained in the original file. If multiple columns exist, the formatting won't be preserved as you see it displayed in Acrobat. When RTF is selected as the file format in the Save As dialog box, the Settings button is inactive. No options exist for RTF exports.

Saving as TIFF

TIFF (Tagged Image File Format) is one of the most popular formats for image files resulting from scans and used in prepress and printing. You can export a PDF as a TIFF image and use it for printing or placing in an application document where the program does not support PDF imports. Settings available for TIFF files saved from Acrobat are shown in Figure 7-30.

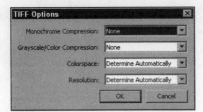

Figure 7-30: When selecting TIFF as the format and clicking the Settings button, the TIFF Options dialog box opens where file attributes similar to Distiller's JobOptions and the PNG format can be assigned.

Options for TIFF formatted files are the same for the compression options as found with Acrobat Distiller, and the options for Colorspace and Resolution are the same as those described for the PNG format.

Extracting Images

Individual images contained on a PDF page can be extracted and saved in one of three formats. When you choose File ⇨ Export ⇨ Extract Images As, a submenu appears offering JPEG, PNG, and TIFF as format options. When you select any one of the three format options, a dialog box appears that is the same as the Save As dialog box with the Settings button active. Clicking the Settings button opens the same Options dialog box as those discussed previously for the respective format.

Images can be selectively determined as to whether they will be exported or not. The Extract Images preference setting discussed earlier in this chapter offers options for the physical size of images that can be excluded when the Extract Images command is used. For extracting all images, open the Extract Images preference dialog box and select the option for No Limit. Other choices eliminate images smaller than fixed choices defined in the preference settings.

Saving PDFs with Security

You can add security to PDF files that can restrict either opening a file or editing a file, as discussed earlier in this chapter as well as Chapter 3. The encryption method used with Acrobat is the RC4 method of security from RSA Corporation. The method may not be important to you, but keep in mind, you have little chance of breaking password security if you lose or forget your passwords. A PDF file can't be opened in any application if the file has been encrypted with security.

Users of earlier versions of Acrobat will remember saving with security was applied in the Save As dialog box. In Acrobat 5.0, security is applied by choosing File ⇨ Document Security. When the menu command is selected, a dialog box opens where the security is determined before selecting either the Save or Save As command. After you open the dialog box, you have three choices appearing in the pull-down menu for Document is secured with, as shown in Figure 7-31.

Figure 7-31: In Acrobat 5.0, security is applied in the Document Security dialog box before you select the Save or Save As command.

The choices include:

✦ **No Security:** If you have a secure document and you want to remove security, you can select the No Security option from the pull-down menu. A dialog box appears asking you to supply the master password before the change can be made. When the file is saved, the security is removed.

✦ **Acrobat Standard Security:** Selecting this option provides you access to the encryption levels discussed in Chapter 5 where the Distiller Security options are covered. When you select Acrobat Standard Security, the Standard Security dialog box appears with a single option different than the dialog boxes reviewed with Acrobat Distiller – Security options. In Figure 7-32, notice the pull-down menu for Encryption Level. In the Distiller Security settings, the encryption level was determined by the compatible Acrobat format that was selected in the General JobOptions dialog box. When you choose File ⇨ Document Security, the security level is determined from the choices in the pull-down menu for Encryption Level. Select either 40-bit or 128-bit encryption from the menu choices. All other options for security handling are the same as those discussed with Acrobat Distiller.

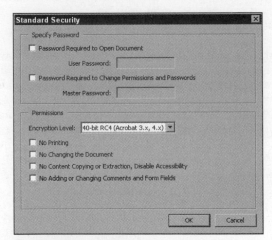

Figure 7-32: The pull-down menu in the Standard Security dialog box determines the Encryption Level for Acrobat Standard Security.

✦ **Acrobat Self-Sign Security:** The methods of digitally signing documents are discussed later in Chapter 14. In order to create a digital signature or to use Self-Sign Security, you need to have a profile created and a list of recipients who will be authorized to receive your PDFs when using Self-Sign Security. These preliminary steps are covered in Chapter 14. For now, be aware that encryption can also be applied with digital signatures. Assuming that you have set up your key and a list of Trusted Certificates, you can select the Acrobat Self-Sign Security option in the Document Security dialog box. When selecting this option, you first need to log in as a user by choosing Tools ➪ Self-Sign Security ➪ Log In. After you've logged in, you can select the Acrobat Self-Sign Security option in the Document Security dialog box. When the menu option is selected, the Self-Sign Security – Encryption dialog box appears. This dialog box displays your recipient list and offers an option to set the user permission for working with your PDF document. A button for User Permissions appears in the dialog box and when selected will open the User Permissions dialog box, as shown in Figure 7-33.

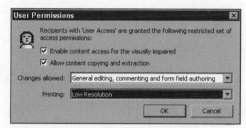

Figure 7-33: Use the User Permissions dialog box to select the security options for the recipient list.

In the dialog box, select the checkboxes and options from the pull-down menus to create encryption. Options available in the dialog box are consistent with the security options discussed earlier in Chapter 5. After applying the restrictions in the User Permissions dialog box, click OK and then click OK in the Self-Sign Security – Encryptions dialog box. When the file is saved with either this level of security or the Acrobat Standard Security, the file will be encrypted. Users of Self-Sign Security need to be among the list of Trusted Certificate holders in order to access the PDF file. The PDF author needs to collect the public certificates from each individual included among the trusted parties.

Note If a warning dialog box appears after you enter a confirmation password, you did not enter it exactly as the original password. If you see the warning dialog box a second time, try to cancel the dialog box and start over—you may have entered the first password in error. Be certain to write your passwords down and store them in a place other than electronically on your hard drive. If your drive crashes and you have a number of passwords on the drive, you may run the risk of never recovering secure files from backup disks.

About Passwords

Following is a list of some important items that you should consider when using security:

✦ Passwords are optional for either field when using Standard Security.

✦ Documents can be opened with either password.

✦ If the master password is used when opening a file, all tools and menu commands can be selected.

✦ Passwords are case-sensitive.

✦ Passwords are limited to 255 characters.

✦ Password-secured files from Acrobat 5.0 with 128-bit encryption cannot be viewed in Acrobat viewers earlier than 5.0. Acrobat 4.0 secured files cannot be viewed in Acrobat viewers prior to version 2.0.

✦ Forgotten passwords cannot be recovered.

✦ Self-Sign Security requires at least one Trusted Certificate to be active among the recipients list.

✦ Profiles cannot be recovered after lost from a hard drive. A backup of all profiles used should be stored safely on two or more external media cartridges.

Summary

✦ Preferences set up the viewer environment. Preferences are uniquely applied to the user environment and many settings have no effect on the PDFs saved from Acrobat.

✦ Whereas preference settings are more global, document properties are document specific. Many document properties items can be saved with the PDF file.

✦ Saving PDF files with the Save As command enables you to save PDFs in many different file formats.

✦ Individual images can be extracted from PDF pages and saved in several different formats.

✦ Security can be provided in several ways. Acrobat Standard Security provides two levels of encryption — either 40-bit or 128-bit. Acrobat Self-Sign Security can apply permissions for a selected group of individuals where the PDF author has obtained their public certificate information.

✦   ✦   ✦

Enhancing PDF Documents

Comments, Text, and Graphics

Acrobat Comment Properties

Acrobat 4.0 introduced us to a new set of features known as Annotations that took the simple Note tool from earlier versions of Acrobat to new levels and much more sophistication. It was a quantum leap in advancing Acrobat with regard to note attachments, page markups, and organizing collected input from co-workers.

The now known *Comment* tools advance yet another quantum leap in Acrobat development. The notes and markup tools have been improved and now they can be shared among workers in new ways by providing common access to content and sharing information in the form of comment notes across networks and the World Wide Web. There's so much to explore with regard to Comments in Acrobat 5.0, I broke it up a little to first handle creating and organizing Comments in this chapter and then look at sharing Comments through collaboration in Chapter 11.

The tools for making comments in Acrobat are grouped into three categories. The first category, the Comment tools, consists of tools for notes, text, sound, stamps, and file attachments. The next group contains the Graphic Markup tools that include the pencil, square, circle, and line tools. Finally, the Text Markup tools are used for text highlights, text strikeout, and text underlining. The tool icons and functions vary greatly among the tools, but most of them all have an associated note where comments can be made in Acrobat and viewed in either Acrobat or Reader.

When comments are created on a document page, they can be used for viewing and exchanging information between workgroups. When the file is printed, the comments can be suppressed or printed as determined by the user. The comments as they appear on a document page are illustrated in Figure 8-1.

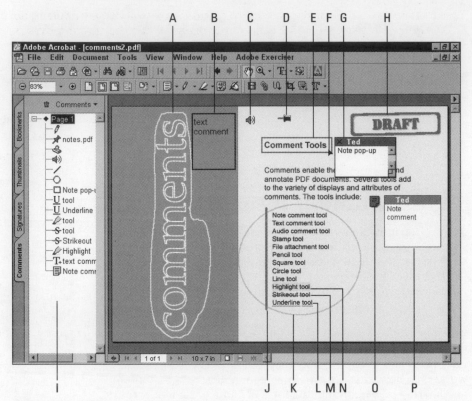

Figure 8-1: All the comment types have unique icon displays or markings. Most of the Comment tools have an associated note where text comments can be user supplied.

In Figure 8-1, the individual items include:

✦ **A Pencil comment:** Free form drawing can mark up an area that you want to comment.

✦ **B Text comment:** Text can be supplied anywhere on the document page. The background can appear transparent or with a background fill. A border can be created around the note area.

✦ **C Sound (Audio) comment:** Sound files or recordings can be contained within the PDF document. Once created, the sound is embedded in the PDF file.

✦ **D File attachment:** External files can be embedded in the PDF from any application document.

✦ **E Square comment:** A square or rectangle can be drawn anywhere on the document page.

✦ **F Current cursor position:** Where the cursor rests above a comment, an associated note window temporarily opens. When the cursor moves out of the comment range, the note collapses.

✦ **G Note pop-up:** From the cursor position, a note pop-up opens the associated note for the comment type. Note pop-up behavior is determined in the comment preferences.

✦ **H Stamp comment:** Preset icons or user defined custom icons can be created to represent Stamp symbols.

✦ **I Comment palette:** When the Document pane is opened and the Comments tab is in the foreground, all comments are displayed in the Comments palette.

✦ **J Line comment:** Straight lines can be drawn on the document page. The line in Figure 8-1 is a vertical line. Straight lines can be drawn and lines can be drawn at any angle.

✦ **K Circle comment:** Circles and elliptical lines can be drawn on the document page.

✦ **L Underline comment:** Click and drag across text with the Underline comment tool and the display appears as underlined text.

✦ **M Strikeout comment:** Text strikeout is created with the Strikeout comment tool.

✦ **N Highlight comment:** Much like a yellow marker, the Highlight comment tool highlights selected text.

✦ **O Note comment icon:** The icon symbol appears when the note window is moved aside.

✦ **P Note comment:** The note comment window is viewed with transparency. Transparency is user defined in the comment preferences.

Assigning color

For all Acrobat color specification of tools and properties, color assignment is handled in the same way as described when using the color swatches noted in earlier chapters. Regardless of whether you specify color in the General Preferences dialog box, any given tool's properties dialog box, or to any content placed on an Acrobat PDF page where color assignment is permitted; selecting color is handled in the same manner.

For all property changes to note comments with regard to color, a context-sensitive menu can be opened by placing the cursor over the comment icon and right-clicking the mouse button (Control + Click on a Mac). When the properties dialog box is opened, a color swatch appears adjacent to the Color setting, as shown in Figure 8-2. Depending on whether you work in Windows or on a Macintosh, the system color palette will appear differently.

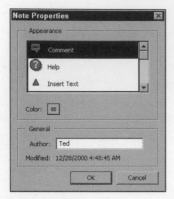

Figure 8-2: The Note Properties dialog box can be opened from a context-sensitive menu command. When opened, color changes to note properties can be made.

Changing color properties in Windows

A color swatch appears with the default color in the preferences dialog box or a properties dialog box. In Windows, click the swatch to open the palette where color selection is made. In Figure 8-3, the Note Properties dialog box is opened and the color swatch is selected.

Figure 8-3: After a color swatch is selected, a palette pops up where preset colors or a custom color can be selected.

In the palette pop-up window, make a selection from one of the preset choices. If you want to use a custom color not available among the presets, click the More Colors text appearing at the bottom of the palette. When you select this item, half of the color palette is exposed. To open the second half of the dialog box, click the Define Custom Colors button. The expanded dialog box appears, as viewed in Figure 8-4.

Any of the items under the Basic colors can be selected as a new color for the properties being adjusted. If another color is desired, click the large color swatch on the right side of the palette. If a different luminosity for a given hue is desired, move the left pointing arrow up or down. When the color value you want appears in the Color|Solid swatch, click OK and then OK again to accept the new color as a choice for the properties. After a color property is changed, it appears as a new default for all note comments reflected in the note title bars and icons.

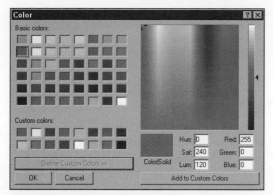

Figure 8-4: When More Colors is selected in the color palette, the Color dialog box opens where custom colors can be selected. Click Define Custom Colors to expand the dialog box.

Changing color properties on the Macintosh

On the Macintosh the same color swatch appears in the Note Properties window. When the swatch is selected, it won't open a palette similar to Windows where several color choices appear in addition to the custom item. On the Macintosh, when you select the color swatch, the system color palette opens without offering preset choices. Click the swatch and the Apple System color palette opens, as shown in Figure 8-5.

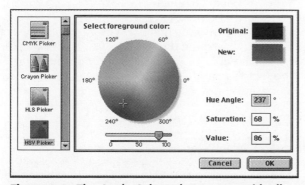

Figure 8-5: The Apple Color palette opens with all the color selection choices available for defining color without opening additional panes.

Along the left side of the palette are different color models that can be selected. When a different model is used, the view on the right side of the palette changes. For specifying color for Note properties or any other custom color assignments, select the HSV Picker item. Colors are subsequently selected by clicking the color wheel on the right side of the palette. The items at the top of the palette display the original color contained in the color swatch when the palette was opened and the new color when selected in the color wheel. After making your choice for a new custom color, click OK.

Using Comment Tools

Comment tools appear collapsed in the Command bar. The Note tool is the default display in the Comments tool group. When the down arrow is selected in the Command bar, the tools contained in this group appear, as shown in Figure 8-6. The tools in this group include the Note tool, the Free Text tool, the Sound Attachment tool, the Stamp tool, and the File Attachment tool. See Table 8-1 later in this chapter for a comparison of the Comment tools.

 Figure 8-6: When the Comment tools are expanded in the tool group, the five tools appear in view in the Command bar.

Creating Note comments

Before using the Note tool to create a note, you may want to first examine the Note preferences, discussed in Chapter 7. If several users are contributing notes to a given file, you may want to pre-assign colors and/or labels individualized for each user. If you change Note preferences while working on a PDF file, the preference changes only affect any notes created subsequent to the preference change. Any existing notes appear with their original attributes.

To create a note, click the Note tool from the Command bar. The cursor changes to the icon displayed at the beginning of this section that enables you to draw a rectangle in the Document pane. Drag open a rectangle and release the mouse button. The note appears where you drew the rectangle and a text cursor appears in the note content area indicating you can now enter text. Notes can be created on a document page, as shown in Figure 8-7, or they can be created outside the document window.

Collapsing, expanding, and deleting notes

In Chapter 6, I demonstrated how to use the /Open true (or false) value pairs with pdfmark to have a note appear as open or closed in the PDF file when distilled with Acrobat Distiller. If the Open key is true, the note will appear expanded, as illustrated in Figure 8-6. To collapse a note, click the small close box in the top-left corner of the note. Collapsed notes can be moved and rearranged in the document window by clicking the icon and dragging it to another location. If the note window is open, you can drag the title bar of the window to relocate it. While the note window is open, you can move the icon associated with the note to another location. These two elements are independent of each other. A moved icon has no effect on the location of the note window and vice versa.

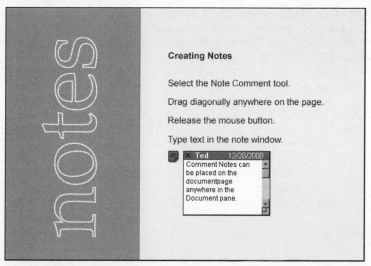

Figure 8-7: To create a Note comment, select the Note tool and drag open a rectangle. After you release the mouse button, a note window opens where text is created.

Aligning the note icon with the note window is handled through a context-sensitive menu command. Open a context-sensitive menu by right-clicking the note icon (Control + Click on a Mac) and select Reset Note Window Location. The top-left corner of the note window moves to the note icon and aligns the top-left corners. You must open the context-sensitive menu while clicking the icon. If you click the note window, different menu commands will appear without an option to align the two elements.

If you want to delete a note from a PDF file, select the note icon. A note can be deleted either when open or when collapsed. With the note icon selected, press the Del key (Delete key on a Mac) on your keyboard or open a context-sensitive menu and select Delete. If all notes or other elements are deselected, the Delete menu command will be grayed out. When a note is deleted, a warning dialog box appears, asking you to confirm the note deletion.

In earlier versions of Acrobat, we had few Undo opportunities by choosing Edit ⇨ Undo. Much of this has changed in Acrobat 5.0. In regard to comment deletions, you can now use the Edit menu and select Undo if a comment is inadvertently deleted.

Note comment icons

The icon representing a Note comment by default appears the same as the icon used in the Note tool displayed in the Command bar. The icon can be changed to another appearance through the Properties menu. In order to change the icon, a Note comment must first be created. Acrobat makes no provision for addressing

Note comment properties before the Note comment icon is on the document page. To change an icon, create a Note comment and then open a context-sensitive menu or choose Edit ⇨ Properties. (If the Properties command is grayed out, you don't have the icon selected.) Be certain the icon is selected before visiting the Edit menu. From the Note Properties dialog box, the icon appearance provides seven choices to represent the appearance, as shown in Figure 8-8.

Figure 8-8: The appearance of the Note comment icon can be changed in the Note Properties dialog box.

Changing the icon appearance has no effect on the note window or the content. These icons are fixed and Acrobat makes no provision for creating custom icons for the Note comments. They are used to help convey a message and add a visual representation that may offer some continuity between the icon and the note message.

Comment note pop-up windows

Note pop-ups are determined in the Comment Preferences dialog box. When you choose Edit ⇨ Preferences ⇨ General and subsequently click the Comments item in the list of preference categories, the item denoted as Automatically Open Note Pop-up appears enabled by default. When enabled, a Note comment window pops up when the cursor is placed over the icon. This behavior occurs when the window is collapsed. Moving the cursor away from the Note comment icon closes the pop-up window. If you want to disable note pop-ups, deselect the checkbox in the preferences dialog box. This behavior is consistent for all comment types that have associated note windows.

Creating Text comments

The Free Text tool creates a text block on the PDF page. Rather than having an icon that can be opened or collapsed to display text, Text comments offer a means of conveying a message in a body of text. Because the annotation contains text, no note window is associated with this type of comment.

Text comments are created by clicking the Free Text tool and dragging open a rectangle in the document window. Just as Note comments, Text comments can also appear on the PDF page or anywhere outside the page and within the Document pane. When the mouse button is released, a blinking I-beam cursor appears in the Text comment rectangle. Text can only be created when the Text comment tool is selected in the Command bar. If another tool is selected, text cannot be entered in the rectangle.

If you want to resize the Text comment, the Hand tool must be used. Select the Hand tool and click inside the Text comment area. Move the cursor to a corner and wait for the cursor to appear as a diagonal line with an arrow at each end, as shown in Figure 8-9. Drag in or out diagonally to reduce or upsize the Text comment area. If the Text comment is to be moved to a different area within the Document pane, use the Hand tool to click anywhere inside the rectangle and drag to another location.

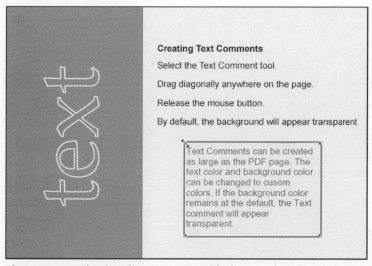

Creating Text Comments

Select the Text Comment tool.

Drag diagonally anywhere on the page.

Release the mouse button.

By default, the background will appear transparent

Text Comments can be created as large as the PDF page. The text color and background color can be changed to cusom colors. If the background color remains at the default, the Text comment will appear transparent.

Figure 8-9: Selecting the comment with the Hand tool and dragging the corners in or out in a diagonal direction can resize the Text comments.

Tip

Acrobat provides no means of creating text, such as a word processor or page layout application. Pages cannot be created in Acrobat through traditional methods. You can, however, create a blank page through Distiller or exports from other applications and insert a blank page in a PDF document. (See Chapter 9 for inserting pages.) A Text comment can be created as large as the PDF page (up to 200 inches by 200 inches). After inserting a page, create a Text comment and the entire page can be filled with text created in Acrobat. As a matter of practice, keep a blank page handy and save it to your Acrobat folder. I keep a blank page on my computer and I call it blank.pdf. Whenever I need a page, I insert this page in a document.

Text comment properties

The FreeText Properties dialog box, shown in Figure 8-10, enables specification of font, font size, and text alignment. Whereas all other comment note properties for font and font size are handled in the General preferences dialog box, Text comment properties for fonts and font sizes are handled in the FreeText Properties dialog box. In addition, you find in this dialog box options for a border frame that can appear around the text block rectangle. The Border Thickness options features choices for border line widths of point sizes ranging from one to seven. If None is selected from the choices, no border appears around the comment.

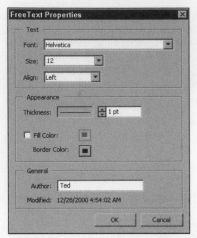

Figure 8-10: In the FreeText Properties dialog box, font, font size, alignment, border attributes, and background color are assigned to Text comments.

The rectangle containing the text comment can be transparent or filled with a color. You make selections for transparency and color within the FreeText Properties dialog box. In order to apply a color fill to the text comment background, select the Fill Color checkbox. To fill the background with a color, enable the checkbox and click the color swatch to open the system color palette where the color selections are made. To eliminate a background color, deselect the Fill Color check box, as illustrated in Figure 8-10.

Creating Sound comments

Sound comments are recorded from within the PDF document. To create a Sound comment, you must have a microphone connected to your computer. Sound comments are created by selecting the Sound Attachment tool in the Acrobat Command bar and clicking in the document window. A click of the mouse button is all that is needed to open the Sound Recorder (Windows) or Record Sound (Macintosh) dialog box (see Figures 8-11 and 8-12). When the dialog box opens, click the record button and speak into the microphone connected to your computer. When you've finished recording the sound, click the OK button. On Windows, the file is saved after you click the OK button. You can determine the directory path by selecting the Choose button and navigate your hard drive where the sound file is to be saved.

Audio comments are saved as a WAV file (.wav) in Windows and as an AIFF (.aiff) file on the Macintosh. If OK/Save is selected in the Sound Comment/Record Sound dialog box, you return to the PDF document window where the sound icon now appears. The Audio comment is embedded in the PDF file when the PDF is saved. As the sound becomes part of the PDF document, you can transport the PDF across platforms without having to include a sound file link. All sound is audible on either platform after saving the file.

Figure 8-11: The Sound Recorder dialog box in Windows opens after you click in the Document pane and select the Sound Attachment tool.

Figure 8-12: You save Audio comments on the Macintosh after you select the OK button in the Record Sound dialog box.

Audio properties

Properties for Sound comments are made available in the same manner as with other annotations. Open a context-sensitive menu and select Properties to open the Sound Properties dialog box shown in Figure 8-13. The Sound Properties dialog box offers selections for adding a text description and editing the author name. By default, the Description field is left blank. You can supply a description containing up to 255 characters that is listed in the Comments tab within the Navigation pane when opened. (See "Using the Comments Palette" later in this chapter.)

Figure 8-13: The Sound Properties dialog box provides choices for author name and a Description field where up to 255 characters can be added to the field box.

Creating Stamp comments

The Stamp tool enables you to add an image icon to a PDF file. In an office environment, the Stamp tool is like a rubber stamp you might slap on a document to indicate it has been approved or confidential, or you might use a stamped signature in place of a hand written signature. When the Stamp tool is used, Acrobat automatically navigates to a directory within the Acrobat Plug-ins folder called Annotations. Inside the Annotations folder is another folder called Stamps. In the Stamps folder resides three PDF files used for custom stamps and another folder where the Standard stamps hold the default icons. All the files are PDF files where different stamp icons can be selected from categories represented by each individual PDF file. These PDF files and their respective pages are the Adobe-supplied stamp images. As PDFs, all the files can be opened in an Acrobat viewer.

When you click and drag open a Stamp comment, by default the last stamp you used appears for the icon symbol. When the Stamp Properties dialog box is opened from a context menu, choices can be selected from categories listed in the Category pull-down menu. A thumbnail on the right side of the dialog box displays the icon used for the selected item, as shown in Figure 8-14. The pull-down menu for Category contains the four categories respective to the PDF files contained in the Stamps folder. When a different category is selected, all the names and their associated thumbnails change.

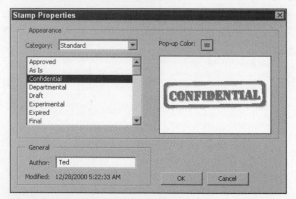

Figure 8-14: Stamp images are selected from among the four PDF files installed with your Acrobat application. You can select a category from among those appearing in the pull-down menu in the Stamp Properties dialog box.

To use the Stamp tool, select the tool in the Command bar, move the cursor to the document window, and drag open a rectangle. When the mouse button is released, the Stamp Properties dialog box appears. When a stamp has been created in the PDF document window, you can supply a text note in the associated note window. Double-click the Stamp icon or open a context-sensitive menu and select Open Note. The text window adheres to the same rules used with Note comments.

Stamp properties

In the Stamp Properties dialog box, you can specify a name in the Author field or the color for the title bar of the associated note as well as the icon to represent the Stamp comment. After a stamp has been created, you can change the image by returning to the Stamp Properties dialog box. Accessing this dialog box is handled the same way as for other annotations. Select the stamp and then choose Edit ➪ Properties or open a context-sensitive menu and select Properties. Selecting the Pop-up Color swatch can modify the color of the note title bar.

Creating custom stamps

Acrobat provides a means for creating user-defined custom stamp icons. You can create images in illustration programs or photo-imaging applications. Whatever program is used to create custom icons, the file eventually needs to be converted to PDF. Use Acrobat Distiller or any of the other methods described in earlier chapters to convert to PDF.

After the PDF file has been created, you must open the file in Acrobat and create a page template. Page templates are created by choosing Tools ➪ Forms ➪ Page Templates. A name must be supplied for the template. After creating a page template, the category is determined by supplying a name or description in the General Document Properties dialog box for the Title field. After all the proper attributes are assigned, the file must then be saved to the Stamps folder. When Acrobat is opened and a Stamp comment is to be made, the new category and associated stamp icons appear in the Stamp Properties dialog box. To understand how creating custom stamps work, take a look at the following steps to create a new category and several stamp icons within the category.

STEPS: Creating Custom Stamps

1. **Create a graphic.** Use your favorite illustration or photo-imaging program to create an icon or illustration. In this example, I use a custom brush from Adobe Illustrator. I want three different icons for my new stamp category, so I create three different shapes, as shown in Figure 8-15.

Figure 8-15: I create my shapes in Adobe Illustrator and apply transparency from the Illustrator Transparency palette for each shape. These three shapes need to be saved as individual PDF files.

2. **Convert to PDF.** If you create an image in a program that exports directly to PDF, use the Export or Save command to convert the file to PDF. If the program does not support exports or saves to PDF, use Acrobat Distiller. Each icon you create must be saved as a separate PDF file.

3. **Create additional icons.** Figure 8-15 shows all the icons I used in my new Stamp file, however each image needs to be saved as a separate file. Create a few more icons and save them as individual PDFs. In my example, I save as PDF from Adobe Illustrator with Acrobat 5.0 compatibility to preserve the transparency.

4. **Combine the PDF pages into a single document.** Open one of the PDF files in Acrobat and choose Document ➪ Insert Pages. In the navigation dialog box, select the files to be inserted. In Windows and the Macintosh, you can select multiple files for page insertion.

5. **Create a document template.** After inserting pages, move to the first page and choose Tools ➪ Forms ➪ Page Templates. The Page Templates window opens.

6. **Provide a template name.** In the Name field in the Page Templates dialog box, enter a descriptive name for your new template file (see Figure 8-16). When the name appears in the Name field box, click the Add button. The name supplied here appears in the Stamp Properties dialog box for this image within a category you identify in the Document Summary dialog box.

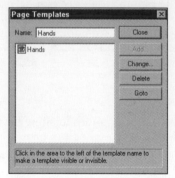

Figure 8-16: Stamp images are selected from a category. The page template name identifies the filename within a given category.

7. **Create additional Page Templates.** Navigate to the second page and create another Page Template. Continue creating additional Page Templates for each individual page in the PDF file. In my example, I use three icons and I create a separate Page Template for each page. When displayed in the Page Templates dialog box, they appear, as shown in Figure 8-17.

8. **Open the Document Summary dialog box.** Categories appear in the Category pull-down menu when the Stamp Properties dialog box is opened. To create a new category, choose File ➪ Document Properties ➪ Summary or press Control/Command + D.

Figure 8-17: Each template is created for each page in the PDF file. When viewed in the Page Templates dialog box, the list box displays the names used for each Page Template.

9. **Supply a name for the category.** Click the cursor in the Title field and type a name for your category. The filename for the PDF is irrespective of the category. What appears in the Title field is displayed in the Category pull-down menu in the Stamp Properties dialog box. Click OK after entering the name (see Figure 8-18).

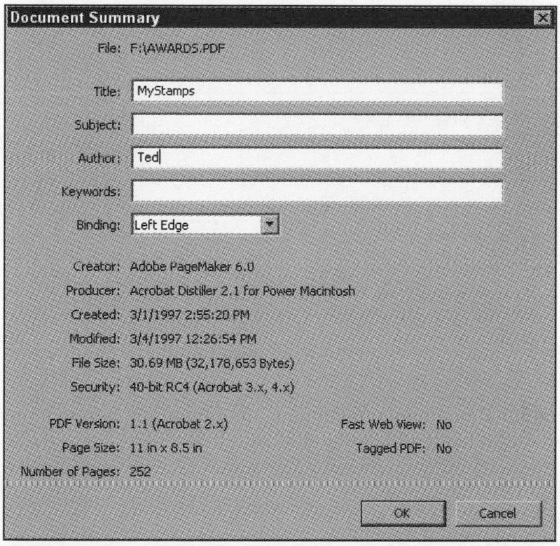

Figure 8-18: Category names in the Stamp Properties dialog box appear from the name you supply in the Title field of the Document Summary dialog box.

10. **Save the PDF file.** Choose File ➪ Save As and save the modified PDF file to the Stamps folder (Acrobat:Plug-ins:Annotations:Stamps). The filename you provide for the PDF file has no effect on the names displayed in the Stamp Properties dialog box.

Note

When you open the Stamp Properties dialog box and select a category from which to choose individual images, you'll notice no navigation dialog box appears. The Category pull-down menu adds names automatically when the PDF file is placed in the Stamps folder with proper assignment of page template and document information. If the PDF file is saved anywhere other than the Stamps folder, you will have no means of navigating to the file.

11. **Open a PDF file.** In order to use the new stamp, a PDF file must be open in Acrobat. Choose File ➪ Open and open a PDF document.

12. **Add a Stamp comment.** Acrobat recognizes your new category without quitting the program. New categories you add to the Stamps folder immediately become available when adding a Stamp comment. To add a Stamp comment, click the Stamp tool in the Command bar. Click and drag open a rectangle. By default, the last stamp used will appear on the page. Select the stamp icon with the Hand tool and open a context menu to open the Stamp Properties dialog box.

13. **Select your new category.** If you performed all the steps correctly, you will see the new category name appear in the Category pop-up menu in the Stamp Properties dialog box. Click the pull-down menu and select the category name. Each Page Template name appears in the list box, as shown in Figure 8-19.

Figure 8-19: The new category name appears in the Category pull-down menu with the list of Page Template names appearing in the list box.

14. **Select the new stamp.** Click any of the names appearing in the list and the icon associated with the name becomes your new stamp icon. When viewed on the document page, the icon can be sized by dragging corner handles to downsize or upsize the icon.

Tip

PDF documents can contain pages of different sizes. If you have several images contained in a single PDF file and some contain more page space than others, you can individually crop pages to different sizes in Acrobat. Click the Crop tool in the Command bar. Navigate to the page to be cropped and use the Crop tool to trim the page close to the edges of the illustration. Be certain to select only the page you desire to crop when the Crop Pages dialog box appears. In addition, pages with different dimensions can be inserted in a PDF, and they hold their dimensions after the insertion. If you have an opportunity to crop a page before insertion, you can perform cropping in the host application.

The properties for stamp icons cannot be changed in regard to color or appearance. Vector objects offer most flexibility when sizing because no distortion occurs no matter how large they are sized. Raster objects created in Adobe Photoshop do pixelate if sized higher than the screen resolution of 72 ppi at 100 percent.

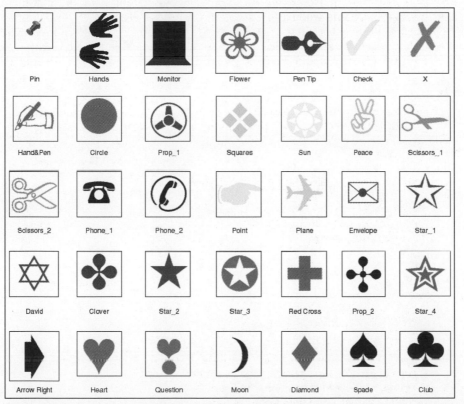

Figure 8-20: I created a PDF file made up of individual characters from the Zapf Dingbats font. On the first page in my new Stamps file, I place all the individual characters on one page and link them to the page where the respective character appears.

Changing Icon Attributes

More flexibility with assigning attributes for custom stamp icons can be obtained by using type font characters as stamp icons. If you use a font, such as Wingdings or Zapf Dingbats, you can change color for the characters from within Acrobat without needing to create another PDF. Individual characters can be placed on separate pages in a layout program for each character that will be included as an individual stamp icon. Export the file to PDF and create a page template for each page. Save the file to your Stamps folder where the Stamp tool can access the file.

If you want to create an index page, all the characters can be placed on a single page with links to the individual pages where the respective characters appear (see Figure 8-20). In Acrobat, you can open the PDF file saved to the Stamps folder, use the Touchup tool to select a character, and then choose Tools ➪ TouchUp ➪ Attributes. In the Text Attributes dialog box, click the text fill color swatch appearing in the lower left corner of the dialog box (see Figure 8-21). The color palette opens where another color can be selected. Choose your color and save the PDF. Because the Stamp tool dynamically enables you to choose new stamp icons without quitting Acrobat, you can immediately use the tool and select the icon in the Stamp properties.

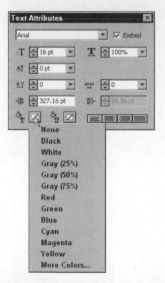

Figure 8-21: If I want to change the color of one of my characters, I open the PDF in Acrobat and click the icon I want to edit. The page opens to where my character appears and I select it with the TouchUp Text tool. I then choose Tools ➪ TouchUp Text ➪ Text Attributes to open the Text Attributes dialog box where I select a new color.

Creating file attachments

The last of the first group of Comment tools in the Acrobat Command bar is the File Attachment tool. File attachments enable you to attach any document file on your hard drive to an open PDF file. After it's attached, the file is embedded in the PDF document. Embedding a file provides other viewer users the capability to view attachments on other computers and across platforms. At first it may appear as though the attachment is a link. However, if you transport the PDF document to another computer and open the annotation, the embedded file will open in the host application. Users on other computers need the original authoring application to view the embedded file.

To use the File Attachment tool, click the tool and click in the document window. The first item appearing is a navigation dialog box. Acrobat opens this dialog box for you to locate a file on your hard drive to be attached and embedded on the PDF page in view when the file attachment is created. After selecting the file to open, click the Select button in the navigation dialog box. The File Attachment Properties dialog box opens where one of four icons can be selected to represent the file attachment. Figure 8-22 displays the icons.

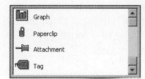

Figure 8-22: In the File Attachment Properties dialog box, you can select one of four icons to represent the file attachment.

After the file attachment is created, the properties menu options available from a context-sensitive menu offers a command unique to this tool. The menu option for Save Embedded File to Disk saves a copy of the embedded file independent of the PDF. This command behaves like a file extraction, however the embedded file still remains with the PDF while a copy of the attached file is saved to disk.

When a file attachment has been created in a PDF document, positioning the cursor over the comment icon displays the name of the file in a tooltip. All file annotations are labeled according to the document name that you specify when you save the file to disk.

Working with Graphic Markup tools

Graphic Markup tools are the electronic equivalent of using a highlighter on paper documents. The Acrobat Command bar has four Graphic Markup tools appearing adjacent to the Comment tools: the Pencil, Square, Circle, and Line tools. To select a tool, click the down pointing arrow to open the tool bar. Select a tool and drag on a document page. All of the tools in this group (see Figure 8-23) have an associated note that appears immediately after releasing the mouse button when the mark is created.

Figure 8-23: Graphic Markup tools are used to mark up PDF files for comments, suggestions, and editing.

Pencil tool

The Pencil tool is used for freeform marking and creating irregular paths. Click the tool in the Acrobat Command bar and draw as you would with a traditional pencil. After completing the mark, an associated note window opens where a Note comment can be created. If you select the mark, a selection rectangle will appear with four corner points. Click and drag the corners to reshape the line. Either the Pencil tool or the Hand tool can be used to click and drag a mark to a new location. Double-clicking the mark will toggle opening and closing the associated note window.

Square tool

Squares and rectangles are used to encompass an area with a rectangular border. Draw a rectangle and release the mouse button. The rectangle is displayed with four handles enabling you to resize and reshape the rectangle. Press the Shift key and then click and drag outward to create a square.

Circle tool

The Circle tool works like the Square tool. The final result is an elliptical shape or circle. Using the same method to create squares with the Square tool creates circles. Use the Shift key when opening a circle to constrain it to a perfect circle.

Line tool

The Line tool is used to draw straight lines on a 360° axis. Use the Shift key to draw diagonal lines at 45-degree and 90-degree angles. When the line is selected, two end points appear on either side of the line. Place the cursor over an end point and drag to resize and/or change the angle.

The Line tool offers some options not available with the other Graphic Markup tools. When the Line Properties dialog box is opened either from the Edit menu or a context-sensitive menu, options for Line Ends appear in the dialog box, as shown in Figure 8-24.

Figure 8-24: The Line tool has options for creating different marks on the head, tail, or both ends of a line. Selections for the style and where the heads will be applied are made in the Line Properties dialog box.

The line ends can be created at the beginning of the line (tail) or the end of the line (head) or they can be placed at both ends. In Figure 8-25, lines have been created with the different line end types for the heads on the left, and both ends on the right side of the figure.

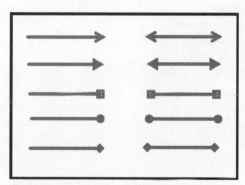

Figure 8-25: Line ends selected from the Line Properties dialog box offer five choices for the head, tail, or both ends of lines.

Graphic Markup tool properties

All of the Graphic Markup tools enable you to create line weights of zero to 12 points also selected from the Line Properties dialog box. Each of the lines can also be created with different colors. To create a dashed line, set the line weight to zero points in the properties dialog box.

Tip   To create line weights and change line attributes not available in the Line Properties dialog box, create the line(s) you want to use in a program, such as Adobe Illustrator and save the file as a PDF. You can create a custom stamp library for different line weights and styles or append pages to an existing custom stamp library. To append pages, choose the Document ➪ Insert Pages command in Acrobat to insert the new page in a custom stamp PDF document. Choose tools ➪ Forms ➪ Page Templates to create a page template. Using the Stamp tool, create a Stamp comment and select the line that you created. You can associate a text window the same as you would when using the Line tool (see Figure 8-26).

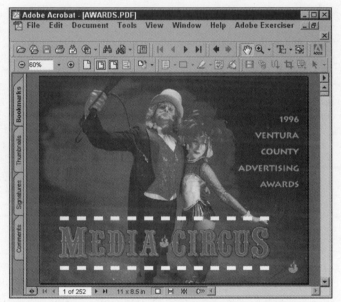

Figure 8-26: I created a 4-point dashed line in Adobe Illustrator and saved the file to PDF format. I then imported the PDF into my custom stamps library by choosing Document ➪ Insert Pages. With the newly inserted page in view, I chose Tools ➪ Forms ➪ Page Templates and named my new image Dashed Line 4 Point. When I created a comment with the Stamp tool, I selected my custom stamps file and chose the name of my new icon from the list in the Stamp Properties dialog box.

Working with Text Markup tools

The last of the Comment tools are the Text Markup tools. Three tools appear in the Text Markup toolbar. The Highlight tool, Strikeout tool, and Underline tool all work with text in a PDF document (see Figure 8-27). When any of the Text Markup tools is positioned in the document window, the cursor changes to an I-beam, indicating text can be selected. To use any of the tools, click and drag across a word, sentence, or through a paragraph. To select a word, just click anywhere on the word. (Acrobat won't select individual characters.) A word within a sentence is the minimum selection that can be made.

 Figure 8-27: Text Markup tools are used to highlight, strikeout, and underline text.

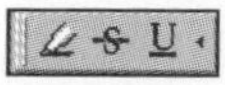

Highlight tool

Using the Highlight tool is like using a highlighter on paper. When you apply the highlight, a transparent display enables you to see the text behind the highlight. Working in Acrobat creates the same results on a monitor display. Selecting the Highlight tool in the Acrobat Command bar and dragging the cursor over a line of text draws highlights. Horizontal movement highlights a line. Drag down to highlight text down the page. The movement of the cursor behaves similarly to the way the cursor moves when the Text Select tool is used, as discussed in Chapter 3. If you want to select a column in a multiple-column document, press the Ctrl key as you drag down the column. Adjacent columns are left undisturbed. Highlighted text won't appear the same on a printed document as you see on-screen. The screen version appears with a transparent overlay. The printed version appears with a rectangle box around the highlighted text.

Strikeout tool

Strikeout text is handled much as it is in applications, such as Microsoft Word. Selecting text is handled the same for all three of the text comment tools. Use the Control/Option key to place a marquee around columns of text as described previously. Horizontal and vertical movement produces the same results as with the other tools.

Underline tool

The last of the Text Markup tools is the Underline tool. This tool enables you to add underlining to text, as the name suggests. The selection of the text is the same as the methods used with the two previous tools and produces the same effects. All three tools support associated notes that can be accessed by double-clicking the comment mark, as shown in Figure 8-28. Note properties are the same for all three tools.

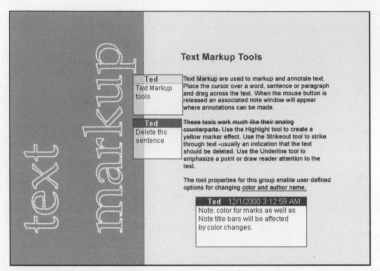

Figure 8-28: The Text Markup tools all have associated notes where comments can be made to further clarify a user's meaning for individual text markups.

Many properties are common between all Comment tools and a few have some distinct differences. For a quick glance at the properties of the comments and markups and what are common or different between them, take a look at Table 8-1.

Table 8-1
Comment and Markup Properties

Tool	Note	Icon	Text Color	Border	Background Fill	Author	Expand/ Collapse	Transparency	Size Icon*
Note	Y	Y	N	N	N	Y	Y	Y	Y
Text	Y	N	Y	Y	Y	Y	N	N	N
Sound	N	N	N	N	N	Y	N	N	N
Stamp	Y	Y	N	N	N	Y	Y	Y	Y
File Attachment	N	Y	N	N	N	Y	N	N	N
Pencil	Y	N	N	N	N	Y	Y	Y	Y
Square	Y	N	N	Y	Y	Y	Y	Y	Y
Circle	Y	N	N	Y	Y	Y	Y	Y	Y

Tool	Note	Icon	Text Color	Border	Background Fill	Author	Expand/ Collapse	Transparency	Size Icon*
Line	Y	N	N	Y	N	Y	Y	Y	Y
Highlight	Y	N	N	N	N	Y	Y	Y	N
Strikeout	Y	N	N	N	N	Y	Y	Y	N
Underline	Y	N	N	N	N	Y	Y	Y	N

* Icon in this regard refers to the mark drawn on the page with the respective tool.

✦ **Note:** The first column in Table 8-1 references the associated note for each comment. The Note Comment tool is itself a note. The appearance of the Note comment is the same for all the other items in Table 8-1 where an associated note is displayed.

✦ **Icon:** When selecting the respective Comment tool, a series of different icons may or may not be used to represent the comment when the note is collapsed or aside the icon. All items identified as Y have several icons that can be selected to represent the appearance of the icon. With regard to the Stamp Comment tool, user-defined custom icons can be created.

✦ **Text Color:** The appearance of the text in the comment note can be adjusted with different color values. Only the text comment provides this feature. (For custom color assignment, refer back to "Assigning Color" earlier in this chapter.)

✦ **Border:** Borders may be invisible or specified in line weights up to 12 points or a dashed line. Lines can be assigned preset or custom colors.

✦ **Background:** The background can be assigned a standard or custom color. Any comments assigned a background color will not appear transparent. The Text Comment tool by default displays transparent. Assigning a color to the background renders an opaque color.

✦ **Author:** The author name can be supplied in the comment properties. A change in author name dynamically appears in associated note title bars.

✦ **Expand/Collapse:** The comment note can be expanded or collapsed. Opening can occur with a context-sensitive menu command or by double-clicking the comment icon. Collapsing the comment note occurs with a context-sensitive menu command or by clicking the close box in the note.

✦ **Transparency:** The associated note can be assigned transparency from the Comment Preferences. The text comment cannot be assigned transparency.

✦ **Size Icon:** The icon or mark drawn on the page can be sized up or down by dragging one of the corner handles.

Common characteristics of comment icons and notes

In addition to the appearance and content of comments, other features are also common across the Comment tools and their content, including the following:

✦ **Context-sensitive menu options:** A context-sensitive menu can be opened when the cursor is placed over any icon and the right mouse button clicked (Control + Click on a Mac).

✦ **Default properties:** Changing defaults, such as font, font size, opacity, and so on in the Comment Preferences changes the default for all comments created in the PDF. Changing individual properties of a comment on the document page changes the current comment and all subsequent comments created (also see Properties dialog box below). Defaults not controlled by note properties remain as identified in the Comment Preferences.

✦ **Delete comment:** Delete all comments by selecting the icon with the Hand tool and striking the Del (Delete on a Mac) key. Other options for deleting comments exist with context-sensitive menus, the Comments palette, and via the Edit menu.

✦ **Filtering:** All comments can be selected in the Filter Comments dialog box. (See Filtering Comments later in this chapter.)

✦ **Listed in Comment palette:** All comment types appear in the Comments palette when the Navigation pane is opened and the Comments tab is selected.

✦ **Maximum characters in a note:** The maximum number of characters contained in an associated note is 5,000.

✦ **Maximum size:** The maximum size for associated notes is 432 pixels wide by 288 pixels high. The Free Text comment can be created as large as the PDF page.

✦ **Move comment:** Select the icon with the Hand tool and drag it around the Document pane to move all comment icons.

✦ **Move comment note:** Dragging the note title bar around the Document pane can move the comment notes.

✦ **Note editing:** Selecting the Hand tool and clicking in the note window edits all associated comment notes. (Text can be edited when many different tools are selected, but some will not enable editing. As a method of consistency, use the Hand tool.) When the Free Text comment needs to be edited, the Free Text comment tool is required.

✦ **Pop-up notes:** When enabled in the Comment Preferences, placing the cursor over the icon of all comments with associated notes opens the note when the note appearance is collapsed. Moving the cursor away from the comment icon collapses the note. This behavior is much like a mouseover call.

✦ **Properties dialog box:** All comments have properties dialog boxes that can be opened with a context-sensitive menu command, choosing Edit ➪ Properties, or pressing Control + I (Command + I on a Mac).

✦ **Reset Note Location:** For all comments with associated notes, the note can be moved with the top left corner of the note registered with the top left corner of the comment icon through a context-sensitive menu option.

✦ **Search:** The content of all comment notes and the Free Text comment note can be searched with the Find Comment command. (See Finding Comment Data later in this chapter.)

✦ **Spell checking:** All comment notes can be spell checked. The Free Text note can be spell checked. (See Spell Checking Comments later in this chapter.)

✦ **Summarizing:** All comments are included in the comment summary according to information about the comment or the note contents. Those comment items that don't have associated notes are listed in the summary without annotation. (See Summarizing Comments later in this chapter.)

Using the Comments Palette

You can imagine that with all the types of comments available, one could easily become lost in a maze of notes and markings. If PDF files are distributed across networks or the Web and input is solicited among many individuals, the number of annotations in a document could easily become confusing. To help develop an organized view for displaying comments, the Comments palette is used. A number of controls are in the Comments palette to help organize, view, summarize, and display comments. To open the Comments palette, click the Show/Hide Navigation pane button in the Command bar or press the F5 key and then click the Comments tab. You can also drag the vertical bar adjacent to the tabs on the right side of the pane to stretch it out. If the Comments tab is not available in the Navigation pane, choose Window ➪ Show Comments. If the Comments appear as a free-floating window when selecting comments from the Window menu, drag the palette to the pane to dock it.

The Comments palette in the Navigation pane displays the comments included in your document. Comments are dynamically placed in the Comments palette as they are created in a PDF. In Acrobat 5.0, you have no need to scan the document to update the palette. From the top-right corner, a palette menu can be opened where menu commands for some comment options appear. Click the down pointing arrow to open the menu. Menu options are the same from this menu as when using a context-sensitive menu when opening it from the Comments palette (see Figure 8-29). If using a context-sensitive menu, be certain to click outside any comments listed in the palette, but within the palette area. If you open a context-sensitive menu while clicking on a comment name in the palette, different menu commands appear (see Figure 8-30).

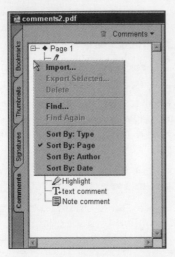

Figure 8-29: When a context-sensitive menu is opened from the Comments palette, the menu appears with options the same as the palette pull-down menu. These options are available when clicking in the palette away from the listed comments.

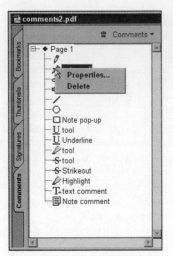

Figure 8-30: If a context-sensitive menu is opened when clicking a comment name, different menu options appear in the pop-up menu.

Menu options exist for the display of the comments in the palette, finding information, and a command for addressing properties. After comments are created in a PDF file, you have many choices for organizing and viewing them.

Note   The Properties command opens the same properties dialog boxes as discussed earlier in this chapter. If you experience difficulty in selecting a comment on the document page, open the Comments tab and select the comment in the list. Open a context-sensitive menu or open the pull-down menu and select Properties. The properties dialog box respective to the selected item opens.

Viewing comments

The display in the Comments palette appears as an outline or file listing similar to your operating system's display. In Windows, the familiar hierarchical structure displays the + (plus) and – (minus) symbols denoting collapsed and expanded views, respectively (see Figure 8-31). Click the plus symbol to expand the list and click the minus symbol to collapse the list. On the Macintosh, you see the right-pointing arrow displayed when the list is collapsed. Click the arrow to the left side of the Comments palette to expand the list. The arrow appears pointing downward when the list is expanded (see Figure 8-32). Click the down arrow to collapse the list.

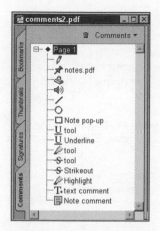

Figure 8-31: Windows display with comments expanded.

Figure 8-32: Macintosh display with comments expanded.

The view in Figures 8-31 and 8-32 display comments according to page. In this example, comments are placed on a single page. With multiple pages, comments are displayed according to page order by default. Sorting comments from menu options displayed in Figure 8-29 can change the order.

When a comment is listed in the Comments palette, any text associated with the comment type displays the first 128 characters contained in the note. In the Comments palette, the width of the palette often is too narrow to display all 128 characters. When the cursor is placed over a comment that contains more text than visible in the palette, a tooltip opens and displays text up to the width of your monitor.

Tip

If you find tooltip displays annoying when browsing comments and selecting them in the Comments palette, you can easily turn them off. Choose Edit ⇨ Preferences ⇨ General and open the Comment settings in the Preferences dialog box. Disable the item Show Comment Tooltips and return to the Document pane. The tooltip displays disappear.

Sorting comments

These four fields can sort comments: Type, Author, Page Number, or Date. Sorts occur in one of two ways: Select the right arrow in the Comments palette and choose one of the sort orders, or open a context-sensitive menu in the Comments palette. Descriptions of the four sort orders are as follows:

✦ **Type:** Comments are sorted according to the type of comment created. The order of the types is sorted alphabetically. (For example, Ellipse precedes Rectangle, and both precede Sound.)

✦ **Author:** The sort order is displayed according to author. All comments created by an author appear nested below the author name. Authors will be sorted alphabetically, as shown in Figure 8-33.

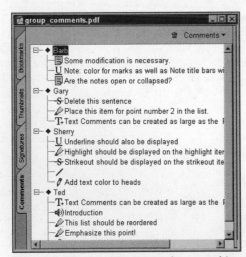

Figure 8-33: Comments can be sorted in four different categories. In this example, the comments are sorted according to the comment author. The comments are grouped according to an alphabetical order by author name.

✦ **Page Number:** Comments are sorted by page number. All comments appearing on page 1 appear listed below the Page 1 category. Page 2 displays another category if comments have been created on the page. If no comments appear, the next page number does not appear in the Comments palette. Only pages containing comments are listed. Regardless of whether the logical page number is used, Acrobat displays page order beginning with the first page in the PDF. If you renumber sections, the order does not conform to the new page numbers.

✦ **Date:** The sort order is displayed according to the date the comment was created. All comments on a given date are nested below the date display in the Comments palette regardless of type, author, or page number.

Navigating comments

The Comments palette can be used as a navigational tool. To open a page where a comment is created, open the Comments palette and view the list. Move the mouse cursor over a comment name and double-click. The page where the comment appears is displayed in the viewer Document pane.

To navigate through comments, you must click a comment name. If you try to double-click any of the category headings (Type, Author, Page Number, or Date), no new page will be displayed. Acrobat does not associate any pages with the category headings.

In the Comments palette, you'll notice the command Select Comment appears on the context-sensitive menu when you right-click (Control + click on a Mac) a comment name. When you choose Select Comment, no navigation occurs. The command is reserved for selecting a comment but not navigating to it. To use this command effectively, first navigate to the page where the comment appears and then open the context-sensitive menu. Choose Select Comment, and the comment appears selected. The use of this command helps if you have difficulty clicking a comment to select it in the Document pane. If the context-sensitive menu is opened without selecting a comment, different menu options will appear.

Finding comment data

If a document contains many different comments, you may want to use the Find Comment search capabilities in Acrobat. Finding information in comments is limited to Acrobat; you can't find comment information in Reader. To use the Find Comments command, open the Comments palette menu or a context-sensitive menu or choose Tools ➪ Comments ➪ Find. Two items are listed for finding information in comments:

✦ **Find:** When Find is selected, the Find Comments dialog box appears. The author name, type, or words contained in a comment note can be searched. When comments are listed in the Comments tab, the Find command becomes active. When the Find Comments dialog box appears, enter the word or words to be searched and click OK.

✦ **Find Again:** After you determine what data are to be searched among the comments in the open document, selecting Find Again searches for the next occurrence meeting the same search criteria as specified the first time you searched for the data using the Find command.

The search criteria used in the Find Comment dialog box is similar to the Find command used in both Reader and Acrobat as explained in Chapter 2. Case-sensitivity, finding backwards from the current page position, and matching whole words are selections in the dialog box that can be used to help narrow the search.

Importing and exporting comments

The commands for importing and exporting comments are available from either the pull-down menu or a context-sensitive menu. Acrobat exports comments in the same order as viewed in the document from which you invoke the Export command. When exporting comments from Acrobat, only the comments are exported. The data on each page is not exported with the comments. As a result, the file sizes for exported comments are considerably smaller than your original PDF documents.

Exported comments are saved as FDF (Forms Data Format) proprietary to Acrobat files. When written as FDF, the data can be imported into any PDF document. The position of the comment and the respective page is fixed. If, for example, you export comments from a three page document and attempt to import comments into a one page document, only the comments from page one of the exported file will be imported into the single page document.

Exporting comments is particularly helpful when distributing a file to many users and asking for input. Each user can export his or her comments, which can then be collected by the PDF author. Subsequently, the export files can all be imported back into the original document. When importing the data, all page sequences and comment types are preserved. For more improved workflow solutions, Acrobat 5.0 now offers the opportunity for workgroups to share comments on servers and through Internet connections. For more information related to collaboration, see Chapter 11.

Before using the Import command from the pull-down menu or the context-sensitive menu, you must have comments exported as an FDF file. When exporting comments, Acrobat exports the comment data and attributes of the comment types only for selected items listed in the Comments palette. Select the comments you want to export, and then choose the Export Selected command from one of the menus. The Export Comments dialog box appears enabling you to find a location on your hard drive and provide a name for the data file. The extension should remain as .fdf when saving the file. When using the Import command from either menu, a dialog box opens and Acrobat recognizes the .fdf files. Select the file to be imported and click the OK button in the Import Comments dialog box.

Deleting comments

You can delete comments by selecting the comment on a page and pressing the Del key (Delete on a Mac) on your keyboard. Deletions can also be performed by using the pull-down menu or a context-sensitive menu and selecting Delete from the menu options. To delete a comment, click the one you want to delete and press the key according to your platform or choose a menu item to delete it. If more than one comment is to be deleted, you can select several comments and use the same keystroke or menu command to delete the selected items. Multiple selections are handled by the following methods:

✦ **Contiguous list selection:** To select multiple comments in the Comments palette in contiguous order, click the first comment, move the cursor to the last comment to be deleted and hold the Shift key down while clicking the mouse button.

✦ **Noncontiguous list selection:** To select multiple comments in the Comments palette in a noncontiguous order, click the first comment, move the cursor to the next comment to be deleted, and hold the Control key down (Command on a Mac) while clicking the mouse button.

If you want to delete all comments from your document, you can use another command. Choose Tools ➪ Comments ➪ Delete All. All the comments created in the document are then deleted.

Multiple Undos

A nice new feature added to Acrobat 5.0 is the ability to use the Edit ➪ Undo frequently. In earlier versions of Acrobat, selecting the Undo command was limited to very few operations. In Acrobat 5.0, the Undo feature has been expanded and now works with many different tool uses and menu commands.

In addition to expanding the use of the Undo command, Acrobat 5.0 has now introduced multiple undos. If you delete a comment, then delete a second and a third comment, you can choose Edit ➪ Undo. Repeat the menu command three times and all the deleted comments are retrieved through the Undo command. When you visit the Edit menu, the Undo command displays what is to be undone. For example, if you delete a strikeout comment, the Edit menu displays Undo Delete Strikeout. When Undo is selected, the Redo item appears in the Edit menu. Redo works the same way. If, for example you delete a note comment and select Undo, the Redo command is displayed as Redo Delete Note.

Comments Menu Commands

The menu options listed in the Comments palette pull-down menu and the context-sensitive menu offer the viewing and organization controls discussed in the previous section. Acrobat provides much more opportunity for organizing comments and offers different display options that occur with additional menu commands. The top-level menu bar supports these options. When you choose Tools ⇨ Comments, the additional menu options are displayed in a submenu. Two items appearing here are in addition to menu options contained in the pull-down menu and the context-sensitive menu. These include the Summarize and Filter commands.

Summarizing comments

When exporting comments, you create a data file where comments are associated with PDF pages. The PDF page however does not export with the data file. In order to see the comments, they need to be imported into a PDF where pages already exist. Most often, importing comments occur in a document from which they were exported. Exporting comments is great if you want to import them in the same location as your original PDF. However, if you want to review a summary of the comment notes, a more efficient means of export is handled with the Summarize command. To access the command, you have to leave the Comments palette and choose Tools ⇨ Comments ⇨ Summarize. When the command is invoked, a dialog box, as shown in Figure 8-34, appears enabling you to choose the sort order for the summary.

Figure 8-34: The Summarize Comments dialog box enables you to create a separate PDF file with the comments summarized according to a sort order made from a pull-down menu.

Depending on the sort order selected from the pull-down menu in the Summarize Comments dialog box, a list of comments appears for all comment types. If, for example, you select Author for the sort order, all comments will be listed for each author beginning with the first page where a given author's comments appear. If more than one comment for a given author is on the same page, the comments are ordered according to date and time. As with the sort order created from the palette or context-sensitive menus, the author names are listed alphabetically.

Summarized comments are helpful when viewing large documents where comments have been contributed by several authors. The summary is concise and occupies only a few pages, depending on the number of contributions. The summary created is a PDF file and appears in the Acrobat viewer immediately after selecting the Summarize command. When the summary is created, it only resides in your computer's random access memory (RAM). If you want to keep the file, it has to be saved to disk. When closing a comment summary, Acrobat opens a warning dialog box if the file has not yet been saved.

In workflows where you have a number of Acrobat Reader users who review documents with the Reader software, be aware that the Reader user cannot summarize comments. If you want to provide Reader users comment summaries, create the summaries as described earlier and append the summarized pages to a PDF file. You can append summarized pages to a file either by inserting pages or by dragging thumbnails from the summarized pages to an open PDF file.

Using the Filter Manager

The Acrobat filter manager is used to individually select comment types and attributes according to author that either appear in the PDF or a summary. When you choose Tools ⇨ Comments ⇨ Filter, the Filter Comments dialog box opens where choices for comment authors and comment types are selected. If you want to have only a selected group of authors with certain comment types listed, the filter manager can accommodate you. Comments can also be listed according to the most recent modification dates. From the Modified pull-down menu, the choices appear, as shown in Figure 8-35.

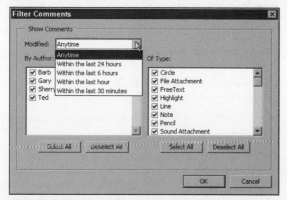

Figure 8-35: The Filter Comments dialog box enables you to isolate comments according to author, type, and a timeframe of when the comments were last modified.

The Filter Manager enables you to selectively determine which comments will be displayed in your document. When you eliminate from view some comment types, the list in the Comments palette is updated to conform to the selections made in the Filter Manager. Furthermore, when you elect to summarize comments, only those listed in the Comments palette are included in the summary.

To get a feel for how comments are created, sorted, managed, and summarized, walk through some steps that you can perform on your computer.

STEPS: Displaying and Summarizing Selective Comments

1. **Open a PDF document.** Use a document with several pages (at least three).

2. **Create comments.** Try to use several different comment types.

3. **Create notes for each comment.** Double-click the comment icon or use the context-sensitive menu and choose Open Note. In the note window, enter a few lines of text.

4. **Change the properties.** Try to create about a dozen different comments. Change the author field several times, producing several notes for additional authors. You can use the Edit ➪ Properties command or a context-sensitive menu. When the Properties dialog box appears, change the author name field.

5. **Summarize the comments.** Choose Tools ➪ Comments ➪ Summarize. Choose a sort order from the pull-down menu and click OK in the Summarize Comments dialog box. A PDF document is created and opened in Acrobat.

6. **Select the original file.** Choose Window ➪ *filename*, where *filename* is the name of the original PDF you opened to create the comments.

7. **Open the Filter Comments dialog box.** To open the Filter Comments, choose Tools ➪ Comments ➪ Filter.

8. **Eliminate two authors.** To eliminate two of the four authors you identified when the comments were created, click the author names for those authors you want to eliminate. The check mark to the left of the author name disappears.

9. **Eliminate comment types.** On the right side of the Filter Comments dialog box, all comment types are listed. Disable the checkboxes for several items. The default for the Modified pull-down menu options is Anytime. Leave Anytime as the menu choice and then click OK in the dialog box.

10. **Summarize the comments.** Choose Tools ➪ Comments ➪ Summarize or press Control + Shift + T (Command + Shift + T on a Mac).

Compare the difference between the first summary and the last. You should see only the comments associated with authors that remained active in the Comments Filter dialog box. Only those comment types that were active in the Comments Filter are displayed in the Comments palette and the summary.

Spell checking comments

A nice new feature for spell checking has been added to Acrobat 5.0. Spell checking won't work on body text or any type created prior to distillation. Spell checking only works with comments and form fields. Type you create in Acrobat with any comment can be spell checked; and even though spell checking is limited to comments and form fields, the Acrobat spell checker is impressive.

Language support is multi-lingual as specified in the preferences. The default language installed with Acrobat will, by default, be the dictionary used with spell checking. You can add to the dictionaries in the General preferences and you can also create a custom dictionary for terms common to your business.

To check spelling on either comments or form fields, select the Spell Check Form Fields and Comments tool in the Acrobat Command bar, or choose Tools ⇨ Spelling ⇨ Check Form Fields and Comments, or press the F7 key on your keyboard. The Acrobat Check Spelling dialog box appears, as shown in Figure 8-36.

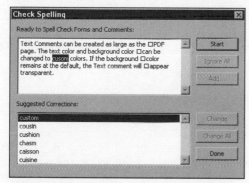

Figure 8-36: The Check Spelling dialog box enables you to change misspelled words or add new words to a custom dictionary.

The Acrobat spell checker works similarly to other application spell checkers. Choose Ignore to continue the check without changing a word. Choose Change to change a single occurrence of a word with the selected word from the Suggested Corrections list or Change All for all occurrences found in the document. If Acrobat encounters a word not found in its dictionary, but you know the word is spelled correctly, you can add it to a custom dictionary. Click the Add button and a dialog box, such as the one shown in Figure 8-37 opens.

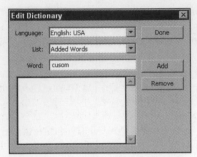

Figure 8-37: The Edit Dictionary dialog box enables you to add new words to a custom dictionary.

One very nice feature with the Acrobat spell checking features is the ability to remove a word from a dictionary. If you inadvertently click a button that adds a word in error, you can find it in the dictionary and delete it. Enter the word in the field box and click the Remove button. Words are added in much the same manner. By default, a word Acrobat doesn't understand is placed in the field box when you select the Add button. You can change the field contents by typing in the Word field box after the Edit Dictionary dialog box appears. Click the Add button in this dialog box when certain the word is spelled correctly.

Editing Text

Creating text in note windows is one of the few means of adding text to PDF files. Acrobat is not a layout or word processing program and doesn't come close to functioning like those applications without the use of third-party plug-ins. If you need to create copy on a page in a PDF document, most often you will want to return to the authoring application, set the type, and then redistill the file. Whereas earlier versions of Acrobat offered little in regard to adding text to the PDF page, Acrobat 5.0 provides much more functionality in this area.

Before moving on to examining how text can be edited in Acrobat, let me start by telling you text editing with Acrobat tools is intended to only slightly modify documents. In some cases, you may be able to correct typographical errors, but reworking a paragraph of text is out of the question. Another matter to deal with in editing text is the availability of fonts. If fonts are subset in the PDF file, characters needed for the font may not be available. If an embedded font is not installed in your system, the font will need to be unembedded in order to edit the text. In such cases, precise font matching is often a problem.

Understanding some of the limitations with the text editing capabilities of Acrobat, Acrobat 5.0 has added many new features where workarounds and text editing can be performed. In this regard, some improved text editing features in Acrobat 5.0 include:

✦ **Text comments for body copy:** The Free Text comment tool can be used to create body copy. Paragraph styles and formatting is limited, but paragraphs of text can be placed over copy on PDF pages. The background for the Text comment can be changed to match the background color of the PDF page. In this regard, using this tool is like pasting a label over existing text to hide it. This method can be used as a quick workaround where you may not have the time or resources to create a new PDF file.

✦ **Text can be added to the PDF page:** A new text block can be added to a PDF page. Unlike previous versions of Acrobat, you can now create raw text in Acrobat 5.0. Text is limited to single lines and no paragraph control can be applied to the lines created.

✦ **Undo works with text editing:** The multiple levels of Undo discussed earlier in this chapter aren't available for text editing. Acrobat 5.0 has, however, provided a single level of Undo when editing text with the TouchUp Text tool.

✦ **Remove embedding:** Acrobat 5.0 now offers a means of unembedding a font in the Text Attributes dialog box. No longer are you prevented from editing text with subsetted characters not available in the embedded font.

✦ **Rotated text editing:** Acrobat 5.0 now offers text editing for rotated text. Single lines of text can be edited consistent with horizontal editing with the TouchUp Text tool.

✦ **Text on a path:** Text on a path can be edited. Unlike other TouchUp Text tool features for editing lines of text, only individual characters can be edited for text created on paths.

✦ **Vertical font editing:** Vertical font editing can be performed similarly to horizontal font editing. Baseline shifts for horizontal text is created in up/down directions while vertical font usage is shifted left/right when adjusting baselines.

Using the TouchUp Text tool

The tool used for text editing in Acrobat is the TouchUp Text tool. Use of the tool is limited to editing single lines of text. Paragraphs with multiple lines are not recognized by Acrobat when using the tool. Paragraph attributes, such as tabs often present problems. When you select the TouchUp Text tool and click in a line of text, the boundaries of the text block appear with a rectangular border, as shown in Figure 8-38.

Figure 8-38: Click over a word of character with the TouchUp Text tool and the text block containing that word or character appears within a border. **Photo/Artwork: Rick Hustead.**

Acrobat may display a warning dialog box indicating there is hidden information in the document when using the TouchUp Text tool. Acrobat can reference the document attributes with information that is hidden from the user. If you elect to proceed, the hidden information will be removed. An example of hidden information would be the text block formatting for character positions. If you create a document with tabs, for example, Acrobat uses a different means to describe where the text is tabbed. Because tabs are not available when creating text in Acrobat, if you proceed from this point, you can potentially encounter problems where the characters will be displayed in a tabbed line of text and you'll lose all the tab attributes.

Note   Earlier versions of Acrobat required using a modifier key when editing text behind a link button. Acrobat 5.0 eliminates the need for using modifier keys. Acrobat assumes you want to edit text when the TouchUp Text tool is used. If a link button is placed over text, Acrobat will not execute a link action when the TouchUp Text tool is used. Clicking with the TouchUp Text tool over a link will select any text behind the link.

Font handing

One of the great features of using Acrobat is the ability to embed all fonts and images in the PDF file. When a font is embedded and you need to edit a line of text, special attention and care needs to be employed. If an embedded font needs to be unembedded in order to change font attributes, the entire font in the PDF file will be affected. When using the TouchUp Text tool and clicking a line of text, a warning dialog box appears if you attempt to edit a font not installed on your system. Figure 8-39 displays the warning dialog box that opens in such cases.

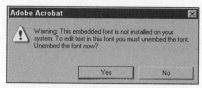

Figure 8-39: When the TouchUp Text tool is clicked on a line of text embedded in the PDF and the font is not installed in the system, a warning dialog box appears.

If you select Yes in the dialog box displayed in Figure 8-39, the font used throughout the document will be unembedded. Acrobat enables you to unembed any embedded font in the PDF file. To re-embed the font, it must be installed on your system.

Caution   In order to legally change attributes of fonts in a PDF document, you must own a copy of the font to be edited or have permission from the font manufacturer.

Moving text

When you select text with the TouchUp Text tool, a rectangular border appears around the text. On the left side of the text border are line markers appearing as a down and up arrow. Line markers are visible by default when you select a line of text. If the markers are not visible, choose Tools ➪ TouchUp ➪ Show Line Markers. To move text, position the cursor above a line marker. Click and drag the mouse left or right. You cannot position text up or down with the TouchUp text tool. To move text vertically on the document page, click the TouchUp Object tool from the Command bar. As an object, the text line can be moved anywhere on the page.

Fitting text to a selection

You can choose to fit the text to a selected area that either stretches the text or condenses it to the area you select. If you change a word in a single line and choose to fit the text to the selection, it may appear as though a second text block is created separately from the original text block. The display is misleading because all the text remains in a single line. To fit text to a selection, first select text in the line then choose Tools ➪ TouchUp ➪ Fit Text to Selection or use a context-sensitive menu and select the same menu command.

Text attributes

You can change many text attributes by using the Text Attributes palette, shown in Figure 8-40. To open the Text Attributes palette, choose Tools ➪ TouchUp ➪ Text Attributes or use a context-sensitive menu and select Attributes from the pop-up menu.

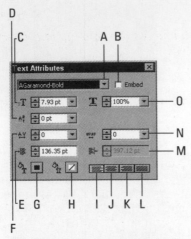

Figure 8-40: The Text Attributes palette contains options for changing font attributes.

✦ **A** **Font selection:** A pull-down menu displays all fonts loaded in your system. From the menu, select the font to be used when creating new text or editing an existing line of text.

✦ **B** **Embed:** A font can be unembedded by clicking the checkbox in this dialog box the same as if selecting Yes in the warning dialog box in Figure 8-37. If a line of text is added to a PDF page or a font is unembedded, the font can be embedded by selecting the checkbox.

✦ **C** **Text size:** The font point size can be changed by selecting the pull-down menu and making a selection from the fixed values or by entering a value in the field box.

✦ **D** **Baseline offset:** Offsets text vertically above or below the text baseline.

✦ **E** **Character spacing:** Condenses or expands the distance between characters.

✦ **F** **Left line tab:** Moves the text line for the left side of the line left or right when the arrows are selected or a value is entered in the field box.

✦ **G**   **Text fill color:** Select the color swatch to open the color palette where preset or custom colors can be selected.

✦ **H**   **Text stroke color:** Another color palette is used to specify colors to be applied to a text outline.

✦ **I**   **Left justify:** Click the icon to left justify text.

✦ **J**   **Center justify:** Click the icon to align text centered within the selection rectangle.

✦ **K**   **Right justify:** Click the icon to right justify text.

✦ **L**   **Full justification:** Click the last icon to fully justify the text.

✦ **M**   **Right line tab:** Moves the text line for the right side of the line left or right when the arrows are selected or a value is entered in the field box.

✦ **N**   **Word spacing:** Adjusts the spacing between words.

✦ **O**   **Text X-scale:** Horizontally scales text from 80 percent to 120 percent sizes from the pull-down menu choices. Values entered in the field box can be supplied for sizes ranging between .01 percent and 32767 percent.

All of the above items are contained in the Text Attributes palette. The palette can remain open while editing text in Acrobat. In order to employ any attribute changes for text characters, be certain to select the text, and then make selections from the palette options.

Text editing controls

Moving around text blocks in Acrobat can be simplified by using keystrokes on your keyboard. Following is a list of keystrokes and how they relate to text editing:

✦ **Click and drag** across a line of text to select it.

✦ **Double-click** a word to select it.

✦ **Triple-click** in a line of text to select the line (Macintosh only).

✦ **Shift + click** to select text from the first cursor position to the second click position.

✦ Use **Shift + right arrow** to select one character to the right; the selection is extended as long as the Shift key is pressed.

✦ Press **Shift + left arrow** to select one character to the left; the selection is extended as long as the Shift key is pressed.

✦ The **up arrow** moves the cursor to the preceding line of text.

✦ The **down arrow** moves the cursor to the following line of text.

✦ **Control/Command + A** selects all the text in a line.

✦ **Del key** deletes one character after cursor position or all selected text.

✦ **Backspace** (Delete on a Mac) deletes one character to the left of cursor position or all selected text.

✦ **Pressing any key when text is selected** deletes the current selection and replaces the text with the keystroke.

✦ **Pressing the right mouse button** (Windows) opens a context-sensitive menu where the commands Select Line, Fit Text to Selection, Delete, Cut, Copy, Paste, and Attributes are available.

✦ **Control + clicking** a text block (Macintosh) opens a context-sensitive menu with the same choices as right-clicking in Windows.

✦ **Edit ➪ Clear** deletes selected text.

✦ **Edit ➪ Deselect All** deselects all the selected text.

External editors

To ease the burden of text editing in Acrobat, external editors can sometimes be used without having to redistill the file. Text blocks contained on individual pages can be edited in an external editor and, when saved, will update the PDF file. External editing is handled with the TouchUp Object tool. Before using the tool however, you must first let Acrobat know what editor will be used. Determining the editor is handled in the General Preferences dialog box.

Choose Edit ➪ Preferences ➪ General to open the General Preferences dialog box. Along the list on the left side of the dialog box, select TouchUp. The second button appearing in the dialog box is used for objects. In Acrobat terms, *objects* are vector art objects and text. Click this button to open the Select Page/Object Editor dialog box. From this dialog box, you can navigate your hard drive and select the editor you want to use. Select an editor in the dialog box and click the Open button.

Editing Text In Adobe Illustrator

One caveat when using Adobe Illustrator or any other program where a PDF is opened from yet not saved as PDF from Illustrator 9 is that text will be broken up. Paragraphs are not preserved and every line of text within a paragraph will have multiple groups of characters with no common order. To edit the text as it first appears will create problems with word wraps and text flow. In a program such as Adobe Illustrator, you can reform the text block where all the characters and lines will be contained in normal paragraph style. After using the Edit Object command and using Adobe Illustrator as your external editor, select all the text by striking Control + A (Command + A on a Mac). Copy the text (Control/Command + A). Click the Text tool and drag open a rectangular text block. Press Control/Command + V to paste the text in the new text frame. All the text will be pasted as a contiguous block where word wrap, indents, and paragraph styles can be applied (see Figure 8-41). When using the Edit Object command, size the text block to match the original size of the text block, and then delete the original text. Save the file and the text is dynamically updated in the PDF.

The editor you select must conform to acceptable editors compatible with Acrobat. In as much as you may be tempted to use a text editor, Acrobat only maintains compatibility with PostScript editing programs, such as Adobe Illustrator. Compatibility with Illustrator is perhaps best used with either text or objects.

If a dialog box appears informing you of a format incompatibility, Acrobat doesn't support the editor that you selected in the preferences for external editing. You need to return to the preferences and select a different editor. When an acceptable editor is used, the text appears in a document window. The file must still remain open in Acrobat while the external editing is being performed. If you quit the Acrobat session, no changes will occur in the PDF document.

After finishing your edits, select Save from the File menu of your editor. If you select Save As and write a new file, the edited text won't be updated in Acrobat. When external editing is performed, Acrobat uses a temporary file to hold the information in memory. This file needs to remain alive and should be updated with the Save command. When you quit the external editor after saving, Acrobat completes the update.

Object Linking and Embedding

PDF files can be handled by any container application supporting Object Linking and Embedding (OLE). A program such as Microsoft Word can have PDF files represented as links from the application document to the PDF. Once placed in the container application, PDFs can be externally edited in Acrobat and easily updated because they are linked to the application document.

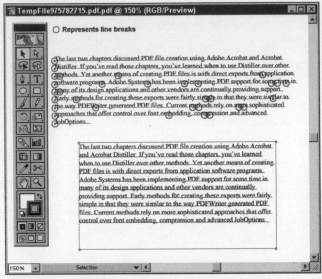

Figure 8-41: The top body of text is exported from Acrobat. The circles within the text body represent line breaks or breaks in the text. When the text was selected, copied, and pasted into the new text block below, all the line breaks were eliminated and the text was reformed into a contiguous body.

With regard to text editing, the entire body of text within a PDF file can be copied to the clipboard and pasted into a program supporting OLE. Choose File ➪ Copy File to Clipboard to place all the text in the open document on the clipboard. In an application program with OLE support, such as Microsoft Word, create a new document and choose Edit ➪ Paste Special. The Paste Special dialog box appears, as shown in Figure 8-42.

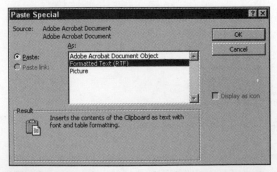

Figure 8-42: When an application program supports Object Linking and Embedding (OLE), the Paste Special command opens a dialog box where options for the format of the pasted information can be made.

To paste an object, select the Adobe Acrobat Document Object item in the dialog box. Pasting with this option interprets the file as an object. As an object, no text editing can be performed. When Formatted Text (RTF) is selected, the text is pasted into the application document. Formatting retains all text attributes and, as such, can be edited. If a block of text needs editing, you can complete editing in a word processor, and then subsequently create a new PDF page. With the Acrobat Replace Pages command, you can then replace the original page with the newly edited page (see Chapter 9). This procedure works well for text only pages, but with graphic objects, a little more work is involved.

TouchUp order

The last tool appearing among the TouchUp tools is the TouchUp Order tool. By default, the tool is inactive unless you are working on a structured PDF file. In order to preserve the structure in a PDF, it needs to be exported from applications that support structured content, as discussed back in Chapter 6.

Click the tool from the Acrobat Command bar. When the tool is selected and a PDF page with structure is viewed in the Document pane, the structural order is displayed, as viewed in Figure 8-43.

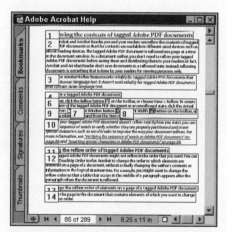

Figure 8-43: When the TouchUp Order tool is selected and a structured PDF is in view, the order of structured elements is displayed with a number in the top left corner of each structure item.

To change the order of structured elements, click the number appearing in the top left corner of each text block. You can start with the text block to be the first to appear in a new order and then successively click the text blocks that follow the new order. If you need to start again, click any tool, and then select the TouchUp

Order tool again from the Acrobat Command bar. Additional arrangements can also be made from choices available in a context menu. Open a context-sensitive menu by selecting a text block and right-clicking the mouse button (Windows) or Control + click (Macintosh). After assigning the new order, click the Reflow tool in the Acrobat Command bar to reflow the text.

Working with table data (Windows)

The structure of text in a PDF document can be further preserved where tables and columns of text are involved. If table cells containing data need to be imported into a program, such as Microsoft Excel, or newspaper columns of text need to be imported into Microsoft Word, using the table formatting features of Acrobat preserves data integrity. As of this writing, support for handling table data in this section only applies to Acrobat running under Windows.

Table data can be exported in a number of formats that are described with the Table/Formatted Text preferences in Chapter 7. When working with table data, be certain to check the preferences against those options discussed in Chapter 7. After establishing preferences, click the Table/Formatted Text Select tool from the Acrobat Command bar. To use the tool, click and drag around the data to be exported. Like all other tools, specific options are available for the tool in a context-sensitive menu. When the context-sensitive menu is opened, choices for handling the data include:

✦ **Copy:** The area within the selection rectangle determines what data is copied to the clipboard.

✦ **Save As:** The data within the selection rectangle can be saved as a file in one of four formats. Choose from ANSI (American National Standards Institute), OEM (original equipment manufacturer), Unicode, or RTF. To avoid problems with symbols and high ASCII characters, avoid OEM and save in one of the other three formats.

✦ **Clear:** The data within the selection rectangle remains unaffected. The Clear command only eliminates the selection rectangle.

✦ **Text (Flow):** The Text command opens a submenu where two items appear, the first of which is Flow. This option disregards PDF line breaks and flows the text into a column format. Paragraph breaks are preserved. The format may be used with columnar text similar to newspapers.

✦ **Text (Preserve Line Breaks):** Keeps the line breaks as you view them in the PDF document as well as original line breaks created in the authoring program prior to PDF conversion. This option may be used with multiple columns and headings that are aligned differently. When the RTF format is specified, horizontal formatting of columns is preserved.

✦ **Table:** Use this option for bona fide tables where cell data needs to be preserved. Exporting to Microsoft Excel may be one good example of table data placed in individual cells.

✦ **Horizontal:** The same as preference options discussed in Chapter 7, Horizontal is used with Roman fonts and horizontal formats.

✦ **Vertical:** Also a preference item discussed in the previous chapter, Vertical is used with vertically displayed fonts, such as Japanese characters.

Drag and drop exports

Table data can be saved from the menu command discussed in the previous section, copied and pasted into editing applications, and can also be dragged and dropped from Acrobat to Windows programs. When using the drag and drop method of exporting the data, the format for data received by the destination document defaults to RTF.

The process is simple. Click the Table/Formatted Text Select tool from the Acrobat Command bar and open a rectangle on the PDF page. Don't be concerned about precise placement of the selection marquee. The rectangle can be readjusted after a rectangle has been drawn and you release the mouse button. Place the cursor over any corner and drag the handles diagonally to size the rectangle up or down. As soon as the data has been selected, click and drag from the Acrobat document to an open document in the receiving application. Both windows need to be in view and the receiver application needs to have a document page in view — either containing data or a blank page. Release the mouse button, and the data is dropped into the application document window, as shown in Figures 8-44 and 8-45.

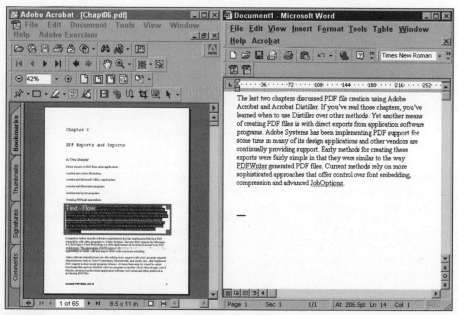

Figure 8-44: A body of text was defined as a table in Acrobat and dragged and dropped to a new document page in Microsoft Word.

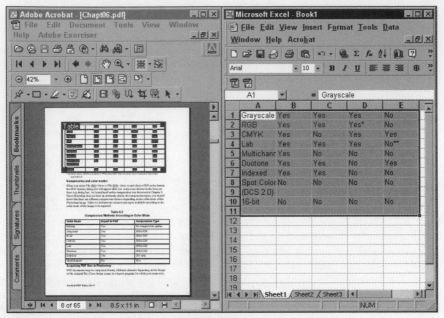

Figure 8-45: In this example, a table is dragged and dropped to Microsoft Excel. All data from the rows and columns are placed in individual cells.

Note Acrobat has traditionally offered more features in new releases for Windows users than Macintosh users upon the first release of a new version. Table formatted text features are available for Windows and may not be available for Macintosh users in the early release. Adobe makes every effort to keep cross-platform compliance with all their products and quite often adds more features for one platform version or another with maintenance upgrades. If using a Macintosh, keep visiting the Adobe Web site where you can find the latest upgrade information. As soon as a maintenance upgrade is available, you can download it from the Adobe Web site (www.adobe.com).

Tip For Macintosh users who want to export data to Microsoft Excel, use the Column Select tool and marquee the data to be exported. Copy the data to the clipboard and open Microsoft Word. Excel won't interpret the pasted data as a table if you attempt to paste directly into Excel. Word, on the other hand, preserves most of the data as a table. Paste the clipboard contents into Word. Now in table format from Word, recopy the data and paste it into an Excel spreadsheet. The data may need a little editing, but you won't need to parse the data to get it into individual cells.

Working with Graphics Editors

You can move graphics on a PDF page and edit graphics with the same tool discussed above. Also enabled in preferences, Acrobat makes a distinction between an image editor and an object editor. When working with text or vector art objects, the object editor is selected from the Choose Page/Object Editor button. The Image Editor button enables navigation to find the image editor of choice. Adobe Photoshop will be the image editor of choice for most people and it is fully supported by Acrobat.

Chapter 3 demonstrated how to use the Graphics Select tool in Acrobat Reader. The same tool exists in Acrobat, and the way it's used in Acrobat is the same as it is handled in Reader. For external editing, the TouchUp Object tool offers much more flexibility.

TouchUp Object tool commands

Various attribute choices for the TouchUp object tool appear in a context-sensitive menu. You have no special menu commands as the tool usage is straightforward and relatively uncomplicated. When using the TouchUp Object tool, it's important to remember that an object must be selected in order to invoke an action, such as editing an object. Click the tool from the Acrobat Command bar and click an object in the document page. An object can be either a graphic image element or a body of text. When you open a context-sensitive menu, the options appear as shown in Figure 8-46.

Figure 8-46: Context menu options for the TouchUp Object include several ways of handling, copying, and pasting image data.

✦ **Cut:** Cuts the selected contents out of the PDF page and places them on the clipboard.

✦ **Copy:** The traditional copy command places the selected contents on the clipboard.

✦ **Paste:** Pastes contents of the clipboard on the page viewed in the Document pane. When an object or objects have been copied and pasted back to the same PDF document, they are pasted to the same page location as where they originated. When pasted to a different PDF document, they are pasted in the lower left corner of the page.

✦ **Paste in Front:** Pastes the clipboard contents in front of selected object(s). When transparent elements have been copied and pasted in front of other objects the transparent effect is preserved.

✦ **Paste in Back:** Pastes the clipboard contents in back of a selected object. When transparent elements have been used in the PDF, the pasted object behind a transparent object is displayed with transparency in tact.

✦ **Delete:** Deletes the selected object(s).

✦ **Select All:** All elements including text are selected.

✦ **Select None:** Deselects any selected elements.

✦ **Delete Clip:** Any clipping that may occur when sizing elements, such as text, restores the image data without any clipping.

✦ **Edit Object:** Like the TouchUp Text tool, this command launches the external editing application. With objects, image editors, such as Photoshop, are launched and the image placed in a new document window. If more than one object is selected, the menu command appears as Edit Objects, indicating all objects will be placed on the image editor document page.

Selecting objects

The TouchUp Object tool offers much more flexibility in regard to selecting data than the TouchUp Text tool. Whereas the TouchUp Text tool can only select a single line of text, the TouchUp Object tool can select multiple objects. The Select All command in the context-sensitive menu selects all data appearing on a given page. If the tool is positioned over an object and the mouse button clicked, the object beneath the cursor is selected.

For multiple object selection, click the TouchUp Object tool from the Command bar and drag the cursor through the objects to be selected. Acrobat doesn't need to completely surround objects with a marquee. Simply dragging the cursor through multiple objects in a horizontal or vertical plane selects all objects within the path.

If a background color appears on the page, Acrobat sees it as an object. You can handle object selections in several ways if you want multiple objects selected in the foreground while leaving the background element deselected. First, the background can be moved with the TouchUp Object tool to a temporary position and out of the way of the foreground items to be selected. Drag through the objects after moving the background to select them. Secondly, you can select multiple objects and hold the Shift key down to deselect individual items. In this case, dragging through foreground and background elements to select them, then hold the shift key down and click the background to deselect it.

Deselecting items can be handled by the context-sensitive menu command mentioned previously or click the cursor outside the selected items. To deselect individual items, hold the shift key down while clicking successively on selected items.

Tip

If a number of objects need to be selected among a maze of other objects, you can delete items then return to the original page. Select individual objects and press the Del key (Delete on a Mac). When all the unwanted items are deleted, drag the cursor through the items to be selected or use the context-sensitive menu command Select All. Copy the contents to the clipboard and then choose File ⇨ Revert. The page is restored to its original view before deleting any objects.

External object editing

When an object is selected, choose Edit Object from the context-sensitive menu or hold down the Control key (Windows) or Option key (Macintosh) and double-click the mouse button. Either action produces the same result. At this point, you momentarily lose control of your computer. By default, Acrobat launches Adobe Illustrator 9 (8 or 7 are also supported) if installed on your computer when vector objects are selected. For raster-based objects, the default is Adobe Photoshop 6 (5.5 and 5.0 are also supported). If you have earlier versions of either application, they won't be compatible with Acrobat.

Note

When Adobe Photoshop version 5.5 and lower is installed on your computer, a special plug-in from the Acrobat installer CD needs to be placed in the Photoshop plug-ins folder. During installation, Acrobat prompts you for the Photoshop folder and installs the necessary components. When you install Photoshop 6, no special components are needed. If you have both Photoshop 6 and an earlier version of Photoshop on your computer, the installer will prompt you for only the folders where Photoshop versions lower than 6 reside. Don't worry about needing to tell the installer where Photoshop 6 is located. Acrobat 5 and Photoshop 6 work seamlessly together without any special configuration.

When either Illustrator or Photoshop is launched, the object selected in the PDF document appears in the application window for the program launched. As you work in either Illustrator or Photoshop, you can make any editing changes you would normally make before the file was converted to PDF. If the file has been protected with encryption at any level, the Edit Image command won't be available. Neither using the context-sensitive menu nor double clicking the object will enable you to open the PDF in an external editor.

Using the Acrobat Edit Image command is better suited for modifying images than copying and pasting data. When you copy data and edit an image, the page must then be produced as a PDF file. Acrobat won't let you paste image data from Photoshop back into the PDF page. When Edit Image is used, the PDF document is dynamically updated if any object edits are made.

 Tip   Copying and pasting data between PDF files is permitted in Acrobat 5.0. If you don't have a source image contained within a PDF where Edit Image can be accessed, you can copy and paste between PDF files. In Photoshop, edit an image and save it as PDF. Open the PDF and select the image with the TouchUp Object tool. Copy the selection to the clipboard. Open the destination document and select a paste option from a context-sensitive menu.

We looked at text editing with Adobe Illustrator earlier in this chapter. Now, take a moment and follow some steps on editing an image in Photoshop when using the Edit Image command.

STEPS: Using Edit Image with Adobe Photoshop

1. **Open a PDF file.** Use a PDF file of your choice. If you do not have a file handy, create a page in a page layout application with a graphic image from either Adobe Illustrator or Adobe Photoshop. Print the file to disk and distill it in Acrobat Distiller. Depending on what version of Photoshop you have, you may also be able to edit an image from a captured Web page.

2. **Verify preferences.** Choose Edit ⇨ Preferences ⇨ General. In the Preferences dialog box. Click TouchUp and be certain the image editing program you intend to use appears listed in the dialog box. If it does not, click the Choose Image Editor button and navigate to your image editor. Be certain the editor of choice is compatible with Acrobat 5.0.

3. **Select the object.** Use the TouchUp Object tool and select the image you want to edit.

4. **Select Edit Object.** Choose either the context-sensitive menu command for Edit Object or hold the Control key (Windows) or Option key (Macintosh) down while double-clicking the selected object.

5. **Edit your image.** Perform some editing tasks that are easily observable in Acrobat, such as applying a filter, changing color, and so on. In many cases, you may need to change a color mode. Although not visible at times, it may be a task you will perform frequently. In my example, I changed from RGB to CMYK color and applied a filter to add some film grain to the image (see Figure 8-47).

Note

When opening a file in Photoshop, you may encounter a dialog box asking you how to handle color information. If using Photoshop 5.5, select the option for leaving color unchanged. If using Photoshop 6.0, select the item to discard the color information. If you are using profile management in Photoshop, the profile used during your editing session will be embedded in the file when it is saved again and exports to Acrobat.

Figure 8-47: In Adobe Photoshop, I convert my color mode from RGB to CMYK color and apply the Film Grain filter to give the image an older appearance.

6. **Choose File ⇨ Save.** Be certain to click the Save button. If you provide another name for the image, it won't be updated properly in Acrobat. The Save command saves a temporary file to the location where the PDF document was opened.

7. **Quit the application.** After saving, quit the application where you edited your image. You are returned to Acrobat, and your newly edited image appears in the PDF file. (See Figure 8-48.)

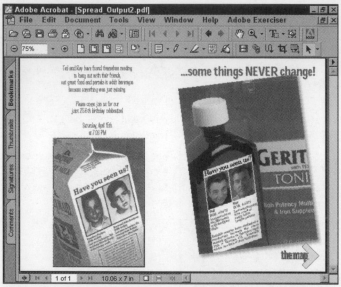

Figure 8-48: After saving my file in Photoshop, I close the document and return to Acrobat. My image file is updated in the PDF.

Summary

✦ Comments can be developed from among three major categories: Comment tools, Graphic Markup tools, and Text Markup tools.

✦ Most comments created in Acrobat have associated notes where descriptions of comments can be supplied.

✦ Comments all have Properties dialog boxes in which unique options can be defined for the comment type.

✦ Comments can be exported from and imported back into PDF files. In addition, comment summaries can be created that immediately open as new PDF documents.

✦ The Comments palette lists all the comments in a document. Double-clicking a comment in the palette moves you to the page where the comment appears.

✦ Comments can be sorted by Type, Author, Page Number, and Date.

✦ The Filter Comments dialog box enables you to select the comments you want to view in the PDF document. When selected, comments are eliminated from view and the comment summary only lists the comments visible in the document.

✦ The TouchUp Text tool is used for minor edits to text in a PDF file. Text can be altered only one line at a time, although many different text attributes can be changed through the Text Attributes palette. Text can be edited in an external editor and dynamically updated in the PDF file.

✦ Raw text can now be created on a PDF page from within Acrobat 5.0.

✦ Text can be spell checked for all comment contents and form fields.

✦ Table formatted text can be preserved and exported to other application programs. The feature is supported only on Windows in the first product release.

✦ The TouchUp Object tool enables you to select and move graphic elements on a PDF page. When you choose the Edit Image command, the selected image appears in an editing program where changes can be made. When the file is saved from the editing program, the PDF page is dynamically updated to reflect the edits.

✦   ✦   ✦

Articles, Bookmarks, and Thumbnails

Working with Articles

Acrobat offers a feature to link text blocks within a PDF file for easy navigation through columns of text, known as *article threads*. User-specified ranges of text can be linked together to form an article. Articles help you navigate through a PDF file, enabling you to read continuing sequences of paragraphs throughout a document.

Working with articles is particularly helpful when you view PDF files on the World Wide Web. With article threads, you can download specific pages of a PDF file in a Web browser, one page at a time without having to wait for an entire file to download. Therefore, if you have a column or group of paragraphs of text that begins on page 1 and continues on page 54, an article thread can assist you in jumping from page 1 to page 54.

Article viewing and navigation

In the following text, an icon may appear occasionally to help you easily identify a tool in the Acrobat Command bar with the topic being discussed. As you browse this section and the remaining chapters, note the tool icon as references to specific tools addressed in the body text.

When you first open a PDF document, you want to determine if articles are present in the file. If articles are included in the PDF, you need to know a few basics on navigating through an article. To determine if articles exist in a PDF file, choose Window ➪ Articles. A palette opens with tabs for Articles and Destinations, as shown in Figure 9-1. If you want to move the Articles palette to the Navigation Pane, click the tab and drag to the top of the open Navigation Pane. The Articles palette can remain in the Navigation pane for all subsequent Acrobat sessions as long as you leave it docked in the pane when quitting Acrobat.

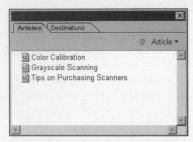

Figure 9-1: When you choose Window ➪ Articles, a palette opens with the Articles tab displayed.

When the Articles palette is in view, any articles existing in the PDF file are displayed in the palette list. If you select the Article tool from the Acrobat Toolbar, the article definition boundaries are displayed. In Figure 9-2, the Article tool is selected. The defined article is contained within rectangular boxes. If another tool is selected in the Command bar, the rectangles disappear.

Figure 9-2: If an article appears on a page and the Article tool is selected in the Command bar, the article boundaries will appear around text used to define the article.

Article properties

The Article properties are contained in a dialog box accessible by clicking an article with the Article tool. To open the Article Properties dialog box, choose Edit ⇨ Properties or open a context-sensitive menu by right-clicking (Control + Click on a Mac) and select Properties from the pop-up menu. Context-sensitive menus can be opened from either the Articles palette or by clicking one of the article boundaries on the document page.

The Properties dialog box is informational. When you view Properties, information supplied at the time the article was created is displayed for four data fields. The Title, Subject, Author, and Keywords fields are the same as those found in the Document Properties dialog boxes. In as much as the data for these fields is identical to that found in document information, Acrobat Search does not take advantage of the article properties information. When you use properties, they are designed to help you find information about an article before jumping to the page where the article is contained. All the fields can be edited when the Article Properties dialog box is opened, as shown in Figure 9-3. You can at any time change the data in the fields.

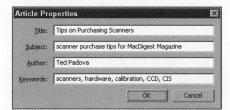

Figure 9-3: The Article Properties dialog box displays user-supplied information for Title, Subject, Author, and Keyword fields. These fields are not searchable through Acrobat Search.

Viewing articles

Before moving about a document to explore articles, the first item you should always check is the maximum view defined in the General Preferences when Display settings is selected. The default magnification view is 800 percent. When articles are viewed, this zoom may be too high for comfortable viewing. Depending on your monitor size and your vision, you may find zooms of even 200 percent to be too large or too small. If you use a small monitor, a 200 percent zoom will usually lose columns adjacent to the column being read. Find a comfort zone for your own viewing preferences and set them up in the General Preferences Display settings dialog box.

As soon as the zoom is established, open the Articles palette by selecting Window ➪ Articles. The Articles palette can remain as an individual palette, or you can drop it into the Navigation pane. The palette pull-down menu in the Articles palette offers only one option. If you choose Hide After Use from the palette pull-down menu, the palette will disappear. If you want to have the palette remain but want more viewing area in the document, dock the palette in the Navigation pane.

When articles are displayed in the palette, double-click an article to jump to the first view in the thread. Acrobat places in view the top corner where the article begins. You immediately see a right-pointing arrow blink on the left side of the first line of text. As soon as an article is in view, click the Hand tool and position the cursor over the article. The cursor changes to a hand with an arrow pointing down. As you read articles, the cursor changes according to the direction Acrobat takes you when reading an article. For example, if viewing a column backward or up instead of down, the cursor changes display to inform you which direction will be navigated. The different cursor views are shown in Figure 9-4.

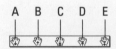

Figure 9-4: Different cursors are used when viewing articles to inform you ahead of time the direction to be navigated.

To help navigation with the Article tool, several keyboard modifiers assist you when using the mouse. From Figure 9-4, the cursor changes according to the modifier keys listed here:

- ✦ **A Click:** First click zooms to the Max Fit Visible preference setting. When the mouse cursor is placed at the end of a column, the cursor displays a down arrow. Click at the end of an article, and the view takes you to the beginning of the next column. Figure 9-4 displays the cursor icon when appearing over the end of a column.

- ✦ **B Shift + click:** Moves backward or up a column. The cursor display appears, as shown in Figure 9-4.

- ✦ **C Alt/Option + click:** Moves to the beginning of the article.

- ✦ **D Control/Option + Shift + click:** Moves to the end of an article.

- ✦ **E Control/Command + Shift + click:** When the cursor is placed over a link, the link is ignored and the article navigation moves the same as the first entry in this list.

- ✦ **Return or Enter:** Moves forward down the column or to the top of the next column.

- ✦ **Shift + Return or Enter:** Moves up or to the previous column.

Defining articles

Articles are defined by drawing rectangular boxes around the text that establish the article definition. While using the Article tool, the rectangular boxes are visible. When the tool is not active, the rectangular boxes become invisible.

Click and drag open a rectangle surrounding the column to appear as the first column in the article. When the mouse button is released, the rectangular box is visible. At each corner and side appears a handle that can be used to reshape the rectangle. An article number is visible at the top of the rectangle, as shown in Figure 9-5. The lower-right corner contains a plus (+) symbol. The number appearing at the top of each box indicates the article number in the document (first article, second article, and so on) and the column order for the article. Therefore, a number, such as 2-3, would represent the second article in the PDF file and the third column for the second article. The second digit indicates the order of forward movement as the article is read. The plus symbol appearing in the lower-right corner for each box indicates the article thread is continued. The plus symbol at the bottom right of the rectangle is also used for linking. If you want to return to Acrobat after deselecting the Article tool, you can continue to add more columns after reselecting the tool. Click the plus symbol, and Acrobat knows that you want to extend the article thread.

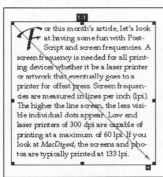

Figure 9-5: The Article tool creates article threads by dragging in a diagonal direction and surrounding the text to be contained within the thread. When the mouse button is released, the article number and column number appear at the top of the rectangle.

Tip

Article threads can be created at the time the PDF file is either exported or distilled with Acrobat Distiller. Most layout applications support creating articles prior to export to PDF. In some cases, you may want to have a single article thread used to help user navigation through your document. Identify an article in one of the programs discussed in Chapter 6, and then export to PDF.

Ending an article thread

When you reach the end of the article, Acrobat needs to know if you want to finish creating the thread. To end an article thread, press Return, Enter, or Esc. Acrobat prompts you with a dialog box for supplying the Title, Subject, Author, and Keyword fields for the article properties. This dialog box appears immediately after defining an article. Supplying the information at the time the dialog box is opened is a good idea. The task is completed, and you won't need to worry about returning to the Article Properties dialog box for last minute clean up.

Deleting articles

If an article has been created, you may want to delete a portion of the article thread or the entire article. To delete either, select the Article tool in the Acrobat Toolbar and click a rectangle box where an article has been defined. Press the Backspace (Delete) key on your keyboard or open a context-sensitive menu and select Delete from the menu options. A dialog box appears that provides options for deleting the currently selected box or the entire article, as shown in Figure 9-6.

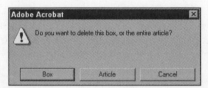

Figure 9-6: The Delete Article dialog box enables you to choose between deleting an article segment or the entire article.

If the Box button is selected, the deletion will eliminate the box within the article thread that you selected when the Backspace (Delete) key was pressed on the keyboard. Clicking the Article button deletes all boxes used to define the article thread.

Combining articles

At times you may want to join two articles to create a single article. The reader can then continue a path through all contents of the former two articles, which are now in a single thread. To join two articles, you must first have them defined in the PDF document. Move to the last column of the first article and click the plus symbol in the last box. This click loads the Article tool. Next, move to the beginning of the article to be joined to the first article and Control/Option + click inside the first box. While the modifier key is pressed, the cursor icon changes, as illustrated in Figure 9-7.

Figure 9-7: When the Control/Option key is pressed, the cursor changes to an icon informing you that the selected articles will join.

The numbering at the top of each box in the second article changes. For example, if you have two articles, the first numbered 1-1, 1-2, 1-3, and the second article numbered 2-1, 2-2, the new numbering for the second article will be 1-4 and 1-5. Article 2 takes on the attributes of Article 1 and assumes the next order of the columns. In addition, the properties identified in the second column will be lost. Because the continuation of the thread is from Article 1, all attributes for Article 1 supersede those of Article 2.

Tip If you want to combine two articles and assume the properties of a given article, always start with the article attributes to be retained. For example, in the preceding case, begin with article 2. Select the plus symbol at the end of the last column and click Control/Option + click in the first box for Article 1. When the two articles become combined, the attributes of Article 2 are retained.

Working with Bookmarks

Bookmarks work the way a table of contents does in PDF documents. Bookmarks can be created from layout programs, as mentioned in Chapter 6, or they can be created in Acrobat. Whereas tables of contents in analog publications are static, bookmarks in Acrobat viewers are dynamic. They enable you to jump to sections and views within an open document or links to files stored on a computer or server.

Bookmarks are viewed in the Navigation pane. Open a PDF file, click the Show/Hide Navigation pane icon in the Command bar or drag open the Navigation pane, and bookmarks appear as the default view. If no bookmarks are included in the document, the window appears empty. The Navigation pane lists bookmarks individually, or you may see them nested in groups. The display looks similar to what you'd see for comments discussed in Chapter 8. A plus symbol (Windows) or right-pointing arrow (Macintosh) indicates the bookmarks are collapsed. Clicking the icon expands bookmarks. The Bookmarks palette contains icons and menu options, as shown in Figure 9-8.

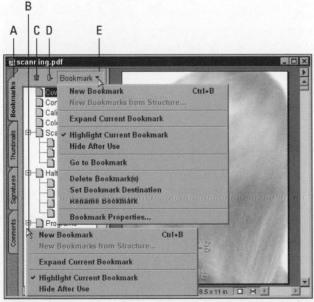

Figure 9-8: The Bookmarks palette contains icons and menu commands where bookmark attributes are selected.

✦ **A   Bookmarks tab:** This tab displays the palette when selected. If another tab is displayed in the Navigation pane, click Bookmarks to bring the tab to the foreground. When a bookmark is selected in the palette and a context-sensitive menu is opened, the menu options are different than those listed in the palette pull-down menu. If a context-sensitive menu is opened from the palette away from bookmarks, the menu options will appear the same as those listed in the pull-down menu.

✦ **B   New Bookmark:** When selecting the New Bookmark icon, a bookmark is created in the palette capturing the current zoom level. Subsequently clicking the bookmark returns you to the page and zoom level when the bookmark was created.

✦ **C   Delete Bookmark:** The trash icon is used to delete a bookmark. Individual or multiple bookmarks can be deleted. When a bookmark is deleted, it has no effect on the page contents. (Note: the exception is when deleting tagged bookmarks explained later in this chapter.)

✦ **D   Expand Current Bookmark:** When a bookmark is collapsed, clicking this icon expands the bookmarks to display all child bookmarks below the parent bookmark.

✦ **E   Palette pull-down menu:** Clicking the down arrow opens the palette menu. A context-sensitive menu opened in the Bookmarks palette and away from the bookmark names displays the same menu options.

All the palettes in the Navigation pane offer different displays when clicking in an open area within a palette. Similar to this behavior, palette menus also appear differently depending on whether an item is selected or no selection is made. With regard to bookmarks, the palette menu options listed in Figure 9-8 will change to those shown in Figure 9-9 after a bookmark is selected and the palette menu is opened.

Figure 9-9: When a bookmark is selected in the Bookmark palette, the menu options are expanded and offer additional commands.

Adding and deleting bookmarks

Bookmarks are added to PDF files in several ways. Regardless of the tool or command used to create a bookmark, you should first navigate to the page and view before creating it. Creating bookmarks is like capturing a page view. When the bookmark is created, it is associated with the page and current zoom level displayed in the Document pane. Therefore, if you want to have page 22 marked with the page fitting within the window, you go to page 22, select Fit in Window from the View menu, and then click the New Bookmark icon in the palette.

Bookmarks can also be created by pressing Control/Command + B or bringing up a context-sensitive menu in the bookmark list window. By default, the name is Untitled. Untitled is highlighted, so that you can immediately provide a descriptive name for the new bookmark. When finished naming a bookmark, press the Enter or Return key.

Deleting bookmarks is also handled in several ways. When you want to delete a bookmark, select it and press the Backspace (Delete) key on your keyboard. You can also use the context-sensitive menu or the Trash icon in the Bookmark's palette. Regardless of which method you use, if the Skip Edit Warnings setting is enabled in the General Preferences Options settings dialog box, the bookmark is deleted without warning.

Ordering bookmarks

Bookmarks created in a document appear in the order they are created, regardless of the page order. For example, if you create a bookmark on page 15, and then create another on page 12, the bookmarks appear with page 15 listed before page 12 in the bookmark list. At times you may want to have the bookmarks list displayed according to page order. Bookmarks may also appear more organized if they are nested in groups. If you have a category and a list of items to fit within that category, you may want to create a hierarchy that will expand or collapse on selection of the plus symbol (right arrow on a Mac) discussed earlier in this chapter. Fortunately, Acrobat enables you to change the order without recreating the current bookmark order. In addition, you can categorize the bookmarks in groups.

To reorder a bookmark, select the page icon adjacent to the bookmark name in the list and drag it up or down. A highlight bar represented by a horizontal line appears when you drag to a location where the bookmark may be relocated, as shown in Figure 9-10. To nest a child bookmark below a parent bookmark, drag up or down and slightly to the right, as shown in Figure 9-11. Wait for the highlight bar to appear before releasing the mouse button.

Although Acrobat 5.0 offers many more opportunities to Undo the last edit, you'll find the Edit ⇨ Undo command not accessible when creating or moving bookmarks. If a bookmark is inadvertently moved to the wrong location, select it and move it where you want to have it appear. The same holds true for creating bookmarks. If you inadvertently create a bookmark, you cannot Undo the operation. Select the bookmark to be deleted and follow one of the steps listed earlier for removing bookmarks.

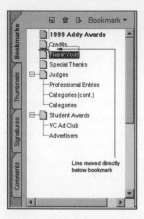

Figure 9-10: A bookmark repositioned directly below another bookmark displays a highlight bar after Acrobat accepts the new location.

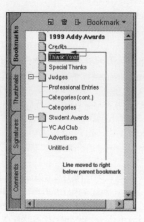

Figure 9-11: To make a child bookmark nested below a parent, move the bookmark slightly to the right until you see the highlight bar.

If you have a parent bookmark with several child bookmarks nested below it, you can move the parent to a new location. Drag the parent bookmark, and all subordinate bookmarks below it move with the parent. If you want to remove a subordinate bookmark from a nest, click and drag the bookmark to the left and either down or up to the location desired. Multiple nesting is also available with bookmark organization. A bookmark can be subordinate to another bookmark that is itself nested under a parent bookmark. To subordinate a bookmark under a child bookmark, use the same method as described previously for creating the first order of subordinates. As you drag right and up slightly, you can nest bookmarks at several levels.

Multiple bookmarks can also be relocated. To select several bookmarks, Shift + click each bookmark to be included in the group. As you hold the Shift key down, you can add more bookmarks to the selection. If you click one bookmark at the top or bottom of a list and Shift + click, all bookmarks between the two will also become selected. For a non-contiguous selection, Control + click (Command + click on a Mac). Once selected, drag one of the bookmarks to a new location in the list. It doesn't matter which bookmark is dragged—their selected order will remain in effect.

Tip

When the Navigation pane is closed, a bookmark can be created and the Navigation pane opened in one step. Create the bookmark by pressing Control/Command + B on the page that you want to bookmark. The Navigation pane opens and your bookmark, named Untitled, appears. The bookmark is created after the last bookmark listed in the Navigation pane.

By default, new bookmarks appear at the end of a bookmark list. If you want to place a bookmark within a series of bookmarks, select the bookmark that you want the new bookmark to follow. When you select New Bookmark from the Bookmarks palette or press Control/Command + B, the new bookmark appears after the one you selected.

Renaming bookmarks

If you create a bookmark and want to change the bookmark name at a later time, select the bookmark to be edited in the Bookmarks palette. From the palette menu, select Rename Bookmark. Acrobat highlights the name in the Bookmarks palette. Type a new name and press the Return/Enter key on your keyboard.

Note

Selecting the name of a bookmark in the Bookmark palette displays the page view for the associated bookmark. Even though the bookmark name is highlighted, you won't be able to edit the name until you select Rename Bookmark from a context-sensitive menu opened from the selected bookmark or select the menu command in the palette menu.

Structured bookmarks

Structured bookmarks retain document structure in files generated from Microsoft Word and Web pages. Microsoft Word headings and certain Web page content, such as uniform resource locators (URLs) for links contain such structure. When pages are converted to PDFs, the file structure is converted to bookmarks. Structured bookmarks can be used to navigate PDF pages, reorganize the pages, and delete pages. Conversion of files containing tables, images, HTML table cells, and other such items can be bookmarked with a structured bookmark. More on using structured bookmarks appears in Chapter 11 where I discuss tagged bookmarks and Web pages.

Bookmark properties

Many more options for bookmark navigation exist with settings available for bookmark properties. Accessing the Bookmark Properties dialog box is handled by first selecting the bookmark in the bookmark list. If a page action is associated with the bookmark, click the right mouse button (Control key on a Mac) while selecting the bookmark. When the context-sensitive menu opens, select Properties from the menu. Or select a bookmark and then choose Edit ➪ Properties. Either way, the Bookmark Properties dialog box is accessed, you can choose from a number of options for the type of bookmark property, as shown in Figure 9-12. For now, I'll restrict the discussion to the Open File option on this menu. (The remaining options are discussed in Chapter 10.) Select Open File from the Type pop-up menu.

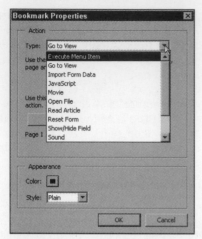

Figure 9-12: The Bookmark Properties dialog box enables you to define a number of different actions that can be associated with bookmarks.

When Open File is selected from the Type pop-up menu, the button below Type appears as Select File. Click this button and a navigation dialog box appears, enabling you to select a file. After you find a file to be opened, select the file and click the Select button in the navigation dialog box and then click OK in the Bookmark Properties dialog box. When you return to the PDF document, click the bookmark and the file identified opens. If the option Open Cross-Document Links in Same Window is enabled in the General Preferences Options settings dialog box, Acrobat will prompt you to save your file if not yet saved. After you click Save, the file is saved and then closed. The selected file subsequently opens. If you want to keep both documents open, disable the Open Cross-Document Links in Same Window preference setting.

Bookmarks are like creating links in PDF files. The many properties associated with bookmarks enable you to maximize viewing options for screen displays, Web pages, and CD-ROM replication. All the properties associated with the Link tool and form fields that are covered in detail in Chapter 10 can be assigned to bookmarks. For a thorough review of the options available to you, study Chapter 10 with an eye toward applying link actions equally between link buttons and bookmarks.

Working with Thumbnails

Thumbnails are mini-views of PDF pages that can be displayed in two sizes. Thumbnails are not only views of the pages, but are also navigational links and can be used in ordering your pages. When used as a tool for ordering pages, thumbnails work like a slide organizer in which you can see all the slides and move them around. As you saw how to reorganize bookmarks earlier in this chapter, you know that moving bookmarks around has no effect on page order. Thumbnails, on the other hand, retain links to pages, and moving thumbnails changes the page order of a document.

Thumbnails in Acrobat 5.0 are created on the fly when not embedded in a document. If you have a large PDF file with many pages, a short delay may be experienced when you open the Thumbnails palette. During an editing session, you can elect to embed the thumbnails that will speed up the screen redraws and later unembed them before saving the file. If you elect to keep the thumbnails embedded in the file, they will add approximately 3K per page, thus increasing file size.

Viewing and navigation are not the only benefits to working with thumbnails. Acrobat provides you with a marvelous page editor in the form of context-sensitive menu and palette menu commands that can be used to edit pages in PDF files in many ways. When you select the Thumbnails tab in the Navigation pane and open the palette menu, the options are displayed as shown in Figure 9-13.

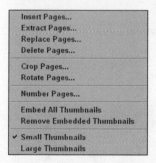

Figure 9-13: Thumbnail palette menu options provide many commands for editing pages in PDF documents.

Creating and deleting thumbnails

If you want to embed thumbnails in a PDF file, select the Embed All Thumbnails command from the palette menu or a context-sensitive menu. Thumbnails can also be created by batch-processing PDF files, at the time of distillation, for a folder of multiple PDF files. When you choose File Batch Processing ➪ Edit Batch Sequences, a dialog box opens containing an option for creating thumbnails. In Distiller's General Job Options, you also have an option for creating thumbnails. When a PDF document is opened in Acrobat, you can use either the palette menu or a context-sensitive menu to create thumbnails. All said, Acrobat provides many different ways to embed thumbnails.

You can delete thumbnails from PDF documents either individually in Acrobat or by using the Edit Batch Sequences command. If your work environment is such that you do a lot of editing in Acrobat and often use thumbnails, you may want to create them during distillation. Working with a lot of page editing on long documents will speed up the screen refreshes when thumbnails are embedded. After you finish up the jobs and want to post PDF files on the Web or create CD-ROMs, you can batch-process the files for optimization and delete the thumbnails. When the Edit Batch Sequences is run, multiple files can be optimized and have the thumbnails removed.

Regardless of whether the thumbnail is embedded, you can navigate the PDF document by double-clicking a thumbnail to jump to the respective page. You can also change views in the Thumbnail palette. The small rectangle displays a handle in the lower-right corner. Drag the handle to reshape the rectangle, and the view corresponds to the rectangle size.

Depending on page content, you may often want to use viewing Small Thumbnails by selecting the option in a menu. When small thumbnails are viewed, more page icons appear in the Navigation pane. You can open up the Navigation pane as wide as your monitor can handle (see Figure 9-14). In such a view, you can move thumbnails around and reorder the page sequence.

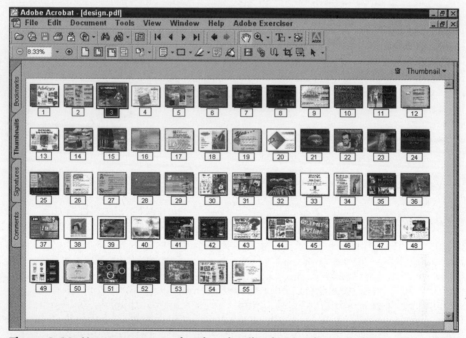

Figure 9-14: You can open up the Thumbnail palette as large as the monitor width. When small thumbnails are viewed, the display appears like a slide sorter.

Tip

For a super slide sorter, open the Thumbnails palette and view thumbnails as Large Thumbnails. Place the mouse cursor over the vertical bar to the right of the thumbnails palette and drag to the right of your monitor screen. Press F8 and F9 to hide the menu bar and Command bar and resize the viewing window to fit the screen size. When displayed as large thumbnails, you should be able to see detail in the images and can sort pages by selecting and dragging the thumbnails to new positions.

Organizing pages with thumbnails

Thumbnails offer page-editing tasks either from selecting options in a context-sensitive menu or palette menu shown previously in Figure 9-13, or by working directly with the thumbnail icons in the Thumbnails palette. The many page editing tasks you can perform are described as follows.

Reordering pages

To reorder pages by using a drag-and-drop method, open the Navigation pane and click the Thumbnails tab to bring the palette forward. Select the page you want to reorder and drag it anywhere among the other thumbnails. A vertical highlight bar appears where the page is be relocated. When pages are reordered, all the links on the page are preserved.

Copying pages

Pages can be copied within a PDF document or between two open PDF documents. To copy a page with thumbnails, hold the Control/Option key down as you drag a page to a new location in the same PDF file. Release the mouse button when you see the vertical highlight bar appear at the desired location. To copy a page between two documents, open the PDF files and view them tiled either vertically or horizontally. The Thumbnails palette must be in view on both PDF documents. To copy a page from one PDF document to another, click and drag the thumbnail from one file to the Thumbnail palette in the other document. The vertical highlight bar appears and the cursor changes, as shown in Figure 9-15. After the vertical bar is positioned at the desired location, release the mouse button, and the page drops into position.

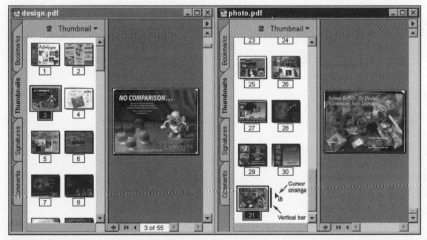

Figure 9-15: If thumbnails are viewed in a single column, dragging a thumbnail to a new location or copying between documents displays a horizontal line where the thumbnail is be placed.

Removing pages

The previous example behaves like a copy-and-paste sequence. You can also create a cut-and-paste action whereby the page is deleted from one PDF document and copied to another. To remove a page and place it in another PDF file, hold the Control/Option key down and then click and drag the page to another Thumbnail palette in another file. The page is deleted from the original file and copied to the second file.

Caution   Be certain not to confuse the modifier keys. If Control/Option + click + drag is used with a PDF file in view, the page will be copied. If using the same keys between two documents, the page is deleted from the file of origin and copied to the destination file.

To delete a page with the Thumbnails palette, use a context-sensitive menu or the palette menu. Select a single thumbnail or Shift + click to select multiple thumbnails in a contiguous order (Control/Command + click for a non-contiguous order) and select Delete Pages from the menu command. When the menu command is selected, a dialog box opens, as shown in Figure 9-16.

Figure 9-16: When deleting pages from the thumbnails menu, a confirmation dialog box opens.

In the Delete Pages dialog box, the default is the selected pages marked for deletion. You can make a change in the dialog box by selecting the From button and entering a contiguous page number range in the field box.

Editing Pages

In this context, *editing pages* refers to the PDF page as an entity and not the page contents. Rather than look at changing individual elements on a page, this section examines some of the features for structuring pages as an extension of the commands found in the Thumbnails palette. Page editing discussed here relates to the insertion, extraction, and replacement of PDF pages. In addition, cropping, rotating, and page numbering are covered.

Before you go about creating a huge PDF document with links and buttons, understanding how Acrobat structures a page and related links is imperative. Bookmarks and other links are specified within a PDF document as user defined navigation. Acrobat handles thumbnails and the link to the respective pages. You have no choice with a link from a thumbnail to a page.

With regard to links and bookmarks, think of Acrobat as having two layers. One layer contains the page and its contents, and the layer hovering over the page contents is where all the links appear. When viewing a PDF file, you don't see the layers independent of page content. This said, when you delete a page, all the links to the page are lost. Acrobat makes no provision to go to the page following a deleted page that may be the target view of a link. Therefore, if you set up a bookmark to page 4 and later delete page 4, the bookmark has no place to go. Such links are commonly referred to as *dead links*.

When editing pages in Acrobat, you can choose to insert a page, delete a page, extract a page, and replace a page. If you understand the page structure, you'll know when to use one option versus another. Each of the options, described as follows, is accessed by choices available in the Thumbnails palette menu, by selecting commands from the Document menu, or by using a context-sensitive menu while clicking a thumbnail in the Thumbnails palette.

✦ **Insert Pages:** When you select this option, the Select File to Insert dialog box opens where the file to be inserted can be selected. When selected, the Insert Pages dialog box opens enabling you to choose the location for the insertion regardless of the current page viewed (see Figure 9-17). You can choose to insert a page either before or after the page in view, within a page range, or before or after the first or last page. Inserted pages do not affect any links in your document. All the pages are *pushed* left or right depending on whether you select the Before or After option. If you attempt to insert a page in a secure PDF document, Acrobat will prompt you for a password. This action applies to all the options listed here.

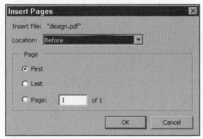

Figure 9-17: The Insert Pages dialog box enables you to locate the page that will precede or follow another page that you specify.

✦ **Delete Pages:** When you delete a page, you delete not only its contents but also its links. If a bookmark or other link is targeted for the deleted page, all links to the page will be inoperable. When creating a presentation in Acrobat with multiple pages, you must exercise care when deleting pages to be certain no links are made to or from the page.

✦ **Extract Pages:** Extracting a page is like copying it and then pasting it into a new PDF document. Extracting pages has no effect on bookmarks or links. The new PDF page created in the new PDF document will not retain any of the links of the page from which it was extracted.

✦ **Replace Pages:** This option only affects the contents of a PDF page — the link layer is unaffected. If you have links going to or from the replaced page, all links will be preserved. When editing PDF documents where page contents need to be changed, redistilled, and inserted in the final document, always use the Replace Page command.

Cropping pages

Acrobat has a tool in the Command bar for cropping pages (shown here). You can select the tool and draw a marquee in the document window to define the crop region, or the Crop Pages command can be selected from either the Thumbnails palette menu or by using the context-sensitive menu. Regardless of which manner you select to crop pages, Acrobat opens a dialog box that can provide you some additional choices for cropping pages (see Figure 9-18).

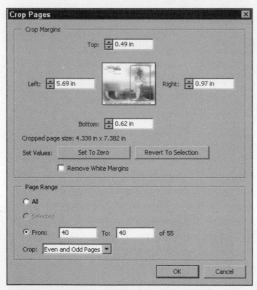

Figure 9-18: The Crop Pages dialog box displays a thumbnail image of the document page and offers options for crop margins and page ranges.

If the Crop tool from the Acrobat Command bar is not used, the crop dimensions can be specified in the dialog box. When the Crop tool is used, the cursor changes to a scissors icon when moved inside the marquee created with the tool. After you click the mouse button, the Crop Pages dialog box opens. On selecting either of the other two methods, the Crop Pages dialog box opens. The Crop Pages dialog box offers several options from which to choose when cropping pages:

✦ **Margins:** Choices for margins are available for each side of the page. In the field boxes for each side, you can use the up or down arrows and watch a preview in the thumbnail at the top of the dialog box. As you click the up or down arrow, the margin line is displayed in the thumbnail. If you want to supply numeric values, enter them in the field boxes.

The margins unit of measure is determined in the General Preferences dialog box in the Display settings. If you need to work back and forth between different units of measure, open the Info palette from the Window menu. Select the desired units of measure, and then open the Crop Pages dialog box. The units will dynamically reflect the same units specified in the Info palette.

✦ **Set to Zero:** Resets the crop margins to zero. If you change the dimensions with either of the preceding settings and want to regain the original dimensions of the crop boundary when the tool was first used, click the Set to Zero button. From here you can redefine the margins. This button behaves much like a Reset button in other image editing programs.

✦ **Revert To Selection:** If you drag open a crop range and open the dialog box, then fiddle with the margins or click the Set to Zero button, the crop rectangle will be restored to the size when the dialog box was opened. That is, to your original crop area. The view displays the crop area within the current page. In other words, the thumbnail preview displays the entire page with the crop area indicated by a red rectangle.

✦ **Remove White margins:** Acrobat makes an effort to eliminate white space on the page outside any visible data. Acrobat's interpretation is confined to true white space. If a slight bit of gray appears as a border, it will not be cropped.

When creating PDFs for slide presentations or screen views, you may occasionally have an unwanted white border around the pages. This appearance may result from creating pages in layout or illustration programs when the image data doesn't precisely match the page size. To polish up the pages and eliminate any white lines, choose Document ⇨ Crop Pages. In the Crop Pages dialog box, select Remove White Margins and then select All for the page range. When the pages are cropped, the excess white lines are removed.

✦ **Page Range:** Pages identified for cropping can be handled in the Page Range options. If All is selected, all pages in the PDF file will be cropped as defined. Specific pages can be targeted for cropping by entering values in the Pages from and To field boxes. Choices for Even and Odd Pages, Even Pages Only, and Odd Pages Only are selected from the Crop pull-down menu.

Cropping pages does not eliminate data from the PDF document even when resaved. If you crop a page, the printed page will appear as it is viewed on-screen with the data cropped. If you return to the Crop Pages dialog box either after cropping or after saving and reopening the file and select Set To Zero, the PDF page will be restored to the original size even after you have saved the PDF after cropping.

Tip

If you want to eliminate the excess data retained from the cropping tool, you can use either Adobe Photoshop 6.0 or Adobe Illustrator 9.0. Both programs will honor the cropped regions of PDF files cropped in Acrobat. When a cropped page is opened in either program, resave as a PDF. Open the PDF in Acrobat. When you use the Crop tool and select the Set To Zero button, you'll notice the page has no data remaining outside the page dimension. The new file size saved from Photoshop or Illustrator results in a smaller file size due to elimination of the excess data.

At times it may be helpful to crop a range of pages to the same dimensions of another page. You may upon occasion have a document with the precise page size needed and want to crop all pages in a second file to the same size as your template file. To understand how such a task might be approached, look at the steps used to crop a PDF file to the same dimensions as another PDF file:

STEPS: Cropping a PDF File to the Same Dimensions as a Second File

1. **Open a PDF.** Open a multiple page PDF file that needs to be cropped to the dimensions of a second file.

2. **Insert a page.** Choose Document ⇨ Insert Pages and insert the page that contains the dimensions for the page cropping. If the second document contains multiple pages, select one page to insert in your file. Insert the page at the beginning of your file.

3. **Open the Info palette and determine the page size.** In this regard, move to the inserted page, select the crop tool and draw a rectangle around the page. While the Info palette is open, examine the readout in the Info palette. In my example, I used a page that reads W: 5.06 and H: 5.03.

4. **Cancel the crop tool.** The crop tool was used to assess the dimensions on the first page. To eliminate the crop tool boundary, press the Esc key on your keyboard.

5. **Draw the crop boundary on the second page.** Draw the crop tool boundary from the top left corner of the first page in the series of pages to crop. As you open up the rectangle, observe the Info palette, and rest the lower right handle to the same dimensions as the first page size. In my example, I started at the top left corner of the page and moved the lower right handle to W: 5.06 and H: 5.03.

6. **Locate the crop position.** While the crop rectangle is visible on the page, you can relocate it to the desired position by clicking inside the rectangle and dragging around the page. Move the rectangle to the desired position.

7. **Crop the pages.** Double-click the mouse button inside the crop rectangle or press the Enter key on the Num keypad. In the Crop dialog box, select the page range from two to the number of pages in the document.

8. **Delete the first page.** When finished cropping all pages, choose Document ➪ Delete Pages and delete the first page.

All the pages in the document will be cropped to the size of the page you inserted into the file. Cropping pages by using this method can be helpful when distributing files for CD-ROM replication and Web page viewing. Unlike printed documents, screen views often don't adhere to standard sizes.

Rotating pages

PDF documents can contain many pages with different page sizes. You can have a business card, a letter-sized page, a tabloid page, and a huge poster, all contained in the same file. Depending on the authoring program of an original document, at times there may be some problems with pages appearing rotated or physically inverted. At other times, you may want to print duplexed material and may need to rotate a page 180-degrees to accommodate two-sided printing. Regardless of whether you want to overcome a limitation or suit a design need, Acrobat enables you to control page rotations.

Rotating pages is handled in either the Document ➪ Rotate Pages menu command or by using the Thumbnails palette menus. When you select Rotate Pages through any of these methods, the Rotate Pages dialog box appears. The direction of rotation is determined in a pull-down menu that enables you to rotate either clockwise or counterclockwise. Among the options in the Rotate Pages dialog box shown in Figure 9-19 are:

✦ **Direction:** Three choices appear from the pull-down menu. Select from clockwise, counterclockwise, or 180-degree rotations.

✦ **Page Range:** Select from a defined range or all pages in the open document.

✦ **Rotate:** The pull-down menu for Rotate offers selections for Even and Odd pages, Even Pages Only, or Odd Pages Only.

✦ **Orientation:** The last pull-down menu offers choices for Portrait, Landscape or Pages of Any Orientation.

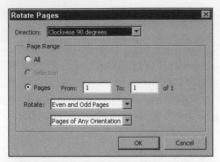

Figure 9-19: The Rotate Pages dialog box offers options for rotating pages in a range or by selecting even or odd pages. The Even/Odd choices can be helpful when printing to devices requiring page rotations for duplexing.

Understanding Destinations

Destinations work similarly to bookmarks. The advantage in using destinations is the capability to sort the destination names by either the name or page number. Another great advantage in using destinations is when creating links to destinations, as I discuss in Chapter 10.

Unlike bookmarks, destinations do not have properties. You can't create actions associated with the destination as you can with bookmarks, and destinations only work within a PDF document, not across multiple PDF files.

Destinations are made visible in the Destinations palette. To open the palette, choose Window ➪ Destinations. The palette has some similar attributes as the other palettes covered in this chapter. The palette contains icons for actions, such as trashing a destination, creating a new destination, and scanning the document for destinations included in the file. To determine whether destinations exist, open the Destinations palette by choosing Window ➪ Destinations and click the Scan document icon in the palette status bar. Acrobat scans the document and lists all destinations in the palette.

Creating destinations

Creating a destination works the same as creating bookmarks. First zoom to the view on a document page you want to define as a destination. When the page and view are specified, click the Create new destination icon in the Destinations palette.

Acrobat automatically names the destination Untitled. The destination name should be descriptive of the location. Enter the text you want to call the destination and press the Return or Enter key on your keyboard.

Caution If you design files that are to be viewed by users of Acrobat Reader, be aware that the Reader user cannot see any destinations created in your PDF files. No Destinations palette exists in Acrobat Reader. If you want the Reader user to select links to other pages in a file, be certain to create bookmarks instead of destinations.

Creating destinations can also be handled in the palette menu appearing in the Destinations palette or by using a context-sensitive menu. If you use a context-sensitive menu, be certain to click in an empty area of the Destinations palette. If you open the context-sensitive menu on a destination name, you won't see the New Destination command appear. Renaming destinations can be handled by opening the context-sensitive menu while clicking a destination name. Navigating to new pages, selecting the desired view, and selecting the New Destination command subsequently create additional destinations. As each destination is named, the corresponding page number appears in the Destinations palette.

Sorting destinations

As destinations are created, they are listed in the Destinations palette. Every time you open a PDF file containing destinations, you need to click the Scan document icon in the status bar or select Scan Document from the palette menu in the Destinations palette. When the destinations appear, you can choose to display the list according to an alphabetical order or according to the page number associated with the destination. To sort destinations according to name, click Name, which appears below the palette tab. To sort by page number, click Page, which is adjacent to Name in the palette. Acrobat sorts the list accordingly.

Depending on how you last sorted destinations, any new destination names appear according to the last sorted order. For example, if your current view is according to page number, and you create a new destination on page 100 called *aardvark*, the name will appear after page 99 in the list. When you re-sort according to name, *aardvark* will appear at the top of your list.

Destinations as well as articles, bookmarks, and thumbnails discussed earlier in this chapter are all used as tools for linking PDF pages to other PDF pages. In some cases the links can be made to other PDF documents. Consider this chapter, in part, an introduction to hypertext links. In the next chapter the flexibility and power of Acrobat and its many ways to create and use hypertext links is explained in greater detail.

Summary

✦ Article threads facilitate navigation across a body of text in a PDF file. Articles can be created with Acrobat and viewed in any Acrobat viewer.

✦ Articles can be joined after they have been created. Article properties help identify key information related to the article contents.

✦ Bookmarks in PDF documents are like tables of contents with links to the pages where they are created. Bookmarks can link to a page or a specific view, or be assigned to many different link actions.

✦ Acrobat 5.0 creates thumbnail images on the fly when the Thumbnails palette is opened. Thumbnails are represented in two sizes in the Thumbnails palette.

✦ Thumbnails can assist the PDF author in manipulating and editing page orders. Thumbnails can be dragged and dropped between PDF files to insert, copy, and remove pages.

✦ Pages can be inserted, deleted, extracted, and replaced in a PDF file either by using a menu command or the Thumbnails palette. When pages are deleted, links to the pages are removed. When pages are replaced, all links to and from the page are preserved.

✦ Destinations work like bookmarks where links to pages and views within a PDF file can be created. Destinations can be sorted by name or page number. Only Acrobat users can use destinations.

✦   ✦   ✦

Hypertext References

About Hypertext Links

"Okay Scotty, beam us over." Ahh . . . if Kirk had only used Acrobat, just think of what the Star Date Logs would have looked like. Why, the whole Star Fleet Command would have been on a PDF workflow. Well, maybe hypertext links are not quite the same as traveling at warp speed, but in our own little world, links in Acrobat enable us to navigate the PDF universe. The celestial bodies of PDF planets can be explored via links, page actions, sounds, movies, and JavaScripts. Links in Acrobat can have many different action types. You can simply jump to a new location or view or add more sophistication through associated menu commands, scripts, data handling, and launching external applications. In short, buttons and links add an enormous variety to how you may navigate and view PDF documents on monitors and via the World Wide Web.

If you've read through the last few chapters, your first glimpse of links appeared in Chapter 8 where I discussed Comments and linking to pages containing comments from the Comments palette. In the last chapter, we discovered additional links with bookmarks and thumbnails. In addition to Comments, bookmarks, and thumbnail links, Acrobat affords many other opportunities to create links and link actions. This chapter covers tools found in the Acrobat Command bar, menu commands, and palettes used specifically for creating links.

Link actions

A *link action* is the result of executing a defined task. The task is identified within the properties of a particular link and most often associated with the movement of the mouse cursor. A link action can occur when the mouse button is clicked, released, or moved over a button. Links can be created with the Link tool, Movie tool, Form tool, bookmarks, destinations, and page actions.

Most often, links and buttons have associated actions. However, creating a link with no associated action is possible. A situation in which this type of link is helpful is when you want to use a bookmark as a space holder where a title, subsection, or section heading appears. The bookmark name will appear in the bookmark list, but no action will occur when the bookmark is selected. All other action types invoke a step or series of steps that are executed when the button is either selected or approached by the mouse cursor.

Link properties

Choices for action types are handled in a Properties dialog box. From this dialog box, you can make choices for different action types and attributes of the associated link. The edit mode for a particular type of link becomes active when a link tool is selected in the Acrobat Command bar. After selecting either the Link tool, Movie tool, or Form tool, the respective Properties dialog box is accessed by choosing Edit ⇨ Properties or by opening a context-sensitive menu. By default, when new links are created, the Properties dialog box opens when the mouse button is released.

Selecting the respective tool and double-clicking the link rectangle can also access link properties. You create links by selecting a link tool and drawing a rectangle around the area where the link button *hot spot* (the area where the link action can be selected) will be defined. When the Hand tool is placed within the rectangle drawn to define the link periphery and the mouse button is clicked, the link action is invoked. When a link tool is selected in the Acrobat Command bar, all link rectangles created respective to the link type are displayed. Clicking a given link with the respective tool selects it.

Removing links

To delete a link from the PDF document, select the link with the respective link tool and then press the Backspace/Delete key. Links can also be deleted through a menu choice in a context-sensitive menu or by choosing Edit ⇨ Clear. If the Skip Edit Warnings option is disabled in the General Preferences Options dialog box, a warning dialog will appear before the link is deleted.

Link environment

Links reside on a layer independent of the PDF page contents. When a link is created, it is associated with the page but behaves like an independent element. As independent page elements, links can be repositioned and moved about a page. If a page is deleted from a PDF document, the page contents and the associated links are removed from the file. When using the Replace Pages command (as discussed in Chapter 9), the page contents will be replaced, and also, all links on the replaced page and their actions will be preserved. This is particularly important when you create PDF documents with links to and from pages. If you inadvertently delete a link, all navigation to and from the link will be lost.

Buttons created with the Link tool and Movie tool cannot be copied and pasted in a PDF document. Form fields can be copied and pasted in the same document or between different PDF documents. When a movie is "imported" into a PDF document, the movie file is linked to the PDF file that must remain in its original location to be found on the source drive. Sound files imported into PDF documents are converted and embedded in the PDF file. Therefore, when transferring PDF files with movie clips, both the PDF and movie file must be transported together. PDF files with sound clips embedded in the document don't require transport of the original sound file.

Creating Links

Navigational buttons and link actions are created with the Link tool from the Acrobat Command bar. The area defined for the button will be the hot spot. To invoke a link action, use the Hand tool and move the cursor over the button. When the cursor enters the defined area for the link, the Hand tool cursor icon changes to a hand with the forefinger pointing upward. Whenever this cursor view appears, you know a link action will be activated on the click of the mouse button.

To create a button, select the Link tool from the Acrobat Command bar and draw a rectangle in the document window. When the mouse button is released, the Properties dialog box opens and the link rectangle is hidden beneath the dialog box. Close the dialog box and the rectangle displays four handles, one appearing at each corner. The handles are used to reshape the rectangle. While in the edit mode (that is, the Link tool remains selected), you can place the cursor inside the rectangle and drag it around the document to relocate it.

If you want to create a button and immediately return to the navigation mode, select the Control/Option key and click the Link tool in the Command bar. After creating the link and setting the properties, you exit the edit mode and return to viewing mode. In edit mode, when the Link tool is selected in the Command bar, all links created on the PDF page appear with rectangular borders, as shown in Figure 10-1.

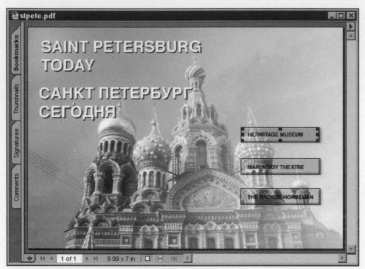

Figure 10-1: When the Link tool is selected in the Acrobat Command bar, all links are displayed with rectangular borders. A selected link appears with handles on the sides and corners, as shown in the first link.

When the Link tool is used to draw the rectangle and the mouse button is released, the Link Properties dialog box appears. The Link Properties dialog box is where actions associated with the link are specified.

Link properties

Acrobat affords you many options for creating link actions that you can select from the Link Properties dialog box. Among the many choices for link actions, you also have choices for modifying the appearance of the link rectangle and specifying the highlight view that appears when the link is selected. To open the Link Properties dialog box, click the Link tool from the Acrobat Command bar, draw a rectangle, and release the mouse button. The Link Properties dialog box opens immediately, as shown in Figure 10-2.

The Link Properties dialog box contains all the properties available for the link display and link action. The first attributes in the dialog box relate to the appearance of the link rectangle:

Figure 10-2: After drawing a rectangle with the Link tool and releasing the mouse button, the Link Properties dialog box opens.

✦ **Invisible Rectangle:** When the link is drawn, the link rectangle only appears in the edit mode. When you return to the navigation mode, the rectangle disappears. To display the link rectangles, you need to click the Link tool in the Command bar. Below the Invisible Rectangle option appear four pull-down menus. If Invisible Rectangle is selected, only the Highlight option is available. The Highlight option includes the following:

- **None:** When the link is selected, no highlight is displayed.

- **Invert:** When the link is selected, the reverse color of the link contents appear as the highlight. The mousedown action displays the highlight that informs the user the button is selected. If you click down and drag the mouse away from the button, the highlight disappears.

- **Outline:** The mousedown action on the link displays a rectangle border similar to the view that you see when the Link tool is selected from the Command bar.

- **Inset:** On the mousedown action, the link looks like an embossed or recessed button, slightly offset.

✦ **Visible Rectangle:** When the Visible Rectangle option is selected from the Type pull-down menu, the pull-down menus for Width, Color, and Style become available in the Link Properties dialog box. A visible rectangle appears in the document dialog box when you return to the navigation mode. To set the attributes of the rectangle border, choose from one of the three pull-down menus in the Appearance section of the dialog box:

- **Width:** The choices Thin, Medium, and Thick are available from the pull-down menu. The keyline border is displayed with a rule thickness as determined by these choices.

- **Color:** Preset color choices for the outline border are available from the pop-up menu as well as the Custom option that enables you to specify a particular color (Windows) or the System color palette (Macintosh). When choosing Custom on Windows, the system color palette opens where custom color selection is made.

- **Style:** The pull-down menu offers two choices. Select from either solid or dashed lines.

After you make choices for the options that relate to the link button's appearance, the next step is to select the particular link action to be associated with the link. A number of different actions reside within the Type pull-down menu under the Action section of the Link Properties dialog box, as shown in Figure 10-3. As all the actions are discussed in the following section, keep in mind the Action Type is selected from this pull-down menu.

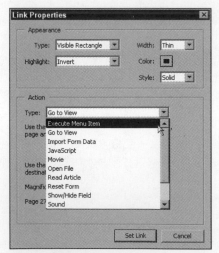

Figure 10-3: The actions associated with link buttons are established from choices made in the pull-down menu for the Action Type.

Execute Menu Item

A link action can execute a menu selection. Just about every menu command is available in the Execute Menu Item dialog box, including commands for bookmarks, thumbnails, articles, and destinations. When Execute Menu Item is selected from the pull-down menu for the Action type, the button in the lower portion of the Link Properties dialog box displays the label Edit Menu Item. Click this button, and the Acrobat menu items are displayed in another dialog box (Windows) titled Menu Item Selection (Windows), or Menu Item (Macintosh). On the Macintosh, menu item selections are made from the top-level menu bar and not within a dialog box. The Menu Item Selection dialog box on Windows lists the menus and menu items available from the Acrobat menu bar. On the Macintosh, be aware that menu item selections made in the top-level menu bar are assigned to the link action while the Menu Item dialog box is open.

Choose a menu and scroll down to the desired command. When the command is selected, click OK in the Menu Item Selection/Menu Item dialog box to return to the Link Properties dialog box. Click Set Link in the Link Properties dialog box, and the menu command will be associated with the link. As an example, if you want to create a link that will navigate to the first page in the document, the selection in the Menu Item Selection/Menu Item dialog box appears, as shown in Figure 10-4.

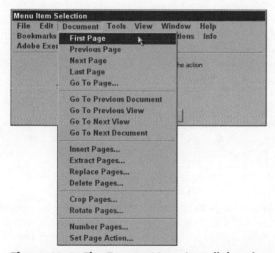

Figure 10-4: The Execute Menu Item link action enables you to execute any menu item appearing in the Menu Item Selection dialog box (Windows) or choices from the top-level menu bar (Macintosh). In this example, the First Page command from the Document menu is selected.

One example of using the Execute Menu Item command may be to navigate a PDF document. Rather than having end users access Acrobat viewer navigation tools, you can create navigational buttons on document pages. When using the Document menu commands, buttons can be created to move around the PDF document. The Open command in the File menu can be used to open additional PDF files. Through a series of links, users won't need to access tools when viewing your authored documents.

Go to View

Go to View is a common link action used frequently when preparing PDF files for screen viewing. The Go to View action type works similarly to the bookmark feature discussed in Chapter 9. To create a button that navigates to another page, another view, or another page and new view, select Go to View from the Action Type pull-down menu. While the Link Properties dialog box is open, navigate to another page and/or view using the Command bar tools or keyboard modifiers. Select the desired view magnification from the menu options or status bar and then click the Set Link button. Acrobat then returns to the page where the link was created. If you use the Control/Option key when selecting the Link tool, you will be ready to test the button by moving the cursor inside the link rectangle and clicking.

Tip   With any kind of link that opens a new view, creating the link action is a very easy process. Always keep in mind that first a link button is created on a page where the Link Properties dialog box is opened. While the dialog box is open, you have complete navigation control within the PDF file as well as access to all menu commands. The second step in associating the link button with the action is to navigate to the desired view. When the view you want appears, click the Set Link button in the Link Properties dialog box.

Magnification options are available from the pull-down menu for Magnification when the Go to View option is selected. The magnification items are the same as those discussed in earlier chapters. What's important to remember is to first navigate to the desired page and view before you click the Set Link button.

Import Form Data

When the Import Form Data option on the Action Type pull-down menu is selected, the Select File button appears, enabling you to select the file from which the data will be imported. This action type works with forms, which I cover in Chapter 13.

JavaScript

JavaScript adds a great opportunity for making PDF documents interactive and dynamic. JavaScripting can be applied to link button actions as well as form fields as I discuss in Chapter 13 and more advanced JavaScripting in Chapter 19. When the JavaScript action type is selected, an Edit button appears in the Link Properties dialog box. Click the Edit button, and the JavaScript Edit dialog box opens. You can type the code in the dialog box or copy and paste JavaScript code from a text editor. In Figure 10-5, a simple JavaScript entered in the JavaScript Edit dialog box takes the user to the first page in the PDF file.

Figure 10-5: JavaScript code is supplied in the JavaScript Edit dialog box. The code in this example executes a go to first page action.

Movie

To select the Movie action type, a movie must be present in the PDF file. Movies are not imported with this command; they are imported with the Movie tool discussed later in this chapter. After a movie is contained in a PDF file, you can create a button that invokes one of four action types when the button is selected. These options are available in a pull-down menu named Select Operation. You may choose to play a movie, stop a movie, pause the movie during play, and have it resume after it has been paused. If more than one movie is contained in the document, you can select which movie will be associated with the action from the Select Movie pop-up menu.

Open File

Open File works differently from using the Execute Menu Item option and choosing the File ⇨ Open command. When File ⇨ Open is chosen, only PDF documents can be opened. If you use the Link Properties dialog box and choose Open File, any application document can be opened. Acrobat launches the host application and opens the document. For example, if you want to open a Microsoft Word file, you can select the Word document by clicking the Select File button in the Link Properties dialog box. When the link is invoked, Microsoft Word is launched and the document is opened in Word. Using this action type requires you to have the host application installed on your computer.

Read Article

On specifying Read Article as the action type for a particular link, the Select Article dialog box opens. If no articles are present in the PDF document, you won't be able to use this link action. When articles are present, select the article you want to associate with the link from the listed articles, as shown in Figure 10-6. When the link is selected in the navigation mode, Acrobat opens the page where the article appears. In addition, the cursor changes to the Article tool that enables continuation in reading the selected article.

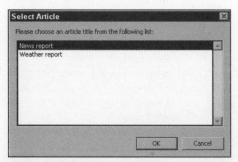

Figure 10-6: After selecting the Read Article option, the Select Article dialog box opens, enabling you to select the article that you want associated with the link. All articles contained in the PDF are listed in the Select Article dialog box.

Reset Form

The Reset Form link action relates to PDF documents with form fields. When a form is filled out, you can reset the form that removes all the data contained in the form fields. Acrobat provides an opportunity to clear the data from all fields or those fields you identify individually. A Field Selection dialog box opens, enabling you to select the fields to clear. (The Field Selection dialog box is covered in more detail in Chapter 13.)

Show/Hide Field

Also related to forms in Acrobat, the Show/Hide Field type enables the user to hide selected fields. Forms can be created to permit users to fill out selected data and preserve some fields where data is not to be completed by the end user. If a field has been hidden, it can be made visible by returning to the Show/Hide Fields dialog box. Within this dialog box, the options for hiding and showing fields are enabled through radio buttons.

Sound

A button can be created to play a sound in a PDF document. When the Sound type is chosen, a dialog box appears enabling you to navigate to the sound to be imported. Acrobat pauses a moment while the sound is converted. After imported in the PDF, the sound can be played across platforms. The button is associated with the sound import so that when the button is selected, the sound plays.

Submit Form

Form and comment data contained in PDF documents can be distributed on the World Wide Web. When a user completes a form or comments, the data can be submitted to a uniform resource locator (URL) as a Form Data File (FDF), hypertext transfer markup language (HTML), extensible markup language (XML) data, or the complete PDF file with the form data. The PDF author can then collect and process the data. Using form and comment data with Web servers has some requirements that you need to work out with the Internet Service Provider (ISP) that hosts your Web site. If you use forms on PDF Web pages, you'll want to include a button that, when clicked, will submit the data after the user completes the form. Using the Submit Form type enables you to identify the URL where the data is to be submitted and determine which data type will be exported from the PDF document. If comments are to be submitted, a checkbox enabling comment submissions appears in the dialog box. When identifying URLs, be certain to use the complete URL address similar to the one displayed in Figure 10-7.

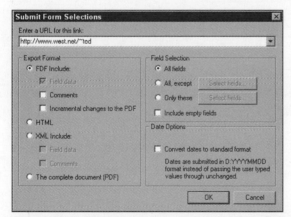

Figure 10-7: The Submit Form link enables you to submit form and comment data to a particular URL on the World Wide Web. The complete URL address needs to be supplied in the Submit Form Selections dialog box.

World Wide Web Link

The World Wide Web Link option enables you to associate a link action to a Web address. Web links can be contained in PDF documents viewed on-screen or within a PDF page on the World Wide Web. If a Web link is contained in a PDF document, selecting the link will launch the browser configured with Acrobat and establish a Web connection. Acrobat remains open in the background while the Web browser is viewed in the foreground. Like the Submit Form requirements mentioned previously, always use the complete URL to identify a Web address.

None

Buttons with no associated link action produce no effect. You may use this type of action with bookmarks, as explained earlier in this chapter.

Linking to files

Creating links add some interactivity to your PDF designs. Without having to learn complex programming code for interactive presentations, Acrobat provides a simple and effective means for creating dynamic presentations. In addition, you can add some functional applications for file management with Acrobat through the use of links. One particular application for link actions that I use is cataloging documents on external media cartridges or CD-ROMs. I often take a screen shot of a directory or folder on a media cartridge before I replicate a CD-ROM. The screen shot is imported into Acrobat where links to the files are made. When the link is selected, the document opens in the application used to create the file. In addition, I add information related to the document, such as purpose, creation date, and comments about the contents. The following steps explain how to organize such documents.

STEPS: Creating Links in a PDF Document

1. **Assemble files in a folder and capture the screen.** Organize files in a folder either by icon view or as a list. When the organization appears as you like, capture the screen with a utility, such as Corel Capture (Windows) or Mainstay Capture on the Macintosh (or press Command + Shift + 4 on a Mac) and marquee the area to be captured.

   Macintosh users can easily capture a dialog box by pressing the Caps Lock key on the keyboard and then pressing Cmd + Shift + 4. The cursor changes to a circle or "target" icon. Click inside the open folder dialog box you want to capture. The screen capture includes the folder dialog box and the contents. In addition, Mac users can also use the Print Window command from the File menu when a folder is opened and in view on the Desktop. Print the window as a PostScript file and distill the PostScript file in Acrobat Distiller.

2. **Convert to PDF.** Open Acrobat and choose File ➪ Open as Adobe PDF. If you capture the entire screen, you may want to crop the image in a program, such as Adobe Photoshop before importing or use the Crop tool in Acrobat after

converting to PDF. Any of the capture formats would be acceptable to Acrobat to convert to PDF. In my example, I captured an open folder on the Desktop that contains some sample Acrobat forms.

3. **Create a link.** For any file type other than PDF, use the Link tool from the Acrobat Command bar to draw a rectangle around the file icon or name.

4. **Define the properties and establish the link attributes.** Determine what appearance you want the link to have. In my example, I want a keyline to appear around the document icons. For the appearance type, I select Visible Rectangle and change the appropriate option settings to specify a red, medium-width border (see Figure 10-8). For all non-PDF file types, use the Open File action from the Type pull-down menu choices.

Figure 10-8: I draw a link rectangle around the first icon in my screen capture on (Windows). I set the Action Type to Open File.

5. **Set the link action.** If the file you link to is not a PDF document and you use Open File as the Link Action, click the Select File button in the Link Properties dialog box. In my example, I select a PDF file on my hard drive contained in the folder where the screen dump was taken. After identifying the file to open, click the Set Link button to close the Properties dialog box.

6. **Create a comment.** For this example, I use the Note tool and create a comment that provides some information about the file, as shown in Figure 10-9. When the notes are collapsed, moving the cursor over a note opens the note pop-up displaying the comments. After creating all the comments in a tight space as the screen shot in Figure 10-9, using note pop-up windows helps eliminate some clutter.

Tip   Graphic designers who archive client files can add a list of all the fonts used in the note window for each respective file. When the mouse cursor is placed over the Note comment, the pop-up note window displays the note and your font list. If you need to load fonts in your system, you can use a utility, such as Extensis Suitcase or ATM Deluxe. Load the necessary fonts and then return to the link and select it.

Figure 10-9: A note is created with the Note tool. The associated note window opens where comments can be made.

If you want to create a link to a PDF document, rather than selecting the Open File link action as described in the preceding example, you can choose Go to View from the Action Type pull-down menu. While the Properties dialog box remains open, choose File ➪ Open from the Acrobat menu bar and then open the PDF document. Select the desired view magnification and click Set Link in the Link Properties dialog box. This method enables you to open a PDF file and set the view magnification. This method only works with PDF documents. For all other document files, you need to use the Open File link action.

Tip   The Acrobat new Find Comment command helps locate information contained in note comments. You can create a button on the PDF page to open the Find Comment dialog box. Select Execute Menu Item as the Action Type. Click the Edit Menu Item in the Link Properties dialog box and click the Menu Item Selection/ Menu Item dialog box, and then choose Tools ➪ Comments ➪ Find from the menu commands. Set the link and a simple click of this button opens the Find Comment dialog box. As another method of finding information fast, you can create a comment summary, as explained in Chapter 8. After creating the summary, save the file from Acrobat, then choose Document ➪ Insert Pages to append the summary to the screen shot.

Each of the link properties works with buttons that you create on PDF pages. The actions associated with the buttons need to have a response from the end user to invoke an action. At times, you may want to have your PDF pages automatically executed without user input. In some cases, creating a page action may be more desirable to implement the views you want to have displayed.

Text links

Fidgeting around text characters, words, and short lines can be a pain when using the Link tool. Constant resizing and aligning the rectangle to create the hot spot for the link button can get a little tedious if you have many links to create from text blocks. Tables of contents or indexes can be a challenge and very time consuming. Fortunately, Acrobat provides an easy method for handling links from text.

To create a link, hold the Control key (Option on a Mac) down while the Link tool is selected. The cursor changes to an I-beam enabling you to select text. Drag across the text. When the mouse button is released, a link rectangle is drawn around the selected text and the Link Properties dialog box opens, as shown in Figure 10-10.

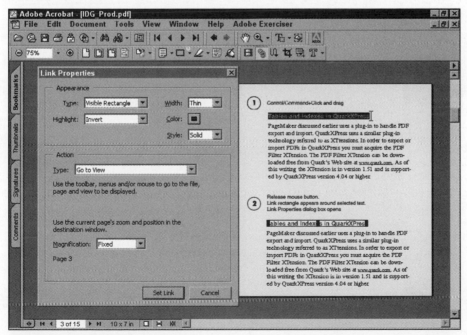

Figure 10-10: With the Link tool selected, hold the Control/Option key down and drag across the text (1). Release the mouse button. A link rectangle is created around the text and the Link Properties dialog box opens (2).

Establish the properties in the dialog box and you're ready to create another selection. Continue moving through the document page with the same method and link rectangles can be created swiftly without struggling with sizing and alignment.

Tip   Adobe Photoshop 6.0 preserves type created on layers when saved from Photoshop to PDF format. If creating links from text placed on an image file in Photoshop, be certain to avoid rasterizing type layers. You can select the type using the Control/Option key as described previously when creating links. Photoshop 6 files can be saved to PDF while preserving type and vector objects as was explained in Chapter 6.

The Link tool offers some great flexibility in regard to the kinds of links to be created and the attributes assigned to links. Almost any action Acrobat is capable of executing can be performed with a single click of a button created with the Link tool. However, you have some limitations. In a production workflow, using the Link tool suffers from lack of automation and repetition. Several functions you can't do with the Link tool include:

✦ **Duplicate links:** Acrobat makes no provision for duplicating links.

✦ **Copy/paste links:** Acrobat does not permit copying and pasting links.

✦ **Multiple selections of links:** Links cannot be selected in multiples. Only a single link can be selected at one time. Therefore, property changes need to be individually applied to each link.

✦ **Custom icon displays:** Acrobat only permits setting attributes for link borders and colors as a custom icon display. No other means of creating an icon for the link is available with the Link tool. No embossing or other effects can be applied to the rectangle borders.

✦ **Background fills:** The link rectangles drawn with the Link tool have no means of assigning color for a background fill.

✦ **Text within links rectangles:** Acrobat does not offer an option to create text within the link rectangle link.

✦ **Batch processing:** No means of automation is afforded when creating links. No batch commands exist for creating links on multiple pages for the same action. An example of what might be used in automating link development is a button on every page that navigates to the next page.

If duplication of links or a need for creating custom icon displays for buttons is required, you can use another means of creating links in PDF documents. All the attributes for link properties can also be applied to buttons created from form fields.

Form fields as links

Chapter 13 is dedicated to working with Acrobat forms and using the Form tool. In addition to providing many opportunities for working with form fields, the Form tool can also be used as a link tool. As a link tool, it overcomes many limitations noted previously. For example, form fields can be duplicated, copied, and pasted within and between PDF documents, and they support custom icon displays. As you look at the use of the Form tool in this chapter, think of it as another means of creating link buttons. In Chapter 13, you look at the tool in regard to creating data fields for forms.

All the attribute assignments available with the Link tool are equally available with the Form tool. Links to the World Wide Web, JavaScripts, setting views, executing menu commands, and so forth can be assigned as actions to a form field. To use the Form tool, click it in the Acrobat Command bar and drag open a rectangle just like creating a link button. After you release the mouse button, the Field Properties dialog box opens.

Form field properties

In the Field Properties dialog box, the first item to deal with is determining the type of field to be created. Because we're restricting this example to buttons, the form field to be created is a button. In the Field Properties dialog box, select Button from the Type pull-down menu, as shown in Figure 10-11.

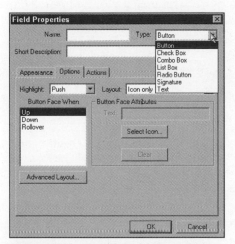

Figure 10-11: In the Field Properties dialog box, select Button from the Type pull-down menu. This selection assigns the field properties to a link button.

One essential item necessary with form fields is supplying a field name for each field created. In the Name field box, enter a name. If you want to create a button that will open the next page in a PDF document, you may enter a descriptive name, such as next.

When Button is selected from the type pull-down menu, the dialog box changes and reduces the number of tabs from six to three. The three tabs offer attribute choices for the following:

✦ **Appearance:** A border color, background color, and style can be used to display the button. All selections are made from the color swatches and pull-down menus for the Border area of the Appearance dialog box. A selection can be made for creating a beveled button by choosing Beveled from the Style pull-down menu. In the Text area of the dialog box, text fonts and point sizes can be selected from fonts installed on your system. Text can be displayed for button contents. Whatever assignment is made here determines text attributes when text is entered in the Options dialog box.

✦ **Options:** Button displays and highlights are determined in the dialog box that opens when the Options tab is selected. In the previous example, the word Next can be supplied in the Text field box under Button face Attributes, as shown in Figure 10-12.

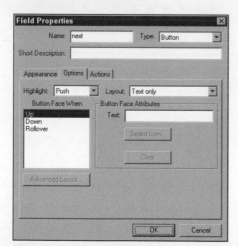

Figure 10-12: Text is entered in the Text field box in the Options tab of the Field Properties dialog box. The text attributes for font appearance are established in the Appearance tab.

✦ **Actions:** The button action is defined in the Actions dialog box. Click the Actions tab in the Field Properties dialog box and select the Add button to open the Add an Action dialog box. Options from the pull-down menu in the Add an Action dialog box are the same as those available for Link properties.

Duplicating form fields

After assigning attributes to a form field, the field can be copied and pasted in the same PDF document on the same page, on another page, or between PDF files. Select the field with the Form tool and choose Edit ➪ Copy (Control/Command + C) to copy the field to the clipboard. After it's on the clipboard, the field can be pasted (Control/Command + V) on any page while it remains on the clipboard.

Tip

Using the mouse and a modifier key can also duplicate form fields. Select the form field with the Form tool, hold the Control key (Option on a Mac) down, and drag away from the selected field. The duplicated field will have the same name and attributes as the original field. To constrain movement, first click the form field with the Form tool and then depress the Control key (Option on a Mac) and Shift key. Drag away from the selected field and the direction is constrained to a horizontal or vertical movement.

If you have a large document containing several hundred pages, then Acrobat provides a means of duplicating the form field and its associated action over a range of pages. To duplicate a field, choose Tools ➪ Forms ➪ Fields ➪ Duplicate. The Duplicate command is nested among a bunch of submenus. After you finally get to the command and select it, the Duplicate Field dialog box opens, as shown in Figure 10-13.

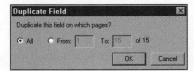

Figure 10-13: The Duplicate Field dialog box enables you to duplicate a selected field across all pages or a range of pages.

In the Duplicate Field dialog box, you may have a field selected on page one and want to duplicate the field for the remaining pages. In Figure 10-13, the dialog box is opened from a fifteen-page document. If I want to duplicate my *next* button on the remaining pages, I would select From in the dialog box and enter the range in the two field boxes. When fields are duplicated, the duplicate field boxes appear at the same location coordinates as the original on all successive pages.

The same kind of button can be created for visiting a previous page. You can use either JavaScript or execute a menu item in the Add an Action dialog box. If the Previous and Next button are both selected, the Duplicate Field dialog box can be used to duplicate both fields across a range of pages specified in the dialog box.

Field buttons can also be created with the same appearance as links that appear invisible. If an icon exists on the PDF page and you want to create a hot spot for a button without a border or icon, deselect the Appearance items for Border Color and Background Color. The Option items should reflect no text and no icon. When all the attributes are set, the field appears invisible when the Hand tool is selected. Moving the cursor over the field displays the hand with the forefinger pointing upward indicating a link is present. When the mouse button is clicked, the action associated with the field is executed.

Custom icons

Form fields can also be assigned custom icons for field buttons as well as mouseover events. Rather than using text to display field contents, any PDF file can be imported as a field button. Attribute assignments are provided in the same manner as discussed earlier in this chapter. If you want to include both text and an icon, Acrobat offers many options for how the icon and respective text will appear. All the options for using icons or icons and text are handled in the Options dialog box.

To use icons for button types, they must first be created and saved as PDF files. Acrobat won't let you import image icons saved in other formats. If you have a number of GIF images used for Web pages and want to use the same icons in your PDF documents, use the Open as PDF command and convert them to PDF. You can use either a single page PDF or a multiple page PDF. The Options dialog box enables you to scroll pages in multiple-page PDFs to select an icon from different pages.

All of this description probably seems a bit esoteric if you haven't used form fields as link buttons, so take a look at some real world examples by following steps to create a button with an icon display. To follow the steps, you need a PDF file with some images that can be used as icons. Either two single-page PDF files or a multiple-page PDF file will work. In this example, we use a rollover effect that changes the icon from the default appearance to another icon when the mouse is moved over the field. In this regard, you want two icons that appear with some kind of similarity.

STEPS: Creating Form Field Link Buttons with Custom Icons

1. **Open a PDF file.** For this example, I use a PDF file with multiple pages. I want to create a link button that opens the first page in the document and have the same button appear on all pages. When selected from any page, the button action opens the first page — much like a home button. Navigate to the second page of the PDF document to create the first link to the home page.

2. **Create the form field.** Select the Form tool from the Acrobat Command bar. Click and drag open a rectangle. When the mouse button is released, the Field Properties dialog box opens.

3. **Select the field type and name the field.** The first item to set in the Field Properties dialog box is to select the field type from the Type pull-down menu. This field is a button, so select Button from the menu options. Enter a name for the field. In this example, I name my button home and enter it in the Name field box at the top of the Field Properties dialog box.

4. **Set the appearance.** Click the Appearance tab in the Field Properties dialog box and deselect checkboxes for Border Color and Background Color. Under the Text item, choose a font for the display of text and a point size. In my example, I use Helvetica for the font and 12 points for the size (see Figure 10-14). If you select Auto, Acrobat auto sizes the font according to the size of the field box. As the size of the field becomes larger, the point size becomes larger. Text is not necessary because we are using an icon for the button display. However, adding text to the icon can offer some descriptive information about what will happen after the button is selected. In this example, I use text to be displayed along with the icon.

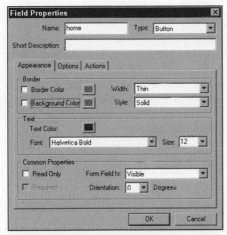

Figure 10-14: The Appearance settings are established to eliminate any border or background color in the field box. The font and point size determine text attributes when text is added to the icon display.

5. **Determine the layout.** Click the Options tab and select Icon top, text bottom from the Layout pull-down menu. This setting allows text to be entered below the icon that will be imported into the form field (see Figure 10-15).

6. **Select the icon.** After you select the Layout option from the pull-down menu and Icon appears as one of the choices (in this case Icon top, text bottom), the Select button becomes active (see Figure 10-15). Click the button and then click the Browse button to navigate to the PDF where the icon appears. Select the PDF to be used as the icon and click Select in the Open dialog box. Click OK in the Select Appearance dialog box and the icon is displayed in the Options settings in the Field Properties.

7. **Add text to the display.** Because I selected Icon top, text bottom, the Text field box becomes active. Enter text in the field box, as shown in Figure 10-15.

Figure 10-15: The Options settings enable you to import an icon for the field box and create text assigned to the top, bottom, sides, or over the icon. In this example, text is selected to appear below the icon.

8. **Add a rollover effect.** When the mouse is moved over the field, the icon changes forewarning the user that the button will invoke an action. The effect is a rollover, much like the same effect used in Web page design. To create the rollover, select Rollover in the Button Face When list. Click Select Icon and navigate to the PDF or page where the second icon appears. Follow the same steps in the prior section to import the icon. In my example, I use the same icon with a different color and a slight drop shadow to distinguish the two icons, as shown in Figure 10-16.

9. **Set the action.** Click the Actions tab and select Add an Action. The default selection is Mouse Up when the field box is selected. Leave this selection as the default. When the Add an Action dialog box appears, select Execute Menu Item from the pull-down menu. Select the Edit Menu Item to open the Edit Menu Items/Menu Item dialog box. Choose Document ➪ First Page and then click OK. Click Set Action and then click OK in the Field Properties dialog box.

Note

When the field box is drawn on the PDF page, it can be resized after setting the attributes. To reshape a field box, click the Form tool and click a field rectangle appearing on the page. Select any one of the four corner handles and move one of them to reshape the rectangle.

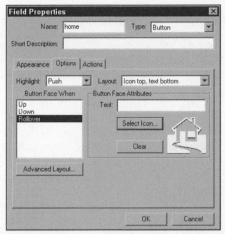

Figure 10-16: I select Rollover from the Button Face When list and click the Select Icon button. When my second icon is selected, a thumbnail preview appears in the dialog box.

10. **Test the button.** If the field properties have been properly assigned, you should see the icon change when the mouse cursor is positioned over the form field (see Figure 10-17). Click the Hand tool and click the icon. The icon should change and after the mouse button is clicked, the first page in the document should open.

Figure 10-17: When the Hand tool is selected and the cursor is not within the field boundaries, the default icon is displayed. When the cursor is moved over the field box (right side of figure), the rollover effect appears with the second icon identified in the Options properties.

11. **Duplicate the field.** Go back to the page where the icon was created and select it with the Form tool. Choose Tools ➪ Forms ➪ Fields ➪ Duplicate. Because the home page and page 2 don't need a button, click the From button in the Duplicate field dialog box and enter 3 in the first field box. Enter the last page number in the second field box. After you click OK, all fields will be copied to the remaining pages at the same location coordinates where the first button was created. Clicking the button on any subsequent page takes the user to the home page.

Creating Page Actions

Page actions invoke a link action when the page is viewed in a PDF document. A page action does not require the user to click a button or issue a command for the action to execute. Page actions can be supplied on any page in a PDF document. Most often you may find page actions helpful when viewing the first page in a file. An example of a page action may be when you want to display a credit page, and then have the document jump to the contents page for the user to select links to other pages. The contents page displays momentarily and then scrolls to the next page in the document. Another use of a page action may be to play a sound or movie. When assigning a sound or movie to play with the open page action, they will automatically play when the file is opened. A page action may also be assigned to closing a PDF file. You may want to have another PDF document open when one file closes.

Navigation and playing sounds and movies are only a few examples of associating a page action with a PDF page. When creating page actions, you have available to you all the link actions found in the Link Properties dialog box discussed earlier in this chapter. Menu commands, URL links, JavaScript, and so on are all available with page actions. And page actions can be applied to any page in a PDF when the page is either opened or closed.

To create a page action, select the Document menu and choose Set Page Action. A dialog box opens that enables you to select either a Page Open or Page Close item for invoking the page action, as shown in Figure 10-18. If Page Open is selected, the action type will be employed when the PDF page opens. Page Close executes the action when the page is closed. You first determine which item invokes the action by selecting it and then clicking the Add button in the Page Actions dialog box. Unlike the Properties dialog box for Links, you cannot navigate pages while the Page Actions dialog box is open. If you want to use a page action to scroll to another page, you must do so through the Execute Menu Item command instead of navigating to a page and setting the link. The one item not available among the action types for page actions is the Go to View action. Therefore, any magnification levels for page viewing must be applied with the Execute Menu Item action.

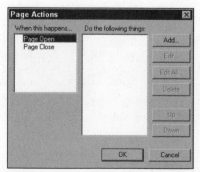

Figure 10-18: When setting page actions, first select either Page Open or Page Close and then click the Add button to identify the action type.

Editing page actions

Care must be exercised when setting page actions on pages in a PDF file. If you set a page action to a page with an action type that moves to another page, you won't be able to return to the page where the action type was created. Even when looking at pages in a continuous or facing pages view, the page where the action has been created cannot be selected if its page action is set to move to another page. If the page is selected, the action will be invoked, thus moving to another page.

Other types of actions where the page remains in view can be edited by choosing Document ➪ Set Page Action. If you want to remove an action, select it in the Do the following things list and click the Delete button (see Figure 10-19). To edit an action, select the action type in the list and click the Edit button. Clicking the Edit button opens the Edit an Action dialog box where you can change the action type.

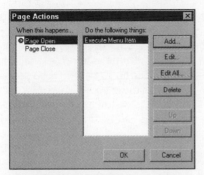

Figure 10-19: To delete a page action, select the action in the Do the following things list in the Page Actions dialog box and click the Delete button.

Tip

To remove a page action that jumps to another page, select Extract Pages from the Document menu. In the Extract Pages dialog box, select Delete Pages After Extracting. The extracted page appears in Acrobat. Choose Document ➪ Set Page Action and delete the action type from the Page Actions dialog box. Because the extracted page is a single page PDF and has nowhere to go, you can edit the page action. Save the extracted page to disk. Select the original document from the Window menu, choose Document ➪ Insert Pages, and insert the saved file back into your original document.

Using transitions with page actions

One effective use of page actions is to introduce transition effects. Transitions are available when you view PDF documents in Full Screen mode and scroll pages with the transitions applied. If you want to view a PDF file without the Full Screen mode in effect, you can create transitions with pdfmark. While in the normal viewing mode, any transitions associated with pages when the file was distilled with pdfmark annotations will be viewed. One circumstance where such an effect might be useful is in creating an opening page with a credit or company logo that uses a transition effect when jumping from the credit page to the second page in the document. Creating such an effect is a two-step process. First, you use a pdfmark annotation and distill a PostScript file with the transition. Next, you create a page action in Acrobat that moves the user to the second page after the transition effect. Take a closer look at how you may work through this example by following some steps.

Note To perform the steps, you need some EPS files to create transition effects. Acrobat shipped with EPS files for creating page transitions that were installed on the Acrobat 3.0 installer CD-ROM. When Acrobat 4.0 shipped, these files were eliminated from the CD-ROM. As yet, we're not certain if the transition files will ship with Acrobat 5.0. If you do not find a transitions folder on the CD-ROM, you can acquire them on the Web. You can perform a search on the Web for Acrobat transitions or navigate to my Web site at: `www.west.net/~ted/transition.html`. This page has a link to where the transition files can be downloaded.

STEPS: Creating Transitions with pdfmark

1. **Create a document in a layout application.** For this example, create a document with multiple pages in a program, such as Adobe PageMaker or QuarkXPress. The document should have several pages so that the first page can accept a page action that moves the user to the second page in the file.

2. **Import a transition effect.** See the note above for acquiring the transition files. If not found on the Acrobat installer CD-ROM, download them from the Internet. From the different transition effects, import one of the EPS files into your layout.

Note To see a sample of the transition effects, open one of the sample PDF documents in Acrobat and scroll through the pages. The sample PDF documents are contained in the Transitions archive when you download the file.

3. **Print the file to disk as a PostScript file.** After importing the transition on the desired page, print the file to disk as a PostScript file. If using Adobe PageMaker, you can choose File ⇨ Export ⇨ Adobe PDF. For this example, I include the glitter transition (`GLTR_0.EPS`) on page 1 in a PageMaker file.

4. **Distill the PostScript file.** Open Acrobat Distiller or select Distill now in the Adobe PageMaker Export Adobe PDF dialog box and distill the PostScript file. For this example, you can use the Screen Job Options in Acrobat Distiller.

5. **View the PDF document.** Open the PDF document created with Acrobat Distiller in Acrobat. After the transition is completed, the page is displayed in the viewer, as illustrated in Figure 10-20.

Figure 10-20: I created a credit page that includes a ghosted-back version of my company logo and a transition effect imported into PageMaker. After I set a page action, this page is momentarily displayed after the PDF file is opened and then the page action opens the next page in my file.

To display the page momentarily and then move to the second page in the document, set a page action to go to the next page.

STEPS: Creating a Page Action

1. **Create a page action.** Using the PDF document described in the preceding example, choose Document ⇨ Set Page Action. In the Page Actions dialog box, select Page Open and click the Add button to open the Add an Action dialog box. In this dialog box, select Execute Menu Item.

2. **Select the menu item for navigating the page.** In the Execute Menu Item dialog box, click the Edit Menu Item button and choose Document ⇨ Next Page. Click OK to accept the choice and return to the Add an Action dialog box. The item that you select is identified in the dialog box adjacent to Execute, as shown in Figure 10-21.

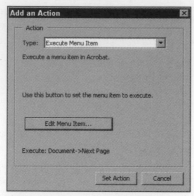

Figure 10-21: After I choose Document ⇨ Next Page, the menu selection item is identified in the dialog box. If the identified item is different from what you want, return to the menus and make the proper selection.

3. **Accept the changes and return to the document window.** Click Set Action after making the selection, and you return to the Page Actions dialog box. Click OK to return to the PDF document window.

4. **Save the file and reopen it.** Save your new edits and close the file. Choose File ⇨ Open and open the saved file. If all the edits you made were correct, you should see a glimpse of the first page with the transition applied and then the second page will open.

You can create an animated effect with the above example by applying page actions to several pages. In Photoshop, open a file, such as the logo suggested above. Apply a fill of white at opacity percentages of 20, 40, 60, and 80 percent to the duplicates of the original file. Set a page action to each page, and the logo first opens with a strong, ghosted effect. Then move through the pages until the last page with no ghosting appears.

Nesting page actions

Page actions are not limited to a single action type. You can add additional page actions to the list in the Page Actions dialog box. After adding an action, select either the Page Open or Page Close item and click Add to add another action. If you want to jump to a view upon opening a page and then return to another view when leaving the page, you can add actions for both the Page Open and Page Close items. Acrobat jumps to the view you associate with the action when the page is opened. After you move from the page to another page, the view level you associate with the Page Close item is displayed.

Multiple page actions can be applied to either or both the Page Open and/or Page Close items. When applying multiple page actions, be certain to think through your work. If you attempt to create actions that conflict with each other, Acrobat will use the last action type associated with the page. In some cases, you may not see an action type if it is overridden in the page display.

Setting the open view

In Chapter 2, I covered information related to document properties and opening pages in different views. For detail on the items related to page viewing when opening a PDF file in an Acrobat viewer, look back at Chapter 2. One item mentioned in regard to opening files in different views, however, deserves repetition. With the page actions and execute menu options, you may be tempted to open PDF files in a Fit in Window or Actual Size view handled by page actions and execute menu commands. If you recall from Chapter 2, PDFs can be opened in different views when choosing File ⇨ Document Properties ⇨ Open. The Document Open Options dialog box enables you to select a view when the file opens. Among the choices are Fit in Window, Fit Width, Fit Visible, and other zoom magnifications. In Figure 10-22, I set the magnification level to Fit in Window.

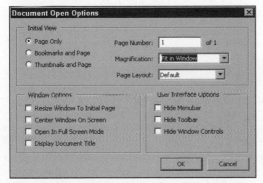

Figure 10-22: In the Document Open Options dialog box, the Fit in Window magnification opens a PDF and fits the page within the open Document pane.

If you elect to use a page action to set the opening view, a momentary display of the default view will appear before the page action is executed. If you want the page open view to appear smooth without the display of the default view prior to the page action view, always use the Document Open Options dialog box for setting the open view.

Named Destinations

Links created with the Link tool offer you opportunity to link to different pages and views in separate documents. The means of creating these links and views is handled the same as any link action related to page views. You first create the link in the source document. While the Link Properties dialog box is open, you use the Acrobat menus to open a second file, navigate to a specific page, set the view from tools or menu commands, and finally click the Set Link button in the Link Properties dialog box. Linking to files in this manner is great for files that you know won't be edited by adding or deleting pages.

But, what happens when you delete a page where the link is associated? Frustrating, isn't it? You quickly learn that links are fixed to specific pages. If a link is associated with a given page and the page is subsequently deleted, the link will no longer function. To resolve this problem, Acrobat provides another means of creating links with Named Destinations.

Unlike links, destinations are not fixed to a target page. They are linked to the file destination. If, for example, a destination is defined as page 2, then the link will open page 2. Acrobat doesn't care what the page contents are, it just knows that page 2 will be the final destination. If you delete page 2 in a multiple page document, the new page 2 becomes the new destination. If all pages are deleted but the first page, then page 1 becomes the destination. Regardless of the number of pages added or deleted in the destination document, Acrobat won't let you down. When using Named Destinations, links won't die like links created with the Link tool.

Destination tools

Before you move about creating destinations, first start by examining the tools used to create them. Destinations are created, organized, and appear within the Destinations palette. To open the palette, choose Window ➪ Destinations.

If you want to use the Destinations palette frequently in an Acrobat session, the tab can be dragged away from the palette and placed in the Navigation pane. As a tab in the Navigation pane, it is visible and easily accessible until you remove it by dragging it out of the pane.

The palette contains a few icons and a pull-down menu, as shown in Figure 10-23. In addition, context-sensitive menus offer several menu options. When selecting a destination name in the palette opens a context-sensitive menu, the options are different than opening a context-sensitive menu from an empty area within the palette window.

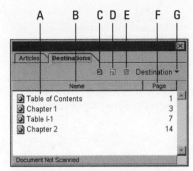

Figure 10-23: Selecting the Destinations command opens the Destinations palette from the Window menu. Several icons and a list of destinations when created appear in the palette.

All destinations are created, edited, and managed through this palette and the options include:

✦ **A** **Destinations list:** When destinations are created, they are listed in the palette.

✦ **B** **Name:** Name appearing in the palette is a button. When selected, the destinations are sorted alphabetically according to name.

✦ **C** **Scan Document:** The icon appearing first on the top-right side of the palette is used to scan the open document for any existing destinations. Destinations don't dynamically appear when you open a PDF where they are contained. You must first scan the document to see them listed in the palette. From the pull-down menu, a menu command appears for Scan Document and creates the same action. Another option for scanning a document is also found when opening a context-sensitive menu away from destination names.

✦ **D** **New Destination:** The second icon, as well as menu options similar to those listed previously, is used to create new destinations. Just as using the Link tool or bookmarks described in Chapter 9, the current page view becomes the destination when a new destination is created.

✦ **E** **Delete:** The trash can icon in the palette as well as a menu command available when opening a context-sensitive menu on a selected destination deletes the destination.

✦ **F** **Page:** Page is also a button. When selected, the destinations are sorted according to page number and order on the page.

✦ **G Pull-down menu:** Just as other Acrobat palettes, a pull-down menu offers menu options for other commands. With destinations, the palette menu commands are limited to Scan Document and New Destination.

✦ **Go to Destination:** If you select a destination name and open a context-sensitive menu, the first menu choice is Go to Destination, as shown in Figure 10-24. Keep in mind this context-sensitive menu offers this option only when the menu is opened when a destination is selected. When the command is invoked, Acrobat opens the destination page.

✦ **Set Destination:** If the current destination view is not what you want, navigate to the desired page and view and click Set Destination. The destination is modified to display the current view when the destination is selected.

✦ **Rename:** A destination name can be changed from any of those listed in the palette. Select Rename and the text for the destination name becomes high-lighted enabling you to edit the name.

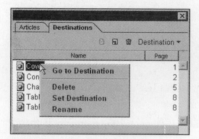

Figure 10-24: When Named Destinations have been created, selecting a destination and opening a context-sensitive menu offers additional menu options not contained in the pull-down menu.

Creating links to destinations

Whereas links offer much opportunity with assigning attributes, such as setting different action types and linking to separate PDF documents, destinations have no attribute assignments and cannot link to other documents. All the destinations created only work within the document from which they were created. To use destinations to be linked to separate document files, you need to use both the Link tool and the Destinations palette. Left alone to create destinations for page navigation in a PDF and displaying different views, the behavior would not be much different than working with bookmarks described in Chapter 9. However, destinations combined with links support some great editing features in Acrobat. To become thoroughly familiar with using links and destinations together, follow some steps to create links to destinations.

STEPS: Creating Links to Named Destinations

1. **Open a multiple page PDF.** For this example, open a PDF file with multiple pages. In my example, I use a PDF file with 40 pages.

2. **Scan Destinations.** If the Destinations palette is not open, choose Window ➪ Destinations. In the Destinations palette, click the Scan Document icon or use the palette pull-down menu and select Scan Document. Before any destinations can be created, the document must first be scanned for destinations.

3. **Create destinations.** Destinations are created just like bookmarks. Go to a page and view and then select New Destination from the palette icon, pull-down menu, or context-sensitive menu. Name your destination. Create several destinations with different views.

4. **Open a second PDF.** After Destinations have been created, open a second file to be used to link to the destinations. A table of contents, index page, or outline may be used in real world cases.

5. **Create a link.** Select the Link tool and use the modifier key (Control/Option) to select text or create a link rectangle that will link the item you select to one of the destinations created in the first document.

6. **Link to a destination.** When the link is created, the Link Properties dialog box appears. Keep the dialog box open while you search for a destination. If the destinations aren't visible in the palette, scan the document again. In the destinations list, select the destination to link to and click the Set Link button in the Link Properties dialog box (see Figure 10-25).

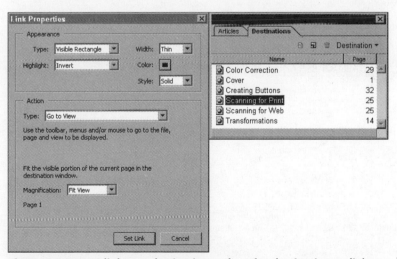

Figure 10-25: To link to a destination, select the destination to link to in the Destinations palette and then click the Set Link button in the Link Properties dialog box.

Note   If monitor space is limited, you can toggle back and forth between documents by selecting the Window menu and choosing the document to view at the bottom of the menu. While the Link Properties dialog box is open, you have complete navigation control in Acrobat. Use tools and menu commands to navigate to locations or documents before setting the link in the Link Properties dialog box.

Create several more destinations with different views to acquire a little experience. After the destinations have been created and the links established, any page editing in the destination document will not disable the links. If the order gets disturbed, you can revisit the Destinations palette and reset the destinations. However, you needn't worry about the links. No matter what you do to redefine a destination, the links to the destinations will remain intact.

Importing Sound and Video

Acrobat supports integrating sound and video files in PDFs. Sounds are embedded in PDF files similar to file attachments while movie clips are linked to PDF files. Links created from bookmarks, links, form field buttons, and page actions can be instructed to play sounds and movies. To use these interactive elements with Acrobat, the file formats must be compatible with those formats supported by Acrobat.

Table 10-1 shows the file formats for Windows and Macintosh formats supported by Acrobat. After Acrobat has converted a sound file, the sounds can be played in a PDF file on either platform.

Table 10-1 Page Navigation Keyboard Modifiers		
File Type	**Windows**	**Mac**
Sound	AIF QuickTime* WAV	AIFF Sound Mover (FSSD)** System 7 sound files** QuickTime
Movie	AVI QuickTime*	QuickTime*

* Apple QuickTime v4.0 or greater is recommended by Adobe Systems for use with Acrobat 5.0. The Adobe Acrobat installer CD-ROM contains QuickTime installation for Windows.

** These formats are converted to QuickTime before they are played in Acrobat.

Because movie files are linked to PDF documents, you need to be certain the linked files are compliant with the platform in which you intend the files to be viewed. Apple QuickTime, which is available on the installer CD-ROM for both Windows and Macintosh computers, can be viewed on either platform as long as QuickTime is installed. Macintosh users typically have QuickTime installed because it comes with the operating system installer. Windows users need to install QuickTime from the Acrobat installer CD-ROM.

Audio Video Interleave (AVI) format is native to Windows machines. If you have video files saved in AVI format, Macintosh users will not be able to view these files on their Macs unless they upgrade to QuickTime 3.0 or later. If you have files saved in AVI format and want to enable cross-platform use for users with earlier versions of QuickTime, you can use a video editor, such as Adobe Premiere to export the video in a QuickTime format compatible for all users.

Importing sound files

Earlier in this chapter, I mentioned using a link to activate a sound in a PDF document. Sounds can be handled in several ways and with several link types. You can, for example, import a sound via the Movie tool and set a page action to play a sound, create a link button, or create a bookmark to a sound. When sound files are imported into PDF files, they will be embedded and become part of the PDF document. After they are embedded, the sound files can be played on either platform.

When you use a page action, any sound added to your file will not be page dependent — that is, the sound will be heard on all pages as you scroll through the PDF file. The sound begins playing on opening the page where the sound import page action has been identified and continues to play until completion. Pressing the Esc key does not stop the sound, nor does the sound stop when the file is closed. Setting a page action to play a sound won't require a user selection to invoke the action — play will be automatic. The only way to stop the sound is to quit Acrobat.

To import sound in Acrobat via a page action, choose Document ➪ Set Page Action. Select Page Open and click the Add button. When the Add an Action dialog box appears, as shown in Figure 10-26, select Sound from the Type pull-down menu and click the Select Sound button. A navigation dialog box appears enabling you to identify the sound file. When you select the sound file, Acrobat pauses momentarily while it converts the sound. After it's converted in Acrobat, the sound is embedded in the document and can be transported across platforms.

If you elect to use the Link tool and select Sound from the Link Properties dialog box, the user will need to click the link button to activate the sound. If a sound file is imported via a link, the sound can be stopped in the middle of play by pressing the Esc key on the keyboard. Bookmarks are handled in the same manner. Create a new bookmark and select Sound for the Action Type in the properties dialog box. The bookmark behavior with respect to playing and stopping sounds is the same as when using links.

Figure 10-26: To associate a page action with a sound file, select Sound from the Action Type pull-down menu. Click the Select Sound button to locate the sound file on your hard drive.

Tip

For recording sounds on your computer, you need to acquire a sound editing application and a microphone attached to the computer. If you don't have a commercial application for recording and editing sounds, you can find many suitable sound editing applications as freeware or shareware on the Internet. Use a Web site where you download public domain software and invoke a search for finding sound editors. Windows users can find many applications at: www.freeware.com and Mac users can find editors at: www.macupdate.com.

Importing movies

The Movie tool in the Acrobat Command bar is used to import movies. To import a movie, you create a movie link similar to other links. Select the Movie tool from the Command bar and click the mouse button or click and drag open a rectangle. When you release the mouse button, the Movie Properties dialog box appears. In the Movie Properties dialog box, shown in Figure 10-27, you can select from a number of attributes for how the movie is to be displayed and the types of play actions that can occur with the movie file.

Tip

After you click the mouse button, the imported movie is placed in the PDF document at the size the movie file was originally created. The spot where you click the PDF page is where the movie frames are centered. If you click and drag with the Movie tool, invariably the movie appears at a different size than it was created, resulting in a distorted view. Use a 100 percent view of the PDF page and click without dragging to import the movie. View the size on-screen to determine how large the movie file will be displayed.

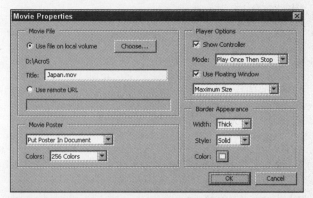

Figure 10-27: The Movie Properties dialog box provides attribute settings for the display and play actions of movie files.

Movie File

The first item in the Movie Properties dialog box displays the name of the movie file you import in Acrobat. The Title field displays the filename. Above the filename appears the directory path for the linked file. Because movie files are linked to PDF documents, the directory path can help you manage your movie imports. If the file is relocated on your hard drive, you will need to redirect Acrobat to the location of the linked file.

Use Remote URL enables you to enter a URL where a movie clip can be found. If placing PDF files on Web servers, the movie file must accompany the PDF and a pointer to the movie clip must be made. When posting PDFs on the Web you can instruct Acrobat viewers to find movie clips on a server where the movie file resides or different URL locations.

Player Options

Player Options enable you to choose between displaying the controller for a movie file or hiding the controller. When the controller is visible, as shown in Figure 10-28, buttons for playing the movie, stopping play, setting the volume, and scrolling through the movie frames will appear. The controller becomes visible while the movie is in play. When not playing, the controller disappears.

 **Figure 10-28:** While a movie is playing, the controller is visible when the Show Controller option is enabled in the Movie Properties dialog box.

Mode

The Mode option offers choices from a pull-down menu for the play action. You can elect to play the movie, and then stop when the film clip reaches the last frame by selecting the Play Once then Stop option. After finishing the last frame, the display eliminates the controller and returns to the first frame in the movie. Play Once, Stay Open is the second choice available from the pull-down menu. When the film clip reaches the end, the controller remains in view and the movie is stopped at the last frame. Repeat Play plays the clip from beginning to end and then continues to replay the movie. Such a choice may be used when setting up a kiosk where you want to play the clip continuously. The final choice is Back and Forth. After the clip completes the play, it plays backward from end to beginning. When the clip comes back to the beginning, it plays forward again, then back, and so on.

Use Floating Window

If this option is enabled, a floating window will display the movie clip centered on your monitor screen irrespective of where the movie clip rectangle is drawn in the PDF document (see Figure 10-29). When choosing a floating window as your movie display, you can choose a size for the floating window from the pull-down menu appearing below the Floating Window checkbox. Size options are available for ratios according to the size of the originally created movie clip. $\frac{1}{4}$x size displays the movie clip at one-fourth the actual size, whereas 2x displays the movie at twice the actual size. For almost all circumstances, a 1x choice is the best view. Movies displayed at larger sizes are pixelated when viewed.

Figure 10-29: Floating windows appear as separate windows in which the movie is played independent of the movie link.

Movie Poster

The display of a stopped movie is called a *movie poster*. The movie poster is typically the first frame in the film clip. You can choose from three options for poster display. Don't Show Poster eliminates the video frame from view while the movie is stopped. The second option, Put Poster in Document, displays the first or halted frame in the film clip. When this option is selected, you can choose the color bit depth for the video display. Choosing 256 colors displays the movie in 8-bit color. You may want to use this option when the end user views videos on 8-bit monitors. Selecting Millions of colors from the pull-down menu displays the video clip in 24-bit color. You can manually choose from either color views when you've selected Put Poster in Document. If either of the other two choices from the first pull-down menu are selected, you won't have a choice for the color bit depth. Choosing the Retrieve Poster from Movie option in the first pull-down menu displays the poster with the color bit depth used in the movie file.

Tip
When the movie poster is hidden, the rectangle drawn with the Movie tool is the hot spot for playing the movie. At times, the user may not intuitively know where to click to play the film clip. You can create a hot spot covering the entire PDF page by drawing the Movie rectangle around the document page. Choose Don't Show Poster and enable the Floating Window option so that the movie will not appear degraded. No matter where the cursor rests on the page, the movie icon will be displayed, informing the user a movie file can be played. If an icon is desired, you can create an icon for a movie by shrinking the movie link to the size of a custom thumbnail and choose the Put Poster in Document option. Drawing a keyline around the movie poster can help the end user find the hot spot to click. When using such an icon view of the movie poster, choose the Use Floating Window option for the video clip display.

Border appearance

Borders can be drawn around the film clip when the Use Floating Window option is not active. Floating windows have a keyline automatically drawn around the poster; however, you can't control the line weight or color. If a floating window is not used, you can create a keyline border in one of three sizes available from the Width pull-down menu. First select one of the width options — Thin, Medium, or Thick — and then select a style for the lines, such as dashed or solid. The Color pull-down menu enables you to select from preset colors or choose a custom color. When the Custom option is selected, the system color palette appears enabling you to make a color choice. The Invisible choice displays no keyline border.

After specifying options in the Movie Properties window, the choices made become new defaults for all subsequent movies imported in your Acrobat session. Acrobat 5.0 eliminates a need to save preferences. When you quit Acrobat and relaunch the program, the last settings made in the Movie Properties will still reflect the new default settings.

If developing many PDF documents with links, you'll need to think out your design very carefully. Individual links on PDF pages can take some time, as each page will require individual authoring. You can cut down the time by using pdfmark annotations, as I explained in Chapter 6 in the context of creating navigational buttons and link actions. Navigational buttons, as explained in Chapter 6, can be added to master pages in layout programs. You can also add links to documents in Acrobat and use the Replace Pages command when common links will be used across many different PDF files. Short of these examples, your PDF workflow may require extensive editing when custom links are used.

Summary

✦ Hypertext links add interactivity to PDF documents for screen and presentation designs.

✦ Links can be created for different views within a PDF document, across PDF documents, and to document files from other authoring programs.

✦ Links can be made to execute most of the menu commands available in Acrobat.

✦ The Link Properties dialog box provides different attribute settings for determining link choices, views, and link button displays.

✦ Form fields can be created as link buttons. Unlike links, form fields can be duplicated, copied, and pasted and can have custom icon displays for buttons.

✦ Page actions can be established to invoke an action or series of actions when opening and closing pages.

✦ Links can be created to Named Destinations. Destinations are linked to locations in PDF files and remain active even when pages are deleted.

✦ Sounds can be imported into PDF files and played via links or page actions.

✦ A movie clip is a linked file in Acrobat and requires the movie file to accompany the PDF document to be viewed. Apple QuickTime movies can be displayed across Mac and Windows platforms.

✦　　✦　　✦

Acrobat Publishing

Acrobat and the Web

PDF and the Web

Throughout this book, the use of PDF files on the Web is addressed. As I discussed in Chapter 4, you can download selected Web pages or entire Web sites and have all the hypertext markup language (HTML) pages converted to PDF. In Chapter 8, I talked about Comments and hinted at collaboration through exchanging comments on Web servers. In Chapter 12, I talk about eBooks, and where would an eBook be if it weren't for the Web? In Chapter 19, I talk about Acrobat form data being submitted to Web servers. In short, the Web plays a major role with much of your Acrobat activity. You can work effectively on a local computer or internal network without accessing the Web, but Acrobat extends its arsenal of tools to aid you in global performance with PDF file exchanges through all the features consistent with Web usage. In this chapter, I cover the Web activity by first looking at PDF viewing in Web browsers. I also examine comment exchanges from within Web browsers, and we take a peek at structured bookmarks from pages captured off the Web.

Viewing PDFs in a browser

A Web browser can be configured for handling PDFs on Web servers in several ways. You can opt to view a PDF directly in an HTML file where the PDF appears as if it was actually created as HTML. You can save a PDF file to disk rather than view it from a Web connection and then later view it in an Acrobat viewer. A file can be viewed outside the Web browser in an Acrobat Viewer window, and you can view a PDF file through the use of an Acrobat viewer directly inside a Web page. The latter is called inline viewing. You'll immediately notice an inline view in your Web browser when the Acrobat tools appear below the browser tools. This form of PDF viewing off the Web is the most common, so I'll keep the discussion of viewing PDFs from the Internet to inline viewing.

Opening PDFs in a browser cannot be accomplished by opening a file as you would an HTML document. You need to specify a uniform resource locator (URL) and filename to view the PDF directly in the browser. For example, logging on to `www.provider.com/file.pdf` would result in the display of the PDF page inside the browser window. As mentioned earlier, this is referred to as inline viewing—an example of which appears in Figure 11-1.

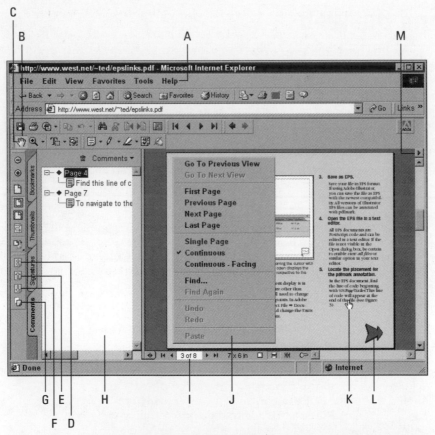

Figure 11-1: Inline viewing displays the PDF file inside the Web browser with access to many Acrobat tools, as shown here in Microsoft Internet Explorer.

The important items to observe with PDFs displayed as inline views from Figure 11-1 include:

✦ **A** The browser menu bar and tools are accessible with inline viewing. All the browser features work the same when viewing a PDF as when viewing HTML Web pages.

✦ **B** The Acrobat Command bar displays all tools functional within the browser. If viewing with Acrobat Reader as the Acrobat viewer, the Save tool will save a copy of the PDF. Comment tools, selection tools, spell checking, and the other tools shown in the viewer Command bar are all active with inline views.

✦ **C** Toolbars can be relocated to the left side of the document window.

✦ **D** Tools for online comments appear when the PDF is viewed in a browser. The first tool in the toolbar is the Show Comments tool. Click this tool to show any comments updated by other users who are sharing comments with you.

✦ **E** The Upload and Download tool synchronizes comments and simultaneously uploads new comments that you have added and downloads new comments from other users.

✦ **F** The download Comment tool downloads any new comments added by other users.

✦ **G** The upload Comments tool uploads new comments that you create on the file being shared.

✦ **H** The Navigation pane is active and all palette items are accessible including bookmarks linked to pages, thumbnails linked to pages, comments linked to comment items, and digital signature displays. Comments used for collaboration are displayed when uploaded or downloaded to and from a server.

✦ **I** Status bar items appear at the bottom of the Browser view. Page navigation and displays are active when working with inline PDFs.

✦ **J** Context-sensitive menus are supported with inline viewing.

✦ **K** If article threads have been created, they will be active.

✦ **L** Navigational buttons and links created in the PDF file are active in the browser.

✦ **M** A fly-away menu offers options for displaying the Document Summary and addressing preferences.

Note Inline viewing can be performed with either Acrobat or Acrobat Reader. Navigation and viewing options are the same for both viewers. However, the tools used for online collaboration in regard to exchanging comments are only available with Acrobat. Acrobat Reader has no provision to upload or download comments from a network server or Web server.

Inline viewing requires proper configuration with components provided with the Acrobat installer CD-ROM and configuration of your Web browser. By default, any necessary plug-ins will be installed for Web browsers. Be certain to install your Web browser before you install Acrobat. If inline viewing is not the default when you view PDF files in your Web browser, you may need to configure the browser's helper applications. Be certain to review the applications in the browser preferences and select the viewer plug-in for handling PDFs.

Sending PDFs across the Internet

At times you may be interested in working with file exchanges between colleagues and using the Internet for sending files. PDFs can be hosted on Web servers where users can download pages or you may be interested in sending PDFs to others via e-mail attachments. Any PDF file can be sent as an e-mail attachment through the same means as you send other attachments. In addition to the same methods that you use for other documents, Acrobat offers you a simple means for sending mail attachments. Choose File ➪ Send Mail and the current PDF in view will be attached to an e-mail. Acrobat automatically launches your default e-mail application and attaches the file in view in the Navigation pane. Type your message, click Send, and the PDF travels along with the e-mail.

Tip

For sharing PDF files among a community of users, you can send an e-mail message to users in your group and identify a URL where the users can download PDF files. Create a Web page with PDF links and a short description of each file. As you update PDFs, you can post them on the Web page. Users then have an option for downloading individual files they need. E-mail messages sent to users will be transferred much faster, especially when the files are large and many files need to be distributed.

Sharing Comments on Servers

Acrobat 5.0 introduces collaboration in the form of dynamically sharing all of the comment types discussed in Chapter 8 on network and Web servers. To share comments on either type of server, you must use a Web browser and you must have Acrobat installed on your computer. The fundamental structure of comment sharing requires a PDF document to be present at a location on a network server or URL where work group members have access. As comments are added to the PDF file, the data is stored in individual Form Data File (FDF) files. The associated FDF data can be viewed and shared among users. An individual may delete or amend his/her own data, but won't be able to delete the data submitted by other users. Tools shown in Figure 11-1 are uniquely added to the Acrobat Command bar when PDFs are viewed within a Web browser. These tools enable you to upload and download the FDF data that can be shared among workgroup members.

Comments on Web servers

Regardless of whether you elect to share comments on Web servers or on a local area network, you need to configure Acrobat and your Web browser properly. Configuration first starts with Acrobat. Choose Edit ➪ Preferences ➪ General and click Online Comments in the left pane in the Preferences dialog box. The first item to address is the Server Type by choosing an option from the pull-down menu shown in Figure 11-2 (Windows) and Figure 11-3 (Macintosh).

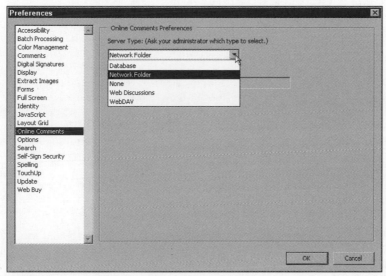

Figure 11-2: The Online Comments preferences are used to determine the server type to be established for sharing comments. On Windows, you have five options for the server type.

For any comments shared on Web servers, you'll need specific information from your Web administrator on how to set up the preferences and the URL to be used for those connection types that require a URL address. Database (Windows), Web Discussions (Windows), and WebDav will need special attention that requires assistance from your Web administrator. You'll also find some helpful information on the Acrobat installer CD-ROM and the Adobe Web site to help you configure your connection properly. If Web Discussions (Windows) is selected from the menu options, you need to also perform some configuration in Microsoft Internet Explorer.

As soon as the connection type has been configured properly, you won't need to return to the Preferences dialog box. Until you change preferences, they will be active for all your online collaboration.

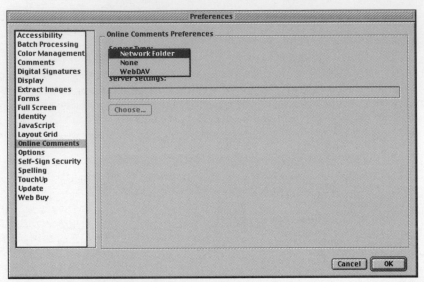

Figure 11-3: The Online Comments preferences on the Macintosh offer three server type connections.

Comments on local area networks

Configuration for sharing comments on local servers requires no special assistance from network administrators. You can create a folder or directory on a server and identify the folder that will be shared among users. For network collaboration, select the Network Folder menu command shown in Figure 11-2 (Windows) and Figure 11-3 (Macintosh). A Choose button directly below the Server Type pull-down menu enables you to navigate your server and find the file to be used for collaboration. A PDF file must first reside in the shared folder before you can use the Choose option. If you change server settings, you'll need to return to the preferences. However, if you add more PDFs to the folder, you can leave the preferences alone and select different files for sharing comments.

Sharing comments

After the configuration has been set up in Acrobat, open your Web browser and navigate to the location where the PDF file to be shared is located. Sharing comments can only be performed from within the Web browser. For browser types, be certain to use the most recent versions of either Netscape or Microsoft Internet Explorer.

You can use any of the Comment tools among the tool groups in the Acrobat Command bar that appear inside the browser window. After adding a comment, click the Upload Comment tool in the Acrobat Command bar. If you want to view recent additions from other users in your group, click the Download Comment tool. To synchronize uploading and downloading comments, click the Upload and Download Comment tool.

 Caution If you create a comment and quit your browser or you navigate to another page before uploading new comments, Acrobat will automatically upload them for you. This feature is handy, but it can also create problems if you have any second thoughts about sending a comment. Before you create a comment, be certain to think it out and only add those you intend to submit to avoid inadvertently sending the wrong comments.

To delete a comment, you can use a context-sensitive menu from either the Navigation pane where the comments are displayed or select the comment in the Document pane. When the context-sensitive menu opens, select Delete. You can also address properties by opening a context-sensitive menu. If you want to change author name or select a different icon for the comment appearance, options are available in the comment properties. If you want to use the Stamp tool, all of the stamps accessible from Acrobat are also available from within the Web browser.

Working offline

Acrobat also offers you an opportunity to work offline when sharing comments on any kind of server. You may not have an Internet connection or network connection and want to organize comments and then submit them later. To work offline, you need to have a copy of the PDF used among your workgroup. Copy the file to your local hard drive. After making comments, from within Acrobat choose File ➪ Resume Commenting Online. Acrobat will launch your Web browser and update the data file where your comments are stored.

Working with Web Links

Any Web addresses contained in the text of a PDF document can be created as hot links to the URL specified in the Web link. For links from text to be functional, the complete URL address must be supplied in the text. This behavior is different than specifying a link button described in Chapter 10. If creating a link, you can select any text on the page and the URL is specified in the Link Properties dialog box. When you create Web links from text, the copy contained in the PDF becomes the link.

To create Web links, choose Tools ➪ Local Web Addresses ➪ Create Web Links from URLs in text. Acrobat will open the Create Web Links dialog box shown in Figure 11-4. In the dialog box, you can make decisions for the pages to be identified where the links will be created. Select All to create Web links from all pages in the PDF. The From button enables you to supply page ranges in the two field boxes.

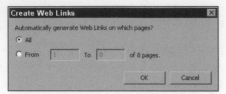

Figure 11-4: The Create Web Links dialog box enables you to determine what pages will be used for identifying Web links and converting them to hypertext links.

Acrobat can also globally remove Web links from all pages or a specified page range. To remove Web links, choose Tools ➪ Local Web Addresses ➪ Remove Web Links from document. The same options are available in the Remove Web Links dialog box as those found in the Create Web Links dialog box.

Tip   Creating Web links can only be performed on text that has been properly identi-fied in the text of the PDF file. If you need to add a Web link, you can easily create the text in Acrobat without having to return to the authoring program. Click the TouchUp Text tool in the Acrobat Command bar. Hold the Control key (Option key on a Mac) down and click. A new text block will be placed on the document page. Type the URL for the Web link and deselect the text by selecting the Hand tool and click in the Document pane. Choose Tools ➪ Local Web Addresses @@ Create web links from URLs in Text. Acrobat will create the Web link from the URL you added to the document.

When a Web link is selected in Acrobat, a dialog box opens by default asking whether you want to view the Web link in Acrobat or in a Web browser. The choices are made available in the Specify Weblink Behavior dialog box that opens when you click a link. (See Figure 11-5.)

Figure 11-5: When you click a Web link, Acrobat prompts you as to whether you want to open the Web link in Acrobat or a Web browser.

If you select Acrobat, the Open Web Page command will be executed and the URL specified in the link will convert the Web page to PDF. The new PDF page will be appended to the document in view when the link was selected. If you select In Web Browser, Acrobat will launch your default Web browser and open the link location in the browser. The behavior of whether to open the URL link in Acrobat or your Web browser can be toggled by holding the Shift key down when you click the link.

Tip   If you want the Web link URL to open in Acrobat but open as a separate document without appending to the open file, press the Control key (Command key on a Mac) and click the link button.

Working with Captured Web Sites

In Chapter 4, I covered using Web Capture to convert HTML files and Web pages to PDF. In this chapter, we'll take off from using the Open Web Page command and look at files after they have been converted to PDF. If the Add PDF Tags checkbox is enabled when you download Web pages with the Open Web Page command, Acrobat will create structured or *tagged* bookmarks automatically. (The Add PDF Tags option is found under the Conversion settings in the Open Web Page dialog box.) Tagged bookmarks offer you additional editing capabilities in Acrobat as well as adding structure to the PDF file. Among other things, you can use the Bookmarks palette in the Navigation pane to organize and delete the bookmarks along with the associated pages. This option is not available with standard bookmarks.

If you examine the Bookmarks palette after downloading Web pages with the Add PDF Tags option enabled, the bookmarks will appear with two different icons. The first icon appearing in the bookmark list is a standard bookmark with no destination. No view is associated with the bookmark. It represents the top level of the bookmarks created when downloading a site. Bookmarks below the parent bookmarks are tagged bookmarks and appear with a different icon, as shown in Figure 11-6.

Figure 11-6: When Add PDF tags is enabled in the Conversion Settings dialog box for Web Capture, tagged bookmarks are added to the converted Web pages.

When the list of bookmarks is expanded, the child bookmarks will be displayed in a nested order. Each of the tagged bookmarks is associated with a view on the page where the bookmark is linked. To move a bookmark, you can drag up or down in the bookmark palette just like using standard bookmarks. If you want to reorder the bookmarks and the associated pages, hold the Control key (Command key on a Mac) and drag up or down. The pages will follow the same order as the bookmarks.

Tagged bookmark menu options

Tagged bookmarks offer some additional menu commands available through either the palette menu or a context menu. The additional features available with tagged bookmarks not available with standard bookmarks include:

✦ **Print Page(s):** You can execute a print command from the tagged bookmark menus. Either the current page or selected pages in the Bookmarks palette will be printed. Contiguous selections can be made by Shift-clicking the bookmark names or Control + Click (Command + Click on a Mac) for noncontiguous selections.

✦ **Delete Page(s):** Tagged bookmarks enable you to delete a range of bookmarks and the pages associated with each bookmark. Like printed pages, either contiguous or noncontiguous selections can be made.

✦ **Extract Page(s):** Pages can be extracted from the current file in either a contiguous or noncontiguous order. The extracted pages will appear in a single PDF file. Bookmarks associated with the extracted pages will not appear in the new file.

✦ **Append Next Level:** Additional Web pages can be downloaded and appended to the open PDF file. If you later decide to add additional levels to a captured Web site, select the Append Next Level from the context menu.

✦ **View Weblinks:** Like the same option available when capturing Web pages, the View Weblinks command opens the Select Page Links to Download dialog box (see Figure 11-7.) Whereas the View Weblinks command in the Web Capture submenu only lists Web links on the open page, tagged bookmarks enable you to select multiple bookmarks and view all links associated with all of the selected pages.

✦ **Open Page in Web Browser:** Any selected tagged bookmark can have the associated page opened in a Web browser. Only a single page can appear in the Web browser; therefore, if more than one bookmark is selected, the menu option will be grayed out.

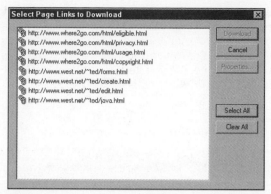

Figure 11-7: The View Weblinks command enables you to select multiple tagged bookmarks and view all Web links associated with the selected pages.

PDF Structure with tagged bookmarks

PDF structure is added to Web page files downloaded with the Open Web Page command. Structured content for accessibility is the same as found with applications, such as Microsoft Word discussed in Chapter 6. When you add the PDF tags and capture a Web site, all the structure tags and form field tags will be contained within the PDF file. In Figure 11-8, I downloaded several pages from the Where2Go.com Web site.

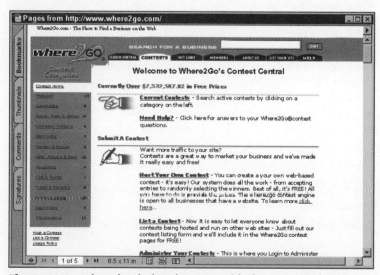

Figure 11-8: I downloaded Web pages with the Open Web Page command on the Where2Go.com Web site.

In Figure 11-9, I opened the Forms palette after the PDF from Figure 11-8 appeared in Acrobat. Each of the button fields contained in the Web pages converted to PDF are linked to the content structure.

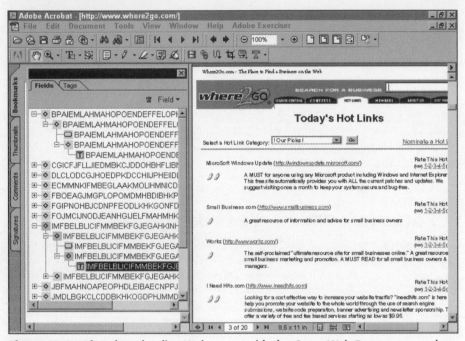

Figure 11-9: After downloading Web pages with the Open Web Page command on the Where2Go.com Web site, the Forms palette opens and the structured content for all the buttons appear in the palette list.

Summary

✦ PDFs can be viewed inside the Web browser window. This kind of display is called inline viewing.

✦ PDFs can be sent as e-mail attachments executed from within Acrobat by using the Send Mail command.

✦ When PDFs are viewed inline in Web browsers, additional tools used for online collaboration appear in the Acrobat Command bar.

✦ Sharing comments can be accomplished on local area networks and on Web servers.

✦ Web pages can be captured with tagged bookmarks and PDF structure.

✦   ✦   ✦

PDF and eBooks

Heading Toward Digital Content

Let's take a journey back in time. Imagine yourself strolling your Silicon Valley neighborhood one day and you stop at the sound of some busy shuffling from a neighbor's garage. Careful not to soil your polyester green leisure suit, you walk through a scattered mess of electronic parts. Two young men approach you and talk of their vision of changing the world. They tell you that one day, computers will be on the desk of every child in school, every household in Western society, and in every imaginable workplace. You smile politely and walk away thinking about the absurdity of it all.

That same year, you take a business trip and stop by a little house where a handful of people are working on various electronic gadgets. You meet a young man who dropped out of Harvard University, and he tells you that one day the richest companies in the world will be producing software for computers owned by the masses. You walk away with your lava lamp tucked under your arm thinking about the absurdity of it all.

A decade later, you unwrap your new Hayes 300 baud modem, log on to CompuServe, and check your messages. A colleague writes that one day soon business in Western culture will be conducted electronically. As the century ends, more investment money will be devoted to electronic commerce than any other industry. Laughing at the absurdity of it all, one click and you're offline.

By the year 2001, you kick yourself for missing the investment opportunities of years' past. In search of new directions, you study the journals and online information centers to find reports on the future of content and distribution of information. You're sitting in the middle of the information age predicted decades ago by Mead and Cooley and wonder where it's all going. The reports speak of the distribution of electronic content that will eventually force a near extinction of printed matter. Everything from textbooks to leisure reading will be purchased and exchanged electronically. Will you see the vision or dismiss it all as absurd?

The predictions

The software giants are not only predicting the evolution of distributed electronic works, they're trying very hard to make it happen. In selling their new products, both hardware and software companies are supporting a vision of the way people will seek out and obtain information beginning now and continuing rapidly through the next few decades. Predictions expect the sale of eBooks and other eMatter to exceed over $1 billion U.S. dollars by the year 2005; printed newspapers and magazines will become near extinct by the end of the decade; and before the end of two decades, over 90 percent of printed matter will be hosted online electronically.

Perhaps you may think that these predictions are pie in the sky dreams by radicals, but stop and think for a moment about some sound arguments that might make a little sense. In education, schools are constantly plagued with rising costs of textbook revisions. Add up all of the textbook budgets in the schools and electronic distribution seems like it could be a viable solution. Within a few years, electronic reading devices will cost so little, a school district could afford to give each student a reader with all the money saved on their textbook budgets. This, of course, depends on whether the textbook publishers pass on production and distribution savings to the schools. Think of one day when people can hold all their textbooks, research, and related content from elementary school through a doctoral program on a single electronic device.

The rapid pace of Western culture has produced a society of people who constantly seek immediate gratification. Even FedEx shipments seem to take too long for some people. Imagine being able to take a European vacation and dock your eBook reader midflight to download a language program, a restaurant guide, and a tour book. Or stop and think about the research that you need to write for a business plan or proposal. You log online and the electronic content is assembled on the fly for the exact information you need. At the local coffee shop, you dock your reader to a station, swipe a credit card, and download the magazines and journals to read while drinking your latte. At the local bookstore, the shelves are all bare. You place your book orders and they are printed and bound on demand.

All of these predictions and many others touted by the technology leaders may seem a little far-fetched to today's adult population. The comfort level of those who grew up with textbooks and printed novels might be awkward for both academic and leisure reading on electronic displays. But the next generation of young people is now growing up with comfort zones more adaptable to computer screens and LCD displays than printed matter. If you think it won't happen, you may some day wish you hadn't thought it all absurd.

eMatter

Stephen King's successful novella, *Riding the Bullet*, caught the attention of the media and popularized some awareness of electronic distribution of fiction works. Web sites created for distribution of eMatter have been growing in numbers in recent years while traditional retail book sites now all host sections where eBooks are available for purchase. Some of the more prestigious sites require published works to be formally published by a reputable publisher while others will accept any work to host online. Both nonfiction and fiction works have been exploding in numbers across the many Web sites where eMatter can be purchased.

eMatter is simply a body of work sold or distributed in electronic form. It may or may not be sold in printed form. If you are an aspiring author and Hungry Minds or Prentice-Hall hasn't given you a go ahead, you can find Web sites that will host your work and handle all the commerce. As an author, you can receive royalty payments ranging from 15 percent to over 70 percent depending on the rates determined by the company that you elect to use to distribute your works. As an author, you usually have the right to determine the retail cost and most often you are not required to engage in exclusive contracts with a single vendor.

For the consumer, you can browse the Internet and find information in both nonfiction and fiction categories. The more advanced Web sites will display bestseller items, book reviews from readers, and a synopsis of each work they host. Some sites enable you to create a virtual library where you can access your purchased works that are stored on the company's Web site. With a password entry you can log on to the Web site and review or download your purchased works. Some Web sites offer a unique means of creating content for you from selections of their hosted work. You may want a report on a particular event and specific people related to the event—for example, individuals and their participation in key political events. The Web host would assemble the content dynamically and make it available as a single work for you to download.

eCommerce

From a commercial viewpoint, there are some considerations for those who want to author works and those who want to sell and distribute works. As an author, you'll want to look at the Web site that you want to use for selling your eMatter in terms of design, accessibility, marketing, and methods of completing transactions. The particulars of your contract and methods of payment will be of concern, but how your work is eventually sold will be an equally important consideration. If you are a developer or own a commerce site, you'll want to consider some factors related to all the concerns of authors and consumers. If you're a consumer and not concerned with author rights or enterprise management, you still will have some interest in knowing how products are sold and some particulars of completing transactions.

Following are some factors that will be important for providers, resellers, and consumers:

✦ **Completing transactions:** In a report titled "Instant Access" by Tony McKinley, which is hosted on the Adobe Web site in their ePaper Columns category, a market researcher was quoted as saying that today on the Web over 95 percent of people who start a transaction fail to complete them. This sounds like a staggering figure, but to validate at least part of the claim, you might look at your own history and probably find many instances where you started a transaction on a Web site and failed to complete it. There are, no doubt, a number of reasons why consumers fail to complete transactions. One of the first areas to examine or polish on a commercial Web site is the ease for completing transactions. If a transaction is complicated and bothersome, people won't stick around to figure it out. Unnecessary information, slow transaction progress, wading through multiple Web pages, complicated forms, forms and JavaScripts that don't work or lock up a computer, and so forth, are potentially some reasons people don't complete transactions.

✦ **Knowing the market:** The largest spending group of goods and services in the U.S. today by age group is the boomer population. The purchasing behavior of this group is: They never saved, they spent all they earned, and they will need to continue working after age sixty-five. Economists predict this population will inherit over 12 trillion dollars in the next decade and a half. What they'll do with the money, according to past behavior, is go out and spend it all. Knowing the population and knowing their buying habits, what turns them on, and what turns them off is greatly beneficial for content developers and resellers. In 1999, this age group averaged $40 in purchases in new computer hardware; yet in the same year, this group was the fastest growing age group of new Web surfers. They're not likely to have fast Internet connections and their level of technical skill as a group is lower than the 17 to 25 age group. For anyone desiring to sell anything on a Web site, be certain to check it out for simplicity and speed. You want to market to this group — they'll spend far more dollars than any other age group.

✦ **Personal information:** Cornell University published reports from their geriatric studies in the sixties regarding the willingness of their respondents answering survey questions. The studies reported that of all questions posed to their target groups, the overwhelming majority refused to answer questions related to family income. In recent studies, over 92 percent of all age groups engaged in completing transactions on the Web are somewhat to greatly concerned about distribution of personal information. The minute the boomer population hits a site where personal information is collected in order to complete a transaction, they'll immediately jump off to another site. If you want to sell your product, avoid collecting any kind of information not necessary to complete the transaction — especially questions related to income levels.

✦ **Intuitive forms:** The design of forms, whether they be HTML or PDF, should be straightforward and intuitive. Forms should be designed with an eye to prevent user error. When possible, be certain to control options as much as can be implemented in the form. The fewer errors the user can create in filling out a form, the more likely they will complete a transaction.

✦ **Passwords:** The absolute nightmare for users with less than sophisticated skills is accessing sites with a password. Many Web sites use unnecessary passwords to keep identifying information on returning clients even though the consumer still has to enter all credit card information back into a form when performing a transaction. Users don't often use the same password for all sites visited. They forget a password, log on at different workstations between office and home, and often have to meet different criteria for creating passwords between different sites. In attempting to complete a transaction, they'll get frustrated with trying to remember a password just to get into a site and will rapidly leave. If you're a content developer, avoid any site that requires a password for entry when it is not essential for a consumer. You'll complete many more purchases from the boomers.

✦ **Navigation and search:** For anyone interested in selling or acquiring eMatter, the obvious single most important factor is finding it. You can have the greatest novel or software manual hosted on a Web site; but if people can't find it, it won't sell. Sites that are complicated and make searching difficult for finding information by category and content should be avoided. If a consumer can't get to their area of interest within two mouse clicks, a good many will leave the site and try to find something elsewhere.

✦ **Disabling navigation:** Users typically go to a site from a search engine. If they find a site attractive and worthwhile, they may bookmark it and return again. If on a mission to find content from a search result, they'll want to return to the search list. One of the absolute insulting programming pitfalls is disrupting navigation. If the site is worthwhile, the user will return. There's absolutely no need to force someone to stay on a site. Many users will avoid the site in the future if they have to struggle to continue their navigation. Content providers should avoid any site where the protocols have been compromised.

Without a doubt, many more considerations need to be examined for those buying and selling eMatter. Content developers and consumers should review site design appearance, category listings, market awareness, integrity of product, and other factors that come to mind. The previous list is intended as a starting point to become aware of factors that can greatly impact online purchases.

eBooks

With regard to eBook distribution, the largest category of downloadable content without cost is fiction works. Works in the public domain are distributed free to users from Web sites trying to promote more mass appeal for supporting eBooks. In terms of sales, the category changes to nonfiction works.

If you are an aspiring content developer, you'll probably see more success if you assemble nonfiction works. Novelists have a great opportunity for getting a lifelong ambition of publishing a novel out, but in most cases you won't see much return. It will probably take some time for people to cozy up to an eBook reader at night. Nonfiction, particularly works related to professional interests, has much greater appeal. Software guides and manuals are a natural for displays on computer monitors and LCD panels. Research and reference works are also good candidates for the eBook market. I wouldn't discourage anyone who wants to begin a publishing career if you want to produce a novel, just be realistic in your expectations.

If we assume for a moment that nonfiction works are potentially more lucrative, then designing a nonfiction eBook will have some special considerations over designing a fiction book. Adult fiction works usually have to accommodate only text as a design issue. Nonfiction work often includes figures, charts, diagrams or other image elements. Hypertext links that might be made to the Web could be a consideration and some degree of interactivity will also be important with eBooks. For potential content developers, look at some issues that need to be considered when authoring nonfiction work that will be sold as eBooks.

Preliminary assumptions

Before the content is finalized for distribution, some preliminary issues need to be considered regarding the audience, mechanisms for display, and target markets. Understanding some of these preliminaries will help guide you in using the proper application for authoring a publication. Some issues to consider include:

✦ **Audience:** Will part of your target market reach people with visual and motion challenges? If so, you'll need to be concerned with developing content that meets accessibility standards. Ultimately the best program available to you for developing structured content is Microsoft Word. If accessibility is not an issue or at least not an issue for the first edition, then applications supporting exports that can get the final publication into a standard for eBook publications needs to be used.

✦ **Consumer tools:** What device(s) should the eBook support? In this book, examples are restricted to the PDF format. Other eBook formats support different display devices. The Microsoft Reader, discussed later in this chapter, is growing in popularity and supports displays on hand-held devices as well as computers. Design and layout is much more limited with the Microsoft Reader format than using Acrobat PDF. Determining the hardware needs to display your works will dictate the design of your publications. In some cases, you may want to support multiple formats.

✦ **Distribution limitations:** Digital rights protection often limits the end user's ability to print the content in order to protect copyrights. This restriction is not always the case. If the work will be restricted to screen viewing, then some design requirements for image resolutions will be less than for works that intend to be printed. If the work permits printing hard copy, the font usage may be different than publications read on screens. If you are an author, you may not have the choice for whether an end user may be able to print your works. This decision may be determined by the Web service hosting your files. Be certain to check with sources where you expect to sell your work before completing the design and layout.

✦ **Platform access:** Will the work be distributed for cross-platform users? In as much as PDF can be ported across platforms, some eCommerce sites haven't resolved encryption methods for Macintosh users. You can find Web sites that host eBooks in PDF format available only for Windows users. If you want more distribution exposure, you may need to either use a different format or choose a different distributor.

✦ **Participate in marketing:** Content developers need to resolve themselves to active participation in marketing their works. This is critical for anyone who wants to sell eMatter. As I said earlier, you may have the greatest publication in the world online; but if people don't know it's there, it won't sell. Presume for a moment you decide to publish your life-long ambition of a story about Charlie the Cheshire. Why every cat lover in the world would just love this story. If this is true, then you'll see many more sales if *Cat Fancy* magazine posts links to the content reseller than links directed from the Adobe ePaper Web pages. Today, marketing eMatter is probably the single easiest product to market. You just need to research all the Web sites interested in your product and make arrangements for them to host excerpts of your work and direct consumers to where the work can be purchased.

Designing eBooks

The accuracy of the content, editing, reviews, and like matters are required for all publications whether they be books or eMatter. Many Web sites don't have standards for publishing works and permit authors to throw up anything they desire to sell. Other sites have editing and layout standards that must be met in order for the publication to be listed in their inventory. As a matter of practice, it's essential to have any work listed for resale to be thoroughly edited and reviewed. After we get past the spell checking, grammar, and technical reviews, some design issues should be addressed for online publications. These issues include:

✦ **PDF Structure:** If you want complete accessibility, then creating the layout in Microsoft Word will be your best choice. Layouts in Word can accommodate many design features found in layout applications. If accessibility is not important, then use one of the design applications mentioned in Chapter 6 that support exporting bookmarks and articles.

✦ **Display size:** Analog works are most often published in portrait formats. Monitors are viewed in Landscape formats. The orientation and size of the work to be displayed on computer screens should be appropriate for 14- to 15-inch monitors with text point sizes easily legible with a Fit in Window view. Aspect ratios of 1.33:1 are consistent with 640x480 screen dimensions. Consider using this aspect ratio for your landscape designs.

✦ **Fonts:** For screen displays, a sans serif font will be a better choice especially if you have a need for smaller font sizes appearing in captions, charts or tables. If the file is to be printed, a serif font would be better to use for body copy. For almost all readers, a point size of 14 to 20 points should be considered. The higher point sizes will offer viewers with smaller monitors and slight vision problems a comfortable display for type.

Adding Graphics to PDF Layouts

If you use Microsoft Word and export the file as PDF and then want to import graphics from non-supported file formats, you can take any image file and convert it to PDF. After it's in PDF format, you can then import the image in a form field with a simple JavaScript routine. The layout of the Word file needs to accommodate margins where you want to place graphics and captions because you won't be able to insert images between lines of text.

In the PDF file, create a button form field and select JavaScript as the action type in the Add An Action dialog box. Enter the code:

```
event.target.buttonImportIcon();
```

You can copy and paste the form fields and provide a separate name for the field each time it is pasted. When you select the button, a dialog box will appear where you can browse your hard drive and select the PDF file to import. Captions can be created either with additional form fields or by adding text with the TouchUp Text tool. Acrobat's not a layout application, but using a simple workaround such as this can provide more flexibility in designing pages.

✦ **Layout:** One of the first design lessons for new aspiring designers in graphic design classes is to honor white space. For anyone not schooled in design, the tendency is to crowd the margins and run text to the edges. If you're not a designer, look at samples both in print and eMatter and study the layouts for space considerations. If you have a lot of text on a page, especially landscape pages, use multiple column formats for text. No more than 12 to 15 words across a single column should be used with ample white space appearing between columns.

✦ **Color:** Avoid using color for backgrounds with text appearing in the foreground. Contrast is important if you have any text on a page with graphics including the cover page. Be certain no distracting elements appear when text is placed on a page.

✦ **Interactivity:** Analog books are static while eBooks can be very dynamic. Be certain all the bookmarks, destinations, article threads, links, and form field buttons all work properly. With Acrobat 5.0, thumbnails are created on the fly, so be certain to not embed them in the PDF file to keep the file size smaller. When links are created over text, use a color for all text items not defined with visible borders. Some clue needs to be provided to a user that a link can be accessed.

✦ **Security:** A site hosting your eMatter may handle Security. If the Web site that you intend to use doesn't provide security for encrypting PDFs, then you need to decide whether you want to let them host your material. If you do elect to use a site that doesn't encrypt PDF files, then add your own security for preventing printing and changing the document if so desired.

Tip

If you sell your works from your own Web site and the number of sales doesn't warrant the purchase of an enterprise management solution, you can create a security system individually for each file sold to a user. Create a comment or use the Document Summary and supply individual purchasers' credit card number, expiration date, name, and billing address in a text note or in the Author and Key Word fields in the Document Summary. Secure the file with a master password. Users will be very unlikely to freely distribute documents that contain their credit card numbers and identifying information.

✦ **File size:** Unfortunately there isn't a standard rule for the size of the files that will be downloaded. As an example, I would suggest keeping file sizes between three to five megabytes. Keep in mind not all consumers will have ISDN or DSL connections. Before uploading a file, be certain to enable Save For Fast Web View and use a Batch Sequence to optimize the file. If printing is not allowed, be certain to have all images downsampled to 72 ppi.

✦ **Page count:** One of the truly great advantages of eBooks is the ability to publish short works between 25 to 75 pages. Traditional publishers won't touch books running these lengths. Printed publications have minimum requirements for page length in order to make a publication saleable. If you have a topic that deserves several hundred pages, break the work up into multiple short volumes. Each volume in a series can be affordably priced for the consumer and the file size and download times will be easier to manage.

eBooks are a relatively new commodity item and we have much to learn in terms of development and marketing. No single formula currently exists for developing the ideal book or reaching the ideal market. As a new industry, the best thing you can do is run tests and listen to feedback from users. The more you do, the more you'll learn what works best for your audience and market.

Web Buy

The previous section was concerned with creating eMatter and marketing work on commercial sites. For the end user, the item of most interest is how to acquire eBooks. When purchases are made for PDF content and file encryption is needed, the best source for protecting PDF works is Acrobat PDF Merchant. When files have been encrypted and a server hosts PDFs using the Acrobat PDF Merchant enterprise solution, users acquire PDFs via Acrobat Web Buy. On the commerce side, an enterprise solution is needed. Adobe PDF Merchant is a server-side solution that enables individual encryption for each document downloaded. The encryption method uses serial numbers from a computer's hardware storage devices. If a user distributes an eBook purchased with this encryption, the PDF will launch the Web site where the content can be purchased. All access to the PDF will be denied for anyone viewing the PDF on any device other than the ones used for the encryption.

Configuring Web Buy

Configuration for Web Buy needs to be properly set up in the General Preferences, as discussed in Chapter 7. Review the chapter and look at the help files distributed with Acrobat. The world of eCommerce and eBooks is changing rapidly. For current information and updating your Web Buy plug-in be certain to frequent the Adobe Web site and log on to `www.adobe.com/epaper/ebooks`. All the information updates for purchasing eBooks with Web Buy will be contained in this area of the Adobe Web site.

Downloading eBooks

After the preferences are established for the hardware identifiers in the General Preferences dialog box, you're ready to access eMatter from Web sites that support Adobe Web Buy. To test your configuration and practice working with Web Buy, you can log on to Web sites that offer eBooks in the public domain. Adobe hosts several eBooks available as free downloads with Web Buy found at: `www.adobe/com/epaper/ebooks/freebooks.html`. Keep in mind that Web addresses change. If you find the pages moved or renamed, search the Adobe Web site to find where the eBook section is located.

Setting up Web Buy

Log on to a Web site and find a book in the public domain to try out your Web Buy service. Both Acrobat and Reader support Web Buy. Use of Web Buy requires that a merchant has used the Adobe secure PDF technology to encrypt the file. When PDFs are downloaded with Web Buy, two files will be downloaded. The PDF file is the content you want to acquire, and the license file enables you to access the content. License files have the same name as the PDF with a RMF extension. Each time you want to open a PDF acquired through Web Buy, Acrobat needs to locate this file in order to unlock the PDF. The RMF file contains information related to the security imposed on the file. If the author has prevented printing or changing the PDF, the RMF file will contain the security handling. If you want to examine the security imposed on a file, open the Document Security dialog box.

When you find a book to acquire, click the link to commence the download. In my following example, I logged on to the Adobe Web site and downloaded a PDF of selected poems by William Shakespeare. The file will download to your computer and be saved to a temporary directory. Figure 12-1 displays the progress dialog box as the file is downloaded.

Figure 12-1: While the file is downloaded through the Web browser, the browser progress dialog box is displayed.

Unlocking Web Buy documents

The PDF file resides on your computer but it cannot be read until you unlock it. If you don't have a security file or Acrobat cannot find a previously downloaded file, you need to tell Acrobat where to go to find the security file. If the file exists on your computer, click the Find License button in the Acrobat Web Buy dialog box shown in Figure 12-2. This dialog box opens when the PDF is opened in Acrobat and the security file cannot be found.

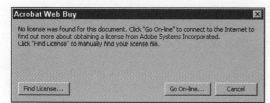

Figure 12-2: A warning dialog box opens if the PDF merchant does not have a record of what hardware serial number will be used to encrypt the PDF file.

The Go On-line button enables you to find the security file from the Web site where the PDF was downloaded. Click this button and your Web browser will be launched and the URL where the security file is stored will be found. Acrobat opens a second dialog box warning you that information will be sent to the merchant. In the Acrobat Web Buy dialog box, you can select a button to display the details of the information Acrobat will send. Figure 12-3 shows the detail of information used for submitting the computer System ID that I used when downloading the Shakespeare poems collection.

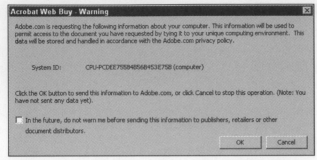

Figure 12-3: A warning dialog box displays the identifier information to be sent to the merchant when downloading a PDF with Web Buy.

Click OK and another warning dialog box appears informing you the information will be sent to an unsecured server. The momentary transfer of the serial number will be sent unencrypted. Click OK again in this dialog box and the merchant page is displayed in the Web browser. In my example, the Adobe Web page for online ordering appeared where my name and e-mail address were supplied, as shown in Figure 12-4.

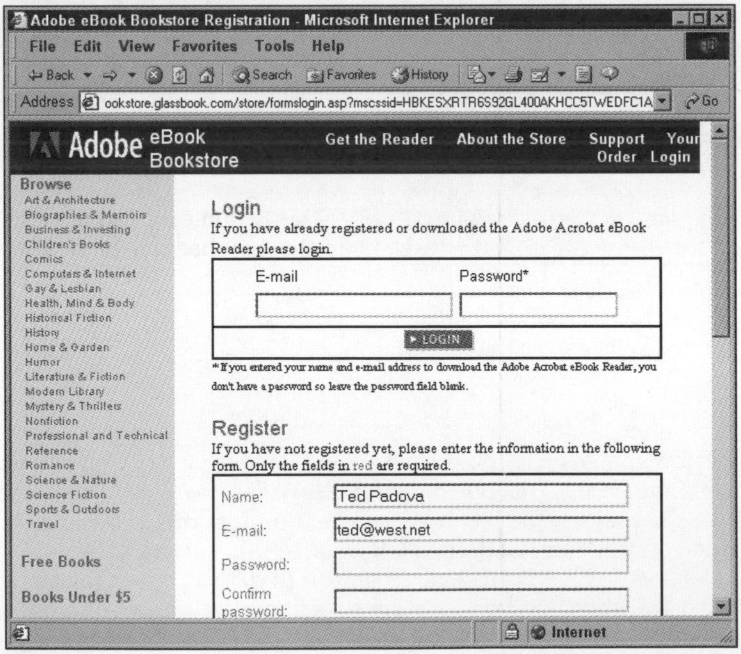

Figure 12-4: When acquiring eMatter from the Adobe Web site with Web Buy, an online form needs to be completed in order to unlock PDFs downloaded from this site.

At this point, the file has been downloaded and the unlocking mechanism has been established.

Note   Every purchase or download you make with Web Buy requires you to download the PDF and the security file. Security files are separate for each PDF and unique for the respective file. When downloading files with Web Buy you need to use the Go On-line button in the Acrobat Web Buy dialog box each time you download a file to acquire the associated security file.

Viewing Web Buy PDFs

If you selected a PDF to be downloaded, the next operation Acrobat performs is yet another warning. Before Web Buy can be used, Acrobat needs to dismiss all non-certified plug-ins. The warning dialog box for Acrobat Web Buy appears, as shown in Figure 12-5.

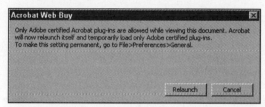

Figure 12-5: Only Certified Plug-ins can be loaded when Web Buy is used. Acrobat informs you it will temporarily unload non-certified plug-ins and relaunch the program.

When you select Relaunch, Acrobat will first quit, disable non-certified plug-ins, and then relaunch. At this point the document opens in the Acrobat viewer, as shown in Figure 12-6.

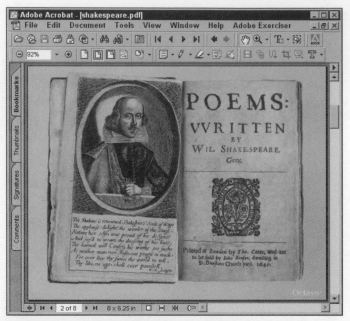

Figure 12-6: After downloading the eBook and establishing the unlocking key, the PDF opens in an Acrobat viewer.

When you view the location where the key was saved, the display appears, as shown in Figure 12-7. The file type will be RMF and a key will appear on the icon display. This file is the key file and not the PDF. If you relocate the file, use the Find License button in the Acrobat Web Buy dialog box that opens when the PDF is opened. The license file also contains information about the hardware encryption. If you move the PDF and the license file to another computer without the hardware identifier, the PDF can't be opened. The Acrobat Web Buy dialog box will open and another user can click the Go On-line button to obtain a license.

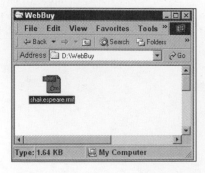

Figure 12-7: The key data file is saved to the location that you determine in the Web Buy preferences dialog box. When viewed, the file icon displays a key on the PDF icon.

eBook Readers

The term *eBook Reader* can be a little confusing at times. In a generic sense, the term may be used to describe different entities. A hardware device dedicated to perform the task of displaying eBooks is often described as an eBook reader. Many consumer electronics companies and new companies developed to produce these devices have begun to proliferate. eBook readers are also referred to as software supporting eBooks on computers, laptops, dedicated eBook readers, and hand-held devices. With regard to the software, two products are the primary contenders in this market.

Microsoft Reader (Windows)

Microsoft Reader is a free downloadable software product designed to display files created for the Reader software on computers and other devices mentioned above. Microsoft got the early jump on the software release and for some time it was the only contender in the market. The Reader is the display mechanism for content created and saved in a format acceptable to the Reader software. To create content, you need another application called ReaderWorks. The ReaderWorks software available from Microsoft is used for creating files acceptable to the Reader. The ReaderWorks software comes in two flavors. ReaderWorks Standard is a freely downloadable application available from the Microsoft Web site. The ReaderWorks Publisher software requires purchase. If you intend to distribute eBooks commercially, you'll need to purchase the commercial edition to add all the necessary bells and whistles to your eBooks.

When you log on to the Microsoft Web site and download the Microsoft Reader software, a series of dialog boxes will guide you through installation. A one-time registration is required. After completing registration, the Reader will be accessible on the device where you install it. The activation screen appearing at the end of your installation, as shown in Figure 12-8, confirms installation.

The Reader Software can display links, bookmarks, read back text from an open book, highlight text passages, and it permits authoring comments. The downside to the Microsoft Reader for PDF file authors is it doesn't support the PDF format in its current iteration. Furthermore, the Reader Software is currently released for Windows users. Cross-platform compliance has not been developed as of this writing.

Figure 12-8: After successfully installing the Microsoft Reader Software, an activation screen confirms installation.

Acrobat eBook Reader

Now to get your tongue tied up a little more, the Acrobat eBook Reader is not Acrobat Reader. Acrobat eBook Reader is the counterpart to the Microsoft Reader. As such, the Acrobat eBook Reader is a software application designed for displays and navigation of eBooks. The Adobe product overcomes the limitations of the Microsoft Reader with support for PDF files and it is a cross-platform product. To acquire the Acrobat eBook Reader, log on to the Adobe Web site and download a copy for the platform you use. Another version of the product is also available and it requires purchase. When you buy the Acrobat eBook Plus Reader, a full version of the *American Heritage Dictionary of the English Language* is included as well as options for sharing eBooks when authorized by publishers.

The Microsoft product described previously is a marvelous tool for displaying eBooks on computer systems and hand-held devices. The Microsoft Reader is feature-rich and relatively easy to use. Without offering too much bias, I have to say that the Adobe product is something to get very excited about. Its sleek design and ease of importing PDF files with structured content makes the task of viewing eBooks saved in PDF format a much easier task than working with the Microsoft Reader.

To add PDF files to your library, click the Open File button on the Reader display. The Adobe product supports PDF, HTML, and EBX (a voucher file model allowing end users to share content). When a new file has been opened, an icon appears on the default cover page of the reader, as shown in Figure 12-9. This page and new pages, added by opening additional files, is the user library.

Figure 12-9: When new files are opened in the Acrobat eBook Reader software, an icon representing the first page of the file is displayed in the user library.

As soon as they're in the library, files can be read or voice activation can read the contents of any file opened in the reader. No special authoring is required for voice activation. Navigational buttons are not necessary when viewing PDF files. The reader automatically moves pages when the page is clicked with the mouse button.

PDF Goes Palm (Windows)

For some time the Microsoft Reader was advantaged for users of hand-held devices. Content could be developed for small Personal Desk Accessory (PDA) devices where you could scroll through pages of a novel, report, eBook, or any kind of content created for displays on these devices. Not to be excluded from this market, Adobe has developed a version of Acrobat Reader to be used with Palm hand-held devices. PDFs can be created and ported to hand held devices complete with bookmarks, document information, graphics, and comments.

The Adobe Acrobat Reader for Palm OS is a product distributed similar to the Acrobat Reader software. You can download the Reader for Palm OS from the Adobe Web site. As of this writing, the software is only available for Windows users. Mac users will want to frequent the Adobe Web site, because a Macintosh version should appear soon.

When you download the software, two important components will be installed when you run the Acrobat Reader Palm OS installer. The Acrobat Palm Desktop is the control software that will download the Acrobat Reader for Palm OS software to your Palm Device when you launch the application and synchronize your Palm Device with your computer. The Reader software and a PDF help file will be downloaded to the hand-held device when you synchronize the device with your computer.

Installing the Acrobat Reader for Palm OS (Windows)

Installation of the Acrobat Reader for the Palm OS is a simple and painless process. When you install the software downloaded from the Adobe Web site, the Acrobat Palm Desktop is installed in the Start menu. Launch the application and the Adobe Acrobat reader for the Palm OS dialog box appears, as shown in Figure 12-10.

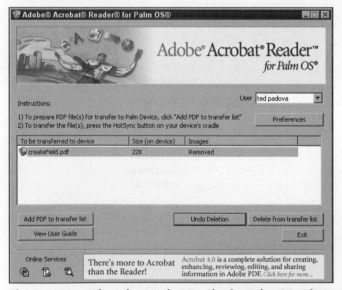

Figure 12-10: When the Acrobat Reader for Palm OS software is installed and you open the Acrobat palm Desktop application, the Adobe Acrobat Reader for Palm OS dialog box appears.

When you first enable a HotSync by connecting your Palm Device to the hotsync cradle and press the HotSync button, Acrobat Reader for Palm OS automatically is installed on your hand-held device. A dialog box displays the install status as the software is ported from your computer to the Palm Device, as shown in Figure 12-11.

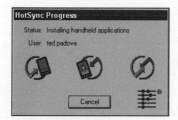

Figure 12-11: A status dialog box appears when the Palm Device and the computer are synchronized displaying the download progress of the Acrobat Reader for Palm OS transferring from your computer to the Palm Device.

When installation is complete, remove your Palm Device from the hotsync cradle and tap the Home button on the Palm desktop. If all the applications are not visible, select the pull-down menu from the top-right corner of the device and select All. Acrobat Reader should be viewed on the display screen among your other applications. Click the Acrobat Reader icon and Acrobat Reader for Palm OS loads into memory. A single PDF file is installed when you first install the file. By default, you should see the help file listed on the display screen. Tap the file and you'll see the contents within the Reader application.

Adding PDFs to your Palm Device (Windows)

From the Adobe Acrobat Reader for Palm OS dialog box on your computer, you add PDF files by clicking the Add PDF to transfer list (refer back to Figure 12-10). When a PDF file is added to this list, you have some options to select from the Preferences dialog box that opens when you click the Add PDF to transfer list button. You will have an option to eliminate images from the PDF file in order to keep the file sizes smaller or you can elect to keep images at full size.

When the option for handling images is made, click the Finish button in the dialog box. The file is then prepared for delivery to the Palm Device. A dialog box, as shown in Figure 12-12, displays the progress for reformatting the PDF for the Palm OS. When completed, you need to resync your Palm Device by placing it in the hotsync cradle. The PDF will then be ported to your hand-held device.

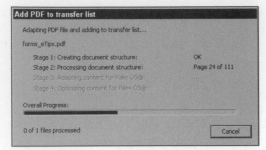

Figure 12-12: As a PDF file is being prepared for transfer from your computer to the Palm hand-held device, a dialog box displays the progress for preparing the PDF to transfer.

Viewing PDFs on your Palm Device (Windows)

As PDFs are added to your Palm Device, they appear in a list under a menu item appearing as Acrobat Reader. Tap a PDF listed under the Acrobat Reader menu and the PDF selected opens. If bookmarks have been created in the original PDF, you can display bookmarks by tapping the Menu button on your Palm Device. When menus are visible, tap the Document menu. From the menu items displayed, tap Show Table of Contents. Any bookmarks saved with the file will appear in a list. You can then tap on a bookmark and jump to the page associated with the bookmark.

Like any other documents on your Palm Device, dragging or tapping the scroll bars scrolls the pages. In addition to the traditional views common on all Palm Devices, you can also view comments saved with the PDF file and also view the Document Summary. These options are also available by making the respective choices after tapping the Document menu.

Summary

✦ eMatter is a body of work most often hosted on Web sites and made available to end users for downloading. The work can be books, papers, articles, and almost any other content developed for electronic distribution.

✦ eCommerce Web sites sell author works and handle distribution of eMatter.

✦ eBooks are predicted by technology leaders to rise in growth over the next few decades. Although not completely replacing printed books, eBooks are expected by some leaders to reduce the number of printed works while increasing popularity with digital works.

✦ Acrobat Web Buy enables authors and distributors of eBooks protection against copyright infringement. Web Buy requires locking a PDF file with Adobe secure PDF technology at the commerce server and unlocking PDF files at the user's computer.

✦ Both Microsoft Corporation and Adobe Systems offer software applications for viewing eBooks on computers and laptops. Microsoft Reader is a Windows-only application and does not support PDF formats. The Acrobat eBook Reader from Adobe is cross-platform compliant and supports PDFs.

✦ Acrobat Reader for Palm hand-held devices enables you to download and view PDFs on Palm Devices. PDFs ported to Palm Devices can retain bookmarks, comments, and document information.

✦   ✦   ✦

Working with Forms

What Are Acrobat Forms?

Forms in Acrobat are PDF files with data fields that can contain user-supplied data. In Acrobat, you can use text string fields, numeric fields, date fields, calculation fields, signature fields, and a variety of custom fields created with JavaScripts. The advantage of using forms in Acrobat is that it enables you to maintain design integrity. Rather than using a database manager, which may limit your ability to control fonts and graphics, Acrobat can preserve all the design attributes of a document while behaving as a data manager. In this chapter, you get the opportunity to explore creating, modifying, and using forms.

Forms are created and filled out in Acrobat. The Acrobat Reader software can edit field data, but there are no provisions for saving the edited form, nor is there an opportunity to export form data without the aid of third party solutions. In developing PDF workflows for a company or organization, all users expected to complete forms in Acrobat need to be individually or site licensed for the Acrobat software or Acrobat Business Tools or seek other software solutions from third party manufacturers.

The one element to keep in mind regarding Acrobat and forms is that a form in the context of PDF is not a paper form scanned in as an image and saved as PDF. Tons of these so-called "forms" are around offices and the Internet. The documents originated as forms, but hopefully by the time you understand all the features available to you with Acrobat, you'll understand these scanned documents can hardly be called forms. Simply put, forms are scanned images. The power of Acrobat gives you the tools to create *smart forms*. These forms can be dynamic, intuitive, and interactive; and save both you and the end user much time in providing and collecting information.

Understanding Form Fields

Forms use different types of data fields that can hold data, act as buttons that invoke actions, and call scripts to execute a series of actions. Form fields can assume different appearances as well as possess the capability to include graphic icons and images to represent hot links that invoke actions. Acrobat forms are more than a static data filing system — they can be as vivid and dynamic as your imagination. When designing a form in Acrobat, you are well advised to plan your work ahead of time. As you shall see, with the many different choices available for field contents and appearances, creating form fields offers an enormous number of options.

Form contents

To learn how forms function in Acrobat, you need to understand how forms are developed and, ultimately, how you will go about creating forms. Because Acrobat cannot be effectively used as a layout application, nor can it be used to objects and design elements, creation of a form begins in another application. You can use illustration or layout software for designing a form that ultimately is converted to PDF. In Acrobat, the form data fields are created with the Form tool, and options are selected from the Field Properties window. Form fields can be of several different types:

✦ **Button:** A button is usually designed in an illustration or layout application as a graphic element and saved as a PDF file. When you create the field in Acrobat, you add the button as a transparent item so that the original design element appears as though it's the item executing the action. (Creating a form field with a custom button was introduced in Chapter 10.)

✦ **Checkbox:** Checkboxes typically appear in groups to offer the user a selection of choices. Yes and no items or a group of checkboxes may be created for multiple choice selections.

✦ **Combo Box:** When you view an Acrobat form, you may see an arrow similar to the arrows appearing in palette menus. Such an arrow in a PDF form indicates the presence of a combo box. When you click the arrow, a pull-down menu appears containing two or more choices.

✦ **List Box:** A list box displays a box with scroll bars, much like windows you see in application software documents. As you scroll through a list box, you can make a choice of one of the alternatives available by selecting it.

✦ **Radio Button:** Radio buttons perform the same function in PDF forms as they do in the dialog boxes of other applications. Usually you have two or more choices for a category. When you click a radio button, it enables the associated option, a bullet (or other symbol you choose) is placed inside the circular shape, and any other radio button in the group is turned off.

✦ **Signature:** Digital signatures can be applied to fields, PDF pages, and PDF documents. A digital signature can be used to lock out fields on a form.

✦ **Text:** Text fields are boxes in which the end user types text or numeric data when the form is filled out.

All these form field types are available to you when you create a form in Acrobat. From the end user point of view, one needs to examine a form and understand how to make choices for the field types in order to accurately complete a form. Fortunately, Acrobat field types relate similarly to the metaphors used by most applications designed with a graphic user interface. An example of an Acrobat form with several form field types is shown in Figure 13-1.

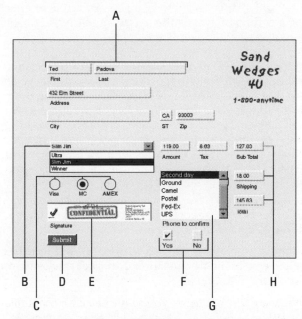

Figure 13-1: Different field types include: A) Text fields; B) Combo Box; C) Radio Button; D) Button; E) Signature; F) Checkbox; G) List Box; H) Text fields.

 Text fields contain both text and numbers.

Navigating text fields

As you view the form shown in Figure 13-1, notice that it contains several text fields, a combo box, a list box, and a least one each of the other field types. To fill out a text field, you need to click the Hand tool, place the cursor over the field, and click the mouse button. When you click, a blinking I-beam cursor will appear, indicating text can be added by typing on your keyboard.

To navigate to the next field for more text entry, you can make one of two choices: Click in the second field or press the Tab key on your keyboard. When you press the Tab key, the cursor jumps to the next logical field, according to an order you specify in Acrobat when you design the form. Be certain the Hand tool is selected and a cursor appears in a field box when you press the Tab key. If you have any other tool selected, tabbing through fields and data entry is possible, however, using the mouse will perform an edit respective to the tool selected in the Command bar.

When selecting from choices in radio button or checkbox fields, click in the radio button or checkbox. The display will change to show a small solid circle or check mark within a box. When using a combo box, click the arrow appearing in the field and select from one of several pull-down menu choices.

When you finish completing a form, you will usually submit the data. This can be accomplished in one of several ways: exporting the form as data, sending the data to an Internet server, exporting to a Form Data File (FDF), or simply saving the filled-out PDF form under a new name so that the original form, serving as a template, remains without any field entries. Forms can include buttons to execute actions similar to those specified by the Execute Menu Item command that appears when creating hypertext links (see Chapter 10). When designing a form, you will often include a button for the user to click that will export the data through one of the export methods just listed.

Form field navigation keystrokes

As mentioned earlier in this chapter, to move to the next field you need to either click in the field or press the Tab key. Following is a list of other keystrokes that can help you move through forms to complete them:

✦ **Shift + Tab:** Moves to the previous field.

✦ **Esc:** Ends text entry.

✦ **Return:** Ends text entry.

✦ **Shift + click:** Ends text entry.

✦ **Double-click a word in a field:** Selects the word.

✦ **Control/Command + A:** Selects all the text in a field.

✦ **Left/right arrow keys:** Moves the cursor one character at a time left or right.

✦ **Up arrow:** Moves to the beginning of the text field.

✦ **Down arrow:** Moves to the end of the text field.

✦ **Up/Down arrow with Combo and List boxes selected:** Moves up and down the list. When the list is collapsed, the Down arrow opens the list.

✦ **Control/Command tab:** Accepts new entry and exits all fields. The next Tab places the cursor in the first field.

In this example, Acrobat is used. Because Reader users cannot save or export data, form data can only be submitted from hard copy if the user has not purchased Acrobat. Forms can be completed in Reader and printed. The printed copy can then be faxed or filed.

Creating Forms

Now that you know something about filling out a form, move on to creating a form and setting up the form fields in Acrobat. Creating forms in Acrobat begins with a template or PDF document and requires use of the Form tool. With the Form tool, you can create actions very similar to those created with the Link tool (see Chapter 10). Rather than creating a link to a view or page, the Form tool creates a data link whereby data fields are identified and choices for expressing the data are defined.

To help create precise placement of data fields, the Grids and Guides attributes should be defined in the Preferences dialog box. Major and minor gridlines can be identified in the Layout Grid dialog box by choosing Edit ➪ Preferences ➪ General and select Layout Grid in the Preferences dialog box. Showing Grid and Snap to Grid are enabled by selecting the View menu and choosing the respective option. When creating forms, it can be helpful to show the forms grid and use the snap to feature. In some cases, if you have a template created from an illustration or layout program, you may want to turn the grids off. All will depend on whether the template lines match your grid.

All the form field types are created with the Form tool. Click the tool in the Acrobat Command bar and draw a rectangle. When the Snap to Forms Grid option is enabled, the rectangle created will snap to the gridlines. The moment you release the mouse button after drawing a rectangle, the Field Properties window will appear.

Field properties

The field properties have six general categories that include Appearance, Options, Actions, Format, Validate, and Calculate. The Appearance tab is displayed by default. The items in the default window relate to the appearance for the form type you have selected from the pull-down menu in the upper-right corner of the Field Properties window. The Type pull-down menu in the Field Properties window identifies several types of fields that can be used in your form. As you scroll through the tabs in the Field Properties window, different options can be selected for the type of field you create. Options will vary according to the field type that you select from the Type pull-down menu. All options above the tabs are independent of the tab options. Some choices need to be made before you go about scrolling through the tabs and selecting different options. The first choice is to provide a name for the field created.

Naming fields

The Name item in the dialog box enables you to enter a name for the field. The name that appears here will be used to provide a name for the field irrespective of the field contents. You can identify your field name as anything you like. In practice, using an identifier that closely resembles the contents of the field is best — something such as *First* or *First Name*. You could use any other identifier, such as *1*, *F1*, *First Field*, and so on. The name you enter will be used to identify the field when the data is exported or imported. If you use forms for the Web or import data into other PDF forms, the Name field will play an important role in setting up the proper import and export criteria. It's critical that you understand the importance of field names and keep naming conventions and case-sensitivity consistent among files and applications.

Tip   When naming fields the most important detail to remember when creating names is to be consistent. Case-sensitivity is important in regard to importing and exporting data. Always use the same case for all fields.

Type

The types of fields available for use in PDF forms are accessed from the Type pull-down menu on the top right of the Properties window, as shown in Figure 13-2. Click the pull-down menu to see the available choices.

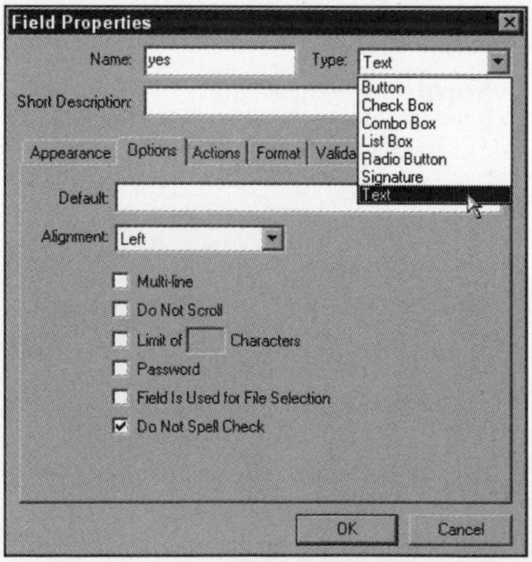

Figure 13-2: The Field Properties window enables you to identify the attributes for form fields. Here the pull-down menu for the various field types is open.

A brief description of the form types was discussed earlier in this chapter. The default field type is Text. Text is a generic field that can accept data in the form of alphanumeric characters. After naming a field, choose from the pull-down menu the field type you want to create.

Short description

As previously stated, the Name item in the Field Properties window identifies a particular field and plays an important part in the import and export of forms. You must supply a field name when creating a field. Short Description, located beneath the Name item, is optional. When you add a descriptor to this field, the field name you supply will appear as a tool tip. The Short Description field can be helpful to the user when completing the form. For example, you could name a field that you want to be the field in which users type in their first name as *name.1*. In the Short Description field, enter the text *First Name*. Then when a user moves the cursor over the field box, First Name will appear as a tool tip. As the mouse cursor encounters fields, the tool tip changes to the short description supplied for the respective field.

Appearance

The Appearance tab relates to the form field appearance. Much like links, you can create a rectangle in a form with the rectangle border either invisible or visible. When made visible, you have access to border attribute options as well as options for the text appearance, as listed here:

✦ **Border Color:** The keyline created for a field can be made visible with a rectangular border appearing in a color selected from the color swatch adjacent to the Border Color option. To specify a border color, enable the option and click the color swatch. When the swatch is selected, choose a color from the preset colors (Windows only) or a custom color.

✦ **Background Color:** The field box can include a background color. If you want the field box to be displayed in a color, enable this option, click the color swatch next to it, and choose a color the same way you would for the border. When the checkbox is disabled, the background will appear transparent, and the field name will be visible in the field box. If you want to eliminate the field name, choose a color for the Background.

✦ **Width:** The Width options include the same options available for link rectangles. Select the pull-down menu and choose from Thin, Medium, or Thick.

✦ **Style:** There are five style types to choose from this pull-down menu. The Solid option displays the border as a keyline at the width specified in the Width setting. Dashed displays a dashed line; Beveled appears as a box with a beveled edge; Inset makes the field look recessed; and Underline eliminates the keyline and supplies an underline for the text across the width of the field box. See Figure 13-3 for an example of these style types.

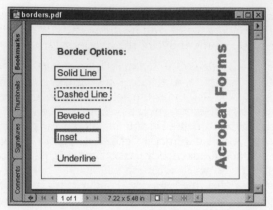

Figure 13-3: Five options for choosing a border
style are available in the Field Properties window.

✦ **Text Color:** The text appearing for the field name defaults to black. If you identify a color for text by selecting the swatch adjacent to Text Color, the field
contents supplied by the end user changes to the color chosen. The field
name, however, remains black.

✦ **Font:** From the pull-down menu, select a font for the field data. All the fonts
installed in your system will be accessible from the pull-down menu. When
designing forms, try to use Sans Serif fonts. They will display better on-screen
than Serif fonts.

When designing forms for cross-platform use, use one of the Base 14 fonts. Custom
fonts loaded in your system may not be available to other users. Using the true Base
14 fonts of Courier, Times, Helvetica, or Zapf Dingbats is important in form fields that
display text. If you use fonts such as Arial, even though Arial will be installed across
platforms, the text will not appear in Acrobat viewers lower than 5.0. Using a font
such as Arial will appear across platforms only in Acrobat viewers 5.0 or greater.

✦ **Size:** Depending on the size of the form fields that you create, you may need to
choose a different point size for the text. The default is Auto, which automatically adjusts point size according to the height of the field box. Choices for manually setting the point size for text range between two and 144 points.

✦ **Read Only:** Below the text attribute choices are the Common Properties settings. The first item is Read Only. When Read Only is selected, the field does
not accept user input — it "locks" the field box. If no background color is used,
the name of the field will appear within the field box. Likewise, the border
color and style will also appear. If a background color is used, the field name
will not be visible. In either case, no cursor can be placed inside the field box,
and no entries can be made. Read Only may be used to display information in
a field where no user input is required. Or you may create a series of forms
where given users may not be requested to fill in some data fields, in which
case this option comes in handy.

✦ **Required:** When the Required option is enabled, the form data won't be submitted until all required fields are completed. You might use this field option for something such as a digital signature or Social Security number field.

✦ **Form Field is:** Several options for displaying individual fields are available from this pull-down menu. The default is Visible, which displays the field and permits entry. The second choice is Hidden, which hides the field from view and does not print the field when the form is output to hard copy. The third item is Visible but doesn't print, which makes the field visible on-screen and enables user entry, but will not print the field to hard copy. The last item is Hidden but printable, which hides the field data but permits printing the field on hard copy.

Regardless of what choice you make for the field type, the Appearance tab will contain most of the items discussed in the preceding list. Subtle changes to options may include different defaults as you select from the Type pull-down menu. For example, the default font for the various form types is Helvetica. However, when you specify the Radio Button type, the font will default to Zapf Dingbats. For the most part, Appearance options are consistent with the field types used. The other tab settings options, however, will change depending on which type is selected.

Options

The Options tab provides selections for specific attributes for the field to be created. Options settings are dependent on the field type selected from the Type pull-down menu. Options tab attributes for each of the types are described here.

Text options

When Text is selected from the Type pull-down menu and the Options tab is clicked, the Field Properties window appears, as illustrated in Figure 13-4.

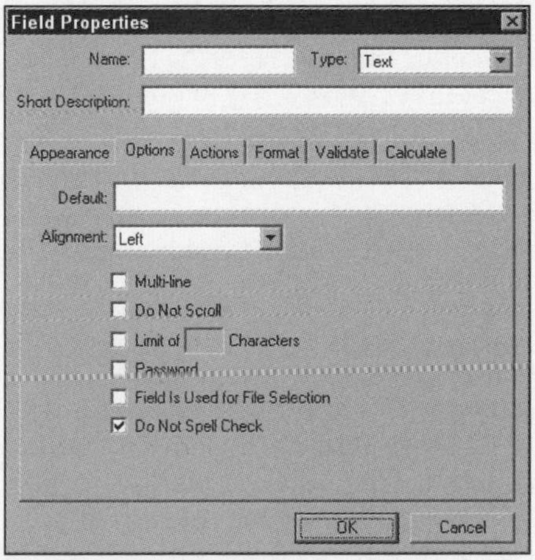

Figure 13-4: The Options settings for Text field properties

Each of the attribute settings listed here are optional when creating text fields:

✦ **Default:** The Default field in the Field Properties dialog box can be left blank, or you can enter text that will appear in the field when viewing the form. The Default item has nothing to do with the name of the field. This option can be used to provide helpful information when the user fills out the form data. If no text is entered in the Default field, when you return to the form, the first field will appear empty. If you enter text in the Default field, the text that you enter will appear inside the field box when you return to the form.

✦ **Alignment:** The Alignment pull-down menu has two functions. First, any text entered in the Default field will be aligned according to the option that you specify from the pull-down menu choices. Alignment choices include Left, Centered, and Right. Secondly, regardless of whether text is used in the Default field, when the end user fills out the form, the cursor will be positioned at the alignment specified in the Field Properties window. Therefore, if you select Centered from the Alignment options, the text entered when filling out the form will be centered within the field box.

✦ **Multi-line:** If your text field contains more than one line of text, select the Multi-line option. When you press the Return key after entering a line of text, the cursor will appear on the second line, ready for text entry. Multi-line text fields may be used, for example, as an address field to accommodate a second address line.

✦ **Do Not Scroll:** To be used in conjunction with the Multi-line attribute, when enabled, no scrolling will be permitted. If the field contents are larger than the field box, the user won't be able to scroll to see the remaining text.

✦ **Limit of [__] Characters:** The box for this option provides for user character limits for a given field. If you want the user to specify something in a date field, for example, where the field would be expressed as *mm/dd/yy*, you may use a limit of eight characters. If the user attempts to go beyond the limit, a warning beep will sound.

✦ **Password:** When this option is enabled, all the text entered in the field will appear as a series of asterisks when the user fills in the form. The field is not secure in the sense that you must have a given password to complete the form; it merely protects the data entry from being seen by an onlooker.

✦ **Field is Used for File Selection:** This option allows a file path to be the field's value. The data file will be submitted along with the form. A JavaScript action can be associated with the field that will open a dialog box where a file selection can be made.

✦ **Do Not Spell Check:** Spell checking is available for notes and form fields. When the checkbox is enabled, the field will not be spell checked. This can be helpful so that the spell checker doesn't get caught up with stopping at proper names, unique identifiers, and abbreviations.

Checkbox and radio button options

Checkboxes and radio buttons have two data options for Export Value: Yes (on) or Off. When a mark is placed in the form field, the default will be Yes (or on). When no check is placed in the field box, the data will be read as Off. From the options available for checkboxes or radio buttons, you can choose a style for the check mark or radio button from the available pull-down menu choices. Checkboxes and radio buttons have identical choices for appearance attributes. (See Figure 13-5.)

Figure 13-5: The Options settings for checkbox fields include a pull-down menu for the style of the check mark to be used and an identifier for the data value exported. The same choices are also available for radio buttons.

In the Options tab for the checkboxes or radio buttons, the item denoted as Default is Checked when enabled, will place a mark in all data fields that have been identified with this default. When the user fills out a form, he or she would need to click a checkbox or radio button field to toggle the check mark on and off. Among the different marks applied to the field boxes are six different characters shown in Figure 13-6.

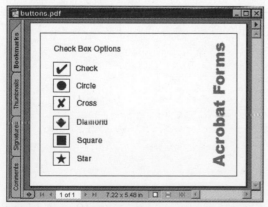

Figure 13-6: Six icon options are available for checkboxes and radio buttons.

Combo box and list box options

Combo boxes enable you to create form fields where a list of selections appears in a scrollable window. The user completing a form can make a selection from the list. A list box is similar to the combo box in that it presents a list that is also scrollable when some items are hidden. However, the list for a combo box only displays one item at a time from the scrollable list, whereas a list box will display as many items as can appear in the form field. Figure 13-7 illustrates the differences between a combo box and a list box.

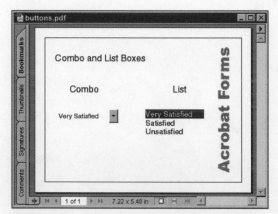

Figure 13-7: A combo box and a list box are displayed beside each other. The combo box items can be viewed and scrolled by selecting the down arrow.

The data exported with the file will include the selected item from the combo box or list box. When creating a form, restricting a user to specific items from which to choose is often preferred over allowing open-ended comment lines. Restricting data choices to a few options makes it easier to analyze and categorize the final data. When the combo box or list box is selected from the Type pull-down menu, and you click the Options tab, the Options window enables you to define various field attributes, as shown in Figure 13-8.

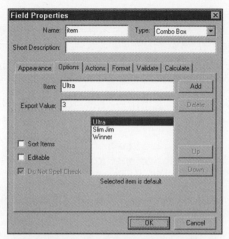

Figure 13-8: The Options settings for combo boxes provide an opportunity to specify how items in the combo box are listed and the export values associated with each item.

The field attributes found in the Options window include the following:

✦ **Item:** The name of an entry that you want to appear in the scrollable list is entered in the Item field. This value can be identical to the export value, or a different name than the export value name can be used.

✦ **Export Value:** When the data is exported, the name entered in this field box will be the value appearing in the exported data file. As an example, let's say you created a consumer satisfaction survey form. In that form, the user may choose from list items, such as Very Satisfied, Satisfied, and Unsatisfied, and you've specified the export values for these items to be 1, 2, and 3, respectively. When the data is analyzed, the frequency of the three items would be tabulated and defined in a legend as 1=Very Satisfied, 2=Satisfied, and 3=Unsatisfied.

✦ **Add:** After the Item and Export Values have been entered, clicking the Add button will place the Item in a list box appearing below the Export Value field. After adding an item, you can return to the Item field and define a new item and, in turn, a new export value.

✦ **Delete:** If an item has been added to the list and you want to delete it, first select the item in the list. Click the Delete button to remove it from the list.

✦ **Up/Down:** Items are placed in the list according to the order in which they are entered. The order displayed in the list will be shown in the combo box or list box when you return to the PDF document. If you want to reorganize items, select the item in the list and click the Up or Down button to move one level up or down, respectively. To enable the Up and Down buttons, the Sort Items option must be disabled.

✦ **Sort Items:** When checked, the list will be alphabetically sorted in ascending order. As new items are added to the list, the new fields will be dynamically sorted while the option is enabled.

✦ **Editable (Combo Box only):** The items listed in the Options tab are fixed in the combo box on the Acrobat form by default. If Editable is selected, the user can change all items in the combo box. Acrobat makes no provision for some items to be edited and others not. The Editable option is not available for list boxes. When you create a list box, the data items cannot be changed.

✦ **Do Not Spell Check (Combo Box only):** The same manner of spell checking discussed earlier in this chapter is available for combo boxes but not list boxes.

✦ **Multiple Selection (List Box only):** Any number of options can be selected by using modifier keys and clicking the list items. Use Shift + click for contiguous selections and Control/Command + click for non contiguous selections.

Button options

Buttons differ from all other fields when it comes to appearance. You can create and use custom icons for button displays, as I discussed in Chapter 10. Rather than entering data or toggling a data field, buttons typically execute an action. You may use a button to clear a form, export data, or import data from a data file into the current form. When the Button type is selected, the Options tab attributes changes to those shown in Figure 13-9.

Figure 13-9: The Options tab for the Button field properties include highlight settings and three options for mouse behavior — Up, Down, and Rollover.

When the Button type is selected, you can make choices from the Options tab for the highlight view of the button, the behavior of the mouse cursor, and choices for text and icon views. The Options attributes for buttons are as follows:

✦ **Highlight:** The Highlight options affect the view when the button is clicked. The None option specifies no highlight when it is selected. Invert momentarily inverts the colors of the button when selected. Outline displays a keyline border around the button, and Push makes the button appear to move in on Mouse Down and out on Mouse Up.

✦ **Button Face When:** The three choices on this list become available when a highlight option has been specified. Up displays the highlight action when the mouse button is released. Down displays the highlight action when the mouse button is pressed. Rollover offers an opportunity to use a second icon; when the mouse cursor moves over the button without clicking, the image changes to the second icon you choose.

✦ **Layout:** Several views are available for displaying a button with or without the field name that you provide in the Name field. The choices from the pull-down menu for layout offer options for displaying a button icon with text (specified in the Text field within the Button Face Attributes section) appearing at the top, bottom, left, or right side of the icon. Figure 13-10 illustrates the different Layout options.

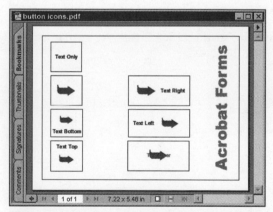

Figure 13-10: The Layout options include (from top-left down): Text Only; Icon Only; Icon Top, Text Bottom; Text Top, Icon Bottom. Beginning top right are: Icon Left, Text Right; Text Left, Icon Right; and Text over icon.

✦ **Select Icon:** When an icon is used for a button display, click Select Icon to open the Select Appearance dialog box. In this dialog box, a Browse button will open a navigation dialog box where you can locate a file to be used as a button. The file must be a PDF document. The size of the PDF can be as small as the actual icon size or a letter-size page or larger. Acrobat automatically scales the image to fit within the form field rectangle drawn with the Form tool. When an icon is selected, the icon will be displayed as a thumbnail in the Select Appearance dialog box.

An icon library can be easily created from drawings using a font, such as Zapf Dingbats, Wingdings, or patterns and drawings from an illustration program. Create or place images on several pages in a layout application. Distill the file to create a multiple-page PDF document. When selecting an icon to be used from the PDF file, the Select Appearance dialog box enables you to scroll pages. Each icon will be viewed in the thumbnail. When the desired icon is displayed, click the OK button. The image viewed in the thumbnail will be used as the icon.

✦ **Clear:** When an icon is selected, clicking the Clear button eliminates it. Clear will eliminate the icon only. The text identified in the Button Face Attributes section will remain.

✦ **Advanced Layout:** Clicking the Advanced Layout button opens the Icon Placement dialog box that provides attributes related to scaling an icon (see Figure 13-11). You can specify that the icon always be scaled, never be scaled, scaled down when it is too big to fit in the form field, or scaled up when it is too small to fit in the form field. The How to Scale option offers choices between proportional and non-proportional scaling. Sliders provide a visual scaling reference for positioning the icon.

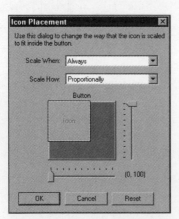

Figure 13-11: The Icon Placement dialog box offers options for positioning and scaling icons.

Actions

The Actions tab, shown in Figure 13-12, enables you to set an action when you click the field, when the cursor appears over a field, and when the cursor exits a field; or, you can have no action associated with the field.

Figure 13-12: The Actions tab provides options for invoking an action dependent on the mouse behavior.

The mouse behavior items in the Actions tab are as follows:

✦ **Mouse Up:** When the user releases the mouse button, the action is invoked.

✦ **Mouse Down:** When the user presses the mouse button, the action is invoked.

✦ **Mouse Enter:** When the user moves the mouse cursor over the field, the action is invoked.

✦ **Mouse Exit:** When the user moves the mouse cursor away from the field, the action is invoked.

✦ **On Focus:** Specifies moving into the field boundaries through mouse movement or by tabbing to the field.

✦ **On Blur:** Specifies moving away from the field boundaries through mouse movement or by tabbing to the field.

Actions for the cursor movements are similar to those discussed in the context of creating links in Chapter 10. You can specify menu commands and deal with some specific items for working with forms. Clicking the Add button in the Actions tab accesses all the actions.

The action will be associated with the mouse cursor option selected when you click Add. The default is Mouse Up, so that when Mouse Up is selected, the action will be invoked when the mouse button is released.

Caution

If you elect to select options other than Mouse Up, there will be times when the other options will complicate filling in form fields with end users. Just about any program dealing with link buttons has adopted the Mouse Up response to invoke an action. Many users will often click down, think about what they are doing, and then move the mouse away without releasing the button. This behavior enables the user to change his/her mind at the last minute. If you deviate from the adopted standard, it can be annoying for the user. Effective uses for other choices for mouse behavior may be for functions, such as opening help menus, tool tips, or playing sounds.

After you click the Add button, the Add an Action dialog box appears. The actions listed in this dialog box are the same as those in the Link Properties dialog box discussed in Chapter 10. Turn back to Chapter 10 for examples of how the following action types work: Execute Menu Item, Go to View, Movie, Open File, Read Article, Sound, World Wide Web Link, and None. Action items, such as JavaScript, Submit Form, Show/Hide Field, Import Form Data, and Reset Form relate more specifically to the task of creating a form. We start with Import Data and Reset Form in the next section and then move on to the others later in this chapter.

Import Form Data

You can export the raw data from a PDF file that creates a Form Data File (FDF) that can later be imported into other PDF forms. To import data, you can use a menu command or set an action on a field and execute the Import Form Data command. Data can be imported locally on your hard drive. Rather than retyping the data in each form, you can import the same fields into new forms where the field names match. Therefore, if a form contains field names, such as First, Last, Address, City, State, and so on, all common field names from the exported data will be imported into the current form. Acrobat ignores those field names without exact matches.

PDF Workflow

The Import Form Data command enables you to develop forms for an office environment or Web server where the same data used can easily be included in several documents. In designing forms, it is essential that you use the same field names for all common data. If you import data and some fields remain blank, recheck your field names. Any part of a form design or action can be edited to correct errors.

Reset Form

This is a handy action for forms that need to be cleared of data and resubmitted. When the Reset Form action is invoked, all the data fields are cleared. When you use this action, it's best to associate it with Mouse Up to prevent accidental cursor movements that may clear the data and require the user to begin over again. Reset Form can also be used with the Set Page Action command. If you want a form to be reset every time the file is opened, the latter will be a better choice than creating a button. Regardless of where you identify the action, it will be performed in the same manner.

The Acrobat Data Search

When a data file is identified for an import action, Acrobat will look to the location you specified when creating the action. Acrobat also searches other directories for the data. On the Macintosh, Acrobat looks to the Reader and System:Preferences directories for the data file. On Windows, Acrobat looks to the Acrobat directory, Reader directory, current directory, and the Windows directory. If Acrobat cannot find the data file, a warning dialog box will appear containing a Browse button to prompt the user to locate the data file.

The Reset Form command offers an option for clearing the entire form or selected fields. Selected fields are handy when you have either/or options, such as fields for identifying gender. When *male* is selected, the form field for *female* can be cleared and vice versa.

Format

The tabs, Appearance and Actions, are available for all field types. Options attributes change and are available for all field types but digital signatures. The Options choices vary significantly depending on which field type is used. For a quick glance at the tab options according to field type, take a look at Table 13-1.

Table 13-1
Tab Options for Field Types in the Field Properties Window

Field Type	Appearance	Options	Actions	Format	Validate Change	Calculate	Selection Change	Signed
Button	X	X	X					
CheckBox	X	X	X					
Combo Box	X	X	X	X	X	X		
List Box	X	X	X				X	
Radio Button	X	X	X					
Signature	X		X					X
Text	X	X	X	X	X	X		

As illustrated in Table 13-1, the Format, Validate Change, and Calculate tab options are only available for Combo Box and Text field types. To access the Format tab, select either of these field types. The Format options are the same for both types.

When the Format tab is clicked, Acrobat displays multiple choices for formatting either combo box or text fields, as shown in Figure 13-13. To define a format, select from the Category list displayed in the window. As each item is selected, various options pertaining to the selected category appear on the right side of the window.

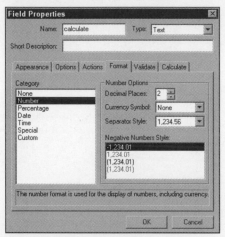

Figure 13-13: When either Combo Box or Text is chosen as the field type, the Format tab appears. Format options provide selections from seven categories.

The Category list displays seven choices for format category:

✦ **None:** No options are available when None is selected. Select this item to use Acrobat defaults for the field type.

✦ **Number:** Options for display of a numeric field include defining the number of decimal places, specifying any currency symbols used to express currency fields, and indicating how the digits will be separated (for example, by commas or by decimal points). The Negative Numbers Style list provides choices for displaying negative numbers that can include parentheses or a different display color.

✦ **Percentage:** The number of decimal places you want to display for percentages is available from the Decimal Places field when Percentage is selected as a category. Acrobat accepts values from zero to 12 decimal places. Choices for Separator Style are the same as those available with the Number category.

✦ **Date:** The date choices offer different selections for month, day, year, and time formats.

✦ **Time:** If you want to eliminate the date and identify only time, the Time category enables you to do so, offering choices to express time in standard and 24-hour units.

✦ **Special:** The Special category offers formatting selections for Social Security number, zip code, extended zip codes, and phone numbers.

✦ **Custom:** Custom formatting can be edited by using JavaScript. To edit the JavaScript code, click the Edit button and create a custom format script. Another dialog box will open where the code is created.

Validate

Validate can help ensure proper information is completed in a form. If a value must be within a certain minimum and maximum range, check the radio button for validating the data within the accepted values (see Figure 13-14). The field boxes are used to enter the minimum and maximum values. If the user attempts to enter a value outside the specified range, a warning dialog box appears informing the user the values entered on the form are unacceptable.

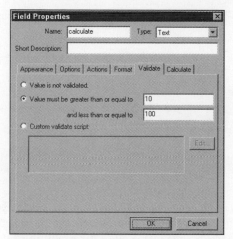

Figure 13-14: Validate can be used with Combo Box and Text field types to ensure acceptable responses from user supplied values.

The Custom validate script radio button enables you to enter JavaScript code. Scripts that you may want to include in this window would be those for validating comparative data fields. A password, for example, may need to be validated. If the response does not meet the condition, the user will be denied entry for supplying information in the field.

Calculate

The Calculate tab in the Field Properties window enables you to calculate two or more data fields (see Figure 13-15). A good example of when calculations may be used is to figure out sales tax. A subtotal field can add together the contents of multiple fields, and a tax rate field can be specified. If the form is submitted to different areas where tax rates vary, you can set up multiple fields for choosing a tax rate or an open text field — the contents of which can be supplied by the user. The tax rate would be multiplied by the subtotal to calculate the tax amount.

Figure 13-15: The Calculate tab offers options for calculating fields for summing data, multiplying data, and finding the average, minimum, and maximum values for selected fields.

If you want to calculate tax and add the tax to the subtotal, you can use JavaScript code to make the calculations and place the resultant data in a single field box. The Custom calculation script enables you to enter JavaScript code for creating custom calculations.

Selection change

The Selection Change tab, as shown in Figure 13-16, is only available for the List Box field type. If a list box item is selected and then a new item from the list is selected, JavaScript code can be programmed to execute an action when the change is made. Just as the other dialog boxes, clicking the Edit button opens a dialog box where the JavaScript code is created.

There are a variety of uses for the Selection Change option. You may want to create a form for consumer response from a given product — for example, an automobile.

Depending on information preceding the list box selection, some options may not be available. For example, a user specifies for "four-door automobile" as one of the form choices; and then from a list, the user selects "convertible." If the manufacturer does not offer a convertible for four-door automobiles, through use of the appropriate JavaScript code in the Selection Change tab, the user would be informed this selection cannot be made based on previous information supplied in the form. The displayed warning could include information on alternate selections that can be made.

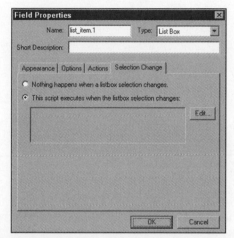

Figure 13-16: The Selection Change tab is only available for List Box field types. When using a Selection Change option, you need to program JavaScript code to reflect the action to be made when a change in selection occurs.

Signature fields

Digital signatures enable you to create a field that is filled in with a signature. The Signed tab, shown in Figure 13-17, offers options for behavior with digital signatures as follows:

✦ **Nothing happens when the signature field is signed:** As the item description suggests, the field will be signed but no action will take place upon signing.

✦ **Mark as read-only:** When signed, all or selected fields can be locked which results in Read Only fields.

✦ **This script executes when the signature is signed:** A custom JavaScript can be provided that can execute upon signing.

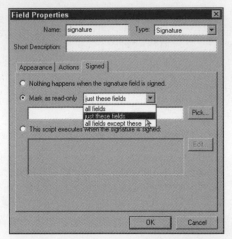

Figure 13-17: The Signed tab offers options for signature fields where a digital signature can be defined for a field and actions associated with applying a signature are established.

Digital signatures may appear as secured data fields, and they can also be used to indicate approval from users or PDF authors. Actions commonly associated with signatures on forms can individually lock out selected data fields. To create a digital signature field, use the Form tool and select Signature from the Type pull-down menu. For setting up digital signatures and understanding more related to them, look at Chapter 14.

Editing fields

For purposes of explanation, I use the term *editing fields* to mean dealing with field duplication, deleting fields, and modifying field attributes. After a field has been created on a PDF page, you may want to alter its size, position, or attributes. Editing form fields in Acrobat is made possible by using one of several menu commands or returning to the Field Properties window.

To edit a form field's properties, use the Form tool from the Acrobat Command bar and double-click the field rectangle. The Field Properties window reappears. You can also use a context-sensitive menu. At the bottom of the context-sensitive menu appears the Properties command. Select Properties to open the Field Properties dialog box. To select multiple fields, Shift + click each field to be selected with the Form tool. When multiple fields are selected and Properties is chosen from the context-sensitive menu, the appearance for the selected fields can be changed. For example, if you use a keyline border for the selected fields, the border style and color can be changed simultaneously for multiple fields. Options and scripts however, cannot be changed when multiple fields are selected and the Field Properties dialog box is opened.

If the fields you want to select are located next to each other or many fields are to be selected, use the Control key (Windows) or Command key (Macintosh) and drag with the Form tool to place a marquee around the fields to be selected. When the mouse button is released, the fields inside the marquee and any fields intersected by the marquee will be selected. The marquee does not need to completely surround fields for selection — just include a part of the field box within the marquee.

Duplicating fields

You can duplicate a field by selecting it and holding down the Control/Option key while clicking and dragging the field box. Fields can also be copied and pasted on a PDF page, between PDF pages, and between PDF documents. Select a field or multiple fields and then choose Edit ➪ Copy. Move to another page or open another PDF document and choose Edit ➪ Paste. The field names and attributes will be pasted on a new page.

Moving fields

Fields can be relocated on the PDF page by clicking the Form tool in the Acrobat Command bar, and then clicking and dragging the field to a new location. To constrain the angle of movement, select a field with the Form tool, press the Shift key, and drag the field to a new location. For precise movement, use the arrow keys to move a field box left, right, up, or down.

Deleting fields

Fields can be deleted from the PDF document in two ways. Select the field and press the Backspace key (Windows) or Delete key (Macintosh). You can also select the field and then choose Edit ➪ Clear. In either case, Acrobat prompts you with a confirmation dialog box. Be certain the Skip Edit Warnings option is disabled in the Options settings of the Preferences dialog box to view confirmation dialog boxes.

Aligning fields

Even when the grids are viewed on the PDF page, aligning fields can sometimes be challenging. Acrobat simplifies field alignment by offering menu commands for aligning the field rectangles at the left, right, top, and bottom sides as well as for specifying horizontal and vertical alignment on the PDF page. To align fields, select two or more fields and then choose Tools ➪ Forms ➪ Fields ➪ Align. The options for left, right, top, bottom, horizontal, and vertical alignment appear in a submenu. The same commands are also available in a context-sensitive menu. Acrobat will align fields according to the first field selected (the anchor field). This is to say, the first field's vertical position will be used to align all subsequently selected fields to the same vertical position. The same holds true for left, right, and top-alignment positions. When using the horizontal and vertical alignments, the first field selected will determine the center alignment position for all subsequently selected fields. All fields will be center-aligned either vertically or horizontally to the anchor field.

Tip Fields are aligned to an anchor field when multiple fields are selected and you use the align, center, distribute, and size commands. The anchor field appears with a red border while the remaining selected fields are blue. If you want to change the anchor (the field to be used for alignment, sizing, and so on), click the desired field while all fields are selected. Selecting a new field among those selected will reassign the anchor field and not deselect any of the selected fields.

You can distribute fields on a PDF page by selecting multiple fields and choosing Distribute from the Tools ➪ Forms ➪ Fields ➪ Distribute menu or the context-sensitive menu. Select either Horizontal or Vertical for the distribution type. The first field selected (anchor field) will determine the starting point for distribution.

Center alignment is another menu command found on both the menus just discussed. A single field will be centered in the PDF page either horizontally, vertically, or both horizontally and vertically, depending on the menu choice made. If multiple fields are selected, the alignment options will take into account the extreme positions of the field boxes and center the selected fields as a group on the PDF page.

Sizing fields

Field rectangles can be sized to a common physical size. Once again, the anchor field determines the size attributes for the remaining fields selected. To size fields, select multiple field boxes and then choose Tools ➪ Forms ➪ Fields ➪ Size or use the context-sensitive menu. Size changes can be made horizontally, vertically, or both horizontally and vertically. To size field boxes individually in small increments, hold the Shift key down and move the arrow keys. The left and right arrow keys will size the field boxes horizontally, while the up and down arrow keys will size the field boxes vertically.

Setting field tab orders

When you design a form and create form fields, Acrobat records the sequence of the field order beginning with the first field you create and continue in logical order through the last field created. The first field becomes Field 1, the next Field 2, and so on. This sequence dictates the *field tab order*—which is the order of fields the user will move through when tabbing through the form. If you move a field from one spot to another in the document, Acrobat does not change the order relative to location. In many cases, you will want to reorder the fields to facilitate easy movement through the fields when tabbing through the document. To change field tab order, use the Tools ➪ Forms ➪ Fields ➪ Set Tab Order command or select the same command from a context-sensitive menu. When Set Tab Order is selected, the form fields will appear in the document window with the tab order indicated by number on each field, as shown in Figure 13-18.

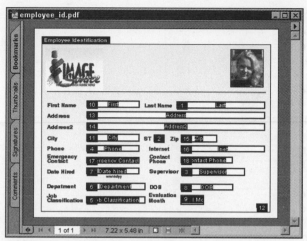

Figure 13-18: When Set Tab Order is selected, the fields are displayed with a number that describes the tab order. Here, the order is without a logical flow that will result in a more complicated means for tabbing through fields.

Tip Tabbing through fields works in both the user mode and the edit mode. While creating a PDF form where fields need to be edited, click the Form tool from the Acrobat Command bar. Edit a field and click OK in the Field Properties dialog box. Press the Tab key to move to the next field then press the Enter/Return key to open the Field Properties dialog box.

After selecting Set Tab Order, the cursor appears as a selection arrow with the # symbol. To reorder the tabs, click the field that you want to appear as number 1, and then click the field you want to appear as number 2, and so on — successively clicking each field following a logical order. As you click each field, Acrobat will dynamically update the display to reflect the order that you select. If a mistake is made, click the cursor outside a field and choose Set Tab Order again. Clicking outside a field box deselects the tab order mode. Figure 13-19 illustrates the previous figure reordered.

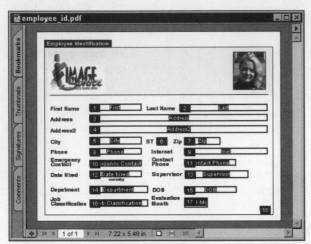

Figure 13-19: The order for the tabs was changed to reflect a more logical flow for the user to complete the form. Pressing the Tab key after completing a field entry sends the user to the next successively numbered field.

Tip

If you want to begin in the middle of a sequence, for example starting at a field numbered 10 and reorder the fields from that point, hold the Control key down (Option on a Mac) and click the beginning number. The first click tells Acrobat where you want to begin reordering numbers. The next click you make will be the next number in the sequence based on the number you selected. In this case Control/Option clicking on number 10 and then clicking the next field will number it as 11.

Setting calculation order

As you design a form, there will often be times when you create a field that requires a calculation and later create another field that needs to create a calculation before the first calculation can be made. For example, suppose you create a form that contains a field for sales tax and a total amount after sales tax. Further suppose you forgot to include a shipping charge. If you create the shipping charge after the total field has been created, the calculations will need to be reordered. Acrobat performs calculations in the order in which the fields are created.

To change the calculation order, choose Tools ➪ Forms ➪ Set Calculation Order. Acrobat will open a dialog box enabling you to move fields up or down a list to restructure the order.

Using the Fields Palette

New to Acrobat 5.0 is the Fields palette. As you work with forms, the palette will list all form fields throughout the PDF. To view the palette, choose Window ➪ Fields. If no fields have yet been added to a document, the palette will appear empty. As you add new fields, each field will be listed in the palette. Figure 13-20 shows the Fields listed according to type.

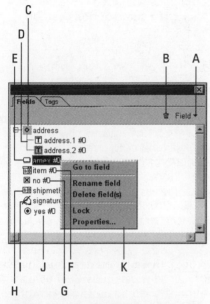

Figure 13-20: The Fields palette dynamically displays all new fields added to a PDF form.

In Figure 13-20, the items identified in the palette include:

- ✦ **A** **Palette menu:** The pull-down menu includes three menu commands. Fields open a submenu and lists the same options you have available when choosing Tools ➪ Forms ➪ Fields. Page Templates open the Page Templates dialog box (use of Page Templates is included later in this chapter). The last item is the command used to set the field calculation order as described earlier.

- ✦ **B** **Trash icon:** Select a field in the palette and click the trash icon to delete it.

- ✦ **C** **Expand/collapse field group:** When fields are named parent/child names, such as field.1, field.2, field.3, and so on, they will be grouped in the parent categories. The icon displayed in the palette for expanding and collapsing the group is the same used for comments discussed in Chapter 8. In Figure 13-20, two fields are displayed in the expanded list.

✦ **D   Text field:** Each field is listed with an icon according to field type. The two icons listed in the first group are text fields.

✦ **E through J:** The remaining field types displayed with their respective icons include: E) Button; F) Combo Box; G) CheckBox; H) List Box; I) Signature; J) Radio Button.

✦ **K   Context-sensitive menu:** When a field is selected in the palette, a context-sensitive menu opens. Among choices in the context-sensitive menu are commands for locking fields, navigating to them, and renaming fields. Access through the palette for some of these commands will often be easier than opening a field's properties dialog box where the same options can be selected.

Naming Fields

Using proper naming conventions will mean the difference between creating some complex forms in a short time or gobbling up every bit of your waking moments. Imagine for a moment that you have a form with several columns of data and twenty or more rows. Each column will be calculated with a total field at the bottom. Constructing the form by drawing individual form fields will require you to enter a unique name in the properties dialog box for each field created. Acrobat will use the last settings from a form field set up in the Properties dialog box so that you won't need to address all the tabs. But you will need to supply a name, click OK, and open up another properties dialog box.

At the time you need to create the calculation field, the method described previously will also extend your design time. Identifying all those individual fields will take some time; and if you use a JavaScript routine, it will be more aggravating. As an alternative, look at how you might create a form in an easier fashion by following some steps:

STEPS: Creating Form Fields from Calculations

1. **Open a PDF file designed to be a form.** If you don't have a form handy, you can use a blank page for the example or open the golf.pdf file from the Tutorial:forms folder on the CD-ROM accompanying this book. For my example, I make reference to the golf.pdf file.

2. **Create a field for the first column.** In my example, I select the Form tool from the Acrobat Command bar and drag open a rectangle in the first row of the first column, as shown in Figure 13-21. In the Field Properties dialog box, choose Text for the type and number for the format. The Appearance options can be any you desire.

3. **Name the field.** Provide a name for the field. The name can be of any name you choose. In my example, I choose price as the name for my field.

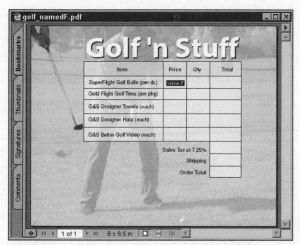

Figure 13-21: The first field is created in the first column and first row. The field is named price.

4. **Duplicate the field.** You could create a new field with the Form tool, but it will be much easier to simply duplicate the field and change the name. Click the field and press the Control key down (Option key on a Mac). Press the Shift key and drag to the right to duplicate the field and constrain the angle of movement.

The sequence of the mouse clicks and modifier keys is important when duplicating fields by clicking and dragging. First click the field and then press the Control/Option key. The cursor will change to two arrowheads. While the mouse button and the Control/Option key are depressed, press the Shift key and then drag away in the direction where the duplicate field will rest.

5. **Open the Properties dialog box.** The new field created must have a different name. In my example, the second column is a quantity column, therefore, I named my field *qty*. All the attributes of the properties will be duplicated with the field. Thus, they will all be text fields and the format will be a number. Likewise whatever appearance settings you identified for the first field will also be duplicated.

6. **Create a third field.** Duplicate the step above to create a third field. Open the Field Properties dialog box and change the name. In my example I used *total* for the third field.

7. **Select the fields.** In this regard, we need to use a different modifier key to create the selection. On Windows, press the Shift key down, on the Macintosh press the Command key and drag a marquee around the fields to be selected. These modifier keys inform Acrobat that you are not just selecting multiple fields, but you are selecting them for duplication.

8. **Drag the marquee center handle.** When the mouse button is released after creating a selection, a marquee will appear as a dashed line around the fields with handles at each corner and the middle of the top and bottom of the rectangle. Hold the Control/Command key down and drag the center bottom handle down the number of rows to be duplicated. In my example, I dragged the handle down to create five rows, as shown in Figure 13-22.

9. **Press Enter/Return.** When the rows appear, as shown in Figure 13-22, press the Enter/Return key. Acrobat will create the duplicate fields and provide a unique name for each field. All the parent names will remain the same while child names will be represented from 0 to 4. That is to say the first field *price* will be renamed price.0, price.1, price.2, and so on. The same holds true for qty and total.

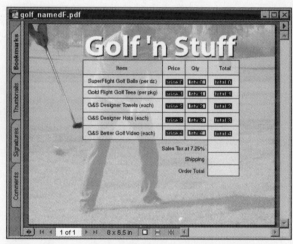

Figure 13-22: After selecting the fields with the Shift/Command key, hold the Control/Command key down and drag the center bottom handle down the number of rows to create.

For columnar data, Acrobat 5.0 can help you create many rows and columns of form fields in a fraction of time compared to individually creating fields. You may need to return to the fields to polish up alignment, but creating fields with Acrobat's auto field generation methods is a new welcomed addition for forms designers.

Importing and Exporting Form Data

The field boxes in an Acrobat form are placeholders for data. After data have been entered in a form, it can be exported. When the data are exported from Acrobat, it is written to a new file as a Form Data File (FDF). These files can be imported in a PDF document or managed in an application that can recognize the FDF format.

When submitting data to a Web server, the server must have a Common Gateway Interface (CGI) application that can collect and route the data to a database. Using form data on the Web requires advanced programming skills and use of the Adobe FDF Toolkit. You can acquire more information about this via the Web, at `http://beta1.adobe.com/ada/acrosdk`. On the Adobe Web site, you'll find samples of CGIs and information for contacting the Adobe Developer Support program. For a brief introduction to working with FDF and exporting to Web servers, look over Chapter 19.

Exporting data

If you intend to export data to a Web site or intranet, you would add to your form a button used to execute a Submit action. Either a hypertext link or a form field can handle this action type. To collect the data, the Web server must have on it a Common gateway Interface (CGI) application that will be used to collect and route the data. Assuming you obtain assistance from a Web administrator for developing such an application, the only factor you would need to know is the URL for the site where the data will be submitted.

The other means for exporting data can be handled locally on your computer or network. Exporting form data can be performed directly from a menu command or by developing a form field with a button to execute the Export command. In most cases, the latter would be used for forms distributed to users. To define an action to export data, create a form field. The field can be a text field or a button. For the action, click the Actions tab in the Field Properties dialog box, select Mouse Up, and click the Add button. Select Execute Menu Item from the Action Type pull-down menu. In the Menu Item Selection dialog box (Windows) or from the top-level menu (Macintosh), choose File ➪ Export ➪ Form Data. Click OK and then click Set Action and finally click OK in the Field Properties dialog box. After the user clicks the field used to export data, a navigation dialog box appears, prompting to save the file and supply a name and location.

When the data are saved, it will be written to disk as a FDF file. The format is not recognized by data managers and needs to be parsed. Therefore, using the data other than in PDF files will need special programming. With regard to PDF files, however, the data can be imported into a PDF document where common fields share the same names and formats.

Importing data

Importing data is handled in a similar manner as exporting it. You can select the appropriate command in the File menu or create a form or hypertext link to import data. Acrobat will recognize FDFs and import from those files the fields that meet the same conditions as the fields in the PDF document to which you are importing. When the field or button is selected, a navigation dialog box will prompt you to identify the file to be imported. When using a form field button to import data, the Select File button in the Add an Action tab enables you to identify the file to be imported. When using a hypertext link, the same button appears in the Link Properties window.

A Little Bit of Java

JavaScript is what I say. With JavaScript you can create dynamic documents for not only forms but also many other uses. JavaScript can help you add flare and pizzazz to your PDF files. With respect to forms, using JavaScript will often be essential to perform the necessary calculations that you want. This section offers you a brief introduction to using JavaScript by example. The contents of this chapter are intended to only offer the novice some examples that can be easily duplicated without much description for understanding what's going on. For more sophisticated uses and some sound reasoning for coding forms, look at Chapter 19.

Before I begin to explain some coding, let me start by making a few suggestions to the novice user who may find the programming aspects of Acrobat confusing and beyond your reach. For those who haven't coded a single line, you can easily search and find samples of code used in Acrobat forms that can be copied and pasted into your designs. Search the Internet and find PDF forms that are not secure and enable you to examine the code. If, for example, you need a calculation for sales tax, you can find many examples of forms where a sales tax calculation is coded in a form field. You can copy and paste fields into your designs and most often will only need to change a variable name to make it work. As a starting point, review the files I have included in both the forms folder and eBooks folder on the CD-ROM accompanying this book. You'll find many JavaScripts that can be analyzed to further understand a little bit of programming. Poke around and experiment and you'll find some worthwhile aids on PDF forms already created for you.

Tip   Create a blank page in a program and convert it to PDF. On the PDF blank page, you can paste JavaScript form fields and add comments as to what the JavaScript will do. A collection of common scripts will make your task easier when it comes time to code a new form. Open the template file and search through the comments to find the routine that you want for a given task. Copy the form field complete with the JavaScript and paste it into your new form design. Test it out and make changes that may be needed to get the routines to work in your form.

JavaScript calculations

Going back to the form created earlier in this chapter, assume that you want to create a sum of a total column and add sales tax, shipping, and a grand total. For the sales tax, we can create a field that will hold a sum of values from the rows in each column. The field can be placed anywhere on the form and be hidden from the user. It would be a temporary field used only to hold a sum. The sum field would then be used to calculate the sales tax.

To create a temporary field, drag open the form tool, and the Properties dialog box will open. I call this field *subtotal*. Select Text as the field type and select number in the Format tab. Click the Calculate tab and the dialog box will appear, as shown in

Figure 13-23. To perform the calculation for the sum of the rows, select Sum from the pull-down menu for *Value is the* field. In the earlier exercise, the total field names were identified as total.n where *n* was the numeric extension of the field name. By using field names where the root is the same and only the extension is different, we can instruct Acrobat to sum the root name. In this case, sum *total*. For the field to be hidden from the user, select the Appearance tab and choose *Hidden* from the *Form Field is* pull-down menu at the bottom of the dialog box.

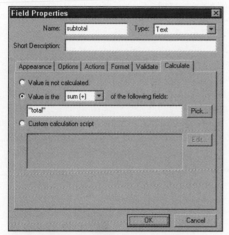

Figure 13-23: To sum the fields, I select Sum from the Value in the pull-down menu and enter "total" in the field box. When my field names were identified as total.1, total.2, total.3, and so on, I only need to use the root name to calculate a sum for all the fields with the common root.

```
var f=this.getField("subtotal");
event.value=Math.round(f.value*7.25)/100
```

The first line of code, the variable name as f, gets the contents of the subtotal field. The second line of code performs the calculation for variable f to compute sales tax for a tax rate of 7.25 percent. If you want to duplicate the code for one of your forms, change the tax rate accordingly. Variable names and proper syntax for coding JavaScript in Acrobat are detailed in a separate manual that ships with the Application. You can review the manual by selecting the Help menu and choose the Acrobat JavaScript Guide menu command.

Math operations

One of the limitations of the Calculate tab is the availability of a few simple math operations. The sum and product of numbers are available but if you want to subtract or divide, you need to use some JavaScript. For subtraction, you need to first define the variables and then compute the math. An example of subtracting one value from another is:

var a = this.getField("field.1");

var b = this.getField("field.2");

event.value = a.value - b.value

For division use the following code:

var a = this.getField("field.1");

var b = this.getField("field.2");

event.value = a.value / b.value

As I mentioned earlier in this chapter, if you create a template and place all the math operations and other commonly used scripts on some PDF pages, you can immediately have access to the code that escapes memory when you design a form.

Working with Page Templates

Page Templates were first introduced in Chapter 8 when I covered creating custom stamps. One very useful tool available to you with page templates and JavaScript is the ability to create new pages from a template page. The template can be either visible or invisible to the user as you determine. If your template contains data fields, a document level JavaScript will need to be developed, so each new page will be created with unique field names. The JavaScript code will need to increment field names so that they remain unique on each page. A sample script for achieving this is shown in Figure 13-24.

The "newpage" item is a template in my PDF file. The JavaScript is added to the document by choosing Tools ➪ JavaScript ➪ Document JavaScripts. In the JavaScript Functions dialog box, provide a name for the Script Name field and click Add. Another dialog box will appear where your JavaScript code can be written.

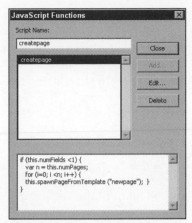

Figure 13-24: A document level JavaScript is needed to increment the pages so that all fields on the page will be unique when the new page is created from a template.

Creating a page template

To create a page template, open a PDF form that you want to use as a template. Ideally you may have a cover page and a second page where the form appears. Navigate to the form and choose Tools ➪ Forms ➪ Page Templates. In the Page Templates dialog box, provide a name in the Name field and click the Add button. Acrobat will open a confirmation dialog box asking you if you want the current page viewed to be used as the template. Click OK and your page template is created. When returned to the Page Templates dialog box, you have an option to make the template visible or invisible. The eye icon at the left of the template name indicates the template will be visible, as shown in Figure 13-25. Click the eye icon to hide the template. Most often, hiding the template is a good idea so that it won't be accidentally mistaken for a new page. To hide the template, you must have at least two pages in the PDF. At least one page needs to be visible at all times.

Figure 13-25: Page Templates can be made visible or invisible by clicking the icon to the left of the template name.

Spawning a page from a template

To create new pages from your template, create a button on your home page. Either a link button or form field can be used. In the Properties dialog box for adding an action, choose JavaScript as the action type. In the JavaScript Edit dialog box enter the following code:

```
this.spawnPageFromTemplate(newpage);
```

The code within the parentheses is the name of the template. In my example, I created a template called newpage. This action will spawn a page from my template. As another item for the action type, you can instruct Acrobat to go to the newly created page. Just add another action and use the Execute Menu Item to go to the last page in the file. When the page is created, the view will jump to the last page.

Spawning pages from a template could be used for a variety of purposes. You can create additional pages for forms, create a virtual memo pad with Text Note fields, store collections of images that are imported with buttons from new pages, and many other uses.

JavaScript and page navigation

Sometimes it's handier to create links to pages with JavaScript than creating link buttons and navigating views. An index may be a good example of using form field buttons and JavaScript. If you have a list of all page numbers and want to create links to the pages from an index, then you could easily duplicate form fields and edit the page numbers. This method will move much faster than creating individual link buttons and browsing the PDF for the right views.

To navigate to a page with JavaScript, create a form field with a button as the field type. In the Add An Action dialog box, select JavaScript. Click the Edit button. When the JavaScript Edit dialog box opens, enter the following code:

```
this.pageNum=(n);
```

In the above line of code, n is equal to the page number. One thing to keep in mind is JavaScript will see the pages numbered beginning with zero (0). Therefore, navigating to page one would be:

```
this.pageNum=(0);
```

For use with index links, create the first form field and duplicate it. You can use index.1 as the first field and then duplicate and press the plus (+) key to increment each duplicated field. After creating all links, you can use a single editor window for editing all JavaScripts in your document. Choose Tools ➪ JavaScript ➪ Edit All JavaScripts. A dialog box appears, as shown in Figure 13-26.

Figure 13-26: In the JavaScript Edit dialog box, all JavaScripts in the PDF are displayed and can be edited.

Obviously, it would be better to export to PDF from a layout program that supports index generation and links exported before the PDF is opened in Acrobat. However, when manual methods need to be performed, you can cut some time by using the above example when workarounds are needed.

JavaScript and destinations

I created a little form not so long ago for my insurance agent. I took photos of all my major household items for my homeowner's coverage and created a form template where the photos were imported and the data fields supplied information on the purchase date, price and location in my house. After all the pages were added, I wanted to create an easy navigation to each item. In this case, I used JavaScript and destinations. The opening page of the PDF is shown in Figure 13-27.

The first task in creating my pop-up menus shown in Figure 13-27 was to create destinations. Each page in the PDF needed a new destination. I opened the Destinations palette and scanned the document. I then began at the second page and selected New Destination at a Fit in Window view. Scrolling pages and adding a new destination created the remaining Destinations. Each destination name was added according to the item on the page.

To create the links to the destinations, I used a form field button. In the Add An Action tab, I selected JavaScript and opened the JavaScript Edit dialog box. The code to create the pop-up menus and links to the destinations appears in Figure 13-28.

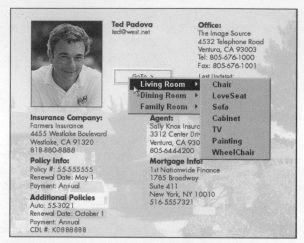

Figure 13-27: A pop-up menu displays individual items linked by JavaScripted code to named destinations.

Figure 13-28: The JavaScript code lists a category name first, followed by the named destinations for each group within each group of brackets.

If I decide to add a new page, editing the code is a simple matter of copy and paste. I can create a new category by copying and pasting an existing category and then editing the category name and page name. The first item appearing between the sets of brackets is the category name that appears for the three categories in

Figure 13-27. Each name in quotes after the category name is the respective destination. For a more thorough understanding of the fields used and the JavaScripts created in this example, you can open the `insurance.pdf` file in the Tutorial:forms folder on the CD accompanying this book. Open the Field Properties dialog boxes for each form field and examine the JavaScripts.

Importing images

Using JavaScript and all the great tools that you have with Acrobat can create some marvelous workarounds. Acrobat was never intended to be a layout program, but there are a number of workarounds that you can use to actually create layouts, new pages, and elements, such as text from scratch. Ideally it is best when you perform all these duties in a program designed for such purposes. However, with forms, sometimes a layout application just won't be practical and, at times you'll need to update forms with elements that need to be imported into the page design. In this regard, importing images can often be a viable need. Fortunately with a simple JavaScript routine, you can import images into any PDF document.

Going back to my insurance form, I need to import a digital camera photo for each new page added to the PDF. Because these pages are spawned from a template, the form design will never see a layout program and all work needs to be performed in Acrobat. Figure 13-29 shows a sample page containing data.

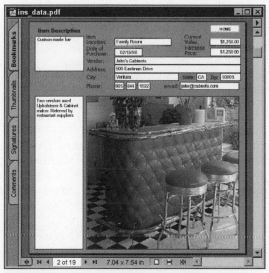

Figure 13-29: The image in the form needs to be imported when each page is created from the template.

To import an image, the file format must be consistent with the Open as Adobe PDF command. All the image formats discussed in Chapter 4 are compatible for importing into a form field. To create a button that will execute an action to import an image use the following code in the JavaScript Edit dialog box:

```
event.target.buttonImportIcon();
```

Use a button field type and when clicked back in the viewing mode, a navigation dialog box will open enabling you to browse your hard drive to find an image to import.

Help menus

Help pop-up menus can assist users in filling out forms. When creating a help menu by following this next example, be certain to first create the help information, and then the button to open the help window. You can use a multi-line form field and enter all the text needed for the help information. View the field on-screen and verify all the information appears as you like it. In the Field Properties dialog box in the Appearance options, select Hidden from the Form Field pull-down menu.

The next step is to create a button that will open the help text window. For a button type field, open the JavaScript Edit dialog box and enter the following code:

```
var h1 = this.getField("helpwindow");

var bDirty = this.dirty;

h1.hidden = false;

this.dirty = bDirty;
```

The helpwindow item is the name of the field where the text was created. You can use a Mouse Enter action instead of a Mouse Up action to display the help text. This kind of help will reduce clutter in a form because the only time the help text is visible is when a user places the cursor over and the area logically positioned to open the help text. Figure 13-30 shows an example of a help text field. For examples in creating help menus, look over the forms located in the Tutorial:forms folder on the CD accompanying this book.

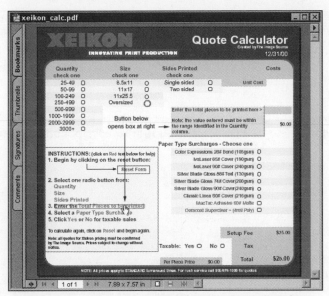

Figure 13-30: When the mouse cursor approaches the text below the down arrow, the help window in the direction of the right arrow opens.

Summary

✦ Acrobat forms are not scanned images. They are dynamic and can include interactive elements, data fields, buttons, and JavaScripts.

✦ Data fields can be created from many different field types including Buttons, Checkboxes, Combo Boxes, List Boxes, Radio Buttons, Signatures, and Text.

✦ All data field attributes are handled in the Field Properties window. Properties can be described for the field by selecting the tabs labeled Appearance, Options, Actions, Calculations, or other tabs associated with specific field types.

✦ Editing fields can be accomplished with menu commands and using context-sensitive menus. Acrobat has several editing commands used for aligning fields, distributing fields, and centering fields on a PDF page.

✦ The Fields palette dynamically lists all forms created in a PDF file. The palette menus and options can be of much assistance in creating and editing PDF forms.

✦ Field names need to be unique for each field created in a form. By using root names and extensions, form design and calculations can reduce the amount of time needed to create forms.

✦ Data can be exported from a PDF document to Web servers and Form Data Files (FDFs). FDF data can be imported into other PDF files with matching field names.

✦ More functionality with many field types can be created with JavaScripts. The Field Properties window enables the user to supply JavaScript code for several field types.

✦   ✦   ✦

Authentication and Archiving

Authenticating PDFs

We haven't yet arrived, but we are moving closer to a time
when digitally signing documents is acceptable in the legal
arena. When you stop and think about it, a digitally signed
document is far more reliable than a personal signature.
Forging a digital signature would be much more complicated
than forging signed papers. In this chapter, I discuss digital
signatures and authenticating documents, comparing PDFs for
reliable content, and then move on to archiving files on
CD-ROM.

In Chapter 7, digital signature preferences were described and
securing PDF files with digital signatures was covered. As yet,
the actual creation of a digital signature has not been
addressed. For setting up the digital signature preferences,
look back at Chapter 7.

The vast amount of possibilities and complexity of digital signatures requires a little more study beyond the description
contained in this book. Many opportunities are available to
you in creating signature handlers and setting up a signature
program for your company or organization. In this chapter, we
look at the default handler available with the Adobe Self-Sign
signature handler for basic signing purposes. On the Acrobat
installation CD-ROM, you also have the Acrobat Entrust
Security for use with the public key introduced by Entrust
Technologies Limited. Look through the documentation on
the CD-ROM for more information on using alternative
handlers.

Understanding digital signatures

The first detail that you need to know to understand how digital signatures are created and used is how to set up a *signature handler*. Acrobat won't let you sign a document until you have identified a handler and created a personal password for digitally signing documents. This task is on your end. The security related to your signature is a private key used by you and known only to you for digitally signing files.

The second detail to understand about signatures is use of the *public key*. A public key is one that you provide to other users in the form of a certificate or one that they provide to you in order to share digitally signed documents. To do this, you must send your public key or acquire a public key from another user in order to access documents signed with security or verify authenticity of a digitally signed document. The public key you work with, albeit one you send or receive, limits access for only public viewing among shared users. Public keys won't compromise your private key profile and only those people you elect to share your public key will be able to access a file when you use self-sign security.

The next factor to understand is that you can sign a document for public viewing without anyone having a public key if you choose to do so. The file will be displayed showing a digital signature. Another user, however, cannot determine the authenticity for the signature unless he or she has the public key to authenticate the signature.

Finally, what you see appearing in the digital signature field is not the password protected profile within the signature handler. What appears on-screen is a representation that you use to display a signature. It can be a graphic, a scanned signature, or your name. The signature profile will remain invisible and accessible for viewing only when accessed with your password. If your password remains with you, you will be the only one who can see the profile.

Creating a profile

To begin using digital signatures, you must first create a profile. Profiles can be created through either the Tools ⇨ Digital Signatures ⇨ Sign Document or the Tools ⇨ Self-Sign ⇨ Log In menu commands. You can also select the Digital Signature tool in the Acrobat Command bar. Regardless of which method you use, if you have not yet created a user profile, Acrobat will prompt you to create one before you can digitally sign a document.

To simplify the process, open a PDF file and select the Digital Signature tool. Click and drag open a rectangle. A dialog box will open for the Self-Sign Security Log In. If you do not have a profile on your system, the fields in the dialog box will be empty, as shown in Figure 14-1. To create a new profile, click the New User Profile button.

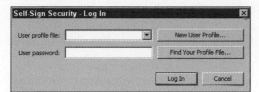

Figure 14-1: If no digital signature profile has yet been created, the User profile file field box in the Self-Sign Security Log In dialog box will be empty.

When you click the New User Profile button the Create New User dialog box appears. In this dialog box, you establish the name to be used for the profile, some company identifying information, and your password, as shown in Figure 14-2.

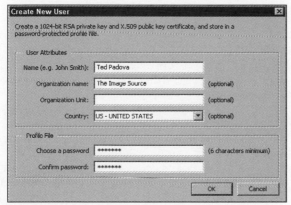

Figure 14-2: The Create New User dialog box is where your password for access to your profile is established.

Click OK in this dialog box and Acrobat then opens a navigation dialog box where you can determine directory path and filename for the profile. By default, the profile will be saved in the Adobe Acrobat folder. If you want to use another folder, navigate through your hard drive and select a location for the profile to be saved. Before you actually define profile attributes, Acrobat will save the profile. If you do nothing more, the profile will still be saved using the default settings for the profile attributes.

Note | If you save your profiles to another folder and Acrobat cannot find them, click the Find Your Profile File button in the Self-Sign Security Log In dialog box. Acrobat permits you to navigate your hard drive to find the profiles. Be certain to keep them together so that they can be easily found.

The first time you set up your profile you have to make some decisions about the files you sign and the kind of information to be shared. After you complete the required information in the Create New User dialog box and click OK, the Self-Sign Security Alert dialog box opens. In this dialog box, you can immediately log in or establish user settings for the profile. Click the button for User Settings and the Self-Sign Security – User Settings for (Your Name) will open, as shown in Figure 14-3. Further reference to this dialog box shall be called the User Settings dialog box.

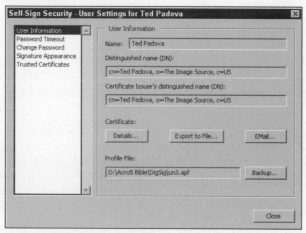

Figure 14-3: User settings specific to the profile can be established in the Self-Sign Security – User Settings dialog box.

In the User Settings dialog box, several options offer you information about your certificate and the kind of information that you want to distribute. The dialog box appearing in 14-3 contains a list on the left side of the dialog box and some buttons on the right used to open additional dialog boxes. The settings include:

✦ **Details:** Like all the buttons on the opening page of the dialog box, Details are only accessible when the User Information is selected from the list at the left side of the dialog box. Clicking Details opens a dialog box where information about your certificate is contained.

✦ **Export to File:** When you select the Export to File button, a file is written that can be shared with users you want to open your digitally signed secure documents or verify authenticity. A file will be written to disk, and the certificate fingerprint appears on-screen. The intent of the fingerprint information is to share with your public certificate holders. You can make a telephone call to another user, e-mail or write to them and provide the certificate fingerprints. Figure 14-4 shows a sample Export Certificate.

Figure 14-4: The Export Certificate contains fingerprints intended to be shared with your community certificate holders. This information does not compromise your private certificate.

✦ **EMail:** When clicking the EMail button, the certificate will be e-mailed to the user you want to share the public certificate. Acrobat launches your default e-mail application and automatically attaches the certificate file. Acrobat also automatically creates a message in the e-mail note. A sample of the e-mail message is shown in Figure 14-5.

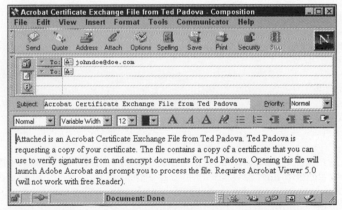

Figure 14-5: Acrobat automatically creates an e-mail message and attaches your public certificate file after selecting the e-mail button in the User Information section of the User Settings dialog box.

Tip

When e-mailing a certificate, anyone intercepting the certificate can open a secured PDF with self-sign security. If you need maximum security and rely on Internet transfers in your work, you may want to use other methods for communicating the certificate finger print information. One easy method is to take a screen shot of the Export Certificate dialog box shown in Figure 14-4. Open the screen shot in Acrobat and save with a standard security password. E-mail the secure PDF file to your intended user. In a phone call with the end user, you can communicate the password to open the PDF file. Anyone who intercepts the PDF won't be able to view the certificate information without the password to access the PDF file.

✦ **Backup:** Backing up certificates is critical. If they're lost, you won't be able to get them back. The button for Backup opens a dialog box where you can save a backup copy. Be certain to use a storage device other than your hard drive and make two backup copies.

✦ **Password Timeout:** By default Acrobat prompts you for a password every time you digitally sign a document. If you open an Acrobat session and create several digital signatures, it may be annoying to keep entering your password. From the dialog box appearing when you select the Password Timeout item in the User Settings dialog box, a pull-down menu will offer many choices for timeout intervals. You can make choices beginning with 30 seconds to 24 hours in fixed increments.

✦ **Change Password:** If you want to change your password, you can do so at any time. Acrobat asks for your current password, so that you'll need to be certain you have it before attempting to change it. Type in the new password and your profile will be updated.

✦ **Signature Appearance:** You can change the appearance from a default view Acrobat provides you when the profile is developed. A company name, scanned signature, or other imported file can be added to the signature display. When you select the Signature Appearance item in the User Settings dialog box for the first time, click New and the Configure Signature Appearance dialog box opens, as shown in Figure 14-6.

In the Configure Signature Appearance dialog box, select the Imported graphic from button and click the PDF file button. The Select Picture dialog box will open permitting navigation to find a PDF file to be imported as the graphic. When you select the graphic to be imported and return to the Configure Signature Appearance dialog box, a preview of the certificate will be displayed in the dialog box as shown in Figure 14-7.

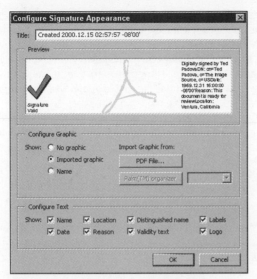

Figure 14-6: The Configure Signature Appearance dialog box enables you to add a graphic image to your signature.

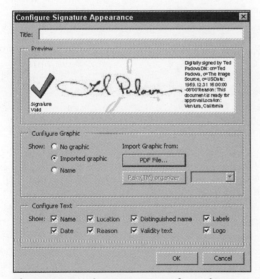

Figure 14-7: I import a scan of my signature in the Select Picture dialog box. After I return to the Configure Signature Appearance dialog box, my signature is added to the certificate display.

Tip

If you sign documents for typical office functions that often are marked with stamps, such as confidential, final, approved, and so on, you can use the Standard stamps file icons. When you click Imported Graphic, navigate to the Acrobat 5.0:Acrobat:Plug-ins:Annotations:Stamps:ENU directory and open the Standard. pdf file. All the stamp icons are accessible by scrolling through the pages. Select the stamp to convey your message and the icon will be displayed in the signature.

✦ **Trusted Certificates:** Trusted Certificates offer you two features. You can develop a list of public certificates from other users and have them listed in the dialog box and you can e-mail a request for a certificate from other users. Select Trusted Certificates in the User Settings dialog box and the view appears, as shown in Figure 14-8.

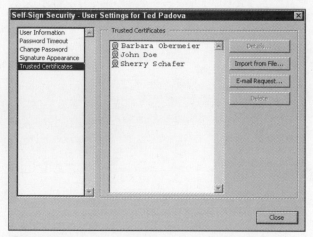

Figure 14-8: Trusted Certificates enable you to list public certificates with people that you exchange documents and affords an option to request certificates from other users.

In Figure 14-8, three user public certificate users have been added. Clicking the Import from File button adds additional users. In order to import a certificate, it must be acquired from a user. To request a certificate, click the E-mail Request button. A dialog box shown in Figure 14-9 appears.

When you click the E-mail button, your default e-mail application is launched by Acrobat and sent to the user specified in the To field. Quit the e-mail program and you are returned to the User Settings dialog box.

Figure 14-9: Pressing the E-mail button opens a dialog box where Acrobat provides a message requesting a public certificate from another user. You can supply the e-mail address (To field) and a phone number or other contact information for verification.

Remember that when you first supplied your name, identifying information, and password, Acrobat already saved your profile. If you make changes in the User Settings, you can save the settings and all subsequent use of the signature will have the attributes you assign when you save the User Settings changes. Every time you sign a document you have an opportunity to revisit the User Settings dialog box and make changes for any documents you sign.

Signing a document

The first time you use the Digital Signature tool and address the User Settings, you are logged in as a user and Acrobat assumes that you want to sign a document. Regardless of whether you first create a new profile or whether you use a previous profile to sign a document, the Self-Sign Security – Sign Document dialog box opens when using the Digital Signature tool. If creating a new profile, you open this dialog box by clicking OK in the User Settings dialog box. To show additional options in the dialog box, click the Show Options button and Acrobat expands the dialog box shown in Figure 14-10.

Figure 14-10: The Self-Sign Security –
Sign Document dialog box opens
every time you digitally sign a
document. When the Show Options
button is selected, additional attributes
associated with the signature can
be identified.

If you have a profile created and want to sign a document, the first dialog box that
will open is the Self-Sign Security – Alert dialog box, as shown in Figure 14-11. The
button for User Settings opens the User Settings dialog box discussed above where
you can toggle through the settings and adjust your profile for the options noted
earlier.

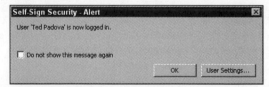

Figure 14-11: If a profile has been created
and you use the Digital Signature tool to sign
a document, this dialog box opens. You can
change the user settings by clicking the User
Settings button. After you click OK, the Self-Sign
Security – Sign Document dialog box opens.

If user settings are not to be changed, click the OK button and the dialog box in
Figure 14-10 opens. Note that Acrobat assumes that you want to sign a document
whether you create a new profile or whether you use the Digital Signature tool to
create a signature. In either case, you'll eventually wind up at the dialog box shown

in Figure 14-10. In this dialog box, you determine specific attributes about the document to be signed. Whereas the User Settings apply to attributes regarding your signature, the settings in Figure 14-10 apply to the document you sign. Every time you want to sign a document, the dialog box will open. Specific options related to the Sign Document settings include:

✦ **Confirm Password:** Acrobat requires you to confirm your password at any time you want to sign a document. Enter your password in the field box.

✦ **Hide Options:** All the options below the password confirmation can be hidden. All subsequent signing will display the dialog box without the other options. If you want to bring them back, the Hide Options button will change to Show Options. Click Show Options, and the dialog box will expand to display the other options.

✦ **Reason for signing document:** From the pull-down menu are several menu options used for describing the reason you are signing the document. Pick from one of the choices and the properties for the signature will reflect the reason chosen for signing the document.

✦ **Location:** This item is optional. You can enter a physical location of where you signed the document (that is, your city name).

✦ **Your contact information:** Phone number, e-mail address, or similar information can be added in this field.

✦ **Signature Appearance:** From the pull-down menu, any appearance items you created in the User Settings dialog box, such as a logo or signature scan are available from the menu choices. If no selection is made from the other menu choices, your name as it was defined in the Create New User dialog box appears in the signature.

✦ **Preview:** A preview of the signature appearance opens in another dialog box. If you use several appearance items for your signatures, click Preview to be certain you are using the right image.

✦ **New:** When the button is selected, the Configure Signature Appearance dialog box opens. You can add a new appearance image through the same steps mentioned earlier.

✦ **Save:** Save updates the open document and adds the signature.

✦ **Save As:** If Save As is selected, a navigation dialog box opens and the file can be saved under a new name. The original file remains unsigned.

✦ **Cancel:** If you select Cancel, the file will not be signed.

Logging in as a user

Acrobat will log you in as a user when the Digital Signature tool is used and you drag open a rectangle to create a signature. You can log in as a user and define the User Settings without signing a document. Logging in can also be performed if no PDF file is open in the Document pane. Choose Tools ➪ Self-Sign Security ➪ Log In.

The Self-Sign Security – Log In dialog box opens where you can select a profile and also address the User Settings. Acrobat will keep you logged in under the same profile until you either quit Acrobat or log out by choosing Tools ⇨ Self-Sign Security ⇨ Log Out. The same menu also offers an option to open the User Settings dialog box after you have logged in. If during a session you want to change settings, you can open the User Settings dialog box and change settings at any time. If you use several profiles, you can also choose to log in as a different user through the same menu.

Blind signatures

You can also create a blind signature that will enable you to sign a document without the appearance of the certificate. Choose Tools ⇨ Digital Signatures ⇨ Invisibly Sign Document. The same dialog box for Self-Sign Security – Sign Document opens. The attribute assignments are identical to those discussed earlier. When the document contains an invisible signature, the area where the signature was created will be invisible to the user.

Verifying signatures

The purpose of signing a document is among other things a means of authenticating a document. After a document has been signed and distributed, the signature needs verification. In order for another user to determine authenticity of your signatures, they will need the public certificate explained earlier in this chapter.

You can add a public certificate to your Trusted Certificate holders in the User Settings dialog box, in which case you can open and verify signatures from those who have sent you their public certificates. If you haven't yet added a certificate to your Trusted Certificate list in the User Settings dialog box, Acrobat can add it for you. Click a signature in a PDF file and the Self-Sign Security – Validation Status dialog box opens. In this dialog box, a button for Verify Identity appears. Click the button and Acrobat opens the Verify Identity dialog box, as shown in Figure 14-12. If you want to add the certificate holder to your list of Trusted Certificates, click the Add to List button.

If you place the signed PDF file and the public certificate in the same directory, Acrobat will automatically find the certificate and enable you to verify the signature and subsequently add the certificate to your Trusted Certificates list. When certificates appear on your screen, an icon is displayed on the signature field. According to whether the signature has been validated, the icon will appear with different views, as shown in Figure 4-13.

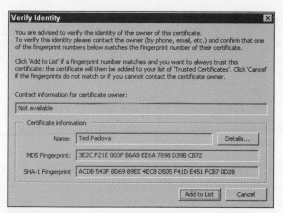

Figure 14-12: If you haven't added a certificate to your Trusted Certificate list in the User Settings dialog box and clicked a digital signature, Acrobat opens the Verify Identity dialog box where Verify Settings can be selected. In order to verify the signature, Acrobat must be able to locate the matching public certificate.

Figure 14-13: Verification status is displayed with different icons.

> ✦ **A** The field is signed but the validity is unknown.
>
> ✦ **B** The field is signed but not verified.
>
> ✦ **C** An X placed over the signature indicates the user certificate was either invalid or unavailable.
>
> ✦ **D** A check mark indicates the certificate is partially verified.
>
> ✦ **E** The document is unsigned. The signature field is empty.
>
> ✦ **F** The signature is verified.

Deleting and clearing signatures

Signatures can be deleted and the signature field can be cleared. When you clear a signature, you remove the certificate display and the signature will appear much like an invisible signature. To delete a signature, first select it and then choose Tools ➪ Digital Signatures ➪ Clear Signature Field. Selecting Clear All Signature Fields from the same menu can clear all signatures. A context menu opened on any signature field also offers the same options.

Digital Signatures palette

The Navigation pane contains a tab for digital signatures. You can open the pane and view all signatures contained within the open PDF file. When a given digital signature has been expanded in the palette, the identity information will be nested below the signature name, as shown in Figure 14-14. Context-sensitive menus in this palette behave similarly to context-sensitive menus in other palettes. Open a context-sensitive menu on the signature field name and the options will appear the same as when a context-sensitive menu is opened from the digital signature on the document page.

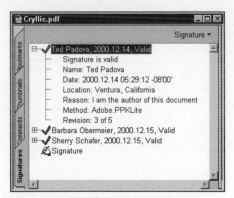

Figure 14-14: The Digital Signatures palette in the Navigation pane displays all signatures in the PDF file. When a signature is expanded in the palette, certificate and revision information appear.

Digital Signatures properties

From either the Digital Signatures palette context-sensitive menu or a context-sensitive menu opened from the signature on the document page, the Properties menu command opens the Self-Sign Security – Properties dialog box. The information in the dialog box contains the data regarding the signature and the properties assigned to the signature when it was signed. This information is consistent with the same information supplied in the Sign Document dialog box viewed in Figure 14-10 earlier in this chapter.

Comparing Documents

Two commands are designed for comparing two different versions of documents. The Compare menu items listed under the Tools menu provide options for comparing two PDF files with minute to gross differences. An additional item for comparing documents is contained in the Tools ➪ Digital Signatures submenu. Both commands enable you to view differences in the content of a PDF with regard to images, text, and changes according to the last time a file was signed.

Compare two documents

To compare pages for differences with text or any visual difference choose Tools ➪ Compare ➪ Two documents. Acrobat opens the Compare Documents dialog box, as shown in Figure 14-15.

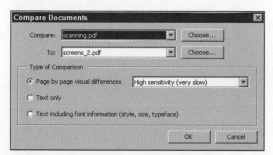

Figure 14-15: The Compare Documents dialog box is used to compare text and visual differences between two PDF files.

In the Compare Documents dialog box settings include:

✦ **Compare/To:** The two field boxes at the top of the dialog box show the files being compared. If you have one open file, click the Choose button and search your hard disk for the second file to open for the comparison.

✦ **Page by page visual differences:** Three items are available to choose from the pull-down menu. High sensitivity is the most precise comparison. Any pixels differing between the compared documents will be reported. Normal sensitivity displays differences between documents with visual differences on-screen in image data. Low sensitivity reports gross differences between documents. The speed for the comparison is respective to the degree of sensitivity with High being the slowest to process and Low being the fastest.

✦ **Text only:** Compares only text in the document for exact character matches without regard to text styles or image data.

✦ **Text including font information (style, size, typeface):** As the name implies, any type differences including type styles will be reported.

When a comparison is made between two documents, the results are reported in a file with double-sided facing pages. One document will appear on the left side of the screen and the other on the right in a vertical page view. The first pages viewed appear with a report of the total differences found between the files. This first page is added to both documents and is used as a header page to display the page names and differences for information purposes. Following the first pages are the remaining pages in the documents. As you scroll through the pages, annotations will be made on the pages where differences are found. In Figure 14-16, the pencil lines show the found differences.

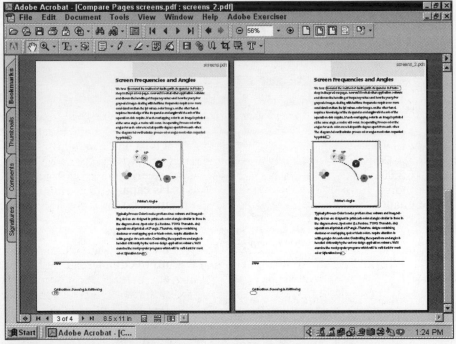

Figure 14-16: All pages where differences are found will be displayed with markings around the data differing between the documents.

Tip

By default, Acrobat creates comment notes associated with all the pencil markings denoting found differences. If you review documents where comments need to be made regarding different document versions, you can easily use the associated notes created by Acrobat. Open the Navigation pane and double-click a comment to open the note window on the document page. Enter your text and close the note. Moving through the Comment palette you can quickly add annotations to the compared differences.

Comparing signed documents

The compare function also works with signed documents. You may at times have a version of a file with a signed version and need to compare the documents for determining any differences. Choose Tools ➪ Compare ➪ Two Versions Within a Signed Document. By default, the page in view will be identified in the dialog box for the first field. In the second field, enter a name or browse your hard drive to find the document to run the comparison. The dialog box options are the same as those discussed above with comparing two documents.

CD-ROM Publishing

You may or may not have a need to archive data that has been digitally signed. Regardless of whether you need to authenticate documents, you probably will have many uses for storing valuable information in a cost-effective way. One of the most cost-effective means of publishing large volumes of data and information is through a CD-ROM. CD-ROMs are inexpensive (under $1.00 each when replicated in volumes of 500 to 1,000) and can be distributed much more easily than printed documents. Furthermore, the volume of information a CD-ROM is capable of containing is exceptionally large when you consider the file compression and storage requirements of PDF files.

CD-ROMs can be created individually with a personal CD-R or in volume for commercial use at a CD-ROM replication center. In regard to commercial reproduction, the original CD-ROM is referred to as a *CD Master*, and in replication houses, the process of duplicating the original CD-ROM is referred to as *mastering*. From the master, the duplicate CDs are developed, and this process is referred to as replication. When you place an order at a CD-ROM replication service center, they will master the CD, which will cost you a mastering fee, and then replicate it according to the number of copies you want to receive. After the CD-ROM has been mastered, you can reorder additional copies without paying the mastering fee again. If you change any of the CD contents for subsequent orders, you will incur another mastering fee.

Planning the content design for commercial distribution

Because the CD-ROM mastering will be the most expensive part of your replication process, you'll want to determine all the contents to be included on your CD ahead of time. Several elements should be on your CD in addition to your PDF files and the directories you create for them.

Welcome file

When the CD-ROM is opened on a PC desktop, you'll want the user to see a README or Welcome file. This file should be immediately accessible and visible when the CD is opened on the desktop. If you have Acrobat PDF files on the CD, the user may not be able to read any of them until the Acrobat Reader is installed. The Welcome file can guide the user through the installation process. On the Adobe Acrobat Reader installer CD, you'll find README files for the Macintosh, Windows, and UNIX systems. These README files can be used as templates for creating your Welcome file. The Acrobat Reader CD-ROM is a *hybrid CD*, which means a Macintosh, Windows, or UNIX computer can read it.

PDF Welcome file

The text files should be limited to a brief description of the contents on your CD-ROM and simply guide the user to complete the Reader installation. You'll want to get the end user into Reader as soon as possible because you have much more opportunity for providing information in a PDF file than in a text file. The first file the user opens should be a Welcome PDF document that should serve as a central navigator for all your CD contents. You can include multiple files and folders on the CD without the user having to search through them if the navigation is simple and logical in the PDF files. The hypertext references can be used to access all your PDF files. If you are distributing a CD to people who may not be familiar with Acrobat Reader, you may want to include a brief description of how PDF navigation is handled in Reader. In doing so, you'll want to keep the instruction simple and restricted to only a few tools and keystrokes. Don't bother with all the viewing options. Users will soon learn some navigation features on their own.

Preparing files

When you plan on developing a CD-ROM for distribution to clients, consumers, or employees of a company, you need to always keep in mind your personal logic may not be shared by the masses. If you plan as you create, users may run into problems when they attempt to browse your CD contents. The first step in preparing PDF files for distribution on CD-ROM is to plan it out carefully and ensure the flow and navigation is easy and makes sense to the novice computer user. There's probably nothing more irritating to the end user than to wind up in some remote PDF location and not know how to go back to the path she or he was following. (Remember, the Acrobat Go to Previous View button may not be familiar to some users.)

Draw a diagram

Before you begin a project, draw a flow chart describing all the PDF files to be created and the folder hierarchy that you intend to use. The end user may never know when a new file is opened or another page in the same file is used. You should also be aware that some users may change preference settings and disable the Open Cross Document Links in Same Window checkbox in the Options category of the Preferences dialog box. If this item is disabled, the end user will wind up with several open documents on-screen. You can plan ahead by setting page actions to close files regardless of how the preferences are set. A flow chart will help you identify the page actions and overall structure of the PDF organization.

Optimizing files

As you create PDFs for distribution on CD-ROM, you should employ all optimizing tasks for the files that you create. You have two specific items to deal with when preparing your files. In Acrobat Catalog, you will always want the Optimize for CD-ROM option enabled in the Index Default preferences. As a last task to perform, run a batch sequence for optimization and fast Web view.

Font issues

During your PDF development, you should double-check some sample files on a few different computers. When you distill files in Acrobat Distiller and use any font outside the Base 13 font sets, you should embed the fonts during the distillation. Be certain to print the files to disk as PostScript files, and then use Acrobat Distiller to convert them to PDF if your authoring program doesn't export to PDF with font embedding.

Double-check a few PDF files containing a sampling of all the fonts that you intend to use on both a Macintosh and in Windows before creating all your PDF files. Also, be certain to comply with licensing requirements when embedding fonts. If uncertain whether a particular font manufacturer permits font embedding in PDF files, contact the vendor and ask for permission.

Color issues

When you create a PDF document on one platform and view the file on another platform, you may see great disparity in color viewing. The range of 256 colors in the system palette on each machine only has a maximum of 216 colors that are common across platforms. For colors specified in illustration programs, you should use colors within the 216-color palette that are common to cross-platform viewing. When using Photoshop images, you can employ the color handling features of Photoshop to embed profiles or export the images in a GIF89a format with a color palette drawn from the 216 colors. Be certain to view some files with colors you intend to use and some sample photos on two platforms before completing your project. For CD-ROM viewing, be certain your working color space is sRGB.

File naming

File naming is of particular importance to Macintosh users. If you write a CD-ROM for cross-platform use, you will want to keep all the file naming conventions within ISO 9660 standards for folder names. To be safe, be certain both folder and file-names have from one to eight characters (using only alphanumeric characters), a dot, and a one to three-character extension. Macintosh users should avoid preceding a filename with blank spaces or including spaces within the name of the file. When blank spaces are desired, use an underscore (file_doc.txt).

Supplying the data

How your CD-ROM is organized should be determined by you and not left to the replication center. I strongly recommend that you do not use low-capacity storage disks in a situation where you need several disks for your CD contents, and then send those disks to the replication house to be copied to a single source. Find a service bureau that can put all your files on a Jaz cartridge, or write a single CD that appears exactly as you intend to have it mastered. Having all files copied to a single source allows you to organize the files and folders without leaving this organization to the replication center. If you have a CD-R, you can write all your files to a CD in the order and hierarchy you want them to be replicated and deliver the CD to the replication center.

Folders and icons

The views that you save with your files will appear the same on the CD-ROM as they do on your computer. If you want to have your folders viewed as a list, you should display all of the folders in a list view before the data is submitted to the replication center. Icon views should be set before the master data disk is sent to the replication center. On the Macintosh, you should place your folder windows in the top-left corner of the screen. If your design was created on a 20-inch monitor and the folder appears in the lower-right corner, the end user may not see the folder on a 13-inch monitor.

Folders should also be opened or closed according to how you want them to appear. If all your folders are opened and you send off your data disk to be replicated, when you receive your CDs back from the service center, all the folders will appear opened. The best way to organize your folders and views is to open them one at a time, view them in the desired view, and size the folder window to the desired size. Close each folder after the views have been set and close or open the final disk. The last step depends on whether you want the CD icon to appear on a desktop or a window to be opened that shows the root directory of the CD.

CD authoring software will optimize files on the fly during the CD replication process. It is, however, a good idea to optimize a disk before you send it off to the service center. If you have a utility program that optimizes and defragments files, use it on the final data disk before you send it to the replication center.

Distribution of the Acrobat Reader Software

Adobe Systems grants you license and distribution rights for the Acrobat Reader software. You can freely distribute the Reader software as long as you comply with licensing and restriction guidelines developed by Adobe Systems. You can include the Reader installer on the CD-ROM you replicate and distribute to others as long as you follow the licensing requirements.

Tip   As an added benefit for users, you can create a Web page that links to the Adobe Web site where the download page for the free Reader software appears. Users who may browse your CD-ROM after another release of the Reader software might want to install a more recent version. By including the Reader installer and a Web page with a link to the Adobe site, you offer the end user a choice of options for installing the program.

Adobe License Agreement

All distribution of the Adobe Acrobat Reader software requires that you also include the licensing information supplied with the Reader installer when distributing the program for Macintosh, Windows, and UNIX.

Reader and Search

If you create a search index with Acrobat Catalog, be certain to include the Reader + Search installer. You may find two separate installers for Reader. If the Search plug-in is not installed, the end user won't be able to search your index file.

Registering as a Reader distributor

Adobe Systems has provided you with a great opportunity to freely distribute the Reader software so that end users may see the files you develop on your CD-ROM. Adobe encourages the distribution of the Reader software and likes to keep track of the distributors and the projects they develop with Acrobat PDF files. You gain some benefits by registering with Adobe Systems on their Web site at www.adobe.com/acrobat/acrodist.html.

Caution   Policies and authorizations are subject to change. As of this writing, the Reader application can be freely distributed as long as the guidelines set forth by Adobe Systems are followed. As all new product introductions are released, be certain to check with the manufacturer for any changes in distribution rights and current authorizations.

Summary

✦ Acrobat PDF files can be encrypted with digital signatures.

✦ A signature handler can be created for private use and a public key can be sent to other users for reviewing authored PDF files.

✦ PDF files can be compared in Acrobat for any discrepancies. Compared files will be marked with pencil comments where the discrepancies exist.

✦ PDF files intended for CD-ROM replication should be optimized. As a final step in transferring files to external media, use the Batch Sequence command in Acrobat to optimize PDFs.

✦ Adobe Systems grants you permission for distribution of the Acrobat Reader software as long as you comply with their distribution and licensing requirements.

✦   ✦   ✦

Cataloging and Scanning

Creating Search Indexes with Acrobat Catalog

Understanding Acrobat Catalog

Acrobat Catalog is used to search indexes of PDF files. Catalog was a separate executable program in all of the earlier versions of Adobe Acrobat. Now in version 5.0, Catalog is a plug-in accessible from within Acrobat. Versions of Catalog prior to Acrobat Catalog 5.0 enabled users to launch Catalog and let it remain in the background updating search indexes at user specified intervals. The new version of Acrobat Catalog eliminates network interval updating and requires individual user attendance at a workstation to perform routine updates.

To launch Acrobat Catalog from within Acrobat choose Tools ⇨ Catalog. Catalog is robust and provides many options for creating and modifying indexes. After a search index is created, any user can access the search index in Reader or Acrobat to find words using all of Acrobat Search's features within a collection of PDF files. In this chapter, you see how to work with Catalog for creating search indexes and optimizing searches for dedicated computers, networks, and CD-ROM collections.

Structure of Catalog files

When you produce an index with Acrobat Catalog, Catalog creates several files and folders automatically. The index file by default will have a .pdx extension. You should get in the habit of using this extension for all index files to keep them organized and recognizable. Indexes can be created inside folders, drive partitions, or on entire hard drives. On the Macintosh, indexes can be created from remote workstations. When a search index has been created, a total of nine subfolders are created by Catalog when the index is produced (see Figure 15-1). Each of these subfolders must remain intact in order to use an index for searching with Acrobat Search. If you eliminate or relocate individual folders, Acrobat Search won't be able to use the index file.

Figure 15-1: When an index file is created by Catalog, nine folders are also created. These folders must be included in the same folder as the index file when using Acrobat Search.

Hierarchy of indexed files

You can index a file, folder, or hard drive. When you identify a folder to index, Catalog includes all PDF files inside the given folder and all nested folders inside the target folder. Therefore, you can index all the PDF documents contained in several levels of folders. Catalog will include for indexing all the PDF documents within the identified folder and all PDF documents in folders nested below the root folder. Several root folders can also be indexed and all subfolders below each individual root folder will also be included in the index.

Relocating indexes

You can move an index and the subfolders to another hard drive or server, or write the index and subfolders to a CD-ROM. When you move an index file, you need to move all subfolders with the index file in order to perform searches on the index. If you fail to copy the index and all related folders, the index will not work with Acrobat Search.

Preparing PDFs for Indexing

Regardless of whether you create a few indexes for personal use or create and organize volumes of PDFs and multiple indexes, there are many considerations to address before creating an index with Catalog. The advance time and planning you take before creating search indexes will save much time over having to manually edit files and rebuild indexes.

Preparation involves creating PDFs with all the necessary information to facilitate searches. All searchable Document Summary information needs to be supplied in the PDF documents at the time of distillation or by modifying PDFs in Acrobat before you begin working with Catalog. For workgroups and multiple user access to search indexes, this information needs to be clear and consistent. Other factors, such as naming conventions, location of files, and optimizing performance should all be thought out and planned ahead of time before you create an index file.

Document Summary

Document Summary information should be supplied in all PDF files to be searched. As discussed in Chapter 2, all document summary data are searchable. Spending time creating document summaries and defining the field types for consistent organization will facilitate searches performed by multiple users.

The first of the planning steps is to develop a flow chart or outline of company information and the documents that will be categorized. This organization may or may not be implemented where you intend to develop a PDF workflow. If your information flow is already in place, you may need to make some modifications to coordinate nomenclature and document identity with the document summary items in Acrobat.

Document summaries contained in the Title, Subject, Author, and Keywords fields should be consistent and intuitive. They should also follow a hierarchy consistent with the company's organizational structure and workflow. The document summary items should be mapped out and defined. When preparing files for indexing, consider the following:

✦ **Title:** Title information might be thought of as the root of an outline — the parent statement if you will. Descriptive titles should be used to help users narrow searches within specific categories.

✦ **Subject:** If the title field is the parent item in an outline format, the Subject would be a child item nested directly below the title. Subjects might be considered as subsets of titles. When creating document summaries, be consistent. Don't use subject and title or subject and keyword information back and forth with different documents. If an item, such as employee grievances, is listed as a subject in some PDFs and then listed as keywords in other documents, the end users will become confused with the order and searches will become unnecessarily complicated.

✦ **Author:** Avoid using proper names for the Author field. Personnel change in companies and roles among employees change. Identify the author of PDF documents according to departments, work groups, facilities, and so on.

✦ **Keywords:** If you have a forms identification system in place, be certain to use form numbers and identity as part of the keywords field. You might start the keywords field with a form number and then add additional keywords to help narrow searches. Be consistent and always start the keywords field with forms or document numbers.

To illustrate some examples, take a look at Table 15-1.

	Table 15-1		
	Document Summary Examples		
Title	*Subject*	*Author*	*Keywords*
Descriptive Titles Titles may be considered specific to workgroup tasks.	**Subsection of Title** Subjects may be thought of as child outline items nested below the parent Title items — a subset of the Titles.	**Department Names** Don't use employee names in organizations; employees change, departments usually remain.	**Document Numbers** Forms ID numbers, internal filing numbers, and so on, can be supplied in the Keyword fields.
Employee Policies	Vacation Leave	Human Resources	D-101, HR32A
FDA Compliance	Software Validation	Quality Assurance	SOP-114, QA-182
Curriculum	Humanities	English Department	Plan 2010
Receivables	Collection Policy	Accounting	F-8102, M-5433
eCommerce	Products	Marketing	M-1051, e-117A

Tip   Legacy PDF files used in an organization may have been created without a Document Summary or you may reorganize PDFs and want to change document summaries. You can create a Batch Sequence to change multiple PDF files and run the sequence. Organize PDFs in a folder where the document summary will be edited. In the Edit Sequence dialog box, select the items to change and edit each document summary item to be changed. Run the sequence, and an entire folder of PDFs will be updated.

File structure

The content, filenames, and location of PDFs to be cataloged contribute to file structure items. All issues related to file structure must be thought out and appropriately designed for the audience that you intend to support. Among the important considerations are:

✦ **File naming conventions:** Names provided for the PDF files are critical for distributing documents among users. If filenames get truncated, then either Acrobat Search or the end user will have difficulty finding a document when performing a search. This is of special concern to Macintosh users who want to distribute documents across platforms. As a matter of safeguard, the best precaution to take is always use standard DOS file naming conventions. The standard eight-character filename with no more than three character file extensions (`filename.ext`), will always work regardless of platform.

✦ **Folder names:** Folder names should follow the same conventions as filenames. For Macintosh users, if you want to keep filenames longer than standard DOS names, you must limit folder names to eight characters and no more than a three-character file extension for cross-platform compliance.

✦ **File and folder name identity:** Avoid using ASCII characters from 133 to 159 for any file or folder name. Acrobat Catalog does not support extended characters in this range. (Figure 15-2 lists the characters to avoid.)

133	à	139	ï	144	É	149	ò	154	Ü
134	å	140	î	145	æ	150	û	156	£
135	ç	141	ì	146	Æ	151	ù	157	¥
136	ê	142	Ä	147	ô	152	_	158	_
137	ë	143	Å	148	ö	153	Ö	159	ƒ
138	è								

Figure 15-2: When providing names for files and folders to be cataloged, avoid using extended characters from ASCII 133 to ASCII 159. Acrobat Catalog does not support these characters.

✦ **Folder organization:** Folders to be cataloged should have a logical hierarchy. Copy all files to be cataloged to a single folder or a single folder with nested folders in the same path. When nesting folders, be certain to keep the number of nested folders to a minimum. Deeply nested folders will slow down searches and path names longer than 256 characters will create problems.

✦ **Folder locations:** For Windows users, location of folders must be contained on a local hard drive or a network server volume. Although Macintosh users can catalog information across computer workstations, it would be advisable to create separate indexes for files contained on separate drives. Any files moved to different locations will make searches inoperable.

✦ **PDF structure:** All the file naming listed above should be handled before creating links and attaching files. If filenames are changed after the PDF structure has been developed, many links will become inoperable. Be certain to complete all editing in the PDF documents before cataloging files.

Optimizing performance

Searches can be performed very fast if you take a little time in creating the proper structure and organization. If you don't avoid some pitfalls with the way that you organize files, then searches will be performed much slower. A few considerations to be made include:

✦ **Optimize PDF files:** Optimization should be performed on all PDF files as one of the last steps in your workflow. Use the Allow Fast Web View found in the Options category in the Preferences dialog box and run the Batch Sequence for Optimize Space. When the Batch Sequence is run, all invalid bookmarks, links, and destinations will be removed. Optimization is especially important for searches to be performed from CD-ROM files.

✦ **Break up long PDF files:** Books, reports, essays, and other documents that contain many pages should be broken up into multiple PDF files. If you have books that will be cataloged, break up the books into separate chapters. Acrobat Search will run much faster when finding information from several small files. It will slow down when searching through long documents.

Tip

Books, reports, and manuals can be broken up into separate files and structured in a way that they will still appear to the end user as a single document. Assuming a user reads through a file in a linear fashion, you can create links to open and close pages without user intervention. Create navigational buttons to move forward and back through document pages. On the last page of each chapter, use the navigation button to open the next chapter. Also on the last page of each chapter, create a Page Action that will close the current document when the page is closed (See Chapter 10 for creating links and Page Actions). If the end user disables Open Cross-Document Links In Same Window in the Options category in the Preferences, the open file will still close after the last page is closed. All the chapters can be linked from a table of contents where any chapter can be opened. If you give your design some thought, browsing the contents of books will appear to the end user no different than reading a book in the analog world.

Creating search help

You can have multiple indexes for various uses and different workgroups. Personnel may use one index for department matters, another for company wide information, and perhaps another for a research library. When searching information, all relevant keywords will appear from indexes loaded in the Acrobat Index Selection dialog box. When using multiple indexes, employees may forget the structure of document summaries and knowing what index would be needed for a given search.

Readme files and index help files can be created where key information about what search words may be used to find document summaries. You can create a single PDF file, text files, or multiple files that serve as help. Figure 15-3 shows an example of a PDF help file that might be used to find documents related to a company's personnel policies, procedures, and forms.

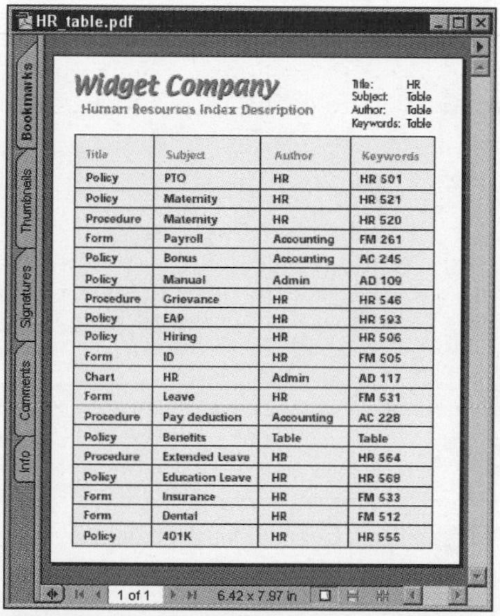

Widget Company
Human Resources Index Description

Title: HR
Subject: Table
Author: Table
Keywords: Table

Title	Subject	Author	Keywords
Policy	PTO	HR	HR 501
Policy	Maternity	HR	HR 521
Procedure	Maternity	HR	HR 520
Form	Payroll	Accounting	FM 261
Policy	Bonus	Accounting	AC 245
Policy	Manual	Admin	AD 109
Procedure	Grievance	HR	HR 546
Policy	EAP	HR	HR 593
Policy	Hiring	HR	HR 506
Form	ID	HR	FM 505
Chart	HR	Admin	AD 117
Form	Leave	HR	FM 531
Procedure	Pay deduction	Accounting	AC 228
Policy	Benefits	Table	Table
Procedure	Extended Leave	HR	HR 564
Policy	Education Leave	HR	HR 568
Form	Insurance	HR	FM 533
Form	Dental	HR	FM 512
Policy	401K	HR	HR 555

Figure 15-3: A PDF help file can assist users in knowing what keywords need to be used for the Title, Subject, Author, and Keywords fields.

In the top-right corner of Figure 15-3, the document summary for the help file is listed. The title fields for this company example are broken into categories for policies, procedures, forms, and charts. The subject fields break down the title categories into specific personnel items and the author field contains the department that authored the documents. Form numbers appear for all keywords fields.

Tip

When creating help files that guide a user for searching document information, use a common identifier in the Subject, Author, and Keywords fields reserved for only finding help files. In Figure 15-3, the identifier is *Table*. Whenever a user searches for the word table in the Author field, the only returns in the Search Results dialog box will be help files. When using the Title and Author field together, a user can find a specific help file for a given department. In the previous example, the Title is *HR* and the Author is *Table*. When these words are searched for the document information, the help file for the HR department will be returned in the Search Results. If you reserve keywords for the document summary fields, any employee can easily find information by remembering only a few keywords.

Setting Catalog Preferences

In earlier versions of Acrobat, Windows and Macintosh computers handled preferences differently. Now in Acrobat 5.0, preference options are identical for both platforms and are selected from a button in the Acrobat Catalog dialog box. To access preferences, open Acrobat Catalog from within Acrobat by choosing Tools ➪ Catalog. The Adobe Catalog dialog box shown in Figure 15-4 opens.

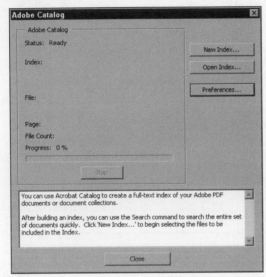

Figure 15-4: You can access Acrobat Catalog by opening Acrobat and choosing the Tools ➪ Catalog menu command.

In Acrobat Catalog, a button is displayed for preferences. Click this button to open the Catalog Preferences dialog box. The first of the preference items includes the General preferences, as shown in Figure 15-5.

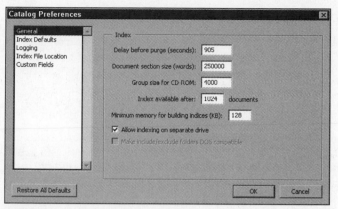

Figure 15-5: The General Preferences is displayed when the Catalog Preferences dialog box is opened.

General Preferences

The General Preferences are opened by default. These items include:

✦ **Delay before purge (seconds):** Purging involves eliminating unnecessary information from an index. I cover purging in more detail a little later and discuss why it is performed. For now, note the setting you see identified as Delay before purge (seconds) is a user-definable item that sets up a warning for when a purge will begin. If users on your network are conducting a search, a warning dialog box will appear before the purge begins. The default time for when the warning is posted prior to the purge is 905 seconds, or roughly 15 minutes. You can determine another time period and change the setting as desired.

✦ **Document section size (words):** This item is limited to the amount of memory installed on your computer. If you have 32MB of free RAM available, the maximum document section size you can use is 3,200,000 (or 3.2 million) words. The amount of memory required to process a document is approximately ten times the number of words in the document. For faster updates, use the largest size your computer can handle. The acceptable range is 5,000 to 1,000,000.

✦ **Group size for CD-ROM:** This setting has to do with the reliability of the total number of documents indexed. The maximum recommended is 4000. Catalog permits ranges up to 64,000,000; however, any number above 4000 may be unreliable.

✦ **Index available after [_] documents:** This setting will be dependent on the size of your index and how soon you may want users to access an index after updating it. When you have small index files and want fast searches, set the number to 1024. If you have large index files and want to have quick access to partial indexes, set the number to 100 or lower. If you need to perform a thorough re-indexing of many large index files, set the number higher than 1024 and let it run overnight on your computer. Catalog will accept a range between 16 and 4000 PDF documents to be indexed in a single file.

✦ **Minimum memory for building indexes (KB):** Catalog will assess memory at the beginning of an index build. If the percentage of memory used in the disk cache falls below the amount specified in the field box, the build will be stopped. The range of disk cache memory that can be used is between 64 and 2048K.

✦ **Allow indexing on separate drive:** On the Macintosh, you can index files on different drives or on a network server. If you plan to create index files on remote systems, you should plan your organization well and not move the indexes. Doing so may create problems in accessing an index. If you want to perform such a task, you need to enable this option.

✦ **Make include/exclude folders DOS compatible:** If you are a Macintosh user who wants your files to be shared by Windows users and you want to build a cross-platform index, all your folders need to be named with standard MS-DOS naming conventions (that is, a filename of up to eight characters with an extension of up to three characters). If you have folders that do not conform to MS-DOS conventions, this option will exclude the folders from the index. Filenames within the folders do not need to conform to standard DOS-compatible names.

Index Defaults

The second category in the Catalog Preferences dialog box is Index Defaults, which includes several items for determining the contents of the index file (see Figure 15-6). You also find optimizing controls and compatibility options in these settings.

✦ **Do not include numbers:** The size of your index files relates dramatically to the speed of updating indexes and performing searches. To speed up both processes, you can exclude some information from the index file. By enabling the Do not include numbers option, you can reduce file size from 10 to 20 percent. If numbers are excluded from the index, you will not be able to perform searches for numbers.

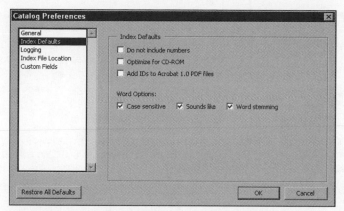

Figure 15-6: The Index Defaults category provides options that determine content attributes of the index file.

✦ **Optimize for CD-ROM:** When you choose this option, the searches performed on an index file contained on a CD-ROM will finish much faster. This option can also speed up searches of indexes on your hard drive. When a file is modified, and you perform a search, a warning dialog box will appear informing you the index has been changed. You need to choose to use the index by signifying so in the warning dialog box. When you optimize for CD-ROM, activating a search will prevent such warning dialog boxes from appearing.

✦ **Add IDs to Acrobat 1.0 PDF files:** Earlier versions of Acrobat Distiller and PDFWriter did not include document identifiers as were later added to Acrobat Pro in Version 2.0. If you want these identifiers added to PDF files created with either Distiller or PDFWriter from the earlier versions, enable this option.

✦ **Word Options:** As discussed in Chapter 2, search options provide additional capabilities for narrowing down the search. These include searching by case-sensitivity, synonyms, and roots of words. If you feel these options are not necessary, you can choose to exclude any one, two, or all of the options by clearing the respective checkbox. When any of these items are excluded from the index file, they will be disabled when performing a search in an Acrobat viewer.

Logging

When an index is created, Catalog creates a text file known as a *log file*. The log file records the progress of creating the index. The log file also contains a date and time stamp for when the index was created. Any errors encountered will be written to the log file. Figure 15-7 shows the choices for logging preferences.

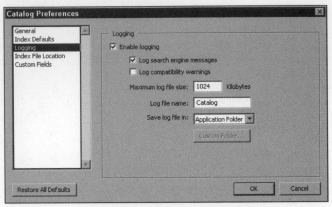

Figure 15-7: Choices for location and filename are established, among other options, in the Logging category of the Catalog Preferences dialog box.

✦ **Enable logging:** The Enable Logging option is the first item in the dialog box. When this option is turned on, a log file will be written. If you disable this option, a log file will not be written. The two options under Enable logging let you include or exclude search engine messages and compatibility warnings.

✦ **Log search engine messages:** Messages regarding the search engine will be written to the log file. Improprieties and invalid items will be included.

✦ **Log compatibility warnings:** Compatibility items found with any discrepancy will be included in the log file. By default the item is unchecked. If you want to examine compatibility problems in the log file, enable the checkbox.

✦ **Maximum log file size:** The default file size for the log file is 1MB. When the log file grows to a size larger than what is specified in this field box, the file will automatically be deleted. The auto-deletion is provided so that you don't have a random file on your hard drive grow to extreme sizes. After the log file is deleted, a new log file is created. You can specify a log file size in the range of 16 to 16,384KB.

✦ **Log file name:** The default name for the log file is Catalog. If you want to use another name, enter it in this field box.

✦ **Save log file in:** By default, the log file is located in the Acrobat application folder. From the pull-down menu you have additional choices. Index Folder selected from the pull-down menu saves the log file in the index folder created with your index. Custom Folder enables you to designate any folder on your hard drive where the log file will be saved. Select Custom Folder from the pull-down menu and the Custom Folder button below the menu will be activated. Click this button and a navigation dialog box will open where you can designate a folder and location where the log file will be saved.

Index File location

The index file is the file that will be created by Catalog and subsequently loaded in the Acrobat Search Indexes dialog box. This preference setting, shown in Figure 15-8, enables you to establish a name and location for where the new file will be saved.

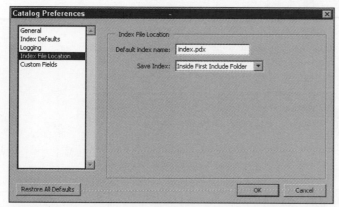

Figure 15-8: The name and location for the index file created by Catalog are established in the Index File Location preferences.

✦ **Default index name:** By default, the filename for the index file will be index.pdx. Any name can be provided for the index name, but it would be advisable to keep the name within standard DOS file naming conventions and use the .pdx extension.

✦ **Save Index:** The location of the index file can be placed in either the same file as the root directories for the catalog elements or outside the folder where these other folders reside. Choices are made for the two options by making a selection from the pull-down menu.

Custom Fields

The Custom Fields preferences, shown in Figure 15-9, are used when customizing Acrobat with the Acrobat Software Development Kit. This item is intended for programmers who want to add special features to Acrobat. To make changes to the Custom Fields settings, you should have a strong command of the PDF format. The options for Custom Fields include:

✦ **Field Name:** The name for the custom field is supplied in the Field Name box.

✦ **Field Type:** An integer field that can accept values between 0 and 65,535 appears as the default field type. Other choices from the pull-down menu include Date (for a date field), and String (a string of text).

✦ **Add:** When Add is selected, the custom field is added to the list box.

✦ **Remove:** To remove a custom field, select it in the list box and click the Remove button.

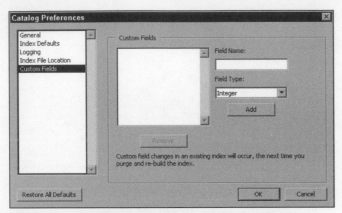

Figure 15-9: Adding Custom Fields requires a strong knowledge of the PDF format and programming skill. Custom data fields can be added to Acrobat with the Acrobat Software Development Kit.

Support for programmers writing extensions, plug-ins and working with the Software Development Kit is provided by Adobe Systems. For developers who want to use the support program, you need to become a member of the Adobe Solutions Network (ASN) Developer Program. For more information about ASN and SDK, log on to the Adobe Web site at: http://partners.adobe.com/asn/developer.

Restoring Defaults

A button appears in all preference dialog boxes at the lower left of the Catalog Preferences dialog box. When you click Restore Defaults, Catalog will prompt you with a warning dialog box. If you accept the change by clicking OK in the warning dialog box, all of the preference settings will be restored to default preferences. In essence, it's like starting over. After the defaults have been restored, you'll need to revisit any preference settings and make changes where needed.

Creating an Index

When creating an index, it is always a good idea to review your preference settings. Be certain to toggle through the various dialog boxes and make your settings choices. Before creating index files, you should also make a habit of reviewing the folder where the PDFs to be indexed reside. Be certain all the files intended to be indexed are contained in the same directory or subdirectories for the designated index location. Also, be certain to double-check all the items listed earlier for preparing files properly.

Creating a new index is handled in Catalog by clicking the New Index button in the Acrobat Catalog dialog box. When the button is selected, the New Index Definition dialog box opens, as shown in Figure 15-10.

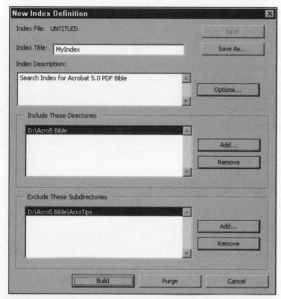

Figure 15-10: The New Index Definition dialog box is used to define the definitions for the Index file and provides the means for selecting the directory where the index will be created.

Index Title

The title that you place in this field will be a title for the index, but not the name of the file you build. The name you enter here does not need to conform to any naming conventions, because it won't be the saved filename. The title will be viewed in the Search Results window when a search is performed. The more descriptive the name, the easier it will be for users to find the information for which they are searching. For simplicity, Figure 15-10 shows the Index Title as MyIndex. In a real world situation, you might use a title that describes the PDF categories that have been indexed. An example would be: *Accounting Summaries prior to Y2K* — or some similar kind of category.

Index Description

You can supply as many as 255 characters in the Index Description field. Descriptive names and keywords should be provided so that the end user knows what this particular index contains. Index descriptions should be thought of as adding more information to the items mentioned earlier in this chapter regarding document information. Descriptions can further help narrow searches where multiple indexes may be created for individual departments.

Include These Directories

If you add nothing in this field, Catalog won't build an index because it won't know where to look for the PDF files to be included in the index. Adding the directory path(s) is critical before you begin to build the index. Notice the Add button on the right side of the dialog box in Figure 15-10. After you click Add, a navigation dialog box appears, enabling you to identify the directory where the PDFs to be indexed are located. Many directories can be added to the Include Directories list. These directories can be in different locations on your hard drive. When a given directory is selected, all subfolders will also be indexed for all directory locations. When the directories have been identified, the directory path and folder name will appear in the Include directories field.

Exclude These Subdirectories

If you have files in a subdirectory within the directory you are indexing and want to exclude the subdirectory, you can do so in the Exclude Directories field. The folder names and directory paths of excluded directories will appear in that field. In Figure 15-10, notice I have included my folder as D:\Acro5 Bible and my excluded folder is D:\Acro5 Bible\AcroTips. In this example, all the files in the Acro5 Bible folder will be cataloged and any subfolders within this directory except the AcroTips folder.

Options

To the right of the Index Description box is a button labeled Options. Click this button and the Options dialog box appears where you can choose to make exclusions from the index file (see Figure 15-11). Some of these options are similar to those discussed in the context of the Preference settings. Any edits you make here will supersede any preferences.

Words not to include in the index

You may have words, such as *the*, *a*, *an*, *of*, and so on, that would typically not be used in a search. You can choose to exclude such words by typing the word in the Word field box and clicking the Add button in the Options dialog box. To eliminate a word after it has been added, select the word and click the Remove button. Keep in mind every time you add a word, you are actually adding it to a list of words to be excluded.

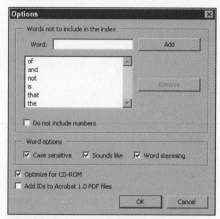

Figure 15-11: Clicking the Options button adjacent to Index Description opens the Options dialog box. Here the various word options can be enabled and made available when using Acrobat Search.

Do not include numbers

Below the settings for exclusion of words is an option for excluding numbers. By selecting the Do not include numbers option, you can reduce the file size, especially if data containing many numbers is part of the PDF file(s) to be indexed. Keep in mind, though, if numbers are excluded, Acrobat Search won't find numeric values. This setting will also supersede any choices made in the preferences.

Word options

The Word options section in this dialog box present the same choices as discussed in Chapter 2 in the context of Acrobat Search. If you want to eliminate these options, you can deselect any or all of the checkboxes. Search indexes will be smaller when deselecting these items and eliminating any words listed above for exclusion. You will also be able to search faster through your PDF contents. Try to give some thought on what search criteria is needed and exclude as much as you can that you know will not be needed for users searching the index.

Optimize for CD-ROM

The Optimize for CD-ROM option is included here, as well as in the Catalog Preferences Index Defaults dialog box. This option is disabled by default. If you want to optimize the search of an index on CD-ROM, enable this option. Like the preceding settings, if you enable this option, it will supersede the preference setting in the Preferences dialog box.

Add IDs to Acrobat 1.0 PDF files

Once again, this setting is the same as you find for Index Defaults in the Catalog Preferences dialog box. Because Acrobat is now in Version 5.0, it may be rare to find a need to add the IDs for Acrobat 1.0 files. If you have older files, it would be best to batch-process the older PDFs by saving them out of Acrobat 5.0. As software changes, many previous formats will not be supported with recent updates. To ensure against obsolescence, update older documents to newer file formats.

After determining Options settings, click OK in the Options dialog box, and you are returned to the New Index Definition dialog box. Before building an index, information must be provided for one more important option. At this point, Catalog does not yet know what files are going to be indexed.

Removing directories

A folder can be deleted from either the Include Directories or Exclude Directories list. To remove a folder, select the name of the folder in the respective list and click the Remove button adjacent to the list box.

Building the index

After all the attributes for the index definition have been set, the index file is ready to be created. Clicking the Build button in the New Index Definition dialog box creates indexes (see Figure 15-10). When this button is selected, Acrobat Catalog will open a navigation dialog box where the index file location can be determined (see Figure 15-12).

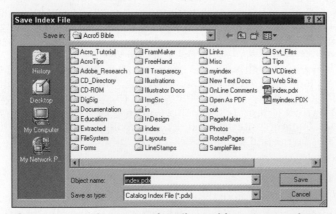

Figure 15-12: The Save Index File enables you to navigate your hard drive to designate a location for the index file.

When you establish the location and click the Save button in the Save Index File dialog box, the index will begin its build. During the index creation, Catalog opens a dialog box where a status bar will display the build progress, as shown in Figure 15-13.

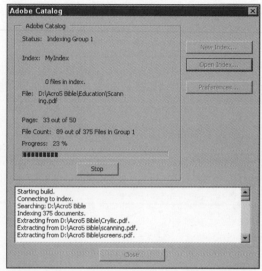

Figure 15-13: As an index file is built, Catalog displays the progress and list files it reads to be included in the index.

The location that you instruct Catalog to save your index file can be any location on your hard drive regardless of where the files being indexed reside. When making choices for where the index file will be saved, the two options available to you are inside the index folder or outside the index folder. Catalog will create the index folder automatically when the build is executed at the location you specify in this dialog box. As you create builds, keep in mind that the location determined in the Save Index File dialog box will instruct Acrobat where the folder for the index files is created. Where the index file resides respective to this folder is handled in the Index File Location settings within the Catalog Preferences dialog box.

Purging data

A button adjacent to the Build button in the New Index Definition dialog box is used for purging data. As indexes are maintained and rebuilt, you will need to perform routine maintenance and purge the data. A purge will not delete the index file; it simply recovers the space used in the index for outdated information. Purging is particularly useful when you remove PDF files from a folder and the search items are no longer needed. Before purging data, it's a good idea to review your preference settings and observe the Time Before Purge (seconds) field box. The Default is 905 seconds, which means Catalog will wait 15 minutes and 5 seconds before purging data. The delay is adjustable for users in workgroups who may be accessing an index file to be purged. While the file is open, the purge cannot be performed. A warning dialog box appears to users when a purge has been invoked (see Figure 15-14). By default, users have over 15 minutes before the purge begins, which should be ample time to quit searches and move on to other tasks.

If you are working in an independent environment and have no other users sharing files on a network, you may want to reduce the amount of time in the Time Before Purge (seconds) field box so that you don't have to wait for Catalog to begin purging data.

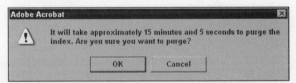

Figure 15-14: When beginning a purge, Acrobat opens a warning dialog box informing you of the amount of time it will take to begin the purge.

Tip   When changing options for adding or eliminating words, numbers and word options from indexes, first open the index.pdx file and purge the data. Set your new preferences in the Catalog Preferences dialog box and rebuild the index. Any items deleted will now be added to the index or any items you want to eliminate will subsequently be eliminated from the index.

After purging data in an index file, select the Open Index menu in the Acrobat Catalog dialog box and choose the Build option again. Catalog will rebuild the index. Index files that are purged after data has been removed provide for smaller file sizes and faster searches.

Using Index Files

After an index has been created, it will be ready for use with Acrobat Search. Index files can be located anywhere on your hard drive or server. To use a new index file, choose Edit ➪ Search ➪ Select Indexes. In the Index Selection dialog box, a new index is selected by clicking the Add button. The dialog box also offers a description of indexes that cannot be found, are currently not loaded, and those that have been added or remain active, as shown in Figure 15-15.

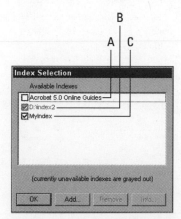

Figure 15-15: The Index Selection dialog box is used to load index files. In the dialog box, a display shows all current active indexes that can be used for searching.

The symbols to the left of each index name give you an indication of the index availability. In Figure 15-15, the checkbox displays indicate:

✦ **A**   The index is available but not currently loaded. When performing a search, Acrobat Search does not use this index file.

✦ **B**   Acrobat lost the directory path for this index or the subfolders have been moved to a new location. To reconnect Acrobat Search to the index file, select the grayed out item and click the Remove button. Click the Add button and find the index file.

✦ **C**   The index is loaded and ready for use.

To view the index description that you supplied in the New Index Definition dialog box, click the Info button in the Index Selection dialog box. Another dialog box opens where information about the index file is displayed, as shown in Figure 15-16.

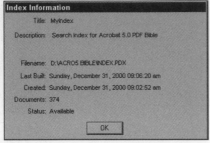

Figure 15-16: The Index Information dialog box displays the index description information supplied in the New Index Definition dialog box when the index was built. Additional information, such as creation date and the date of the last build is also made available.

Summary

✦ Acrobat Catalog is a plug-in used for creating search index files.

✦ Before creating an index, PDF files should include document summary information, be optimized and structured, and be labeled with proper naming conventions.

✦ Creating custom help files can be useful when creating index files for multiple users.

✦ Catalog preferences should be reviewed before building an index. Preferences help determine what information will be contained in the search index.

✦ An index is made available from the Index Selection dialog box. The index selection dialog box will display all available indexes and show any files that cannot be recognized by Acrobat Search.

✦   ✦   ✦

Scanning in Acrobat

Acrobat and Scanners

If you haven't gotten your fill of Acrobat features thus far, then hold on — here you have the opportunity to explore more of what you can do by taking a look at scanning and capturing pages. Among other things, Acrobat enables you to use a plug-in, called Acrobat Scan, for accessing a desktop scanner. After the scanned image is created, you can capture the scanned page and have all the text read through an optical character recognition (OCR) program, such as Acrobat Capture (see Chapter 17 for more on Acrobat Capture).

Acrobat Scan is a plug-in module that enables you to access your scanner without leaving the Acrobat program. To work properly, the Scan plug-in needs to be installed in your Acrobat plug-in folder, and the scanner needs to be configured by accessing the Scan plug-in in Acrobat. After a paper document is scanned and appears in Acrobat, Acrobat Capture converts the scanned image to text via OCR software. In earlier versions of Acrobat, Acrobat Capture was installed along with Acrobat Scan when you installed Acrobat. In Version 5.0, the Paper Capture command that was used to access Acrobat Capture has been eliminated from the program. Acrobat Capture remains a separate software application and requires a separate purchase.

Accessing a scanner

Your scanner must be properly attached to your computer and capable of working independently of Acrobat. Be certain the scanner manufacturer's software for scanning images is properly operating before attempting to scan in Acrobat. Access to your scanner is made through the aid of either the

Automatic Scanner Interface Standard (ISIS) software or a TWAIN (Technology With An Important Name) scanner module.

ISIS software (Windows)

Adobe supplies ISIS software for Windows. (The ISIS software is not available to Macintosh users.) With ISIS, you need to have the profile available for your particular scanner, or you'll need to use the TWAIN software. To determine whether the profile for your software is available, choose File ⇨ Import ⇨ Scan. The Adobe Acrobat Scan dialog box appears offering several options. (See Figures 16-1 and 16-2.)

✦ **Device:** Your scanner device or scanner application software should appear on this pull-down menu. If it is not visible, recheck your scanner installation to ensure that it is properly installed.

✦ **Format:** If your scanner and software permit double-sided scanning, you can select Double sided from the pull-down menu. If not, the default format is Single sided. Leave the default choice if your scanner does not have double-sided capabilities.

✦ **Open New PDF Document:** When no file is open, you can access the Scan plug-in. Any scanned page will be converted to PDF and opened in the Document pane.

✦ **Append To Current Document:** If a PDF file is open, scanned pages will be appended after the last page in the document. Regardless of the page in view, the appended page will be added after the last page.

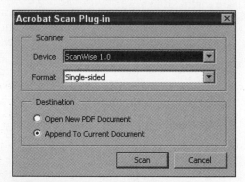

Figure 16-1: The Acrobat Scan Plug-in dialog box in Windows enables you to specify your scanner and format from pull-down menus.

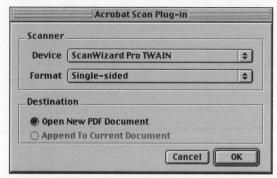

Figure 16-2: The Acrobat Scan Plug-in dialog box on the Macintosh offers the same user controls as Windows.

TWAIN software

TWAIN software is manufacturer supplied and should be available on the floppy disk or CD-ROM that you receive with your scanner. In Windows, the TWAIN files are stored in the \WINNT\twain_32 folder. When you install scanner software, the TWAIN driver should find the proper folder through the installer routine.

On the Macintosh, you have two files for TWAIN, and they both belong in the Preferences folder inside your System folder. They should also be inside a TWAIN folder, which resides inside the Preferences folder. When the TWAIN components are installed in the Preferences folder, your scanner name should appear in the Acrobat Scan Plug-in dialog box, as shown in Figure 16-2. From the pull-down menu, the name of your scanner will be listed as an option. If more than one scanner is installed, you can select from the available choices. If only a single scanner is attached to your computer, the default will select your current scanner.

Many scanner manufacturers produce equipment but use third-party developers to write the software. Adobe has certainly not tested the Acrobat Scan plug-in with all scanner manufacturers and all software developers. Theoretically, the TWAIN software should work in all cases. If you have problems accessing your scanner from within Acrobat, but can perform scans in Photoshop, then you most likely have a problem with the TWAIN software. If this is the case, contact your scanner manufacturer and see if they have an upgrade or if you can get some technical support. In many cases, you can download upgrades for registered software on the Internet.

HP AccuPage software (Windows)

Hewlett-Packard developed the HP AccuPage software to optimize scans for OCR and text scanning. The HP AccuPage software works with the ISIS profile, which is available by installing the driver from the Acrobat CD-ROM. If you have an HP scanner supporting the technology, be certain to install the driver. Errors listed as exceptions in Acrobat Capture will be much fewer than with traditional grayscale scanning.

Scanning Basics

At this point you should have your scanner and Acrobat Scan configured properly. Before I discuss how to use Acrobat Scan, take a moment to understand some of the essential issues to deal with in performing clean, accurate scans. Several items need to be discussed: first, the hardware and hardware-related issues; second, the types of scans to be produced; and third, the document preparation for which the scan will be made. A few moments here will save you much time in producing the best scans that you can expect from your equipment.

The first hardware item is your scanner. The single most important issue with scanner hardware is keeping the platen clean. If you have dust and dirt on the glass, these particles will appear in your scans. Keep the platen clean and use a lint-free cloth to clean the glass. If you use a solvent, always apply the solvent to the cloth and not the scanner glass.

The second hardware item to consider is your computer. When running Acrobat and the Scan plug-in, try to allocate as much memory as you can spare to Acrobat. If you have multiple applications open simultaneously and subsequently experience crashes, then by all means try using Acrobat alone when performing scans. Also related to your computer is the hard drive free space. Double-check the free space on your computer's hard drive before attempting to scan. Scans will eat up memory fast, so be certain you have ample space before engaging in a scanning session.

Understand your scanner and the technology used to manufacture the device. Flatbed consumer-grade scanners often use charge coupled devices (CCDs), tiny little sensors placed along a horizontal plane in number equal to the optical resolution of your scanner. Therefore, a 600-dpi scanner has 600 CCDs per inch. Each of these sensors will pick up a pixel when the scanner pass is made.

Less expensive scanners that you can find today in the less than $100 price range are CIS scanners. These scanners use contact image sensors instead of CCDs. They may be well suited to scan text but you'll have to test the results to determine if the scanner performs efficiently. In many cases, the low cost CIS scanners can produce text scans that work well with Acrobat Capture.

Understanding Acrobat scan types

You can produce several types of scans with your Acrobat Scan plug-in. Each of the scans that you produce will have different requirements and need some special attention when scanning.

Text recognition

If you scan directly in Acrobat, more often than not, your requirements will be for text and OCR scanning. Given the fact that PDF pages are usually created in applications, such as layout, illustration, and photo editing software, it would be rare to attempt to create PDF documents for final proofs by scanning them into Acrobat. If you compose a layout, you're more than likely going to use Photoshop as the scanning source, as it will enable you to enhance and optimize your image quality. The area Acrobat excels in is the creation of search indexes from text-heavy documents. In such a case, using Acrobat enables you to have easy access to your stored PDFs, and you can find information fast. For this situation, you would use the Scan plug-in and then the Capture software to recognize the text. When scanning text, you want to follow a few simple rules.

Image mode

Image modes range from 1-bit line art or black-and-white scans to 24-bit color. The higher the bit-depth, the larger the file size. For text scans, you only need 1-bit line art to recognize text. If your scanner software has a line art mode, use it to perform scans for text recognition.

Resolution

Resolution for text recognition needs to be high enough for good, clean scanning and tight pixels on the edges of characters, but not as high as you would need for output to high-end devices. As a general rule, you can scan normal body text at 300 dpi. Large text sizes might be sufficiently scanned at 200 dpi. For small text of eight points or lower, you may want to raise the resolution to 600 dpi. In many cases, you need to run some tests for the target resolution for your particular type of scanner, software, and typical documents scanned. The maximum resolution supported by Acrobat is 600 dpi.

Grayscale scanning

Once again, scanning images is often the task of Photoshop. However, you may find grayscale scanning necessary or helpful when scanning for text recognition. The most important attribute of a scanned image for OCR software is sharp contrast between the text and the background. If your line art scans aren't producing enough contrast, try scanning in grayscale and apply contrast settings in your software before completing the scan. Many software applications provide controls for brightness and contrast settings. Most software will display previews of the adjustments you make, which greatly speeds up the entire process.

Grayscale Photos

If you want to scan photographic images in grayscale, be certain to lower the resolution. Try 200 dpi or lower. You should plan on testing resolutions to achieve the lowest possible resolution that will maintain a good quality image. If you scan grayscale images in Acrobat, they should be for screen view only. To create PDF files that will ultimately be printed, you should use Photoshop and a layout or illustration application, and then either export to PDF, as described in Chapter 6 or print a PostScript file and distill with Acrobat Distiller.

Color Photos

Color images occupy the largest file sizes and should almost always not be scanned using Acrobat Scan. If you use a color image for text recognition, you can optimize the image in several ways by either printing the image to a PostScript file and distilling the file with Distiller's compression settings or by replacing an image with a grayscale or color scan that you create in Photoshop. In either case, you should be prepared to not leave the original scanned image in the PDF file. The size burden defeats much of the purpose of the PDF format.

Color scanning

If you have color documents and want to capture text from the pages, you may want to use a color mode if you can build up enough contrast during the scan. Large type in color images can be effectively recognized in 200 dpi scans.

Preparing a document

Just as your scans can benefit from paying careful attention to your scanner, exercising a little care with the source material can help produce clean scans. Bits of dust, improperly aligned pages, poor contrast, and degraded originals will affect your ability to create scans capable of being read without many errors by Acrobat Capture. A little time in preparation before scanning will save you much time in trying to clean up poorly scanned images.

Photocopying originals

Sometimes you can improve on the contrast adjustments by photocopying original documents. If you can improve image and text contrast by photocopying material, try some experiments to test your results. If you have large, bulky material, photocopies placed on the scanner bed will ultimately result in better scans.

Straight alignment

If you have documents with frayed edges or pages torn from a magazine, then you should trim the edges and make them parallel to the text in the page. Precise placement of pages on the scanner bed will facilitate clean scans. Even though Acrobat has a recognition capability within a 7-degree rotation, the straighter the page, the better the results.

Tip

A method that I use with all flatbed scanning is to place the source material in a jig I created from posterboard. If a standard 8.5 by 11 page is your source material, get a large piece of posterboard that extends past the edges of the scanner lid on the sides and bottom. Use a T-square and align a standard size page parallel to the top. Mark the edges where a cut out will be made in the center of the posterboard. Cut out the marked area and use the waste as a lid on the posterboard. You can tape the top so that it will open much like your scanner lid. The cut out area will be your template where pages will be placed and ready to be scanned. Place the template under the scanner lid and preview a scan. If the preview is not straight, you can move the posterboard because the edges extend beyond the scanner lid. After the preview appears straight, tape the posterboard to the scanner. As you open the scanner lid, subsequently open the jig lid and place a page in the cut out area. Every scan you perform will have all the pages aligned precisely. The lid on the jig will prevent the pages from rising in the cut out space and keep them flat against the platen.

Try to remember the axiom "garbage in, garbage out" when you approach any kind of scanning. The better the source material, the better your scanned results will appear. Exercise a little care in the beginning, and you'll find your Acrobat scanning sessions will move along much faster.

Memory Configurations

When using Acrobat for scanning, you have two considerations with memory requirements. You must have enough RAM to operate both Acrobat Scan and Acrobat Capture, and you must have enough hard disk space for work files to be created during the scan. Each of the memory requirements must be satisfied to work efficiently when you attempt scanning.

Macintosh memory requirements

The total RAM recommended to run Acrobat on the Macintosh is 31MB. When you add the Scan plug-in, the memory requirements grow another 8.8MB. Therefore, the total memory to run Acrobat Scan is almost 40MB.

Assessing memory

On the Macintosh, your first step to determine whether you can run Acrobat Scan is to assess how much available RAM you have after your system starts. From the Desktop, choose Apple ➪ About This Computer. The About This Computer dialog box that appears will inform you if you have enough free memory to run your applications, as shown in Figure 16-3. Look for the item designated Largest Unused Block. If the amount of free memory does not exceed 40MB of free RAM, you'll need to use virtual memory.

Virtual memory

To allocate more RAM for applications, you can use virtual memory. Virtual memory uses a portion of the free hard drive space and treats that portion of free space as an extension of RAM. Virtual memory will never operate as fast as RAM, but you may need to use it if your hardware is not sufficient to run Acrobat Scan. Refer to your system manual for configuring your computer with virtual memory.

Figure 16-3: From the Desktop, choose Apple ➪ About This Computer and look at the largest unused block to determine the amount of free memory.

Allocating memory to Acrobat

On the Macintosh, you need to allocate enough RAM to an application in order to take advantage of using more RAM than allocated with the default installation. By default, software manufacturers have preset allocations of memory assigned to a software application. In order to increase the memory assigned to the application, you will need to manually make that assignment.

You should have a minimum of more than 40MB free when setting the preferred size to 40MB. I like to allow at least 1MB of latitude between the computer's available memory and the maximum size assigned to an application. If you have more available RAM, then by all means try to allocate more memory to Acrobat. The preceding is only a guideline for the most conservative assignment with limited hardware memory.

Hard disk space

The other memory issue of concern is the amount of free hard drive space after you assign virtual memory. Whether virtual memory is assigned or not, you do need ample space for creating scans in Acrobat. When you scan an image with Acrobat Scan, the file is saved to your hard drive in PDF form. When you then invoke Acrobat Capture to recognize text, Capture will require some working space on your hard drive. The average amount of required space will be approximately three times the file size. Hence, if your scan is 5MB, 15MB of free space will be required. If you intend to scan with resolutions of 300 dpi, you'll need to compensate for larger image sizes. For almost all circumstances, as a minimum, you need at least 15MB of free hard disk space.

Windows memory requirements

Adobe recommends a Pentium-class processor and 64MB of RAM for Windows 95, 98, Windows NT, and Windows 2000 of system memory. Application memory requirements in Windows are similar to those discussed for the Macintosh. Windows users don't need to be concerned with assigning memory to specific applications, but those users do need to work with allocating virtual memory to foreground applications of which the open application will take advantage.

Assessing memory

You probably know how much RAM you currently have installed on your own personal computer. If you're working on an office system or shared computer, you may not be aware of how much RAM is installed. In Windows 95, 98, 2000, or NT, by default, your system will be named My Computer. If the name has been changed, you should see the icon for your system, bearing the changed name, in the top-left corner of your screen. Right-click the icon and select Properties from the pop-up menu. The System Properties dialog box appears, as shown in Figure 16-4.

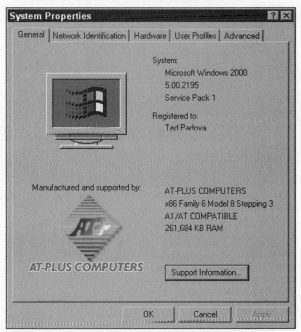

Figure 16-4: Right-click the computer hard drive to open a pop-up menu. Select Properties from the menu to open the System Properties dialog box where the amount of memory is displayed.

You should see a view similar to the one displayed in Figure 16-4. In the bottom of the dialog box, note the total amount of installed RAM on the computer. You should have at least 64MB of RAM installed and preferably 128MB. If you're running Windows 2000, anything less than 128MB will be a problem when running Acrobat and Scan.

Virtual memory

Virtual memory is adjusted by clicking the Performance tab in the System Properties dialog box or the Performance Options dialog box accessed through the Advanced options in Windows 2000. Notice the item identified as Virtual Memory and the button to the right-labeled Change for System Properties as might be viewed in Windows NT (see Figure 16-5). In Figure 16-6, the Performance Options are displayed from Windows 2000.

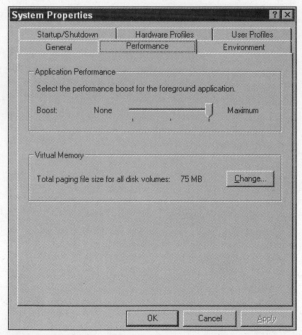

Figure 16-5: For virtual memory configurations in Windows NT, click the Performance tab in the System Properties dialog box and then click the Change button to assign a different amount of virtual memory.

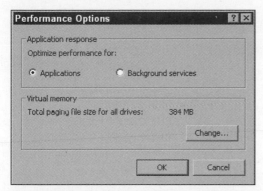

Figure 16-6: For virtual memory configurations in Windows 2000, click the Performance Options in the Advanced tab and then click the Change button in the Performance Options dialog box.

If you have multiple drives or partitions, you can assign a virtual memory space to any of the drives or partitions. In the example shown in Figure 16-7, two drives appear in the dialog box when the Change button was selected. To change the virtual memory, select the drive for the virtual memory space and enter a value in the Initial Size (MB) field. For the Maximum Size (MB) field, enter a higher value. When the values have been entered, click the Set button in the Virtual Memory dialog box.

Allocating memory to Acrobat

The Performance settings also include an adjustment for application performance. You'll see a slider with adjustments ranging from None to Maximum in Windows NT, and in Windows 2000, you'll see a radio button for Applications. These settings apply to any software loaded in Windows. Background tasks take secondary position over the foreground application. If you move the slider to the far right, the foreground application will take advantage of all the memory Windows can provide it. On Windows 2000, be certain the Applications radio button is selected. When working in Acrobat and Acrobat Scan, you should keep the performance boost for the foreground application to a maximum if you are using only the minimum memory requirements. For those who have 128MB of RAM or more, you won't need to bother with changing virtual memory.

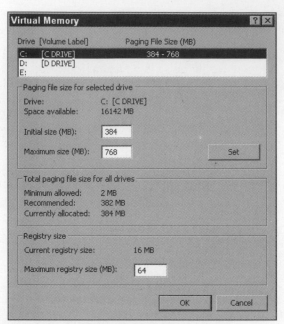

Figure 16-7: Changing virtual memory in Windows 2000 is handled in the Virtual Memory dialog box, which is accessed by clicking the Change button in the Performance Options dialog box.

Hard disk space

Hard drive free space will be of equal concern to Windows users as it is Macintosh users. To determine how much free space you have on your hard drive(s), select the System Properties again. You should see the available drive(s). If you have only one hard drive and a single partition, only one drive letter will appear. Note the area designated Free Space. Be certain you have enough free working space available on your hard drive. Like the Macintosh users, you'll need 15MB of free hard disk space as a minimum.

Using Acrobat Scan

When you perform a scan with Acrobat Scan, the scanned image appears as a PDF document in Acrobat. You can choose to leave the scan as an image and save it as a PDF file. However, to do nothing more than scan images with Acrobat Scan would be less efficient than scanning images in Photoshop and saving the Photoshop image as a PDF file. Acrobat Scan is only half of the equation related to scanning in Acrobat. The real power of using Acrobat for scanning images lies in its capability to convert all scanned text into readable and searchable text with Acrobat Capture. Raw image files with no text are referred to in Acrobat terms as PDF Image Only files. When you distill documents with Acrobat Distiller or capture scanned pages with the Capture plug-in, the files contain text that can be indexed, searched, and selected. These files are known in Acrobat terms as PDF Normal documents. When Acrobat Scan is used to import a scan into Acrobat, the file will be a PDF Image Only document.

Scanning images

After you verify proper configuration for both your scanner and computer hardware and prepare your document, the rest of the scanning process is easy. To scan an image with Acrobat Scan, choose File ⇨ Import ⇨ Scan. The Acrobat Scan Plug-in dialog box discussed earlier will appear. Select the proper Device and format choices from the pop-up menus. Make a decision for opening the file in a new document window or appending it to an existing file.

Acrobat Scan opens the scanner plug-in from your device manufacturer. You should have a clear understanding of the various options available in the scanning software for adjustments made before scanning images. If you have contrast and brightness adjustments in the application, you may need to perform tests on which adjustments work well when scanning for text recognition. Typically, sharp contrast will always be a criterion when scanning for optical character recognition. One scanner I use on my Macintosh is a LaCie Silver Scanner IV. When the Scan button is selected in the Acrobat Scan Plug-in dialog box, my Silver Scanner software appears, as shown in Figure 16-8. From this window I make changes for image resolution, color mode, and preview selections. Brightness controls are made from a menu appearing when the Silver Scanner software is opened.

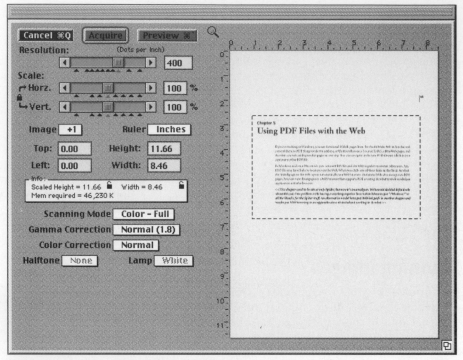

Figure 16-8: From this window, I make changes for image resolution, color mode, and preview selections when using the Silver Scanner IV.

On Windows, I have a low end Agfa SnapScan 1212 installed on my PC. The software is a bit less sophisticated than the Silver Scanner software, but does provide some options for contrast and brightness controls, as shown in Figure 16-9.

When adjustments are made in the scanning software, click a preview button if your scanning software supports a preview. Examine the alignment and contrast. Adjust the margins for the scan area and click the appropriate button to begin scanning. When the scanning is completed, the Acrobat Scan Plug-in dialog box appears enabling you to continue scanning, as shown in Figure 16-10. You can choose to replace the source material with another page and continue scanning or click the Done button to terminate scanning. If Next is selected, your scanner software dialog box reappears. You can change resolutions, create another preview, and adjust brightness before continuing.

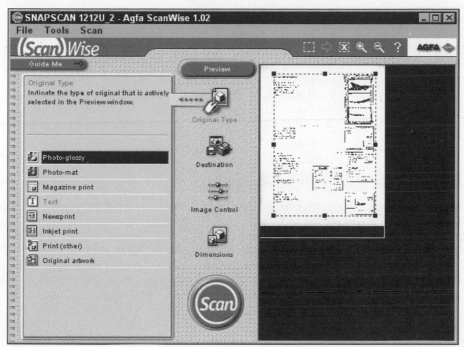

Figure 16-9: The Agfa SnapScan 1212 is a low end CIS scanner. The software provides brightness controls that help produce good scans for OCR recognition with Acrobat Capture.

Figure 16-10: After completing a scan, Acrobat opens the Acrobat Scan Plug-in dialog box, prompting you to either continue or terminate scanning.

After you finish scanning, click the Done button in the second dialog box. If you scanned several pages, they will appear in the same document. After you have the scan imported as a PDF Image Only file, you can use Acrobat Capture to convert the scan to a PDF Normal image or Original Image with Hidden Text. Both of these terms will be explained in the next chapter.

Workflow Solutions

Scanning individual pages for limited use can easily be handled by the methods described previously in this chapter. As you scan documents with the methods thus far explained, you need to attend to feeding papers under the scanner lid and clicking the Next button after each individual scan. If large numbers of papers need to be converted to digital content, then you'll probably want to explore other solutions. Depending on how much money you want to spend there are a few options available to you.

Automatic document feeders

Some scanners can accommodate automatic document feeders. If your workflow demands scanning volumes of papers, you'll be much advantaged in acquiring a good scanner with an automatic document feeder. When scanning with Acrobat Scan, the scanned pages will successively be appended to the PDF. Therefore, you can leave a stack of papers in the scanner feeder and leave it unattended. Scanning can be performed automatically overnight. When you return to your computer, the PDF file would be ready for saving and have the text converted with Acrobat Capture. The only down side to this operation is if your computer crashes, you'll loose everything because Acrobat won't save your PDF on the fly as new pages are appended.

A more expensive solution, but not out of the question for workflows needing automated means of capturing pages, is to purchase the Adobe stand-alone product Adobe Acrobat Capture. Combined with a scanner and document feeder, the conversion of scanned images to text is handled in one single operation. The cost of adding the stand-alone Capture product is $699 U.S. as of this writing.

Batch sequencing

If an automatic document feeder is not in your office, you can leave the task of converting pages with Acrobat Capture to semi-attended operation. To do so, you'll need a multi-page PDF file in order to make it all worthwhile. If there are multiple scanners at your workplace, files can be scanned as individual pages in either PDF format or any of the other Acrobat acceptable image formats discussed back in Chapter 4. The most common formats would be in either PDF or TIFF. If scanning through a Photoshop plug-in, users of Photoshop 4.0 and above can save in PDF format. Dedicated scanner software without the use of Photoshop can most often save in the TIFF format.

Assuming that you have many individual PDF or TIFF pages, you'll want to have each page appended in a single PDF document. When a single file is used, you'll still need to be at the computer to click the Next button, but you won't need to Open and Save files independently. To get all those independent files into a single PDF, you'll want to use one of the new batch sequence commands by Acrobat. To gain more understanding of using a batch sequence to combine individual pages into a single PDF file, look at the steps used to produce the file.

STEPS: Creating a Batch Sequence for Appending Pages in a PDF

1. **Copy all your image files to be appended to a single folder.** The file types can be Acrobat PDF, TIFF, or other image formats that can be recognized by Acrobat when using the Open as PDF command.

2. **Create an output folder.** Although not necessary, it would be best to create a folder on your hard drive where the new PDF will be saved. If something goes awry with the batch sequence and a file is not produced, you'll immediately notice when observing a folder with no contents.

3. **Name a new sequence.** Choose File ➪ Batch Processing ➪ Edit Batch Sequences. The Batch Sequences dialog box will appear where the sequence options can be determined. The first task is to click the New Sequence button to open the Name Sequence dialog box, as shown in Figure 16-11. Provide a name and click OK.

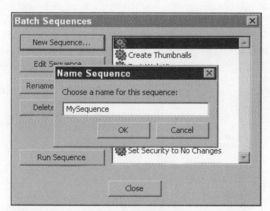

Figure 16-11: In the Batch Sequences dialog box, click the New Sequence button to open the Name Sequence dialog box.

4. **Add a sequence.** In the Batch Edit Sequence for the new sequence name that you provided, click the Select Commands button. The Edit Sequence dialog box opens, as shown in Figure 16-12. Scroll the list of commands and find the Insert Pages item. Click the Add button to add it to your new sequence.

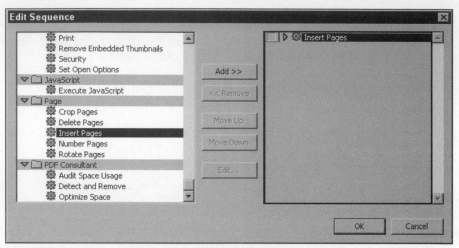

Figure 16-12: In the Edit Sequence dialog box, select the sequence to be used in your batch and click the Add button to add it to your new sequence.

5. **Select the files to be processed by the sequence command(s).** When the sequence appears on the right side of the Edit Sequence dialog box, double-click the sequence name. In this example, I added Insert Pages and double-clicked the item. A navigation dialog box opens. Navigate to the folder where you saved your files and select all of them, as shown in Figure 16-13. Click the Select button and the Insert Pages dialog box appears.

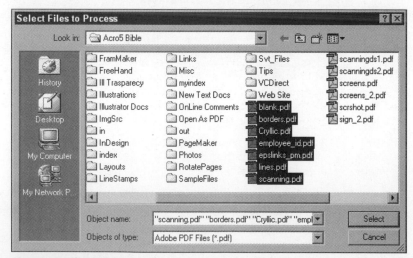

Figure 16-13: Select the files to be processed by the sequence command and click the Select button.

6. **Select the insert pages attributes.** Pages can be inserted before or after current pages, the last page, first page, or within a page range. From the pull-down menu, select After and click the Last button, as shown in Figure 16-14. Click OK when the settings have been made. You are returned to the Edit Sequence dialog box. Click OK again and you are returned to the Batch Edit Sequence dialog box.

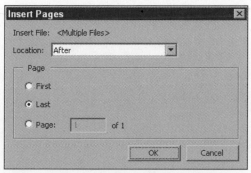

Figure 16-14: The Insert Pages attributes have been set up to insert pages after the last page in the document. Each page appended is added at the end of the file.

7. **Select a destination folder for the new file.** When returned to the Batch Edit Sequence dialog box, select Specific Folder from the Select output location pop-up menu. The Choose button becomes active when the choice has been made, as shown in Figure 16-15. Click the Choose button and navigate to the folder that you created for the output.

8. **Run the Sequence.** When you leave the Batch Edit Sequence dialog box by clicking OK, the Batch Sequences dialog box appears. In the dialog box is a button for Run Sequence. Click the button to run the new batch command and the Run Sequence Confirmation dialog box appears. Click OK in this dialog box and the sequence will run.

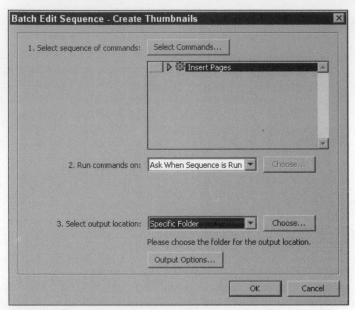

Figure 16-15: Select Specific Folder from the pull-down menu for Select output location. The Choose button becomes active enabling you to select it and assign the folder where the new file will be saved.

A final confirmation dialog box will appear. In this dialog box, click OK, and a progress bar will display the progress as the command is executed. In this particular example, all files originally selected will be appended to the first PDF file in the selected group.

By using a batch command to add all the pages together in a single PDF document you can acquire multiple files from multiple users scanning pages. The conversion of the image files to text can be processed on a single file or several files with multiple pages on different computers. Attended operation after each page is scanned is needed. However, you can easily sit at your desk and click the Next button while performing other business without thinking about saving and opening independent files. If you purchase Acrobat Capture, the conversion of image files to test can be performed automatically on the entire document and left to work overnight unattended.

Using Acrobat Scan with Digital Cameras

Acrobat Scan can also be used with digital cameras. In order to acquire images from a digital camera, you must have an acceptable TWAIN driver. If you don't have one on your camera's installation CD-ROM, you'll need to visit the manufacturer's Web site. With a proper TWAIN driver installed, choose File ➪ Import ➪ Scan. The camera can be attached by cable to your computer or from a device that supports the memory cards used by your camera.

Images from digital cameras are typically saved in JPEG format and can be imported and converted to PDF from within Acrobat. In many cases you'll probably opt for other methods of handling digital camera images, especially when any editing needs to be performed on the images. Acrobat can provide a simple solution by acquiring the image and subsequently using the Send Mail command to attach your PDF to an e-mail message. This makes for a single step operation of acquiring the image and sending it off to your colleagues, friends, or family.

With regard to Acrobat Capture, you can use a digital camera, some controlled lighting, and a copy stand to photograph paper documents. With a little ingenuity and some supplies purchased at a home improvement center, you can create a work setup where photographing papers with a digital camera will move along much faster than scanning them. Acrobat Scan can be used to acquire the images, or the files can be appended to a single PDF document using the steps noted above and subsequently captured with Acrobat Capture.

Summary

✦ Acrobat Scan uses ISIS software for Windows or TWAIN software for either Macintosh or Windows. ISIS software is distributed on the Acrobat Installer CD-ROM, and TWAIN software is acquired from a scanner manufacturer.

✦ When preparing documents for scanning in Acrobat, proper preparation of the scanner and documents will improve the quality of the scans. The scanner platen should be clean, the documents should be straight, and the contrast should be sharp.

✦ System memory requirements are critical when using Acrobat Scan. Be certain to allocate enough memory to the program and clear enough hard drive space to accommodate scans.

✦ When scanning images in Acrobat, use the scanning software to establish resolution, image mode, and brightness controls before scanning. Test your results thoroughly to create a formula that works well for the type of documents that you scan.

✦ Workflow automation can be greatly improved by purchasing the Adobe stand-alone product Adobe Acrobat Capture. When using Adobe Acrobat Capture with a scanner supporting a document feeder, the scanning and capturing can be performed with unattended operation. PDF files can be assembled with a batch command to support multiple page capturing.

✦ Digital cameras are supported by the Acrobat Scan plug-in. Images can be acquired only when the proper TWAIN software has been installed.

✦   ✦   ✦

Converting Scans to Text

Using Acrobat Capture (Windows)

In the last chapter, I discussed scanning images into Acrobat. After a file is either scanned into Acrobat or opened as a PDF file by using the File ➪ Open as Adobe PDF command, the page can be converted to text through an OCR (optical character recognition) conversion. Acrobat Scan retains the data as image data. In order to convert image data to text, you need to use Acrobat Capture. Acrobat Capture is not a plug-in, but rather an executable application that you need to purchase apart from your Acrobat software. (In earlier versions of Acrobat, Paper Capture was included as part of the Acrobat suite of software. Now in Version 5.0, Acrobat Capture requires a separate purchase.)

Note   In Acrobat 4, Acrobat Capture was referred to as Paper Capture in the Tools menu and the Preferences submenu. This term was introduced to avoid confusion with Web Capture. If using Acrobat 4.0x, the Capture Server was the name of the application launched to perform the OCR conversion. If you have Acrobat 4.x and capture pages with the Capture plug-in, the capture suspects will be acknowledged in Acrobat 5.0.

Acrobat Capture requirements

Acrobat Capture requires proper installation and a few conditions must be met for it to launch and properly perform the OCR conversion. If you fail to adhere to the following requirements, the Capture Server may not launch.

✦ **Font limitations:** If the total number of installed fonts in your system exceeds 128, you will receive an error message while launching Capture. If you encounter problems with warning dialog boxes related to fonts, uninstall some fonts and try to launch Capture again.

✦ **Font requirements:** When Acrobat is installed, a number of fonts will be installed on your system. Acrobat will operate with the Base 13 fonts, Adobe Sans Serif, and Adobe Serif fonts. Acrobat Capture, however, requires additional fonts to create recognized characters during operation. If you remove any of the fonts installed with Acrobat, Capture may not be able to recognize text in the document that you attempt to capture. For Macintosh users, be certain to avoid using font management utilities for the Acrobat fonts. If you use Suitcase, MasterJuggler, or ATM Deluxe for loading and disabling fonts from a fonts folder, don't manage the Acrobat fonts with these utilities. Leave the Acrobat fonts in your System:Fonts folder. The same holds true for Windows users — leave the fonts located in the default installed directory.

✦ **Dictionaries:** Eight dictionaries are in the Capture folder for text recognition in eight different languages. U.S. English is one of the dictionaries. Additionally, a custom dictionary is accessible where words can be added for individual user needs.

Paper Capture preferences (Acrobat 4.0 users)

If you upgraded to Acrobat 5.0 and want to use the Paper Capture options in Acrobat 4.0, you can leave both applications installed on your hard drive. In this regard, you can perform OCR conversions, then open your PDFs in Acrobat 5.0 and correct all the suspected words. In Acrobat 4.0, to address preferences for Capture, choose File ➪ Preferences ➪ Paper Capture. In the Acrobat Capture Preferences dialog box, options enable you to select a supported language; the output format for the captured page; and a directory for temporary files.

✦ **Primary OCR Language:** By default, Acrobat will install multiple languages in the Capture folder. Eight different language dictionaries are included during installation. If you scan documents from any of the supported languages, select the appropriate language in the pop-up menu in the Acrobat Capture Preferences dialog box.

✦ **PDF Output Style:** You have two choices for PDF Output Style. Normal scans the text in the image, and the scanned text is converted to text characters appearing in the document when viewed in an Acrobat viewer. When you select Original Image with Hidden Text, the appearance of the scanned image does not change. Text will be supplied on a hidden layer that gives you the capability of creating indexes and performing searches. Use this option when you don't want to change a document's appearance, but you do want to be able to search the text of that document. Something on the order of a legal document or a certificate might be an example of such a document.

Tip

If you keep files as Original Image with Hidden Text as a final PDF, the file sizes will be much larger than text files converted to PDF. If only a few graphics need to remain on a page and the original text is not needed, you can reduce file sizes by eliminating the original scanned image. To do so, create a layout with the graphics you want to keep and place them in their original positions. Open the file you captured and choose File ➪ Save As ➪ Rich Text Format (RTF). After they're exported as

RTF, you can import the text and finish the layout in your application of choice. Export to PDF or print to disk and distill a PostScript file. The final size of the newly created PDFs will be much smaller.

✦ **Downsample Images:** This option enables or disables downsampling of images. When the checkbox is enabled, images are downsampled as follows:

- **Black and White:** Black-and-white images are downsampled to 200 dpi. If the line art mode was used and the scan resolution was 300 dpi, the image won't be downsampled.

- **Grayscale and Color:** These types of images are downsampled to 150 dpi. If an image was scanned as grayscale or color at a resolution of 225 or less, the image will not be downsampled.

✦ **Location for Temporary Files:** In Windows, select the directory Capture will use for temporary space while converting the PDF page(s) to one of the formats listed previously.

Custom dictionaries (Acrobat 4.0 users)

The custom dictionary resides in the Capture folder and is labeled `Custdict.spl`. To add words to the dictionary, you must have a text editor or word processor. When you attempt to open the file in a program such as Microsoft Word, a dialog box appears prompting you to identify the file format. Use Text Only as the file format option. If you can't open the file in your editor, try to use Windows WordPad or another text editor. With the file open, you should see a list of words added to the custom dictionary.

To add a word, you can place the new word in alphabetical order by placing the cursor to the right of the word preceding your new word and pressing the Return key. Enter the word and double-check the spelling. Save the file as Text Only. If you decide to edit the Custom Dictionary, always make a backup copy of the last saved version. If the new save becomes corrupted or doesn't work, reinstall the last working version of the dictionary.

 Words in the custom dictionary must be in alphabetical order and each word must be on a separate line. You need to manually find the alphabetical location and enter the word in proper order. Use a carriage return after entering the new word(s) in the alphabetical list.

Capturing a Page

After the file is scanned and preferences are established, the PDF page(s) is ready to be converted to text. When you capture a page with Acrobat Capture, the text will be converted from an image file to a rich text file. The text can be edited with the TouchUp Text tool in Acrobat, which was covered in Chapter 8. Acrobat Capture enables you to convert a single page or multiple pages during a single operation.

Capture Suspects

After Paper Capture used with Acrobat 4 or the Acrobat Capture software completes its task, the page is converted to text. However, not all text may have been recognized by Capture. To see if any words have been misunderstood, you need to look at the Capture Suspects. In Acrobat, suspect words do not appear until you choose Tools ⇨ TouchUp ⇨ Show Capture Suspects. After the command is selected, the PDF page in view is displayed with red borders to indicate suspects (see Figure 17-1). A Capture Suspect displays because Capture was not certain whether the suspected word had a match in the Capture dictionary. You can choose to accept the guess Capture provides or edit the text to correct it. All of the editing of Capture Suspects is accomplished with the TouchUp Text tool.

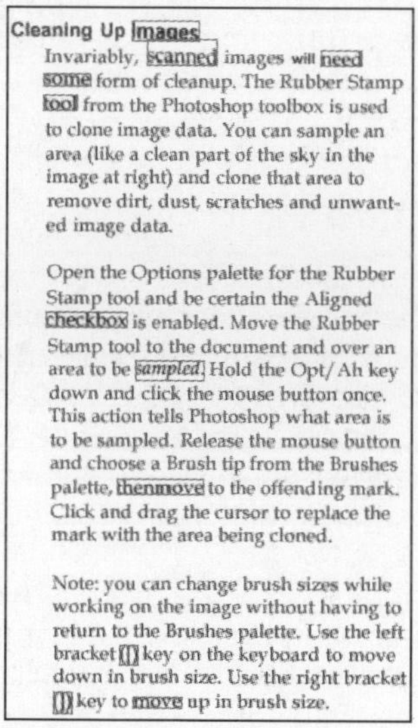

Figure 17-1: I capture a page in Acrobat and choose Tools ⇨ TouchUp ⇨ Show Capture Suspects to display all the suspected words.

When you select the first suspect with the TouchUp Text tool, a window appears, as illustrated in Figure 17-2. The window displays the original scanned text and two buttons. The buttons offer choices for Accept (TAB) and Next (Ctrl/Command + H). If you select the first option, any text you have edited will be changed, and you will be sent to the next suspect. Next leaves the currently selected suspect as it appears and moves to the next suspected word. If you edit the suspect and click Next, the edit will not be accepted and the text will return to the original suspect. To make a change, you need to edit the text and click the Accept button.

Figure 17-2: When I select Stamp and examine the text on the page, I find the text to be interpreted correctly. I click the Next button to move to the next suspect.

When you view the document and see the marked suspects, Capture only displays the items in question. Capture's interpretation of the suspect is only revealed when you select the suspect. Therefore, if a word is identified as a suspect, Capture's interpretation is not yet displayed. When a word is selected by pressing Tab or clicking the TouchUp Text tool, Capture's interpretation is revealed. What's important to note here is that you won't know how the word has been interpreted until it is selected.

You want to commit the keyboard modifiers to memory when correcting suspects. In Windows and on the Macintosh, Accept (TAB) is invoked with the Tab key. Acrobat helps you keep the key modifier in mind by indicating so in the dialog box. Next is applied with Control + H in Windows and Command + H on the Macintosh. If you select Accept, Acrobat will change the word to the suspect interpretation. If you select Next, then you assume Capture's interpretation is not correct and you want to leave the text as it was originally interpreted by Capture.

To correct the suspect, you can enter the text while the suspect is selected, or position the cursor inside the selection and press the Backspace key, or enter text from the cursor position.

If you want to develop a workflow in an office environment, you may want to have the function of scanning documents performed on several machines and use other computers to capture suspected words. Acrobat can import images that are not in PDF form. Therefore, you can scan images in software other than Photoshop and save your files in a format, such as TIFF. Acrobat can import TIFF images via the Open as Adobe PDF menu command. In addition, all the other formats acceptable to Acrobat can likewise be opened, as I explained in Chapter 4. After they're scanned, you can set up workstations or servers to import images and save them as PDF files. The PDF files can be routed to workstations capturing pages. In this scenario, you won't need to purchase Acrobat for all your computers, and the time saved will be significant.

Using Paper Capture Online

If your workflow requires only scanning a few pages periodically for text conversion, you have another alternative for capturing the page and converting the scan to text. When you choose Tools ➪ Paper Capture Online, your Web browser launches and the Adobe Create Adobe PDF Online Web page becomes the selected URL. From this Web page, you can follow instructions to upload scanned images and have Adobe Systems perform the capture. When the file is returned to you, you can view the capture suspects and edit them in the same manner as described earlier.

For Macintosh users, the Paper Capture Online service is currently your only alternative. Because Acrobat Capture 3.0 is only available for Windows, you don't have the option to purchase the stand-alone application. If you upgraded from Acrobat 4.0 to Acrobat 5.0, you can use the Paper Capture features in Acrobat 4.0.

Paper Capture Online can be tested by uploading files and taking advantage of the free trial offered by Adobe. Three files can be used for the trial. After the trial period, you can subscribe to the online service for a monthly or annual fee.

Summary

✦ Acrobat Capture is a stand-alone application for optical character recognition used for converting scanned images into editable text.

✦ Text can be captured and saved as a PDF Normal image, which will modify the text appearance of the original scan. Text can be captured and saved using the Original Image with Hidden Text option, which preserves the scan appearance and contains a text layer independent of the scan. The latter format can be used where document integrity is necessary for legal and archival purposes.

✦ Capture Suspects are used to correct interpretation problems when Paper Capture does not properly identify a word. Text editing is performed with the TouchUp Text tool. When changes to text are made, the Tab key is used to accept changes and move on to the next suspect.

✦ Paper Capture Online is a Web hosted service provided by Adobe Systems to offer low cost optical character recognition services.

✦   ✦   ✦

Advanced Acrobat Applications

Printing and Digital Prepress

Printing PDF Files

One of the features that has traditionally been underdeveloped in Acrobat is printing. Compared to high-end design applications, Acrobat has not offered us much for printing files with any degree of sophistication. Other than desktop printing, we have had to rely on third-party applications or workarounds. Now in Version 5.0, we are not quite there, but the newest release has implemented many new printing features.

To understand how to print PDF files, we need to look at the Acrobat Print dialog box. Like any other application, printing is accessed by choosing File ➪ Print or by clicking the Print tool in the Acrobat Command bar. When the Print dialog box opens, you'll immediately notice all the new changes implemented with Acrobat printing as shown in Figure 18-1 (Windows) and Figure 18-2 (Macintosh).

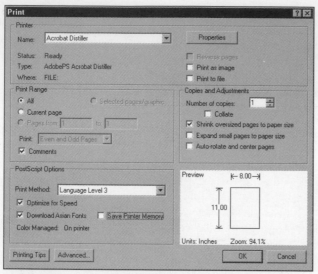

Figure 18-1: The Print dialog box in Acrobat 5.0 offers many new printing controls. In Windows, all printing features are accessed in a single dialog box.

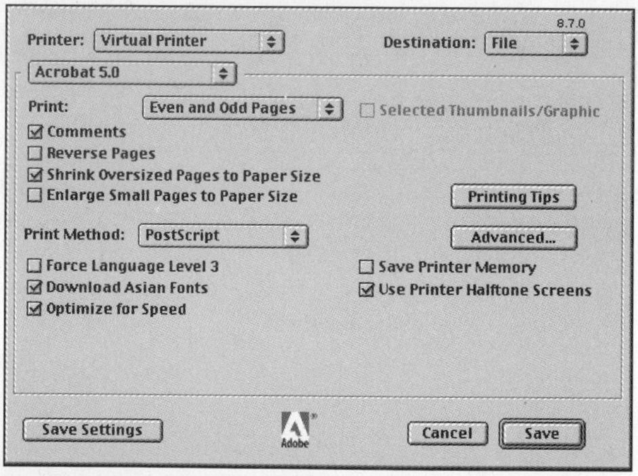

Figure 18-2: The Macintosh Print dialog box contains similar features as Windows. The additional items not appearing in the Print dialog box are contained in other dialog boxes accessed through the printer driver.

Among the many options that you have available in the Print dialog box include the following:

✦ **Name (Windows)/Printer (Macintosh):** From the pull-down menu, all installed printers appear.

✦ **Properties (Windows):** Specific to each printer are properties that enable you to choose various page sizes, font handling, and page orientation.

✦ **Destination (Macintosh):** The destination choices are either Printer or File. When printing to devices, be certain to choose Printer.

✦ **Reverse pages (Windows):** Pages can be printed from last to first when the checkbox is enabled. If you want to print two-sided copy on laser printers, you can print all odd pages front to back, and then print even pages back to front with the Reverse pages checkbox enabled. For Reverse Pages on Macintosh, select Acrobat 5.0 from the pull-down menu directly below the Printer pull-down menu. Reverse Pages appears as a checkbox below the Print item in the dialog box.

✦ **Print as image (Windows)/Print Method (Macintosh):** In Windows, the option is a checkbox directly below the Reverse Pages checkbox. On Macintosh, select the pull-down menu for Print Method. Print as Image prints the file as a bitmap. You can use this option if you experience printing problems when printing the alternate setting of PostScript. If using a PostScript printer, the file will often print with poor text quality and strong anti-aliased effects.

✦ **Print to file:** Leave this option disabled. You should have your printer online and print the PDF directly to the device. Printing to file would be redundant, as you could download the original PostScript file directly to your printer before the file is distilled. On Macintosh, the File option is selected from the pull-down menu for Destination.

✦ **Print Range (Windows):** The range of pages is specified in the Print dialog box in Windows. On the Macintosh, the page range is determined in the General settings of the Printer driver accessed by selecting the pull-down menu below the Printer item described previously.

✦ **Print (Even and Odd Pages):** From the pull-down menu you can select from Even, Odd, or Even and Odd pages.

✦ **Selected pages/graphic (Windows); Selected Thumbnails/Graphic (Macintosh):** This checkbox handles two different items. You can select Thumbnails in either contiguous groups or non-contiguous groups (Control/Command + Click to select non-contiguous pages) and print the selected pages. If you use the Graphics Select tool, you can print the selected image area while ignoring all data outside the selection.

✦ **Comments:** For printing files as proofs for imaging, deselect the option to print annotations. If Comments is selected, comment notes will print. Deselecting Comments in the Print dialog box, but enabling Print Comment Pop-ups in the General Preferences dialog box will print the comment icons.

✦ **Number of Copies:** In Windows, you can specify the number of copies to print in the Print dialog box. On the Macintosh, the number of copies is determined in the General dialog box.

✦ **Collate:** When using double-sided printing, collate prints pages in proper order. This option for Macintosh is in the General dialog box.

✦ **Shrink oversized pages to paper size:** PDF files can accommodate many different page sizes in the same document. When checked, this option ensures that all pages will be printed to the paper size without clipping. Oversized pages are shrunk to fit the page.

✦ **Expand small pages to paper size:** Any pages smaller than other pages in a document will be upsized to fit the printed page. If using smaller pages with raster images, the image quality will suffer as the page size is enlarged if resolution is not sufficient for the output size.

✦ **Auto-rotate and center pages (Windows):** If the document contains Landscape and Portrait pages, all pages will print properly when the checkbox is enabled. This is a rare feature with other applications software. Acrobat will compensate for page orientation on the fly as pages are printed.

✦ **Print Method (Windows):** Some devices may not offer options for the print method. If a PostScript printer is used, Acrobat may automatically choose the PostScript method for your printer. If you have a PostScript 3 printer, you may have a choice for selecting PostScript Level 2 or PostScript 3. If the choice is made available, choose the method corresponding to the level of your printer.

✦ **Print Method (Macintosh):** This option may be a bit confusing when comparing the two platforms. Print Method for the Macintosh was mentioned previously when the Print as Image item was discussed. For the PostScript options on the Macintosh, use the Page Setup dialog box from the File menu before accessing the Print dialog box. In the Page Setup dialog box, select PostScript Options from the pull-down menu to open a dialog box, as shown in Figure 18-3. The PostScript Options dialog box offers other settings that will be important to you when printing to PostScript devices. Be certain to uncheck the checkboxes for the first three items listed under Image & Text. These checkboxes will anti-alias text and graphics and place tiny pixels unnecessarily around all data elements. Printing will take longer and quality may suffer when printing to PostScript devices if these items are enabled.

✦ **Download Asian Fonts:** If Asian fonts are not installed on your printer and the fonts are not embedded in the PDF, you need to check this option when using character sets from Far East languages. If you do not have the fonts installed on the printer and fonts are not embedded, font substitution will be used.

✦ **Save Printer Memory:** When checked, all fonts on a given page will be downloaded to the printer before the document begins printing. Printer memory is actually conserved by handling font downloading in this manner. If left unchecked, the print job may be smaller, but the amount of memory needed to image the print may be greater.

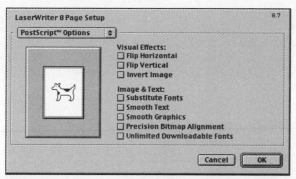

Figure 18-3: On the Macintosh, deselect the checkboxes for the first three items under the Image & Text category. Printing to PostScript devices is more efficient and saves print time.

✦ **Use Printer Halftone Screens (Macintosh):** If the PostScript file has been prepared with a higher screening than accommodated by the printer, and the distillation included the PostScript file screening, be certain to enable this option with laser printers. If the screening is higher than can be accommodated by the device, the images will appear muddy. If using continuous tone printers, such as desktop color devices, this option will have no effect whether enabled or not.

✦ **Preview (Windows):** A thumbnail preview is displayed in the Print dialog box. The current page size will be shown according to the page size selected from the Properties dialog box.

Tip

If you have a low-end PostScript printer that has limited RAM, PostScript errors may be encountered when too many fonts are downloaded to the printer during printing. If enabling the Save Printer Memory checkbox does not eliminate printing problems, try printing fewer pages when printing the file. If the problem persists, try printing one page at a time. Downloading fewer fonts to the printer may eliminate a RAM overload.

Printing tips

From the Print dialog box, the Printing Tips button in the Print dialog box launches your Web browser and connects you to the Adobe Web site and opens a page where printing issues are listed. You can find print tips and how to resolve problems by browsing the Web pages. The information is updated regularly, so be certain to check the Web site periodically before placing a tech call. Chances are, some problems you experience in printing PDFs will be contained within these Web pages.

Advanced options

Another button for opening a dialog box for advanced settings is contained in the Print dialog box. Click the Advanced button to open the Print Settings dialog box. Figure 18-4 shows the Print Settings dialog box for Windows and Figure 18-5 shows the same dialog box for the Macintosh.

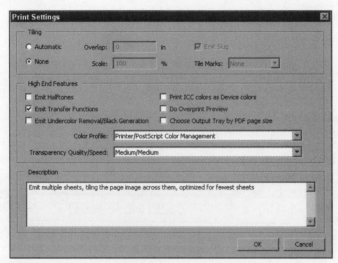

Figure 18-4: The Print Settings dialog box in Windows offers additional features for printing PDFs.

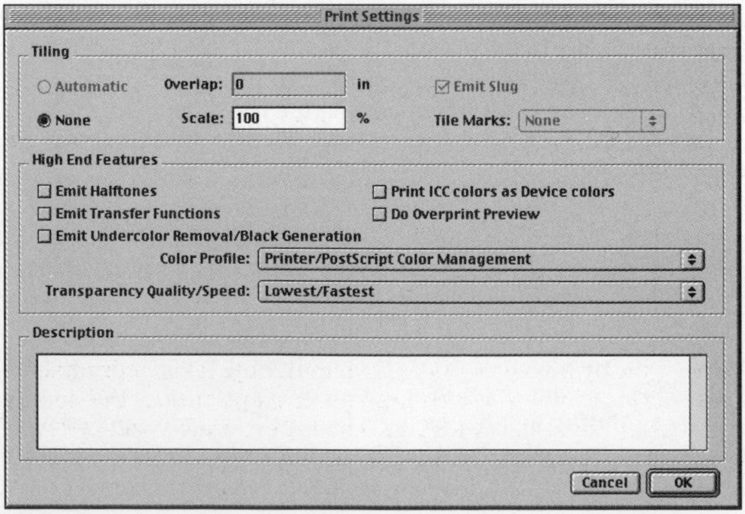

Figure 18-5: The Macintosh Print Settings dialog box offers the same options as found in Windows.

✦ **Tiling:** If printing page sizes larger than can be accommodated by your printer, you can print actual size pages by tiling them. If Automatic is selected, Acrobat will print the pages with as much data as can be handled on each tiled page. You can specify the amount of overlap and a scaling value. Each page will be printed with a slug outside the tile marks. If you don't want the slug printed, enable the checkbox. If tile marks are to be excluded, select None from the pull-down menu options.

✦ **Emit Halftones:** If halftone frequencies are embedded in the PDF, Emit Halftones will eliminate them and print with a frequency controlled at the printer. High-end devices can have frequencies controlled through printer default settings.

✦ **Emit Transfer Functions:** If you set up custom transfer functions in Photoshop and embed them in the Photoshop file, Emit Transfer Functions will eliminate them if preserved in the PDF.

✦ **Emit Undercolor Removal/Black Generation:** Likewise, any undercolor removal settings contained in Photoshop images will be eliminated when the checkbox is enabled.

✦ **Print ICC colors as Device colors:** When enabled, ICC profiles will not be sent to the printer. The color profiles from the printer for grays, RGB (red, green, black), and CMYK (cyan, magenta, yellow, black) will be used.

✦ **Do Overprint Preview:** A simulated color blending for composite color prints will display overprint results. This is a handy feature to preview before sending the file off for color separations. When previewing overprints, the print time will increase.

✦ **Choose Output Tray by PDF page size (Windows):** Paper sizes will be determined from the page size of the PDF file and not the paper size selected in the Properties dialog box (Page Setup on a Mac). This option only works with printers that have multiple paper trays.

✦ **Color Profile:** Options from a pull-down menu enable you to select color profiles installed on your system. When choosing a profile, the color space from the profile information will be used for the print job and override the device profile. Two other options exist in addition to profiles installed on your computer. The top item in the pull-down menu is Same As Source (No Color Management). If this selection is made, no color management system will be used. The second option is Printer/PostScript Color Management. When selected, this option will disregard the ICC profiles installed on your computer and manage the color at the printer's RIP.

✦ **Transparency Quality/Speed:** When transparent objects are contained in the PDF, printing quality can be selected from several options. As the quality increases, the print time will slow down. The lowest quality will rasterize the file and simulate all transparent effects. The highest quality will maintain all vector objects and transparent appearances, but the print time will take much longer.

✦ **Description:** The open field box at the bottom of the dialog box is a help window. As you select items in the Print Settings dialog box, the window contents will change to display a description of the selected item. When selecting the previous Transparency item, for example, each choice made from the pull-down menu will tell you what to expect from the respective choices.

Printing to Desktop Devices

Desktop printing devices can be either PostScript or non-PostScript printers. Many low-end desktop color printers do not ship with a PostScript interpreter. The color printers you can purchase for $600 or less will typically not be PostScript printers. Many of these printers can be outfitted with a software PostScript raster image processor (RIP). If you haven't purchased a PostScript RIP for a desktop color printer, you can often print PDF documents without the use of PostScript. There are many different models of non-PostScript printers, and each model ships with a different printer driver. It is important to review the printer documentation to understand the different options available in both the Print Setup/Page Setup and Print dialog boxes. Depending on the printing device and software shipped with the printer, choices for various print options will vary significantly.

Printing to non-PostScript devices

Desktop color printers are continuous tone devices, so that you need not worry about screening when printing the PDF. Other choices may be available for using device profiles and special attributes for ink choices, page sizes, and dithering. If the printer driver permits choices for the print method, you may have a selection to choose PostScript or Print as Image. If the PostScript method does not produce the print, try using the Print as Image method. Some errors generated while printing a PDF can be overcome by one or more of the following:

✦ **Print one page at a time:** In a multi-page PDF file, try printing one page at a time. If the print buffer gets overloaded, you may experience problems.

✦ **Disable Shrink Oversized Pages to Paper Size:** If Shrink Oversized Pages to Page Size is enabled, it will require more processing time to reduce the image size. Try turning this option off when printing. To print oversized pages, you can crop the pages to your output size in Acrobat before printing or use the Graphics Select tool to select an area to print.

✦ **Use fewer fonts in the native file:** Font downloads and substitutions can overload the printer memory. If you experience problems with multiple fonts, try reducing the number of fonts in the authoring application and redistill the file.

✦ **Downsample images:** Be certain to sample images at optimum sizes for the device. Because desktop printers are continuous tone, you can't follow rules for image sizes related to frequencies. Most color desktop printers will have a recommended file resolution to be used. Downsample images to the recommended sizes or lower when printing PDF files.

If using a desktop color printer for proofing files to be printed on high-end devices, print a PostScript file from your authoring application to disk. Use Distiller's JobOptions and downsample to levels appropriate for your desktop color printer. If the proof looks right, redistill the same PostScript file with JobOptions recommended by your service center.

✦ **Rasterize the PDF in Photoshop:** If PostScript is difficult to print, you can rasterize the PDF in Photoshop. Desktop color printers print raster images usually without a problem. Open the PDF in Photoshop and rasterize to the image resolution optimized for the printer.

✦ **Convert images to the proper color mode:** Some desktop color printers may prefer RGB images as opposed to CMYK. If the printer uses RGB, save the Photoshop files as RGB TIFFs and distill the PostScript file. If the same document is to be printed at an imaging center, two files will need to be produced. Be certain the high-end output PDF file uses CMYK images from the authoring application.

Regardless of the device used, you'll need to become familiar with the driver software and run some tests. Also, if you have an Internet connection, be certain to visit the Web site for your printer manufacturer. Many drivers are updated regularly, and the latest printer driver can often be downloaded from the manufacturer's Web site.

Printing to PostScript devices

Most laser printers are PostScript printers. Some of the printing problems experienced with the non-PostScript printers can often be overcome by printing to a PostScript device. This is not necessarily always true and sometimes you may have to deal with a few workarounds. But, it is safe to say that more often than not, you'll have fewer problems with PostScript than non-PostScript printing.

If you have a desktop color printer, you may have at least one excellent option available as a low cost solution for using a PostScript RIP with your printer. Adobe PressReady is a marvelous product that offers an incredibly accurate means for proofing color for high-end output. In addition to the color proofing, you get a PostScript 3 software RIP. I say you may have an option because not all printers are supported. You need to check the Adobe Web site to see if PressReady supports your printer. As of this writing, the product has a street value of only $99. The downside regarding PressReady is that Adobe has made announcements for no further development of the product. We may soon see PressReady abandoned. If you can get your hands on a copy, it will be worth the money for as long as you can use it.

If you've suffered from anti-aliased edges on type and vector objects, Adobe PressReady will solve printing problems when using non-PostScript color printers. Smooth tones and elimination of dithering of vector objects and gradients will be surprising if you haven't used this product.

Printing to High-end Devices

When files are printed to imaging devices at service centers, the controls for page sizes, screening, rotations, emulsion, and other such attributes require the use of a PostScript Printer Description (PPD) file. Acrobat does not permit PPD selection in the Print dialog box. Therefore, high-end imaging requires printing through other means. You have two choices when PPD selection is required. Either export the PDF as an EPS file that ultimately will be printed from another program, or use a third-party plug-in to print from within Acrobat.

Exporting EPS files

Acrobat offers an option to create an EPS file from within the application. EPS files exported from Acrobat will appear as though they were created in an EPS authoring application, such as Adobe Illustrator or Macromedia FreeHand. The exported file will contain all the file attributes of the PDF, including embedded fonts and image links. To export an EPS file from Acrobat, choose File ➪ Save As and then select Encapsulated PostScript from the Save as type (Windows) or Format (Macintosh) pull-down menu. Click the Settings button in the Save As dialog box to open the Encapsulated PostScript dialog box, as shown in Figure 18-6.

Attribute choices are made for language level and the content of the EPS file. Among the choices are font embedding, screening, and color handling. Make all the necessary choices in this dialog box and click OK. When the file is exported, you can choose to have all the pages saved as EPS files as per the page ranges selected in the Encapsulated PostScript dialog box. If multiple pages are saved as EPS, each page will be saved as a separate file.

Tip   Whereas printing PostScript files are best handled by using binary encoding and PostScript Level 2, in almost all cases, exporting EPS files will require ASCII and PostScript Level I. Use these settings as a default when placing EPS files in other applications. Macintosh users who want to port EPS files across platforms should enable TIFF for the preview option in the Encapsulated PostScript dialog box. If PICT previews are used across platforms, the file will appear as a gray box.

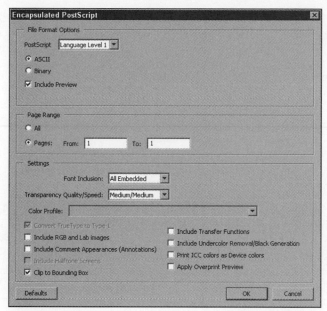

Figure 18-6: The Encapsulated PostScript settings offer attribute choices for the data to be contained in the EPS file.

The Include Halftone Screens option preserve the halftone screen only if it was embedded in the PDF file. If the Include Halftone Screen option is disabled, screening can be controlled in the application from which the resultant EPS is printed.

The EPS file created from exporting to EPS will appear as though you created it from an illustration program. The file will print, separate, and accept the print specifications entered from the program that ultimately prints the file. You can choose to use a layout, illustration, or color-separating program for printing.

Several advantages exist when printing EPS files from a layout application. You can specify printer type and PPD, image output resolution, paper sizes, and halftone frequencies. When all the printing attributes are established, you can print the file to any device where these controls are necessary.

Tip

If you export multiple page EPS files and need perfect registration when separating them in other applications, you can use features in programs that will place one page exactly in the same position as other pages. For QuarkXPress, create a master page and create a picture box around the page sufficient enough to accommodate bleeds if necessary. On each page, use the same master and the Get Picture command. Press Control/Command + M to center the image. In programs, such as PageMaker and InDesign, place the first image on a page. Duplicate the page, select the graphic and choose File ➪ Place. In the Place dialog box, select Replace Existing Image or Replace Selected Item. The new image placement will be perfectly registered in all of the programs.

Plug-ins supporting printing

Third-party manufacturers have special add-on software that makes many printing attributes available without your needing to export a file as EPS. A plug-in designed for high-end output of PDF files is Crackerjack from Lantana Research Corporation. More information about Crackerjack can be obtained from the Lantana Web site at www.lantanarips.com.

Crackerjack performs all the tasks necessary for printing PDFs directly from within Acrobat. Crackerjack is a plug-in that loads when Acrobat is launched and becomes available through a menu command. When accessing the plug-in, a Print dialog box will appear, enabling you to select a PPD and perform all the print selections needed for imaging.

Another solution is Adobe InProduction. InProduction offers all the printing control that you need for printing color separations and output to high-end devices. One nice feature available with InProduction is remapping color. If a file contains two different spot colors that should be printed on the same plate, InProduction provides a means of remapping one color to another to correctly separate the file.

Printing to PostScript 3 devices

One of the great benefits of PDF and PostScript 3 is direct imaging of PDF files. Rather than working through the PostScript interpreter, PDFs can be passed through the interpreter directly to a PostScript 3 RIP. These RIPs are not exclusively found at imaging centers. Many new desktop models are being introduced with PostScript 3. In order to submit a PDF to a PostScript 3 RIP, the device manufacturer needs to supply a utility for sending the PDF to the RIP or support the delivery of PDF files to hot folders.

The ability to accept PDFs directly at the RIP requires an updated interpreter. Adobe has been involved in updating interpreters for PostScript RIPs for some time, but not all interpreters have been upgraded to accept either PDF Version 1.3 or 1.4. If your RIP crashes when PDFs are sent directly to the RIP, it's most likely due to a problem with the interpreter. You can overcome the problem by distilling the file with Acrobat 3.0 compatibility.

Printing Color Separations

PDFs designed for color separation require some knowledge of separating documents, the device that will produce the separation, and the level of PostScript used. For the PDF author, you need to be certain all color is properly defined in your document before sending it off to the imaging center. If you're a technician at a service center, then you probably have to handle many different workarounds to get files to print properly.

For the author of a PDF file, you have a few general rules to follow when preparing files for color separations or any kind of high-end device printing. Among your standard operating procedures, you should follow a few simple guidelines:

✦ **Proper color mode:** For color separations to be produced as process color (Cyan, Magenta, Yellow, Black), be certain all elements in the authored file have a CMYK color specification. RGB images will not separate properly and won't be converted on the fly with many separation methods used by imaging centers. With regard to spot color separations, you need to be certain all color is specified properly. If you have a Pantone 185 CV and a Pantone 185 CVC color contained in the PDF, the computer will see these as two different colors and print two different plates.

✦ **Use the Acrobat Distiller PPD:** When printing PostScript files or using Distiller in the background, as a default you should always use the Acrobat Distiller PPD when a PPD selection is available. In some cases, use of device PPDs will not render a PDF suitable for printing. Unless instructed by an imaging center to use a specific PPD, this option should always be your default. In addition, be certain to use the most recent Distiller PPD. If you have older versions of Acrobat on your computer, you may have several versions of the Distiller PPD. Be certain to check and verify using the most recent PPD.

✦ **Acquire Job Options from the service center:** You should check with your service center and see if they have developed a set of Job Options for their printing devices. Service centers may prefer Acrobat 3.0 format to Acrobat 5.0 format compatibilities. If they have a set of Job Options available, copy them to your Distiller Settings folder and use them for the jobs that you submit.

✦ **Sample all images at print requirements:** In the authoring program, import images at a 1:1 ratio and sampled at the output resolution requirements. Don't rely on Distiller's JobOptions to downsample images. This can lead to longer distillation times and slow down your workflow.

✦ **Minimize font conversion to outlines:** Always embed fonts where licensing permits and avoid globally converting fonts to outlines. Reserve font conversion to outlines for only those fonts that you know create problems. Converting all fonts to outlines will greatly increase printing times.

✦ **Submit color composites to imaging centers:** All the PDF files you submit to a service center should be composite images. If you pre-separate files, the imaging center will have trouble obtaining the right angles for each plate to be printed. In addition, you'll prevent technicians from creating workarounds that they may be able to exercise to correct printing problems.

Soft proofing color separations

Regardless of whether you print process or spot color separations, the beauty of using Acrobat is in viewing on your monitor a close rendition of what will appear on printed plates. If colors don't separate properly, you can easily see the problems. For the PDF author and imaging technician, soft proofing can be a time saver and ultimately save you money.

For the PDF author, you know the final file that you submit to the imaging center must be a composite image. Therefore, soft proofing only involves producing a temporary file you create to verify all colors are properly produced on the right plates. In addition, you can check for the page size accuracy, how overprints will be produced, and if crop marks and bleeds are all properly set up.

From your authoring program, print a file as separations. Distill the PostScript file with Acrobat Distiller and open the PDF in Acrobat. Each color separation will be contained on a separate page. If you print process separations, you should have four pages. For spot color, you should have a separate page for each spot value. If the number of pages exceeds the number of colors you expect, then you know there will be a problem correctly separating your file. In Figure 18-7, I printed a file as separations and viewed the converted PDF in Acrobat. The thumbnail view shows five color plates.

Figure 18-7: Viewing a separated file in Acrobat shows the number of plates that will be printed. If this file is to be process color, an extra plate was improperly assigned a spot color value.

Soft proofing color

A discussion of color management and calibrations could take another several chapters to explain thoroughly. Because I don't have the space to provide you a thorough detail of color management and using color profiles, I have to refer you to the Help file installed with your Acrobat installation. The Help file is excellent and will get you started with color management if you don't currently have a system in place in your workflow.

As a starting point for those who are unfamiliar with all the terms of color management, such as color gamut, ICC profile, device independent color, and so on, let me draw your attention to a few menu commands that can be helpful in proofing color before printing your PDF files.

When soft proofing color for printing on CMYK devices or color separations, choose View ➪ Proof Setup ➪ Custom. A dialog box opens where you can make a choice for your color proofing space, as shown in Figure 18-8. The pull-down menu displays profiles installed with Acrobat and any others you may have created from programs, such as Photoshop.

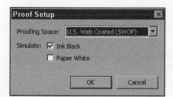

Figure 18-8: The Proof Setup dialog box enables you to select a proofing space from the installed color profiles to be used for soft proofing color.

As a simple jumpstart for those not yet versed in color handling, select a color profile, such as U.S. Web Coated (SWOP) from the menu choices. This profile displays all the color on the PDF pages in a CMYK gamut that will more closely represent the color you can expect when printing color separations.

After selecting the profile from the Proof Setup dialog box, you need to address another menu command for viewing the color mapped to the profile that you selected. Choose View ➪ Proof Colors. When a check mark is placed aside the Proof Colors menu item, Acrobat will display on your monitor how the colors in your document would be mapped to the gamut from the profile selected in the Proof Setup.

What's important here is to understand how the soft proofing on-screen works. The remaining tasks of creating a color management system and calibrating monitor views to devices is where you need to dig into the literature and learn how to set up profiles for your output devices.

In addition to viewing color spaces, Acrobat 5.0 has introduced a means of viewing overprints. You might assign some colors in a document to overprint, while other colors will knock out. If unfamiliar with separating color, imagine a yellow object where type appears in black and a cyan object is placed over the yellow. The type will *overprint* and the cyan object will *knockout*. If you look at the yellow separation, the type won't appear on the plate because it overprints. The cyan object will appear as a hole in the yellow object because it knocks out.

When designing illustrated art and manually assigning overprints, an error can easily be created, especially if you duplicate objects and don't exercise care in changing appropriate attributes. You may, for example, inadvertently assign an overprint that should be knocked out.

To preview knockouts and overprints, open a PDF file and choose View ➪ Overprint Preview. The view in Acrobat displays all your overprints in terms of how the composite image will be printed. Colors not assigned an overprint appear at their assigned values. Those colors where overprints have been assigned appear with a color blend of the objects. For example, a cyan object on top of a yellow object where the cyan overprints the yellow will show the image with a blend of the two colors. In this example, the cyan object will appear green when overprinted.

Workarounds for correcting separation problems

The two most common problems imaging centers experience when printing client files for color separations is improper color modes for raster images and improper naming conventions for spot color. Even if you are the author of a PDF document to be submitted to a service center, knowing how to easily correct these problems can save you time. For the imaging center technician, the workarounds are essential in almost any production environment.

For color images that have not been converted to CMYK from RGB modes, you can easily create a color conversion after the PDF file has been created. Select an image with the TouchUp Object tool and open a context menu. Select Edit Object from the menu choices and the default image editor opens the selected image. By default, if you have Adobe Photoshop installed, the image will open in Photoshop. You can convert the mode from RGB, save the file and return to the PDF. The image will be dynamically updated and separate properly.

If spot colors have been improperly defined in the authoring application, you can easily return to the application and change the miss assigned values to the correct color assignments. For simple color changes, this method works well. But presume you have a complex vector image with many layers and different objects where the colors need to be changed; or, for the imaging center that doesn't want to take the time working through a client's design to find all the elements that need to have color reassigned. A simple solution can solve your problem and it is best described by following some steps:

STEPS: Remapping Spot Color

1. **Create a file with two spot colors and add a third color.** In a layout or illustration program, create some simple graphics that have two different spot values. Then add a third object and define the color with a third value.

2. **Print the file to disk as a composite image.** For this step, we don't want to print separations. You can soft proof the job by printing separations to verify the colors will all fall on a separate plate. But, to correct the problem, we need a composite color image.

3. **Open the PostScript file in a text editor.** PostScript files are ASCII text. They can be edited in a text editor and saved back out as a text file that can be distilled with Acrobat Distiller.

4. **Search and replace to change the color name.** Using the text editor's search and replace features, find the color that is improperly assigned. In the Replace dialog box, enter the color name to find and the color name to replace all found occurrences. (See Figure 18-9.)

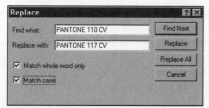

Figure 18-9: Using a text editor's replace feature, find the color name to change and enter the color name to remap the color.

5. **Save the file.** After creating the change, save the file as text only.

6. **Distill with Acrobat Distiller.** Distill the text file with Distiller. Be certain all the Job Options are set to the output requirements that you desire.

7. **Export to EPS.** Choose File ➪ Save As and choose EPS as the format. You can use a plug-in to print the file to disk or use the EPS file and return to your separating application.

8. **Print the file as a separation to disk.** In order to soft proof the file, we need to create a separation and preview it in Acrobat.

9. **Distill the separated file.** Distill the PostScript file with Acrobat Distiller and preview the pages in Acrobat. If you changed the color names accurately in the text editor, all colors will be remapped to the new values, and you should only see the number of plates you want to appear in your final output.

If all works as you expect, remember you need to return to the composite color file and send it off to the imaging center. By using a few workarounds, Acrobat can be a great time saver and efficient workhorse for resolving many printing problems.

Large Format Inkjet Printing

Some large format inkjet printers render better color results from RGB images than CMYK. If sending files off to a service center for oversized printing, you need to check with the service center personnel regarding what color mode they recommend you use for their devices. Regardless of the color mode, the one problem many people often face is creating files with sufficient resolution to support large format printing. Whether it is a commercial ad or a family photo, pumping up a digital image 300, 400, 800 percent or more will often lead to poor image quality and severe file degradation.

At the onset, let me say that capturing a 72 pixels per inch (ppi) image off the Web and outputting it at 30 x 40 inches will never result in anything more than mush. You can't do it, so don't try. You do have some alternatives though with files that have been digitized at higher resolutions and need to be upsized for larger output. A good example is when using a digital camera or acquiring a Kodak PhotoCD image.

A digital camera of 2.1 megapixels produces an image approximately 4 x 5 inches at 300 ppi. Because a digital camera image can't be rescanned for higher resolution, you're stuck with the image at the size the camera produces it. If you want to make a 30 x 40 color print, the image will need to be resampled in a program, such as Photoshop. Left alone to the Photoshop algorithm, the results will be less desirable than some other alternatives available to you. One nifty utility I have found that works very well is Genuine Fractals by the Altamira Group (`www.altamira-group.com`).

Genuine Fractals is a Photoshop plug-in designed to resample images with excellent results. (See Figure 18-10.) I have successfully upsized digital camera images from a 2.1 megapixel camera to sizes over 30 x 36 inches. If upsizing images for larger output is something you need, take a look at this Photoshop plug-in.

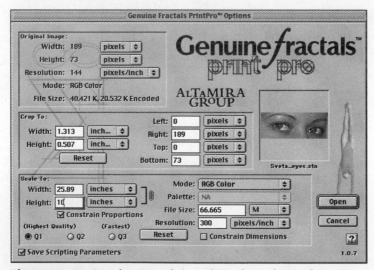

Figure 18-10: Genuine Fractals is a Photoshop plug-in that uses sophisticated algorithms to impressively upscale raster-based images.

If your need is to print nothing more than a large TIFF image, then you would have little use for Acrobat. If, however, you need to print files with images and text or other art elements, then PDF will be of great value to you. Be certain to first provide enough resolution for the raster images before converting to PDF. From an authoring application you can print at scaling sizes larger than the layout and use the Acrobat Distiller PPD. When distilled in Acrobat Distiller, you will have a preview of the final print at actual size. Through the compression of Acrobat, many large format prints can be sent to service centers via an Internet connection.

Scaling can sometimes lead to misaligned elements and problems with type floating on the document page. When you distill a PostScript file and preview the results in Acrobat, these problems will often be apparent. Together with soft proofing the color, Acrobat PDFs can be your best source of previewing output for large format inkjet printers.

Summary

✦ Acrobat 5.0 has introduced many sophisticated printing controls. Although screening and color separations are not available with Acrobat 5.0, you have many attribute choices for printing composite files to desktop printing devices.

✦ For non-PostScript printers, Acrobat has several options available to help print difficult files. As a low cost solution for acquiring a PostScript RIP, Adobe PressReady offers an excellent solution.

✦ PDFs can be sent directly to PostScript 3 devices. To image PDFs on PostScript 3 printers, a software utility or support for hot folders is needed to send the file to the device.

✦ For professional printing, you can acquire third party plug-ins or purchase Adobe InProduction. If neither is available to you, you can export PDFs to Encapsulated PostScript files and use other application's software for controlling halftone frequencies and printing color separations.

✦ Acrobat offers many opportunities to create workarounds for improperly designed files. You can convert color modes and remap spot colors to correct problems and soft proof the results with Acrobat.

✦ Acrobat PDFs created for large format inkjet printers can provide image previews for upscaled images at actual size with accurate results.

✦   ✦   ✦

Programming

What Is Acrobat JavaScript?

Adobe Acrobat has offered the ability to attach JavaScript code to PDF documents for several years. But with the advent of Version 5.0 of Acrobat (and Reader), the product's JavaScript capabilities have undergone significant expansion, making it possible to do some truly spectacular things in PDF. What's more, although JavaScript *authoring* is available only in Acrobat, users of Reader are not at all restricted in their ability to see and use JavaScript-powered document features. The entire world of PDF users benefit from the enhanced functionality afforded by JavaScript.

You already saw (in Chapter 13) how JavaScript can be used to add interactivity to PDF forms. JavaScript's capabilities go far beyond this, however. With the aid of JavaScript, PDF documents can form the basis for powerful stand-alone applications that can perform SQL (Structured Query Language) queries into databases, obtain information from the Web, send e-mail, control other PDF documents remotely, and much more. In addition, you can use JavaScript to exercise fine control not only over a PDF document's appearance but the viewing environment (that is, Acrobat or Reader) itself.

With Version 5.0 of Acrobat, Adobe has officially adopted the term *Acrobat JavaScript* to refer to the version of JavaScript used in Acrobat. This term is to distinguish it from other implementations used in other products, such as Web browsers. What makes Acrobat JavaScript different? Let's back up a moment and first talk about JavaScript. You may have heard of JavaScript in connection with HTML pages. JavaScript, originally developed by Netscape, is a general-purpose, object-oriented programming language that can do many of the same things that other programming languages (such as C and Pascal) can do. Unlike C or Pascal, however, JavaScript is not a compiled language but an *interpreted* language. This means the executable part of a program written in

JavaScript is just plain text (rather than a specially prepared binary module, or *executable*). The good part about this is that JavaScript programs can be written by using any text editor, and because no extra "compilation" steps must be taken before a JavaScript program can be run, development of working scripts is a quick process. If you have an idea, you can test it quickly in JavaScript. Another good thing about scripting languages that use text files is that they are inherently cross-platform, because a text file is always a text file no matter what kind of machine it's on, whereas binary executables are platform-dependent.

Note   Don't confuse JavaScript with Java. The latter is not a scripting language but a highly evolved, comparatively complex object-based language developed by Sun Microsystems.

Acrobat JavaScript is actually a superset of *core JavaScript*. At root, every implementation of JavaScript builds on a core set of features described in the ECMA-262 standard. (ECMA is short for the European Computer Manufacturers Association, a standards body that oversees changes to the language.) These core features cover elements, such as the language's basic syntax, data primitives, and built-in objects. Core JavaScript's built-in objects include items, such as the Date object as well as String, Array, and Function objects. Core features are called "core" because they are common to all implementations of the language.

Companies that implement JavaScript in their products are free to extend the language in ways that are appropriate to the environment in which the language will be used. Hence, for example, makers of Web browsers have added browser-based extensions to the language (comprising features, such as Document and Window objects), to facilitate the manipulation of Web page contents. Some producers of server software, likewise, have created *server* extensions to make possible certain operations (such as file I/O) that are appropriate in a server environment. Adding extensions to the language simply means adding new features: for example, new objects that have new methods and/or properties. Because these features are specific to a given implementation, they are not core language components. You can't use Server Side JavaScript (SSJS) methods, for example, in a script running inside a browser; nor browser-specific methods in a script running on a server.

In order to maximize the usefulness of JavaScript in a PDF-viewing environment, Adobe added certain extensions of its own to the core JavaScript language. The result is Acrobat JavaScript. Like any other implementation of JavaScript, Acrobat JavaScript has built-in Date, Array, String, and so forth objects and follows normal JavaScript syntax rules. But in addition to the baseline feature set, Acrobat JavaScript contains additional objects that are designed to allow you to manipulate PDF file elements and the PDF viewing environment. So for example, in Acrobat JavaScript is an Annot object, with methods and properties for manipulating PDF Annotations. There are also objects for Bookmarks, Fields, Events, and much more. Table 19-1 shows a complete listing of all of the Adobe-defined objects available in Acrobat JavaScript.

Table 19-1 **Acrobat JavaScript Objects**	
ADBC Object	Index Object
Annot Object	Plugin Object
App Object	PPKLite Signature Handler Object
Bookmark Object	Report Object
Collab Object	Search Object
Connection Object	Security Object
Console Object	Sound Object
Doc Object	Spell Object
Event Object	Statement Object
Field Object	Template Object
Fullscreen Object	TTS Object
Global Object	Util Object
Identity Object	

The Adobe documentation of the objects shown in Table 19-1 can be found in a file called AcroJS.pdf, which is in the Help subdirectory of your Acrobat installation. The AcroJS.pdf file, otherwise known as the *Acrobat JavaScript Object Specification* (Tech Note No. 5186), constitutes the official Adobe documentation for the Acrobat JavaScript extensions. It gives a detailed listing of all methods and properties applicable to all Adobe-defined objects, with calling conventions, usage examples, and so forth. If you ever have any questions about a particular JavaScript feature or method, you will definitely want to consult AcroJS.pdf, because it's the ultimate authority on such matters.

AcroJS.pdf is around 300 pages long. Obviously, space precludes a comprehensive discussion of the matters covered by AcroJS.pdf in the few pages available here. What I try to do in the sections that follow is build on the foundation laid in Chapter 13, giving additional code examples designed to have you producing useful PDF forms (and PDF-based applications) in as little time as possible. Most of the code examples will be usable "as is" — you do not have to be a JavaScript expert or an experienced programmer to take advantage of the techniques described in this chapter. It will help a great deal, however, if you are already familiar with JavaScript's basic syntax (which is virtually identical to that of the C language) and can refer to a good JavaScript reference from time to time as we go along. The examples given in this chapter will build in complexity, going from relatively simple to quite sophisticated. No matter what your skill level, you should find plenty of relevant material here.

Backward Compatibility

Most of the objects in Table 19-1 (in fact, all of them except the App, Doc, Event, Field, Global, and Util objects) are new to Acrobat 5.0. These additions are an important concern if you are developing PDF forms that will be used by people who have Acrobat Reader 4.0 or 4.05 (or even an earlier version). At some point in the future, it will be safe to use 5.0 features freely, but it takes years for older versions of software to disappear from use. In the meantime, you'll want to check the version number of the user's software before using 5.0 features in your PDF documents. Otherwise, if a person is viewing your document with Acrobat Reader 4.0, say, and a 5.0-only JavaScript method is encountered, your user will see a runtime error message and wonder what's wrong with your file.

The way to check the "viewer version" of your user's software is to inspect the value of app.viewerVersion. (The App object has a property called viewerVersion that contains a number representing the version of the currently running viewer app, which is to say, Acrobat or Acrobat Reader.) You can check the viewer version before executing version-sensitive code by creating the following JavaScript:

```
if (typeof(app.viewerVersion) != "undefined")
  if (app.viewerVersion >= 5.0)  // we can use 5.0 features
  {
    // do something here that requires 5.0 features, such as:
    var ourURL = this.URL;  // get our file's location

    var ourName = ourURL.split("/").pop();  // get our
filename

    // etc.
  }
  else      // can't use 5.0 features? try something else...
    {
    var ourPath = this.path; // path property is 4.0-
compatible
    var ourName = ourPath.split("/").pop();
  }
```

We start by checking to see if the viewerVersion property itself exists (that's what the typeof check is for), because this property was, itself, not present before Version 4.0. All of the code after the first line will be skipped if viewerVersion doesn't exist. (Note that in JavaScript, an entity that doesn't exist is undefined.)

The second line of code checks to see if app.viewerVersion. is greater than or equal to 5.0. (We don't simply want to check if it is equal to 5.0, because somebody with Acrobat 6.0 may someday use our file!) If this condition check succeeds, we go ahead and execute some 5.0-dependent code that obtains the filename of our file. (Remember that the filename may not be what we originally set it to be. The user can always change our file's name.)

Note All code following // is a comment. Any line where these comment references are contained can be eliminated and will have no effect on running the routine accurately. It is, however, good programming practice to include comments for your own reference when needing to return to the code for updates and debugging.

If you're curious how the code works: The URL property of the Doc object is new for Acrobat 5.0. It doesn't exist in prior versions. In 5.0+, this property contains a string that holds the fully qualified Uniform Resource Locator of our file, which will start with a protocol, such as "http:" or "file:" and end with the name of the file. In between, there will be path information identifying any subdirectories that lead to our file. The subdirectory names will be separated by forward slashes, in accordance with ordinary URL rules: for example, http://www.domain.com/catalog.pdf. To get the file name by itself, we apply the String method split() to the URL string, which returns an array containing whatever substrings could be obtained by splitting the source string on a given delimiter. In this instance, we've specified a delimiter of "/" (forward slash). The final item in the array that split() hands us will be the filename; and we conveniently obtain it by applying the pop() method to the array.

Note This code will run into problems if the URL or path happens to contain form data appended to it, as in http://www.domain.com/abc.pdf?query=name& priority=1. In this case, your filename will actually have a question mark and potentially quite a few parameters attached to it. You can get rid of this "trailing junk" quite easily, of course, by applying the split() and pop() technique once again, only this time using the question mark as the delimiter for splitting.

What if the user doesn't have Version 5.0 or greater? We can get our file's name from the information stored in the Doc object's path property, which is available in Version 4.0 or later of Acrobat and Reader. The difference between URL and path is that the former will always begin with a protocol identifier, such as "http:" or "file:" whereas the latter will not.

What about checking for JavaScript?

Acrobat's JavaScript capabilities rely on the presence of the AcroForm plug-in. In theory, it's possible for a user of Acrobat or Acrobat Reader to remove the plug-in and still view files. It is also possible for someone with an early version of Acrobat (or Acrobat Reader) to have no JavaScript capability whatsoever. How do you check for this?

You have no way to use JavaScript to check to see if the user has a JavaScript-safe version of Acrobat or Reader, for the (hopefully obvious) reason that you need to have JavaScript in the viewing environment, already, in order to run any kind of JavaScript-based check of the environment. The bottom line is that you can do nothing to prevent a user of Acrobat Reader 3.0 (who has no JavaScript capability) from seeing an error message when he or she opens your JavaScript-powered PDF document. Your PDF file will still be viewable in a no-JavaScript version of Reader, but it will generate an error dialog box initially, on opening. The user will simply be told that he or she lacks the plug-in necessary to use the JavaScript features found in the file. After the user dismisses this dialog box, the file can be viewed. (Hopefully, the user will get the hint and go download a more up-to-date version of Reader!)

Checking for Acrobat versus Acrobat Reader

The great thing about using JavaScript in PDF is that most scripts work equally well in Acrobat or Acrobat Reader: Your user does not have to own the full commercial version of Acrobat in order to enjoy the interactivity features made possible by JavaScript. There are, however, a few exceptions to this rule. Some JavaScript properties and methods (mainly those that involve saving a file) are not available in Reader and will generate an error if used in Reader. For example, the `mailForm()` method, defined on the Doc object, exports FDF (form data, in Forms Data Format) from the current PDF document and e-mails it to one or more recipients. But because this method involves saving a file (something only Acrobat, not Reader, can do), its use is not supported in Reader. A Reader user can open and view a PDF document that references the `mailForm()` method, but the method will not produce any action when invoked from Reader.

Fortunately, the number of Acrobat JavaScript methods that are Reader-disabled is small, and they are all documented in `AcroJS.pdf`. The code examples shown in the remainder of this chapter use mainly universally-applicable Acrobat JavaScript methods. Still, in your own programming, you may occasionally find it useful (or even essential) to use Reader-disabled methods of one sort or another. Before you do, you should check to see whether your document is being viewed inside Acrobat Reader; and if so, issue an alert to let the user know that the feature in question is unavailable in Reader. One way to do that is with the following code:

```
// We want to check to see if the user is viewing
// our file with Reader (as opposed to Acrobat)

if (typeof(app.viewerType) != "undefined")
    if (app.viewerType == "Reader")
        {
            var msg = "This feature requires the full \
                    version of Acrobat. Sorry!";
            app.alert(msg);
        }
    else {
        // call method that requires Acrobat
        }
```

The `viewerType` property of the App object (as explained in `AcroJS.pdf`) can return one of two possible values, depending on the viewing environment: "Reader" if the user is using Reader, and "Exchange" (Acrobat's old name) if the user is using Acrobat. By inspecting this property's value at runtime, you can determine whether your document is being viewed in Acrobat Reader, and if so, spare the user from seeing error messages generated by calls to Reader-disabled JavaScript features.

What Can I Do with Acrobat JavaScript?

You may be wondering what sorts of magic you can do with JavaScript in a PDF document. We've already talked about some of the forms-related elements that you can do with JavaScript in Chapter 13. In a forms context, JavaScript is extremely useful for functions, such as binding field dependencies (for example, calculating subtotals from individual field values) and validating user input. But JavaScript brings many other capabilities as well. For example, you can use Acrobat JavaScript to:

✦ **Control the appearance of form fields:** You can change the text font, color, field background color, bounding-box color and type, and other appearance characteristics of form fields at view time. (You can also change the read-only attribute of a field dynamically.) In Acrobat 5.0, creating new form fields is also possible, and controlling their placement on the page, programmatically.

✦ **Control the viewing environment:** You can jump to a given page, set the zoom magnification, make toolbars visible or not visible, create new bookmarks or annotations (in Acrobat 5.0 or higher), and so forth on-the-fly.

✦ **Allow the user to go out to the Web:** Using the getURL() method of the Doc object, you can cause the user's browser to launch (if it's not already running) and make a new URL display in the browser.

✦ **Control the submission of forms:** You can use JavaScript to process and/or filter user-entered data, and then submit it (via HTTP POST or GET) to a given URL. In Acrobat (not Reader), you can also send form data or entire PDF documents as e-mail.

✦ **Open and Close PDF and other documents:** Acrobat 5.0 offers new methods for opening and closing documents on a local disk.

✦ **Execute menu commands:** Using the App object's execMenuItem() method, you can programmatically execute almost any Acrobat or Reader menu command. (The exceptions are Save As and Quit, which are not reachable.)

✦ **Intercept user keystrokes in real time:** This capability (which is important for validating user input in forms) is demonstrated in an example below.

✦ **Control one PDF document from another:** Suppose you have an "order form" document and a handful of catalogs in PDF. The user can click a button ("Order This Item Now") on page 37 of Catalog No. 1 and have the relevant pricing information appear, automatically, in the Order Form document. An example of how to do this is shown later in this chapter.

✦ **Make Acrobat (or Reader) "speak" text strings via the Windows Text-to-Speech (TTS) engine:** This accessibility feature has actually been in Acrobat JavaScript since version 4.05 but was not fully documented until now. It is a separate feature from audio annotations; but you can also use Acrobat JavaScript to play audio files embedded in a PDF document.

✦ **Conduct advanced text searches:** You can use JavaScript to set up searches that harness the power of the Acrobat Search plug-in (and index files), with or without specifying stemming and sounds like attributes, and so on.

✦ **Delete or reorder pages in a document:** When this technique is combined with opening/closing PDFs remotely, it can be a powerful way to custom assemble entirely new PDF documents.

✦ **Spellcheck a document programmatically:** This feature is a new as of Acrobat 5.0, and it requires Acrobat (in other words, it is disabled in Reader).

✦ **Generate reports:** Acrobat 5.0 now offers (through a Report object) JavaScript methods that can create text (and horizontal rules) on a page, and generate new pages quickly.

✦ **Reach into relational databases with SQL queries:** Acrobat 5.0 introduces a new capability called ADBC: Acrobat Database Connectivity. Using Connection and Statement objects, a custom script can establish a connection to a relational database (MS Access, Sybase, and so on.) and perform queries into the database using standard Structured Query Language. A brief example of this is shown later in the chapter.

✦ **Create basic animations similar to GIF89a:** With creative use of JavaScript, a PDF author can create both page-flip animations as well as animations that move icons around the page in real time. (The key is to use a core-JavaScript method called setInterval.)

✦ **Create PDF stand-alone applications:** Combining the power of JavaScript (and the new objects and methods of Acrobat) with the flexible form-creation features of Acrobat, you can create powerful stand-alone applications that use PDF as the Graphical User Interface. For example, you could create a mortgage interest calculator; a search-engine registration tool; an HTML editor; database applications; personal-information manager apps; and more.

These are just some of the sorts of capabilities made possible by Acrobat JavaScript. The list of possibilities is endless, limited only by your imagination.

What Can't Acrobat JavaScript Do?

There are, of course, some functions that Acrobat JavaScript can't do, such as open a new browser window, create (or manipulate) an HTML page, or make use of DOM (Document Object Model) methods. The reason for these limitations should be obvious: Acrobat JavaScript executes (or "lives") inside Acrobat or Acrobat Reader, not the browser. A more programmerly way of putting it is that Acrobat JavaScript is scoped to the PDF environment, not any other environment. Acrobat doesn't know about Web pages, nor should it be expected to. Conversely, a Web browser that supports JavaScript or JScript can't be expected to know about the workings of PDF documents. The runtime interpreter that makes Web-page JavaScript work doesn't reside in Acrobat and doesn't use Acrobat extensions to the language; it lives in the browser. So it should come as no surprise that you can't use app.viewerVersion in a Web page, any more than you can call Window object methods from inside a PDF document.

After the distinction between the browser environment and the PDF environment becomes clear in your mind, you'll have no trouble understanding what the respective capabilities and limitations are of the two JavaScript environments.

Where Can I Attach JavaScript Code to PDF?

Acrobat follows a philosophy of letting the PDF author attach JavaScript code to the parts of the PDF document that will actually be affected by it. Thus, a close association is between, for example, form fields and the scripts that modify those fields. From a design standpoint, this is good, because it enforces a discipline that makes possible good separation of functional units. This is a common paradigm in object-oriented design: Code that modifies a given object is usually best scoped (or attached) to that object.

The flip side of this architectural strategy is that code can potentially be scattered all over a document, making it hard to manage. Fortunately, with version 5.0, Acrobat has introduced an excellent tool for dealing with this. A "code-dump" feature is accessible via Tools ⇨ JavaScript ⇨ Edit All JavaScripts, that displays all of the scripts contained in a given PDF document in one window with automatically generated headers that relate each portion of each script to the part of the document to which it belongs. For example, Figure 19-1 shows the code dump that was generated using this command for one of the author's files. The file in question contains just one script, which executes only when the document is being closed. The script puts an alert window on the screen showing the current date and time.

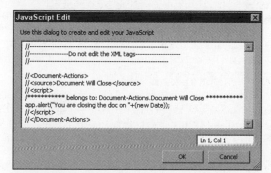

Figure 19-1: The Tools ⇨ JavaScript ⇨ Edit All JavaScripts command displays all of a document's scripts in one window, letting you see at a glance which scripts apply to which parts of the document.

The code dump window contains a number of automatically generated comment lines. JavaScript supports two styles of comments: The C++ style, in which everything on a line following a double-slash, //, is a comment; and the older ANSI C style of wrapping comments in /* and */. In the code dump, the older style of comment is used for showing "belongs to" information (in other words, information relating the code to the part of the document it affects). The double-slash type of comment is used for other information. You'll notice, for example, that every script is wrapped in XML tags. Acrobat automatically generates these tags. You shouldn't concern yourself with them; and in fact, you're warned at the top of the code listing not to edit the XML tags. The tags are for the internal use of Acrobat.

Note   If you were to try to make a true XML file out of the code window's contents, you would have to add an appropriate XML header at the top of the file, such as `<?xml version="1.0" encoding="UTF-8"?>`, wrap the file contents with root tags, remove the C++ comments (or place them in CDATA sections), and put all JavaScript code blocks in CDATA sections, because JavaScript makes extensive use of angle brackets (greater-than and less-than symbols), which are reserved for tag usage in XML. In other words, don't let the Adobe XML tags fool you: The code dump that Acrobat gives you is a long way from being a well-formed XML file.

You can use the code dump window as an edit window, where you can create and/or edit JavaScript code affecting any part of your PDF document. As a practical matter, however, you probably should not rely on this window as your primary editing window, because mentally keeping track of all the individual scripts and how they affect individual parts of the document is hard. A more practical tactic is to edit scripts in place, right at the spot(s) where they're needed; in other words, at various attach points around the document.

Where, then, can you attach scripts to a PDF file? In all of the following places:

✦ **Form field event handlers:** Every time you create a field using the Form tool, you can attach scripts to that field. Use the Actions tab of the Field Properties dialog box. In the left-hand part of the Actions tab (see Figure 13-13 in Chapter 13), you can choose from one of six event handlers: Mouse Up, Mouse Down, Mouse Enter, Mouse Exit, On Focus, and On Blur. Select one of these options and then create a JavaScript action. The script becomes associated with the event in question.

✦ **Document level:** Access to document-level (or top-level) scripts is via Tools ⇨ JavaScript ⇨ Document JavaScripts. Scripts created at this level are available from any place in the PDF document, so that if field scripts, for example, need to share functions among each other, the shared functions can (and should) go at this level.

✦ **Document Actions:** Access to Document Action code is via Tools ⇨ JavaScript ⇨ Set Document Actions, which causes the Document Actions dialog box shown in Figure 19-2 to appear. In essence, this dialog box exposes handlers for document-level events, such as Close, Save, and Print. The handlers that contain the word "Will" let you execute a JavaScript Action *before* the event in question takes place; those containing "Did" let you execute a script *after* the event takes place. These handlers are new for Acrobat 5.0.

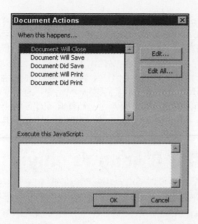

Figure 19-2: The Tools ⇨ JavaScript ⇨ Set Document Actions command brings up the Document Actions dialog box that lets you associate JavaScript with various document-related events.

✦ **Page actions:** Access to Page Actions occurs via Document ⇨ Set Page Action in the Acrobat main menu bar. The Page Actions dialog box allows you to associate JavaScripts with Page Open as well as Page Close events. This means you can create scripts that apply just to specific pages in a document and have those scripts execute just when a page first opens or is about to close. This function can be handy if, for example, you have a graphic on a given page that looks best at one particular magnification (such as 125 percent). You can attach a Page Open script for that page that does something such as:

```
if (this.zoom != 125)
    this.zoom = 125; // set zoom to 125%
```

You can also save the reader's initial zoom setting in a global variable, and then attach a corresponding Page Close script that resets the user's old zoom setting when the user leaves that page to go to another page.

✦ **Bookmarks:** If you highlight any bookmark and open a context menu, then select Properties, you will see a drop down menu for Actions, which lets you associate any of the standard Acrobat Actions (including JavaScript) with a particular bookmark. This means that you can have a script execute whenever the user clicks a bookmark.

✦ **External files:** You can place a plain-text file, ending with the extension .js, in your JavaScripts folder (under the Acrobat folder, or the folder containing Acrobat itself), and any JavaScript code that exists in that file will be loaded and executed when Acrobat starts up. This is extremely handy when you have large code libraries that need to be shared across multiple PDF files. It is obviously a tactic designed for use on local hard drives, not for JavaScript code that will be distributed across the Internet (unless you can rely on your users to know how to download and install .js files). When code is stored in a separate file from the PDF document(s) it acts on, file management becomes an issue. Bear this in mind when using .js files.

✦ **FDF files:** Not many people know it, but you can import JavaScript into a PDF file by placing code inside a Forms Data Format file. Unfortunately, Acrobat won't help you do this because the Acrobat Export to FDF feature does not write any of a field's associated scripts to the FDF file; only the field data gets exported. So to use this technique, you have to hand-edit your FDF file(s). This feature is for advanced users only.

Tip

Basically, you have to find the FDF file's Fields dictionary and add an /AA (Additional Actions) entry to the dictionary, containing your code. See the example file called `thankyou.fdf` on the accompanying CD-ROM and consult the PDF Reference Manual for details regarding AA syntax and FDF file construction.

Using an external code editor (Windows only)

Beginning with Acrobat 5.0, you can specify an external editor for use in creating or modifying your Acrobat JavaScript code. (You're no longer limited to using the Acrobat somewhat klutzy built-in code editor, which lacks auto-indent, syntax coloring, global search/replace, find, print, and certain other features that you may have become accustomed to working with in a code editor.) In the Acrobat main menu bar, choose Edit ➪ Preferences ➪ General (or use Control/Command + K) and select JavaScript from the Navigation pane, as shown in Figure 19-3. In the detail pane under JavaScript Editor, select the radio button titled External Editor and then click the Choose... button and navigate to your favorite editor on your local disk (whether it's Microsoft Word, Notepad, or whatever). Dismiss the Preferences dialog box. Now whenever you access any JavaScript code anywhere in your PDF document, Acrobat will launch into your favorite editing program, display your code in a window in that program, and bring the code window to the front. After you make your changes or finish entering new code, just close the edit window; you'll be asked whether you want to save a temporary file. Answer Yes. The code will be incorporated into your PDF file in the same spot it would normally go if you were using the Acrobat built-in JavaScript editor.

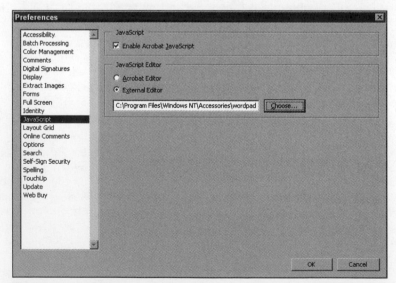

Figure 19-3: External JavaScript editors are selected from the General Preferences dialog box and the JavaScript section.

Tip For Macintosh users, you can use an external editor, such as BBEdit Lite from BareBones Software to create your scripts. After editing in a text editor window, copy the contents and paste in the JavaScript Edit window in Acrobat. Dragging the lower right corner of the window to accommodate more viewing space can expand the Acrobat internal editor on both platforms.

Is my code visible to others?

If you have a need to keep your source code away from prying eyes, fear not: Acrobat can hide your scripts from view by others. First, you should know that in no case does Acrobat Reader ever expose raw JavaScript to end users; the Field Properties dialog box, for example, is accessible only to owners of Acrobat. But even Acrobat owners can be kept from viewing your JavaScript code. All you have to do is use the Document Security command under the File menu to set a master (admin-level) password, under Password Required to Change Permissions and Passwords, and then check the security checkbox that says No Adding or Changing Comments and Form Fields, as shown in Figure 19-4. Save the file after the security has been enabled. The next time anybody opens your PDF document in Acrobat, all access to JavaScript code editing will be forbidden: Menu items, such as Tools ⇨ JavaScript ⇨ Edit All JavaScripts will be grayed out, the Form tool won't work, and so on. Not only that, but if somebody tries to "hack into" your file with a text editor, your JavaScript is still safe: After the security setting has been used, all JavaScript is encrypted. Your code is as secure as Acrobat security can make it.

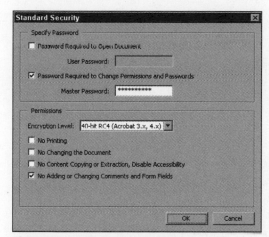

Figure 19-4: When you prevent users from changing forms, all the JavaScript code is inaccessible to anyone who doesn't know the master password.

Realtime Keystroke Filtering

In the sections that follow, we'll go through some real-world Acrobat JavaScript examples to give you an idea of what's possible. The examples vary in complexity from rudimentary to (eventually) quite advanced. Sample documents can be found on the CD-ROM accompanying this book. To begin with an example, first start with what is known in Acrobat terms as *realtime keystroke filtering*.

A basic requirement for many online forms is that user input be monitored for validation purposes. For example, you may have a text-entry requirement, for a given text field, of no non-numeric characters. (Maybe you're asking for the user's age, or credit card number, and so forth.) How can you alert the user that he or she has entered non-allowed characters? One way is to examine the contents of the text-entry field after the user completes a field entry, perhaps using a script attached to the field's On Blur handler, so that when the user leaves that field, you can inspect the value stored in `getField(fieldname).value`. The problem with this technique is that if you wait until the user is finished to flag him or her, it may be necessary for the user to go back and do quite a bit of retyping. The user may curse your form as being poorly designed. And he or she may be right!

There's a better way to handle this kind of situation. It involves intercepting the user's keystrokes as he or she enters them; and flagging non-allowed characters immediately, the instant they're typed. How can you set this up? The key is to select the Format tab of the Field Properties dialog box and choose Custom in the list on the left (see Figure 19-5).

Figure 19-5: The Format tab of the Field Properties dialog box lets you assign a custom keystroke script to a text field.

Notice the area in the lower right where it says Custom Keystroke Script. If you click the Edit button next to that label, you can create a script that inspects individual keystrokes as they are typed, but before they are committed to the field.

It's important to understand that because a text field's value is not fully determined until the field loses focus, there is no way we can hope to gain access to the user's keystrokes via the getField() method. Keystroke filtering has to occur at the event level. Fortunately, Acrobat JavaScript provides an Event object with methods and properties that can help us here. The change property of the Event object is what we want, because it always holds the value of whatever is currently being appended to the text field's contents, be it a keystroke or the value of a Paste operation. (Remember, the user can always try to Paste values into a field. He or she might not actually type them in.) If we're simply interested in inspecting individual keystrokes (not Pasted text), we can just inspect event.change. But that's not usually what you want. What if you're trying to prevent the entry of a multi-character value, such as "year"? What if the user pastes "ye" into the field, followed by pasting "ar"? How would you detect that?

It turns out we really need to inspect the entire contents of the field. And that, in turn, consists of the existing content plus the value about to be typed or pasted. The existing content is available to us via event.value; the to-be-appended (just typed, or just pasted) value is in event.change.

Suppose we want to prevent the user from entering "year" as part of his or her text-field entry. One way to do this would be to put event.value and event.change into a string variable, and then apply the String object's match() method to inspect the string for a match against the forbidden value:

```
var forbidden = "year";
var str = event.value + event.change;
var illegal = str.match(forbidden);
if (illegal) // a non-null value was returned!
{
  app.alert("The value '"+ illegal +"' is not allowed.");
  event.rc = false;  // disallow the change!
}
```

The match() method is a built-in method of the core JavaScript String object. (It is available in every implementation of JavaScript.) It inspects the string value on which it's called (in this case, the string stored in our str variable) for any matches against the value passed as an argument (in this case, the value of our forbidden variable). If no match is found, the method returns null. On the other hand, if the argument value occurs anywhere in the source string, the match() method returns an array of information. (The zeroth value of the array is the matched text. See any good book on JavaScript for more information about the match method.) That means any hit returns a non-null value. We rely on this in performing our check.

If an illegal value has been entered (whether by typing or by pasting), the user sees an alert dialog box that (in this example) says "The value 'year' is not allowed." Then, we disallow the entry of the illegal text by setting the rc property of the Event object to false. The rc property (which you can think of as meaning "Ready to Commit") is a Boolean read/write value. If it is true, whatever is contained in event.change will be appended to event.value in preparation for the next keystroke (or paste operation), which is to say, the next event. This means the user's data will be committed to the field. If we set event.change to false, however, we are telling Acrobat not to let the value in event.change be committed. And sure enough, the user's keystrokes don't show up in the text field.

Tip   The String object's `match()` method will take a RegExp (regular expression) object or regex literal as an argument value. This gives the method exceptional power and versatility. If you're not familiar with regular expressions, consult any good Perl reference or see Jeffrey Friedl's *Mastering Regular Expressions* (O'Reilly, 1997); or look around on the Web for a good regex tutorial. Regular expressions are powerful pattern-matching tools. They come in very handy in situations such as the one we've just been talking about.

See the file called `Keystrok.pdf` on the CD-ROM that accompanies this book for a working example of this technique. Feel free to experiment with the code in it.

Working with Dates

Calculations involving dates are common in JavaScript-powered forms. This is no less true for PDF forms than for HTML forms. Sometimes all you are really interested in is making sure that the date the user entered is formatted according to your needs. Other times, you may be interested in finding the difference (in days, weeks, or hours) between two dates. Or you may have more complex requirements. Fortunately, core JavaScript offers a great deal of built-in capability for manipulating dates, via the core Date object.

Like all core (built-in) JavaScript objects, the Date object has a constructor. The constructor can be used in several different ways, depending on what kinds of arguments you want to give it, but the simplest way to use the Date constructor is simply to give it no arguments. Try this simple experiment: In Acrobat, bring up the JavaScript Console window by typing Control + J (Macintosh users note the modifier is Control + J) or by choosing Tools ➪ JavaScript ➪ Console. Type new Date and press Enter on the numeric keypad of your keyboard. You should a window, such as Figure 19-6 (but with the current date showing).

Tip   You can execute any line of JavaScript code from the JavaScript console window at any time: Just type code into the window, position the cursor anywhere in the line that you want to execute, and press Enter on the numeric keypad.

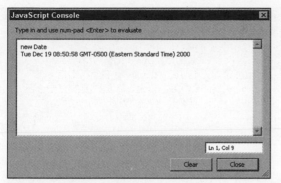

Figure 19-6: If you type the words new Date into the JavaScript Console and press Enter (on the numeric keypad), you should see a date string containing today's date.

JavaScript doesn't require parentheses on a constructor when no arguments are being passed; hence, it's perfectly acceptable to call new Date instead of new Date(). Executing the call to the constructor causes the constructor to return a Date object, which in turn is evaluated as a String. The current date is thus shown as a date string (consisting of day of the week, month, day, hour:minute:second, offset from Greenwich Mean Time, and year). This is not really how a Date object works internally, however. Internally, dates are numbers. To prove it, try this: Enter the following line in the JavaScript console and execute it:

```
0 + ( new Date )
```

You should see a value similar to 977234502169 appear under the line of code after it executes. This huge number represents the number of milliseconds that have elapsed since midnight, January 1, 1970. Adding zero to the new Date statement puts the date in a numeric context. (You can achieve the same effect if you multiply the Date object by one.) The JavaScript interpreter thinks you want the Date object to behave as a number, so that it obligingly evaluates the date as a millisecond value.

After you understand that dates are really millisecond values, date arithmetic becomes much easier. Say for example, you want to know how long a user looked at a given page in a PDF document. You need to know the time the page was first opened and the time it was closed. All you really need to do is make two calls to the Date constructor (once from a Page Open action, and again from a Page Closed action), then take the difference between the two values; and convert the answer from milliseconds to the desired combination of seconds, minutes, and so on. The Page Open script would simply store the current time into a global variable:

```
global.start = new Date; // store as global
```

About Global Variables

Sometimes you want variables to be shared between functions or between event handlers associated with form fields. But variables associated with a field or function are not automatically exposed to other fields or functions. To make a variable visible from all spots in a PDF document, you have to create it as a *global variable*. You have two ways to do this, depending on the exact degree of exposure you want to give the variable. A *document-level* global is visible to all JavaScript routines in a given document (but not visible to scripts in other documents). You can create a doc-level global as this:

```
this.myVariable = "This is a doc-level string
variable.";
```

Remember that the keyword this is a reference to the current Doc object (the foreground PDF document in Acrobat). Attaching myVariable to the Doc object gives that variable global scope within the document.

To create a variable that has truly global scope across all open documents, attach it to the Global object:

```
global.myGlobal = "This variable is visible
everywhere.";
```

The variable myGlobal is usable from any point in any document; it is truly global in scope. (But to use it, you must always prepend global. to it.) To make a Global property persistent across Acrobat sessions, call the setPersistent() method on it:

```
global.setPersistent("myGlobal",true);
```

After this call, the variable myGlobal will exist (for all documents) every time Acrobat (or Reader) is launched. Variables created in this manner are called *persistent* globals, and they are stored on disk in a file called glob.js (in the JavaScript folder under your Acrobat installation). Note that even Acrobat Reader writes data to this file (one of the few cases where Reader writes anything to disk), but only string, Boolean, and number variables can be persisted this way, and only up to a total of 32K of data.

The corresponding Page Close script may look like this:

```
var finish = new Date;
var elapsed = finish - global.start;
elapsed = elapsed/1000;
var msg = "Page was open for " + elapsed + " seconds.";
app.alert(msg);
```

Notice that after subtracting one Date from another, we divide the elapsed time by 1000 to get an answer that's in seconds instead of milliseconds. To convert seconds to minutes, of course, you would divide seconds by 60. But you would probably want to round the answer down using Math.round(), or convert the answer to a string and extract the substring containing everything up to, but not including, the decimal point. (By default, JavaScript treats all numbers as floating-point numbers.)

Putting a Timestamp on a document

Suppose you want to put a timestamp on the first page of a document so that whenever a user loads the document, it displays the current month, day, and year (in a format as July 15, 2001). However, you don't want the date to look like a form field, and you certainly don't want it to be editable if the user clicks inside it. How can you set this up? It's actually pretty easy. Follow these steps:

STEPS: Creating a Timestamp Form Field

1. **Create a Text Field.** Start by creating a text field (we'll call it timeStamp) on the page where you want the date to show. Use the Form tool to drag out the outline of the date area, and then set the desired typeface, point size, and so forth using the Appearance tab of the Field Properties dialog box. Make sure to uncheck the Border Color and Background Color boxes, but *do* check Read Only. This prevents the field from being editable by the user. Supply a name for the field. In my example I use timestamp.

2. **Close the Field Properties dialog box**. The field will initially be invisible, because it contains no text. Click the OK button in the Field Properties dialog box.

3. **Create a Page Action.** Now go to the Document menu and select Set Page Action and then Page Open. Add a JavaScript action that looks like:

```
var today = util.printd("mmmm d, yyyy", new Date());
this.getField('timeStamp').value = today;
```

4. **Save the file.** After saving the PDF, close the file. The Page Action will only be executed when we open the document.

5. **Open the file.** Now open the document and check to see if the timestamp looks the way you want it to. It should show the month (spelled out) followed by the day (with no leading zeros) and a comma, and then the full year, for example, August 30, 2001.

Our code uses the Util object's `printd()` method to format a Date object the way we want it. This method is well documented in `AcroJS.pdf`. Suffice it to say, you can easily format a date in any manner you want using `printd()`.

 Tip

The core JavaScript built-in Date object has over three dozen predefined convenience methods built into it to make your life easier when working with dates. Space precludes a discussion of those methods here, but be sure to consult any good JavaScript reference to find out more about those methods, which can come in handy.

Working with Open Documents

One the most powerful capabilities of Acrobat JavaScript involves the ability to use one PDF document to manipulate other open PDF documents remotely. For example, say you have several catalogs (each one a PDF file) along with a PDF order form, and you'd like to have information transfer automatically from a catalog page to the order form when the user clicks a button. This type of cross-document control is easily possible with Acrobat JavaScript, especially with Acrobat 5.0. Prior to version 5.0, you could do cross-document manipulation of field data, but it was a bit awkward to set up. The problem is, you need access to each document's Doc object in order to be able to reach inside documents remotely. With versions of Acrobat prior to 5.0, there was no function that you could call that would enumerate documents or hand you a list of Doc object references. Therefore, you had to make sure that each document would broadcast its Doc object reference via a global variable at document-open time. That is, each document had to do something such as

```
var global.documentA = this; // store doc handle in global
```

That way, later on, if you wanted to obtain a reference to Field_A remotely from Document B, you could call a line of code from Document B that might look like

```
var remoteField = global.documentA.getField('Field A');
```

In this example, Field A exists in Document A. But its value is available to Document B, through the global called documentA (whose value was set when Document A first opened). One of the qualities that make this sort of control awkward is that all of the participating documents have to somehow know in advance what the convention will be for storing Doc object references (that is, what the names of the globals are). Also, you can never quite be sure which documents are open and which are closed. Knowing about closed documents is important because any attempt to use a Doc object reference to a closed document in your JavaScript will result in a runtime error.

With Acrobat 5.0, details are much simpler for the programmer who wants to control PDF documents remotely, because the App object now includes a property called activeDocs, which is simply a JavaScript array that contains a list of Doc object references for all open PDF documents. Just as any array, activeDocs has a *length* property, which means you can iterate through all available Doc object references just by looping through activeDocs until length docs have been encountered.

For example, say that you want to display a list of all open PDF documents in an alert dialog box. You can do it by attaching the following code to the mouse-up event of a button:

```
function getFileName( pdf )
{
    return pdf.path.split("/").pop();
}
```

```
var docNames = [ ]; // empty array
var allDocs = app.activeDocs; // get all Doc objects
for (var j = 0; j < allDocs.length; j++)
{
    var theName = getFileName( allDocs[j] );
    docNames.push("\r"); // CR for formatting
    docNames.push( theName );
}
app.alert( docNames ); // display names
```

We start by declaring a one-line function that, given a Doc object reference, returns the name of the associated file, based on the path information for the file. (See the section "Backward Compatibility" earlier in this chapter.) Next, we declare an empty array (docNames) that will later hold the complete array of filenames of all open PDF docs. Then we declare a variable, allDocs, that receives all open file-names via the App object's activeDocs array. This variable simplifies our typing a bit and increases the code's readability.

The for statement sets up a loop that cycles through all open files. Using our counter variable (j), we index into allDocs to get a Doc object reference, and then use that as an argument to our custom function, getFileName. For formatting pur-poses (so that in our alert dialog box, we see one filename per line, instead of all the filenames run together), we stuff a carriage return into the docNames array (that's what \r means); and then we stuff the name of the file. The loop continues until all filenames have been found. Finally, app.alert() is called to display our names to the screen in an alert dialog box.

In a real-world situation where you may need to have five specific files open at once, you could use code similar to the previous example to generate a list of file-names and check each one against a master list to see if all files are present and accounted for. If any needed file was not present, you could prompt the user (or better yet, use the App object's openDoc method to try to open the document pro-grammatically, and then prompt the user if the doc couldn't be opened).

To see an example of remote document manipulation in action, check out the files named Slavedoc.pdf and Control.pdf on the CD-ROM that accompanies this book.

Checking to see if a document is open

Prior to Acrobat 5.0, operating on remote documents using Doc object references hard-coded to globals could be a bit dangerous. After all, a user might choose to close a given document, without telling you, at any time. But using a closed docu-ment's Doc object handle could generate an error. Unless the global variable con-taining that document's Doc object reference is somehow zeroed out when the document closes (and unless you're careful to check each object reference for being non-null before using it), you could get into serious trouble very easily. This is less of a problem in Acrobat 5.0, because the activeDocs property of the App object always contains an up-to-date list of open documents. The key is to check this list, and obtain a usable document reference every time you need to manipulate a given document.

Say for example that you want to obtain a handle to a document by name. That is, given the name of a document, you want to check to see if that document is currently open; and if so, you want a Doc object reference to it so that you can (for example) grab form-field data from it. You can do this with a custom function that looks like the following:

```
function getDoc( name ) {
    for (var i = 0; i < app.activeDocs.length; i++)
        if (getFilename(app.activeDocs[i]) == name)
            return app.activeDocs[i];
    return null;
}
```

Note the function relies on our earlier custom function, getFileName(). You simply set up a loop and iterate through all values of app.activeDocs. If we find a PDF whose name exactly matches whatever is stored in name, we return the Doc object for that document. Otherwise, we return null.

To use this function in a script that expects to manipulate the value of a text field called Field A in a remote document called Catalog.pdf, we could do:

```
var docObj = getDoc("Catalog.pdf"); // try to get doc object
if (docObj != null) // if it exists, use it
{
    var fieldValue = docObj.getField('Field A').value;
    // do sometime with Field A value . . .
}
else app.alert("The file Catalog.pdf is not open.");
```

Of course, before using the above code (which relies on Acrobat 5.0 features), it would be wise to check to see if Acrobat 5.0 (or Reader 5.0) is present, and fail gracefully (that is, warn the user that Acrobat 5.0 is required; then skip over the 5.0-dependent code) rather than subject the user to runtime error messages. (See "Backward Compatibility" earlier in this chapter for suggestions on how to do this.)

Collating pages from other PDF documents

Say that you have a catalog of company offerings, featuring one offering per page. You've received an inquiry from a customer who is interested in items 3, 7, and 9 from the main catalog. You want to send him or her a document consisting of a thank you letter followed by pages 3, 7, and 9 from Catalog.pdf. This document is easy to set up using Acrobat 5.0, because starting with Version 5.0, Acrobat JavaScript includes an insertPages() method designed to let you pluck pages from remote documents more-or-less at will and insert them into other documents.

The insertPages() method, which is called on the Doc object, takes four parameters. The first parameter is the zero-based index of the page after which you want new content inserted. (Acrobat JavaScript uses zero-based numbering of pages, which means that the first page in a document is always numbered zero; the second page is 1; the third page is 2; and so on) The bottom line is that if you want new pages inserted after page one of your source document, you supply zero as the first parameter to insertPages(). The second parameter (or argument) is the path to the source document: the document from which pages will be taken. You can use a relative path, or a complete path (such as the path property of an open document). The third parameter is the starting page (again, zero-based) of the selection in the source document, and the fourth parameter is the ending page of your selection.

Continuing with the previous example, assume that the thank-you letter is in Thanks.pdf and the source document (from which we'll grab pages) is Catalog.pdf. We need Doc object references to both documents; so we'll rely on our previously defined custom function getDoc() to obtain those. Then it's a simple matter to use the insertPages() method to get pages 3, 7, and 9 from the catalog and append them to Thanks.pdf. We can then use the mailDoc() method to e-mail the finished document (containing the thank you plus new pages) to our customer at joedoe@domain.com.

```
// NOTE: getDoc() is a custom function that we wrote!
// (see further above for source)
var customDoc = getDoc("Thanks.pdf");
var catalog = getDoc("Catalog.pdf");
customDoc.insertPages(0,catalog.path,2); // insert p. 3
customDoc.insertPages(0,catalog.path,6); // insert p. 7
customDoc.insertPages(0,catalog.path,8); // insert p. 9
customDoc.mailDoc(false,"joedoe@domain.com"); // mail it
```

The mailDoc() method will attempt to e-mail the PDF document specified by the calling Doc object (in this case, customDoc) to the address supplied in the second parameter. If the first parameter is false, Acrobat will try to do everything without putting up any dialog boxes. (The PDF will be sent as a file attachment to an empty e-mail.) Otherwise, if the first parameter is true, you will see a "compose new message" window in your favorite e-mail program before the message goes out.

Notice, again, how zero-based page indexing works. To append page 3 of Catalog.pdf to Thanks.pdf, we must specify a page offset of 2. To append page 7, we specify an offset of 6. (I know, it looks goofy. But this is how programming works.)

Incidentally, you should note that the mailDoc() method is one of those that work only in Acrobat (not Reader). If you try to execute it from Reader, nothing will happen. See AcroJS.pdf for more information.

Roundtrip CGI

One of the things JavaScript is most often used for is validating and manipulating online forms. This fact is no less true for Acrobat JavaScript than for JavaScript in HTML forms.

A forms session usually begins with a user encountering a form in the browser while navigating a Web site. The user fills out the form online, and then clicks a button (usually labeled "Submit") to send the form data back to the Web site. A CGI script on the Web site processes the form data and optionally sends back some kind of acknowledgement. This kind of interaction is known by the general name of "roundtrip CGI," which implies a back-and-forth exchange of information via the Web, all in one session.

CGI, which stands for Common Gateway Interface, is an agreed-upon standard for handling interactions between Web users and scripts or programs on a server. Some CGI programs are written in C or Java; others are written in a scripting language, such as Perl or Python. But it's important to note that CGI is not a language in itself. It's merely a protocol for making client/server interactions work. PDF forms can participate in CGI sessions just like forms created in HTML. The server doesn't know or care that the user is using PDF; all that matters is that chunks of data are arriving at the server via HTTP (HyperText Transfer Protocol). A CGI script is designed to handle those chunks of data.

As an illustration, suppose a certain PDF form has five text-entry fields, plus three buttons (Reset, Help, and Submit), and you want the user to be able to send all of the form data to the server when he or she clicks the Submit button; but you require all five fields to contain data (empty fields are not allowed), yet no field must have more than 36 characters' worth of information. Obviously, your CGI script could check for these requirements at the server, but prompting the user to correct any problems would require an extra roundtrip to the client machine and back (which is wasteful of time, energy, and bandwidth). It would be much better to check the data on the client's side, before sending it. How can we set this up in PDF?

The first thing to do in this situation is make sure the Submit button in your PDF document is not linked to a Submit Form action. Instead, link it to a JavaScript action. (If you allow it to be linked to a Submit Form action, the data will go out before you've had a chance to check it.) The JavaScript action for the Submit button can look like this:

```
// First, define a custom function that validates
// user input:

function checkField( aField )
{
    if (aField.value == "") // empty field
    {
```

```
        var msg = "No fields can be left empty.";
        app.alert(msg);
        return 0;
    }
    if (aField.value.length > 36)
    {
        var msg = "A field is too long (limit 36 chars).";
        app.alert(msg);
        return 0;
    }
    return 1; // on success, return a non-false value

} // end of function
// - - - - PREPROCESSING BEGINS HERE - - - -

var okToSubmit = true; // sentinel value

// loop over all fields:
for (var j = 0; j < this.numFields; j++)
{
    var fieldname = this.getNthFieldName(j);
    var theField = this.getField(fieldname);
    if (theField.type != 'text')
        continue; // get past button fields
    var valid =  checkField( theField );
    if (!valid) // valid == 0? Halt!
    {
        okToSubmit = false;  // set flag
        break;   // exit loop prematurely
    }

} // normal end of loop

var ourURL = "http://www.domain.com/cgi-bin/process.pl";
if (okToSubmit) // are we good to go?
    this.submitForm(ourURL, false);
```

We start by defining a custom function, checkField(), which inspects the value of the passed-in field object to be sure the field is not empty and does not exceed 36 characters in length. If the field contents are okay, this function returns 1; otherwise it flags the user with an appropriate error message and returns zero.

Actual processing begins just below the comment line that says Preprocessing Begins Here. Most of the 18 lines of code under this section are devoted to checking text fields one-by-one for correctness before submitting (or not submitting) the form data to our CGI script, which is called process.pl and is located at http:// www.domain.com/cgi-bin/process.pl. We start by declaring a sentinel variable, okToSubmit, that, in the end, will contain false if for some reason we shouldn't sub-mit the form, and true otherwise. Then we loop over all fields in the form, using the numFields property of the Doc object and the getNthFieldName() method (both of which are, of course, documented in AcroJS.pdf). This is a good illustration of the fact that it's not necessary to know the names of the fields in a PDF form in order to inspect them. You can iterate through all fields programmatically. In our case, we're only interested in text fields, so we make that check (inspecting the type property of the field) midway through the loop. Remember that we're iterating through all fields in the PDF form, but three of them are buttons! There is no need to check the correctness of the value of a button, so if we encounter something that is not a text field, we simply use the continue statement to go on to the next iteration of the loop.

The return value from checkField(), stored in a local variable called valid, tells us whether the field is non-empty and less than or equal to 36 characters long. If valid is zero, it will evaluate to false in the conditional statement; hence the expression !valid will be true if valid is zero. This is a common programming idiom. Some people find this makes for more readable code, because the expression if (!valid) translates, literally, to: "If *not* valid..." In any event, a field that isn't valid causes us to use the JavaScript break statement to terminate the loop immediately, with a sentinel value of false. (The sentinel variable okToSubmit keeps track of whether to submit the form or not.)

In the end, we use the submitForm() method of the Doc object to submit valid form data to our URL. The submitForm() method, which is present in Acrobat 4.0 and up, can take up to 13 arguments in Acrobat 5.0, depending on whether you want to submit data as XML, include annotations in exported data, incorporate security measures, and so on. Most of the arguments are optional; many are not supported in Acrobat 4.0; and some are not supported at all in Reader. AcroJS.pdf devotes a lengthy discussion (as you'd expect) to this method, so be sure and consult the Adobe documentation if you want to become intimately familiar with it. For our purposes, we're simply interested in the first two arguments: the destination URL and a Boolean indicating whether data should be submitted as FDF (Forms Data Format) or in HTML format. By setting the Boolean parameter to false, we are telling Acrobat to emulate an HTML Web form in its handling of outgoing data. This is important, because it means we can use the same CGI script (at the server) to handle incoming data from a PDF form or from an HTML form. The script won't know the difference.

Handling data at the server

You can write a CGI script to handle PDF form data the same way you would write one to handle HTML form data. In our case, though, we'd like to be able to send a PDF response (a thank you or order confirmation) back to the user after receiving the data at the server. The easiest way to do this is to generate a custom FDF file and send that as the response. The FDF can point, internally, to a PDF shell document at another URL; the shell document will be fetched automatically, and Acrobat (or Reader) will merge our FDF data into the shell doc automatically. The result is that a seemingly custom-made PDF document gets loaded into the user's browser (see Figure 19-7).

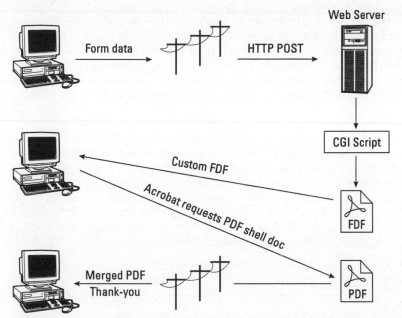

Figure 19-7: Data from a PDF form can be processed by a CGI script on the server just like data from any other Web form. To generate a custom PDF response, the script can create a small FDF document on the fly, containing a pointer to a PDF shell document. Acrobat requests the shell doc automatically and merges the FDF data into it, ultimately displaying the result in the user's browser.

Note When Acrobat (or Reader) loads an FDF file, it looks for an / F key inside the file, the value of which is a Uniform Resource Locator to a PDF file. If the PDF file associated with that URL is not already loaded, the viewing app (Reader or Acrobat) will try to fetch the file from the local disk system or the Web, as appropriate, using the URL. After the file has been found and loaded, the data from the FDF is merged into the PDF file and the result is displayed on-screen. Of course, if the viewing app is Reader, the combined data-plus-PDF cannot be saved to a storage device. Reader provides read-only services.

Creating the shell document is easy: Just design a nice-looking one-page PDF document and add a text field (using the Acrobat Form tool) to the middle of it. Call the text field "ReplyMessage", for example. Give it the appearance attributes (typeface, type size, color, and so on) that you would like; and make the field read-only so that no one will click in it and think it's a form. Name the document Reply.pdf, save it, and store it on your Web site in a directory that's public.

A typical FDF file looks like the following:

```
%FDF-1.2
%'"__
1 0 obj % Begin object
<< /FDF
    << /F (http://www.domain.com/public/Reply.pdf)
       /Fields
       [
         <<
             /V (Type Your Name Here.)
             /T (Name)
         >>

         <<
             /V (Type Your Street Address Here.)
             /T (Street)
         >>

         % . . . more Value/Title pairs
       ]
    >>
>>
endobj % End object
trailer
<<
/Root 1 0 R
>>
%%EOF
```

The internal syntax for FDF is much the same as for PDF, which means the percent symbol (%) serves as the beginning of a comment; Acrobat ignores everything to the right of the percent sign. Spaces and line endings are also ignored. The detailed syntax here is not important. What's important is to notice that there are /V and /T pairs corresponding to the value (V) and title (T) of every form field inside the destination PDF document. (In this case, there are two fields, named Name and Street.) You should also notice that the destination PDF document (the shell doc) has its URL stored next to a /F (file) tag. This is where Acrobat or Reader will go to try to find the PDF document that needs this data merged in.

Our tactic will simply be to write a CGI script in Perl (although it could be any language) that will fetch incoming form data and write out a custom FDF file containing a dynamically generated reply message. The following short Perl script, process.pl, shows how to do this, assuming the form data includes a field called userName containing (what else?) the user's name.

```
#!/usr/bin/perl
# -------------- SCRIPT: process.pl
use CGI;

$msg = "Thank you, ";  # start the thank-you message
```

```
$msg .= param('userName');  # append the person's name
$msg .= ", for your order."; # finish the sentence

$fdf = GenerateFDF($msg); # generate FDF

$len = length($fdf); # get the length

# serve out the FDF header, with content-length:
print header(-type=>'application/vnd.fdf',
            -Content_length=>$len);

print $fdf;  # serve out the FDF itself
exit;        # finished

#-----------------------------------------------
sub GenerateFDF {

my ($fieldValue) = ($_[0]);

$fdfString =<<END_FDF;
%FDF-1.2
%'"__
1 0 obj
<<
/FDF
/Fields [ << /V ($fieldValue) /T (ReplyMessage)>> ]
/F (http://www.domain.com/public/Reply.pdf)
>>
>>
endobj
trailer
<<
/Root 1 0 R
>>
%%EOF
END_FDF
```

The 40-line script is fairly easy to interpret, even if you don't know Perl. We start by building the custom thank-you message, into which we insert the user's name. (The .= symbol is a way of concatenating strings in Perl.) Because we're using the standard CGI package that ships with Perl, we can obtain form field values very easily using the param() function. A custom subroutine called GenerateFDF() builds a small, custom FDF file for us (containing our thank you message, passed as a parameter), as a Perl string. The rest is a matter of using Perl's print operator to send text back to the user via HTTP. In order for the user's browser to know that we're sending an FDF file, we have to first send an HTTP header containing the mimetype for FDF, which is 'application/vnd.fdf'. We also go to the trouble of sending content-length info in the header (which some browsers need). After printing the body of the FDF file, we're done.

The user's browser, seeing the FDF mimetype info, responds by handing the incoming FDF file to Acrobat or Reader, while Acrobat (in turn) looks up the PDF file stored at `www.domain.com/public/Reply.pdf`, and then loads it and merges the FDF data (that is, our thank you message) into that file before displaying it in the user's browser. The user sees a custom-generated PDF document, with a custom thank you message, which causes him to slap his head and exclaim: "How neat is that?"

Note When adapting the previous code for your own use, be certain to remember to change `ReplyMessage` to the name of the text field in your shell document; and change the URL stored after `/F` to correspond to the URL of your shell doc.

By building on this technique, you can generate some very sophisticated (and impressive-looking) PDF acknowledgements as part of your CGI sessions. Bear in mind that the shell document (`Reply.pdf` in this case) is itself a form, which means that if you want to design text fields into it (along with a Submit button), you can easily extend this technique to encompass multi-part, extended CGI sessions with the user. Where you go with it is totally up to your imagination.

Database Access via ADBC

Recognizing the pivotal importance of database access in business applications, Adobe wisely decided to incorporate database connectivity into Acrobat with the release of version 5.0. Thanks to the new ADBC (Acrobat DataBase Connectivity) plug-in by Acrobat JavaScript creating JavaScript-powered PDF forms that present a user-friendly front end to relational database systems is now possible. Extremely powerful PDF database applications are possible because of the *SQL binding* built into ADBC. (SQL stands for Structured Query Language, the lingua franca of data retrieval.) It's safe to say that ADBC will give an enormous boost to PDF at the enterprise level, because of the critical importance of database access in business.

Unfortunately, database connectivity is an unavoidably elaborate subject, and a comprehensive discussion of how ADBC works would fill a book by itself. In the pages that follow, I won't have room to present anything more than an abbreviated run-through of ADBC concepts. But fear not: You will see plenty of working code that you can cut and paste into your own projects; and you'll be able to find additional examples on the CD accompanying this book. (Look for a file called `ADBCdemo.pdf`.) We don't have space to waste, so let's hit the ground running.

Basic architecture

Getting an overall understanding of how database access via ADBC works is important. ADBC, which requires Acrobat (not Reader) as well as the `ADBC.api` plug-in (check your Plug_ins folder), works in a manner similar to the Microsoft Open DataBase Connectivity (ODBC) model. Under the ODBC model, databases created in diverse software environments can be manipulated via a standard, platform-independent application programming interface (API), using *drivers* (software utilities with no user interface) whose purpose is to handle proprietary interactions behind the scenes so that the database user doesn't have to worry about anything but ODBC-defined behaviors. Almost all database-software vendors offer ODBC drivers for their databases, so that any given database can be reached by multiple users on multiple platforms, using multiple (diverse) host programs. ADBC likewise isolates the end user from the ugly low-level details of dealing with many types of relational databases, exposing only a common set of features via a common interface. With ADBC (as with ODBC), you can "reach into" a relational database using ordinary SQL queries. As long as you know Structured Query Language, and as long as your database is accessible via a suitable ODBC driver, it doesn't matter whose software created the database, or on what machine.

Figure 19-8 shows the relationship (in terms of flow of control) between the various software pieces involved in handling Acrobat database connectivity.

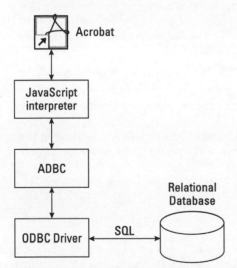

Figure 19-8: Acrobat database connectivity relies on communication between the Acrobat JavaScript interpreter, the ADBC plug-in, and the ODBC driver for your particular database system, in order to read and write data (via SQL) from a relational database.

Acrobat JavaScript defines several new-for-5.0 objects that play an essential role in database connectivity:

✦ **ADBC Object:** This object has two methods, called `getDataSourceList()` and newConnection(). The former returns an array containing a DataSourceInfo object (see the next entry) for every available database in the system. The `newConnection()` method allows you to obtain a Connection object that defines session behavior.

✦ **DataSourceInfo Object:** This object, returned by the ADBC object's `getDataSourceList()` method, has just two properties: name and description. These properties contain strings describing a given DSN (Data Source Name), or database.

✦ **Connection Object:** The Connection object encapsulates session behavior. It provides methods for creating Statement objects (see next entry), enumerating tables, and enumerating column lists within tables.

✦ **Statement Object:** The Statement object allows you to execute SQL queries against a database and get column and row information of various sorts, plus inspect columnCount and rowCount status values generated by SQL calls.

✦ **Column Object:** The Column object, which is returned by the `getColumn()` method of the Statement object, encapsulates data associated with a particular column in a given row in a table. The name and value properties of this object are useful in identifying data of interest.

✦ **ColumnInfo Object:** This object holds basic information (such as name, description, data type, and so on) about a particular column in a table. The `getColumnList()` method of the Connection object returns an array of ColumnInfo objects.

✦ **Row Object:** The Row object is returned by the `getRow()` method of the Statement object. It has one property, the columnArray property, which points to an array of Column objects.

✦ **TableInfo Object:** This object is returned by the `getTableList()` method of the Connection object. It holds general information about a table within a database, such as the name of the table and a short description (if available).

At first blush, this may seem like a rather complicated list, but in fact each object is just a wrapper for some very basic database-related features, and the relationships between objects are actually quite natural and intuitive. The interrelationships will become clearer if we look at some code examples.

Bear in mind that the whole point of connecting to a database via ADBC is to be able to make queries via SQL. Everything we do will ultimately be aimed at this goal. Through SQL, you can do just about any kind of database manipulation that you might need to do, whether it involves reading or writing data. Obviously, a detailed discussion of SQL basics is beyond the scope of this book and you should consult a good SQL text if you need to know more about that subject. For our purposes, only a tiny amount of SQL will be needed, because all we're going to do here is illustrate some general techniques to get you started.

A word about DSNs

In order for a database to be visible to ADBC, it must be available under a Data Source Name (DSN) on your system. The DSN is simply an arbitrary string that associates a given database file (which could be a file created by Microsoft Access, for example, or Sybase Adaptive Server Anywhere, and so forth) with a given ODBC driver. The DSN may be a User DSN (in which case it will be visible only to you, on your machine) or a System DSN (in which case all users of your system can see the database, even across networks). Either one will work for ADBC.

On Windows machines, you can assign DSNs to database files using the ODBC Data Source utility in the Control Panels folder. On Macintosh, look for ODBC Setup in the Mac Control Panel folder.

Quick code example

Just so you can see how uncomplicated the whole process of using ADBC can be, run through a quick code example that gets information from a known data source. We will assume that a DSN by the name of "MyTestDB" exists on the local machine. In addition, we'll assume that we want to inspect the first available table in MyTestDB so as to develop a list of all the column names in that table. Our goal will be to display all column names in an alert dialog box. We can do all this in about eight lines of JavaScript (if we sacrifice error-checking code in the name of clarity):

```
var myConnection =
    ADBC.newConnection("MyTestDB");  // open a connection

var myTables = myConnection.getTableList(); // get table info

var theTableName = myTables[0].name; // get name of first table

            // now obtain column info for that table:
var myColumnList = myConnection.getColumnList(theTableName);

// prepare a list of names of columns
var theNames = "";

for (var i = 0; i < myColumnList.length; i++)
    theNames += myColumnList[i].name + "\r";

app.alert(theNames); // display the names
```

The easiest way to test this code is to type it into the JavaScript Console window, highlight (select) all of it, and then press the Enter key on the numeric keypad (which executes the selected code). Assuming you have a database on your system that's registered under the DSN "MyTestDB", you should see an alert window (perhaps similar to Figure 19-9) pop up containing the column headings for all columns in the first table of that database. Each column name is on a separate line.

Figure 19-9: The result of our "Quick Code Example" with all column names of the first table in MyTestDB.

Look at what we did. First, we opened a connection to the database with `ADBC.newConnection()`. Then we called the connection's `getTableList()` method, which simply returns a JavaScript array containing TableInfo Objects corresponding to all the tables in "MyTestDB." Because we're only interested in the first table, we inspect the zeroth item of the array, specifically the name property of that item. We need the table name as an argument to the Connection object's `getColumnList()` method. After we've called the `getColumnList()` method, we have an array of ColumnInfo objects stored in a local variable, `myColumnList`. What we're interested in is the name property of each ColumnInfo object. To get those names, we must iterate through all members of the ColumnInfo array; hence the `"for i"` loop, which concatenates names (and carriage returns) into a single string. Finally, we display the string in an alert.

Obtaining data via an SQL query

The previous code example is a good one if you don't know the name of the first table in your database or the names of the columns in that table. But in reality, you probably will know the name of the table (and the names of the columns) if you are going to execute SQL queries of the type:

```
SELECT Name, Address, City, State FROM "Customers"
```

In this query, for example, we're interested in obtaining data from the columns named Name, Address, City, and State in the table called `"Customers"`. It's a little awkward (though by no means impossible) to construct a statement like this programmatically, in JavaScript, using table and column names looked up at runtime. Real-world SQL statements tend to use hard-coded values for factors, such as column and table names.

So let's pose a slightly different problem. Suppose we want to execute the above SQL query against the Customers table of `MyTestDB` (which may or may not be the first table in that database). How can we do that in JavaScript? We start, as before, by opening a connection to the database:

```
var myConnection =
    ADBC.newConnection("MyTestDB");  // open a connection
```

Next, we have to create a Statement object:

```
var myStatement =
    myConnection.newStatement();  // create Statement object
```

For convenience, we'll store the SQL query as a JavaScript string. Notice that we escape the quotation marks around the table name using backslashes:

```
var mySQL = "SELECT Name, Address, City, State FROM
\"Customers\"";
```

Finally, we execute the query:

```
myStatement.execute(mySQL);
```

What does this statement actually do? It tells the JavaScript interpreter to go ask the ODBC driver to query the database and obtain a result set, which in this case will consist of the requested columns from all rows in the table. The returned data set becomes part of the Statement object. How do we get at each row of data? This is where it gets a bit tricky. We have to ask for each row of data in the following way:

```
var success = myStatement.nextRow(); // returns a Boolean
if (success)
    var myRowObject = myStatement.getRow();
```

The Statement object's `nextRow()` method must always be called before processing any row of data (even the first row). But the return value from `nextRow()` is just a Boolean value indicating whether the next row could be obtained. (Maybe it doesn't exist.) If the next row does exist and is obtainable, you must then call `getRow()` to obtain it as a Row object. In the above case, we store the returned Row object in the local variable `myRowObject`. To loop through all available Row objects in the result set, we could set up a while loop that looks like:

```
while(myStatement.nextRow() == true) {

  myRowObject = myStatement.getRow();
  // ... do something with the data

  } // end of loop
```

Working with row objects

At this point you may be wondering how to get at the column data obtained via an SQL query. If you're guessing that this data may be reachable via the Row object, you'd be right. The Row object, as the name implies, contains all the information in a single row of data (consistent with any constraints you may have imposed in your SQL statement). Every Row object has a columnArray property, which is just a JavaScript array filled with Column objects (see Table 19-2).

	Table 19-2: Column Object Properties	
Property	**Access**	**Description**
columnNum	R	The number identifying the column's place in the Statement from which the Column was obtained.
name	R	The name of the column.
type	R	The SQL Type (data type) of the data. This can be one of 19 predefined types (documented in AcroJS.pdf).
typeName	R	A database dependent string representing the data type. This property may give useful information about user-defined data types.
value	R/W	The value of the data in the column in whatever format the data was originally received in.

To iterate through the column values contained in one row of table data, you could do copy the following. Remember that because the columnArray is just an ordinary JavaScript array, it has a length property.

```
var theColumns = myRowData.columnArray; // get column array

for (var i = 0; i < theColumns.length; i++) // loop over length
{
    if (theColumns[i].name == "Name")
        // do something with theColumns[i].value

    if (theColumns[i].name == "Address")
        // do something with theColumns[i].value

    // etc.
}
```

In many cases, of course, it will be simpler (if you know the column names) just to grab values directly from columns by name. It turns out that although the Row object begins life with just one property, the columnArray, it has additional properties after a result set has been returned to a Statement object. The additional properties are Column objects that have names corresponding to the headings of the columns you requested. So in the previous example, you can alternatively do:

```
var customerAddress = myRowData.Address.value;

// ... do something with customerAddress

var customerCity = myRowData.City.value;

// ... do something with customerCity

// etc.
```

To summarize: Our SQL statement generated Row objects, which we must access using `nextRow()` and `getRow()`. Each Row object has a bunch of Column objects attached as properties; and those properties have names, such as "`Name`," "`Address`," "`City`," and so forth. Because each property refers to a Column object, we must use the value property to find the object's data value. (Simple, right?)

Don't worry too much right now if this all seems a tad murky. It will begin to crystallize for you as you begin working with live code. It will help, too, if you pick apart the example file called ADBCdemo.pdf on the CD-ROM accompanying this book. That file contains working ADBC code (attached to GUI elements; in other words, form widgets) that's guaranteed to stimulate your imagination and keep you going in the right direction(s).

Of course, in the space available here we've only been able to scrape a small handful of frost off a very large iceberg. As you know if you've developed database applications before, crafting well behaved, reliable, user-friendly database management forms is a difficult challenge (particularly in an HTTP environment, where session state is difficult to track). A great deal of thought and effort need to be devoted to details, such as user interface design, data validation, error checking, security administration, state management, transaction management (via SQL commit and rollback verbs), and so on. What PDF brings to this picture is an opportunity for the database application designer to take advantage of exceptional graphic appeal, security, application stability, cross-platform interoperability, and programming power (via Acrobat JavaScript) in database forms that might otherwise be far too unwieldy to implement in HTML, far too sluggish-performing in Java, or far too platform-dependent in a 4GL (fourth-generation language) app. With Acrobat 5.0, it can truly be said that new opportunities await the JavaScript forms developer.

Summary

✦ Acrobat JavaScript is a powerful extension of the JavaScript language, incorporating all of the core functionality of ECMA-262 while also providing scores of objects, methods, and properties tailored to the PDF environment.

✦ JavaScript-powered PDF documents can be viewed in Reader as well as Acrobat. Many features are backward-compatible to Acrobat/Reader version 4.0 (or earlier, in a few cases). Until Version 5.0 is widespread, however, you should be careful about using 5.0-dependent features. Also, you should consult `AcroJS.pdf` to find out which features are disabled in Reader. Fortunately, only a few are.

✦ Acrobat JavaScript can be used for far more than just data validation in forms. Even a PDF document that contains no form fields at all can contain a significant amount of JavaScript.

✦ Acrobat JavaScript doesn't know anything about HTML pages, nor does JavaScript inside an HTML page know anything about PDF. By and large, the PDF and HTML worlds do not overlap where JavaScript is concerned.

✦ When you set security options in a PDF file, you are encrypting not only the file's text contents but also any JavaScript it contains. Therefore, if you don't want your JavaScript code to be available for inspection, it doesn't have to be.

✦ With Acrobat 5.0 running under Windows, using an external code editor when writing JavaScript for PDF is possible.

✦ Acrobat 5.0 produces a comprehensive code listing (or "code dump") of all JavaScript in a given PDF file, which can be an incredibly useful element for troubleshooting and debugging.

✦ The JavaScript Console window is a good place to test scripts: Just enter the script, select it (highlight it with the mouse), and press the Enter key on the numeric keypad to execute the code immediately.

✦ JavaScript can easily be used to inspect a user's keystrokes as they are happening, and block illegal keystrokes in real time.

✦ One PDF document can control another PDF document remotely by using JavaScript.

✦ PDF Web forms can participate in CGI sessions using the same CGI scripts that work for HTML forms.

✦ A CGI script that generates a small, custom FDF file can make an attractive PDF "response document" appear in the user's browser.

✦ ADBC (Acrobat Database Connectivity) opens up new vistas for form designers by allowing easy, cross-platform access to relational databases. Using JavaScript, you can design sophisticated PDF forms that execute SQL queries against databases (a truly exciting and powerful capability).

✦   ✦   ✦

Using Plug-Ins

Understanding Plug-ins

Adobe Acrobat supports a plug-in architecture. But don't
think that all of these third-party add-ons are inexpensive little items that you want to run out and purchase. Some are
incredibly expensive. XTensions for QuarkXPress can run into
many thousands of dollars, and some for Acrobat can be
equally expensive. Before you purchase a particular plug-in
for Acrobat, you can often find a demonstration version that
will run for a limited amount of time after you install it. Other
demo versions may disable a few features, but offer you
enough usable commands to thoroughly test them. If a demo
version is not available for a costly plug-in, be certain to
research it well. You can often find information on the Web.
Visiting trade shows where products are demonstrated can
also be helpful.

You will find some plug-ins supplied by Adobe Systems on the
installer CD-ROM as well as some demonstration plug-ins from
third-party manufacturers. You can visit the Adobe Web site at
www.adobe.com/acrobat for updated announcements on
available plug-ins as well as some demonstration utilities you
can download. In addition, you'll find several demonstration
third-party plug-ins on the CD-ROM accompanying this book.

Installing plug-ins

Plug-ins developed by third-party manufacturers often use an
installer application. You can double-click the installer, which
will automatically decompress and save the necessary files to
the proper locations on your computer. Most often the location will be the Acrobat:Plug-ins folder. However, some plug-
ins are designed to work with Acrobat and other applications,
or they may need to install some system resources, so installation of other files may be in different locations on your computer. If the manufacturer supplies an installer application,
using the installer is best instead of copying files to the
Acrobat Plug-ins folder.

On Windows, double-click the installer application or use the Run command from the status bar to install a plug-in. In most recent versions of installer applications, double-clicking launches the installer application for Windows. Either method you choose, however, will work. On the Macintosh, you may also encounter an installer application for third party tools. When an installer is provided, double-click on the installer icon. Follow the directions in the installer dialog box to complete installation.

Plug-ins may be supplied by manufacturers without an installer application. If this is the case, you will often find a ReadMe file contained on the installer disk or CD-ROM. If a ReadMe file is supplied, be certain to review the installation instructions. There may be files that need to be stored in special folders on your hard drive, and the ReadMe file will describe these to you. If the manufacturer does not supply an installer, then you will likely need to copy some files to the Acrobat Plug-ins folder on your hard drive. When the Acrobat folder is opened on your hard drive, the Plug-ins folder will appear in the next level. Opening the Plug-ins folder, shown in Figure 20-1 on Windows, will display subfolders containing individual plug-ins as well as plug-ins installed without subfolders. By default, plug-ins installed on a Macintosh will be installed in individual folders.

Figure 20-1: Plug-ins installed on Windows are stored individually or in separate folders in the Acrobat:Plug-ins folder.

If you acquire a plug-in without an installer or documentation, then the plug-in will need to be copied to the Acrobat:Plug-ins folder. When copying plug-ins to this folder, copy the folder if one exists. Acrobat recognizes nested folders for plug-in usage. If several files exist for the plug-in, it will be difficult to manage your files and know exactly which files relate to which plug-ins. Therefore, copy the folder supplied by the manufacturer with all the resources contained therein to the Acrobat:Plug-ins directory.

If a plug-in is supplied by a manufacturer without a folder and only as a single item, you can copy it directly to the Plug-ins folder. You can also create a folder and place the single plug-in inside this folder. This method is a matter of personal preference. I prefer to handle plug-ins this way so that I don't forget that a plug-in contains no other files, and this method helps keep my Acrobat plug-ins organized. If you make a folder and copy the plug-in to a new folder, test it out. If Acrobat can't find the plug-in, then relocate it to the Plug-ins folder level.

Plug-in conflicts

Software releases at the *point zero level* (that is, 3.0, 4.0, 5.0, and so on) often have bugs when a manufacturer ships them out the door. Personally, I find Adobe applications very solid when shipped in the final version. Upon the release of Acrobat 5.0, the program went through an extensive beta period before it was finally shipped. However, no manufacturer can expect to find all bugs and inconsistencies when a program is shipped. In the case of Acrobat, many plug-ins are being shipped with the application program. Add the first release version of all the Acrobat components to the new or updated software offered by many plug-in manufacturers, you most definitely will find problems. Sometimes the problems can lead to system crashes, irregular behavior, or rendering a program nonfunctional. Plug-in installations can lead to problems with the performance of Acrobat. At times, you may find a conflict between plug-ins or between Acrobat and a third-party plug-in.

Diagnosing plug-in conflicts

Finding conflicts with plug-ins is not always an easy task. The first thing to look at when Acrobat misbehaves is the last plug-in installed. When installing plug-ins, keep a record of the installation order. It will often help to know exactly which application was installed last on your computer. If you know a plug-in was installed and then Acrobat experienced problems, remove the offending plug-in folder from the Acrobat:Plug-ins folder. You can simply relocate this folder to another folder on your hard drive without trashing it. If an uninstaller has been supplied with the plug-in by a third-party manufacturer, de-install the plug-in. Sometimes installers will copy hidden files to your computer. This is particularly true for Windows users. If a .dll file has been installed in the Windows directory, unless you're a tech head, you'll never find it. Use the uninstall application if one exists.

When Acrobat is launched, it will read all the plug-ins before opening the Acrobat window. If Acrobat is launched, and the program freezes, it may relate to a plug-in problem. Watch the splash screen as Acrobat reads the plug-ins. It may display a plug-in name when it halts. Try to remove the offending plug-in as noted previously.

If Reader is installed on your computer along with Acrobat and you experience problems, you may have a conflict with Acrobat attempting to read two plug-ins of the same type. Remove Reader from the Acrobat folder if you find the two programs installed in the same folder. Relaunch Acrobat after removing Reader to see if the problem is resolved.

If all the preceding attempts fail, you may need to isolate the problem by removing all plug-ins from the Acrobat:Plug-ins folder, and then add a few at a time to isolate the problem. For example, remove all plug-ins, bring three or four back to the plug-in folder, and then launch Acrobat. If everything works, quit Acrobat, move a few more plug-ins to the plug-in folder, and relaunch Acrobat. Continue this operation until you narrow down the problem. Before you attempt to reinstall Acrobat, it is a good idea to try to isolate the problem. Reinstallation won't tell you anything about where the problem existed, and you may return to it by installing additional plug-ins. Use the reinstallation method as a last resort.

 Tip   To verify a problem with a plug-in when Acrobat freezes upon launching, you can temporarily disable all plug-ins without removing them from the plug-in folder. Hold the Shift key down and double-click the Acrobat program icon. When Acrobat launches, it will bypass loading all plug-ins.

One more issue that is equally important when experiencing problems is to use the current version of Acrobat. While third-party manufacturers are updating their software, Adobe will be recording all problems reported as bugs. Whenever a software product is released, you can soon expect a *point zero one release* (for example, 5.01) to soon follow. Updates usually fix bugs found after the first release of a product. When Acrobat Distiller 3.0 was released, I remember having much difficulty running it on a Macintosh without constant crashes. By the time release 3.02 appeared, it ran flawlessly. You can check for current releases and bug fixes by visiting the Adobe Web site. Be certain to use the most updated version of the software and check out the Adobe Web site before attempting to reinstall the program.

Plug-in documentation

Manufacturers of software, especially plug-in manufacturers, usually supply their product documentation in Acrobat format. Whenever you see a PDF file accompanying a new release, be certain to review the document. The PDF document can be a compilation of last-minute notes, or it could be an entire user manual. All supported documentation can often help you understand the application usage and how to avoid problems.

If Acrobat is installed with an installer application, you may have ReadMe files and PDFs all stored in the plug-in folder. These files won't be needed to operate the program, and they can be relocated on your hard drive (or removed) if you choose to do so.

When installing several plug-ins, keeping track of the documentation can sometimes be overwhelming. To organize your documentation when it is supplied in PDF documents, create a folder on your hard drive for Acrobat documentation. Create a catalog of all the PDF files and rebuild the catalog as new PDFs are added to the folder. When you need to find information related to a particular feature, open Acrobat and use Acrobat Search for finding the keyword(s) supplied in the Query dialog box. You can combine all the help files shipped with Acrobat along with your plug-in PDFs in the same catalog for easy access.

Disabling plug-ins

At times you may want to temporarily disable a plug-in. If you deinstall the plug-in or delete it from your hard drive, you'll need to reinstall at a later time. Deleting plug-ins is much more difficult to manage and requires more time than simply disabling them. An easy method for keeping track of your Acrobat plug-ins is to create a folder and name it Disabled, Disabled Folder, or Disabled Plug-ins. Whatever name you prefer can be used. Move the plug-in to the Disabled folder and keep this folder inside the Acrobat folder. You must, however, keep the Disabled folder at the Acrobat level or in another location on your computer. Acrobat can find plug-ins in nested folders, so if the Disabled folder resides inside the Acrobat:Plug-ins folder, it will locate the plug-ins therein. I find keeping my Disabled folder at the Acrobat folder level to work well because I know at a quick glance these plug-ins belong to Acrobat and not another application.

Using Third-Party Plug-ins and Applications

Third-party manufacturers have created many plug-ins for Adobe Acrobat and there are many related applications designed to work with Acrobat or support the Portable Document Format. As Acrobat becomes more prolific with computer users, we can expect many new developers and more plug-ins to add to the amazing features of Acrobat. In addition to plug-ins, some stand-alone applications are designed to work with Acrobat and PDF files. It would be beyond the scope of this volume to list all plug-ins manufactured for Acrobat or applications used to work in concert with PDF documents.

A number of demonstration plug-ins are available on the accompanying CD-ROM. Most of the plug-ins are fully functioning for a limited time or may limit a single feature. Software developers are continually upgrading their products and adding new plug-ins and applications to work with Acrobat. In Table 20-1, I list some of the more popular manufacturers who offer demonstration versions of their products. If the product is contained on the accompanying CD-ROM, you may first want to visit the Web site for the manufacturer to ensure that you are using the most updated version. Also, you may want to bookmark this table for future visits to the listed Web sites to investigate new developments.

Table 20-1

Third-party Manufacturers Offering Demonstration Software on Internet Web Sites

Manufacturer	Product	Platform	Acrobat Plug-in	Stand-alone Application/ Other Non–Plug-in	Web Address
Ambia Software	Aerial	Win	X		www.ambia.com or www.infodata.com
	Compose	Win	X		
	Re:mark	Win	X		
Avenza Software, Inc.	pdfPlus	Win	X		www.avenza.com
BCL Computers	Magellan	Win	X		www.bcl-computers.com
	Freebird	Win	X		
	Jade	Win	X		
	Drake	Win	X		
Brook House, Ltd.	BatchPrint PDF	Win		X	www.brookhouse.co.uk
	Homer	Win	X		
	ShowMe	Win	X		
	PDF-Assistant	Win	X		
Callas Software	pdfToolbox	Mac/Win	X		www.callas.de
	pdfOutputPro	Mac/Win	X		
	pdfPreview	Win	X		
Consolidated Technical Services, Inc.	SpiffyPop	Win	X		www.contechinc.com

Manufacturer	Product	Platform	Acrobat Plug-in	Stand-alone Application/ Other Non–Plug-in	Web Address
Dionis	Ari's Crop Helper	Mac/Win	X		
	Ari's Link Checker	Mac/Win	X		
	Ari's Print Helper	Mac/Win	X		
	Ari's Ruler	Mac/Win	X		
	Ari's PDF Splitter	Mac/Win	X		
	Ari's Toolbox	Mac/Win	X		www.dionis.com
Easy Software Products	HTMLDOC	Win		X	www.easysw.com
Enfocus Software	Certify PDF	Mac/Win	X		www.enfocus.com
	PitStop	Mac/Win	X		
	PowerUp	Mac/Win	X		
	WebPerfect PDF	Mac/Win	X		
Extensis Software, Inc.	Collect Pro*	Mac	X	X	www.extensis.com
	Preflight Pro	Mac	X	X	
	Preflight Online	Mac/Win		X	
	QX-Tools	Mac	X	X	
FileOpen Systems, Inc.	FileOpen Publisher	Mac/Win	X	X	www.fileopen.com
	FileOpen Personal Publisher	Mac/Win	X		
	FileOpen Web Publisher	Mac/Win		X	
Handmade Software	Image Alchemy PS	Mac/Win		X	www.handmade.com
Iceni Technology	Argus 3.0 XP	Win		X	www.iceni.com
	Gemini	Mac/Win	X		

Continued

Table 20-1 *(continued)*

Manufacturer	Product	Platform	Acrobat Plug-in	Stand-alone Application/ Other Non–Plug-in	Web Address
Informative Graphics Corp.	Myriad	Win		X	www.infograph.com
Lantana Research	Crackerjack	Mac/Win	X		www.lantanarips.com
	PDF Bellhop	Mac/Win	X		
	PDF Imageworks	Mac/Win	X		
	PDF Librarian	Mac/Win	X		
	PDF Valet	Mac/Win	X		
Markzware USA	FlightCheck	Mac/Win		X	www.markzware.com
	MarkzNet	Mac/Win		X	
	MarkzScout	Mac/Win		X	
Merlin Open Systems	Name It	Mac/Win	X		www.merlin-os.co.uk
	Name It Launcher	Mac/Win	X		
	Index Fixer	Win	X		
	Multi-Index	Mac/Win	X		
	Options	Mac/Win	X		
	Date Stamp	Win		X	
	Search Results Printer	Mac/Win	X		
	View Info	Mac/Win	X		
One Vision, Inc.	Asura	Mac/Win		X	www.onevision.com
	Solvero	Mac/Win		X	
Page Technology Marketing, Inc.	FormView	Win		X	www.pcltools.com

Manufacturer	Product	Platform	Acrobat Plug-in	Stand-alone Application/ Other Non–Plug-in	Web Address
PDF Solutions, Ltd.	Clonelinks	Win	X		www.pdf-solutions.com
	Bookmark Counter	Win	X		
PrePress-Consulting	Distiller Tools	Mac/Win		X	www.prepress.ch
Quark, Inc.	PDF Import/Export	Mac/Win		X	www.quark.com
Quite Software	Quite a Box of Tricks	Mac/Win	X		www.quite.com
	Quite Imposing	Mac/Win	X		
	Quite Imposing Plus	Mac/Win	X		
A Round Table Solution	ARTS Duplex	Win	X		www.roundtable.com.au
	ARTS Import	Win	X		
	ARTS Joust	Win	X		
	ARTS Security	Win	X		
	ARTS Split	Win	X		
	ARTS ThumbOpt	Win	X		
	ARTS PDFWorkshop	Win	X		
TechPool Software	Transverter Pro	Mac/Win		X	www.techpool.com
Ultimate Technographics	Impostrip	Mac/Win NT		X	www.ultimate-tech.com
	IMPress	Mac		X	
	Trapeze	Mac/Win NT		X	
	UltimateFlow	Mac/Win NT		X	
Visual Software	pcl2pdf	Win		X	www.visual.co.uk
xman Software	xToolsOne	Mac/Win	X		www.xman.com
Zeon Corporation	DocuCom	Win		X	www.zeon.com.tw

* Functions as both a stand-alone application and plug-in.

Table 20-1 is not to be construed as all-inclusive. There are many more manufacturers with current products or products under development. In addition, companies do fall or get acquired by other companies. As of this writing, the products listed are respective to the manufacturers producing them. However, to stay current and find updated information, frequent the planetPDF Web site at `www.planetpdf.com` for a comprehensive list updated regularly. In addition, the planetPDF store sells most of the Acrobat plug-ins available through reseller channels.

Summary

✦ Adobe Acrobat uses a plug-in architecture to expand program features and enable third-party developers a means of offering expanded solutions with the Portable Document Format.

✦ Many of the tools by Acrobat are made available through plug-ins installed during the installation of Acrobat.

✦ Plug-ins for Acrobat can be nested in folders, but those nested folders must be installed in the Plug-in folder.

✦ Disabling plug-ins may be required when there are conflicts that prohibit Acrobat from operating correctly. Plug-ins can be disabled by removing them from the Plug-ins folder.

✦ A great many third-party distributors of plug-ins develop products to enhance performance of Acrobat and add specialized features.

✦ If you have Acrobat and related third-party products, you should plan on making routine visits to the manufacturers' Web sites to keep on top of the latest updates and upgrades.

✦   ✦   ✦

Using the CD-ROM

Contents

The enclosed CD-ROM at the back of the book contains five folders. The CD-ROM is hybrid and can be read by both Macintosh and Windows computers. Macintosh users need System 8.0 or above. Windows users need Windows 95, Windows 98, Windows 2000, or Windows NT. (The CD-ROM will not function properly with Windows 3.1.) To gain access to the CD-ROM contents, follow these steps:

1. Insert the CD-ROM in your CD drive and wait a few moments until the CD icon appears.

2. Double-click the icon to open the CD-ROM that displays a window where all five folders will appear.

The folders and their contents include:

✦ Adobe Acrobat Reader 5.0 software

✦ Documents

✦ The entire text of this book in PDF documents

✦ Tutorial PDF documents

✦ Macintosh demonstration plug-ins and applications

✦ Windows demonstration plug-ins and applications

Adobe Acrobat Reader 5.0

The Adobe Acrobat Reader installers appear inside the **Acrobat** folder. A Macintosh and Windows version of Reader is inside this folder. In addition to the installers are readme files and licensing agreements. Please take time to read the licensing information distributed by Adobe Systems. The readme files will provide installation instructions for installing Acrobat Reader on your computer. Follow the guidelines for installation. Distribution of the Reader installer is prohibited unless all licensing agreements and distribution guidelines are followed.

Documents

The folder labeled **Documents** contains articles, product information, and some sample eBooks. Among the eBooks are a few public domain publications that are currently distributed on several Web sites. From BookVirtual, you'll find an eBook version of *Alice's Adventures in Wonderland* and William Shakespeare's *Hamlet*. In addition, there are some excerpts of my recent eBooks related to Adobe Acrobat in this folder.

There are many Web sites and individuals distributing information on Acrobat, PDF, and various solutions that Acrobat provides. Some individuals and companies distribute information free to users and visitors of to their Web sites. The *Acumen Journal* is a monthly publication available as free downloads. A few samples of the monthly newsletter are contained in the Documents folder.

Acrobat 5 PDF Bible

The entire text of this book has been converted to PDF files, complete with a search index. You can review pages and sections of the book while working in Acrobat. Search on keywords using the search options discussed in Chapter 2. Before attempting to search for information, however, you'll need to load the search index contained in the **PDFBible** folder. (Loading search indexes is also explained in Chapter 2.) As you come to the Steps sections in the *Acrobat 5 PDF Bible*, you can toggle open windows in Acrobat and review the steps needed to follow a sequence of activities to produce the results for the concepts described.

Tutorial PDFs

Within the **Tutorial** folder, you'll find PDF files and one Adobe Illustrator .ai file that can be used with exercises where they are referenced in the book. Inside this folder are two additional folders. The **Images** folder contains several different image file formats that can be used with exercises referenced in the text. The **Forms** folder includes sample PDF forms where you can browse the form fields and understand some of the JavaScript used in the forms. When a given form is included as part of an exercise step, the form will be located in this folder.

Macintosh Software

Third-party manufacturers offer a number of demonstration plug-ins and applications. In some cases, plug-ins can be copied to the Acrobat plug-ins directory and other items require launching the installer application. Opening the folder and double-clicking on the installer icon can launch all installers. Distribution of the software on the CD-ROM is prohibited without authorized permission of the developer. Many software products may be upgraded by the time you first attempt to install the applications. Before installation, explore the developer's Web site to see if a newer upgrade is available for download. These are located in the **Software** folder.

For more detail on the plug-ins or applications listed in the following pages, look at Chapter 18 where summaries of the respective items are explained. The following applications or plug-ins are identified by manufacturer:

✦ **Callas Software (Callas).** pdfToolbox is available from Callas Software. Five plug-ins can be copied to the Acrobat Plug-ins folder. You can make a folder and name it Callas or pdfToolbox and copy the plug-ins inside the folder. This folder must reside inside your Acrobat Plug-ins folder. The pdfToolbox folder also includes pdfBatchMeister, which is an executable application. This application can be copied to any folder on your hard drive. It does not require installing it in the Acrobat Plug-ins folder. In the pdfPrefs folder, you'll find several PDF files where instructions are provided.

✦ **Dionis (AriToolbox).** Acrobat plug-ins are included in the folder for Ari's Bookmark Tool, PDF Splitter, Ari's Link Tool, Ari's Link Checker, and Ari's Ruler. Each of the items is an Acrobat plug-in and needs to be copied to the Acrobat Plug-ins folder.

✦ **Enfocus Software (Enfocus).** Demo versions of PitStop, PowerUp, and WebPerfect. The first three items are Acrobat plug-ins and Tailor is an executable application. The plug-ins use an installer application. Double-click the installer to expand the archive. Copy the plug-ins to the Acrobat Plug-ins folder when ready to use.

✦ **Iceni Technology (Iceni).** Gemini 3.0 is provided. Copy the plug-in to the Acrobat Plug-ins folder.

✦ **CreoScitex, Inc. (CreoSci).** PDF Embedder is included. Copy the plug-in to the Acrobat Plug-ins folder.

✦ **Lantana Research (Lantana).** Crackerjack and PDF Image Works are available. Double-click the installer and copy the respective plug-in to the Acrobat Plug-ins folder.

✦ **Markzware (Markzware).** MarkzScout and FlightCheck are available as executable applications. Double-click the installer icons and follow the directions in the dialog boxes for installation.

✦ **PubSTec Corporation (PubStec).** A number of different plug-ins are contained in this folder. Copy the plug-ins to the Acrobat Plug-ins folder.

✦ **Quite Software (Quite).** Quite a box of tricks, Quite Imposing and Quite Imposing Plus are all plug-ins that can be dropped in the Acrobat Plug-ins folder.

Windows Software

Windows applications may be an .exe file, which is an executable application; an Acrobat .api plug-in; or you may need to run a setup file from the Windows status bar or double-click the setup file. When readme files are provided in the directory for a product, be certain to read the file in Windows NotePad or a text editor. All products are prohibited from distribution without authorization from the manufacturer. As with the Macintosh applications mentioned earlier in this appendix, explore the developer's Web site before attempting to install the applications. Upgrades may be available. Many of the installers for the products contained on the CD-ROM have licensing agreements noted in the installer dialog boxes. Installation will assume that you agree to the manufacturer's licensing agreement. These are located in the **Software** folder.

For more detail on the plug-ins or applications listed in the following pages, look at Chapter 18 where summaries of the respective items are explained. The Windows applications include:

✦ **Ari's Toolbox (Dionis).** Ari's Bookmark Tool, PDF Splitter, Ari's Link Tool, Ari's Link Checker, and Ari's Ruler are available. Copy the .api files to the Acrobat Plug-ins folder.

✦ **BCL Computers (BCL).** Freebird, Jade, and Magellan are offered by BCL Computers. Run the .exe file to expand and install the applications.

✦ **BrookHouse Limited (BrookHse).** Homer, BatchPrint PDF, and ShowMe demo versions are offered by Brook House Publishing. Homer and ShowMe are Acrobat plug-ins and BatchPrint is a stand-alone application. Run the installer files to install the applications.

✦ **ComputerStream (Comstr).** PDF Protector is available. Double-click the Pprote.zip file to expand it. The plug-in for PDFProtector is found in the 16bit or 32bit folder for respective use with 16bit or 32bit operating systems. Drag the Pprot32.api (or Pprot16.api file) to the Acrobat Plug-ins folder.

✦ **Easy Software (EasySW).** HtmlDoc is available. Run the htmldoc-1_7-windows.exe file and follow the installation guidelines.

✦ **Enfocus (Enfocus).** Pitstop Professional, PitStop Server, PowerUp, and WebPerfect are installer applications. Run the installer by double-clicking the respective application and follow the installation guidelines.

- ✦ **WebBase Inc. (ExpForm):** If seeking an enterprise solution for forms management with Acrobat and Acrobat Reader, look at the demo version of ExperForms. Follow the link included on the CD-ROM to download the latest version. A companion PDF explaining WebBase and ExperForms is also included for further explanation of the vendor's products. The PDF is located in the 'Documents' Directory.

- ✦ **FileOpen (FileOpen).** PDFPublisher is available. Run the fo_eval.exe program and follow the installation guidelines.

- ✦ **Iceni Technology (Iceni).** Gemini 3.0 is available. Double-click the zipped file to expand it. Run the Setup.exe file to install Gemini. Expanded folders will include manuals and user guides.

- ✦ **Image Solutions (ImageSol).** ICopy and ISIToolbox are Acrobat plug-ins that can be copied to the Acrobat Plug-ins folder.

- ✦ **Lantana Research (Lantana).** Crackerjack and PDF Image Works are Acrobat plug-ins. Run the .exe files and follow installation directions.

- ✦ **Markzware (Markzwre).** Markzscout.exe is an installer application. Double-click the .exe file and follow installation directions.

- ✦ **Merlin Open Systems (Merlin).** NameIt, NameIt Launcher, and Date Stamp are available. Run the setup.exe files and follow installation instructions.

- ✦ **pdfSolutions (pdfSolut).** Copy the CloneLink.api file to the Acrobat Plug-ins folder.

- ✦ **PubSTec Corporation (PubStec).** A number of different plug-ins are contained in this folder. Copy the plug-ins to the Acrobat Plug-ins folder.

- ✦ **A Roundtable Solution (RndTable).** Nine installer applications are contained in the folder. Double-click each .exe file and follow installation directions.

- ✦ **Tangent Software (Tangent).** Simple PDF is included. Read the simplePDF document and run the Simplepd.exe file to complete installation.

- ✦ **Visual Software (Visual).** pcl2pdf is a stand-alone application that will convert PCL files to PDF. Run the installer utility to use the demo version.

- ✦ **Zeon Corporation (Zeon).** DocucomPDF RIP and DocucomPDF Core are used to convert any application document to PDF and supports multiple languages including Far Eastern. Run the installers to complete installation.

✦   ✦   ✦

Index

Continued

Continued

Continued

Continued

Continued

Continued

Hungry Minds, Inc.
End-User License Agreement

READ THIS. You should carefully read these terms and conditions before opening the software packet(s) included with this book ("Book"). This is a license agreement ("Agreement") between you and Hungry Minds, Inc. ("HMI"). By opening the accompanying software packet(s), you acknowledge that you have read and accept the following terms and conditions. If you do not agree and do not want to be bound by such terms and conditions, promptly return the Book and the unopened software packet(s) to the place you obtained them for a full refund.

1. **License Grant.** HMI grants to you (either an individual or entity) a nonexclusive license to use one copy of the enclosed software program(s) (collectively, the "Software") solely for your own personal or business purposes on a single computer (whether a standard computer or a workstation component of a multi-user network). The Software is in use on a computer when it is loaded into temporary memory (RAM) or installed into permanent memory (hard disk, CD-ROM, or other storage device). HMI reserves all rights not expressly granted herein.

2. **Ownership.** HMI is the owner of all right, title, and interest, including copyright, in and to the compilation of the Software recorded on the disk(s) or CD-ROM ("Software Media"). Copyright to the individual programs recorded on the Software Media is owned by the author or other authorized copyright owner of each program. Ownership of the Software and all proprietary rights relating thereto remain with HMI and its licensers.

3. **Restrictions on Use and Transfer.**

   (a) You may only (i) make one copy of the Software for backup or archival purposes, or (ii) transfer the Software to a single hard disk, provided that you keep the original for backup or archival purposes. You may not (i) rent or lease the Software, (ii) copy or reproduce the Software through a LAN or other network system or through any computer subscriber system or bulletin-board system, or (iii) modify, adapt, or create derivative works based on the Software.

   (b) You may not reverse engineer, decompile, or disassemble the Software. You may transfer the Software and user documentation on a permanent basis, provided that the transferee agrees to accept the terms and conditions of this Agreement and you retain no copies. If the Software is an update or has been updated, any transfer must include the most recent update and all prior versions.

4. **Restrictions on Use of Individual Programs.** You must follow the individual requirements and restrictions detailed for each individual program in the *Using the CD-ROM* appendix of this Book. These limitations are also contained in the individual license agreements recorded on the Software Media. These limitations may include a requirement that after using the program for a specified period of time, the user must pay a registration fee or discontinue use. By opening the Software packet(s), you will be agreeing to abide by the licenses and restrictions for these individual programs that are detailed in the *Using the CD-ROM* appendix and on the Software Media. None of the material on this Software Media or listed in this Book may ever be redistributed, in original or modified form, for commercial purposes.

5. Limited Warranty.

(a) HMI warrants that the Software and Software Media are free from defects in materials and workmanship under normal use for a period of sixty (60) days from the date of purchase of this Book. If HMI receives notification within the warranty period of defects in materials or workmanship, HMI will replace the defective Software Media.

(b) **HMI AND THE AUTHOR OF THE BOOK DISCLAIM ALL OTHER WARRANTIES, EXPRESS OR IMPLIED, INCLUDING WITHOUT LIMITATION IMPLIED WARRANTIES OF MERCHANTABILITY AND FITNESS FOR A PARTICULAR PURPOSE, WITH RESPECT TO THE SOFTWARE, THE PROGRAMS, THE SOURCE CODE CONTAINED THEREIN, AND/OR THE TECHNIQUES DESCRIBED IN THIS BOOK. HMI DOES NOT WARRANT THAT THE FUNCTIONS CONTAINED IN THE SOFTWARE WILL MEET YOUR REQUIREMENTS OR THAT THE OPERATION OF THE SOFTWARE WILL BE ERROR FREE.**

(c) This limited warranty gives you specific legal rights, and you may have other rights that vary from jurisdiction to jurisdiction.

6. Remedies.

(a) HMI's entire liability and your exclusive remedy for defects in materials and workmanship shall be limited to replacement of the Software Media, which may be returned to HMI with a copy of your receipt at the following address: Software Media Fulfillment Department, Attn.: *Adobe® Acrobat® 5 PDF Bible*, Hungry Minds, Inc., 10475 Crosspoint Blvd., Indianapolis, IN 46256, or call 1-800-762-2974. Please allow four to six weeks for delivery. This Limited Warranty is void if failure of the Software Media has resulted from accident, abuse, or misapplication. Any replacement Software Media will be warranted for the remainder of the original warranty period or thirty (30) days, whichever is longer.

(b) In no event shall HMI or the author be liable for any damages whatsoever (including without limitation damages for loss of business profits, business interruption, loss of business information, or any other pecuniary loss) arising from the use of or inability to use the Book or the Software, even if HMI has been advised of the possibility of such damages.

(c) Because some jurisdictions do not allow the exclusion or limitation of liability for consequential or incidental damages, the above limitation or exclusion may not apply to you.

7. U.S. Government Restricted Rights. Use, duplication, or disclosure of the Software for or on behalf of the United States of America, its agencies and/or instrumentalities (the "U.S. Government") is subject to restrictions as stated in paragraph (c)(1)(ii) of the Rights in Technical Data and Computer Software clause of DFARS 252.227-7013, or subparagraphs (c) (1) and (2) of the Commercial Computer Software - Restricted Rights clause at FAR 52.227-19, and in similar clauses in the NASA FAR supplement, as applicable.

8. General. This Agreement constitutes the entire understanding of the parties and revokes and supersedes all prior agreements, oral or written, between them and may not be modified or amended except in a writing signed by both parties hereto that specifically refers to this Agreement. This Agreement shall take precedence over any other documents that may be in conflict herewith. If any one or more provisions contained in this Agreement are held by any court or tribunal to be invalid, illegal, or otherwise unenforceable, each and every other provision shall remain in full force and effect.

CD-ROM Installation Instructions

How to Install the CD-ROM

The enclosed CD-ROM at the back of the book contains five folders. The CD-ROM is hybrid and can be read by both Macintosh and Windows computers. Macintosh users need System 8.0 or above. Windows users need Windows 95, Windows 98, Windows 2000, Windows Me, or Windows NT. (The CD-ROM will not function properly with Windows 3.1.) To gain access to the CD-ROM contents, follow these steps:

1. Insert the CD-ROM in your CD drive and wait a few moments until the CD icon appears.

2. Double-click the icon to open the CD-ROM, which then displays a window where all five folders will appear.

Refer to the appendix for information on the files contained on the CD-ROM.